SCRIPTING DEFIANCE

Four Sociological Vignettes

SCRIPTING DEFIANCE

Four Sociological Vignettes

SUMANGALA DAMODARAN
WIEBKE KEIM
AMRITA PANDE
ARI SITAS
NICOS TRIMIKLINIOTIS

with
Gaëtan Cliquennois
Jan-Louise Lewin
Javier Perez
and
Sepideh Azari, Dina Dabo, Anubhav Sengupta,
Abdallah Grifat, Sofia Saeed

Tulika Books

Published by
Tulika Books
44 (first floor), Shahpur Jat, New Delhi 110 049, India
www.tulikabooks.in

First published in India in 2022

© The Authors 2022

ISBN: 978-81-950559-1-3

Printed at Chaman Enterprises, New Delhi

Contents

Preface

This was a long journey with many people who did not complete all the way to the finishing line. Yet, Yorim Spoelder, Zandi Sherman, Bianca Tame, Bruno Monteiro, Asanda Benya, Faisal Garba, Manuela Boatca, Jose Tomás Elgorriaga Kunze and Ana Ceceña contributed to the discussions with gusto. Such discussions happened on the back of other workshops and conferences, so we would like to thank SAGE (Sociétés, Acteurs, Gouvernement en Europe) and CRNS (Le Centre national de la recherche scientifique) at the University of Strasbourg, the Global Studies Programme, University of Cape Town, and the University of Nicosia for their hospitality. We would also like to thank Rosemary Sebastian Tharakan for the remarkable editing work on the final manuscript and Ruth Sack for her work on getting the permissions for the artworks that have been used. An enormous thanks goes to Claudia Honegger and Nandini Sundar for agreeing to be critical readers of the first draft of this volume. We hope our revisions rise to their standards!

Introduction

I

Our 'time was/is out of joint', 'disarticulated, dislocated, undone, beside itself, deranged, off its hinges, disjointed, disadjusted, *aus den Fugen, aus den Fugen gehen . . .*' (Derrida 1997: 23). Jacques Derrida had borrowed from Shakespeare's *Hamlet*, this sense of time being out of joint, to start his controversial volume, *Spectres of Marx*. It was a playful and daring evocation. For Derrida, the rise of a neo-Hegelian and Christian messianism and other religiosities, the ideas of an end of history and neoliberalism, had made this period a time of a deep cultural crisis, demanding an assertion in turn of a 'weak messianism' of justice, a new international, an 'untimely link, without status, without title, and without a name . . .', out of joint, 'without coordination, without party, without country, without national community . . .' (ibid.: 85).

He also left us with a provocation, that 'pardoning' and reconciliation would be a futile task. As he advanced in *Le Siecle et la Pardon* (Derrida 2001), even though his admiration of Nelson Mandela was consistent and even predated his release from prison, the project of reconciliation was flawed as pardoning by proxies or third parties defeated the very idea of pardoning itself. It would not redress injustice. It would involve, as argued in *The Mandela Decade* (Sitas 2010), an erasure of many unresolved traumas, ever-threatening to burst through the membrane of social cohesion. So why do we start with Derrida and his hauntings: a time out of joint, irreconcilable and frighteningly unjust? The idea of using the notion of a world out of joint rather than an expression of a disjointed time was toyed with when we tried to find a title for the recent Immanuel Wallerstein-led project and book about historical and contemporary world polarizations that gave birth to our first volume, *Gauging and Engaging Deviance* (Sitas *et al.* 2014).

For Wallerstein, the world was out of joint because it was in the midst of a 'structural crisis' which involved 'a series of chaotic and wild fluctuations of everything – the markets, the geo-political alliances, the stability of state boundaries. . . . Uncertainty even in the short run, became chronic' (Wallerstein 2015: 167). It runs in and through our work, an 'anomalic phase', with moral panics escalating and without obvious 'fixers' on the horizon. This is a terminal crisis of the world capitalist system itself for Wallerstein, a system that was *articulated and systematized*, from the fifteenth century onwards, in and through European hegemony.

Such dominance in the affairs of the world has been rehearsed often by the Braudellian world systems school (Wallerstein 1974, 2000, 2015; Chase-Dunn 1991; and Arrighi 2007, amongst others).[1] In this context a hegemonic power *systematizes, articulates* and *immunizes*: in the former case it turns all seeming or real contrariness into a differentiated *subsystem*, it pronounces stories of success, and in the latter case, it creates the immunizing capacities to neutralize 'risks' and perceived 'deviance'.

It is not that the USA did not try and fix the 'anomalic phase' in the world system that Britain put together in the late nineteenth century and the Soviets attempted to tear up in the early twentieth. After the Second World War, the USA took over the relay stick and the mantle and tried to act as any hegemon should – what is known in popular parlance as the 'Washington Consensus' was a remarkable effort: the 'reconfiguration' of the post-Second World War capitalist economy under US hegemony in the shadow of a bipolar world and in the context of decolonization was a major challenge.[2]

What created the sense of 'out of joint'-ness was the failure of the USA to fix this phase despite its explicit victory in the Cold War, despite its self-serving market fundamentalism and military/political interventions and prowess that created a conflagration it could not withdraw from. The triumphalism of the end of history has been muted, the veracity of its economic models has been in crisis since the world's meltdown in 2008 and yet its insistence perpetuates the structural crisis alluded to above.

The list of tensions is long: the fossil fuel primacy of its economic success is straining the discussions on carbon emissions and climate change, its contradictory messages vis-à-vis labour rights and the deregulation of labour regimes, the funding of all forms of alternatives in other countries – from human rights NGOs and pro-democracy movements to neo-Nazi and neo-religious movements, to its definition of rogue states and its defence often of the indefensible in the Middle East, to its funding of anything from neoliberal to new-left ideas, to the making of the dollar as the universal currency, to the General Agreement on Tariffs and Trade (GATT) and the double standards of the World Trade Organization (WTO), to a range of rationalizations that emphasize what is good for the USA is good for the world.

Despite that, it seems as though US hegemony is on the decline and the rhetoric has shifted; it is not about a clash of civilizations but about the encouragement of clashes within civilizations: democratic liberals in Russia and China, ISIS in the Middle East through proxies, right-wing networks (religious and secular) in Latin America and US-trained dissenters in Africa. And within the USA, racial animosities and violence. It is as if the manufacture of instability has become an unalterable constant.

If we follow the Wallersteinian logic of booms and slumps, Nietzsche would have been the philosopher of crisis of the European project in the late nineteenth century, Heidegger of the 1930s and now, the nexus of Leo Strauss, Harold Bloom, Samuel Huntington and Francis Fukuyama would be the contemporary heirs. Nietzsche was bemoaning in 1888

> the victory of Chandala values, the evangel preached to the poor, and lowly, the rebellion of everything downtrodden, wretched, ill-constituted, underprivileged against the 'race'-undying Chandala revenge as the religion of love! A perpetual rage against the herd, democracy, the feminine- and the well-being dreamed of by shop keepers, Christians, cows, women, Englishmen and other democrats. (Nietzsche 1974: 92)

What do we do now with expressions like 'the spiritual decline of the earth' as Heidegger stated in 1935, 'the darkening of the world, the flight of the gods, the destruction of the earth, the transformation of men into a mass . . .' and the mission of Germany 'to move itself and thereby the history of the West . . . into the primordial realm of the powers of being . . . where . . . the beginning must be begun again, more radically, with all the strangeness, darkness, insecurity that attend a true beginning' (Heidegger [1935] 1973: 38–39)?

Ironically, Derrida was of the same philosophical mettle, a convinced Nietzchean and Heideggerian, but his radical deconstruction took him too far: his critique of the logocentrism of the Abrahamic tradition, the Eurocentrism of modernity's thought, had opened up the space both for post-coloniality and Euroscepticism. He had become an heir of Adorno rather than Schmidt, concerned with Europe's narcissism and racism. He demanded the waning of Europe as 'headland and heading of world civilization' (Derrida 1997: 20) and preferred a borderless and post-national space anywhere.

Our first volume, *Gauging and Engaging Deviance*, was born out of the sense of 'out-of-joint'-ness and already hinted at Another Sociology or An Other Sociology: instead of the monologue about the binary of European modernity and its traditional backwoods, it tried to create an observatory that was more generous and inclusive. It sought to revisit modernity as an entanglement visible from all vantage points of the planet. In this it joined a growing chorus about the limits of classical sociology, its Eurocentrism, its inability to understand a world before European hegemony and by implication the inevitability to misunderstand its very own 'take-off'.

The volume refused to provide a mere critique/deconstruction of the discipline's Eurocentricity – a flaw castigated by Andre Gunder Frank (1998) in his controversial *ReOrient*, as its inability to look at the world without a 'European streetlight'. It went on to provide a historically informed counter-narrative of the entanglement and a new bagful of concepts. Starting from the seventeenth century, it explored the booms and busts of the emerging world capitalist system, its anomalic phases, the moral panics around a range of deviances and deviants, and sketched out a range of alterities.

We left the reader with a trove of moral panics that animate perceived and quite real forms of deviance. Though we challenged many sociological orthodoxies, we found ourselves in a serious conversation and argument with Michel Foucault. We differed on his idea of an endless play of dominations and argued that indeed there is much freedom and equality (however fragile) that we owe to deviant Black slaves in rebellion and to levellers – women, workers and plenty others; we disagreed on his take on the constitution of the 'subject' and the 'human' and his historical lineages that are too close to a European narrative of emergence.

But like that 'other time' of perceived crisis, the 1930s, the 'out of joint'-ness of our times that Derrida intoned about had Adorno's prescient warning: 'most urgent need today appears to be the need for something solid. The need inspires the ontologists; it is what they adjust to. Its right lies in the will of the people to be safe from being buried by a historical dynamic they feel helpless against' (Adorno 1966: 93). That was then the rise of authoritarian movements, of fascism, the Heidegger moment, the Holocaust, Mordor. The new moral panics and the authoritarian turn are not a mere repetition of that past but there is a jagged line from Heidegger to the neocons and the post-Reagan world because once more the need for 'something solid' is very much part of the narrative.

The contemporary indifference to human beings and their suffering has been stunning; the moralization of 'good' and 'bad' suffering has been debilitating. The callousness of dislocation, the refugee impasse, each moment of moral hesitancy killed off part of the pulse of rectitude, part of any emancipatory potential. Listening recently to Homi Bhabha's (2018) argument for a new moral code based on a 'future conditional' rooted on the self-knowledge that those refugee bodies could be us or indeed are us, perhaps sooner than we think, was a sturdy step away from the processes that reduce all of us to an Agambenian 'bare life' (Agamben 2005).

In this volume, our commitment to deep historical lineages of the modern endure, but we avoided revisiting the seventeenth and eighteenth centuries in a systematic way because we found ourselves repeating the substantive points made in the first volume.[3]

In the midst of completing this, the pandemic struck. The authors were caught by their conceptions tugging at their shirt- and blouse-sleeves. Is this the end of the capitalist world system as we know it? Is it enough, as Narendra Modi intoned, to stop being anti-national and to bang pots and pans to ward off the virus and admire the country's air force dropping flower petals to honour health workers? Was it the time to have a disdain for scientists and secular academics, would yoga and the Vedas save the day? Should we, as Bolsonaro stated, stop behaving like a 'country of fags' and get on with our herds? Have the powers that be invented the virus to reduce us to compliant forms of bare life at a moment when movement after movement was shaking the status quo?

II

In *Gauging and Engaging Deviance*, we wrote: 'virus carriers, foreign migrants, terrorists, traffickers, and rogues keep the media working, the panic sustained, and the world on tenterhooks . . .' (Sitas *et al.* 2014: 220). We could have not imagined the scale nor the depth of the panic and global state of emergency against what we termed as 'miasmic deviants' when we concluded our chapter then, and how those final words of the book written would speak so much for the present moment.

To recap: in the first volume we dealt with four types of deviance since 1600 on a planetary scale: behavourial, articulatory, existential and miasmic. We had taken an entangled and historical perspective on global cycles of deviance and its identification, classification, management, confinement or extermination, in parallel to the global cycles of capitalism as put forth by our world systems analysis-oriented colleagues.

The initial outline of three categories of deviance – existential, by what one is; behavioural, by what one does; articulatory, by what one signifies – had at a later stage of our work been completed by a fourth one of a slightly different nature: miasmic deviance. It was so obvious as a response to the moral panics around the HIV/AIDS crisis. Crudely put: what you did, what you expressed/signified, who you were and what was thought you carried inside you could get you into trouble. The term 'miasmic' was to cover all those cases of deviants who were considered such because they carried, consciously or unconsciously, the toxic, viral or otherwise contagious substances that are likely to contaminate their social environment. We wrote about its presence from the seventeenth century's plagues, so ably described by Daniel Defoe then, to the *cordons sanitaire* of colonial settlements, all the way to the HIV/AIDS pandemic of the recent period.

The miasmic deviants of the Covid-19 pandemic are everywhere: those who knowingly or unknowingly carry the virus; those who are flirting with virus carriers; those who aid and abet the spread of it; those people (classes, races, ethnicities, clans or congregations and clustering) who may be or are incubating it; those 'others' who most obviously will be carriers of it; those who behave in a certain way that encourages its spread; those who celebrate those who do so; those activities that allow the spread of viruses full stop. There are adjacent 'folk devils', doctors of Evil who manufacture viruses, the Chinese, the Americans, exploiters of the need for protection – vaccine and pharmacological culprits, charlatans, the deep state, Bill Gates and other servants of Lucifer.[4]

Why is this virus so dominant in the world of public opinion and power? There are other major threats to humanity at a global scale that have not generated anything similar to the political reactions to the virus. Simulations of the outcomes of climate change, for instance, look more frightening than any statistic modelling of the pandemic, where some proponents for decisive reaction still speak of a rather banal disease.[5] And we have never seen a daily live count of death victims of the climate crisis. It appears that classical civilizational diseases like malnutrition, stress, pollution increase immensely the mortality of the virus, but attempts to remedy those health problems related to ordinary life under global capitalism have hardly come forth. The coronavirus had strange origins, to start with, in other species like bats and pangolins before it reached humans. And once it swapped over into our species, it had the potential for moral panic as we have known it throughout the long history of deviance. Anyone could become a danger for anyone else.

The miasmic deviance, already in a somewhat inchoate form, is now being shaped by the forces of the intertwined global 'state(s) of exception' coupled with what Bauman called the 'liquid fear' (2000) of the info-panic or better, to coin a phrase, an 'info-demic'.

We had already spent some time in the previous volume discussing the work of Giorgio Agamben and his idea of a 'state of exception' that allowed an insight into how refugees were dealt with, how unwanted migrants were controlled and how people involved or suspected to be involved in acts of terror were encamped. We also addressed new media and their role in creating 'metanarratives of disturbance' through their multiplication of images, graphemes, opinions and often lies in their sway (Sitas *et al.* 2014: 194). Both processes have been overactive in the current period, reducing what occurred before into a morbid dress rehearsal.

The catastrophic coincidence between 'globalization' and neoliberalism made sure that the very international mobility so celebrated twenty years ago was the classy passage for the virus into a multiplicity of destinations from the markets of Wuhan, and the underfunding or cuts of public institutions made sure that hospitals would be overwhelmed by hundreds of thousands gasping for air and exhausted by fever and unknown side effects.

But beyond the biomedical strain, the virus provided the alibi for any individual, social ensemble, socio-economic interest and cultural formation to articulate anything from prejudice to fact, from attempted panic to solution. It is a dispositional anarchy channelled or attempted to be channelled through social, political and often religious interests. And, given the new media's sway, we witness the use of the digital translocal sphere as a space of shrill or calm refection.

In turn, the state, which was already 'back in' by the late 2000s to deal with what we had termed an 'anomalic phase' of threats and of collapsing economies and financial systems, was now occupying centre stage as a response to the spread of the coronavirus. Governments had been already speaking in epidemiological metaphors for some time: in September 2008, when Lehman Brothers collapsed, as most parts of the world went into severe recession – reflected in the declining financial health of households, firms, banks and governments – the language that came from epidemiology spread rapidly. Financial markets, it was reluctantly acknowledged even by gurus of economic deregulation like Jagdish Bhagwati, were subject to 'herd behaviour', 'bandwagon effects', 'manias and panics' and 'contagion' that led to crashes. Controls on pervasive financialization and opening up, it was argued, both by Keynesians and proponents of the post-Washington Consensus, were necessary, as well as the recognition that financialization and its effects could send what economists call the 'real economy' (or the realms of physical production, consumption and livelihoods) into a downward tailspin that would be very difficult to escape from.

In other words, borrowing terms from epidemiology, the idea that reckless financial liberalization premised on the idea that individuals should have access to any financial asset that they would want from any part of the world (in that sense premised on the so-called expansion of freedoms of the individual) could have disastrous and lasting consequences for the 'real lives' of people appeared, even if reluctantly, in the liberal discourse. From Joseph Stiglitz to Abhijit Banerjee, the reworked role of the state was seen from within the liberal discourse as needing to tame markets and 'protect' the poor through social protection measures and 'inclusive growth' strategies (Duflo and Banerjee 2011).

The responses to the Great Recession, however, in most cases, did not extend its generosity to improve livelihoods or deal with precarity and growing inequalities. Measures ensured bailout packages for banks, a deepening of labour market deregulation to ostensibly 'improve' productivity and efficiency, and a further tightening of the controls on entry and exit into labour markets. The politics of bailouts won over the politics of demand expansion and employment generation (save in China), making this a long anomalic phase even as 'fixing' happened partially.

With the outbreak of the corona crisis, even as the world continued to be suffering the impact of the 2008 recession, what did the so-called assertion of the nation state and its increased responsibility to its citizens mean?

States were already in crisis management mode anyway. Take the twenty-five most populous countries in the world accounting for more than 70 per cent of the world's people: seventeen were experiencing the strains of declining growth, twelve were experiencing major internal upheavals and challenges.[6] The USA led through belligerence, populism and pluck, and cultivated a deep political divide between its Republican and Democratic leadership and a serious economic rift with China, abandoning pretences at world leadership or hegemony and assuming a quarrelsome and offensive street language. Most difficult for state authorities was a growing chasm and a distrust between those whom they governed and governance systems. Corruption and cronyism, explicit favour for captains of industry and commerce and their advantages, a popular 'us and them' was proliferating: the elites, the 1 per cent, the 'they' of power. What was articulated early by sociologists like Ulrich Beck as a mistrust of expert systems in risk societies was at a high point when the virus struck. And so it was too in the 'developing world', about expert systems in and around the Organization for Economic Co-operation and Development (OECD), development advisers, the World Bank, the International Monetary Fund (IMF) and even the World Health Organization (WHO).

Ironically, it was to epidemiology and to the medical model that governments turned, surrendering the social to the viral, even though the consequences would rend the social fabric. Even though the WHO proved to be a teetering viral panopticon by declaring an epidemic emergency in the third week of January following China's decisive intervention. This was followed by South Korea, Vietnam and New Zealand. There was a lag and a seeming hesitation as the majority of countries only moved towards lockdown by mid-March. With some of them already awash with viral cases and some catching the spread early, the shrill reporting of cases gained immense ground. The first deaths (after Wuhan and China) were registered in Vietnam and in the Philippines. Italy, Germany, France, the United Kingdom and the USA registered their first ones during the third week of February. What predominated was a new language of war, a new frontier against the invisible enemy.

It was not surprising that for the defence against such a virus one spoke of war. Emergency measures obligated life in conditions of curfew. But a war with an invisible enemy that can lurk in every other person was and is the most absurd of wars. It was, in reality, a civil war. The enemy was not outside, it was within.

But the virus's invisibility and spread privileged institutions that had the monopoly of clairvoyance in its first phase: the scientist and epidemiologist on the one hand, and the mandarins of surveillance systems on the other. And, given the fact that the unsuspecting hosts developed drastic pulmonary symptoms, it brought along the primacy of the hospital and the medical model of dealing with and treating contagion. Since the mandarins of surveillance were embedded in state apparatuses and interstate protocols, states needed to act following epidemiological rather than sociological pathways in concert with digital service providers. Most scientific institutions have been promulgating an idea of the 'republic of science' in the last decade; what the contagion brought forth was the elevation of science in the epicentres of power in a proclaimed new war – this 'state of exception' has resulted in the birth of new ideas for a hygiene regime, or how to reorganize the biopolitics of societies.

There were always countervailing tendencies: the weakened WHO was listened to by most but there were significant detractors. As Wang Hui (2020) explicated, China's leadership combined the idea of a 'people' and of 'total war' in its response. The former was phrased in Mao's language as a state of mobilization, the latter in Lenin's as a total mobilization of resources to deal with the task. One by one, the countries of the Global North abandoned their initial denialism about the problem 'out there', 'far way' in China. This was replaced by new regimes of exception and derogation of rights, marking a new cycle of restrictive and suppressive processes. One by one, borders were closed, new bordering and restrictive controls were erected, regimes of emergency were suspended indefinitely, as was free movement of the European and other integrated areas. Within countries, let us say Brazil and the USA, there were tensions between the central government and provincial states, whereas the centre in China overrode all provincial autonomy. And while at first science was part of each war room or command council, the minute the extreme lockdown was relaxed, political interests and major lobbies took over to manage the tension between lives and livelihoods.

In opposition to Agamben's argument, the reality or rumour of a deadly virus brought conditional compliance because the right to be protected from it, its habitat and its hosts – such compliance and surrender, was conditional. It also generated its opposite, defiance, especially among right-wing constituencies who responded to fearmongering and mistrust of governments and their scientific advisors. Agamben's intervention when speaking of 'the invention of the epidemic'[7] prior to its mass spread in Europe caused concern about how those in power would use and abuse this as another opportunity for the proliferation of another 'state of exception' (Agamben 2020a, Agamben 2020b, Agamben 2020c).[8] Yet, Agamben's far-fetched 'invention' was far off the mark. He admitted later that he aimed 'not to give opinions on anything but bare life', sacrificing 'practically everything – the normal conditions of life, social relationships, work, even friendships, affections, and religious and political convictions – to the danger of getting sick' (Agamben 2020b). The gravity of the disease raises the ethical and political consequences of the epidemic, social re-engineering in the guise of necessary 'social distancing', and a media-led social celebratory about 'going digital' and 'staying at home'. Agamben asked: 'What do human relationships become in a country that habituates itself to live in this way for who knows how long?' Amid the paralysis of the fear and panic in Italy, he noted that 'our society no longer believes in freedom. And what is a society that has no value other than survival?' (ibid.: 2). Indeed, governments and their expert systems, informed by power blocs around them, came to institutionalize 'states of exception' in a cascading order of force and decisiveness.

There are few scholars and public intellectuals who shied away from pronouncing on the pandemic, from Slavoj Žižek highlighting aspects of a new communism on the ascendance even in the heart of neoliberal polities, to the end of capitalism as a social system. Jürgen Habermas's more sober injunction was that 'we must act in explicit knowledge of our non-knowledge' (Habermas 2020). With her metaphor 'pandemic as a portal', Arundhati Roy has written of the current situation as a gateway between one world and the next: as the virus brought 'the engine of capitalism to a juddering halt', it exposed the fault lines of our systems.[9] As the Northern liberal democracies, US, Italy, France and Spain, flail, and countries like India and Brazil make the pandemic a convenient excuse to strengthen their fascist acts, war is declared on this virus and our deviants both metaphorically and literally. In this so-called 'war zone', the healthcare and essential workers in farms, mines and shops become soldiers and martyrs to be disposed of, whenever necessary, along with migrants, slum dwellers and other such unruly bodies. War becomes a convenient metaphor for capitalism's lack of care, where debilitating demands can be made on workers without an ounce of reciprocity – collateral damage in a perennial war zone. War allows for tanks, rubber bullets, surveillance and policing to be prioritized over provision of healthcare, basic income grants and food security.

The war metaphor also makes invisible the fact that the majority of pandemic 'warriors', whether healthcare workers, nurses, sanitary workers, farmworkers, teachers or parents, are not the masculine soldier but, in the main, women. It exposes not just the deficiencies of the market and state systems, but affirms that these deficient systems have been limping along because of the unpaid and unrecognized labour of women.

The burden is gendered, one, because unlike the recession of 2008–09, which initially hit 'male-dominated' industries, for instance finance and construction, the pandemic is likely to disproportionately affect industries where women are over-represented, like service and retail. The adverse economic effects are compounded since women are more likely to hold insecure and informal jobs, and, in general, earn less (and save less). As critically, what makes the burden unequal is the effect of the pandemic on unpaid childcare responsibilities. As schools, daycare and eldercare centres face closure, women face the added pressures of fulfilling work and care obligations. Further, with greater livelihood insecurity, falling incomes and increasing time being spent at home, the rise in domestic violence that is being documented across the globe accentuates the gendered impact of the pandemic. The pandemic is being written down in history as a crisis in capitalism and production, but in all its true colours, it is ultimately a crisis of social reproduction (Fraser 2016). Some optimistic research is speculating that in the long term, the crisis will alter gender norms and the politics of social reproduction: who lives and what gets acknowledged for creating life worlds, much like it did during the Second World War. The less optimistic scenario emphasizes the necropolitics of Covid-19: the state's ultimate inability to ensure who lives, but its systemic and flagrant power over who dies – the 'other', the deviant and the non-citizen.

In our volume I, we argued that the bubbles of panic are likely to continue in a very long B-phase, no matter how sophisticated the technologies of surveillance and control might have become since the digital and the genetic revolutions, and how much the 227 nation states that constituted the map of the present invest in them. We spoke with certainty about a prolonged 'anomalic phase' in a world which seems incapable of normalizing, but we could not grasp the ascending fixers and moral entrepreneurs. Deviance, for sure, has become exaggerated, made theatrical and immediate by technology, and the theatrical mimicking of supposed ordering is what we are witnessing as well; but the world is in no way 'normalized'.

The coronavirus has thrown a blanket over social polarization, dissent, defiance and discontent that defined the years between 2014 and 2020. Compliance, as we have claimed, is conditional and impossible to sustain. The existing tensions within governmental and civil society responses to the lockdowns and expenditures that are occurring oscillate between restorative and transformative directions, the outcome of which is undecided. What is certain is that the hosts of the virus will continue to be among us for some time to come, but so will the tensions that defined the period.

Precarity and labour conditions had been at the source of a spread of labour action in most of the new workshops in the world – strike waves in Chinese factories; general strikes in the clothing and textile industries of Bangladesh and Pakistan (and their repression); enormous marches by millions of Indian rural and urban workers, culminating in perhaps the largest strike in human history of anything from 170 to 250 million workers; demonstrations of precarious workers everywhere from Spain and Egypt to Greece and Tunisia. Similarly, students' and young people's protests and challenges to the status quo by women, migrants, ethnic and first people constellations, artists and academics in a world that indeed seemed out of joint, multiplied manifold. These mass upsurges in different parts of the world were beginning to challenge various forms of othering and associated notions of deviance that had proliferated under neoliberalism and its associated authoritarianisms.

Whilst the pandemic was unfolding on its full-blown deadly course, many states were witnessing what experts called 'the flattening of the infection and mortality curves'. Hence, many governments went on to declare that the 'first wave' is over, depending on the different phases, according to their assessment of the country's 'return to normalcy', or so they have branded it: after all, it is for sovereign states to declare wars, truces and cessation of hostilities. It is more than apparent that the lockdowns have caused devastating effects on global and national economies, in spite of the beneficial effects in the slowdown of environmental destruction and emission of polluting gas and waste that is accelerating climate change. Covid-19 is proving to be an economic destroyer with much more power than any of its pandemic predecessors we have recently experienced (AIDS, SARS, MERS and Ebola). The comparisons in terms of socio-economic devastation can only be made to catastrophic wars, such as the Second World War or the crisis of the 1930s. According to the IMF, this crisis is estimated to be the worst economic one in 200 years, even though there is still an over-optimistic assumption, which may be not more than wishful thinking, that a speedy recovery will ensue after the end of the pandemic.[10]

During the lockdown process, there has been a massive expansion of inequality. The social and economic magnitude of the inequality is likely to be immense. Even with the most over-optimistic scenario of a miraculous disappearance of the virus, we will not see a 'return' to the world at the point we left it prior to the pandemic. Yet, the 'magical' solution of neoliberal capitalism seems to be more of the same: it is likely to be an accelerated push of more of what we have known in a desperate effort to 'make up' for lost profit, income and time. At least, this is the indication from the way various states are desperately attempting to 'reopen' their economy after the lockdown.

This would be the best moment for a radical shake-up to redress the dismantling of health systems by building them anew, to curtail the destruction of the environment, forests and subjugation of wildlife, and to put a decisive halt to sacrificing everything on the altar of finance-and-debt, and put the nail in the coffin of the powerful food chain and the big pharma which were responsible for the jump of the virus pathogens to human. However, the states, having declared war on this 'invisible enemy', i.e. the 'deviant' virus, which proved capable of threatening and halting, albeit temporarily, the planning and accumulation in the circuits of world capitalism, have now declared that they won the first decisive battle. Workers therefore must go back to work.

The pandemic has thrown a blanket, too, over major patterns of defiance in the contemporary period. In this volume, completed in the midst of the pandemic, we are looking at specific figures of discontent, whose scripts define most of the symbolic resources against systems of domination: the worker, the woman, the student, the artist, the migrant and refugee, the prisoner as a counter-voice, the movements of reaction to their discontent, the movements of authoritative restoration.

III

When the virus struck, we were trying to fathom the rising tides of worker protests in the new industrial epicentres of the world economy. They had shifted decisively to the east with the rise of China, and India in tow, as epicentres of world production. It was a new world of commodities of immense technological refinement and hardship.

The iPhone has been the exemplary commodity of the twenty-first century – it mixes desire and refinement: it is a medium for everything digital and a sign of status for the hands, eyes and ears of the ones who possess it. It is a community in motion with an I/me crafted in its microscopic sinews, a fact that enables the owner to feel like an exalted creator and consumer. It is an enticing thing, a brand that brands, an epicentre of brilliant apps and functions that are 'enhance-able' each year. Ask any of its users. Not only because it is well branded and carries with it the Apple aura do the queues gather at each release in all the major cities of the world. They lust after its reputational prowess, the elegance and the simplicity of its design, and its existence as the centre of the digital constellation. The sociological words used in the past to describe the grip commodities have had in the popular imagination – Marx's fetishism, the Frankfurt School's reification, post-structuralism's enticing simulacra – seem rather archaic for this 'information galaxy' of our interconnected world.

And yet . . . it killed.

Listen to these lines drafted at the cusp of death: 'I will drop like a screw in the dead of night, unnoticed, on the factory floor', wrote Xu Lizhi, a young worker-poet at Foxconn, where the iPhone is made, before he took his life in 2014.

He left behind a small collection of sad poems that endured. 'I want to take another look at the ocean, behold the vastness of tears from half a lifetime / I want to climb another mountain, try to call back the soul that I've lost / I want to touch the sky, feel that blueness so light', he wrote.[11] But before he ended his life, a number of young women workers flew out of their dormitory windows, strange birds in the night, 'forcing' the company to instal rope-nets to catch them. One of them survived; thanks to her and the labour activists who ran to her, the allure of the phone should have dimmed, the phone's lightness to the hand should have gained weight. Yet it didn't: the apps of the 2017, 2018 and 2019 models have been described as sublime.

Lu Zhi's female kin in Shandong work at another lever of enticement: each one in overalls, operating six powerlooms, producing enough silk to cover the world's roads three times over each year – as folklore has it – again, enticing designs that catch the eye and tempt the fingers so we may come to forget the hecatombs and hillocks of silkworms sacrificed in their billions. Perhaps a putrid smell endures after some of the poo is gathered by the workers, for it does make good tea.

We may forget the handloom weavers of Bihar who take their lives, in honour or in debt, who were unable to withstand the power of such mechanical powerlooms. Let us not be misunderstood, the silk looks good and in its name new Silk Roads and Belt Initiatives may be imagined, sometimes overland and sometimes maritime. The narrative gets worse in India – workers who made the alumina products that go into the innards of the gizmos of the digital have taken their lives. More than a thousand garment workers in Tiruppur, Tamil Nadu, have taken their lives. Silk weavers and farmworkers have taken their lives, all producing for the value chains of the new world economy.

Undoubtedly, silk is good for both business and for the work of metaphors, but what has trumped all is yet another material: hazmat fabric! Silk brought back an average of 14 per cent per yuan invested, hazmat brought 22 per cent in 2016.[12] At least, that was the claim by Lakeside Industries. They are manufacturing the hazmat suits that, for example, Nurse Neo Mokone from South Africa wore to fumigate and treat Ebola sufferers in Sierra Leone. You should hear the howls and shrieks when she and her cohort appeared dressed up like that, like the bird surgeons of a medieval plague. Mokone went to West Africa because she felt she had to show how xenophobia was a lie, and as an African nurse she served a calling to duty. She returned to find millions of migrants from the rest of the continent, who had run away from structurally adjusted life worlds, on the run again from her compatriots or hiding in tents. The xenophobic attacks in her homeland sent panics everywhere. They were branded as thieves of the remaining jobs and of the remaining fragments of Mandela's rainbow.

The same fabric made body bags and refugee tents – after all, both Lakeside and du Pont had won the contracts to provide stuff for the 51 to 65 million refugees of our recent times. Humanism's new prisoners made for an enticing market. Just to note in passing: reinforced fabric can be inflated into a boat to cart the new human diaspora across Homer's wine-dark sea.

Back to the body bags: Sarita alias Urmila Ganjoo, the Maoist insurgent killed in Bihar, Mgcineni Noki, the green blanket-clad leader mowed down at Marikana in South Africa, the young man from the favelas of Rio succumbing to rubber bullets in the protests against World Cup expenditure, all ask us to reflect seriously on what we mean by growth, progress and development in the modern world.

There is the irking concern that Immanuel Wallerstein was right: that the world system was spiralling into its final crisis. The polarizations were forcing the vectoral pressures into asymptotes, into crises and the bursting of all bubbles of success. Beyond the aura of consumption, the iPhone and the daisy-cutter bomb, there was conviction that there is another way of wiring things and reconfiguring our life chances. What is the role of sociology in all this?

In this book, we argue that the contours of another sociology are to be found in another archive, one that is made up of significant scripts or narratives of defiance that endured and endure through subaltern people's cultural formations despite and in response to dominant ideas and ideologies. By 'significant' we are hinting that such scripts had and have become 'ideomorphic' (Sitas 2008), that is, they habituate new generations and constitute alternative dispositions. They do articulate a difference, a divergence, a disturbing asymmetry. We argue that such scripts within this archive will help sociology reconstitute itself away from its original mandate: to be part of the 'fixers' (in the language of the first volume), to help the maintenance of social order, to predict and control aberrant behaviour and to create functional individuals and ensembles. Instead, in and through tracing these ideomorphic constellations, we seek to enhance a craft that is more concerned with human flourishing and an understanding of what constrains it.

Furthermore, this volume amplifies a small and varied number of voices and 'scripts' for pragmatic and strategic issues. Pragmatic: we are all limited by our specializations and prior work, and therefore we had to search for repertoires and scripts available to us through networks independent of this one. Each one of us is caught within scholarships and debates defined by our national and international encounters. So, the range of our abilities was much narrower than the ambition this project entailed.

In Vignettes A, Sumangala Damodaran focuses on the 'universal class' of capitalist society,[13] and the historical relationship between freedom and unfreedom. Her narrative starts from what has been seen as an obvious case of 'unfree labour': the silver mines of Potosi, and how resistance and compliance played themselves out and how struggles over control shaped the very system of wage labour itself. It was as clear to Adam Smith that

> the wages of labour, depend everywhere upon the contract usually made between those two parties, whose interests are by no means the same. The workmen desire to get as much, the masters to give as little as possible. The former are disposed to combine in order to raise, the latter in order to lower the wages of labour. (Smith 1974: 169)

Despite the fact that labour was later recognized as the source of all value in a Smithian sense and that contractual freedom was presupposed in much of the political economy literature, it always coexisted with other forms of labour: serfdom, slavery, bondage, indenture and caste derogations. Such forms coexist in new forms of intensity in the contemporary period and constitute important nodes in most value chains. At a time when labour's powers have been weakened through precarity and casualization, struggles over the form and content of freedom are multiplying.

The first part also devotes itself to the emerging archetype of deviance in the contemporary period: the migrant and the refugee. The very figure that is seen in all countries studied in our first volume distorting and threatening ways of life, the figure that has to be controlled, encamped, repatriated, made to work under specific conditions. Nicos Trimikliniotis addressed the European dissensus over refugees and migrants, and showed how undemocratic powers, surveillance and discourse are transforming the emerging fortress. Trimikliniotis here takes us to the very migrant imaginaries as well, their mobile commons and their concrete experiences. Ari Sitas, with the help of Dabo and Azari, explored the imaginaries of African migrants and refugees in the other major destination: South Africa, combining voices and conceptual insights into how we can comprehend everyday forms of resistance, to conclude with a range of articulations that destabilize nation states and borders, insiders and outsiders, indigenes and foreigners.

Vignettes B dives into the forms of transgression that some sections of so-called 'deviants' engage in through their work, activism, circumstances and even their mere existence. Amrita Pande focuses on the perceived transgression of women in and through activities that castigated them as 'loose', most importantly prostitution. Elements of such an exploration had already been touched upon through her important work on surrogacy in India, *Wombs in Labour* (Pande 2014), but now the camera lens has taken on a wider angle in time and place: it gazes at patriarchy's scoundrels in colonial and postcolonial times. It was noted in the previous volume that women's behaviour is seen as highly deviant in the contemporary period, how women were being demonized with new energy in ten of the twenty-eight countries researched between 2009 and 2012.

> In an era when the women's movement has gained more breathing space . . . serious patriarchal backlashes have been underway, defining women's behaviour, demeanour or appearance as deviant and imposing strict social and legal sanctions. Undoubtedly on the avant garde of all this are faith-based reactions that are demanding not only a new piety, but also a new level of control over women's bodies and sexuality. (Sitas *et al.* 2014: 208)

The chapter turns all this on its head, exploring the kind of freedoms that are implied in and through perceived transgression.

The section also takes us to the second major behavioural deviant: the criminal and her/his incarceration. At first Jose Tomas was to be part of this project as he had worked intensively on the circulation of ideas and knowledge and of centres and peripheries in the social sciences. He was arrested, tried and sentenced as being part of and/or aiding and abetting the Basque insurgency. He was then to write from prison as an inmate. This proved to be difficult, if not impossible. This led to the idea of establishing a network of incarcerated sociologists (including those in refugee camps) from the Americas, Africa, Europe and Asia. The idea of a co-written book by them, with us only playing a facilitating role, never materialized just as strains and stresses are experienced by sociologists in countries as we speak. This left Gaetan Cliquennois alone for a while, to bravely take the idea of prisons and prisoners forward into a chapter about their condition and struggles for rights within and outside the very institution. The 'inverted panopticon' produced in and through struggles by those incarcerated and their representatives has had an impact in the nooks and crannies of administered life. Later, when Javier Perez and Jan-Louise Lewin joined the team, the scope of the vignettes got expanded. Javier Perez takes us to the Cape where Coloured inmates articulate their defiance as a continuum of the discord bred during the years of slavery in the seventeenth and early eighteenth centuries. And with Jan-Louise Lewin, we go to the insides of South African prisons to explore queerness and sexuality, and how these both defy norms as well as reinforce them.

In Vignettes C, we look at two main sources of defiant scripts: students and the arts. Where to start presented its own poser as each essay, as you will see later, presupposed the other. We chose also the most familiar to us: 'the' university and its discontents. This exalted institution with its pressures and role in regenerating elites and power, with its contested spaces and issues, gives us an 'in' for three reasons. This is where the philosophical and sociological reflections have occurred about that peculiar 'out there'. It has been the space where young people think and take on the world. It has been also the marker in most accounts of a shift in cultural formation, with Paris 1968 squatting on world history's pedestal, but finally, it is the very same student upsurges that created the tear and then the cultural panic that galvanized the neoconservative counter-revolution. Many democrats and socialists have painted Ronald Reagan as buff, but the truth is far from it: after a close reading of his rise in California, we realized it had the student movement as its alibi, and neoliberalism was not his only strategy.

We were reflecting on these issues as much of the more contemporary disquiet was happening on our campuses. So, from simple dialogues and disagreements, the chapter became a point of tension between its principal authors and a new generation of senior student activists from Palestine, Pakistan and India. Egyptian, Spanish and South African students were there to start with but the actual conflicts and polarizations they were dealing with took over. We hope we have done justice to their notes.

In the next chapter, we find Ari Sitas's work on art and artists and their defiant imaginaries: starting from Paris, the imperial cultural capital of the world, he shows how competing movements wove imaginaries everywhere up to a moment when, during the Second World War, an international of the imagination seemed possible. How the experience fragmented thereafter and how, in the shadow of what Wiebke Keim was describing, new currents came to define defiance in the recent past. Like students, women, migrants, workers, the derogated and captives, artists using their remarkable acuities have created the visual, aural and scripted defiance of our world system.

This volume has severe limitations but like the previous one, it asks of the broader community to respond critically. Can it provide a more complex understanding of historical regimes of derogation?

There were those who were seen as exterminable and as non-people (modernity's problem is that they have survived); there were those who were seen as useful chattel, Black and unfree, broken in and emerging through slavery; there were those who were seen as malleable colonial and tribal subjects; there were those who were seen as non-us and therefore excludable – all these are about variegated forms of self-expression, and within that, different and differing gender-based modulations which demanded a different concept of emancipation, not exactly dialectical but poly-lectical, multi-voiced and unique.

The fourth part presented a more complicated challenge: there was this world 'out of joint' and then the rise of movements of authoritative restoration everywhere. There is though this lethal and toxic balance between movements in Europe as opposed to their mirror movements in the worlds and countries where a political Islam is ever-present. There is a balance which demonizes the 'other' to achieve its own goals, and it is reciprocal and reinforcing. Yet, the respective

'Ordnung' mandarins on both sides are reacting to subdue movements that are all about freedom and equality, and are attempting to impose a normative straitjacket everywhere.

Wiebke Keim started exploring the rise of these movements as a continuation and a departure from her work on National Socialism and the Holocaust in our first volume. She was joined by scholars who were to explore the other worlds of 'Good and Bad Muslims', as Mamdani wrote more than a decade ago (and more specifically, Taliban, Boko Haram and versions of the Khalifate). There were colleagues who were to also take care of the rise of Hindutva. She was left with their notes as the people committed to working on these withdrew because of taxing overwork at their institutions. She turned to provide an extensive account of the rise of fascist and post-fascist movements in Europe, and more specifically France and Germany.

There were withdrawals from the project because of other pressing priorities. One of them left the glaring and unintended gap about the absence of the defiant narratives of first people/nations – modernity's surplus and exterminable people. Without their voices, the very critique of borders and resource banditry, the very rejection of modernity in search of a fair balance between people and nature, an 'eco-ality', is not catered for. In a similar vein, the colonial would have bred the anti-colonial and a range of defiant collectivities – Pan-African, Bolivarian, Black, Bandungian and so on. A sudden withdrawal of another co-traveller left the issue of the demonization of a range of sexualities as yet another yawning gap. Nevertheless, we feel, there is enough here to inaugurate a conversation. There was also a withdrawal of a colleague dealing with the LGBTQIA+ scripts of defiance, leaving another more contemporary yawning gap. We were fortunate that a small aspect of this was dealt with by Jan-Louise Lewin in the context of prison lives.

We do believe that there is enough here to ignite further dialogue and debate.

In conclusion, we felt that human and social rights have become a tick-box abstraction. We needed to go deeper about living rights, something that the arts teach us by refusing the human abstract – something about substantive reconciliation, something like Wang Hui's attempt to salvage Chinese traditions from their cliched interpretation; something like Chizuko Ueno's insistence of atonement about the comfort women of Japanese imperialism; something like Homi Bhabha's future conditional around the death toll of refugees and migrants over their Mediterranean passage; something like Nandini Sundar's rendition of Adivasi dignity in the burning forests of remote India; something like the Dalit's cry for recognition – something not *a priori*, a canon, but something emerging in dialogue and at the same time committed to human flourishing, studying in detail what constrains it.

NOTES

[1] For a discussion and an overview of how Chinese scholars have dealt with the concept of an Asiatic mode of production and Chinese modernity, see Brook (1989).

[2] On the Washington Consensus, see Harvey (2005).

[3] The historical dimension of this work was taken up in new ways by Sumangala Damodaran and Ari Sitas (2016). Their research on one arc of a musical lament of sorrow has been unearthing a vibrant world of interconnections, pathways and sea routes from the seventh to the fifteenth centuries – in these bits of Silk Road, of spice, gold and ivory, it traced and traces trade routes, slaves, slaving and slave rebellions. Through this it deals with the movement of material and symbolic goods, and demands a rethink of historical sociology and historical materialism.

Undoubtedly, that world had its own rhythms. The worlds of the Indian Ocean and of large parts of Afro-Asia have remained on the researcher's back-burner or on the margins of curricula. That the scholarship is increasing is a welcome fact but the need to move beyond case studies has become palpable. There were the rhythms of the monsoon with its radical seasonal reversals, its winds and environmental shifts that moved dhows here and there, and long stays at ports of destination. The bigger canvas was necessary and difficult once one moved outside sociology's conception of a traditional mush. We have been deeply indebted to ambitious archaeologists like Andrew Sherratt (Bauer 2011) who added to the canvas a rich trove of interconnections from 3000 BCE to 1500 CE, from the time of sedentary agrarian social formations, since their secondary products revolution and the emergence of urban nodes, and whose far-flung and long-distance trade punctuated social change.

Within those expanding and contracting worlds there was agency and movement, and within the people on the move there were people in servitude who had a defining role to play. Granted, slavery then was different from the trans-Atlantic one, and granted, the research is still in its early stages – but its volume was significant: males from Africa, the Middle East and Eurasia were forced into plantations, salt and iron mines, public works and reclamations and military service. African slaves or the Zanj were the backbone of one of the most violent and enduring insurrections from 869 to 879, that almost put to an end Abbasid rule and put to the torch Baghdad. Women slaves were forced into sex work, entertainment and performance, and came to define the repertoires of musical composition and performance. And if the tones and semitones of the lament moved through large swathes of lands, it was mainly women in servitude that moved them.

The idea of movement too, historical and contemporary between worlds and social formations, was taken in new directions by the Wiebke Keim-initiated project on the circulation of knowledge and ideas, that culminated in a significant and path-breaking volume involving scholars from all over the world (Keim *et al.* 2014).

[4] The connection between Bill Gates and Lucifer is rife within right-wing and religious fundamentalist groups. There are other dynamics too. Of course, the coronavirus was a perfect excuse to shut out everyone other than the privileged few. The suspension of all basic rights of entry and the refugee convention will all be tested to the limits. Already we are seeing the 'normalization' of pushbacks for refugees branded as mere 'economic migrants' who are essentially 'opportunists' and who do not warrant international protection. What is an even more noxious phenomenon that is eating away humanity is how geopolitics and anti-terrorism are intermingling with border protection: migrants and populations in what is branded as 'mixed populations' are depicted 'non-combatant invaders' directed by powers in hybrid wars against Europe or the USA.

5 J.D. Michel, 'Covid-19 : fin de partie ?!' *Anthropo-logiques*, 18 March 2020, available at http://jdmichel.blog.tdg.ch/apps/print/305096, accessed 24 April 2020.

6 USA, Brazil, Colombia, Mexico, South Africa, DR Congo, Tanzania, Nigeria, Ethiopia, Egypt, Turkey, Russia, Iran, India, Vietnam, Indonesia, Philippines, China, Japan, Bangladesh, Pakistan, United Kingdom, Spain, France, Germany. Data compiled from, *inter alia*, *New York Times*, *O Globo*, *La Prensa*, *News24*, *Le Republique*, *Daily News* (Tanzania), *Daily Post* (Nigeria), *Addis Tribune*, *Egypt Independent*, *Daily Sabah*, *Kommersant*, *Ettelaat*, *Indian Express*, *Viet Nam News*, *Kompas*, *Philippine Daily Inquirer*, *China Daily*, *Asahi Shinbun*, *Daily Jugantor*, *Daily Qudrat*, *Guardian*, *El Pais*, *Le Figaro*, *Frankfurter Allgemeine Zeitung*. Data compiled by the team that has authored the chapter 'Students and Youth' in this volume.

7 Giorgio Agamben, 'L'invenzione di un'epidemia', *Quodlibet*, 26 February 2020, available at https://www.quodlibet.it/giorgio-agamben-l-invenzione-di-un-epidemia, accessed 24 April 2020.

8 The second one, 'Contagion', was rather misplaced given the rising death toll in Italy which exceeded China's and was still rising. What made things worse was that his arguments were made at a time when the USA, UK, Sweden, Netherlands, as well as Brazil and India, were in a state of denialism rather than investing in public health, taking measures to protect ordinary people and preparing so that their systems can cope. His points were about the world to come essentially after the epidemic, and on this his arguments were valid. He also has a second more general concern: 'The other thing, no less disquieting than the first, that the epidemic has caused to appear with clarity is that the state of exception, to which governments have habituated us for some time, has truly become the normal condition. There have been more serious epidemics in the past, but no one ever thought for that reason to declare a state of emergency like the current one, which prevents us even from moving. People have been so habituated to live in conditions of perennial crisis and perennial emergency that they don't seem to notice that their life has been reduced to a purely biological condition and has not only every social and political dimension, but also human and affective. A society that lives in a perennial state of emergency cannot be a free society. We in fact live in a society that has sacrificed freedom to so-called "reasons of security" and has therefore condemned itself to live in a perennial state of fear and insecurity' ('Contagion', *Enough is Enough*, 20 March 2020, available at https://enoughisenough14.org/2020/03/20/giorgio-agamben-contagion/, accessed 24 April 2020).

9 A. Roy, 'The Pandemic is a Portal', *Financial Times*, 3 April 2020, available at https://www.ft.com/content/10d8f5e8-74eb-11ea-95fe-fcd274e920ca, accessed 24 April 2020.

10 'COVID-19: World Economy in 2020 to Suffer Worst Year since 1930s Great Depression, says IMF', *Euronews*, 14 April 2020, available at https://www.euronews.com/2020/04/14/watch-live-international-monetary-fund-gives-world-economic-outlook-briefing-on-covid-19, accessed 24 April 2020.

11 See https://inthesetimes.com/article/lingering-words-from-a-passive-life. For the English translations of his poems, see https://libcom.org.

12 See V. Ocasio and K. Schachter, 'LI Compaby Raising Funds to Boost Hazmat Suit Production for Ebola', *Newsday*, 24 October 2014, available at https://www.newsday.com/business/li-company-raises-funds-to-boost-hazmat-suit-production-for-ebola-1.9542310, accessed 24 April 2020, and K. Gordon, 'Inside the Factory where Ebola Protective Suits are Made', *The Baltimore Sun*, 28 October 2014, available at http://darkroom.baltimoresun.com/2014/10/inside-the-factory-where-ebola-protective-suits-are-made/#7, accessed 24 April 2020.

13 The very agency of emancipation from Proudhon, Marx, Lenin and Lukacs.

VIGNETTES A

Of Workers, Migrants and Refugees

1

Labour's Powers and Questions of Freedom

Sumangala Damodaran

INTRODUCTION

At the turn of the new millennium, a movement of the 'precariat' by a set of workers who called themselves 'Chain Workers' began to take shape in Milan. They used a word derived from Latin (*precator*) which means something obtained by entreaty, begging or prayer, and referring to the condition of the precariat, a supposedly new category of working people. The precariat's experience in labour markets, as the employment of the begging metaphor indicated, was to constantly apply for jobs, scrounge for work opportunities, acquire greater and greater qualifications and degrees, but then submit to whatever terms were offered which would invariably be below acceptable standards. In 2004, a powerful symbol of the conditions of precarity was created in the form of 'San Precario', the patron saint of precarious workers, who, along with 'Santa Graziella' (Graziella is the brand name of a popular Italian folding bicycle), another patron saint who had already been created by the Milanese Critical Mass group, appeared in public together at the Euro May Day celebrations. 'A statue was carried in the streets, preceded by assorted clergy including a cardinal reciting prayers over a loudspeaker, and followed by pious people' (Vani and Marcello 2004) on 29 February of the year, and it was officially declared the Feast Day of San Precario. San Precario, it has been stated,

> . . . is irreverent, mocking and offensive. . . . San Precario is a creation of the precarious intelligence, a free and independent expression that does not refer to any party or union . . . is the patron of who is underpaid, who suffers the pains of an intermittent income and who is oppressed by an uncertain future that is common to us all: sales clerk and programmer, factory worker and researcher.[1]

The Chain Workers also created a fictional fashion stylist called Serpica Naro (an anagram of San Precario) for a hoax during the 2005 Milan Fashion Week.[2] Serpica Naro, described as an 'Anglo-Japanese stylist attentive to street fashion and a genius bursting with distinctive, effervescent, eclectic traits',[3] was created by 200 workers in the fashion industry in Milan and became the virtual embodiment of precarious conditions in the industry in 2005. The workers lodged their protest, or 'capillary agitation' by climbing on to the catwalk that they had constructed.

Some time in 2007, the workers from a trade union of G4S, a giant security multinational corporation (MNC), went out on the streets of Delhi in their uniforms with a begging bowl, in protest against the indignity that they were being subjected to by the terms of their employment with the company. This happened after a protracted peaceful sit-in had resulted in no heed being paid to their demands. The begging metaphor was being employed here again, reinforced by the workers being in uniform, focusing on their precarious and undignified conditions, hardly different from those who were moving from job to job. In this case, the company in question responded by registering a legal case of 'assault' by these workers against the management (Damodaran 2007).[4]

In both the cases above, the metaphor of begging or entreaty was employed to focus on what the workers' existence means in the contemporary world of work, powerfully foregrounding qualitative aspects that have been pointed out in analyses of work and labour. The story of defiance in the modern period is linked inextricably to the story of the working class, its forms of consciousness across time, its organization and its articulation of alternatives, or its 'repertoires of contention' (Tilly 1986, 2006). This is so, even if the working class 'failed' those who expected so much from it; it was to constitute itself as a universal class, as a class that knew what it wanted, and obviously wanted what it knew. Whereas we can spend pages looking at why and how its potential to be an agent for world revolution never fully materialized, we suggest a different take: we shall focus on its role in strengthening notions of equality and freedom and how, despite it not becoming a class for itself, it was a major agent for social change.

How has labour and labouring been structured under capitalism, or what has capitalism's script been about, around work, labour and livelihoods? If, as we will argue in our work, it arose out of the slave factories, the mines, the plantations, based substantially on human degradation, what were the 'unfreedoms' that were attempted to be overcome in the construction of the working class/es in different parts of the capitalist system? What did the emergence of regulations and greater 'freedoms' entail? Does the contemporary period signal a 'retreat to unfreedom' or, in fact, is that freedom itself a myth?

If our focus in this paper is on the working class and its role in enhancing notions of equality and freedom, we would need to address the various elements that constitute labour contracts under capitalism and the idea of freedom of labour. Over time, the ranges of servitude and unfreedom that were worked out and the freedoms that were wrested by the working classes need to be delineated through these processes and mechanisms for understanding the scripts of labour's defiance.

Analytically, we focus on the following points that have been important in both labour control as well as resistance.

1. We eschew the linear narrative of a unified working class coming into its own by way of steadily developing class consciousness. We focus, instead, on a varied working class that has historically played a major role in furthering the notions of freedom.

2. In doing so, we address the various elements that constitute the labour contract under capitalism, and how the idea of freedom of labour is worked with and negotiated across systems with different histories and social mosaics.

3. In between the gross unfreedoms of forced labour and the 'celebratory freedom' of a mobile labour force liberated by the free market, we consider here systems of labour employment and control that have been important signposts of the unfolding narrative and contested trajectory of freedom of labour under capitalism.

4. We would need to qualify neat divisions between categories such as slavery and indenture, precapitalist and capitalist structures, or petty commodity production and full commodity production, in order to identify *continuities* between capitalism and precapitalist systems on the one hand, and *elements* that are worked upon by capital and labour on the other, in negotiating freedom.

5. With the classic 'free' industrial worker at one end of the spectrum and the proliferation of a whole range of systems of labour neo-bondage at the other, what is perhaps generalizable is that wage employment has expanded as a mode of subsistence under a broad range of production and labour contract arrangements that embody different degrees of freedom and unfreedom.

6. Inasmuch as capitalism's script has been about the constitution of the workplace (growth in size, consolidation, dispersion, de-verticalization, etc.) and the varieties of control mechanisms that correspond to different kinds of workplaces and labour processes, it has also been about the body of the worker and the images and the symbols associated with it. If control of the labour process has involved strategies to increase output, productivity and the creation of value, it has also harnessed various mechanisms to devalue the one who labours, most often reflected in or inscribed on the

body of the worker. This devaluation, which becomes possible through the retention or reconstitution of historical forms of degradation, is buttressed by the symbolic figurations of work and the worker. Defiance in turn employs or works through the same symbolic figurations or metaphors associated with work and the worker.

7. We bring into focus, therefore, the social positionings that are contained in working class identities and their deployment in the workings of employment systems, the degrees of freedom or unfreedom that characterize labour's existence, and the entanglements of work lives and social lives.

The paper is divided into two main sections: the first traces historical milestones in the emergence of the wage contract under capitalism from the perspective of the freedom–unfreedom grid, and the second looks at examples of stigmatized and degraded work regimes and understandings of them that underpin the principles of the wage relationship across capitalism's history. We also analyse the tropes that are employed by workers to resist the regimes of degraded work, thus producing defiant scripts.

In a chapter like this, we have to be selective in our narration. As we are committed to take the modern narrative back to the sixteenth century, we have to choose specific areas that throw light on this entanglement of emergence. We shall avoid the simple and Eurocentric way of talking about enclosures, manufacturing, machinofacture, Fordism, post-Fordism in a linear manner. We take up mining and plantations to begin with and the labour practices that emerged in these production systems at the cusp of transitions from the beginning of the sixteenth century.

The Wage Contract, Freedom and Unfreedom

Silver, the Mita System and the Emergence of the Wage Contract

We begin our story with silver mining in Potosi, Bolivia, in the sixteenth century, and the *mita* system of bondage that might have been one of the early examples of forced labour[5] in the service of colonial accumulation in the Americas. The Potosi mines, discovered in 1545, provided the largest deposits of silver to the Spanish empire. In just about a couple of decades after their discovery, in the 1560s, production collapsed due to severe labour shortages and the exhaustion of high-grade ores. The development in 1557 of a mercury amalgamation process for refining low-grade ores and the discovery of mercury at Huancavelica, Peru, in 1563 created hopes for revitalizing Potosi silver production. The aim of the Crown was to revive silver production to levels attained using free labour in the 1550s, before epidemics had substantially reduced labour supply and increased wages. Labour availability for the mines came from the *mita*, a forced labour system instituted by the Spanish Crown – specifically by its representative, Viceroy Francisco de Toledo – in Peru (for mercury mines) and Bolivia (for silver) in 1573. Local elites were responsible for enlisting conscripts from indigenous communities, delivering them to Potosi or Huancavelica and ensuring that they reported regularly for mine duties. If community leaders were unable to provide their allotment of conscripts, *mita* captains required them to pay in silver the sum needed to hire wage labourers. The *mita* required over 200 indigenous communities to send one-seventh of their adult male population, between the ages of 18 and 50, to work in the Potosi silver mines by rotation. Over 12,000 *mita* workers, or *mitayos*, were expected to be in Potosi at any given time, and records show that for several decades such numbers were sustained. The *mita* system was abolished in 1812. At the date of its dissolution, the *mita* had been in force for almost 240 years (M. Smith 2004; Cole 1985).

The Potosi *mita* was not new when it was formalized and expanded by Viceroy Toledo, but was a reconstitution of an existing tributary labour system in the regions where it was modified. It was loosely modelled on a draft labour system which the Incas had imposed on their subject populations (primarily the Aymara Indians, the same group targeted by the Potosi *mita*) in order to ensure sufficient labour for public works projects and seasonal agricultural enterprises. The *mita* provided labour for agriculture, building and road construction, ranching and other tasks, but it was the Potosi *mita* for silver mining that became prominent due to its organization and contribution to colonial accumulation.

Mitayos in Potosi were part of a rather complicated labour system. They performed their *mita* duties in the mines or refineries for one week out of every three during the year they were required to spend in Potosi. This week of labour usually required living on site at a work camp from Monday to Saturday. In other words, the economic and social conditions enforced by the *mita* compelled *mitayos*, if they and their families were to survive, to become long-term labourers in the Potosi silver mining industry.

The workplaces also had another category of free workers, the *mingas*. They were voluntary Indian labourers but most of them ended up in their 'voluntary' occupation due to the deprivations and restrictions of the *mita*.

The two weeks the *mitayos* spent 'resting', *de huelga*, were primarily devoted to finding other sources of income since their wages were not enough to cover the cost of living in Potosi. While some *mitayos* worked in the city selling goods or employed as servants, most returned to the mines during their *de huelga* to work as voluntary labourers, or *mingas*. *Mitayos* who worked as *mingas* while taking *de huelga* were distinct from the *minga* workers who either had their roots in the Yanacona class (those who served the Inca elites) or who had escaped the Potosi *mita*. The *mitayo*-turned-*minga* workers were at a disadvantage in terms of job type, working conditions, treatment by supervisors, pay and the amount of power they held in the employer–employee relationship. *Mitayos* of Potosí usually worked as *apiris* in the periods of 'rest', with the unenviable task of carrying 25-kilogram sacks of ore up rope ladders from the heart of the mine to the surface, distances in some cases of 300 metres. While Toledo's order was that *apiris* should make only two of these trips per day due to the very harsh conditions, by the 1580s, often they would have to make twenty-five trips daily, and by the 1590s, the quota was set at nineteen trips a day. It is not surprising that permanent *mingas* (that is, *mingas* who were not *de huelga mitayos*) refused to do this work. Different jobs meant different working conditions, and as a rule *mitayos* in all phases of silver production worked under much more oppressive conditions than free *mingas*. Most *mitayos* did not come to Potosí alone but with families, and wages covered just about a third of the expenses which included food, clothing, shelter, tributes, levies, hospital fees, funeral services and the costs of travelling back to the home province once the year of service was finished. As the massive levels of production eased off at the end of the sixteenth century, mine owners and *azogueros* (ore refiners) introduced quotas for *mitayos*, refused to pay travel allowances and withheld wages. *Mitayos* would be forced to work until their quota was filled and were often forced to hire *mingas* or even get their wives and children to help them meet their quotas. By the seventeenth century, there was a decrease of easily attainable silver ore for the amalgamation process, a drop in the quality of ore in general, a population decline in Potosí, and these saw mutation of the *mita* from a form of labour for the mines into a source of labour subsidy. This change in the *mita* is exemplified by the *Indios de Faltriquera*, or pocket Indians, whose abuses of the *mita* tended to increase as the productivity of the Potosí mines dropped and the number of *mitayos* reporting to Potosí declined. *Mitayos* were made to bear the brunt for increasing production costs, overextension in construction during boom times, ill-spent profits and the declining quality of silver ore. It was a massive labour subsidy for Spanish mine and mill owners and a major cause for indigenous population decline in a large portion of the Andes, as harsher conditions at the mines and depleting silver reserves intensified employment through the *mita*. The labour subsidy came from the cheapness of *mita* labour in comparison to other freer labour. The intensification of work meant the breaching of quotas for the frequency of the drafting of *mitayos* as well as harsher conditions down in the mines, combined with strict enforcement of quotas for *mitayos* to physically 'show' the attainment of loads of ore extraction. Family members accompanied *mita* workers in their long migrations, turning Potosí into one of the most populous cities in the world and certainly the largest in the Americas, at over 120,000, by the late sixteenth century.

The *mita* system became part of an influential debate during the 1980s between Steve Stern and Immanuel Wallerstein about the nature of the Latin American economy (Stern 1988; Wallerstein 1988). The relationship between *mingas* and *mitayos* with regard to working conditions, wages, living conditions and responses to the *mita* was at the crux of the debate over the question of the degree of agency that the indigenous workers had. Wallerstein suggested that the mine owners retained control over the labour system and that Latin America fit into contemporary global patterns, whereas Stern argued that the *mita* was a unique labour system shaped by Indian agency, where they did have some control over their economic fate.

What is important for our discussion here is that this qualified 'voluntariness' or the system of forced wage labour coexisting alongside employment of free wage labour resembles forms of forced or bonded labour that exist today, for example, in many parts of South Asia.

It is interesting that the forms that *mitayos* employed to resist the system allow for understanding the complex negotiation between the degree of voluntariness in wage employment and forms of control. The Potosi *mita* system turned into a highly oppressive system not only of employment, but it also became a massive labour subsidy for the mine and refinery owners. This was because, with *mitayos* fleeing from their original homelands to escape the draft, cash payments had to be made by *curacas* (Andean lords) to mine owners and *azogueros* to compensate for unaccounted *mitayos*. The important point to note is that better conditions did attract indigenous populations to work in mines, but unhospitable conditions in Potosi created conditions for the generation and perpetuation of the *mita* system (M. Smith 2004).

The responses of the *mitayos* took different forms. *Mitayos* and their families exercised some measure of control over their circumstances by choosing whether or not to comply with the mandatory draft. Many of them went to great lengths to escape the Potosi *mita*. For instance, when Viceroy Duque de la Palata reformed the *mita* to include new geographical regions and formerly exempt communities, the newly subject potential *mitayos* fled to areas outside the viceregal administration. They used every available means to avoid the *mita*. Some avoided further service after the quota was over by remaining in Potosi, because redrafting would need them to return to their villages. Many escaped to other mines or distant places to look for non-*mita* employment. Over time, the double process of large numbers being conscripted to Potosi under the *mita* and of large numbers deserting their *pueblos*, which gave them their customary rights and protection but at the same time bound them down to exploitative labour tribute systems, resulted in large migrations of the communities from which the *mitayos* were recruited. The *mita* system, thus, was one of the important factors that led to the 'depopulation' of what came to be identified as the Toledan *pueblos*. This in turn increased the burden on the *mitayos* who continued to supply labour and the communities that were depopulated by the flight of Indians from the *mita*, and forced to pay replacement fees for them.

By the beginning of the seventeenth century, flight by the *mitayos* and worsening conditions due to the intensification of work had created pressure for the creation of a free, resident labour force; but a free worker was not going to be willing to work under the conditions or wages that the mining employment system offered. The *mita* system, as a result, continued to be in existence until after Simon Bolivar reached Potosi and declared from atop the Cerro Rico, one of the important Potosi mines, that this age of horror was over.

The specific conditions under which the *mitayos* worked – i.e. ill treatment, withholding of wages, deployment in 'other' activities in the mines even when they were supposed to be resting, intensification of the quota of physical production through accusations of stealing, transference of some of the costs of production, like candles for finding their way down the mines, on to the *mitayos*, or transfer or deployment to other areas and mines at will – are the classic features of informal employment systems even in the contemporary period. At the heart of it are the varieties of mechanisms by which the 'freedom' of the worker can be qualified and manipulated, and the quantum of work extracted can be enhanced without commensurate remuneration.

The silver mined in the Americas allowed European powers an entry into the world of Chinese trade and industry: 'At no previous time had so much of this precious metal been circulating in traveller's satchels, on pack animals, in riverboats, and most of all in the cargo holds of Chinese junks and European carracks restlessly plying the waters of the globe' (Brook 2009: 135). Most of it found its way to China partly because, as Timothy Brook insists, 'European merchants had little else to sell in the China market' (ibid.: 160). The silver financed China's own industrious revolution which has been receiving more attention since the Great Divergence debates in economic history.

This world of wealth creation and accumulation experienced by the Ming dynasty was not exactly well-received by many, including members of the power-elite: they saw this period of 'confusions' as a disruptive force. In 1642, Zhang Tao, a prominent gazetteer, was quite explicit:

> One man in hundred is rich, while nine out of ten are impoverished. The poor cannot stand up to the rich who, though few in number are able to control the majority. The lord of silver rules heaven and the god of copper reigns over the earth. Avarice is without limit, flesh injures bone, everything is for personal pleasure, and nothing can be let slip. In dealings with others, everything is recompensed down to 'the last hair'. The demons of treachery stalk. (Brook 1998: 238)

The times of treachery bred tension, strikes and riots as a range of working people questioned authorities through their own moral economies, sensing a gross violation of their communal rights incubating forms of resistance that, according to Ho-Fung Hung, survive to this day (Hung 2011).

We will argue in the second half of the chapter that the characteristics of informal production systems, like the one described above, are also seen in formal contemporary production contexts, utilizing the norms that derive from social structures that supposedly sanction customary relationships/ hierarchies, and the obligations therein, within employment systems. These qualitative features typically hinge on characterizing labour forces as stealthy, lazy, trustworthy or otherwise, in turn justifying the nature of the wage contract.

Sugar, Slaves and Marronage

The latter half of the sixteenth century and the seventeenth century saw the emergence of a production system for a new commodity by Portuguese colonizers in South America, specifically Brazil: sugar. Sugar mills that used the labour of enslaved Africans and local Indians were set up in the Brazilian coasts of Bahia and Pernambuco. The sugar production resulted in profits not only for Portugal, but also Dutch commercial interests based in Holland responsible for refining the sugar. While the Portuguese dedicated themselves to implementing production in the sugar mills, they also started to see increasing incidents of enslaved African and Indian labourers escaping from their control (Carvalho 2007).

It is interesting to consider the case of Palmares and marronage here. In the mid-seventeenth century, colonial chroniclers in Brazil were writing about runaway slaves in settlements referred to as *quilombos*, and especially about Palmares. Palmares, the prototype of the *quilombo* in Brazilian historical and anthropological literature,[6] was a federation of maroon communities whose population was estimated to be anything between 11,000 and 30,000. Although the precise details remain obscure, Palmares itself was created in the late sixteenth century during the period of the Iberian Union (1508–1640), when Portugal was incorporated within the Spanish Crown by rebellious slaves from a large sugar plantation near Porto Calvo on the coast of Pernambuco. Through the period of the Iberian Union, the settlement continuously attracted new settlers.

The Palmares *quilombo* became a settlement that came to be acknowledged by the Portuguese as a powerful and dangerous refuge for escaped labourers by the second decade of the seventeenth century. After the expulsion of the Dutch from Brazil in 1654, and also with the end of the Iberian Union in 1640, the colonial authorities and mill owners concentrated their military forces with the purpose of destroying the Palmares *quilombo*. As a response, the Palmarians started to attack farms along the coast in order to obtain weapons, free more enslaved persons, and take revenge against the mill owners and overseers. In one of the many conflicts, the captain of the infantry, Fernão Carrilho, imprisoned about 200 members of the *quilombo*. Within the *quilombo*, there were disputes between the residents, typified by the differences between Ganga-Zumba, the military chief of the Palmares *quilombo*, and another military leader, Zumbi. Ganga-Zumba tried to negotiate a deal with the governor of Pernambuco, promising that the inhabitants of Palmares would be disarmed if, in exchange, they could have the right over the lands of Palmares and their freedom. Zumbi is said to have led a struggle against Ganga-Zumba and organized Palmares's resistance to the colonial forces. The settlement was finally destroyed after seven years and Zumbi was captured in November 1695 (ibid.).

Similar stories cover the long history of slavery in Brazil. Fugitives often killed or maltreated masters, overseers and members of their families, burned down fields, and stole arms, ammunition and food before escaping to the woods, swamps or mountains.

Ranging from a culturalist approach to *quilombo* studies in the 1930s and 40s, which emphasized the role of *quilombo*s as isolated, alternative communities which sought to reproduce Africa in the Americas and where all members were free and equal, to an interpretation of maroon activity as a kind of class struggle that proclaimed the end of slavery and the creation of an alternative society, the runaways created a powerful form of social organization that focused on freedom.[7] Its members often raided coastal plantations, kidnapped slaves (especially women) and stole cattle. They also traded with travelling merchants, recruited members from indigenous groups and incorporated Europeans who had problems with the law.

The formation of *quilombo*s did not mean a complete withdrawal from the system. Many rebel slaves organized themselves to negotiate from a position of collectivity in the *quilombo*s to obtain better terms of labour and living. Maroons from the Santana plantation in Bahia even produced a 'peace treaty' consisting of several demands relating to the work routine. They also asked that more land be assigned to their subsistence gardens, that planters assist them with selling their produce in the market, that they be given a voice in the appointment of overseers, and that they be allowed to sing and dance any time they chose. Their master did not sign the treaty.

Towards the end of slavery, fugitive slaves often did manage to negotiate their terms of slavery, get access to customary rights and to bigger subsistence gardens. In Rio de Janeiro, they demanded that family members not be separated by sale and that undesired overseers be laid off.

From the sixteenth and seventeenth century examples of mining and plantations we thus see the emergence of the idea of freedom of the worker as an important element of capitalist production, increasingly demanded by workers and continuously manipulated by employers as production systems emerged. These fierce expressions of the demand for freedom would take proper shape under colonialism, but also unfolded in non-colonial contexts.

For Europe, the very trade that silver made possible started off the first stimuli towards breaking with its feudal past. The ascendance, which combined enclosure and poverty, coexisted with another ghastly interregnum – the Atlantic slave trade – at levels that would become unimaginable, bringing with them the first articulations of race, anti-race and a range of eschatological beliefs. Palmares was one nodal point of the slave imaginary, struggles over autonomy, dignity, labour time and a range of cultural manifestations of alterity; the 'slave sublime' was another.

Marronage and slave revolts, and anti-slave networks started denting the system in the nineteenth century (although slavery and slave raiding continued well into the early twentieth century) and coexisted with a range of other forms of bondage and coerced labour. The idea of a 'virgin birth' in Europe's ascendance has made opaque what was absolutely clear to any discerning social and economic historian – the slave factories processing human chattel on the West Coast of Africa were part of the same 'chains' as the cotton plantations of the US South, as much as they were part of the Industrial Revolution in Britain, using 'free' and 'naked' labour power in its 'dark satanic mills'.

And if cotton was to be the heart of industrial capitalism in Britain, this was not unrelated, as Paul Mantoux reminded us, 'from the prohibition of 1700 that the success of English-made cotton goods, as a substitute for Indian fabrics, can be said to date' (Mantoux 1928: 203). However interconnected, consciousness about each other was scant, unless you were part of the sailing masses of the oceanic workforce that would be conscious of all the nodal points though each would be involved in their immediate solidarities. The very concentration of a human mass in the factory system in Europe brought with it ideas of 'wage slavery' and a range of beliefs about an earthly paradise. Around this experience, philosophical notions that this class, as the Young Hegelians thought, had to be the 'universal class' of modernity that would somehow end capitalism, emerged.

Freedom, Bondage, Indenture

Plantation economies, by the end of the eighteenth century, had seen the rise of indenture as a system of employment in the shadow of emancipation debates around slavery in the colonies and when major rebellions were challenging it. The British Parliament passed the Abolition of the Slave Trade Act on 25 March 1807. After the 1807 Act, slaves continued to be held, even if not sold, within the British empire. The abolitionist movement became more active in the 1820s, campaigning against the institution of slavery itself. On 23 August 1833, the Slavery Abolition Act outlawed slavery in the British colonies. The French empire abolished slavery in 1848. The Dutch, who were the last Europeans to abolish slavery, freed their slaves on 1 July 1863.

Various slave rebellions, like the Bussa Rebellion in Barbados during Easter in 1816, the Demerara Revolt in Guyana in August 1823 and the Sam Sharpe Rebellion in Jamaica in December 1831, were key in forcing the transition to freedom of slaves in the Caribbean at a time when ameliorative proposals were being made in Britain. This gave way to widespread rumours, or Emancipation Rumours, that measures were being initiated in metropolitan Britain to grant slaves their freedom but that planters were withholding them. In all three cases, this rumour aided in the agitation for freedom and precipitated rebellion. These rebellions were pivotal to the passing of the Emancipation Act in August 1833. For African slaves on the plantations, the question was how to squeeze freedom out of enduring and oppressive planter practices; for planters, it was how to maintain the plantation system's survival within a 'free' society. As with the *mita*, it was a fine balance between freedom and bondage/coercion/servitude that characterized the indenture contract, which formed the substance of worker revolts too. In all three cases, the uprisings were responded to by hangings, beheadings and 'gibbet'ing of rebel slaves in public view.[8]

The abolition of slavery, thus, was the catalyst for the introduction of the nineteenth-century version of indentured labour, which we take up here. Indentured labour has been defined as involuntary migrant labour – confined, compelled and bound by contract to mostly plantations for specified time periods. Even if historical accounts might want to linearly separate slavery from indenture and freeze the latter as a specific system under colonialism, the actual workings of systems of indenture point to conditions distilled out of different pre-existing forms of bondage in various countries and fluidity along a long continuum of freedom and bondage rather than a discrete system.

We specifically take up the example of the rise of indentured labour in the Caribbean in the backdrop of slave rebellions, and the demand for slaves to be freed and paid wages.

Indentureship was inaugurated by the arrival of the first Indian labourers in the sugar colonies of Mauritius (1834), Guyana (1838) and Trinidad (1845). This was followed by the inception of indentureship in South Africa (1860) and Fiji (1879). Introduced in Mauritius, the indenture system was adopted by other colonies under the same basic principle of penal contract labour. By the time indentureship was abolished in the British empire in 1917, over 1 million Indians had been contracted under this system of labour; the overwhelming majority of this number never returned to India. Indentured labour was introduced in the

French and Dutch colonies of the Caribbean from the 1860s after the success of the system in the British colonies.

More than thirty-five years after the first indentured labourers were brought to Guyana, and just three weeks before the apprenticeship system was about to end, a ship named *Lalla Rukh* carrying 399 British Indians arrived from Calcutta, with the workers having signed a five-year contract to work in a plantation in Suriname. The contract placed the indentured labourer under stringent control and penal sanction, with breach of work conditions attracting criminal proceedings and becoming punishable as breach of contract. More than recruitment itself, the contract and the accompanying laws constituted the unfree elements of indenture. Even if they were supposedly 'free' workers only under a work contract, the possibility of being jailed, physical and social immobility, and competition between free and unfree labourers were strategies for labour control.

A fundamental condition of plantation life was that the indenture contract regulated the terms of employment of labourers and defined the general standard of living since it specified the wage rate, working hours and the type of work, rations, housing and medical attendance. The indenture system, although based on a contractual agreement between employer and labourers, differed from other forms of contractual labour that existed in the seventeenth and eighteenth centuries. Indentured labour derived its authority from various acts regulating relations between masters and servants that were enacted in most colonies, and which were established to set out mutual rights and obligations but, in reality, provided criminal punishment for breaches of contract by workers. For example, in Mauritius, Ordinance No. 16 of 1835 was designed to combat so-called *ëidlenessí* of apprentices and to legislate indentured labour. The contract made punishable by forfeiture of wages or imprisonment with or without hard labour if a servant without reasonable cause neglected or refused to attend work; was guilty of absence, disobedience of orders, insolence, gross neglect of duty or other misconduct in the service of the employer; or quit service before the expiry of the contract. The purpose of this system was on the one hand to provide for a fixed term of service, and on the other, to give employers a blunt instrument of discipline through the penal sanctions.

The process of recruitment was similar for all colonies. Recruitment was carried out by men licensed by the Protector of Emigrants but employed by subagents who manned the up-country depots at which emigrants were assembled prior to their journey to Madras or Calcutta in India, for example, for embarkation. Licensed recruiters often appointed assistants who travelled around the villages to obtain recruits. The indenture contract set a fixed rate of pay for the entire indenture period, without the possibility of bargaining for more. Often, a major proportion of the wages of labourers would be retained by employers until the expiration of the contracts to pay for the return passage of the labourer, even though the contract specified free passage and the payment of full wages.

Contractual terms were not uniform throughout all labour-importing colonies. The experience of the indentured labourers depended on the provisions made in the contract that he or she signed and the way in which it was enforced. With the abolition of slavery, planters and the governments agreed upon a ten-year 'transition' period during which former slaves would work under an employer as free men under the supervision of the state, a kind of 'apprenticeship'. The initial transition from slavery to apprenticeship was supposed to be an intermediate measure that was temporary to move towards full freedom. Apprenticeship, on the one hand, was an important symbol in the advancement of 'civilizational' possibilities for the colonizers, and on the other, an important mechanism, through the idea of the contract and its disciplinary tools, to exert control over time and bodies through power, creating possibilities for numerous forms of bondage ranging from indenture to neo-bondage.

The resistance to indenture, which escalated from the 1860s onwards, reflected worker reaction to the nature of the contract as it was practised in the different colonies. With penal sanctions being used to ensure actual physical control over indentured labour, the contract across colonies limited physical movement and instituted pass systems to keep labour confined. Arbitrariness and elements of force prevalent for indenture got reflected in constant conflicts over work tasks and wages. The contract gave a job guarantee but not a guaranteed wage, because the job task was arbitrarily determined. Arbitrary definitions of 'average workloads' and associated payments allowed planters to reward, punish and control workers.

Stereotypes were constantly used. When planters appealed for replacing former slaves with indentured labourers, the former were characterized as lazy and unreliable. When the first ships from Calcutta arrived, the managers approved of their new labourers by calling them 'industrious'; when they needed a new source of labour, they characterized the Javanese as 'docile'. Soon, however, they viewed immigration as a 'necessary evil': the immigrants belonged to 'scum of the earth' wherever they were recruited and they were as 'vice-ridden' as the Creoles, and Asian docility got transformed to 'primitive monstrosity' (Carter 1996; Lal, Munro and Beechert, eds 1993).

Forms of resistance ranged from indirect and non-violent forms to openly violent ones like foot-dragging, murder and mass uprisings. In the year 1884, there was a major labour revolt at the Zorg en Hoop plantation in Suriname in the West Indies. Indentured workers at the plantation were protesting against unpaid wages, overwork and penal punishments. One of the leaders of the uprising was a young woman worker called Janey Tetary, who had arrived in Suriname with her young son four years before. She was the key organizer of the women workers of the plantation and was shot dead along with six men workers. Tetary's protest was among the earliest of ten significant uprisings during the period of indentured labour by Indian workers in Suriname.

Tetary and her co-workers lost their lives in an armed uprising protesting ill treatment and breaches of contract. Uprisings of indentured labourers took place in 1868, 1873, 1879, 1884, 1891, 1902 and 1908 in different parts of the Caribbean where indenture had been established as a system. The creation of, as well as rebellions against, the system of indentured labour took place between the 1830s and the first decade of the 1910s, after which indenture was abolished as a formal system of employment.

Non-violent forms or passive resistance took the form of neglect of duty, being lazy and indolent, and illegal absence including desertion. Punishments ranged from three weeks to three months of hard labour. Large-scale desertions took place along with strikes against rampant underpayment at the turn of the century, masked by the authorities as deviant behaviour or preferring to steal rather than work. Open resistance took individual forms like arson, murder, destruction of crops/fields, and also large-scale uprisings (Shepherd 1994).

To go back to the comparison between slavery and indenture in historiographical analysis, it is important to note that though perhaps separate as systems of domination, the elements of control over the work process and the worker indicate a continuum of domination that functioned within and adjusted to 'progressive' changes in plantation settings. Further, it is through the tropes of defiance that workers employed that one can understand the nature of this continuum. These examples from early capitalism's history of labour control strategies demonstrate that the degree of freedom of the worker, the nature of work and conditions of work were contested and mediated through various social modalities and customary exclusions and otherings. It is important to reiterate here that recognizing the specificities of such historical systems of employment is necessary to make sense of whole ranges of contemporary bondage systems that base themselves on the unfreedom of workers that is grounded in some prior vulnerability or social othering.

The planetary ascent of Europe through foraging, settlement (land grabs too) and colonialism was unthinkable without coal, steam and the industrial revolution, its machinofacture and the emergence of an industrial proletariat. We owe gratitude to British social and working class historians like Edward P. Thompson, who did not treat the story of labour as a cultural and political force, but made us understand the actual essence of the transition to abstract labour time and clock time. Thompson's remarkable piece on the initial struggles to avoid clock time once resistance against it gets quashed becomes a struggle over its expenditure, its shortening. As he forcefully argued:

the first generation of factory workers were taught by their masters the importance of time; the second generation formed their short-time committees in the ten hour-movement; the third generation struck for overtime or time-and-a half. They had accepted the categories of their employers and learned to fight within them. They had learned their lesson, that time is money, only too well. (Thompson 1980: 390)

Trade unionism in its craft, skilled and/or general forms in Europe and the Americas travelled to the colonial world, and even if they shared the racist attitudes of their employers as whites, they did impose limits on the working day and on working conditions that had to apply to all. The way that this dynamic unfolded was clearest in the South African highveld in the late nineteenth and early twentieth centuries, over the mining revolution that encouraged Britain to impose the gold standard on the world economy.

After the adventures of the British East India Company, Britain had a foothold on the southern tip of Africa through its colonization companies that facilitated settlement in the Western and Eastern Capes and in Natal and its commercial networks seeking advantage against the Dutch and the French. Already, British settlers in Natal had imported indentured labourers from India to work in its sugar plantations before and after the defeat of the Zulu Kingdom in Natal. It was a mediocre and troublesome foothold until the so-called discovery of diamonds in Kimberley and then the so-called discovery of gold on the Witwatersrand, when an explosive transformation and further colonization would be inaugurated. There was gold in abundance in Witwatersrand's seams, so the British imposed it as the monetary standard, leaving silver reeling; they also imposed its price: 25 shillings an ounce.

The abundance had its own snares: the seams went deeper and deeper to reach unimagined depths, and therefore each ounce involved higher and higher costs. The creation of the most ingenuous system of labour exploitation, in the words of John Rex, followed: creating reserves for 'Natives' by the 1870s and pushing all Black indigenes inside them; introducing pass laws to enforce migrancy on the Black majority, imposing a tax that had to be paid in money on each household by 1906; forcing Black labour into single-sex compounds to work in the mines; defining them as pariahs in the land of their birth by 1916 through the Land Act; establishing urban legislation that kept them out of the cities by 1923 and, a year later, defining them as non-employees under the industrial laws of the land and therefore ineligible for trade unionism. Colour bars reserved skilled labour for white workers and entrenched a cheap labour system for Blacks. White workers defended their privilege in job reservation until the 1970s. A divided working class on the basis of race became the reality of labour politics in South Africa.

What many commentators fail to see were, and are, the world system's interconnections: the colonial worlds were not just 'out there' but were an integral part of what we these days call 'value chains'. Even as the USA was trying to perfect modalities of mass production (Taylorism/Fordism) and the Soviets, impressed by scientific management, were trying to emulate the USA's feats, rubber, that was so central to machinofacture, was extracted through the most horrific abuse of power. It is important to re-emphasize the brutality of the system of exploitation the Belgian state inaugurated in the Congo, a system that is short-changed by the banal category of 'forced labour'. Given that rubber grew in abundance in ivy-like plants in the rainforests, villages were given targets, and if these were not met, killings, amputations and untold punishments ensued – enforced by militia that had to return a cut-off hand for each bullet expended. The locals resisted or fled. Both fronts were brutally repressed but their condition started filtering through networks of solidarity. For example, Morel (later to become a Labour Party MP) in Britain in the 1900s became the chief campaigner against all this, gaining dramatic support from liberal, ecclesiastical and socialist networks. His book, *Red Rubber*, in 1906 reached a vast audience. That the Congolese were victims, no doubt, that their resistance was defeated, no doubt, but that their acquiescence meant servility, never. In a song heard on the lower Congo in 1888:

O mother, how unfortunate we are! . . .
The white man has made us work,
We were so happy before the white arrived,
We would like to kill the white man who has made us work
    But the whites have a more powerful fetish than ours,
    The white man is stronger than the black man,
    But the sun will kill the white man,
    But the moon will kill the white man
    But the sorcerer will kill the white man
    But the tiger will kill the white man
    But the crocodile will kill the white man
    But the elephant will kill the white man
    But the river will kill the white man.[9]

There is no doubt that the mine and the plantation in Europe's African possessions only defined the lower ends of their planetary value chains, constructed in a way that always advantaged the North. Those were also the years, 1890s to 1930s, when the emergence of the industrial working class gained force everywhere in the industrializing world. The spectre of communism was more than real and even if the attempted revolutions failed, save in Russia, the mere threat of its proliferation went hand in hand with substantive labour reforms. Until the Great Depression, trade unions managed to push back managerial controls, gain recognition agreements, and enforce collective contracts and bargaining. Even in the USA, which always lacked a labour or socialist party even though it was the first to have a labour one and even invented May Day, in this exceptional space where workers – in Mike Davis's remarkable formulation – have been prisoners of the American dream, industrial unionism (the Congress of Industrial Organizations [CIO]) and collective bargaining enhanced their capacity for mass consumption through productivity deals that escalated the productivity of mass production. Not only was leisure time expanded but the capacity of workers to take part in a consumer cornucopia was magnified.

The world of work got reconfigured decisively in the post-1970s period with the abandonment of the gold standard and the emergence of the dollar as the mirror of all commodities anywhere. There was the wild saga of the oil boom and the petrodollar, there was the profit squeeze and the right-wing challenge of welfare economies and what they termed the 'nanny state'. Even in South Africa, for many the avant-garde of labour militancy, 'the shrinking of the core and the expansion of the non-core and periphery has fractured labour solidarity and weakened the trade unions which are a primary vehicle not only for improving workplace conditions and protecting worker rights, but also for integrating workers into society' (Webster and Von Holt, eds 2005: 10). The age of the digital did not only transform all aspects of life, but supplanted too the solidity of gold with the ephemeral flows of digitalized finance and its flows.

Neo-Bondage in the Contemporary Period: South and Southeast Asia

The contemporary period has been characterized by the proliferation of many forms of employment practices that are referred to as 'modern' forms of unfreedom, 'slavery', 'trafficking', 'bonded labour' and 'forced labour' (for example, by the International Labour Organization [ILO]). Given our discussion above, such unfreedoms would involve varying degrees of being tied to an employer/agent/contractor outside of the formal production/work process and not being able to set or implement temporal limits to the wage relationship, i.e. there can be seen a plethora of ways in which constraints are imposed on a worker's ability to *leave* a particular arrangement even if the point of entry might appear free – in other words, unfreedom at the point of *exit*.

South and Southeast Asia are important locations where various practices of bondage, being characterized by such unfreedom at the point of exit and which continues in old and new forms in the contemporary period, can be understood. Bonded labour is characterized by a creditor–debtor relationship between the employer and the employee which can also involve other members of the family, be of an indefinite duration, and involve adverse contractual stipulations not justified by law or even by the prevailing state of the market.[10] Traditional bondage relations are determined by customary hierarchies. In a country like India, it often involves whole families, with the debt obligation carried over inter-generationally, resulting in families often never being able to get out of debt and hence leading to bondage. Even in non-traditional bonded labour relationships, they are not purely economic contracts, even though employees may enter into them voluntarily because of economic necessity.

There is only a fine line that divides indenture and bondage. Indentured labourers, who were bonded to work in a distant land for a fixed period and became indebted due to their inability to pay the fare, were contractually obliged to repay their debt by providing a specified period of labour. The pledge to repay was formulated in a (written) contract, or indenture, which the labourers supposedly signed voluntarily but after which they had no choice of master or of work and were subject to strict public laws that tied them to their master, who was legally entitled to exploit their labour or to sell them until the contract expired.

In India, where the system of bonded labour and its persistence have been extensively studied, bonded labour did not disappear with legislation banning the practice in 1976 and with the advancement of capitalism in the rural economy, but has, in fact, continued to exist and has taken on new forms – what Jan Breman (1970, 1996) has called 'neo-bondage'. Breman's research on 'footloose labour' in rural western India, spanning over fifty years, showed the gradual replacement of older forms of bondage relations that rested on traditional/customary credit relations by practices at the bottom of both rural and urban informal-sector economies that restrict labour's freedom of movement through indebtedness, which causes labourers to comply with a condition of employment that keeps them entrapped at the worksite. Employers who recruit migrant workers for an entire season for a whole range of economic activities like agricultural work, brick kiln work, sugarcane harvesting, road building, sand digging and working in stone quarries are an important source for binding labour in a relationship of indebtedness through the payment of advance wages ('earnest money'). This advance serves to 'attach' the worker to the employer, in the sense that the worker has to repay the employer in labour if and when desired for a price lower than the going market rate, in a cycle of production that begins at the start of the dry season and ends before the first rainfall. The workers are mobilized at times when they are unable to provide for their subsistence needs due to lack of work and income, typically at the beginning of the monsoon, by recruitment agents who hand out earnest money that commits the recipient to leave the village two or three months later to go and work elsewhere. The relationship thus usually starts with a debt, like in a traditional credit-bondage system, with the worker surrendering his freedom of movement at the point where he accepts the advance. From when the migrants arrive at the worksite, they cannot leave until they have worked off the advance payment. The wage that has been agreed upon, in turn, is paid in a lump sum when he returns home at the end of the season, after a deduction of a weekly amount to cover his daily requirements. Breman argues that while the manner of recruitment and the nature of debt bondage resembles earlier systems of bondage, the agreement is for seasonal employment and not, as with traditional bondage, the start of a relationship that often lasts for life or is carried over across generations. Further, it is only the worker who is bonded and not whole families. The payment of earnest money is purely on the basis of productive capacity and not familial or patronage relations. In this sense, the appearance of 'freedom' at the point of entering the contract remains and it is the economic aspects of the contract that dominate, not non-economic aspects of patronage.

> The army of migrant men, women, and children is immobilized as long as their presence is needed and sent back when the season is over. Their bondage is therefore founded not only in the fact that they receive a payment in advance, but also by the holding back of their wages until the work has been completed. This 'custom,' as the employers call it, is an effective means of pre-empting opposition to the abominable working conditions. The workers withhold protest against the long working days, the pace of the work, the great distance to the fields, the continual moving from place to place, the low grain ration, and so on, for fear of incurring the displeasure of the employer. (Breman 1996: 192)

The relation between 'unfree' labour and capitalism has been the subject of a long-standing theoretical debate, positions ranging from asking whether freely entered contractual relations should really be considered 'unfree' even if characterized by unfreedom after the contract has been entered into, whether 'unfree' labour relations are the result of the persistence of semi-feudal structures or are, in fact, perfectly compatible with capitalism (Lerche 2007; Brass 1999).

Why focus on a category called 'bonded labour', when speaking of 'modern' or 'new' forms of 'slavery', 'trafficking' and 'forced labour' are more in vogue at present? Although referring to different practices and to different discourses originating in different times and in different efforts to combat these practices, the terms are often used interchangeably. For example, the ILO (2005, 2009) considers 'slavery' and 'bonded labour' as a form of 'forced labour', and 'trafficking' as a practice leading to 'forced labour'; the US State Department (2011) calls 'the enslavement of people for purposes of labour exploitation' or 'forced labour', as well as 'bonded labour', a form of 'trafficking'; and Bales (1999) sees 'chattel slavery', 'debt bondage' and 'contract slavery' in modern labour relations as forms of 'new slavery'.

Bonded labour is distinct in terms of the arrangements related to debts and contracts, with debt resulting in bondage. Debt bondage originates in the practice of pawning persons, as opposed to property, for the discharge of a debt. This means that debtors themselves who could not repay their debt or their dependants were transferred into bondage to the creditor as a guarantee for a debt or a security for a loan. Within South and Southeast Asia, pawning one's dependants or oneself, or else entering a very unequal partnership with the creditor who became the patron or master, was a common means of obtaining capital. While debt bondage theoretically presents a temporary form of bondage because it assumes that the bonded labourer would be released after the debt is discharged, in practice it could last the whole lifetime of the labourer and even be transferred inter-generationally when the debt cannot be repaid (under the conditions set by the creditor/employer). In addition, it was very rarely the case that the bondage arrangement would end for a family for generations because of the terms on which the discharge of debt was considered valid.

Through the twentieth century, debt-bonded arrangements have been used as a means to directly recruit labour. Research on Javanese indentured labourers in New Caledonia (Maurer 2010) shows how indentured workers, while working off their initial debt that covered their recruitment and travel expenses, would be obliged to contract new debts to be able to buy subsistence necessities. Being doubly debt-bonded to their employer, many had no choice but to sign on for another term. Znoj (2010) demonstrates, for Indonesia, that traders in rattan who had difficulties finding workers willing to leave for extended periods to work in the jungle used debt-bondage arrangements to create a workforce for the hard and dangerous work of collecting rattan in Kerinci Seblat National Park, Sumatra.

We can see, therefore, the distinction between 'traditional debt bondage', which served to discharge a debt and which typically grew out of patron–client relationships in which economic debt and moral obligation were blended in a multistranded relationship of lasting statutory and personal dependency (Srivastava 2005), and 'modern debt bondage' which facilitated the recruitment of a sufficient amount of 'suitable labour' for emerging capitalist enterprises – plantations, mines or manufacturing workshops – from the late nineteenth and early twentieth centuries, and which continue to exist in contemporary production systems. The ILO identified debt bondage as a form of unfree labour to which poor peasants and indigenous peoples in Asia and Latin America fall victim due to poverty and paucity of employment opportunities.

We have brought up the notion of 'suitable labour' in a general sense here, referring to processes by which cheap labour supplies become available through systems that rely upon older customary arrangements in specific areas, but get reworked to suit the needs of emerging capitalist enterprises or capitalist forms of production. We have also traced continuities in the modalities that characterize employment systems from the sixteenth century onwards by using the freedom–unfreedom grid as a trope that is useful to understand the evolution of or variations in the labour contract under capitalism. However, the idea of 'suitability' goes beyond the act of labour mobilization to encompass the qualitative aspects of employment that draw from social hierarchies and social evaluations of different categories of people who constitute the working classes. Suitability of labour, then, becomes a term imbued with the norms and values associated with social hierarchies, and the mechanisms that result in the mobilization of 'suitable labour' become important scripts to unravel. We do so in the second half of this chapter.

To pull together the discussion in the first half, has the Eurocentric fantasy of capitalism's typical worker being the male, regular factory worker been a mere fancy? Does the working class constitute an example of the incomplete transition to free enterprise capitalism, or is it that the construction of the working classes and its constitutive principles actually question the very characteristics of the supposed/expected transition?

Questions of the degrees of freedom or unfreedom in labour contracts have been considered from the point of view of how they mark distinctions between capitalist and non/pre-capitalist forms of production, and within this, how to understand contemporary forms – for example, of bondage and neo-bondage, the persistence of employment based on race, caste, religion and ethnicity-based stereotypes. The expansion of a formally free and mobile labour force has been a structurally necessary as well as empirically proven underpinning of the world capitalist economy, with several forms of mobility being seen, but it has also been shown through extensive research that labour regimes under capitalism have combined several labour forms of diverse historical origins in complex ways. An important question that arises, then, is whether the persistence of these pre/non-capitalist forms are an aberration or marginal as phenomena. It has been argued by labour studies scholars (for example, in long debates in labour history in India) that the free–unfree distinction is often reduced to binary models of whether labour is free *or* unfree on the one hand, or of complete fluidity along a long continuum from unfreedom to freedom on the other (Ahuja 2013). In the first case, an urge to argue for a binary would relegate several contemporary forms such as neo-bondage to non-capitalist vestiges, soon to be replaced, in appropriate institutional and legal frameworks, by freedom of the worker. In the second case, of arguing for an unfreedom–freedom continuum, where in certain strands of labour, historiographical analysists argue, 'there is an almost endless variety of producers in capitalism, and the intermediate forms between the different categories are fluid rather than sharply defined' (van der Linden, ed. 2008: 22). This takes away from the idea that these often fine differences reflect differing degrees of tension between the urge by workers for freedom and the tendency by capital to restrict it.

What, then, would be a way to look at fine gradations in the freedom –unfreedom grid as an indicator of processes and tendencies in capitalism, and how can defiant scripts allow us to understand the distinctive nature, within capitalism, of the need for unfreedom? Here we point out, as the above discussion on the *mita* system or indenture demonstrates, that it is the ability for withdrawal from work at the workplace that makes the wage contract distinctly marked by time, or temporally limited, and makes workers demand freedom even if the employment system is founded on unfreedom or coercion. Wage labour thus can be understood as possessing 'temporal limits' to the granting of labour use to an employer. Conflicts over the temporal limits, which has been an important element of labour struggles, are not mere negotiations over the 'secondary modalities' of the labour relationship but have to be seen as being constitutive of the wage relationship itself, and connect slavery, indenture, bondage and various other forms that the wage relationship takes under capitalism. The conflict in turn may be manifest in several forms, using symbols from specific social contexts. Maroons, deserters and runaways thus can be seen, with the advent of capitalism, to be pointing towards defining freedom in terms of an opposition to being bound down in an unlimited way, acquiring the ability to withdraw labour and be 'lazy'.

In large parts of the world where capitalism has penetrated deeply but the generalized wage labour relationship has not emerged, rather than thinking of incomplete transitions, it is perhaps better to talk of layered, segmented and varied transitions that hinge on the negotiations between the push towards freedom by the working classes and the need to maintain unfreedoms of various kinds by capital. 'The boundary zone between free and unfree labour as a politically constituted and embattled frontier' (Ahuja 2013: 99), where there is a 'threshold of concrete change' or a 'zone of transformation', marked by milestones in labour freedoms.

STIGMA, STEREOTYPES, VALUE AND LABOUR

Respectable readers of the *Morning Chronicle* and *The Times* in Britain woke up one morning in May 1842 to disturbing reports of trousered women and girls working underground in mines. Harnessed like animals, they dragged heavy carts of coal. In the coming days, increasingly scandalous details from the newly published *Report of the Children's Employment Commission* appeared in newspapers and periodicals across the country. The greatest scandal was not the brutal work which damaged the women's health, but 'revelations' that they worked topless alongside naked men. The commission's report left a bad impression of mining women, largely due to the controversial images that were used to accompany it. For example, a sketch of two topless teenagers sitting crotch to crotch as they were hauled out of the mine in a dangerous manner was used to illustrate safety violations.

In our earlier volume, we analysed the notion of the deviant and his/her deviance as being the basis for othering, and understood deviance as being articulatory, existential, behavioural or miasmic. Specific people or groups of people, we argued, could be declared deviant in one or more than one of these ways, generating moral panics around the perceived deviance. Here, we extend that understanding to examine how the basis for stereotyping that leads to notions of existential or behavioural deviance has historically been employed in labour markets in capitalism.

Like the example at the beginning of this section demonstrates, the entry of women into the labour market has been met with derision and derogation, both in keeping with historically observed patriarchal social norms as well as to sustain regimes of low labour costs. What women's entry into labour markets called attention to was the fact that not only did labour exploitation under capitalism attain a new register, but that this could be justified by the stigma associated with women and their bodies. From gendered understandings of labour market formation, conditions of employment and outcomes for women workers, it is also possible to point towards the critical elements that constitute regimes of derogation based on social identities and their interaction with labour markets.

There is an extensive literature on colour bars and class/colour bars in South Africa's mining revolution. What is argued here is that colour, caste or stigma bars have been part of the organization of work since the beginning of the modern story. Of course, capital can be colour-blind, but in the actual concrete relations of production forms of derogation have been part of the organization of work and the division of labour. The Black Code of 1685 that we discussed extensively in the first volume defined Black slavery's unfreedoms in the French possessions and their plantation economies. The fact that colour or ethnicity could define the suitability of labour has been a constant and shifting terrain of struggle. And we witness, as the legal underpinnings of this order get addressed and transformed through struggle, that they transmute (like in the case of caste) into social underpinnings of the division of labour.

Colonizers in the Americas defined the new identity of the colonized indigenous populations: they were 'Indians' (Quijano 1998: 29). For the populations in question, colonial domination meant being stripped of their original identities (Maya, Aztec, Inca, Ayamara, etc.), losing these identities and in the long run coming to have a common – and pejorative – identity.

The population of African origin, also coming from a wide variety of historical experiences and identities (Bongolese, Bacongo, Yoruba, Ashanti, etc.), was subjected to the same process and made to accept a common and pejorative colonial identity: 'Black'. Forms of labour and kinds of work were in turn ascribed as suitable to these categories of people.

It is our contention here that the 'precariat' of the contemporary global economic system cannot be understood without acknowledging that it is underpinned by regimes of derogation that rely on locally and regionally handed down or constructed systems of stereotyping centred around social identities. We use two tropes, stigma and suitability, already mentioned above, to understand this. Defiant scripts, we argue, can also be understood better if the basis of derogation and its workings can be understood historically.

The relationship between stigma and notions of deviance was brought into prominence in sociology by the work of Goffman (1963), who identified it as a social construction in which people who are distinguished by a 'taint' or 'mark' are viewed as deviant, socially excluded and devalued. He identified three types of stigma: stigma of character traits, physical stigma and stigma of group identity. Since then, a large body of literature that emerged has looked at the impact of stigma on the orientations of 'normal' people toward members of stigmatized groups, the experiences and the self-concepts of members of groups targeted by stigma, the restrictions on access to social- and community-level resources and their responses to such stigma. There have also been innumerable studies on the occupations that are 'tainted' and the strategies that are employed by workers in such occupations to counter the taint, or the protective or mitigating measures that have been taken in many cases. Goffman's 'stigma of group identity' that comes from being of a particular race, nation, religion, etc., is what we focus on in this section, but we argue that, one, mitigating measures, in terms of compensation or protection against discrimination, have come into existence in response to hard struggles by those stigmatized and hence excluded or 'tainted'.

Two, when people are considered tainted due to what they do, the stigma that is associated with such tainting allows for them to be accorded places in occupational hierarchies that reflect the taint-imbued evaluation of their worth. Thus, stigmatized people tend to be relegated to stigmatized occupations or to stigmatized work or tasks within an occupation. Often, therefore, it is not possible to separate the existence of groups of people doing degraded work from their identities as those subjected to social derogation. In turn, the congruence of degraded work with the person who has been historically degraded also allows for inflicting upon them inferior conditions of employment, low wages and various forms of coercion, bondage or other forms of unfree labour.

Thus, there is a close link between stigma, stereotypes and labour regimes across the history of capitalism that has very specific dimensions linked to the creation of value and the process of accumulation. Historically, recruiting slaves, indentured workers or other unfree workers from populations that were subjugated created new forms of surplus extraction for a nascent capitalism where, as we argued in the previous section, physical control over the worker's body and movement created the basis for the extraction of labour power and surplus value.

Mining, a key exemplar of degradation of work and the worker, became newsworthy, as the example of England in the beginning of this section showed, when women entered the mining labour force. The stigma attached to women was emphasized by how dangerous mines were due to their presence. Between the early history of mining in different parts of the world and that in contemporary times, gendered bodies have been subjects of discussion and have been researched a great deal. Women in mining have also produced repertoires of contention/scripts of defiance historically and continue to do so.

In more contemporary analyses of the strategies that are employed to counter stigma associated with particular occupations, particularly a range of jobs considered 'dirty', it is argued that these consist of 'fashioning salutary occupational ideologies, erecting social buffers or insulation against stigma threat and utilizing defensive tactics' (Ashforth and Kreiner 1999: 420). Workers doing 'dirty jobs' like nursing, garbage collection, sex work, etc., thus collectively attempt to counter the stigma associated with their jobs and address the identity threat that they face through campaigns for societal legitimation. For example, such legitimation comes through masculinity, self-sacrifice and heroism, performing a critical service, etc. However, while such strategies by workers are important to recognize and underscore in understanding defiance to stigma, it is necessary to emphasize that social buffers might function, at best, to protect workers against the impact of stigma. If the relegation of particular groups of workers to dirty or stigmatized jobs is justified by the stigma that is related to their identity and also by them being declared as existentially, behaviourally or miasmically deviant, the struggles by workers to counter this is not limited to particular shopfloors but is often part of movements against social discrimination that focus on the stigma itself. Or, it is the indignity of their existence in employment and the symbols of the indignity that are focused upon. Defiant scripts, then, have to be identified both from the smaller struggles that are local or unit-based and from social movements that incisively address stigma itself.

Recent examples of the history of sanitation work, its particular dimensions in India, and of movements against 'untouchability' and its link to employment in India illustrate this.

The workforce engaged in sanitation work has to a great degree come from disadvantaged groups across the world. In the twentieth century, it was the historic Memphis sanitation workers' strike of 1968, in response to the deaths of two workers, Echol Cole and Robert Walker, who were crushed to death by the hydraulic press of the truck they were riding, that became the basis for Martin Luther King Jr.'s 'Mountaintop' speech in support of striking sanitation workers, a few days after which he was assassinated. In the late 1960s, garbage collection was dangerous, brutal and poorly paid, and handled mostly by African-American men. They had to handle materials like tree limbs, broken glass and biological waste that could infect, poison or otherwise injure them. The treatment of African-American sanitation workers became a rallying point to address the ills of segregation. After King's death, even though a deal was reached in Memphis recognizing the workers' union and guaranteeing better wages, more than a half century later, the poor conditions of African-American workers in private employment continue. It has been seen that in different parts of the world, there are different regimes of cleanliness that have created armies of janitorial, sanitation cleaning workers drawn from specific backgrounds in private employment or on contract in public employment, resulting in what Aguiar and Herod call the 'marketization of excretion' (Aguiar and Herod, eds 2006: 7).

In India, sanitation and cleaning work has been done by workers from the poorest and most socially disadvantaged Dalit castes, notably those designated as 'manual scavengers', the work being defined as 'removal of human faeces from streets and cleaning of septic tanks, sewers and gutters'.[11] This practice is still widely prevalent in India, driven not only by class and income divides, but much more by caste and patriarchy. Within such work there is a clear gender divide: women workers, who are paid the lowest, dominate in the cleaning, removal and carrying of faeces from toilets in both rural and urban areas. Men work on cleaning septic tanks, gutters and sewers. Both types of tasks are unpleasant and unhealthy, and even carry severe risks to life. In recent years, the deaths of several workers due to poisoning or drowning while working in sewers and the struggles of an organization representing them, the Safai Karmachari Andolan (Movement of Cleaning/Sanitation Workers), have drawn attention to the degree to which caste-ridden employment persists in sanitation work and the extent to which degrading practices characterize the employment. Also, the pervasiveness of 'untouchability' as a practice and its translation into employment of 'suitable' workers in specific occupations based on caste has been foregrounded in political struggles by Dalit workers. In the case of sanitation work, the struggles of the workers resulted in legislation, the Prohibition of Employment as Manual Scavengers and Their Rehabilitation Act, 2013, which prohibits the construction or maintenance of insanitary toilets and the engagement or employment of anyone as a manual scavenger, and also forbids the employment of workers for hazardous cleaning of a sewer or a septic tank (that is, without adequate safety gear and other precautions) even in emergency situations. Despite the legislation, with poor implementation and little punitive action that would serve as a deterrent being taken against the continuation of the practice, more than a thousand deaths are reported each year and about 1.2 million people are estimated to still be engaged in manual scavenging (Ghosh 2017).[12] Even a 'Clean India Mission (Swachh Bharat Abhiyan)' initiated by the government does little to address the main issues of manual scavengers, resulting in what a prominent leader of the manual scavengers' movement in the country, Bezwada Wilson, refers to as representing 'the interests of the toilet users, not the toilet cleaners'. [13]

Another recent example of defiance against 'untouchability' and its link with employment in India came from a movement in a province of Gujarat that took shape after the public flogging of four young men who were flaying the skin of a dead cow by people who called themselves cow protectors. In certain versions of dominant, ritual Hinduism, the cow, while alive, is bestowed a ritually elevated status as mother, or *gau mata*. But *gau mata*, when dead, is transformed into an object of disgust by those belonging to the higher castes, and all activities related to carcass collection, skinning and flaying dead cattle have historically been done by people belonging to Dalit castes. With the growth of the leather industry from the colonial period and with India turning into an important exporter of raw hides and skins to begin with and then of tanned leather and finished leather goods over the course of the twentieth century, the leather industry has become one of the most important and significantly globalized industries in India. A large part of employment in the industry is of Dalits (from the communities considered 'untouchable') and Muslim men and women, with the carcass collectors, flayers and rural tanners being entirely Dalit and very poor. The lowly social status and working conditions of those engaged in skinning dead cattle, who run into hundreds of thousands of people all over the country, are an important factor in keeping the leather industry a low-cost one. With the rise of right-wing religious fundamentalism under the government in power at the centre in India, attacks against these communities by so-called cow protectors or cow vigilantes, and the violence against the four youths who belonged to Gujarat's traditional cattle-flaying Rohit community who were stripped, beaten and even videographed in public view, resulted in a massive mobilization and uprising of Dalit communities in protest. The protests invoked slogans like 'You love your mother, keep her' and 'You keep the cow's tail, give us land', and made prominent the degree to which social degradation had left Dalit communities involved in industrial production impoverished and landless.

Defiance, in this case as well, made reference directly to the specific stigmas, humiliation and violence that workers in these activities are subjected to, and employed the same metaphors of touch, mother and land that are used in the discourse of 'untouchability'.

When devaluing is systemic, historically sanctioned and, in fact, is reinvented to suit changing production regimes, how is it related to value production under capitalism? In an important contribution that theorizes the relationship between the labour theory of value and degrading gendered and caste-ridden regimes of employment, Mary John (2017) argues that the devaluing of women's work is founded on the stigma attached to women's bodies and the interconnected yet contradictory nature of their engagements with work, and that the labour theory of value should be replaced by a stigma theory of labour. Her argument about the implications of the experience of labour as degradation and not just exploitation, that much of gendered labour, especially of low-caste women in the Indian context, is degrading and in fact inscribed through stigmatic practices on the body of the woman worker, has profound implications since stigma, according to John, cannot be valorized like and as value-producing labour. Thus, if there is a distinctive quality to the degradations based on low-caste status of labour, say, of Dalit men in India, this quality attains a new register when the labouring body is that of a Dalit woman, ridding it of any possibility of being treated with dignity. Therefore, looking at labour as adding 'value', according to John, prevents us from understanding the undervaluation of women's labour and the productive–unproductive, paid–unpaid dichotomies that arise with women's work. This argument can be taken forward for the case of various other forms of social identity as well, identities whose expressions reflect historical otherings. Is it the case, as John argues, that this implies that value is not produced, but only stigma reinforced? Do we need to replace a labour theory of value with a stigma theory of labour?

We have argued, in this chapter, that capitalism's continuous casting and recasting of social identities and its translation into actual terms of the employment contract under varying systems of production rely heavily on symbolic figurations of work and the worker. The symbols, drawing from race, caste or gender stereotypes, that buttress the devaluing of particular kinds of work allow for the accretion of surplus value in the production process. It is precisely these stigma-reinforcing practices in employment that aid the production of value. For, often the attributes producing stigma and stereotypes are recast as the 'suitability' of those workers for particular kinds of labour, producing qualities that are important for sustaining particularities of the production process. It is when the degradations come to the fore, in resistant practices and movements, that the actual mechanisms become apparent, and then, curiously, appear as if antithetical to the 'usual' or 'typical' mechanisms of capitalism. Or, as in John's formulation, it becomes necessary to downplay the conceptual importance of the idea of value production under practices that employ stigma as the basis of employment.

NOTES

[1] 'San Precario, an Introduction', *Designing Economic Cultures*, available at http://www. designingeconomiccultures.net/san-precario/, accessed 12 August 2021. San Precario appeared for the first time in an Ipercoop supermarket in Milan on 29 February 2004, and his consecration is celebrated every year during Euro May Day. The symbol has contributed to the organizing of precarious workers in Italy since then.

[2] 'Serpica Naro, il media sociale', *Serpica Naro*, available at https://www.serpicanaro.com/ serpica-story/serpica-naro-il-media-sociale, accessed 12 August 2021.

[3] Ibid.

[4] The union, by the name of Group 4 Falck Employees Union, which was registered in January 2004, raised an eighteen-point charter of demands with respect to wages, allowances and benefits, which the management considered 'unreasonable'. On many occasions, the union appealed to the management to consider the demands positively and help maintain a peaceful atmosphere in the company. When their demands were not conceded, they issued notices to go on hunger strike and a general strike. The company obtained a stay order from the Delhi High Court restraining any action or agitation by its employees within a radius of 100 metres of the company's office premises and also informed the police about the 'threats' made by the union. The union subsequently started an indefinite *dharna* (sit-in) and also threatened to get action initiated against the company under the Trade Unions Act. Finally, when the union realized that their demands were not being considered even at a minimum level, they issued a letter to the management stating that their members would beg in various places in Delhi in their uniforms and also go on a hunger strike. In response to this, a case was filed in the Delhi High Court against the union for violating the 'code of conduct', and stated that 'any unsavoury act like "begging" in the employer's uniform, which has the potential of undermining and humiliating the employer would scare away customers and mar the image of the security agency . . . the employer is viewed by the public at large with a high level of integrity, and a security guard wearing the uniform of the company is an emblem of a high level of trust. . . . Begging in uniform will make a mockery of the trustworthiness which is personified by the guard wearing the uniform' (Damodaran 2007: 15).

[5] In the contemporary period, the presence and persistence of different kinds of forced labour under capitalism has been specifically noted, defined and legislated against. The ILO tends to look at these in terms of indicators, and emphasizes that the violation and the restriction are matters of degree and are found in many different contexts. The point of emphasizing degree is that forced labour can shade into situations one might want to describe as highly exploitative but not necessarily forced. See 'What is Forced Labour, Modern Slavery and Human Trafficking', *International Labour Organization*, available at https://www.ilo.org/ global/topics/forced-labour/definition/lang--en/index.htm, accessed 12 August 2021.

[6] See Nelson (1987); and S.H. Lara, 'Palmares and Cucaú: Political Dimensions of a Maroon Community in Late Seventeenth-century Brazil', paper presented at 12th Annual Gilder Lehrman Center International Conference, Yale University, New Haven, Connecticut, 29 October 2010.

[7] The historiography of the Palmares *quilombo* was characterized by the creation of specific

binaries: good versus evil, the black man versus the captain of the woods, black people against colonial authority, among others. From 1992, archaeological investigations added evidence on the settlement through the discovery of artifacts from the daily life of the *residents*.

8 D. Geggus, 'Slave Resistance Studies and the Saint Domingue Slave Revolt: Some Preliminary Considerations (Paper #4)', Florida International University FIU Digital Commons, LACC Occasional Papers Series (1981–1990), 1983, available at http://digitalcommons.fiu.edu/laccops, accessed 12 August 2021.

9 C.V. Kolar, 'Resistance in the Congo Free State: 1885–1908', Southern Illinois University Carbondale, 1 June 2015, available at https://opensiuc.lib.siu.edu/uhp_theses/399/, accessed 12 August 2021.

10 R. Srivastava, 'Bonded Labor in India: Its Incidence and Pattern', ILO Working Paper, Cornell University Library, 2005, available at https://hdl.handle.net/1813/99630, accessed 12 August 2021.

11 'The ILO and Manual Scavengers in India: Paving the Long Way towards the Elimination of Discrimination based on Social Origin', International Labour Organization, 18 July 2011, available at https://www.ilo.org/global/about-the-ilo/mission-and-objectives/features/WCMS_159813/lang--en/index.htm, accessed 12 August 2021.

12 J. Ghosh, 'Sanitation Workers in India', International Development Economics Associates, 2017, available at https://www.networkideas.org/news-analysis/2017/09/sanitation-workers-in-india/, accessed 12 August 2021.

13 Srivastava, P., 'Swacchh Bharat Represents Toilet Users, Not Toilet Cleaners', *Governance Now*, 24 August 2016, available at https://www.governancenow.com/views/interview/swachh-bharat-represents-toilet-users-not-cleaners-bezwada-wilson, accessed 12 August 2021.

2

Migration and Asylum

'Dissensus' as a Sociological Concept in European Politics

Nicos Trimikliniotis

Much of sociology was developed on the basis of problematic assumptions about society and migration. It was developed based on distinct societies which correspond more or less to distinct nation states or, more generally, based on logics with a nation-centric frame. This is a highly problematic reading of how we conceptualize migration: we require a reading that takes *the global as the unit of analysis*. One can study migration from different angles, including perceptions, responses from particular localities, regions, national specificities and states. However, to properly explain and understand the complexities of migration one has to move away from a nation-centric approach. Moreover, one must move beyond assumptions about 'order', 'equilibria' and 'consensus' as the basic frames of analysing social formations and processes when reading migration, which again is ingrained in much of the established sociology.

This chapter proposes *dissensus* as an important concept to read the current debates over migration and asylum. Dissensus allows us to have as a starting point, disagreement as the key characteristic of *fragmented* and *divided societies* of today. Dissensus is drawn from Jacques Rancière (2004, 2010a); however, it is necessary to augment and revise the idea to shape it as a *sociological* concept (Trimikliniotis 2020b) by modifying Rancière's philosophical approach and stripping it of elements that allude to any kind of 'anti-sociology' ingrained in his thinking (Toscano 2011). Rancière developed his theory around notions of 'disagreement' and 'dissensus' relating to 'the distribution of the sensible', which goes back to Aristotle, to address the delineation of the boundary between who can talk, who can be represented and counted. This chapter conceptualizes the notion of *dissensus* as a valuable element within the broader, complex and multilayered fragmentations and polarizations that extend beyond the binary exceptional sense which divides 'the Police' (i.e. everyday management and discipline) from 'Politics', as Rancière did. From the outset, it must be stated that the present author does not share the approaches that depict politics as exceptional and rare, including certain radical or critical theories which espouse such readings.

In fact, Rancière later distanced himself from such approaches and sought to revisit his own formulations about 'political rarity', proposing instead a different formulation (Rancière 2014: 157):[1] 'The political is present in all forms of struggle, action and intervention that reassert decision making over the public affairs as anyone's concerns, and as the expression of anyone's equal capacity' (ibid.: 158). This is particularly useful to read the racism and anti-immigration of our era.[2] To utilize the potential and transform this essentially philosophical concept into a sociological formulation, the concept must be adapted as an analytical insight and tool to capture the broader political, sociological and postcolonial spectrum of our times to read migrant-and-asylum related phenomena.

Rancière intervened in public debates critiquing immigration politics as coercive logics of social control by the state, extending his arguments developed in *Hatred of Democracy* which blame the masses for racism, as if what we are witness to are brainless and ignorant masses who are responsible for the rise of racism and xenophobia. This *hatred of democracy* is spreading as elitists refer to 'democracy' pejoratively as 'populism' simply because it threatens *their* order (Rancière 2006). Over the last decade, we have witnessed governments and political parties increasingly using anti-immigrant, anti-Muslim and xenophobic discourses. In France, the prevailing interpretation of the governmental anti-Roma and anti-immigrant policies is that it is mere demagogic political opportunism, a kind of populist pandering to the ignorant 'masses' passions'. Often, this is connected to theories of conspiracies masterminded by far right groupings in Europe and the USA. While there is no doubt that the far right is much more organized than was thought and has developed coordinated international networks, this is not the reason, or at least the main reason, for the rise of anti-immigrant and xenophobic racism, nor can it explain the tendencies of mainstream parties to shift in this direction.

Rancière's argument is attractive, as he explains this as 'a passion from above', which can be thought of as a driver of anti-immigrant racism across Europe and beyond (Rancière 2010b). He speaks of 'cold racism' as 'an intellectual construction', which is 'primarily a creation of the state'.[3] Anti-immigrant racism is seen as the product of immigration *control* obsession generating the logic of security obsession, which in turn engenders *new* anti-immigrant fears, insecurities and moral panics: '[States] seize upon the control of this other circulation as their specific object and the national security that these immigrants threaten as their objective – to say more precisely, the production and management of insecurity. This work is increasingly becoming their purpose and their means of legitimation' (ibid.).

According to Rancière, the essential functions of law are 'an ideological function that provides a subjective figure who is a constant threat to security' and 'a practical function that continually rearranges the frontier between inside and outside, constantly creating floating identities, making those who are inside susceptible to falling outside'. He takes the view that it is the deliberate intention of immigration legislation to construct 'a category of sub-French people firstly intended to create a category of sub-French people, making people who were born on French soil or to French-born parents fall into the category of floating immigrants'. Moreover, the legislation on undocumented immigration intended from the outset 'to make legal "immigrants" fall into the undocumented category [*cela a voulu dire faire tomber dans la catégorie des clandestins des "immigrés" légaux*]', which is the same logic that has allowed the recent use of the notion of 'French of foreign origin'. He extends the application of 'that same logic that is today aimed at the Roma, creating, against the principle of free circulation in the European space, a category of Europeans who are not truly Europeans, just as there are French who are not truly French' (ibid.). For Rancière, racialization is not a contradiction or an unintended consequence of immigration regulation and a rather embarrassing problem of effective manageability of the immigration/integration question, but an intentional policy result:

> In creating these suspended identities, the state isn't embarrassed by the contradictions, like those we have seen in the measure concerning 'immigrants'. On the one hand, it creates discriminatory laws and forms of stigmatization founded on the idea of universal citizenship and equality before the law. This then punishes and/or stigmatizes those whose practices run against the equality and universality of citizenship. But on the other hand, it creates within this citizenship discriminations for all, like that distinguishing the French 'of foreign origin'. So on one side all French are the same, and beware of those who are not; and on the other all are not the same. (Ibid.)

Rancière's analysis of the state is rather blunt, as it does not contain any contradictions or shifts in policy and priorities with little space or potential for struggles to affect the state policies. Moreover, one cannot take the view that there is no racism in the 'masses'. In the past, Marxist and radical studies underplayed or even ignored altogether working-class racism, as demonstrated by Phizacklea and Miles (1980), who tried to take working-class racism seriously.

The contradictions of state processes can be found in the 'management of migration', particularly when it comes to curbing 'illegal immigration', where, despite the state's efforts, undocumented migration continues to grow. States and supranational bodies may be anxious to introduce policies to control migration; however, 'paradoxically, the ability to control migration has shrunk as the desire to do so has increased' (Bhagwati 2003: 99). At the core of anti-immigrant politics is the discourse and political praxis of combating '*illegal* immigration, a subject intimately connected to social phenomena such as racist populism in democratic process and debates regarding social citizenship (Castles 2004). As argued elsewhere, examination of the construction processes of exclusionary citizenship, both European and at the national level via the discourses on undocumented migrant labour, is a process that tends to racialize liberal democracy across Europe. Moreover, this process reproduces an exclusionary Europeanization, as well as novel forms of racist populist mutations present at the core of European nation states and at the European Union (EU) level. Racial anti-immigrant politics and ideologies and the politics of racism are not merely a question of political opportunism; nor are they a marginal phenomenon connected to extreme right-wing groups. Rather, it is a mainstream process at the heart of which lies a racist ideological core in European institutions (Trimikliniotis 2020a, 2020b; Malik 1996, 2009; Fekete 2019). Anti-immigrant and racist ideologies of a populist type contain specific elements of the kind of 'closure' required to marginalize, exclude and devalue the 'Other': the process of 'delineation of the internal boundary' (Anthias and Yuval-Davis 1992: 28) generates what is called 'the authoritarian propensity of this political logic' (Laclau 2005: 197). The discursive construction of the community takes a definite form with the processes of criminalization and illegalization of migrants as the central element of a '*novel* racist populism and populist racism.

The pandemic crisis after the spread of Covid-19 has brought the celebrated 'world on the move' to a standstill. In the fear and panic generated, new global and localized states of hygienic emergency against what we term 'miasmic deviants' (Sitas *et al.* 2014) have generated a more virulent anti-immigrant and xenophobic rhetoric and bordering practices (Trimikliniotis 2020a). As various waves of the pandemic unfold with the mutation of the virus, we witness accentuated processes of exclusion, racialization, marginalization and expulsion of migrants, refugees and 'the damned of the earth' in different parts of the globe. Both new borders and bordering processes are generated, as well as old ones being re-enacted and invigorated. This environment is engendering both 'old' and 'new' forces in Europe and the globe, bringing about the collapse of consensus in politics and generating a 'politics of hate', as well as invigorated forms of solidarity and resistance by enacting new socialities of significant segments of the populations. Dissensus reigns, and migration and asylum are at the heart of these processes (Trimikliniotis 2020a, 2020b). New struggles of resistance are emerging in a system flipping 'out of joint' (Wallerstein 2015) *against* the competing reactionary camps of 'fixers'. On the one hand, the mainstream 'managers' of neoliberal globalization, in their forty-odd years of reign, are essentially calling for *more of the same*. Against them, we have the reactionaries of the 'new' far right calling for 'authoritarian restoration' of the 'old' order: nostalgic of some idealized 'golden age of nation states', a (bizarre) bygone era of 'authentic' national or ethnic 'homogeneity' that has never existed.

Mobility in what Bauman (2000) called 'liquid modernity' is about a mobile capitalist world based on unequal, often oppressive, and exploitative relations, and racialized and gendered differentiations, fragmentations and polarizations. In these contexts, we have the simultaneous emergence of new forms of resistance, solidarities and social imaginaries as praxes of 'real utopias'. We know from immigration history countless examples where resistance functioned as a catalyst for transformation, exchange and enrichment of knowledge, experiences and skills. In fact, the three societies above are such instances. It is therefore inconceivable to portray such societies as if they are suddenly confronted with immigrants unexpectedly, as an event that has 'surprised' or 'shocked'. For years we have been living not just in 'migration societies' but in *post-immigrant societies*, societies which have changed radically because of the presence of immigration that has taken place across the spectrum of life. Countries have been hosting migrant workers, whose financial contribution to GDP growth has been enormous, for decades.

It is thus not surprising that significant segments of the population would presumably identify themselves as active members of a 'post-migrant society'. The term 'post-migrant society' does not denote or imply that one ascribes to or adopts various 'postmodern' notions about the globe, but it aims to take seriously the contributions and debates in various poststructuralist scholarship, a field considered to be valuable:

> Our theorization engages the remarkable advances in theory and empirical research in a critical manner to reach conclusions in the directions of the theory of post-migrant society to ensure that it is properly rooted and embedded in empirical grounding to resonate in the great transformations we are witnessing across the globe. (Parsanoglou, Tsianos and Trimikliniotis, forthcoming)

Even though it is difficult to define 'post-migrants' in a sociological sense, post-migrant situations occur everywhere in our common everyday life, which accordingly express the worldly side of these relationships: post-national spaces of perception and action of lives whose self-relations do not directly refer to migration experiences but are reflected and lived between multiple affiliations and multiple discriminations. In a sense, *we are all post-migrant now*. For example, a third-generation German-Greek woman has never personally been racially discriminated against, as she says, but has experienced and processed the experiences of discrimination of her parents and even her grandparents as part of her post-migrant identity in Germany. The same applies to 'German partners of origin' in binational marriages who have to painfully process the experiences of discrimination of their partners or children in their own lives. We can make similar claims about second- and third-generation Greeks or Turks in the UK, USA, Canada or Australia. Yet many of these will bear witness that they have faced, and are faced with, numerous instances of racism and discrimination that are endemic to and reproduced in different shapes and forms in societies. The major rupture seems to be between the first and second generations of migrants, where the expectations and attitudes of second-generation migrants on how institutions must treat them rises to meet the levels of their peers born from non-migrant parents. These persons live in societies that have over 50 to 100 years of migration history, all post-migrant societies: and the fact that second-generation, even third-generation migrants have the same expectation to be treated equally with dignity and respect is proof in itself that we are living already in a post-migrant society. The same could be said about other European countries with empires or an imperial past (Spain, Portugal, France, Denmark, the Netherlands, etc.). Can we claim that even countries which have relatively recently and with astonishing rapidity been transformed to migration destinations and transit and receiving countries from sending countries have also become post-migrant societies, moving beyond 'migration societies'? This is an empirical question.

The EU is undergoing the bordering process as a re-territorializing place with a renegotiation of borders, boundaries and othering in relation to nation, migration and race (Anthias 2020: 141–75). We are dealing with processes pertaining to 'interrelated aspects of territorializing resource allocations and subordinations' where '"nation", "race" and migration mark important spaces where struggles about where and how borders are placed for control and management of populations and resources are played out' (ibid.: 141). This has been particularly the case after what can be thought of as a 'triple crisis', which combines the economic crisis from 2008, the 'migration and refugee crisis' in 2015–16 and the pandemic crisis since 2020. In the EU today, bordering processes are intensified, and this tends to further politicize and police belonging and hierarchize resources. We are acutely aware how borders are connected to violence and dislocations as boundaries are erected in categorizing the collective 'other': the 'migrant' category then is reimagined and reconstructed in relation to the so-called 'migration and refugee crisis', and the racisms and nativisms, and other associated forms of racialization, are treated as both modes of exclusion and modes of exploitation within new regimes of exceptions generated (Anthias 2020; Trimikliniotis 2020b).

In this sense, the current European *dissensus*, often framed in political discourses as *a fundamental disagreement*, is the connection between national identity and migration and the incorporation of the ethnic/national 'Other' within the boundaries of the 'nation'. In many EU countries there is an increasing tendency in many mainstream discourses to refer to a 'crisis of multiculturalism', which may be read more precisely as a crisis of citizenship in Europe. Similar intolerant discourses are prominent in media and policy debates over migration and migrant integration, which engender and breed old and new forms of racial, ethnic and religious intolerance and hatred. The anti-immigrant right, particularly the virulent neo-Nazis and far right groups, express an intense feeling of being threatened by immigration and the need to reaffirm the 'national heritage' via drastic anti-immigrant action. There is a contagion of generating a sense of 'national emergency' and a siege mentality against 'the enemy' who is depicted as having 'invaded' or 'illegally' entered Europe. This legitimizes the call for 'drastic' acts by vigilante groups, which are portrayed as either 'self-defence' or 'legitimate reaction/retaliation' for the state's alleged failure to take resolute action to 'secure' the nation's survival. There is a new polarization in the public discourse over questions relating to migrants (integration, irregular migration, border control, and to some degree, racism, discrimination and xenophobia), as there is a radicalization by new groups consisting of persons who live a multicultural life and claim the right to the city as a matter of fact – they defend their way of living and a public sphere which is very much their 'everydayness', a crucial feature in their daily lives. Anti-immigration and anti-asylum discourses, political groups and politics across the world are on the rise. Human rights groups have called for a decisive pushback against this racist populist challenge. There is structural *disagreement* or *dissensus* over migration and asylum, i.e. the absence of consensus in Europe with resistance against right-wing anti-immigrant populism (Trimikliniotis 2020b).

There is little doubt that anti-immigrant xenophobia is enjoying an unprecedented surge in Europe. The talk of a *verrechtsing*, i.e. right turn of European politics (Mudde 2013), connected to anti-immigration and anti-Muslimism, and the politics of fear and terror in the era of 'liquid modernity' (Bauman 2000), must be scrutinized. In fact, the rise of the 'third wave of extreme right', which emerged around the mid-1980s (Mudde and Karlwasse 2016), has brought about considerable scholarship of anti-immigrant right-wing populist parties, sometimes called 'right-wing populist', 'radical right populist' or 'xenophobic populist' parties. However, studies show that there has been a resinous rise in anti-immigrant sentiment in many European countries from the late 1980s, i.e. *prior* to the rise of these parties (Mudde 2013; Alonso and Claro da Fonseca 2012). Similarly, empirical studies in the 1990s and 2000s comparing the immigration and integration policies of radical right parties in government show little direct influence of these parties on immigration and integration policies (Akkerman 2012; Alonso and da Fonseca 2012). Studies comparing the record of legislative changes related to citizenship and denizenship, asylum, illegal residence, family reunion and integration show that the policy output of cabinets does not differ much from that of centre-right cabinets. Interestingly, studies show that centre-right parties are mostly responsible for adopting the very same agendas, and implement restrictive and illiberal immigration policies. Some scholars go as far as questioning the presumed significance of radical right parties (Van Kersbergen and Krouwel 2008; Duncan 2010). There is disagreement about whether the policy results would have been significantly different if right-wing parties had remained in opposition. In any case, there is no systematic and comparative assessment of the policy outputs of such parties in power. Moreover, the comparative studies of political parties as evidence have two main problems: first, the evidence collected is based on a rather narrow reading of immigration in electoral strategies and politics, rather than as a broader societal issue that transforms society, including politics; secondly, it is somehow dated (Alonso and da Fonseca 2012; Mudde 2000). Moreover, what is missing is a broader societal perspective drawing more on sociological studies and approaches that reorientate and update the debates towards reading the meaning, use and framing of the migration question. Recently, there has been a renewed interest in the rise of the new right, xenophobia and populism, and this is producing insightful knowledge on ideological shifts and political transformation in anti-immigration agendas, discourses and priorities (Mudde 2013; Fangen and Nilsen 2021; Nissen and Siim 2021).

The victory of Boris Johnson's Conservatives in the snap elections of November 2019, following their failure to agree on how to implement the exit from the EU, is another illustration: the country remains bitterly divided and, despite the Conservative victory in terms of parliamentary seats, there is no wide consent in Parliament. While it was possible for Margaret Thatcher to rule with parliamentary majorities and win over a very divided society, the era of Brexit may well prove more unstable and volatile in what is now a society ingrained in a dissensus, as conditions of intense division and polarization emerged and have been entrenched since the Thatcherite destruction of 'the social' in the UK and Europe, which diminished the room for manoeuvring for governments. We are witnessing the contradictory process of Brexit and its consequences, many of which were very predictable. The process of leaving the EU is a messy affair, and it unleashes economic, social and political forces and phenomena that cannot be contained or managed. For the UK, the continuation of austerity measures in combination with the Brexit transitional measures are likely to generate more poverty and inequality in one of the most unequal societies in Europe. Second, the prevention of the break-up of Britain is highly likely to lead to more authoritarian politics and repression, undermining the legitimacy of the already crisis-ridden democracy and unity of the UK. The third factor of instability is the Boris Johnson phenomenon, which seems to temporarily cover up the deeply rooted contradictions and divisions within the British ruling bloc. The preference of Boris Johnson's Tories and their chaotic politics, which appear to be emulating Donald Trump rather than Jeremy Corbyn's Labour redistribution and radical shape-up, is hardly a sustainable and long-term strategy of stability for British capitalism. Anti-immigration may have been electorally beneficial for the Tories, but it will prove to be a very difficult matter now that they have to deal with the consequences.

Another instance of how anti-immigrant politics are a tool for the New Right is the overwhelming victory of Fidesz,[4] the party of Viktor Orbán in Hungary, indicative of similar processes in many Central European countries. In Hungary, the right-wing anti-immigrant party Fidesz and the far-right Jobbik party together have received 3.5 million out of 5 million votes, as 'Hungary has become a laboratory of illiberal governance' with a party in power whose 'rhetoric is based on identity politics, conspiracy theories and enemy images' (Juhász 2018).

Some explanatory frames often depict such processes of mere populist games as political opportunism by mainstream parties (Lazaridis and Konsta 2015). Whilst this may explain the initial shifts or how mainstream political parties justify their shifts in policy, often preparing the ground for far-right parties to emerge, they underplay the depth and the dangers involved, failing to explain how such processes become societal processes of their own right. More astute approaches illustrate how occupying far-right and xeno-racist positions is something deeper than mere opportunism. Nagy (2016), therefore, explaining the rise of Viktor Orbán's Fidesz in contestation for power with the far-right Jobbik party, argues how the party has 'its own agenda, actually occupy far right positions':

> Instead of engaging the body politic by discussing what would serve the public good and instead of designing the large social systems – taxation and redistribution to municipalities, education, and health care – in dialogue with the stakeholders, a long chain of us versus Other dichotomies have been produced by government propaganda. Neighboring countries with large Hungarian minorities, foreign-owned banks, large multinational food store chains, and partly foreign-owned utility companies all have been targeted as acting against the imagined collective interest of the Hungarian nation. Once those battles were concluded, a new Other and in turn, a new enemy had to be invented. (Ibid.: 1043)

Nagy connects the three key elements, 'securitization, majority identitarian populism and crimmigration', and suggests that Viktor Orbán introduced anti-immigration and anti-refugee rhetoric in 2014 as part of his campaign 'at a time when immigration was a total non-issue in Hungary'. He promised 'rock-hard official and domestic policy not supporting immigration at all' (ibid.: 1040). It is noteworthy that before January 2015, his rhetoric did not include asylum seekers and 'illegal' migrants; it was after the attack on *Charlie Hebdo* in France that Orbán changed his discourse and all migrants and refugees became undesirable: 'Economic immigration is a bad thing in Europe. One should not regard it as useful because it only brings trouble and dangers to the European people, therefore it has to be stopped – this is the Hungarian position' (quoted in ibid.: 1053).

Anti-immigrant and anti-Muslim racism and xenophobia, on the one hand, and how migration has already transformed society engendering new modes of social, economic, political, ideological and cultural formation, on the other, are matters that require further scrutiny. However, one has to question many of the assumptions about the rise of such ideas in politics. In this sense, rather than only reading immigration *within* the established political game, as for instance many political scientists who specialize on the extreme right parties do, this chapter proposes that what is needed is also to start from the exact opposite point. In other words, sociologists and political scientists ought to read politics *within* the social, ideological and cultural transformations, by locating how the immigration and asylum issue is played, mediated and reshaped within the political game, primarily from a political, sociological and critical migration studies perspective. Moreover, contrary to assumptions which take for granted a kind of primacy of parties, organization and governance, it is suggested to embark on an examination of matters from the opposite angle: thus, we take *opposition*, resistance and struggles, i.e. contestation and disagreement. Hence the notion of *dissensus* as the starting point of the current era, rather than *consensus*. After all, the so-called 'consensus politics' ended more than four decades ago and in the end it has proven to be a short interlude of western politics between 1945 and the early 1970s.

Locating Migration and Asylum in the Current EU Sociopolitical Context

We ought to contextualize the emergence of the migration and asylum dissensus in the current historical conjuncture in EU and the globe. This requires that we take stock of the main features of the current sociological and economic context.[5] There is an abundance of empirical data showing the spread and growth of migration across the globe.[6] In 2020, the total number of international migrants residing in the globe was estimated to be 281 million, which was equal to 3.6 per cent of the global population (IOM 2019).[7] In 1990, there were 49.2 million migrants in Europe who made up 6.8 per cent of the population; in 2017, they were 77.9 million or 10.5 per cent. In percentage terms, Europe is far behind the other richer regions of the world, North America (9.8 and 16 per cent) and Oceania (17.5 and 20.7 per cent), as shown in Figure 2.1. Important also are the trends in numbers of international migrants and countries hosting the largest number of migrants (Figure 2.2), as well as the regional distribution and country distributions as shown on the world map in Figure 2.4.

According to the United Nations High Commission for Refugees (UNHCR), by the end of 2020, 82.4 million people worldwide were forcibly displaced. The numbers are growing: in 2016, there were 65.6 million, as against 33.9 million in 1997. While applications for asylum peaked in 2015, the numbers decreased in 2017 as the overall number of persons seeking asylum from non-EU countries during the third quarter of 2017 was 1,64,300 – a number around the levels recorded in 2014.[8] In the first half of 2021, 2,48,000 asylum applications, of which 2,00,000 were first-time applications, were lodged in the EU, 12 per cent more than the level in the same period in 2020 but 26 per cent below pre-Covid levels during the same period in 2019.[9] The UNHCR 2021 figure given in Figure 2.5 is indicative of the rising numbers of refugees in the globe. The UN Global Compact for Safe, Orderly and Regular Migration proposes a '360-degree vision of international migration', and recognizes the need for 'a comprehensive approach' which 'optimizes the overall benefits of migration while addressing risks and challenges for individuals and communities associated with it'.[10]

The EU and national state responses have led to a mixture, often contested, of Europeanized and national state policies on migration and asylum. We are witnessing processes of transformation of the migrant integration debates, as well as processes opening up old and new national and minority questions. The context of crisis and austerity is reshaping the balance of rights and obligations with states and transnational formations such as the EU. Borders seem volatile and sovereignties are being transformed. We are witnessing the emergence of multiple migration regimes, often in the forms of authoritarian 'states of exceptions', regimes of uncertainty and fluidity – in general, we are witnessing the emergence of regimes of lesser rights than those governed by human rights conventions and norms. These are being experimented and reproduced within and outside the EU borders.

Another feature of the current conjuncture is that we are witnessing new polarizations which have emerged as transformations of the old polarizations. Immigration, Islam and terrorism are depicted as interchangeable and immediate threats to 'our way of life'. Multiculturalism, often depicted as 'failed integration', is under attack by conservatives and liberals from the mainstream, many of whom have taken up the agendas of invigorated anti-immigrant populisms, racialized and illiberal politics. The increasing digitalization of the public sphere has facilitated dissemination, ultimately reshaping the debate in Europe and beyond.

Figure 2.1 *Number of international migrants (millions) by region of destination, 2000 and 2017*

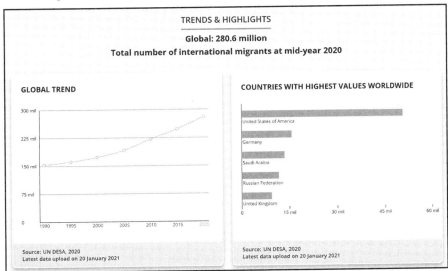

Source: 'International Migrants as a Percentage of Total Population by Major Area of Destination', *United Nations Department of Economic and Social Affairs*, available at http://www.un.org/en/development/desa/population/migration/data/estimates2/estimatesgraphs.shtml?1g1, accessed 9 September 2021.

Figure 2.2 *The trends of international migrants (millions) 1990–2020 and the countries with the highest number of international migrants, 2020*

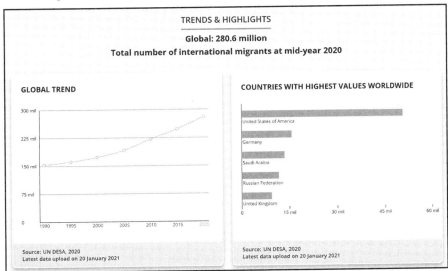

Source: 'Total Number of International Migrants at Mid-Year 2020', *Migration Data Portal*, available at https://www.migrationdataportal.org/international-data?i=stock_abs_&t=2020, accessed 9 February 2022.

Figure 2.3 *The global migrant population – stocks*

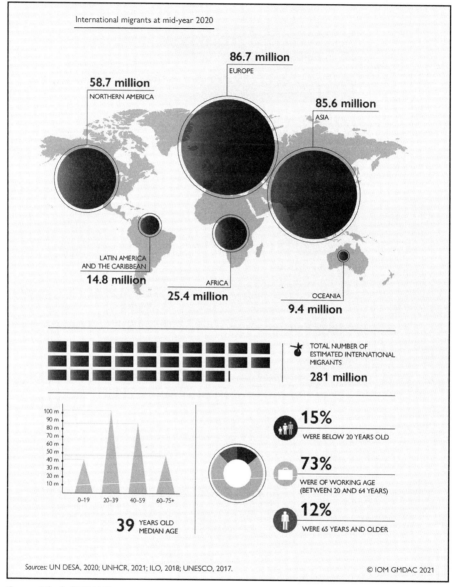

Source: Black (2021).[11]

Figure 2.4 *Total number of international migrants at mid-year 2020, distribution by country*

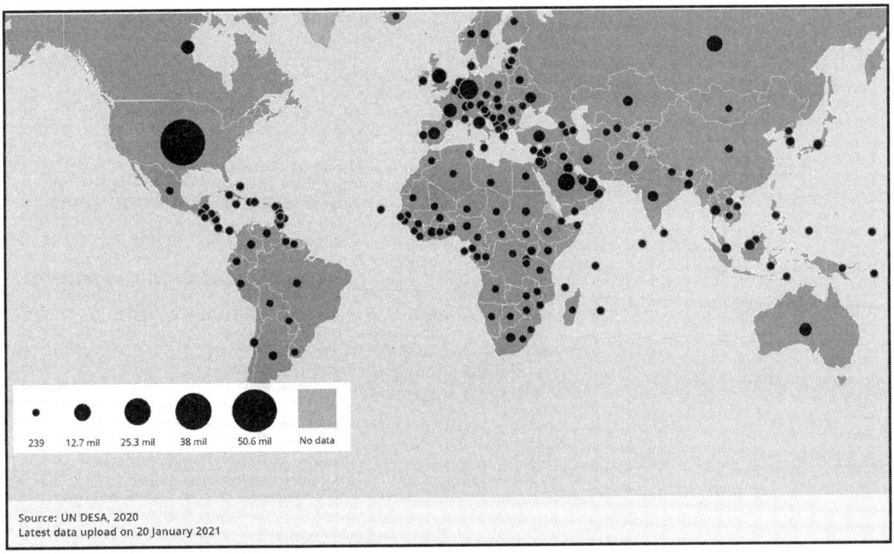

Source: UN DESA, 2020
Latest data upload on 20 January 2021

Source: 'Total Number of International Migrants at Mid-Year 2020', *Migration Data Portal*, available at https://www.migrationdataportal.org/international-data?i=stock_abs_&t=2020, accessed 9 February 2022.

Figure 2.5 *People forcibly displaced: 82.4 million*

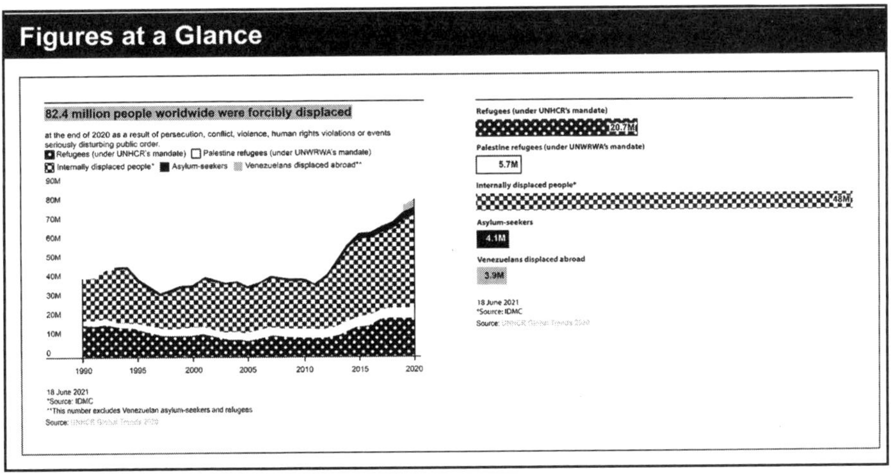

Source: Same as of Figure 2.4.

The challenge for social research is to establish the connections between national, European and global contexts which are historically connected. This is taking place within processes that are increasingly integrated within the EU debates and beyond. Despite efforts to stress the importance of dialogue of cultures, Huntington's (1996) so-called 'clash of civilizations' has become ingrained in global and political agendas as well as social debates. Moreover, the processes of securitization of national identity, whereby ethnic diasporas are construed as a threat to national identity (Huntington 2004),[12] have fed into the debates in most European countries. There has undoubtedly been *Europeanization* (i.e. connected to the EU integration project) and *localization* within particular national contexts of these broader debates. The debates took a concrete form in the context of the question of integration of migrants in the EU via the development of policies to integrate migrants, national action plans for integration, and other integration 'instruments' and 'toolkits'.[13] The logic of the 'clash of civilizations' is feeding into the perception and representation of those migrant and ethnic groups who are considered to belong to the 'other' side – the enemy camp – using ethnic, religious and cultural markers to differentiate and exclude them. Even those measures which are depicted as benign and positively aim at *integrating* migrants, diaspora and other ethnic communities by 'making room' in the receiving country for migrants to fit in, accommodate and adapt (Groenendijk 2004: 113) through alternatives senses of integration generate very different results in society. In fact, the current integration policy framework has 'diverse roles' in the EU context with various actors pushing for different agendas and tension between the security/identity agenda pursued versus the rights-based approach (Mitsilegas 2007). The most serious aspect regarding the subject of tolerance and acceptance as related to this chapter are the restrictive and exclusionary elements contained in the very notions of 'integration' (Groenendijk 2012; Kostakopoulou 2010a, 2010b). The integration packages as understood and implemented today often contain exclusionary, xenophobic, Eurocentric and ethnocentric elements, which pander to and reflect the current anti-immigrant public opinion driven by forces who want to exploit the latest economic crisis.

We are also simultaneously witnessing crucial transformations from the *realities* on the ground, which are related to the ongoing flows as well as the long-term presence of migrants from non-EU countries and from other EU members. Multiculturalism, multireligious practices and multi-ethnicity are a de facto reality that can neither be undone nor can we return to some status quo that existed before. Even more importantly, we are witnessing on the ground the emergence of new solidarities by non-migrants at the opposite side to anti-immigrant, xeno-racist and anti-Muslimism politics. It must be noted, however, that migrants are no uniform and homogeneous group, given the crucial class, gender, ethnic and power-related differentials at play. Characteristic of our epoch are processes of multiplicity, fragmentation and differentiation at all levels. Socio-economic class and status, gender, ethnicity, faith, sexuality and other modes of differentiation are affecting, and are affected by, social and economic policies, and cultural practices and attitudes in a system of differentiated inclusion. At the top end, 'elite' migrants are welcome. In fact, at the very top, a ludicrous global industry has been booming in recent years, as countries offer fast-track modes of acquisition of citizenship or residency to rich investors. However, the vast majority of immigrants do not receive the same warm welcome. At the lower end of the socio-economic spectrum, less esteemed and subaltern migrants do not have the same access to opportunities in Europe, as they are offered differential treatment with numerous obstacles in the path of their integration. The very terms 'integration' and 'multiculturalism' have become divisive and controversial political issues. Nonetheless, the presence of migrants is transforming spaces and belonging via the shared knowledge, affective cooperation, mutual support and care between migrants and non-migrants when they are on the move. The reconstruction of the ontology of the moving people is the mobile commons of migration which opens potentialities for different worlds.

We require a broader frame that contributes towards understanding the complex issue of migration and asylum from a political sociology perspective that draws on migration, border studies and critical legal scholarship, so as to enhance further research and debates in different empirical contexts.

CONCEPTUALIZING MIGRATION BEYOND THE 'SOCIETY-AND-MIGRANTS' APPROACHES

A major stumbling block in explaining and theorizing migration in society is how the object of *society* is defined. The definition of 'society' itself contains problematic assumptions that go to the foundations of modern sociology about distinct 'societies', their characteristics, features and boundaries. Yet, to this day, sociologists continue to fundamentally disagree on *what society is*, as the general basis of any institution or societal process, which is the subject matter of sociology, is hotly debated. The founders of sociology have properly maintained that there is always something in *excess* to merely adding up the individuals that make up society: the sum total exceeds the individual parts added together. This 'something', the *excess*, is the subject of disagreement. The issue cannot be 'resolved', particularly in this day and age, when for such a long time, thankfully, there has been no one 'orthodoxy' dominating the discipline of sociology and the social sciences at large. This is because of the disagreement between different schools of thought, perspectives and approaches, the fragmentation and multiplication of the social sciences, etc. Talk of the 'crisis of sociology' has been ongoing since the 1960s.[14] Even to this day, standard definitions of 'society' often assume that society contains some features considered to be essential elements defining the *differentia specifica* of each society. It is common to define society with reference to some notion of a bounded territory, i.e. corresponding to the unit of nation state. Society can be defined as 'a large group of interacting people in a defined territory, sharing a common culture' (Open Education Sociology Dictionary). Even sophisticated definitions which focus on systemic and structural elements of social relationships seem unable to escape from the limitations of 'bounded territories': Giddens and Sutton define society as 'a group of people living in a bounded territory who share common cultural features such as language, values and basic norms of behaviour' (Giddens and Sutton 2021: 7).[15] While this may make sense with regard to trying to read matters from the point of view of government policies and how the politics of migrations are shaped and negotiated within these territories, given the way polities are organized, it is highly problematic in trying to study and explain migration sociologically. Such approaches may also prevent us from seeking possible solutions that require a broader reading than perspectives within bounded territories. However, as many scholars have pointed out, there is something fundamentally problematic with the foundational assumptions regarding 'societies'. Migration studies are increasingly transcending nation state-centric models by locating matters within the broader context of regional constellations and integration processes, such as the EU, North American Free Trade Agreement (NAFTA), Gulf countries, Middle East, northern Africa, Euro-Mediterranean, South African Development Community (SADC), etc. Overcoming banal nationalism, sedentary bias and 'methodological nationalism' (Castles 2015; Castles, Hass and Miller 2014; Massey *et al.* 1993; Urry 2007, 2016)[16] are essential to properly study migration. The leading sociologist of the world system theory, Immanuel Wallerstein (2000), refers to the problem of the 'unit of analysis'.

The assumptions correspond roughly to the current world as a world of order, balance and equilibrium as the global norm, i.e. a functionalist social system which formed the basis of modern sociology. It is a world organized territorially as a system of distinct nation states which are 'naturally' somehow formed as 'settled' and 'resolved' as 'people in a given territory': it is more or less a world of order, territorially divided between sovereign states where people have exercised their right to self-determination. In this simple orderly schema, there is room for some imperfections and temporary anomalies as disequilibria in transitional periods of disorder. Thus, there may be some unresolved questions here and there, where some boundaries are disputed and some groups, i.e. peoples or nations, are claiming the right to exercise their right to self-determination (let us call this 'paradise' or 'Ithaca'). The schema then is made of distinct 'boxes', with some modifications from outside influences. The norm within each one of these 'boxed' societies is also one of order and equilibrium, unless they are in an incongruous and transitional phase that somehow, with possible 'fine-tuning' and manipulation by those in power within the society or with support from outside, will reach an equilibrium point of rest.

The era of restrictive migration came with the First World War, as the processes of migration faltered due to war. Then came the Great Depression, which halted migration, and then the Second World War. The interwar regime was based on restrictive immigration by most important receiving countries (including the USA). The movements of large populations then were essentially war-related, i.e. refugees and displaced persons rather than labour migrants (Massey *et al.* 2008). The current era is that of post-industrial migration from 1960 onwards, where there is a sharp break with the past: it is no longer an outflow from Europe to a handful of former colonies; immigration has become a global phenomenon. Castles, Hass and Miller (2014) describe the post-Cold War period as the 'age of migration'. Yet, migrants have been seen as something 'outside' to be 'integrated' within. Since the 1930s, 1940s and 1950s, the debates were dominated by the question of 'incorporating' migrants into the societies in which they settled via different social mechanisms: hence we have both sociological theories and social policies of 'assimilation', the 'melting pot' approaches and integration models, multicultural approaches, etc. On the other hand, based on the knowledge produced, an attempt was made to control the 'flow' of migrants, using essentially the 'hydraulics model', i.e. attempting to regulate and manipulate 'entry' into the 'closed system', assuming that we are living in 'boxed territories'. This is how economists tried to understand the circulation of money in different countries before the 'open economy'. These are the theories that were translated or integrated into policy. The most recent debates in the EU regarding the integration of migrants, or the more 'negative' approaches, as articulated in the US Presidential elections of 2020, are indicative. There is no doubt that they contain many of the social elements which are commonsense features regarding the adaptation and accommodation, as well as enabling the access, participation and belonging of migrants. Other approaches are used to control, affect the so-called 'push-and-pull' factors, send 'messages', etc., 'out there'. However, this schema is rather inappropriate in reading society, especially today. Also, it is often misleading and problematic in informing the world view, social and policing policy and assumptions about the world and its future.[17] This, by and large, leads to uncritically accepting the underlying assumptions which are simply passed on to new research projects, while the methodological flaws are never questioned. The way forward is to locate migration studies within a broader understanding of the transformations of society. While some theories of mobility have attempted to open up mainstream sociology to global complexity in the last quarter of century, producing the 'new mobilities paradigm' for the twenty-first century,[18] the problem is that we need to overcome the unit of analysis of the problem ab initio. This was already resolved and well-developed in world system perspectives from the 1960s and 1970s. Migration within the world system has developed further to address immigration in the world; it is certainly a superior theoretical frame at a worldly level to various globalization theories currently in vogue.

Sociologists have come some way to recognize and take up the challenges which affect many aspects of social life. The argument has been made for reading the mobilities as a key to understanding societies in the past, present and future, from the days of the founders of sociology, in different readings. Critical migration and border studies have shown that mobility is at the heart of the processes we are currently witnessing. Moving is not some marginal side-point in society but a crucial factor reshaping it. Mobilities are the means by which the 'social' is spatialized and embedded. It is the complex assembly of mobilities that together make possible different forms of social actions. This is illustrated in this chapter when discussing the implications and future of sociological agendas. The key is to unravel epistemological weight of mobilities in a sociological frame. Attractive within the 'new mobilities paradigm' is the reading that the world is in a *constant disequilibrium*, to be empirically studied, theorized and understood (Sheller and Urry 2006). As underlined by the late Zygmunt Bauman, in the world of 'liquid modernity', 'speed of movement has today become a major, perhaps the paramount, factor of social stratification and the hierarchy of domination' (Bauman 2000: 151).

Our argument, therefore, is that old theoretical sociological schemata cannot be fixed merely by 'adding on' the extras that would just 'fine-tune' any weakness in the system, as if we were to surgically stitch up a wound. What is required is not a serious reassembling of the sociological cannon but a reformulation of the nature of society, the social and sociology, i.e. another sociology. Various sociological theories – some as alternatives, others complementing each other – drawing on different empirical approaches deal with the causes of migration through various studies that examine the impact of migration on receiving and sending societies (Massey *et al.* 1993, 2008; Castles, Hass and Miller 2014, 2015). Most large countries have always been both migration receiving and sending countries. In today's crisis-ridden world, many societies which had been, historically speaking, predominantly sending societies may become receiving societies, and then become both sending and receiving countries.[19]

The issue of mobility is constructed as a 'social problem', as understood, managed, practised and operated in what Foucault called governmentality, or in one of his definitions as those techniques, strategies and rationalities by which society is rendered governable (Foucault 2008) and the kind of knowledge-power on what is considered to be the 'reasoned way of governing best and, at the same time, reflection on the best possible way of governing' (ibid.: 2).[20] In Foucault, these are designated as 'techniques of government' because 'to speak of a technique or art presupposes that the practice in question has been subjected to a certain degree of investigation, critical reflection and calculated refinement' (Walters 2012: 11–12).

Mobilities in this sense, and migration in particular, is a major sociological challenge, not only because migrants and migrations directly impact societies, but also because of knock-on effects and the broader, short-term and longer-term consequences. The reactions, ideas, knowledge and praxis of governance and social responses set in motion social, political, cultural and economic processes by far greater than the direct and immediate consequences of migration. Therefore, the study of these other societal processes is necessary not only to understand the rather narrow but increasingly more important field of migrants and migratory processes, but primarily in order to unlock key features to explaining and understanding modern societies and current and future trends in society. This chapter proposes a reading of migration in the context of global normalizations, deviance and defiance to provide us with the analytical insights to explain and understand these processes. In this context, a *global political sociology* allows us to address the questions of power, governance, bordering and surveillance, as part and parcel of mobilities. As William Walters (2015: 16) argues, Foucault's notion of governmentability is particularly useful in the context of migration and border studies: 'Governmentality affords a valuable perspective precisely because its understanding of power is not wedded to a static concept like the state, nor to any telos of transformation like global governance.' Migration is the most radical and powerful dimension of mobilities, as the transfer of humans, as groups or individuals, is both the result of social transformations and a major cause of further, often unpredictable, transformation (Castles 2015). However, migration must not be seen as unleashed processes of some kind of exogenous global force on to countries via borders. Whilst undoubtedly the current world order seems more unaccountable than before in 'the new architecture of global governance characterized by legal plurality and overlapping sovereignties [which] has facilitated a game of "passing the blame"' (Randeria 2007: 1) between international financial and trade organizations, transnational corporations, states and NGOs, in reality states are active shapers in the process. The so-called 'weak' states, which have significantly less power vis-à-vis 'strong' states, operating as 'cunning states' (ibid.: 2), make this argument in a different policy context with

India as the case study. However, immigration policy and practices in the EU are perhaps an even better instance for the notion of the cunning state which illustrates the point: 'Although inadequate, the state remains indispensable, as its laws and policies play a key role in transposing neoliberal agendas to the national and local levels' (ibid.). Immigration remains one of the most cherished bastions of state sovereignty even within the transnational EU structure. Rather than viewing weak states as mere victims of globalization or of hegemonic international institutions, the notion of the 'cunning state' provides superb lenses via which we may examine the globalized, regionalized and localized processes of immigration politics of control in the context of decoding the scripts of defiance:

> Whereas weak states lack the capacity to protect the interests of vulnerable citizens, cunning states show strength or weakness depending on the domestic interests at stake. 'Cunning' is a weapon of weak states, or, more precisely, of the stronger among subordinate states in the international system. It does not describe a characteristic of state structure or capacities but the changing nature of the relationship of national elites (very often in concert with international institutions) to citizens. The notion of a cunning state is thus a useful way to delineate a range of tactics deployed at various sites of negotiation where a shift in responsibilities and sovereignties occurs. By tracing in concrete cases how the state both appears and disappears, is constructed and dismantled through various kinds of practices of government, it seeks to understand how globalization – as a transnational apparatus, discourse and as a social reality – is (re)produced. (Ibid.: 3)

DEVIANCE, DEFIANCE, MIGRATION AND ASYLUM

The current historical moment has brought back into question the issue of the 'right to have rights'. This Arendtian idea was materialized into an established norm ultimately with institutional mechanisms for monitoring its effective implementation. Even though the first seeds of such norms and mechanisms were established by the League of Nations after the First World War, the moment that gave rise to rights relating to migration and asylum was in the immediate aftermath of the Second World War. After the defeat of Nazism and the experience of the Holocaust in the Second World War, in order to establish the new world order, an essential part of 'the normalization process' that ensued was the development of universal norms to regulate border crossings, asylum and protection of all those in fear of persecution, as defined by the Convention Relating to the Status of Refugees, the Geneva Convention (1951). After all, according to Article 1.1 of the Geneva Convention, a refugee is defined as anyone who:

owing to the well-founded fear of being persecuted for reasons of race, religion, nationality, membership of a particular political group or political opinion, is outside the country of his [sic] nationality and is unable or, owing to such fear, is unwilling to avail himself of the protection of that country; or who, not having a nationality and being outside the country of his [sic] habitual residence as a result of such events, is unable or, owing to such fear, is unwilling to return to it.[21]

The second line of protection for all those whose circumstances did not allow for protection as refugees was of course the Universal Declaration of Human Rights, which protects the universal rights of all humans. However, by the end of the twentieth century, large-scale encampment came to undermine the logic of universal protection of human rights, as the fight against terror is the ongoing legal justification for practices such as torture, captivity and pre-emptive assassinations (Agamben 2005).

The blurring of the line between refugees/asylum seekers and migrants is a poignant element of the panic. The imagery of people-crammed boats and emaciated migrants and adorned with TV commentaries of 'crisis', 'tragedy' and 'disaster' become points of vulnerability and panic. *Der Spiegel*'s pictorial depiction of Germany as 'a massively overcrowded boat' whereby criminal/migrants are responsible for the 'sinking' is but a manifestation of the mainstreaming of the foreigner/criminal equation. The full title of *Spiegel* reads: *The Onslaught of the Poor: The New Mass Migration* (Brinkbäumer 2007; Fekete 2009: 4). The deviant is depicted not only as the *surplus* population but as the *dangerous* population for society as a whole.

The issue is how migrant and forcibly displaced persons are socially and politically located within the notion of 'population', not in the abstract but in the current political and social context. We ought to examine how migrant and refugee groups are categorized as types of *surplus* or *excess* populations, how power is exerted over these populations based on the exercise of 'sovereignty' over a territory and how these impact upon rights. We address both aspects of these complex processes of the *encounter* under these conditions: on the one hand, these processes can be read as Althusserian *interpellations* as a result of being subjected to 'regimes of derogation' (Sitas 2016), 'states of exception' (Schmitt 2005; Agamben 2005), and/or other regimes of ambiguity, lesser or no rights. On the other hand, we must examine how the encounters under these conditions also generate processes of political subjectivization occurring as *defiance*, *resistance* and *solidarity* by rejecting and challenging being treated as surplus, via staging a dissensus (Rancière 2010a), and how this is facilitated by encounters, connectivity and the development of socialities with potentialities for different worlds. However, such a venture must be adapted to fit our sociological enquiry (Trimikliniotis 2020b). Moreover, it requires that we move beyond the encamped, marginalized and excluded refugees and migrants so as to address the wider societal processes characterized by fragmentation, unsettlement and broader societal transformations. The long-term effects of the shrinkage of political space (at an institutional level) as a result of the de-democratization and multiplication of states of exception and derogation of rights go hand in hand with the processes of racialization and exclusionary politics. However, this *shrinkage* of political space has widened the gap between the 'hardening' of institutional forces organized around state processes versus *broader* societal processes: on the one hand, we can observe that on the whole, many institutional forces have become harder, more conservative and in many aspects have shifted in the direction of xenophobia and racism, reflecting, legitimizing and pushing further in the same direction segments of a polarized society whose opinions seem to have moved in this direction. On the other hand, we can observe a move in the polar opposite direction by other segments of the population who both articulate and practise a radical solidarity in contrast to the state-institutional shift to the right. In this sense, the latter shift can be seen as broadening spaces for alternative socialities derived from alliances resulting from the encounters of various types of migrant and refugee populations deemed as 'surplus' populations. This is the result of neoliberal processes over the last forty years as practised by European states (and others in the Global North and those influenced by them) that have made the welfare states vacuous and ineffective, as well as policies of exclusion and marginalization of migrants, asylum seekers and refugees. These often take the form of a social-spatial displacement. Refugees and migrants have encountered other socially displaced populations with precarious, exploited workers and struggling groups, and are living examples of alternative futures in society. There is no consensus but societal dissensus unravelling. The production of this 'excess' resulting from the encounter is theorized as 'excessive socialities' (Papadopoulos, Stephenson and Tsianos 2008; Tsianos 2012) opening up spaces to transcend the states of exception, and derogation of authoritarian regimes and lesser rights not in the direction of postliberal de-democratization but its opposite of 'democratizing democracy' and renewed visions for 'real utopias'.

The findings of Georgiou and Zaborowski (2017)[22] are revealing of the processes of shifts of opinion within six months from July to December 2015, which framed the 'refugee crisis' as a 'migration crisis' to be managed in the way it is dealt with today. The European media reportage started with what the authors describe as 'careful tolerance', which reflected an attempt to 'balance between securitization and humanitarianism' (Georgiou and Zaborowski 2017: 10). The basic story is that 'Europe appeared to want to help refugees more than not but remained careful about negative consequences'. The second period is described as a period of 'ecstatic humanitarianism', which emerged in the aftermath of the photographs of the body of 3-year-old Alan Kurdi. In the last period from November to December 2015, there was a fundamental shift towards 'fear and securitization' after the November Paris attacks. From the emotional stories of 'saving refugees', the discourse shifted to address the 'negative geopolitical consequences of the migrant crisis' and the 'deep in shock' Europe. Eventually, the refugees appeared to be to be blamed.

What followed are various policy measures from the perspective of those in power to restore order in the European Union: reducing the flow became paramount, sorting out those who had entered the EU territory by 'managing' migration and asylum (Chouliaraki and Georgiou 2019). Chouliaraki and Georgiou speak of the 'the humanitarian securitization of European borders', which is based on contradictory and fluid articulations of networks of discourse through these multiple mediations consisting of muddled messages that include 'formations or voices of human rights, security procedures, and solidarity' which make up 'three relatively distinct domains of reception at the border: military securitization, securitized care, and compassionate solidarity' (ibid.: 4).

This is the context whereby the migration and asylum issue must be understood as both *management matter*, as well as a broader process that pertains to *political, ideological* and *social* issues. We must thus understand how the combined effect of population and immigration management and control impacts societies at large. Hence the migration and asylum issues are rearticulated well beyond the various modes and complex processes of management of migrants and asylum seekers. These issues become interwoven with the issue of control and regulation of migrant labour in ageing western societies, the results of integration policies and practices in the context of the economic crisis over the last decade, the ways this is dividing Europe, the rise in intensity and scale of terrorist attacks in many western cities following 11 September 2001, as well as the way migration increases politicized and polarizing societies.

Despite the fact that the flows of asylum seekers in the EU have significantly reduced since 2015, the migration and refugee question became a key issue in many election campaigns over the last five years. The migration debate seems to be dominating elections and politics in many European countries: the last elections in Italy, Netherlands, France, Austria, the Brexit referendum campaign, Hungary, Finland, Germany, Italy, Austria and Finland are illustrations of how it is a crucial issue to be studied and understood in the current conjuncture. On the other hand, we have some crisis-ridden countries where migration was not a hot political issue (Spain, Portugal, Ireland). It is however uncertain how the issue will play out in future elections, given the way it has played in all other EU countries.

Whichever metaphor is adopted, the central argument for the cycles of deviance approach we adopt is that there is a constant contestation manifested in the form of the institutional powers' use of *normalizing processes of ordering*, geared towards suppressing, curtailing and containing the *logics of disruption of the order.* Crises are moments when the normalizing is not working. In this sense, Max Weber's celebrated formulation of the state as the institution with monopoly right to use force, precisely to ensure that *order* is maintained, is the sociological and political foundation of Karl Schmidt's pinning down of the ultimate source of power of the modern capitalist societies: sovereign is the one who can proclaim a state of emergency or state of exception (Schmidt 1994; Agamben 2005). There are important colonial lineages to the current 'age of migration' (Castles, Hass and Miller 2014). First, 'modern' migration can be traced back to colonial times via its historical antecedents (chattel slavery, transmigration, indentured labour). Secondly, the current migratory systems are products of the colonial division of the world and the order it has defined and fought over since. Thirdly, the presence of 'colonials' in the former colonies and the immigration to the more 'developed' world (mostly former colonial powers) has created a multicultural setting within the North and former colonial powers which are redefining the world. So, while in the older days the colonists saw it as their moral duty to 'bring lesser breeds into the law' in the empires they ruled via exemption, during the 1960s, millions of ex-colonial subjects joined Greeks, Turks and Italians as migrant workers in the major European economies of the day. The formal welcoming of darker strangers has been reversed in Europe and the Americas as tides of racism and xenophobia are growing in volume. The growth of an emphasis on social pathologies, 'black pathologies' (Lawrence 1982), myths about 'black criminality' (Gilroy 1987) and the general 'migrant deviance' of darker strangers has resonated in the media and provides a threatened 'insider's' common sense. Papadopoulos and Tsianos may be correct in insisting that 'the spectre of migration will never become a new working class', but the spectral politics of the old *Communist Manifesto* are returning with a vengeance as 'the spectre haunting Europe' today (Papadopoulos and Tsianos 2013: 187).

Towards a Global Political Sociology of Migration and Asylum

In order to properly research the immigration and asylum issue focused on the European debates, one has to go beyond Europe to draw on global comparative contexts and influences. This is the old problem that Wallerstein (2000) referred to as a problem of the 'unit of analysis'. To properly explain the width and the process of a *global* problem such as the emergence of 'the new logics of expulsion', aptly described by Sassen (2014) as a 'savage sorting', one needs a global political sociology. And this despite the fact that expulsions are by definition taking place within a national territory to another, as processes legislated and enforced by national states in exercise of their sovereignty. This is a typical instance of an 'insertion of a global project coming not only from outside but from the inside of the nation', in what amounts to a reassembling of the spatio-temporal matrix of nation states (Sassen 2008: 381). Therefore, what is required is not a *global political sociology* displacing or negating national, regional or local migration and border studies (with sociology as its core), but a process which has begun transforming research in a way that combines national territorial specificities and sovereignties with transnational and global studies, in what is a genuine *global political sociology*. The idea is to examine these in the European, regional and global contexts as these are manifested at national and transnational levels, and how these operate as processes affecting institutions and the public sphere.

Moreover, the complexity of the phenomena of migration and asylum study will bring together several intersecting themes of the debates concerning migration and asylum at the level of political, ideological, social, economic and cultural discourses, which are transforming the public sphere and political institutions in European societies that appear increasingly polarized and divided. This requires that connections are made between four interconnected areas of study: (a) migration, asylum policy management and integration, asylum studies and citizenship; (b) studies on labour, precarity, social divisions and inequality; (c) political and sociological studies of movements, parties and organizations, particularly those examining the xenophobic populism and polarizations; and (d) legal and sociolegal studies of sovereignty, migration, social justice and rights.

What is required is a conceptual framework that brings to the fore the mediating factors connected to political discourses and ideologies to societal transformations over a subject that seems to increasingly influence and divide societies. This will be the basis to construct a theory in current understandings of the migration and asylum issue bridging migration studies and border regime studies, policy and management issues with the study of mainstream and marginal political institutions, parties and organizations.

Several recent events point to the necessity of dealing with the complexity of migration and asylum both as a *management matter* and as a *political*, *ideological* and *social* issue, and thus connecting various aspects from an interdisciplinary perspective. Developments point to the need for sociological explanations for transformations taking place at global, regional, national and local levels. There is an unprecedented rise in the numbers of asylum seekers in the globe, while migrant labour is increasingly required in ageing western societies. The numbers of displaced persons are likely to rise further. In Europe, after the invasion of Russia in Ukraine, the numbers of refugees have been massively rising: from

24 February to 8 March 2022, the UNHCR counted 2,155,271 refugees and estimates that there could be up to 4 million as the conflict escalates and the situation continues.[23]

Social scientists are called upon to creatively use their 'sociological imagination' (Mills [1959] 2017) in a manner that constructively connects the conceptual to empirical aspects of migration and asylum questions in the current reality that draws upon and properly integrates various disciplines. There is no doubt that with each of the scientific fields referred there is a vast amount of scholarship that has advanced to provide the basis for a global political sociology of migration and asylum. However, there are certainly gaps in the published literature, particularly in conceptual and methodological integration that properly unifies and connects distinct areas derived from different specializations. The division of labour and specialization often leads to a problematic fragmentation of knowledge as scholars within their respective fields often do not properly engage in a proper exchange with scholars from other fields. While the existing literature includes important readers connecting disciplines,[24] the disciplinarian specialization results in further fragmentation and specializations rather than encouraging the development of a genuine multidisciplinarian approach – the aim of a *global political sociology of immigration and asylum* would be to transcend this problem.

The goal of global political sociology would be to develop theoretically and empirically in a manner that connects the critiques of anti-immigration politics to the potentialities related to the emergence of alternative social imaginaries based on new forms of livelihoods. It is required that research critically engages with old paradigms of security, belonging and citizenship, labour and politics, to address migration and asylum as scientific dissensus, a fundamental disagreement in the current state of multiple crises.

SURPLUS POPULATION, MIGRATION AND SOCIAL EXCESS

'No registration, no rights', declared the outgoing President of the EU Commission, Jean-Claude Juncker, at the peak of the 'asylum crisis', in the context of justifying emergency responses, such as the 'hotspot approach', of the EU to cope with the crisis. This was no sociolegal analysis of a dilemma about accessing rights of refugees and migrants. It was a declaratory instruction, which essentially stated the following: 'If you are to claim any rights, you are obliged to register.' However, it does not stop there. The implication is that unless they register, i.e. go via the process of identification, assessment and decision by the authorities, they are subject to arrest, detention and deportation. The Arendtian 'right to have rights' passes through registration.

Sociologically and politically, the operation of refugee camps around the globe, outside and within the borders of the EU, is categorizing, sorting and interpolating these populations within populations as *surplus* populations. This takes us back to Karl Marx's critique of Malthus on population. Marx constructed the notion of 'relative surplus population', or the commonly used (and often abused) notion of 'reserve army of labour'. Marx attacked the Malthusian theory of population growth as developed in 1798 in *An Essay on the Principle of Population*, which examined the relationship between population growth and resources, concluding that population growth occurs exponentially. Malthusianism is not without followers today. Various modified versions exist, such as crypto-Malthusianism of the global overpopulation threat, which are combined with environmental and health concerns or overpopulation dangers for Europe connected with immigration from Africa or Asia. These, together with notions such as 'collateral damage' and 'states of exception', 'emergency' and 'scarce resources' and cultural concerns, are remoulding the socio-ideational landscape of policymaking on population and movement control. The analogy Bauman (2011) used in framing the debates for a regime of unequal rights and opportunities is appropriate here: those with power have the luxury to decide what 'eggs' to break so that we can have the kind of 'omelette' that pleases *their* taste.

The population debates, particularly the notion of 'surplus population' of Marx vis-à-vis Malthus, has been replayed throughout the twentieth century and is being replayed in the new millennium: it is now being used to debate the dangers of overpopulation in Europe by the kind of population in terms of ethnicity, culture, religion and culture.[25] In fact, overpopulation in Europe went hand in hand with underdevelopment in Latin America and other 'Third-World' regions in the first attempts to regulate migration at the global level with the establishment of the International Organization for Migration (IOM) in the early 1950s (Parsanoglou 2015; Parsanoglou and Tourgeli 2017). Beyond the neo-Malthusians, such as Ehrlich (1968) and Ehrlich and Ehrlich (2009), there is new impetus for Malthusian-inspired approaches which underlie much of the immigration, asylum and population debates. In his introduction to *Capital*, Ernest Mandel attempted to correct the false picture that attributed to Marx the so-called 'iron law of wages', which assumed an ever-increasing decline of the living standard of the working class who are assumed to reproduce *en masse* (Mandel 1976: 66). This is, according to Mandel, a crude population growth theory of wages which originated with Malthus and, via Ricardo, reached socialists of Marx's generation, such as Ferdinand Lassalle. Against this notion, Marx 'maintained a constant barrage of polemic'. Mandel illustrates this misreading of Marx which assumes that wages will inevitably be depressed due to the 'surplus population'. In fact, Marx had a sophisticated theory of the value of wages which is always mediated via the class struggle. Mandel summarizes

Marx's theory of wages as 'an accumulation of capital wage theory, in opposition to the crude demographic wage theory of the Malthus–Ricardo–Lassalle school', as products struggle in 'long-term movements of wages are a function of the accumulation of capital' (ibid.: 68). The population debates are relevant also to ecology, where the question of 'overpopulation' and drainage of resources on the environment typically depicts the populations of regions other than Europe as posing the most danger: 'excess population' in certain radical ecology and ecofeminist debates takes a Malthusian twist.[26]

Today we are witnessing a dangerous blurring of the demarcation line between displaced persons and migrants, not in the direction of opening up borders for all but in the opposite direction: closing borders and further restricting access to displaced persons (Sitas *et al.* 2014: 189–222). There is an abundance of interactive datasets and maps by the IOM recording arrivals,[27] estimated disappearances and deaths en route,[28] integration, detention, deportations, etc. According to the IOM ('Migrant Deaths and Disappearances',[29] 2021), since 2014, more than 4,000 global fatalities have been recorded annually on migratory routes worldwide. The number of deaths recorded, however, is only a minimum estimate because the majority of migrant deaths go unrecorded. Since 1996, more than 75,000 migrant deaths have been recorded globally. In the Mediterranean, since 2014, the estimated figure of migrant deaths and disappearances is estimated to be 22,931 persons by the IOM but the real figure may be much higher.[30]

Since the pandemic, violating the 'non-refoulement' principle and pushback to refugees in territorial waters have become routine practices. Numerous states are openly using pushbacks in the Mediterranean, violating humanitarian and refugee law (UNHCR 2020a). Italy, Malta, Greece and Cyprus, invoking the exceptional situation of the pandemic, are routinely using pushbacks on sea and land to deter and exclude asylum seekers. The trend in the mainstream media is to attempt to 'normalize' and treat these practices as 'legitimate'. Media headlines concerning the pushback of a boat with Syrians on 30 July 2020 arbitrarily use the terms 'refugees', 'migrants', 'undocumented migrants', even 'illegal migrants', which is legally meaningless and dehumanizing; the UNHCR has issued statements against the use of the term 'illegal migrants' (UNHCR 2020a). Pushbacks are illegal in international and ECHR law (Hruschka 2020). Even in times of crisis, the non-refoulement principle cannot be violated. As the UNHCR (2020a) notes, 'measures may not result in denying them an effective opportunity to seek asylum or result in refoulement'.

Differentiating between terminologies and categories is important because one of the fundamental principles of international law stipulates that refugees must not be returned to face conditions where their lives or freedom are at risk. A refoulement at sea, as well as the prohibition of disembarkation, endangers lives.

Pushbacks and obstructing disembarkation are illegal. If the government has concerns about the spread of the coronavirus, they can perform tests and place refugees in quarantine. The pandemic is no excuse for human rights abuses and for endangering lives (Racism Watch 2020). However, the pandemic has become the most convenient tool for states to violate international law by invoking exceptional conditions (Trimikliniotis 2020a).

Even prior to the deaths in the Mediterranean in 2015, the virtual images of people-crammed boats of persons fleeing were described by TV commentaries in terms of 'crisis', 'tragedy' and 'disaster', which were constitutive elements of the 'moral panic' generated. This was then depicted as more or less analogous to what is happening in Europe and each individual country: essentially a Malthusian overpopulation, depicted pictorially as a massively overcrowded boat, blaming migrants for 'sinking' the country. Even prior to the 2015 'asylum crisis' it was apparent that 'the deviant is depicted not only as *surplus* population but as the *dangerous* population for the good of society as a whole' (Sitas *et al.* 2014: 200). This must be understood in the context of 'a constant contestation manifested in the form of the institutional powers' use of *normalizing processes of ordering*, geared towards suppressing, curtailing, and containing the *logics of disruption of order*' (ibid.; italics in original).

We can schematically sum up a complex set of processes to develop a rudimental theory of 'surplus population' and 'social excess' produced by the encounters, in what we propose as a *sociology/social science of dissensus and encounter* as manifested in the current crisis. Crises ought to be read as moments where normalizing is failing, which result in authoritarian restoration of order by those in power through invoking a state of emergency or state of exception. These invariably mean imposing various measures that suspend basic constitutional and human rights norms democratically won in social struggles. Various historical studies demonstrate that the 'displaced person' and the 'migrant worker' have been targets of shrill moral panics, in the typical schema that Hall *et al.* ([1978] 2013) have so accurately analysed. These are well-known techniques where those in power, or those with the support of or at least with the acquiesce of those in power, often use fear and insecurity about who are treated as deviants (Sitas *et al.* 2016; Sitas *et al.* 2014). Appreciating both the continuities and the ruptures is crucial here, hence one can trace the colonial lineages via different processes and trajectories that take at least three forms:

1. Historical antecedents (chattel slavery; transmigration; indentured labour) with current practices of exploitation, marginalization, differential inclusion and exclusion, i.e. all based on different levels and types of inequality.
2. The current migratory systems are products of the colonial division of the world and the order it has defined and fought over since.

3. There is a multicultural setting within the North and former colonial powers which are remoulding societies as a result of the very presence of 'colonials' in the former colonies and immigration to the more 'developed' world (mostly former colonial powers). The formal welcoming of darker strangers has been reversed in Europe and the Americas as tides of racism and xenophobia are growing in volume.

This book and volume I (Sitas *et al.* 2014) have shown how social pathologies and myths about Black criminality have generated, by the general 'migrant deviance' of darker strangers, what is by and large a media-amplified and distorted threat, a kind of 'commonsense racism'. Of course, the relation between class, ethnicity/race, gender and migration is part of longer, rich debates ensuing since the 1970s and 1980s: identities are indeed 'ambiguous', as Balibar and Wallerstein (1991) insisted. Yet matters cannot be reduced to class, it is not 'all a question of class', nor are they exclusively or even primarily questions of gender or race but are in fact far more complex (Anthias and Yuval-Davis 1992). In the last two decades, scholars have attempted to bring 'intersectionality' and 'translocational belonging' to analytically explain the fluid and contested shifts which however retain the importance of structure (Anthias 2020). Scholars operating from the autonomy of migration perspectives (Papadopoulos and Tsianos 2008, 2012; Mezzadra and Neilson 2013; Trimikliniotis *et al.* 2015) have attempted to bring back social and class debates, but in radicalized forms.

This is the paradox here: displaced persons such as asylum seekers and others who are not recognized as refugees but with some other reason to remain (e.g., those with subsidiary and humanitarian protection), and in many contexts refugees and migrants with temporary status, are *potentially part of* the working class but they can be *potentially* excluded from being counted. In fact, large sections of these persons have different sets of rights: some are detained and incarcerated in detention centres or prisons; others are hosted in reception centres, often very much apart from the rest of city, sometimes far away from the urban centres; other times, they are in industrial places, abandoned by the indigenous working class or abandoned altogether in derelict or old military camps in disuse; some may be denied access to work or enjoy only partial access or are forced to work without a permit; others are deferentially included, for instance, on certain occasions some are used as a 'reserve army of labour', as cheap exploitable and exploited labour; in other cases they are simply detained pending deportation; on other occasions, they are simply abandoned, marginalized and excluded. With such a variety, this is truly an infinite reproduction of 'different forms of existence of relative surplus population', in the ways originally analysed Marx (1976: 794–97). Mezzadra and Neilson (2013), who insist on the 'multiplication of labour' in their 'autonomy of migration work' on cogent grounds, refuse to distinguish between different categories of migrants: they are seen simply as part of the process of the 'multiplication of labour' via the 'method of borders' and bordering the capitalist system. However, in the context of this book, it is essential that we sociologically, politically and legally appreciate the role and processes of categorization, and distinctions pertaining to the status and the positioning of people within the asylum and migration categorizations. It is essential that we take a critical stance against the fragmentation logics that may potentially further deprive these people of solidarity and commonalities, and from developing a common consciousness and praxis of resistance. However, it is essential to also appreciate the specificity of asylum and forceful displacement. Moreover, we can extend the ideas of *multiplication* as *forms of augmentation and reproduction* in the spirit of Marx's original idea of 'the progressive production of a relative surplus population' (ibid.: 781–94), which led to 'different forms of existence of existence of the relative surplus population', understood of course in terms of 'the general law of capitalist accumulation' (ibid.: 794–802). Besides, the meaning of 'refugee' and 'asylum' at the beginning of the twentieth century was rather different from the way it has been 'instrumentalized' since the 1950s in the current world system, the EU and the international law system at the dawn of the twenty-first century. We are witnessing processes whereby the multiplication is not only about labouring *versus* unemployed population but extends to other modes of existence, subsistence and reproduction in the spheres of the symbolic, the cultural and social life that further fragment and divide in multiple ways. While labour remains crucial and at the core of the accumulation processes, it would be misleading to *subordinate* everything to labour and deny other modes of subordination, exploitation, oppression, resistance and escape derived from the analysis of concrete situations. We are to move from abstract categories to concrete situations so as to avoid mechanistic approaches such as a dogmatic application of theory to concrete social reality. Approaches attempting to use Marxian concepts as if these 'concepts would coincide directly a description of the facts' and with 'the categories of sociology' are simply a non-starter, for we are aware that concrete situations are 'more historical and sociological "dense" and complex', and ignoring this amounts to an aberration and distortion of the basic method of scientifically relating 'facts' to 'concept', social reality and abstraction (Balibar 2015: 397–98). These distortions often lead to apologetics for anti-immigration policies and politics, such as Zizek (2016).

The treatment of populations who are otherized generates much greater *social, political and legal outcomes* and effects than *simply as labour*. First, the reality of precarity, for workers who have settlement rights but more so for the unsettled, spreads throughout time and spaces of living, 'exploiting the continuum of everyday life, not simply the workforce' (Tsianos and Papadopoulos 2006).

Second, they are taking part in the broader social reproduction processes and are the prime targeted populations experiencing, by default or design, the transformations of sovereignty, territoriality and citizenship, and their social and political consequences and long-term effects. These are part of wider experimentations in the context of liminal and precarious spaces. Moreover, the encounters with local populations, some in conflict/contest, others in generating antipathy, indifference or sympathy, some by common action and solidarity, are generating new transformation processes. We can thus speak of processes where groups deemed as *surplus* population are at the centre of producing *societal excess* that propels social transformations. Tsianos and Papadopoulos, when discussing the subjectivity of precarious workers, argue that 'an excess of sociability' cannot be properly 'accommodated by the three existing political forms without being neutralized and normalized' (ibid.). The processes that produce 'excessive sociabilities' are even more powerful when it comes to displaced populations. These are structured in the form of struggles, contestations and dissensus challenging the figurations of alterity such as slave, race, caste, migrant other, etc.: they are what Sitas (2016) calls 'freedom's blind spots' where the search for a 'balance' between freedom and equality 'was not inherent as a constitutive part of this so-called modernity – this emerged despite violence, massacres, genocides, bombs and technological wonders based on wars' (ibid.: 123) . There is a long global history that has taken different shapes and forms from the fifteenth century onwards where 'freedom and equality emerged as deviant notions, and emerged out of defiance and struggle'. Sitas's argument is that contrary to 'an enticing parable of unfolding freedom', the reality is very different: 'the real story of the majority world – the primordial encounter in the process of foraging, settlement and colonization'. He describes these encounters of inequality and force as resulting in 'regimes of existential derogation', whose 'racial derogation' is a necessary but not sufficient condition. 'The Other was never an equal will: the Other was seen as a non-person and therefore exterminable; the Other was seen as useful and therefore enslave-able; the Other was seen as a non-us and therefore excludable' (ibid.: 125–26).

From the categories generated as apologetics for plunder and slavery, to classification and codification of difference, to the first category of people deemed to be surplus people, right through to slavery and rejected migrants, Sitas speaks of 'their dialectic of freedom' as 'one of withdrawal, abjection and exclusion' (ibid.: 125). It is essential, however, not to stop here as if it is the end. Sitas connects the struggle of 'the non-us and . . . therefore excluded' to bring matters to date: 'migrants and immigrants, refugees, unwanted minorities, colonial subjects in the colonial motherland (until 1974 in Britain) to the more contemporary forms from Filipino domestic workers and housekeepers to larger and larger refugee cohorts' (ibid.). This is 'the process of articulation and praxis – in transforming material and symbolic conditions, in addressing the sources of suffering, fear and meaning' by collectively responding and insisting on reimagining and recreating the 'we' by articulating and locating 'the horizontal bond that binds us all' (ibid.: 126). There is a way out of Adorno's labyrinth of the dialectic of freedom after the Holocaust, 'to address the "waste products and blind spots that have escaped the dialectic"' (Adorno 1974: 15). Drawing on Thompson (1974), he powerfully argues that 'we must save those moments of emerging self-definition from history's condescension', which does not stop with seeking to safeguard and enshrine formal equality in the constitutional and legal texts. This is the very context which 'impels people to mobilize through such classifications to achieve a semblance of equity'. But it does not stop there: 'in formally abolishing the institutional props that sustained it in law, it cannot do much as such categories and discriminations proliferate in all the planes of sociality'. It is here that new struggles for implementation and new frontiers for imagining begin.

This is illustrated in the volatile shifts of European media reportage, first from 'careful tolerance' towards 'ecstatic humanitarianism', and then the fundamental shift towards 'fear and securitization' after the November Paris attacks (Georgiou and Zaborowski 2017: 8), as the unfolding of a classic moral panic story in society where the digitalized media has accelerated, further distorted and expanded the original moral panic schema (Cohen 1972). However, we can see that while the flows of asylum seekers in the EU have significantly reduced since 2017 to the levels of 2014, the politics of the 'migration-and-refugee' crisis have not subsided but is intensifying. This has solidified trends that existed before, namely, the refugee and migration issue has generated a major political and ideological cleavage in many European societies. In many EU countries, as well as countries bordering or acceding to the EU, the migration and refugee question has become a crucial issue in election campaigns over the last years and is likely to be a major issue in the next elections.

HISTORICAL CATEGORIZATIONS OF SURPLUS POPULATION PROJECTED ON TO SURPLUS MIGRANT POPULATIONS

In the modern era, the categorization of people who are defined as surplus and expendable people, using different justifications, stretches back to the seventeenth-century story of the Black slave, but then was extended to the 'first peoples' in the colonial context (Sitas *et al.* 2014: 52). A significant impetus of the spirit of much of international human rights norms is based on recognition of the wrongs of the past as a result of emancipation, liberation and anti-colonial struggles in the nineteenth and twentieth centuries: these are by and large inscribed as condensations of historic struggles, if we are to extend the Poulantzian logic as a 'condensation' of sociopolitical struggles and Rancierian struggles of 'staging a dissensus' of those uncounted to be counted. Of course, these victories of being counted do not finish with the symbolic victory of recognition but are only new beginnings for struggles. However, the colonial encounter has shaped the wealth, boundaries and peoplehood of Europe and its borders today. Does this colonial encounter speak to the current immigration policy and politics? Does it resonate with the rise of the new far right and anti-immigration waves in Europe and the North in general? Today's identitarian nativism as expounded by the new far right is about reassertion of confidence, the realignment of the European forces of the right is about reasserting and reclaiming the pride of past glory, and denialism is about colonial atrocities and how much of the current global problems are related to colonial and postcolonial relations. However, it extends well beyond that. The colonial logic about 'the deviant other' is very much inscribed within European logics of controlling the crowds at large, and in particular the control of migrants via immigration law and border policies: restricting free movement and 'escape' is the key (Papadopoulos 2008; Mezzadra and Neilson 2015; Trimikliniotis *et al.* 2015; Trimikliniotis, Demetrioun and Stavrou 2016), while also projecting on to the unwanted migrants the same sort of capacities, i.e. surplus, primitive, deviant and thus removable. In the study on the cycles of deviance (Sitas *et al.* 2014: 110), it is discussed how certain behaviour turned into 'existential deviance'. The first element related to 'their relation to nature and to land as pastoralists or hunter-gatherers, or both': the fact that they were 'primitives', 'pagans' and 'tribal' was the justification for rendering them 'surplus people, surplus to requirement and they were most certainly inassimilable "others"'. They were simply 'natives as primitive and removable' who could be 'cleared off the land' (ibid.). The same drive and arrogance that designated the colonial expansion to justify the lands abroad as *terra nullius*, Latin for 'no man's land', now designates the population as 'surplus': their existence is rendered insignificant as if they are nothing and nobody, for they 'do not count' in Rancierian terms – first in the Americas and then in Australia, their territory was simply 'terra nullius' to be grabbed (ibid.).

The colonial lineages of the current 'age of migration' as 'modern' migration can be traced back to the colonial time via its historical antecedents such as chattel slavery, transmigration and indentured labour. In any case, the current migratory systems are products of the colonial division of the world and the order it defined and fought over since. Therefore, the presence of 'colonials' in the former colonies and the immigration to the more 'developed' world (mostly former colonial powers) has created a multicultural setting within the North and former colonial powers, which are redefining the world. During older days the colonists saw it as their moral duty to 'bring lesser breeds into the law' in the empires they ruled via exemption; during the 1960s, millions of ex-colonial subjects joined as exploitable migrant workers, the major European economies of the day. In the twenty-first century, particularly after the 2015 'asylum crisis', the populations from the colonies are deemed surplus, exploitable, potentially deviant and removable, with the upsurge of racism and xenophobia across the globe (Sitas *et al.* 2014). Cheap labour meant high profits, but also acted as a check on labour demands. During the period of economic growth, migrant labour was welcome to produce wealth in the leading industrialized nations; later in the 1990s and early 2000s, in the European periphery such as the southern European countries, migrant labour was cheap labour for servicing tourism, domestic work, and low-status, low-paid jobs that most locals would not do at those wages (Anthias and Lazarides, eds 1999; Triandafyllidou and Gropas 2014). However, this drastically changed as people were defined as 'parasitic surplus populations to be sent back to their home countries' (Sitas *et al.* 2014: 245). Moral panics about the nation state losing control and failing in its role as 'boundary keeper and norm enforcer' within its sovereign territory became more regular and appeared to resonate with disillusioned populations, in a desperate effort at 'policing the crisis' (Hall *et al.* 2013). The signs of the new 'cycle of deviance' that might result in authoritarian solutions eroding democratic rights were there from the new millennium: 'illegal immigrants, asylum seekers, refugees and other categories of unwanted mobile persons are an intractable nemesis for the contemporary state' (Sitas *et al.* 2014). In this context, the potential for another possible world is there because there is the necessary critical mass and the experience drawn from the rise of multiple social movements providing real, living alternatives with social imaginaries that can be built on new civility, autonomy, tolerance and solidarity. A world in crisis is where 'fixers' and 'agents' of change are pushing in opposite directions; such a world is a space of polarization, contestation and dissensus.

CONCLUSION

During the pandemic crisis, the EU overall, as compared to 2015–16, had fewer numbers of asylum applications. Yet, there is an upsurge in anti-refugee and anti-immigrant politics as the new far right is capitalizing on fear and new states of exception are emerging, often leading anti-vax mobilizations. As many countries are blocking routes, and with new and different conflict zones as well as the continuation of old conflicts, some border countries of the EU are facing a larger numbers of applications. Many asylum seekers and migrants do not want to stay in or have not chosen these countries as their destination, but their routes have been blocked. Forced migration leads to fleeing of the masses as today's 'globalized world' or 'world system' is facing unprecedented crises: wars, conflicts, environmental crises, authoritarian regimes, oppression and impoverishment.

The only acceptable democratic response of civilized societies is to welcome and protect these refugees, integrating them equally into society, and not to exclude, repel or expel them. However, we are witnessing new colonial pockets on the EU's south-east border, illegal mass refoulement by land, sea and air, new forms of incarceration and de facto refugee detention, and an effort to externalize and extra-territorialize border controls. With the old 'march-of-progress' modernization theory, one would have expected the gradual demise of anti-immigrant discourse and racist ideologies in democratic and 'developed' societies. Yet, state and non-state institutions, and large segments of the population, seem to be endorsing anti-immigrant discourse and racist ideologies, and there is an effort to create a hostile environment to avert, deter and expel all migrants without differentiation. The pandemic crisis has provided a golden opportunity for invigorated anti-immigration policies, ideologies and practices to create an even more hostile environment for migrants and refugees. But, as discussed in this paper, anti-immigration politics are strongly challenged and there is resistance as we are living in the era of dissensus: the pandemic and post-pandemic mobile commons are the heart of these forces and realities of solidarity, resistance and the social imaginaries that envision transcendence of borders, sovereignties and national citizenships, and thus transformation of society as we know it.

Migration, i.e. geographical mobility, is sometimes depicted as 'one of the processes cascading across the interlinked systems' that various writings depict as 'catastrophic' – others are energy, food, water, governance (Urry 2016: 54). However, warning against the dangers of 'catastrophism' which is part and parcel of the dystopias currently in vogue may obscure the potential for alternatives in the world ahead of us. The rise in global inequalities in income and development acts as a boost to migration; so too the rise in wars and conflicts and disasters, development and global change. This however requires that we address a number of theoretical and methodological issues. Migration as a mass population movement is made up of many aspects which can work in parallel at the same time, sometimes in contradiction and symbiotically at other times. It has a dual function as both part of 'the order of things' (i.e. metaphors of 'safety valve' in capitalist accumulation, profits and wages) and a part of *disorder*, as it causes turbulence, trouble and can unsettle societies, setting in motion transformation processes whose direction and extent are often difficult to predict. There are systemic factors which constantly generate restriction to rights, barriers, borders and fortresses. The movement of populations causes constant turbulence and disruption of order; it alters social relations as the encounters between people cause unchartered transformations. The encounters between migrants and others unleash processes which are uncharted, unrated and uncertain. Another sociology would then develop not only a critical mobility and border regime paradigm, but a new kind of 'sociology of the encounter' just as Althusser spoke of 'philosophy of the encounter', i.e. an 'underground', 'unique' current of 'aleatory' materialism. The focus is thus on the *excess, the surplus* produced as a result of migrant encounters that are also very much a part of the production and reproduction of populations which are characterized in terms of being somehow 'lesser', 'sub' and 'under'. Finally, any future research agenda for another sociology must examine the broader consequences and effects of migration itself. We a need a broader sociological enquiry that looks beyond the immediate issues of managing migration, 'policing the crisis' and being blinded by the different securitization agendas. The implications and short-term and longer-term effects of the responses to immigration issues are often felt afterwards. However, they are often patterned, and with the insights, discipline and tools of the social sciences, they can be rendered predictable. At least, we can begin to think of these effects and consequences.

We have discussed some of the common failings of reading migration and society in many mainstream studies, and then sketched out some of the crucial elements for reassembling a *critical sociological reading of migration as a social phenomenon*. We have argued that this is best understood in the context of *mobilities* rather than perceiving migration as an exogenous force that enters 'society' from outside. Migration is very much part and parcel of the processes of global transformations, in a world possibly in a permanent state of disequilibrium rather than a mere transitional phase. This will allow us to uncover the bases for *another sociology* that is properly rooted and empirically documented in social reality. The research programme and general research agenda regarding migration as stated above is premised on this logic.

NOTES

[1] This can be traced back to Platonic elitist thinking from his *Politeia*.

[2] The present author has developed and used Rancière's *dissensus* in a number of sociological and sociolegal research papers in the past (Trimikliniotis 2012, 2013; Trimikliniotis and Demetriou 2016).

[3] J. Rancière, 'Racism: A Passion from Above', *MR Online*, 23 September 2010, available at https://mronline.org/2010/09/23/racism-a-passion-from-above/, accessed 20 December 2020.

[4] Fidesz stands for Fidesz–Magyar Polgári Szövetség (Fidesz–Hungarian Civic Alliance). 'Fidesz' itself is an acronym for Fiatal Demokraták Szövetsége (Alliance of Young Democrats) (Nagy 2016: 1041).

[5] The author, who is also a legal scholar and trained lawyer, recognizes the importance of retaining the distinction between 'asylum' as *forced* migration and 'migration' as more general movements of populations, which become political issues when they become 'transnational'

(i.e. crossing borders). However, this distinction is not relevant for the purposes of this chapter, without adopting a conflation of 'migration' and 'asylum' as if it were one and the same, as is often framed in political contexts today.

[6] See *Migration Data Portal*, available at https://migrationdataportal.org/?i=stock_abs_&t=2017, accessed 12 April 2018.

[7] International Organization for Migration, *World Migration Report 2020*, 2019, available at https://publications.iom.int/system/files/pdf/wmr_2020.pdf, accessed 20 December 2021.

[8] 'Asylum quarterly report, Third quarter 2017', 12 December 2017, available at http://ec.europa.eu/eurostat/statistics-explained/index.php/Asylum_quarterly_report, accessed 20 December 2021.

[9] 'Statistics on Migration to Europe', European Commission, 10 December 2021, available at https://ec.europa.eu/info/strategy/priorities-2019-2024/promoting-our-european-way-life/statistics-migration-europe_en#asylum, accessed 9 October 2021.

[10] The zero draft of the Global Compact for Safe, Orderly and Regular Migration was adopted by the Heads of State and Government and High Representatives at a meeting in Morocco on 10–11 December 2018. See 'Global Compact for Safe, Orderly and Regular Migration: Zero Draft', Global Compact for Migration, 5 February 2018, available at http://refugeesmigrants.un.org/sites/default/files/180205_gcm_zero_draft_final.pdf, accessed 9 September 2021.

[11] J. Black, *Global Migration Indicators 2021*, International Organization for Migration, Geneva, 2021: 25, available at https://publications.iom.int/system/files/pdf/Global-Migration-Indicators-2021_0.pdf, accessed 9 February 2022.

[12] Huntington (2004) castigated the west's diasporic and increasingly multicultural cities. In this context, national identity is being threatened by the 'global Islamic conspiracy' and the Latino communities in the USA.

[13] For critical reviews, see Pascouau (2012); Pascouau and Strik (2012); Trimikliniotis 2012; Kostakopoulou 2010a, 2010b.

[14] There has been a long debate – on and off since the 1970s – on the subject. See Michael Burawoy's presidential address to the American Sociological Association in 2004 (Burawoy 2005).

[15] This is a very popular and influential introductory text which has grown massively in size and complexity since the first edition appeared in 1989, until its latest ninth edition into a text over 1,081 pages long.

[16] Castles (2015); see also Bakewell (2007) and Goldin, Cameron and Balarajan (2011). The 'sedentary bias', i.e. the assumption that being sedentary is the human norm and movement is the exception, is something that has been predominant even in migration studies.

[17] Castles (2015) illustrates that much of sociology and the social sciences in general and policy research perpetuate such schemata via various ways in which political elites incorporate the social science and research community: 'Political elites have (often over long periods) constructed national models for managing migration and ethno-cultural diversity, with social science often an integral part of this process of construction. Such models range, in the case of our fieldwork countries, from the official Australian acceptance of multiculturalism as a necessary aspect of a nation built through immigration, to the South Korean principle of maintaining cultural homogeneity as an essential basis for social solidarity' (Castles 2015: 11).

[18] Urry (1999, 2003) developed his 'global complexity' as a tool that explains such transformatory processes as mobility, migration; he locates the current transformations relating to the

emergence of the global, the use of metaphors such as networks and fluids, social orderings and power-relations, and examines the implications for theorizing the global.

[19] This is found within the EU; see Trimikliniotis, Demetriou and Stavrou (2016), which examines the mobility of young persons, i.e. within the 25–35 age group, exercising their free movement rights.

[20] See Walters (2012); Mezzadra and Neilson (2013); Kutlay (2014).

[21] UNHCR, *Convention and Protocol Relating to the Status of Refugees*, available at https://www. unhcr.org/3b66c2aa10 m accessed 9 September 2021.

[22] Based on an extensive study of mainstream press coverage of the crisis in the days immediately after three sets of key events (twenty articles per newspaper in a period, 1,200 articles analysed in total) associated with the crisis: (a) Hungary beginning to build a barrier along its border with Serbia; (b) the publication of Alan Kurdi's images; and (c) the November 2015 Paris terrorist attacks.

[23] 'Refugees fleeing Ukraine (since 24 February 2022)', Operational Data Portal: Ukraine Refugee Situation, UNHCR, https://data2.unhcr.org/en/situations/ukraine, accessed 9 March 2022.

[24] See, for instance, Fiddian-Qasmiyeh *et al.*, eds (2014); Juss (2013); Chetail and Bauloz (2014); Triandafyllidou (2016).

[25] See, for instance, Caldwell (2010); Murray (2018).

[26] For a critique of Malthusianism in the ecology debates, see Bellamy-Foster (1998).

[27] 'Flow Migration: Europe', IOM UN Migration, available at https://migration.iom.int/ europe?type=arrivals, accessed 9 September 2021.

[28] 'Missing Migrants: Global', IOM UN Migration, available at https://missingmigrants.iom. int/global-figures/all/csv?eid=13513&return-url=/, accessed 9 September 2021.

[29] 'Migrant Deaths and Disappearances', *Migration Data Portal: The Bigger Picture*, 7 May 2021, available at https://www.migrationdataportal.org/themes/migrant-deaths-and-disappearances#recent-trends, accessed 20 December 2021.

[30] 'Migration within the Mediterranean', Missing Migrants Project, 31 December 2021, available at https://missingmigrants.iom.int/region/mediterranean, accessed 28 November 2021.

3

Scripts of Resilience and Defiance in Migrants' Everyday Encounters

Ari Sitas, with Dina Dabo and Sepideh Azari[1]

'The life I am living in SA for now is not my life.'

'Oh yes, I told them I am political refugee? Yaa, I ran away from hunger.'[2]

If we follow the work of a variety of scholars on the everyday our migrant subjects are confronting, the commonplace and mundane reality – the *quotidian*, as Henri Lefebvre phrased it – are depicted as the drudgery of the everyday in capitalist society, its institutions and streets (Lefebvre 1971, 2002). From the Zimbabwean miners killed underground in the Free State – a province where formal mining has been abandoned, miners who are made to work by illicit syndicates, to those trapped in outrageous conditions on farms in South Africa's hinterland, the drudgery experienced would be obvious.

The argument here runs as follows: the precarity of migrant workers creates conditions of existential unease, a sense of displacement, degendering and disvaluation, which provide the context for unique recoiling and refracting agencies around strategies of survival. The migrants' sheer existence in these often hostile spaces produce defiant forms of self-understanding and behaviour. We shall return to these defiant forms in the last pages of this chapter.

Most of them, whether they work in closed settings like mines and farms, or open ones in the urban informal economy, would be working six days a week, a few even seven days a week. As Etheldreda (Zimbabwe: 2), a farmworker from Zimbabwe, tells: 'When it comes to having free time, I really don't have free time, I am working every day because I am trying to make the money; especially weekends because there is more money on the weekends.'

Work or better 'jobbing' is incessant for all of them: from making beaded or wire artefacts and selling them on street corners to sourcing Chinese commodities to sell at traffic lights, to working on farms or for the tourism and hospitality industry as chefs and waitrons, to providing services within a specific niche community or providing haircare as barbers and hairdressers to making *enjeera* bread for other Ethiopians so thoughts and tastes of 'home' may endure, we could be describing untold hardships. From running a small shop selling cloth in Durban's CBD to walking the streets to sell goods from the rest of the continent, their labour constitutes a key component in the production, exchange and circulation of goods. It is a harsh reality as Pierre (DRC: 4), who has a better deal than many as a barber, asserts: 'I feel pain. There is no one who is happy when you are a foreigner. You are a slave of that country.'

The story of a Rwandese refugee like Simone is more than typical:

> In view of the job that we get here, remember that we are foreigners, as they usually remind us, so we do not need to complain. We do those jobs because we have no other options. If you try to evaluate how hard we do our jobs, like being exposed under the rain and all the hardships we encounter while on duty, truly speaking you would realize that there is no association between our wages and the service done. Another thing is that since all the companies are governed by local citizens, all opportunities which occur are given to them. Foreigners do not benefit from any advantages. (Rwanda: Simone: 3)

Getting a job is hard, very hard (Nigeria: Samantha: 6, Abebi: 7, Adaego: 8, Wole: 9, Japtha: 10, Aderinsola:11; Zimbabwe: Etheldreda: 2), and when you do, the hours are long and arduous:

> The working hours [are] long – seven to seven every day and the money was little. . . . We worked every day but I felt the hours and the conditions put my life in danger and also I was pushing myself a bit too much and my body was straining and I just felt this was not good for me. (Zimbabwe: Joseph: 12)

But 'that is life', whether you are from Zimbabwe or from Ghana. 'For me,' Kwasi (Ghana: 18) asserts, 'I don't have day off, it's only Mondays; even Mondays I open but I don't open early but I don't have a day off for that one, I cannot lie to you. I work here every fucken day. He he he.'

The few who are employed in manufacturing too complain about wages: 'It's not enough because the job that I'm doing is hard job. I'm working with the chemical, I am a machine operator and I am getting that salary seven thousand. My salary is supposed to be maybe twenty thousand but because I am a foreigner I need the job' (Joseph: DRC: 3). However, even a wage like that is quite utopian for most foreign workers. Echoing many others (Rwanda: George: 11; Mozambique: Philemon: 3, Graca: 4, Raul: 5, Sarah: 6, Patricio: 7, Ernestina: 8, Romelus: 9), as Philemon (Mozambique: 3) states, 'In this country is not easy to get money. Seven thousand? Never. It means you suppose to work very hard to get some money. You can work all the times per week and you cannot make enough.'

The story of Joseph (DRC: 3) is also typical of the service and hospitality sector where many are caught in perpetual overwork:

> You cannot find an easy job here in SA [South Africa], like the job I was doing at the restaurant, I used to stand the entire day, and they will allow you one hour break which is too short for such a hard job, when you get home, you already tired. The second job was even harder and could kill because the restaurant was busy and you have to keep moving around. Once has to be strong here, if you are lazy, you are going to suffer.

Stories of hardship and resilience constitute a mosaic of 240 migrants, both men and women, from countries of the African continent, interviewed in and through a broader study of migration conducted in the three major urban areas of South Africa: Johannesburg, Cape Town and Durban.

There is no doubt that the last two decades have witnessed a major change in the division of labour between the city and the country that has created manifold social problems and tensions. In the broader African context, structural adjustment programmes in return for further development aid have created vast strains in villages and rural life. Whatever the strains, the result is vast *migrations* within national borders and beyond them. Furthermore, these recent migrations involve 'de-peasantization' but not 'de-ruralization': the land as an economic activity is being abandoned but not the rural homestead. In fact, most remittances still reach the village in the countryside. Thus, where livelihoods are earned are not where livelihoods are spent.

Also, the capacity of agrarian production in feeding the population of the rapidly growing cities has been declining. By implication, the recently urbanizing populations are experiencing untold forms of discrimination and exclusion, and are facing a lack of social integration/assimilation on the margins of urban life.

We often called ourselves 'fence cutters' when we started working on this project. The humorous description became a palpable reality as the project unfolded. How could such a multinational ensemble of researchers and activists not be fence cutters when studying the 'third African diaspora'? There were respondents and researchers from Nigeria, Ethiopia, Democratic Republic of Congo (DRC), Uganda, Mozambique, Ghana, Somalia, Zimbabwe, Rwanda, Tanzania, India and South Africa. Our subjects come from countries that accounted for 86 per cent of Africa's population, or around 1,15,33,08,000 people!

We believed quite quickly that we had to snap our own mental fences, understand how arbitrary the Berlin-created colonial borders were and how they needed to be cut and what pliers would be appropriate. We also needed to come to terms with one of the world's most important macrostructural challenges as Africans, among other population groups, have been on the move. They have been populating other spaces and turning the wheels of economic life in new ways. If we look at the processes at hand without a discourse of human rights or trope of victimhood, there is quite an overflow of emotion that is being articulated by them: apart from economic hardship and economic compulsion, our participants lived through wars, civil wars, half of them encountered and/or lived in refugee camps (humanism's new prisons) and all except the Ghanaians experienced political strife. And then they experienced xenophobic attacks in South Africa, and their networks tell them they are experiencing xenophobic attacks everywhere: in Europe, Asia, Australia and the Americas. Accounts are filled with descriptions of violence and shattered hope.

There are marked differences in the South African experience from the European. Most important are two facts: asylum seekers or migrants are not placed into camps to start with (they are, if deemed to be deportable, later); furthermore, although targets of xenophobic violence and attacks, there have been no active mobilizations by any political party nor an attempt to create a moral panic about them, save from unmandated officials, local councillors and, in a recent case, from the Zulu king and his royal house. This does not mean that governments and officials are not making their lives very difficult indeed. Most share deep feelings bordering on existential unease, displacement and devaluation. After the xenophobic attacks of 2008, much has been written about the sources of such violent responses by locals, and remarkable policy work has been undertaken by many universities and research centres. What we are concerned with here is to trace the contours of disquiet. We will let their voices and scripts enunciate the parameters of this disquiet and the way they attempt to negotiate their dignity in an everyday sense.

EXISTENTIAL UNEASE

The phenomenological field of the 'everyday' was and is punctuated with the 'shocks' and the exhilarations of the 'urban' that Walter Benjamin described, but also by an existential unease about the potential for violence wherever the migrants moved. 'When the xenophobia came, they were just looting things from foreigners, most of them. And most of them, like the locals, believed that foreigners were taking their jobs. Of which it wasn't like that' (Zimbabwe: Etheldreda: 2). But even if it was not like that, 'they would beat you anyway'. Marta (Ethiopia: 13) emphasized further, 'Since I came to South Africa in 2003 it [violence] happened twice. . . . It is discrimination of foreigners and the South Africans wanting foreigners out of their country.' Whether such shocks were experienced directly or indirectly, the existential unease would form an emotional backdrop woven out of personal experience or stories from others who have had such experiences. As Jonathan (Zimbabwe: 19) stated, '. . . looking at the way we treat people when they visit Zimbabwe and the way Zimbabweans were treated during that time of xenophobia . . . but it really got into me so much even though I'm not one of those people who were persecuted'.

Violence was and is ever-present: Miguel (DRC: 8) recalled immediately how 'at the Johannesburg Park Station, they just attacked me and my friend, told us to go to our country, beat us and took our stuff'. Marcia recounted:

> I was coming from the church and there were a lot of people on the road. Someone touched me from behind. I thought it was someone who knows me, but when I turned I saw a fifteen-year-old boy and he had a black knife and he demanded my phone and I gave it to him. He also took all my money. (Zimbabwe: Marcia: 17)

Giorghis (Ethiopia: 1) added his own woes: 'I lost some of my friends because of crime and I won't forget. [A] couple of years [ago] I lost a lot of money because of xenophobia. That's my negative experience.' Paulo corroborated that above all, the experience of violence and its threat is overwhelming:

> Sometimes my neighbours go to my room and take my things while I am working. They know that I am Mozambican; they do that because I am not South African. If I was South African they wouldn't do such things. Sometimes they take everything in your room and it means that you have to start again from scratch. (Mozambique: Paulo: 19)

Had Abdul (Somalia:12) had a camera, he 'would take pictures of a lot of difficulties that I went through in SA because I remember some of the times when I was hijacked, I remember another time when I was robbed and I remember another time one of my friends was killed in the shop'. Pierre's (DRC: 4) pain facing the South African worlds of Pietermaritzburg, Durban and Pretoria after having run away from the troubles in the Eastern Congo or Marta's (Ethiopia: 13) loss amplifies the 'unease'. They add with a tone of despair: '. . . and we are Black!'

Samantha gives his/her opinion on the xenophobic violence perpetuated against foreigners in South Africa; s/he says:

> . . . for direct answer I would say the whites, the white colonialists have perpetuated this xenophobia action because when you . . . when I first came here, the Blacks here, sometimes the Blacks were telling me they know South Africa to be in Africa, but they don't know any other place in Africa. They think other places is just forest or abandoned land, I mean they are something else and people live in bushes and people don't have good life, and there's war and people are being killed in other

places. Therefore, they are very much better here and all these are put in them by these white colonialists. So instead of them seeing the white colonialists as the threat, they see you the foreigner who come in to try and earn a living as a threat. That's how I see it. Because looking at the economic structure of South Africa, you realize the whites are the most endowed and economic wise they are controlling the economy. Because they own the companies, they have everything, everything that's good in South Africa is for them. (Nigeria: Samantha: 6)

'Ah,' states Marcia (Zimbabwe: 17), a more recent border-crosser from Zimbabwe, 'sometimes your complexion determines you are a foreigner also. Yaah complexion, language, sometimes you fail to speak their language, also determine you are included also or you are foreigner.' There is very little that would distinguish Enoch (Zimbabwe: 6) from locals, the south of Zimbabwe is populated by the same 'Scatterlings' from the difecane[3] exodus during the formation of the Zulu kingdom. On the other hand, perhaps a Somali would be lighter in complexion and a Rwandan, darker. Paulinio, a United Nations' verified refugee, found the streets and what awaited him more than overwhelming:

I live in city, or town, because it is more secure here. I find it difficult for people to stay in townships if they do not speak local South African languages. So you have to live in places where you feel secure, and are really accepted, especially residing with people, who do not mind about your identity. It is quite easy to feel safe when you reside in town. We tried the townships . . . never again. (Rwanda: Paulinio: 14)

Some of the most intense feelings around their treatment were expressed by Somali migrants: 'This word makes me sometimes cry,' asserts Amina,

it is a word that sometimes makes me think, it is a word that makes me sometimes restless. I can sometimes say the person, or the group or the company who came with this idea of xenophobia are people beyond human limits. I can say they are extra-terrestrials. This word, xenophobia, is a word that brings a lot of feelings to the foreigners, especially the Somalis. (Somalia: Amina: 18)

Ahmed agrees:

Phobia means fear, and 'xeno' means people whom you don't know. So, it is fearing the people they don't know, because they don't know us, we came to their country. So, the definition of xenophobia is 'hatred of the Black or people you don't know'. Those guys don't know us, we came to their country, and they attacked us because they don't know us. (Somalia: Ahmed: 3)

Majid adds his take:

I think xenophobia is showing the foreigners that they don't belong to SA and cannot do anything in SA; all they are supposed to do is to leave the country; they are not human beings, they are not Africans; we are not the same as the South Africans, we are not human beings like them. It is like we are nothing good next to them, we are useless. That is what xenophobia is because you just can't come and burn someone's shop, and take them to the police and sometimes burn him to death, it is inhumane, it has never happened in this world. We are not even animals, animals are being taken care of; we are nothing to them. They don't even have the feeling that we are humans. Xenophobia shows to me that we are totally different from them and we are not human beings and they are. (Somalia: Majid: 5)

Amakwerekwere, fraudster, thief, are some of the derogatory names African migrants get called on a daily basis. The prevalence of everyday discrimination, alienation and prejudice is high and intense:

Yeah, it's like there's something in . . . it's like you have a mark on your forehead, you can't remove that mark but you are living with that mark. There is nothing you can do. It's painful for someone to come to find you say 'you are not a South African, you are a foreigner' so you feel pain. So, it's always pain every day. (Beatrice: Rwanda: 1)

A considerable number of respondents perceive xenophobia to be a thing, a doing, a practice, a verb. It is something that is done. The explanations for why 'they do xenophobia' range mainly around scarcity of jobs; that other African working-class migrants are taking jobs from South Africans; African migrants steal/take South African women; the government is not providing for poor South Africans and this frustration over poverty fosters hatred. Hate is a commonly used term/experience that the interviews express: 'They do it because they don't want us in their country and that is very clear' (Rwanda: Simone: 3). 'Xenophobia is a bad treatment by South African people against migrant people. Hate the migrants. They do it because they said we are coming to disturb everything, interfere with their ways of living. But all these have no basis; it is just an excuse to discriminate [against] others' (Menan: Rwanda: 6).

Back to Somali voices that were most affected by attacks in the recent period:

The worst was to have somebody killed in front of me. The xenophobia where more than 1,000 people invaded your property and took what you had worked very hard for, for years and to see old people being hurt. . . . The continued killing of Somalis and you will see and feel how much these people dislike us, how they speak to us and how they treat us. . . . Xenophobia is something which happened to all foreigners and it happened in Johannesburg also, Zimbabweans are affected and so Somalis are part of that and the Somalis are the ones who lose everything in the process. They accuse other foreigners that they took their jobs and that is where it began. (Azad: Somalia:14)

Paulo from Mozambique corroborates in his own, more distant way:

> I can't say that I have been victim of xenophobia as it is, but once, I was beaten here in Protea Glen, because I am not South African, and I had some money with me. I think that is also xenophobia, but it is not like what happened in 2008, because people here in Protea Glen hate Mozambicans; South Africans who are not working hate Mozambicans. Once I was beaten because I was a foreigner and had some money, they call us *Makwerekwere*. (Mozambique: Paulo: 19)

Marcia ran out of words to describe her contradictory predicament:

> Xenophobia is like . . . I don't want to talk about that because it is like . . . when I think . . . some memories about long time back ago, it has been crazy for me; it is like . . . that was not good for us. Because, you think of going back to Zimbabwe, but you tell yourself, 'when I go to Zimbabwe, I have got a problem in Zimbabwe, they chased me away, I am running away from those guys.' It is like you are squeezing yourself, it is like your life is like, you are losing in Zimbabwe, and you are not South African, for South Africans you are taking their jobs. So, I don't know how I can try to express it, but it is like . . . (Marcia: Zimbabwe: 17)

Avicena (Ghana: 15) also emphasized the importance of understanding the language issue: '[South Africans] come, they speak their language and they call us *Amakwerekwere*, that was our name, it is very sad in South Africa. Even yesterday I took a taxi the driver was saying the same thing. They call us names, they don't respect us at all, we are nothing.' Fabrice added her own bit of unease:

> My first experiences were to get used to languages. These languages are very hard to learn. So, I was very concerned with communication, getting used to the weather conditions, familiarize with the city, as the cities of where we come from are very small, but South Africa cities are big. (Rwanda: Fabrice: 10)

Language is used as a tool of exclusion, discrimination and barrier. This is particularly experienced in public transport, on the streets, in the workplace and in hospitals.

The unease is particularly marked in the townships: 'everyone knows that Khayelitsha is risky and those guys who rob people are certainly criminals' (Somalia: Azad: 14). 'I live in cities for safety reasons. It cost a lot, but it is secured than in townships. I only resided in the city' (Rwanda: Fabrice: 10). 'The people who are staying in town are safer than the ones in the townships' (Somalia: Saad: 19). 'You see white area is right and peaceful because where we were staying there were a lot of *tsotsis* [street-level criminals], that is why we moved to town' (Kojo: Ghana: 11).

Indeed, ironically, those in more closed settings who have to dig and harvest whilst living on farms might have less of such an unease, even though the conditions might be grim. As Etheldreda, a Zimbabwean farmworker, states: 'We are all squashed. I think it will surprise my family, I think they will be so surprised because they never thought SA to be like that. . . . They will be surprised to find out that the conditions that we live in are very difficult, sometimes more than in Zimbabwe' (Zimbabwe: Etheldreda: 2).

Such an existential unease would have another dimension: the belief that they are observed and are seen to be the 'other', and that the looks – the 'gaze' in a Sartrean sense (Sartre 1974: 257 ff) or the racial gaze as in Fanon's work ('Look ma, a Negro!' in Fanon 2008: 37) – whether it is a fact or fiction as Blackness in South Africa is the commonest of hues everywhere, exacerbates a sense of difference, of estrangement and a sense that one's body, one's appearance, carries signs that enhances danger (Nettleton and Watson, eds 1998; Zerubavel 2006). It would have a major influence on how individuals present themselves to others so as to manage the impressions made and also to have a sense of control of the outcomes of social interaction. 'I can explain them in a sense that, in South Africa, race plays an important role in ranking people. Therefore, I have realized that in some places it is difficult to reach people, simply as not being a South African, but because you are a foreigner' (Rwanda: Beatrice: 1).

> The road could be filled with about one thousand persons, but the police would come to you specifically and ask you for the papers. Those could be amongst other pictures, which I could capture to show how life is very difficult to foreigners, who reside in South Africa. Imagine to be selected among thousands of people due to your physical appearance or other features and be asked for a paper. (Rwanda: Santa: 19)

As a product of colonialism and apartheid, South Africans are preoccupied, if not obsessed, with phenotypes. Being able to distinguish and group people according to ethnic, racial, national, religious and linguistic groups forms part of everyday preoccupation. Simultaneously, these acts are part of demarcating spaces of belonging and access to resources. Those who fall outside the spaces of belonging do not have immediate rights or access to inclusion and resources.

It would define, using Goffman's (1969) dramaturgical language, how they perform, use props, control their scripts, enter settings, use expressions, create front stages and back stages; how they are managing otherness. When asked how he chose to interact with his South African customers, Ameena, a Somali migrant, responded by saying, 'They [South African customers] are very happy when we speak to them in Xhosa language. We must struggle a bit to learn the language'

(Somalia: Ameena: 16). The alternative is harsh, as she confirms: 'Every night one or two Somalis are killed and robbery takes place. The government doesn't know about it. It is done by criminals.' Another Somali trader adds: 'The shop has been looted, and one of the boys working was shot and became disabled, the boy has gone back to Somalia, hence we vacated and ran away for our lives' (Somalia: Ayesha: 10). Yet another adds, 'But now, it is not wonderful that you might be shot because you are a Somali; people call you a Somali, *Kwerekwere*. You can't pass in the street, in a corridor, in a parking, everywhere; you become like hunted' (Somalia: Amina: 18).

Demarcation of the alien body is through nationality, ethnicity, language, hair texture, body odour, body language, sense of dress, physical features. Each defined group of the 'other' is assigned particular stereotypes, permanent markers of truth. This is particularly marked in relation to officialdom: migrants from the rest of the continent frequently report negative experiences with the Department of Home Affairs and the South African Police Services. The police are notoriously known for their ill treatment of foreign nationals. Incidents where police officers arrest migrants, tear ID documents, physically abuse arrestees and demand bribes are almost expected to be part of everyday life for working-class African migrants.

Below are a few selected excerpts on experiences with the police:

You know, the police see you on the road, ask you so many different kinds of quest-ions. You find that they ask you some questions you don't even have an answer for. And not as if that they are there to do their job or that they are there to protect you, as that should be one of the primary objectives of what they should be doing. The police is just there to even to intimidate you just because you are a foreigner. [. . .] Discrimination of the police, I think that the police have seen that the foreigners are a source of income . . . whereby they believe that they arrest you on the road, you know? You know, many people, many foreigners, Nigerians, so to say, wouldn't like to be having an argument with the police. Talking, you know, it seems as if they are wasting their time. So many of the people tend to give them whatever they have so that they just have their way. So when the policemen see you on the road, you are Nigerian, they think that you are an ATM, a walking ATM. So they want, just want to withdraw money. They just want to take money from you! (Nigeria: Afaro: 15)

The police is the worst department the other night the police break our door beat us all without any reason and when we ask what was the reason they slap at our face, kicked us with their boots and told us, '*Kweri-kweris* shut the fuck up'. (Somalia: Salah: 15)

I can still recall it in a very negative way. I cannot understand how the one who is presumed to protect people would do things that he did. . . . Another experience is related to the police. Bearing in mind the high level of crimes which occur in South Africa, it has come to my attention that only being a foreigner in South Africa increases the risk, due to the fact that you do not [get] fair justice; as being accused of crimes, you have not committed. In other words, the fact of being foreigner might lead you to be judged without being presented to the court. . . . In Durban, the police arrested me for the same issue of papers. This happened during those days that I had to go every morning to the Department of Home Affairs for papers. I told them that I was still waiting for the next day's appointment with the Department of Home Affairs. They could not believe my statement, and they took me back to the Home Affairs. I waited there for the whole day, until the offices closed and I had to go back there the following day. That is how I faced the police in my first days in South Africa. (Rwanda: Beatrice: 1)

The police stopped me before, and they were very nice until they found I was Nigerian and they became harsh. When they notice you are from Nigeria they change the strategy they used to deal with you. (Nigeria: Japhta: 10)

Not receiving assistance from the police when reporting robberies and other criminal activities is common for many African migrants. Similarly, during xenophobic outbreaks, migrants report no assistance from the police.

I can tell you for example what happened to my friend. Imagine someone being held at gunpoint and there is CCTV evidence that they tried to kill him and when the police came they did not do anything, they said you are a foreigner. They said you are a foreigner, they can't do much. To me it's xenophobic because their action because this person is a foreigner is not the same as what they would do if someone's daughter was involved who is South African. (Zimbabwe: Aaron: 10)

Yes, police – they don't like us at all, for them 'migrants' means like a rubbish; for instance, one day in Johannesburg policeman with a uniform asking me a paper and I asking who he is he showed me his police ID and then I give my asylum paper; he cut in pieces my permit and took me to the Yeoville Police Station [in] Johannesburg . . . he asking me money and I refuse to give him that's why this happened. (Ethiopia: Yonas: 15)

'So everywhere I went like I have been to the Home Affairs, public hospital and the municipality office and in all those places priorities are given to the natives' (Ethiopia: Zala: 20). His compatriot Khalil (Ethiopia: 5) added about the police's treatment of him as a foreigner, saying, 'They [the police] are always treating me badly, I don't know why, for them refugee is not a human being.' Fabrice (Rwanda: 10) expanded on this:

Yes, it was the issue of papers. These South Africa police, when they see a foreigner, they immediately associate him with an illegal person. When they see, they start searching you; if you do not have it, maybe you forgot it, they just put you in the police van. If you do not have money to bribe them, you are more likely to spend two or three days in prison.

The mere theme of police behaviour creates a discordant chorus:

So many of the people tend to give them whatever they have so that they just have their way. I didn't have any problem with them; the only problem is that to get the papers took me a little bit of time, because to be recognized as a refugee took me about four years, because some of the officials from the home affairs like money, you have to give them money so that they can approve your file. I didn't use the money, so that took me about four years. Besides that, to open the business was not a problem. (Zimbabwe: Marcia: 17)

Much of this unease and the violence that always feeds it happens in the commute from home to work, on the trains, buses and minibus taxis (Ghana: Avicena: 15; Somalia: Saad: 19). Whereas Somalians may look slightly lighter than locals, the same kind of encounter is shared by Ghanaians and Rwandese:

If you meet with one Black person and when he/she speaks to you in Zulu and you cannot answer that on its own becomes a problem. Even if you try to ask what he/she means in English that becomes like insulting him or her. This shows that the person is telling you that you do not belong here. (Rwanda: Beatrice: 1)

Fabrice elaborates:

For instance, in the taxi if someone asks me something in Zulu and I reply that I don't understand it, that on its own becomes a problem and source of harassment. Even if you try to explain it in English, the person will not want to hear you any more. In they view; they think that everyone is a Zulu, which is wrong. All Black people cannot be Zulu. We have thousands of tribes, maybe they problem is that they do not travel and understand other people and different cultures. They have so much discrimination. (Rwanda: Fabrice: 10)

From the neighbourhood where their kids are not allowed to play with local children (Rwanda: Jacques: 17) to even the mosque where Ghanaian Muslims experience prejudice (Ebrahim: Ghana: 19), discrimination is rife. Alienation and exclusion are the words that come to mind as Aaron explains:

I feel excluded even within my neighbourhood. My neighbourhood is made of people from different countries. As a result, there is a lot of discrimination, especially when they realize that you are a person from another country. They often keep distance from you, and suspect you all the times due to your origin. (Rwanda: Aaron: 18)

Maria continues:

> When one starts to engage a conversation with them in English, it seems that they are disgusted. In general, they do not like foreigners. We just live with them, because there are no other options for a refugee. A refugee is always a refugee, so there is nothing more to do about that. Personally speaking, I can tell you that we do not have a good relationship with local South Africans; and that is not good at all. (Rwanda: Maria: 13)

Beatrice (Rwanda: 1) explains further: 'But there are some problems from sides, foreigners and locals, there is no love from each other. Sometimes, you can live with a neighbour but you will never hear none of them saying hello and [even them] being bored to find out the neighbour is doing.' 'It really worries me', says Aruna (Rwanda: 2). She adds that there is no exclusion *per se* 'but the attitude of some people is not very good'. Majid (Somalia: 5) adds that locals see them as subhuman: 'Xenophobia show to me that we are totally different from them and we are not human beings and they are.'

> In this country, the only people who worry me most are local. Local South Africans can be aggressive when they hear you speaking different language from their mother tongue; they become arrogant, violent and start swearing, as well as mistreating you. The only people who mistreat others because of being foreigner, are mostly local. They do not like foreigners. (Rwanda: Fabrice: 10)

There is also a third element to such 'unease' and it is touched on by quite a few postcolonial urbanists who try and understand the dynamics of cities themselves, replete with nouns that allude to instability, energy, cacophony, improvisation, 'superfluity' and 'excess', in the words of Achille Mbembe (2008), about Johannesburg. Most of the descriptors and concepts are attempts by researchers to name difficult and intangible processes and are rarely derived from the perspective of those who navigate through them. Black working-class South Africans in Durban have used more Zulu-centric metaphors like *iFuku* (state of confusion, chaos) or biblical ones like *uBabeli* (Babel) to describe Durban's inner city, and this is described so in a context where the ethnicity and language of the majority caught in this cityness is Zulu.

'I used to live in Philippi,' Esther (Zimbabwe: 15) emphasizes, and adds:

> there was so much of shooting there and also there was a lot of mugging. You could be mugged and no one would even lift a finger, especially if you are a foreigner, your phone can be taken, you can be body searched, your bag can be taken and no one cares and I used to be very scared.

The reality or stories of xenophobic violence, the imagined or real mark of 'otherness' and the pressures that come from post-apartheid urban spaces are crucial in framing an 'existential unease' that is shared trans-ethnically among foreign migrants. What seems common amongst all the narratives is the feeling of being discriminated against by African brothers and sisters in South Africa. Paulus communicated vividly this sense of restlessness:

When I first arrived in South Africa, I could not imagine seeing people walking without shoes, or people wearing dirty clothes. However, when I first saw them, I was shocked. That was strange to my expectations of South Africa. Another thing was the people here. It looks like everybody is busy, rushing with hours. Unlike in my home country where people get sometimes to chat, socializing and joking, what I have noticed in South Africa is that every time people are in a hurry, running and busy all the times. Actually, that had impressed me a lot because people in South Africa know how to manage their times. (Rwanda: Paulus:7)

Finally, nationality plays a role in the ways in which prejudice, hostility and discrimination are experienced. South African perceptions of stereotypes shape the way in which African migrants are perceived and treated. Zimbabweans are often viewed as border jumpers who come here to steal jobs. Nigerians are conceived of as criminals, drug dealers and fraudsters. Somali shopkeepers (Spaza owners) are seen as a threat to local business and consequently experience high levels of robberies and violent crimes. Refugees and asylum seekers from the Great Lakes are viewed as burdens on scarce state resources.

From the Nigerian interviews, it is evident that the respondents are perceived as fraudsters, drug dealers and as untrustworthy. It is not only the general public that directs these types of stereotypical prejudice towards Nigerians; structural discrimination and police harassment follow the lines of these stereotypes.

The way them are treated, the way they call you names, the way they talk to you, you know, the way they being so mean, arrogant and even at school sometimes, bullying. Pupils like, sort of like, you know you expect some of these things probably maybe from the white but you find it more from the Black people. They see that you are different, 'go back to your country', you know and again it's that if you are Nigerian, they think that every Nigerian on the road is a criminal like the moment you identify yourself as a Nigerian, they see. . . . Because I am Nigerian. Just because I'm a Nigerian, they tell you that everything about a Nigerian is fake. Everything you do is suspicious, you are even guilty before you're even investigated or anything, you know . . . you understand. (Nigeria: Afaro: 15)

Violent attacks, criminal acts and what are often generally termed as xenophobic attacks are most often directed at Somali shopkeepers and Ethiopians.

After I worked for three days, shooting started. The boss went somewhere and left me alone. The thieves came in at the back door and I ran away. They took everything. This was not the only time it happened. It was continuous, there were robberies for about a month. They came back every day. We called the police but they only responded after three hours. We opened a case which was closed again and no further investigation was done. One day three guys came to me and asked me to bring them meat. I realized they were criminals and told them I won't sell anything to them. They starting shooting me so I ran to my neighbours. They vandalized the place. They broke the water pipe off and the shop ran full of water. I called the police. They only opened a case and made no arrests. That's when I decided not to work in the Black area any more so I went to Worcester but things were not better. Guys came into the shop, pointed a gun at me and demanded money from the till. I opened the till, they took everything and hit me with the back of the gun. We reported it to the police but no arrests were made. A friend and I then opened a shop but after three days the same thing happened. People again took everything. They beat us and warned us that next time they will kill us, so we suspected there were South Africans who owned a shop next to us who was behind the attacks. (Abdul: Somalia: 10)

DISPLACEMENT, DEGENDERING, DISVALUATION

Why displacement? It was key for all respondents to be 'homing' but always sensing displacement in the very act. Leaving a home, finding a tentative home, leaving that home, looking out for less 'unease', has most of our respondents on constant move. We are told that whereas Johannesburg offers better prospects for disappearing from the official radar, it is experienced as a harsher homing space. Enoch (Zimbabwe: 6) explained how difficult Johannesburg was, 'Yeah, so we decide to come to Cape Town because the police wasn't a big problem there.' There were too many raids for papers and passports in Johannesburg. He had heard from his networks that Cape Town was less aggressive. Marta (Ethiopia:13) moved to Durban: 'When I was in Johannesburg we could not go out and work and stayed in our place for three days with no food because we were scared of any and many danger.'

Even in Cape Town, finding a living space in town was elusive. Goodwood had spaces rented out to groups of migrants but they were closed down, then five young compatriots moved to Khayelitsha and lived together in a shack. Giorghis (Ethiopia: 1) chose Durban because of security concerns: 'Durban is safe than other place . . . most of villages and locations are not safe.'

Thomas narrated:

They are always asking us money for nothing they use to demand money; they call it a 'business'. Personally, I'm tired of that, totally they are not helpful. . . . Every three month I have been robbed once since I came here in SA. But when you are here in SA it's like a sport to be robbed. For themselves, they are scared of each other, the South Africans. They are scared of each other so what about a foreigner, it's a walkover. So, it depends, because someone can protect you but it's only Jesus. (Zimbabwe: Thomas:1)

He continued to narrate the harsh experiences of being displaced from his home country, yet feeling unsafe in his new-found home in SA: 'So to a foreigner it's a walkover. So, if a South African is even scared of a South African what about a foreigner, it is a walkover.' According to Fabrice (Rwanda:10), language is a major barrier for homing: 'I find it difficult for people to stay in townships if they do not speak local South African languages. So you have to live in places where you feel secure and are really accepted, especially residing with people who do not mind about your identity. It is quite easy to feel safe when you reside in town.'

Beatrice agrees:

It was difficult, especially in terms of communication with the local people. You would require you to speak their mother tongue, Isizulu, and if you spoke to them in another language, it was a problem. That was a serious problem. So, wherever you could go, you had to use sign language in order to communicate with them. It was very challenging. (Rwanda: Beatrice:1)

If the sense of displacement is a strong pressure, so is the desperate attempt to establish new gender roles and relationships. Moving out of your ethnic niche is hard and when you do, there are many issues to navigate, as Marta found out:

. . . like maybe if you have got money or anything. Like maybe, in other words, another experience that I find out that if you take, like, maybe a girl from South Africa, South Africans they don't like foreigners to take their women. Maybe you are a friend to another South African female, they don't like that. Even if you are friends but they just think maybe you are dating they will come for you. (Ethiopia: Marta: 13)

Most people like Marta want to live in enclaves with their compatriots; it guarantees peaceful relations and a more comfortable family life.

But of course, quite a number are with either South African male or female partners. Pierre is married to a local. When asked if he was happier than his compatriots, he laughed and added:

When you've got South African wife or what, that is love. We talking about love. Love and experience of life is not the same things that we are talking about because when you get love, doesn't mean if I'm get South African who love me so which means I can be South African or I will be a South African, no. That one it was because of love, that's why she love me. That's why we are staying together. But it is hard. (DRC: Pierre: 4)

The workplace is pivotal to their experience of pressures. We have already alluded to the fact that they work hard and work long hours. Thomas recounts:

I have my day off but I can, I don't want, because in the saloon when you have a day off is the day the customer coming. So, but I've got my day off . . . if it was a job like you have a full salary but they don't pay us in salary, they pay in commission. If it was in salary I can have a day off but now it's you pay the more you work and the more you wage. So which I say that day you go home and that day there are customers so you losing your money so that's why I'm not taking off. (Zimbabwe: Thomas: 1)

The workplace is a site of exploitation, but also of networking: migrants on the streets and those in repetitive and supervisor-driven work are in a constant search for something better or are helping others find something better. Teresa (Mozambique:11) is a hairdresser. She found her job through connections that her sister cultivated at church. There she was introduced to her future boss, a Cameroonian, who obliged. Networking continues at work because hairdressing is a job that allows for conversations and the exchange of useful 'titbits': 'I have clients who speak Shangaan, Zulu, Ndebele Xhosa and even Portuguese. There are some Mozambicans who come here also for make-up.' Through her job she has helped lots to find other jobs – usually bar work, housework or waitron work.

The experience of networking at work is also echoed by Pierre, who is a barber:

. . . because you know when you are also a barber you meet different types of people. Some of the people will come for a haircut and they will tell you, 'Pierre, I'm looking for a housemaid, you see.' Some of those are friends of mine, they are not employed then I say, no someone is not working then. . . . Laughter. The current job is 100 per cent enjoyable. I get food, access to buy clothes then it's fine. It's reliable, you see. You can't expect much but when you get food, clothes, you get money for transport, I think it's right. (DRC: Pierre: 4)

At leisure times, people prefer their home language, Pierre likes hanging out with his Shona-speaking friends to share jokes and stories from back home, as opposed to the ZimEnglish of his public existence. It is ZimEnglish because it is better than MzansiEnglish.

When asked about how he prefers to communicate with his fellow friends, Carmi (DRC: 13), a Congolese migrant, responded that he sometimes speaks French or Swahili or even Chibemba. He further noted, 'When we met especially when I was in Pietermaritzburg, when we meet together it's too many languages, so we adjust to change to Swahili too. Many too are in English. And Pretoria is the same. Swahili is a dominant language when I'm with my colleague from DRC.'

There are strong stereotypes about the *Kwere*, be it a Nigerian or a Somali migrant. Fredrick speaks of such stereotypes as he recalls his living arrangement in Cape Town. He narrates:

> So the people in Seapoint, they didn't like us. Like the local people who were staying in the vicinity of the lodge, in the vicinity of the lodge. Because they just thought maybe what are these Black people doing here. So where are they getting money to pay for the rentals. Although we were sharing the house so it wasn't that expensive. So one day when we come back from work at night, the police came and started to search us in the house. (Nigeria: Fredrick: 12)

The police found money and arrested them for being involved in drug trafficking. They spent time in jail. In the end they were released, but their community had to fork out money.

Saad (Somalia: 19) exclaims, 'Whenever we go with the taxis the Black people insult us by saying we are *Kwerekwere*s', in concert with quite a few others (Somalia: Ayesha: 10; Majid: 5).

> For example, when you board a taxi and you are the only one who is not from SA, they start talking a lot of 'shit', you cannot accept it, even if you cannot handle it you have to accept it because they will tell you: 'You *kwerekwere*, what are you doing in our country?' There is a lot of arrogance; it is like we are not comparable with South Africans. (Somalia: Saad: 19)

> Among other issues, which sadden us, are often the matters of mistreatments. In most of the cases, a foreigner has no say. Even in the workplaces, a foreigner is treated differently from a local citizen. (Rwanda: Markus: 4)

> I had experienced discrimination during xenophobic attack against foreigners in South Africa. During that event, I was in Johannesburg. I lived in a place close to Alexandra, like one hundred metre[s] away. As such, before going to work I had to catch a taxi from Alexandra to town in Luis Botha Avenue in Johannesburg. There were no, in fact, other taxis to reach the Johannesburg city, besides those of Alexandra. In the meantime, they were burning houses, and killing people in Alexandra. It was even a problem to get in the taxis. Sometimes they could push you and refuse to sit with you. That was when I experienced discrimination in South Africa. (Rwanda: Pontificus: 5)

> The negative here in South Africa, like, people are not friendly here. Especially here in Cape Town where they are not friendly and there's full of racism here. If you

have got a problem like if you wanna see like the racist here in South Africa, just . . . if you find yourself like if you've got a problem then you go to a police, sometimes maybe you, that's where you see that there is a racist here in South Africa. Like, Coloureds and the white people, they don't treat you nice if you are a foreigner. It's very difficult and it's very sad. (Zimbabwe: Enoch: 6)

One of the respondents describes experiences on South Africa's streets:

My experience of neighbours is really very limited because my sister lived in Philippi when I first moved here. We hardly had very much to do with our neighbours; we kept very much to ourselves. Although the people who lived immediately close to us tried to be friendly, but we were very scare[d] because we were foreigners and people knew that we were foreigners. (Ethiopia: Marta: 13)

Another female respondent, speaking of the feeling of insecurity on South African streets as a foreigner, says:

The fact that my husband comes home safe every day is a good thing considering all the bad things that happen in this country on a daily basis. One time he was a victim of a robbery when he was driving. But luckily, he escaped and they managed to take the things he was transporting. For example, in the neighbourhood where I work, there are a lot of robbery going on around the taxi rank. Gunshots and killings happen here as if it is a simple thing and I would have had a record of that. There are threats everywhere in the surrounding area.

So, avoidance and living in isolation in fear is the harsh reality of life for so-called *Kwerekwere* on the streets of South Africa.

Paulinio (Rwanda: 14) states: '. . . because I could be the locals' next target. I might forget to give them one rand by mistake, and the argument might possibly lead them to use knives as a way to resolve the problem. Those events can affect me as well.' 'There is a lot of fear of living anywhere in this country' (Rwanda: Felicita: 12). She continues, 'We don't even go out, I. No, I don't have. We watch TV, we chat, etc. . . . We don't go out.'

Cedric narrates:

Yeah, that is always because police, they are always doing their things because of corruption and what? But from the neighbours, there you can't see there who's the neighbour because we are living in flat so you when you came you enter in your flat you don't know who is staying next to you. Sometime you just meet in the lift, so I don't have any problem with the neighbours. But the police and the other, the community like if you are in the street it's very dangerous. (DRC: Cedric: 10)

The exclusion and sense of avoidance that the African migrants face in South

Africa extend to their children. When asked about what kind of problems their children face in South African schools, one respondent painfully says:

> Hmmm, there are problems because they [other children in school] always tell them your father is a *kwerekwere*. You are not South African because the mother she's a South African. And they always coming and cry about others, They told me at school I'm a *kwerekwere*, that 'you're a *kwerekwere*, what do you say?' I say yeah, it's fine, just leave it like that. Say there is nothing wrong.

While some teach their children to avoid perpetuating conflict in school, other migrants like Agnes try to avoid conflict with the state. She says:

> In fact, when I came here, I didn't have any problems with accommodation because I just moved in with my sister, who was already working here, and she and her friends advised me on what to do. Part of the advices they gave me was that I needed to send my passport back to Zimbabwe, so I gave that passport to the truck driver that go back to Zimbabwe. So, I have already sent my passport back to Zimbabwe as I speak, and when I am done here, I will just cross the border and tell them that I am just a border jumper and I won't have any problem, and my passport will remain clean. (Zimbabwe: Agnes: 20)

How they experience isolation in intimate and large settings, how imagined or real togetherness gets played out – or at least what they have articulated about all this – provides a vivid picture of an unsettled life.

As mentioned above, the main fearsome duo are the police and Home Affairs officials. The treatment of the migrants by both constitutes a painful narrative. Patricio (Mozambique: 7) recalls that it was worse a decade ago:

> I can say that in 2005, up to 2008 and 2009. We experienced many problems here in SA, and now I think that things have changed little bit, because we are no longer arrested. In the past, cops could come three or five times a day, and now they can come two to three times in a month; and sometimes they pass through us and they don't arrest us.

Hospitals have been particularly singled out. Accessing hospital care is in many experiences marked by reluctance and exclusion. Local nurses, it was reported, refuse to address foreign patients in English. Here is Rwandan Loren's experience:

> In the Department of Health I have a bad experience there every time when I go there to ask for a service they don't give a good service. If I ask what I need, I asked in English because I don't know Zulu but when they want to give me the information they tell me in Zulu and when I reply that I do not understand what she saying, so, she started telling me many things. Asking how come I cannot

understand Zulu. While they talking to Indian or white, they talk to them in English. Why they do not force them to speak in Zulu, while they their fellow South Africans? How come they can force us to speak in Zulu? When you ask question, they say 'I don't understand what is going on with migrant people.' . . . For instance, when you go to hospital the Zulu people can't ask you in English they only give you all instructions in Zulu and when you say you don't understand they continue to use only Zulu more times and they tell you that you must know Zulu. Everyone is not a Zulu. They cannot also understand our language and we cannot blame them for that, they either cannot blame us. This attitude for me is what I can call xenophobia. (Rwanda: Loren: 16)

As the time went on, I met with the Zulu people, it was difficult before I could get used to their language, but now I can speak Zulu fluently. Now I can do my job at 100 per cent with anyone, Zulu and foreigners. (Rwanda: Maria: 13)

The main problem exists at healthcare centres like hospital clinics; for example, I am diabetic, if I go other hospitals I don't get medication quickly, sometimes you see Somali pregnant women when they want to give birth no one is attending to them and when you ask the nurses, 'Can [you] please help me?' they respond to you by saying, 'Hey, don't talk shit here, you fucking foreigner.' One of the days I fainted somewhere in Cape Town an ambulance took me to one of the hospitals at Somerset . . . it was night they charged me R. 80. I stayed and waited the whole night, no one attended to me till morning. I went to nurses and asked them am here since last night and am not getting any medical attention. Then that is the time she responded, 'How can I treat you while South African people are in the queue?' That's the time my temper flared and went straight to the counter and pulled my file out there and shouted at them and said to them, 'You pigs who doesn't have respect for other human beings besides yourselves and I will report you.' And they try to manhandle me all of them know plus the security and we shouted . . . then a white guy came out to cool down the situation, he asked me what was the problem. I explained to him and that is time he said he will solve everything and I will get my medication immediately. Then I refused and demanded my money back due to the fact I afraid maybe they will poison me. (Somalia: Brahimi: 7)

Regarding the Department of Health, you might go there, if you are a foreigner, although you might be dying, they hardly help you. So, all those are challenges, which we face in South Africa as foreigners. (Rwanda: Magda: 15)

One day I went to the hospital, as I was involved in an accident with my motor bicycle. They just ignored me, and simply paid attention to the local people (Rwanda: Jacques: 17)

In hospitals, if you go there as a foreigner having flu, there are two things to expect. If you spend a night there, especially in Addington and King Edward hospitals, to come back alive is only by the grace of God. That is, if you have a small problem; you are more likely to die, because none cares about you. Many of our friends have lost their lives there. (Rwanda: Menan: 6)

Yeah, even hospital, even hospital. If you go to the hospital [and] you are a foreigner, you are different; they don't take care of us nicely even pregnant women. Even they don't take care of us foreigners, I don't know South Africans but all I know is that they are not taking good care of us because if you are a foreigner they don't respect you if you got to hospital they [verbally mimicking disrespect in unintelligible words], especially if you don't have the ID, if you are a refugee and you are using the refugee [status], the asylum paper they don't take good care of us and it is not only me people are complaining a lot. (Ghana: Akosua: 13)

The lady shouted at me, yaaah because the way she was talking to the other coloured ladies was different from the way she was talking to me. The problem here, especially in Cape Town, is racism. (Zimbabwe: Jonathan: 19)

I have been to the Home Affairs and the public hospital but the way they see us and treat us is not the same like the natives. When I was at the hospital to give birth there was me and other South Africans and the South Africans were given priorities by the doctors follow up on their cases because the nurses give more attention to them. So everywhere I went like I have been to the Home Affairs, public hospital, and the municipality office and in all those places priorities are given to the natives. (Ethiopia: Zala: 20)

Simone even had to spend time in prison because of the hostility of locals:

They had nothing to discuss with those *Kwerekwere*, and that they hated them and that she wanted the guy to be sent to jail. That thing had deeply touched me; if I rethink how many days I had spent in prison because of injustice, it really hurts me. I had spent seventeen days in prison. This simply indicates that people of this country do not like us, simply because we are foreigners in their land. (Rwanda: Simone: 3)

Recoiling and Refracting Agencies

These considerations bring us back to the research and theorizing that produced the text *Voices that Reason: Theoretical Parables*. The book was nothing but an extended argument for agency: active, recoiling and refracting agency that allowed Black working-class communities to absorb pressures through and constitute subaltern cultural formations. It also touched on the migrant experience of the city, its noise and sound, its tempo – how it involved a panic, a loss, a thrill but also a pressure, a system of chaotic impressions produced by the traffic, the hooters, the laughter, the screams, the noise: 'We all feel', I argued,

> when we visit a new and strange place, that we use peculiar, unconscious, pre-programmed dispositions through which certain signs, speech-patterns, gestures command our attention and draw us towards them. They create sensual affinities, they are familiar, they create a comfort zone; but even when we feel we understand some of them, there are still signs that frighten, signs that make us worry, signs that are incomprehensible. We search for connectivities – instrumental, informational – but we also feel distances and differences, repulsions. (Sitas 2004b: 88)

Migrants were and are not a tabula rasa; their pre-programmed and socialized dispositions vary. Many of our Ethiopian interviewees are from conflict zones. Bess (Zimbabwe: 16) explicitly cites the reason for migration as flight from a political situation: her husband had to flee, so she followed. She describes how she lost many family members in the political unrest of the early 2000s and that to this day they could not return. Many of our Zimbabwean subjects are fleeing political tensions and violence and economic hardship. According to Joseph:

> I left Zimbabwe because the situation was for . . . I think Zimbabwe the situation was I didn't have a job at that time, you see. I'm just sitting at home, the situation of starvation now. Those are certain things that forced me to and politics . . . I want change because ZANU-PF [Zimbabwe African National Union – Patriotic Front] ruled for many years. So, at that time, it's better to vote for MDC [Movement for Democratic Change], for a new party, so that was trouble. (Zimbabwe: Joseph: 12)

DRC, Rwandan and Somali migrants in turn had spent time in refugee camps in many different African countries on their journey to South Africa to find political and economic peace as well as freedom from their war-torn countries. Their experiences and histories matter and like all people, in unconscious and often banal ways, they transpose meanings: that the 'other', the 'local' is feeling or saying this because of an obvious X; they do generalize – that my own beliefs and dispositions are the norm and what the other is doing is normless, wrong or crazy and stereotypical; Xs are like this, because of that. In this context, this then translates into that – for instance, all South African Blacks are criminals and all whites are racists.

Such dispositions are overlaid by the experiential lessons and encounters gleaned from the new spaces they have come to inhabit – on foot, in cars and trains, in streets, in settings that create a world of attractions and repulsions. And such dispositions and experiences move in controlled and predictable spaces, through dangerous settings of a politics of utilitarianism (these people get you this and those people provide access to that), of enticement (these spaces are radiant, attractive, mesmerizing), of comfort (community, church, etc.) or of danger. All of which translate into a negotiated politics of everyday life involving encounters and rituals.

Enoch explained:

. . . because the thing is I don't get a lot of time to like mix and mingle with the local South Africans because they are more like foreigners. So right now, you see, I cannot say they are day-to-day problems but if you are mingle with South Africans, like in the vicinity where there are a lot of South Africans that's when you can feel it that; no these people, they don't like foreigners. Yeah, they are not friendly like other, you know, like the other people from other countries. You see it's easy to get along with someone from Nigeria and Ghana but few South Africans but not everyone. (Zimbabwe: Enoch: 6)

He did try and mingle in the Harare squatter camp in Khayelitsha but his lesson was harsh: 'Because me, I used to live in Khayelitsha.'

Beyond the actual treatment there is also a world of bribes and bribing: 'So for me to get the passport I had to pay, I did not pay exactly 220 cos I had to pay the guy [bribe] at the passport office so that he can make everything quick' (Zimbabwe: Enoch: 6). Giorghis (Ethiopia:1) agreed: 'they always asking me a bribe I should pay. . . . Otherwise they don't give me my paper [permit].' 'Police, they always harassing and asking bribe – that's my negative experience' (Ethiopia: Meron: 16).

Once, police came here and they asked us for passports and since we are working here, we cannot use a passport with a visitor's visa because it's not allowed to use permit of visitors here in South Africa to work here in South Africa. We gave them money and they went away. (Mozambique: Paulo: 19).

Enoch's experience turned ghastly:

The first time I was in Khayelitsha, I went to work and then when I was at work, I was working at night. So somebody burnt my house. . . . Yeah, I was living in a shack, so to my surprise it's only my shack which was burnt compared, like . . . there were some other shacks around but it was only mine it was like burning. So I lost a lot of stuff like money and the passports, many things. (Zimbabwe: Enoch: 6)

Giorghis (Ethiopia: 1), who eked his living in the Durban CBD selling cloth, often wondered about 'them', the locals: 'When I was attacked by a thief, police don't help you swiftly and this is the big problem nationally too. So I understand. And sometimes, we have a problem with the community that is mainly related to our business. We are seen as impostors.' In all the narratives, there is a sense that there is something wrong with South Africans' mentality, their attitudes, and such 'wrongness' is reproduced by those in authority – usually the police and Home Affairs officials. Elizabeth, a student nurse, amplified:

> I would say with the police . . . with the area I stay they are quite familiar with foreigners. They believe that foreigners are mostly engaging in dodgy deals or drugs or something. So they . . . if you are by mistakenly get to have something with the police. I mean I didn't like my first experience with the police because they treat you like you are any other foreigner who is engaged in something dodgy or bad. (Nigeria: Elizabeth: 18)

Despite the discouraging life circumstances and hardships that most of the migrants have faced while residing in South Africa, some of them contend that the country has provided them with opportunities and to a certain extent some positive experiences. For instance, Joseph (DRC: 3) recounted that South Africa is a good country. Despite there being some negative aspects in the living situation, he still believed that with work, a foreigner can make a good life for himself/herself. He further noted that amongst the positive aspects of living and working in South Africa was that 'the business is positive for me, if I can get my things properly and right work, I can go forward, because of the economy and so many things which are happening in SA'. Another respondent, Cedric, narrated:

> Because first I am a cripple if I was in my country I can't do those, like a saloon, to survive. I pay the rent, I've got two kids, I'm supporting of my kids, they are in school. As myself I'm staying in a place where I'm renting without any problem. But if [I] was in the, a country like DRC, I couldn't have survived. (DRC: Cedric: 10)

Here is an amalgam of statements: 'There are more ways to a job, "quite easy" construction especially.' 'They have freedom of expression here, you can make it beyond survival here, once you earn . . . accommodation can be of good quality, they have not put us in camps here.' 'There are good roads and infrastructure, there are lavish malls, there is some good education and once you are in the formal economy there is training.' 'There is no war or fear of wars, police, hospitals, opportunities, envious of the freedoms locals enjoy.' 'Women "have it better" in the jobbing space here than back home.' Indeed, 'The roads are good. There is electricity, water. The scenery is beautiful. Everything is good. But it is not like home.'

As will become obvious, any analysis of such movement has forced active verb concepts into our vocabulary: it became quite difficult to speak of settlement and accommodating. Rather, words like homing, bi-homing, associating, fusing, dealing, friending, negotiating, became thick descriptors. On the terrain of livelihoods, work was unstable, it was not about a job but jobbing, haggling, transacting, and in everyday life, it was about avoiding, huckstering, helping out, taking flight, keeping clear and improvising.

The ever-present threat of extreme violence combined with the more everyday feeling of exclusion and anomie meant that respondents offered a rather ambiguous and complicated notion of home and belonging. While there were ambiguous responses to what is home – 'real', 'imagined', 'here and there' – most did say they missed home. Most were also unsure when and if they would return. There was only one certainty: *'Home is where one goes to die.'*

After all, it was through that shifting and kinetic sense in this enormous diaspora, this interconnected and networked migration, this incessant globalization from 'below', this – dare we say – homelessness, of need and hope, that a new consciousness has been emerging. We listened carefully to how such migrants defined and redefined the idea of 'home' and how the home is 'here' and 'there' and 'nowhere'. It was always an idea and a process: of homing, bi-homing, multi-homing, and there is a sense that unlike Marx's time where the workers of the industrial revolution felt at home when they were not working and when they were working they were not at home, the diasporic proletariat feels at home nowhere – neither at work nor in their homing contexts. And yet the idea of home persists. There is a mix of frank expressions and a poetics of everyday life in their accounts, but also prejudice and invective.

Broadly speaking, there are two dimensions to such an aesthetic: its imaginary and self-expressive nature. On the first count, there are the contours of an imagined community. But this is not the abstracted and horizontal comradeship of a nation but rather an assemblage of concrete clusters of people and networks (local and translocal), ranging from kin, co-villagers, support networks, sometimes intensively ethnic and local, sometimes trans-ethnic and pan-African, sometimes made up of participants of congregations.

They exist on the intersection of two networks that strengthen their resilience: useful networks through reliable locals, landlords, labour brokers and agencies, NGOs and non-profit organizations; and practical networks facilitated through religious communities of the church or the mosque. Also, most importantly, networks of belonging: diasporic through clan and kinship associations across continents, ethnicity- or nationality-based in the local area through which cultural and religious activity flourishes. But also, association that facilitates saving of resources, disseminating information and keeping in touch with the wealthier members of their community who have been successful in having academic, professional or corporate jobs. Furthermore, many of them are active participants in political networks from 'back home', an inevitable fact among refugees.

Church seems to be the only counterweight:

Church and Bible, avoid drinking houses, I think it's God's favour, you know. The thing is, the time when we were staying in, the first time when we came here, there were some of the guys from Zimbabwe. They were staying in Khayelitsha. So we went there, they give us accommodation, all the stuff but . . . and they are the ones who also taught us what to, to like, how to go and sell things at the traffic lights and all those stuff. But there was a difference between me and my brother and those guys. Like, every time whenever they get money, they could go out and drink and all that stuff. They never thought of tomorrow or like thinking of going to church and all those stuff. In other words, they were not focused. They didn't know exactly, what exactly they want here in South Africa. So, personally me, I thank God for my life because He's the One who changes me in my life because I used to pray every time and again. Even until now, I just, the hand of God. It's not that I'm clever that [I] am what I am today but just the grace of God. (Zimbabwe: Bess: 16)

Maria (Rwanda: 13) is also active in the Ethiopian church in Durban. She describes the church as a place where she seeks support. She goes on to say, 'I first share my problem with people in my church that I consider close to me and then if it is bigger then I announce it to the church elders. I never had any problem that made me go to the police.'

But irrespective of actual policies, there is the imagination of *a borderless Africa* that appears frequently in the narratives of our respondents (DRC: Pierre: 4; Ethiopia: Yonas: 15; Mozambique: Ernestina: 8; Rwanda: Tete: 20) – the sense that we are all Africans, divided through conquest and colonialism; we are all Black Africans, discriminated against everywhere. There is this assertion that during the fight against apartheid, all Africans were together in the struggle and now it's time for the South Africans to reciprocate and open up the borders. Etheldreda makes an interesting comment: she feels South Africa and Zimbabwe are not separate countries, so what she and others have done is not really migration:

Yes, they are two different countries but if you look at the historical background you see that it's the same country. Half of the people in Zimbabwe they are Nguni, they came from down here. In our genes some of us we have South African origins because half of Zimbabweans are Ndebeles who are like Zulus. But what I meant is that in the sixties and seventies people were flocking from SA to Zim so now it's the other way round. (Zimbabwe: Etheldreda: 2)

The real non-Africans in this discourse are South African Blacks.

If we draw the contours of this imaginary, it is made up of the following coordinates: there is a social being which is African that is deeply marked by the trauma of racism that shapes both its possible solidarities and patterns of life; this being is shared by most and it is a serious marker of experience. The first modality, therefore, is about the existence of a different African ontology that is uniquely different from the rest. Our understanding of being, beings and social beings is distinct, and that defines an African cosmology, community and alterity.

The second coordinate is the awareness through their networks of the growth of neo-racism in Europe and the tightening of immigration in the North Americas; discrimination in Europe and race-based attacks have been on the increase (Ethiopia: Miriam: 10; Akosua: Ghana: 13, Ebrahim: 19; Nigeria: Adaego: 8, Afaro: 15).

The third coordinate is their exilic and peripatetic existence at home anywhere and nowhere in the world: strategically, instrumentally and substantively. This mobility itself constitutes a part and parcel of their self-understanding. It is not that they have travelled intensely but that they are connected to people in far-flung ways. Also, the fact that one can disappear in Paris within a large enclave of Africanness with limited interaction with locals; the fact that one can similarly try and be invisible in Johannesburg and stay in touch with the fastest growing cities in the world: Lagos, Kinshasa, Addis Ababa and so on. This informs their world views, creates a cosmopolitan consciousness and a sense that locals are just parochial victims. What keeps them in touch are cell phones with roaming access, cheap Bangladeshi call shops, internet cafes run by Ghanaians in Durban, freight and money-moving agencies, hubs where the entire globalized network operates in real time (Nigeria: Samantha: 6; Ghana: Kojo: 11, Avicena: 15; Somalia: Majid: 5).

Fourthly, many feel that multi-ethnicity has to be saved from its political exploitation. The consensus among them is that multi-ethnicity is no problem *per se*, it is its political exploitation that should be avoided. This has been helped by homogenizing tendencies among locals: it doesn't matter what kind of Nigerian you are, you are a Nigerian, a Zimbabwean, a Kenyan. And in the North you are Black or African (Nigeria: Aderinsola: 11; Rwanda: Magda: 15; Zimbabwe: Thomas: 1).

In allowing for generous quotation in this chapter, we wanted to craft a sense of the ways through which this experience of migration is expressed, but we have made sure to protect the identities, locations and workplaces of the respondents. Most of them occupy the bottom rungs of the labour market and are in occupations that have been casualized and informalized; there, they also occupy specific niches that are decorated with ethnic attributes: Congolese for car guards, Zimbabwean women for intimate domestic labour, Mozambicans for construction work – and they respond by playing up to those descriptors to enhance their life-chances. The majority have not responded to trade union organizations nor have they sought to be represented, but they are in conversation with trade union members.

Then, we come to how they have constructed cultural formations (our language) – a negotiated habitus (Bourdieu's language, 1997) or a private world (Goffman's language, 1969). As a Zimbabwean migrant described their living arrangements:

> We live together in small cottages, and we share everything. We share our food, and we also share our problems. It is almost like we are back in Zimbabwe. We speak our language and the bosses are really, really happy with us. Where we have moved now, there is a lot of neighbouring and there are many other Zimbabweans; it is like we live in Zimbabwe in a way. We talk to each other, everybody know who has come and who has gone. That, in a sense, is the neighbouring that I have experienced in SA. (Zimbabwe: Joseph:12)

The spaces of contestation stretch across institutions, cities, suburbs, provinces; it is in these fluid nets of social relations and social actors that the politics of belonging are defined. In the murmurs of the city centres, Home Affairs offices, hospitals, schools, streets and workplaces, economic insecurity is intensified and the 'other', the dark foreigner, disrupts the precarious local social relations. In volatile spaces, sentiments of ubuntu – I am because you are – or the 'rainbow nation' does not exist. In a melting pot of hustling and survival, symbolic violence is the spoken language (Von Holdt 2011).

Finally, there is a deep sense of injustice permeating their experience: asked what kind of pictures they were, are or would be taking on their journeys or in South Africa, apart from a few who said they would be taking pictures of landscapes and verdant beachscapes, the majority were dismissive, disinterested – some very pointed and some angry in their responses. A common narrative was of 'camera for poetic justice': for justice; for exposing police injustice and corruption, harassment by Home Affairs; for exposing xenophobia; for capturing migrants' hardship.

INTERVIEWS

Pseudonyms have been used to protect the identities of the interviewees. Numbers refer to the archived interview sequence of twenty per country.

Democratic Republic of the Congo (DRC): Joseph 3; Pierre 4; Miguel 8; Cedric 10; Carmi 13

Ethiopia: Giorghis 1, Khalil 5, Miriam 10, Marta 13, Yonas 15, Meron 16, Zala 20

Ghana: Kojo 11, Akosua 13, Avicena 15, Kwasi 18, Ebrahim 19

Mozambique: Philemon 3, Graca 4, Raul 5, Sarah 6, Patricio 7, Ernestina 8, Romelus 9, Teresa 11, Paulo 19

Nigeria: Samantha 6, Abebi 7, Adaego 8, Wole 9, Japtha 10, Aderinsola 11, Fredrick 12, Afaro 15, Elizabeth 18

Rwanda: Beatrice 1, Aruna 2, Simone 3, Markus 4, Pontificus 5, Menan 6, Paulus 7, Fabrice 10, George 11, Felicita 12, Maria 13, Paulinio 14, Magda 15, Jacques 17, Aaron 18, Santa 19, Tete 20

Somalia: Ahmed 3, Majid 5, Brahimi 7, Ayesha 10, Abdul 12, Azad 14, Salah 15, Ameena 16, Amina 18, Saad 19

Zimbabwe: Thomas 1, Etheldreda 2, Enoch 6, Aaron 10, Joseph 12, Esther 15, Bess 16, Marcia 17, Jonathan 19, Agnes 20

NOTES

[1] Although drafted by the three, this work involved about thirty established and student scholars exploring a range of areas: intimate labour, integration and non-integration, identity, informal and illicit networks. It involved researchers/activists from all the communities and a mix of academics from South Africa, Ghana, Tanzania, Ethiopia, Zimbabwe, Uganda and the Democratic Republic of the Congo (DRC). The results of the entire study have not been published because sections of the research will create untold vulnerabilities for migrant communities. We agreed to allow for a decade to elapse and then review the prospects of publication. The research was coordinated by Aisha Lorgat, Amrita Pande and I.

[2] Given the number of interviews involved in this chapter, we decided on the following reference methodology: all the interviews are listed at the end of the chapter. They are listed according to the country of origin. Furthermore, there follows a pseudonym and a number. For example, Phineas: 6. The number refers to the way the interview archive has been constructed. So, Phineas would be the sixth archived interview in the African Diaspora Database. Finally, in the text, citations or references would appear as (Zimbabwe: Phineas: 6), or as Phineas (Zimbabwe: 6) said, or according to a Zimbabwean (Phineas: 6), XYZ.

[3] 'Difecane' is the period of violence and war that accompanied the formation of the Zulu kingdom. Southern Zimbabwe was populated/invaded by the Ndebele clans that refused to come under *amaZulu* control. Others moved into Mozambique and Southern Tanzania. The words 'Scatterlings of Africa' were popularized by Johnny Clegg and Sipho Mchunu through their band Juluka.

VIGNETTES B

Of Deviants and Defiance

4

Loose Women, Pleasure Work and Defiant History

Sex Workers and Beer Brewers in India and South Africa

Amrita Pande

They say I'm a beast.
And feast on it. When all along
I thought that's what a woman was.

They say I'm a bitch.
Or witch. I've claimed
the same and never winced.

The mob arrives with stones and sticks
to maim and lame and do me in.
All the same, when I open my mouth,
they wobble like gin. . . .

I like the itch I provoke.
The rustle of rumor
like crinoline.

I am the woman of myth and bullshit.
(True. I authored some of it.)
I built my little house of ill repute.
Brick by brick. Labored,
loved and masoned it.

I live like so.
Heart as sail, ballast, rudder, bow.
Rowdy. Indulgent to excess.
My sin and success –
I think of me to gluttony. . . .

I'm an aim-well,
shoot-sharp,
sharp-tongued,
sharp-thinking,
fast-speaking,
foot-loose,
loose-tongued,
let-loose,
woman-on-the-loose
loose woman.
                    – Sandra Cisernos, 'Loose Woman'

A most enduring verbal expression for prostitution has been to mark it as the world's most ancient profession. This is truly laughable. This saying makes this profession *sui generis*; as if there was a profession when there were none others. The history we are trying to recuperate is a history of the erasure of working women and the emergence of prostitute as the only category of women who work for money. Once the task of the erasure of the working women in complete, the binary is created between the prostitute and the wife – *a woman who does not work.*
                    – Gayatri Chatterjee (2008)

Introduction

Loose women are those whose behaviour and lifestyles do not fit the norm. Their transgressions may vary: being autonomous-minded and free-spirited, brewing spirits, alcoholism, unrestrained sexuality, immoral appearance, or even the ability to be alive without the presence of legitimate menfolk (Hunter 2005; W. Jackson 2013). Despite the elusive nature of the adjective 'loose', loose women are often visualized as sexually unrestrained, or prostitutes, who need to be controlled.

In this chapter, my argument is twofold. One, I build on my earlier works on the new dynamics of intimate labour in the South (Pande 2014, 2017) to argue that the adjective 'loose', a signifier of the stigma attached to certain forms of women's labour, becomes a powerful tool of colonial discipline and control of native women. By focusing on two types of loose women – women who dance, sing and sometimes engage in transactional sex in British India and South Africa, and beer-brewing women in South Africa – I argue that the codification of financially autonomous women as sex workers is not so much about sex and sexuality but primarily about making not just prostitution but women's paid work seem exceptional and ahistorical. The normalizing gaze that the surveillance of prostitution legitimizes can then be effectively deployed to surveil as well as codify all women, especially in so-called 'public spaces'. The prostitute stigma and the dirt associated with this identity are so powerful that women have to constantly distance themselves from this identity, so as to gain the respectability of a non-prostitute (Shah 2003: 75). Unlike the good wife who allegedly has sex only for procreation, prostitutes have sex for money and/ or for pleasure. That is their sin and dirt.

But the dirt associated with a prostitute gets attached to many other gendered and intimate forms of labour. In recent decades, feminist scholars of labour have used the analogy of dirt and intimacy to analyse a gamut of women's work, ranging from sex work to care work, in order to examine the social construction of commodified intimacies (Boris and Parreñas, eds 2010; Pande 2009). For instance, in my earlier works (Pande 2009, 2014, 2020), I have discussed a continuum of work – erotic dancing, salon work, domestic work, nursing, wet nursing, egg provision and even paid pregnancy – which involves touch, physicality or the body fluids of the worker itself, as embodied, dirty and stigmatized labour. The scholarship on intimate labour has been critical in unpacking the socially constructed dichotomy between production and reproduction, public and private, in delineating the heterogeneity of such professions, yet there are also parallels among all such labour organized around dirt, bodies and intimacy. My second ambition in this chapter is to extend and critique this scholarship by arguing that this otherwise rich scholarship has paid inadequate attention to the centrality of *pleasure* in such gendered forms of labour.

Feminist literature on sex work has sought to dissect the binaries wife–prostitute, virgin–whore, good girl–bad girl, embedded in discussions around this topic, but at the same time has reinforced some of them. For instance, the images of suffering and trafficked prostitutes from and in the Global South have become a powerful tool for western feminists to speak for and rescue their injured sisters. The injury of Southern prostitutes becomes a symbol of the universal victimhood of Southern women – the eternal victim as opposed to the liberated western counterpart. Or, as Jo Doezema highlights, the free-versus-forced dichotomy reaffirms another dichotomy, that of empowered, pleasure-seeking sex workers from the Global North, a defiant woman who need not be saved, as opposed to the forced or trafficked prostitute silently and passively toiling away in the squalor of a brothel (Doezema 1998). There is little place for desire or pleasure in the past and present of the loose women in the South.

Pleasure and looseness are two terms that often go together. Leisure, pleasure and such distractions may be opposed by the religious and by proponents of temperance. Excessive pleasure, for some, is a sin. For the colonial powers, control over leisure and recreation was also about utilitarian social engineering (L. Jackson 2019: 4). Drunk workers were not productive enough. A native having fun was one more likely to resist and revolt. How does gender intersect with such pleasure economies? Women consumers of pleasure, whether in Victorian Britain or colonial India and South Africa, were often labelled as belonging to the 'demoralized' working classes of society. When combined, alcohol and sexuality became potent and dangerous ingredients for a loose woman in the making. As A. Lynn Martin (2001: 11) summarizes, 'Men feared the sexuality and the disorderliness of sober women; drinking women escalated their fears'. One has to dig quite deep into the archives to find instances of public drunkenness amongst women. Far more visible in history, however, are women producers of pleasure and debauchery for (mostly) male consumers.

The main protagonists of this chapter, the loose women, are bound together by their involvement in 'pleasure work', or work that is deemed to be primarily for the leisure and pleasure of male consumers, which sometimes may be pleasurable for the workers as well. The stigma, dirt and sometimes panic associated with such work have as much to do with gender and morality as with its intersections with class, caste, race and space. The women who dance, sing, have sex, or brew and serve beer for money, whether in the Mughal courts, present-day dance bars in India, or near mines and *shebeens* in South Africa, are all part of a pleasure economy. Extending the subject of historical and sociological analysis from a 'prostitute' (a figure that has long obsessed colonial archives and social scientists at large) to these pleasure workers has two related ends: (1) to disrupt the framing of prostitution as exceptional (work) and instead bring out the role of colonial laws and archives in making not just prostitution but women's work exceptional; and (2) to shift focus from the functionality of these occupations (another convenient colonial tool) to the desires and motivations, as well as the political, economic and social impacts on the lives of the pleasure workers themselves.

Archiving Loose Women

Social scientists have been obsessed with the figure of the prostitute for more than a century now. For instance, one of the first and most influential social scientific studies on female criminality, Italian criminal anthropologist Cesare Lombroso and Guglielmo Ferrero's 1893 book *La Donna Delinquente* (translated by Rafter and Gibson 2004), compares three groups of women: criminal, prostitutes and 'normal'. Lombroso goes on to show that prostitutes have the smallest cranial capacity of the lot, the heaviest jaws, the most imperfect teeth, making them the most 'degenerate female criminal type'. In fact, he argues, nearly 40 per cent of prostitutes he has studied can be categorized as female 'born criminals' who have a 'passion for evil for evil's sake, an automatic hatred that springs from no external cause. . . . Indeed the criminal propensities of female "born criminals" are more intense and perverse even than those of their male counterparts' (Lombroso and Ferrero 2004: 8). Worth noting is that by prostitute, he sometimes narrowly means 'sex worker', while at other times he uses the term to refer to any woman who experiences sex outside of marriage. Lombroso's work continued to be influential for a while, and although early twentieth-century scholars like Willem Bonger, Mabel Fernald and William Healy rejected his emphasis on biological determinism, studies of female criminality reversed direction in the 1920s and 30s, with authors like Sheldon and Eleanor Glueck (1934: xxiv) concluding in their book *Five Hundred Delinquent Women* that in women, extramarital sexuality is often a sign of biological inferiority and weak intelligence, and for such 'defective delinquents' they had studied, the Gluecks recommend life sentences so that they cannot spread their bad heredity.

Like criminologists, historians are exceptionally keen on the 'prostitute' as a topic of enquiry, especially in conjunction with colonial governmentality. In fact, my initial foray into this topic was to do a comparative history of sex work in British India and some parts of British Africa (more specifically South Africa, Zambia, Uganda and Nigeria). Just a cursory comparison of such records revealed some fascinating parallels in the moral panic created around prostitution in the above-mentioned countries, Although certain categories of women – single women, domestics, 'town women', women who tend to be 'autonomous' from men, women who work outside the home, hold property, travel, brew beer, are 'rowdy' in public, practise medicine – are broadly branded as 'loose women', this classification remains amorphous till the late nineteenth century. Historical writings around prostitution have astutely demonstrated how these labels start being codified and reified very often with colonial anxieties around miscegenation, white slave trade, wars, corruptibility of soldiers, venereal disease, urban migration, mining and development of ports, especially in the early twentieth century.

Although this chronology of codification is in itself fascinating, what piqued my curiosity within this vast scholarship was how the prostitute becomes a central 'prop' for not just colonial domination but also for 'orientalist' social science, wherein sex and sexuality come to define, label and differentiate the colonized from the colonizer as well as the moral from the immoral subaltern. In a classic move of orientalizing that would make even Edward Said proud, this interlinking of colonial coercion and knowledge production achieved two things: it exaggerated the difference between the colonized and the colonizer; at the same time, it homogenized the colonized. Taxonomy and differentiation were necessary but only that which the colonizer created and controlled. Simply put, native women across a whole range of 'looseness' could be classified as prostitutes and sexual deviants in need of colonial control. On the one hand, their sexual looseness could conveniently be connected to their immoral savagery (and pitted against the morality of upper-class European femininity), but at the same time, this would serve as a reprimand for all native women to conform to an amorphous code of morality so as to not be labelled prostitutes. Or, as Chatterjee surmised in the opening quote in this chapter, this effectively created the false binary of the prostitute and the wife – a woman who does not work. Thus, the codification of prostitution in British colonies was not just a reflection of colonial sexual anxieties but more the need to restrain the autonomy of working (native) women at large. And herein lies the key to understanding the colonial codification of 'loose women', whether in the Indian subcontinent or South Africa: while prostitutes needed to be enumerated, regulated and controlled, their qualities seemed amorphous with no proper legal definition of prostitution. The colonial conundrum, in Mary Poovey's words, was: 'one cannot count prostitutes until one defines (describes) prostitution' (Poovey 1993: 18). So what the colonial state, aided by oriental knowledge production, demographers, the census and scientists, needed to do was to claim to know what prostitution looked like, even while a legal definition remained elusive.

This leads me to the second point that piqued my interest – the consequence of this colonial codification and orientalist sociology on the deviant herself. The colonial codification took away from the subaltern woman the ability to define her own occupation. Instead of the rowdy beer brewer or the skilled devadasi, she, in one sweep, became a prostitute. As the prop of colonial power, the female deviant emerged as an exotic and convenient signifier. She was a marker of colonial categories, a metaphor of the 'other' and the extreme of all vices to such an extent that this floating metaphor for colonial lawmakers and postcolonial scholars becomes invisible as a person. Ann Laura Stoler (2009) gives a sharp critique of such archival work where archival activity remains merely extractive rather than ethnographic. She warns us not to view archives as sites of knowledge retrieval but of knowledge production, as monuments of states as well as sites of state ethnography. Colonial archives effectively 'design' histories as they conceal, reveal and reproduce the power of the state. So how does one move from extraction to ethnography in colonial archives? I start by rereading history for a particular group of loose women in order to unravel how the anxiety around financial, and sometimes sexual, autonomy of a certain class of working women made the establishment of the 'prostitute' as a classifiable, identifiable and punishable figure a critical colonial imperative.

Loose Women, Pleasure Work and Prostitutes in British India

In India, a whole spectrum of social historians have written extensively on 'prostitution' in colonial India. Scholars have particularly highlighted how prostitution has been simultaneously defined and tackled as a local, national, imperial and international problem (Legg 2014). Paying attention to these multiple scales, or what geographer Stephen Legg calls the 'international geographies of prostitution', reveals diverse connections between nations, states and colonies. This is what Ann Laura Stoler (2010) reads as 'imperial circuits of sexuality' that linked metropolitan sexual identities and practices to imperial anxieties. Stoler argues that the intimate emerges as a central anxiety of colonial politics, wherein 'the micro-management of sexual arrangements and affective attachments was so critical to the making of colonial categories and deemed so important to the distinction between the ruler and the ruled' (ibid.: 8).

A key moment in the 1850s that had a direct effect on the regulation of prostitution was the Indian 'mutiny', which resulted in a move away from Company Raj to direct governance by the British state and the subsequent codification of India's criminal system and personal law. Within this code, prostitution belonged not to private law that governed all other forms of 'natural' sexualities but was categorized as a public harm and hence under the purview of the 'public' (Shah 2014). Historian Ashwini Tambe succinctly summarizes the reasons for the change in policy: 'To stave off sailors' and soldiers' boredom, to counter anxieties about possible homosexual relations between personnel, and to reinforce imperial dominance through the sexual control of local women' (Tambe 2005: 165). Other scholars have highlighted the intersection of prostitution laws and colonial anxieties around not just proper femininity but also racial purity – how the threat of miscegenation, the anxiety that the Raj may well have to maintain 'native wives' and mixed-race children, all resulted in an extremely punitive system of surveillance and treatment of 'native' prostitutes. The Contagious Diseases Acts in Britain followed a few years later, in 1864.

An obvious and much talked about impetus for the regulations was military, and the imperative to protect troops from dirt, infection and disease, but that was not all. While, till the late nineteenth century, prostitutes were mostly tolerated as a necessary evil, the effects of the Contagious Diseases Acts found these women becoming socially marginalized and their identities increasingly stigmatized. The dirt of the work had infected the worker's identity to such an extent that she was now being blamed for not just spreading infectious diseases, but also for being the cause of overcrowding, unsanitary conditions, for breaking marriages and corrupting young boys.

This period was when other manifestations of the pleasure economy were gaining visibility as well; for instance, radio stations and cinema halls were being introduced in bigger cities in India. These new forms of visible pleasure brought with them dangers of defiance and deviant forms of gender and sexuality. As expected, prostitutes became the most visible and easy target for this general social unrest. This then became the period when prostitutes (interestingly, along with another group of 'dirty workers', the butchers) were to be systematically evicted from the bazaar areas – the central market zones in the city – to the margins (Legg 2014: 59). For instance, in a petition submitted to the Delhi Municipality in support of removing prostitutes (ibid.) from Chawri Bazaar, the commissioner submitted a list of fifty reasons. Prostitutes, the petition argued, not only adversely affected public life but more – these loose women, the petition lamented, were known to fly kites on the roof of their houses, which troubled local gentlemen and violated the purdah of gentle respectable ladies; they spoke too loudly and cracked jokes inappropriate for the ears of the local respectable women. Girls and boys were said to 'lose their character' just by sitting in shops opposite these brothels (ibid.: 62). In essence, the exact nature of the municipality's anxiety was very ambiguous – a trend we will notice in much of the moral panic created around prostitution in late nineteenth- and early twentieth-century British South Africa as well, which I will come to in a later section.

Despite the parallels with other parts of the (British) colonized world, India and its prostitution debate remained somewhat exceptional. In her book *Prostitution, Race and Politics: Policing Venereal Disease in the British Empire*, Philippa Levine (2003) examines four colonial spaces of India, the Strait Settlements, Hong Kong and Queensland, to argue that the Contagious Diseases Acts were a conscious means to dominate across the colonies. But at the same time, she demonstrates that the experience varied from one colony to another. In India, she argues, race, sexuality and prostitution took on a distinct shape. Even though India was not a settler colony, it had a far larger white population than any other colony and was one of the most militarized of the colonies. As a result of the 1857 mutiny, the ratio of British troops to Indian sepoys was increased drastically. The vastness of this colony required a larger and more sustained presence of the army. The cantonments were often surrounded by two kinds of markets or bazaars: the *sadr* bazaar (for local goods) and *laal* bazaar or red market for local women (prostitutes).

In India, the Contagious Diseases Acts were in some respects not new but a continuation of regulatory practices that existed prior to the 1860s. The concept of a 'lock hospital', for instance, set up for the treatment of venereal diseases and often a way for confining prostitutes and keeping them off the streets and from their work, existed as early as the early 1800s. But while the forms of regulation that tackled and treated infections were dated to a previous century, these earlier regulations did not explicitly discourage the business of prostitution. With the emphasis on the Contagious Diseases Acts and the desire to track all prostitutes, the 'governing assumption was that knowing women's whereabouts and having the ability to register, detain, or expel them bodily was desirable' (Levine 2003: 39). By the late nineteenth century, prostitution and venereal diseases (VD) were almost always discussed together, with the entire blame for the spread of VD falling on women's uncontrolled sexuality. This was a disease that spread from women who were sexually active to men who, strangely enough, were not deemed culpable of any crime. While in Hong Kong and Straits Settlements the assumption was that women were forced into prostitution, and hence registration was targeted at the brothel keepers and not individual women, in India, women were expected to come forward and register themselves. Part of the reason was the assumption that the local police force in India was too corrupt to be trusted; it was also deemed logical since historically prostitution was not stigmatized in India. In fact, it was believed that prostitution was a 'designated caste activity, accepted as safeguards to society and are not themselves ashamed of their calling' (ibid.: 53). I will revisit this analysis of prostitution as designated caste activity, and hence the different nature of 'dirt' attached, later in the chapter.

But this 'colonial imperative' of targeting prostitutes was not limited to the colonial powers. The Madonna/whore binary, increasingly being codified by early colonial administrators and medical professionals, was strategically deployed by Indian (male) nationalists in 'outlining their own definitions of respectable female sexuality' (Wald 2009: 1472). In fact this criminalization of women as 'prostitutes' was as essential for reaffirming the power of the male head of household in upper-caste Hindu families and 'in shaping the ideals of Hindu womanhood' (ibid.: 1474). Colonial codes and Hindu Brahmanical practices went hand in hand in ensuring that any public activity or participation in labour outside the home could attach the dirt of prostitution to a woman. Codification of certain women as prostitutes effectively ensured that women stayed within the private space of the home, the space allocated to them.

Similarly, the segregationist policy had an effect not just on the prostitutes themselves but on other women workers in public space, whether or not engaging in transactional sexual practices. The delineation of an exclusive red-light area meant that the rest of the city was demarcated as a 'non red-light area', subjecting not just those who identified as prostitutes but women in all public spaces to the 'normalizing gaze' (Shah 2014: 71). The designation of certain areas, the red-light districts, for the purpose of prostitution laid the spatial foundation for designating prostitution as exceptional, even as many other forms of (gendered) pleasure work continued in the 'non red-light' areas. With designated red-light areas, women in various occupations and in public spaces became subject to this gaze, and any woman not conforming to the norm in the public space could be deemed a 'prostitute'. This discourse, powered by the force of the stigma of prostitution and notions of *izzat* and respectability, as well as the colonial tactics of regulation and confinement, had one long-term effect: 'economic abjection and gender' became a 'single conjoined signifier for prostitution' (ibid.: 73). *In essence, all women, especially those with low class and caste privileges, involved in a livelihood-generating activity in the public space, could be controlled via the threat of being classified as a prostitute.*

The national and the international, the imperial and the local shaped each other around another pivotal moment – the 1920s. This is the time when middle-class morality in India become increasingly intertwined with international anti-trafficking laws, rumours around white slavery and children being abducted into prostitution. The international moral world of protecting and rescuing victims of trafficking shaped the Suppression of Immoral Traffic Act (SITA) introduced in Delhi, Bengal, the United Provinces, Punjab and Burma. Scholars of the various scales of regulations have highlighted the ironic convenience of the acronym SITA: national legislators could draw upon not just the international discourses around suppressing immoral acts like trafficking, but also use the figure of the revered Hindu goddess Sita, the perfect wife, who could be dialectically transposed against the diabolic other woman – the prostitute. This transposition was situated as much in imperial formations as in nationalist masculinities, what Janaki Nair (2008: 223) labels a 'patriarchal compact' between colonial authorities and the (male) intellectual and political leadership in India, yet again proving that Indian men could protect their women from immorality just as the imperial Raj could.

GOLDEN ERA FOR PLEASURE WORK ?
KINGS, COURTS AND THE DEVADASI SYSTEM

Prior to these key events of the 1850s and 1920s, the colonial 'tolerance' of a hierarchy of sex workers, as well as brothels, is well documented. Women's work and transactional sex came together in many other forms of 'looseness', which cannot be easily or linearly defined as prostitution. In the 'golden calm' period of 1800–57, for instance, there were the influential courtesans of the Mughal courts who refused to be seen close to any ordinary street prostitute or those who serviced soldiers (Legg 2014: 55). In his book *The Last Mughal*, William Dalrymple (2009) mentions 'the beauty and coquettishness of Delhi's courtesans' and the

> celebrated Ad Begum who would famously turn up stark naked at parties, but so cleverly painted that no one would notice. . . . Her great rival Nur Bai, was said to be so popular that every night the elephants of the great Mughal Umrah completely blocked the narrow lanes outside her house. (Dalrymple 2009: 81)

In one of the rare works that reveal the voices of the women themselves, especially in encounters with men in power, Sumanta Banerjee (1993) describes the songs and sayings of nineteenth-century prostitutes in Bengal. Unlike the finesse, art and aesthetic skills of the songs of *ganikas* (singers), whether in temples or royal courts, what is worth focusing on here is the bold and robust lyrics, very often a way of 'turning the tables on their male customers'. These sexually explicit songs were sometimes about strategic love (with policemen who could protect them), but often about just pleasure (finding poor but young and sexually adventurous lovers). For instance, in one poem (Banerjee 1993: 2468):

> *Machh khabi to ilish.*
> *Nang dhorbi to pulish.*

> If you want to eat fish, choose hilsa.
> If you want to take a lover, choose a policeman.

Or, more poetically, about a young lover (ibid.):

> *Sadhey ki hoinu, didi, Chhokra nanger boshibhuto?*
> *Taka Paisa daye na botey,*
> *Thapguli daye moneyr matoe*

> It's not for nothing, my dear sister, that I'm loyal to my young lover,
> Although he can't pay me, he gives me the kind of love I desire.

Some others gave insight into the material realities of working with madams and brothels (ibid.: 2469):

> *Bariulee, hisheb metao, Kal jaboe utey.*
> *Emon baler ghar diyecho, Nang jotey na motey.*
> *Ebarjaboe Beleghataye, Nang jotaboe mota-shota,*
> *Kuli-mojur shab bashaboe, Baad deboe na motey.*

> Send me my bills, landlady, and let me clear them.
> I am quitting your place tomorrow.
> No lover ever comes here in any case.
> Now I will go to Beleghata and pick lovers myself, ones who are nice and beefy.
> I will entertain everyone – from porters to labourers – and refuse none.

Banerjee demonstrates the low stigma and, instead, enormous power of some '*beshyas*' in Calcutta, reflected in a survey of forty-four streets in a central area where a tenth of all the houses were owned by *beshyas*. And another report indicates that in north Calcutta there was a prostitute called Moynah Tackooraney (Tackooraney is a historical feudal upper-caste title/last name associated with powerful and property-owning individuals) who owned fourteen straw huts, one upper-roomed house and a mosque. Prostitution was such a commercially viable profession in some parts of nineteenth-century Calcutta that several babu/high-class/aristocratic Bengali families were happy to rent out their residents to prostitutes.

Pleasure workers, later categorized simply as 'prostitutes', can be traced back to centuries before this so-called golden calm in the Mughal period. Portuguese travellers to the Vijayanagara empire (AD 1300–1600) in south India wrote about the *raj ganika* (royal singers), the only ones who had permission to sit by the king and were even allowed to chew betel-nut in his presence (Chatterjee 2008). Another classic and much celebrated example of a related category of pleasure workers is that of devadasis in south India. While some of the contemporary writing on devadasis has erroneously classified them as a singularly exploited group, oppressed by both patriarchy and religion, the history of the devadasi community cannot be placed in a victim/agent binary frame. The codification and reform of devadasis as prostitutes is a particularly interesting one for our argument here as the categories of sexual and religious personhood come together in a critical project of modernity. Devadasi comes from the Sanskrit terms '*deva*' (God) and '*dasi*' (servant or slave). The devadasi system originated between the third and sixth century AD predominantly in south India. Devadasis were women who become 'God's' wives. Through a ritual marriage to a deity, they serviced local temples and their daily occupation depended on their ritual status. They were often skilled singers and dancers, but their rituals could also involve other religious activities, begging and even sex work. Their identity and work were not limited to either the temple or to sex work. In fact, the 'temple focus' on devadasis was directly related to the moral anxieties and urge to label and codify these diverse sets of women in the twentieth century.

The need to codify and reform devadasis and the devadasi system, in the words of anthropologist Lucinda Ramberg (2014), is predicated on ideas about what constitutes proper and improper sexual activity as well as true and false religion. The codification of devadasis may have been a colonial impetus, but the reform of the devadasi system was as much a nationalist project – devadasis offended modern sensibilities of what female sexuality should be for and at the same time challenged 'modern' or enlightened forms of Hinduism. Much as controlling female sexuality and homogenizing the colonized were an impetus for codification of prostitution in north India, eradication of devadasis in south India was as much an impetus for the 'purification' and homogenization of Hinduism as a modern, global religion (ibid.: 257). The two together have tried to erase the variety of sexual economies, ritual duties and performing arts underlying the devadasi system. In *Unfinished Gestures*, Soneji (2012) highlights the heterogeneity of devadasis in Telegu-speaking areas of south India, and describes them as active in politics and cultural spheres way beyond the temple environs. One of the chief consequences of the moral codes, reform programmes and laws, like the Madras Devadasi Act of 1947, that Soneji unpacks was to impose strict gender norms on the devadasi community. But it had another effect: it led to a sudden rise in power of the devadasi community of men. Even as once renowned and skilled female artists were pushed into the margins and disparaged as street prostitutes, the men in the community started laying claims on property and inheritance rights. In fact, in large part due to the marginalization of devadasi women after this Act was passed, some very prominent contemporary male political figures started laying claims on the devadasi lineage.

While the study of devadasis has continued to provoke researchers and scholars from within and outside India, one of the few works written by a devadasi herself merits special attention here, a novel titled *Dasigal Mosavalai Allathu Mathi Petra Minor* (The Treacherous Net of Devadasis or the Minor Grown Wise) by Moovalur Ramamirtham Ammaiyar (1936), translated and analysed by Anandhi S. (1991). This work is a radical departure from both sets of literature that frame these women either as forcibly married to God or romanticize their desires as free-flowing. This work is also worth highlighting because of the critical 'caste corrective' it provides to the otherwise rich literature on the devadasi system.

From as early as AD 1000, devadasis were not just receivers of huge tracts of land and property, but also respected enough to be made trustees and administrators of temple funds (Anandhi 1991). But this 'ritual status', Anandhi argues, did not necessarily confirm their high social status. The notion of dirt and impurity accompanied devadasis despite their 'auspicious' ritual status, and even their own caste community thought of devadasis as a dishonour to their caste. Though sexual services may not have been the sole mandate, many rituals were devised to celebrate the union of these women with God and with other patrons. Here we notice the critical centrality of caste: all the male patrons were Brahmins and other wealthy landlords. While on the one hand these women, often skilled performers, were involved in a heterogenous and diverse set of pleasure activities, some of which brought them immense wealth and fame, on the other hand this pleasure economy cannot be viewed merely through the analytic lens of gender and bodily autonomy. The work was organized and hierarchized by the caste system. Women were required to meet the needs and ensure the pleasure of caste-privileged men.

Although the rituals did not necessarily tie the women down to God or any one patron, their sexual autonomy had its structural limits. Devadasis were not the ultimate victims of religious trafficking, nor were they free to desire any sexual partner of their choice. For instance, the women were often surrounded by male drum players in the temple itself. Sexual union with these musicians was explicitly forbidden and the sexual contract was restricted to landed (and/or high-caste) patrons. Their other celebrated status, wealth, also had its caveats. The land they received as gifts was not 'inherited' as land rights but as ownership of the income earned through this land. In fact, the inheritance of even this income earned was ensured only if the devadasi could provide a female heir, who could then be trained to become a future devadasi. Her economic independence was contingent on her continuing to perpetuate the system as a whole (ibid.).

The lobbying for and against the Devadasi Abolition Bill, 1930 highlights the ironies of the devadasi system. The 'progressive abolitionist' lobby used the predictable chaste woman/wife/good citizen versus bad devadasi analogy to support the Bill. In fact, one of the reform programmes suggested for devadasis was to force them into 'monogamous familial norms', and as incentives, provide employment to potential and willing grooms (ibid.: 740). While the anti-devadasi lobby took a predictable turn, some of the pro-devadasi advocates were more interested in preserving Brahmanical rights. It is no coincidence then that one of the chief supporters of the system, a conservative Brahmin nationalist and one to fight against the Devadasi Abolition Bill, was a defender of Brahmanical hold over temples' property and wealth.

Much like the tale of the prostitute, the past and present lives of devadasis are too complex to be delineated within the victim–agent frame. In the attempt to make visible the fissures and insert the invisible into history and archives by reversing the discourses of vulnerability and trafficking often used in the framing of pleasure work and loose women, my intention is not to glorify a 'golden age' of defiant women. Instead, the argument is that prostitution is not exceptional, it has been historically constructed as exceptional. Working women are not exceptional, they have been made invisible or made exceptional by history. In her book *Street Corner Secret*, Svati Shah writes, 'Whether prostitution begins as a sign of high status (courtesanship) and piety (devadasis), or it has simply existed for all times as it does today, both of these perspectives end up in the same place – the abject commoditization of women's bodies, that they are powerless to interrupt' (Shah 2014: 22). Prostitution is not a totalizing context but part of a complex set of informal, leisure, sexual or pleasure economies that flourished in the British colonies before and during colonization. Understanding how these economies have changed or how their framing and regulation has changed over time assists in deciphering how prostitution is produced as exceptional and ahistorical by the colonial archives and thereafter.

Given the diverse history and distinct lived realities of 'pleasure workers', whether in courts, temples or just flying kites, the use of the term 'prostitution' was not just a tragic social homogenization but also an unfortunate linguistic homogenization (Chatterjee 2008). The terms *'veshya'* (courtesan), *'ganika'* (singer) and *'tawaif'* (from the Arabic root word *'tawf'* which means a traveller/nomad) were associated with a specific type of pleasure worker and distinct forms of artistry which evolved differently across time – a fact that has been erased by the archives. In fact, an investigation into the etymologies of all the Sanskrit and Arabic/Farsi words now associated with the blanket term 'prostitute' reveals a similar tilt towards art and travel – *a creative nomad*. '*Veshya*' (now connoted with prostitute) originates from the Sanskrit root word '*vesh*', which has many sub-meanings related to dwelling, tenancy and dependency. '*Fahesheh*' (same root as *veshya*), which is now a common Farsi word for sex worker, evolved from the much broader term '*Zæn-e-khiabani*' or lady of the street. Somehow, somewhere down the line, the sub-meanings of the root term are dropped because of lack of use and only one of its meanings gets anchored in contemporary language. '*Tawa'if*' (again common in current usage to mean prostitute) derives its roots from '*tawf*' which means to travel, move around, wander. The plural *tawa'if* in Arabic means a special kind of dancing girl. In fact, the Arabic *tawaif* was often a courtesan with exemplary skills in dancing and poetry. What was the effect of this linguistic homogenization and strategic collapsing of all pleasure workers and occupations into the blanket terms 'prostitute' and 'sex work', a woman to be scorned and despised? It was a step towards the erasure of the working woman from history and archives by creating a false binary between the prostitute and the wife – *a woman who does not work* (Chatterjee 2008: 288).

In tune with these wandering women, I now wander into the twenty-first century and the pleasure economy of dance bars. Much like the colonial framing of the related pleasure works of dance, song and sex by women, public policy around pleasure works continues to be informed by hegemonic understandings of gender and morality, but also of labour and public–private spaces. And, as importantly, the policing of this contemporary pleasure economy is driven by the (masculine) state's anxiety over losing control over the labour of these (often lower-caste) women.

Dance Bars and Twenty-First Century Pleasure Economies

On 15 August 2005, ironically the exact day India gained its Independence from British colonial rule in 1947, a law banning dance bars in Mumbai was passed (Bombay Police Amendment Act, 2005). Although in 2013, bar dancers and owners ultimately won their case against the ban, most bars remain closed or have reinvented themselves in some other (often underground) way. The ban affected approximately 75,000 female dancers (Lakkimsetti 2017). The new section (33A) inserted stated that, 'Holding of a performance of dance, of any kind or type, in any eating house, permit room or beer bar is prohibited. All performance licences are cancelled.'[1] The Dance Bar Virodhi Manch (a forum against dance bars) had successfully submitted 1,50,000 signatures to the Maharashtra State Assembly in support of the ban. Flavia Agnes (2006), one of the feminist activists lobbying against the ban, labelled the order the Indian state's 'hypocritical morality'. For instance, one parliamentarian declared, 'We are not Taliban, but somewhere we have to put a stop. The moral policing we do, it is a good thing, but it is not enough . . . we need to do even more of this moral policing.' Agnes went on to lament, 'The "morality" issue had won. The "livelihood" issue had lost' (Agnes 2005: 6).

In preparation for the discussion, media advertisements and signature campaigns held across the city made their focus the Madonna/whore analogy or, in this case, the stay-at-home wife versus the loose woman/bar dancer. One of the popular campaigns was 'Sweety versus Savithri – who will you choose? wherein "Savithri" was the loved and respected moral Indian wife while "Sweety" was the loose woman and "wrecker of middle-class homes"' (Agnes 2005). Politicians and feminists were violently divided around the issue of the ban. Much like the question of prostitution brought to the forefront many of the dilemmas of feminism (Rajan 2003), the dance bar ban became a battleground for feminists from different standpoints. As with the devadasi case, a caste-based corrective to the hegemonic understandings of this ban and the lobbying against or in support of the ban are critical for our analysis. Such an analysis reveals, for instance, the fraught nature of feminist thinking on caste and intimate or sexual labour (Gopal 2012). Radical feminists are often violently against prostitution. While liberal feminists talk of women's rights to choose what they want to do with their bodies, conversations around prostitution can never be about 'women' as one homogenous category. As queer feminist activist Meena Gopal argues for Dalit women:

> The sexual division of labour operates very insidiously for women of the lower castes. Where upper caste women are withdrawn from paid labour to establish the power of caste status and to maintain the boundaries of compulsory heteronormativity, lower caste women are condemned to caste-defined domestic service in upper caste households. (Ibid.: 224)

Some feminists joined hands with the Bar Girls' Union in fighting the ban, but many others, including Dalit feminists, celebrated it as a victory of anti-trafficking issues. Dalit feminists challenged other feminists who claimed that since the majority of bar girls come from traditional entertaining and dancing communities, they must be allowed to carry on their hereditary occupation. They argued, instead, that these class- and caste-privileged feminists failed to recognize this as an instance of 'caste patriarchy', with lower-caste women being forced to provide such entertainment to upper-caste men (Dalwai 2019). For Dalit women, the real battle was not for the right *to work per se* but for the right to work with dignity and self-respect, as well as to say no to 'defiling' and 'dirty' work (like dancing in bars).

The battle for and against the ban revealed another fraught discussion, quite predictable in debates around intimate and sexual labour – private versus public spaces. The Act of 2005 claimed that dance bars flouted the law by allowing public display of obscenity, and were 'likely to deprave, corrupt or injure the public morality or morals' (Mazzarella 2015: 482). But if dancing at bars was indeed public obscenity, what about cabarets and erotic dancing in nightclubs, another regular feature of the Mumbai pleasure industry? In fact the ban was quite clear on what venues were not affected by the ban: any theatre where entry is restricted to members only or a hotel of repute catering to foreign tourists! Places where people paid membership or paid a lot of money became tantamount to private space. People in public places, by default, were assumed to be easy victims of moral corruptibility. But what about the women dancers themselves? What did this work mean for them? For that a short history of this pleasure industry is vital.

Dance bars have been an integral part of the nightlife and pleasure economy of the city of Mumbai. It has been linked to the flow of migrants into the port city, the restaurant industry and the state policy on the sale of liquor (Agnes 2005). In the 1950s, Bombay and Gujarat (from the former Bombay Presidency) were 'dry zones' and restaurants could not serve any alcohol. But after Maharashtra and Gujarat became separate states Maharashtra chose permits over prohibition, with alcohol being served in so-called permit rooms. In the 1970s, the permit rooms and beer bars, in their attempts to outdo one another, started employing dancers to serve as waitresses. This history has interesting parallels with the beer halls and then *shebeen*s in the South African context, which I will come to in a later section. As profits from these dance–drink pleasure spaces boomed, more establishments converted to dance bars, and more women were recruited as dancers. The dance bars are a fascinating example of the heterogeneity as well as idiosyncrasies of the pleasure economy. Women danced, in mostly grungy establishments and mostly clad in saris, to the latest Bollywood numbers. What was particularly titillating for the audience was this unusual combination of the familiar and the exotic where a working-class woman, who appeared to be much like their wives at home, was indulging them with an erotic dance and flirtatious attention. Male clients, primarily working-class migrants and 'non-English-speaking middle-class businessmen' (Puri 2016), bought drinks and watched the dancing, but were not allowed to touch any of the dancers. The display of cash was often in the form of conspicuous amounts of currency notes being thrown at the dancer (a money shower) as an appreciation of her dance and in order to get a few moments of exclusive attention. The state saw all these as manifestations of a corruptible and naive male working class who were ready to shower their hard-earned money on women who were not even that scantily dressed! In essence, these irrational male symptoms 'fuelled anxieties not only about the overindulgences of masculinity but also about women amassing vast amounts of money merely (!) by dancing' (ibid.: 314). The state was not the only anxious party. One of the strongest pro-ban lobbying was by middle-class women, who feared two things: one, men (namely their husbands) getting attracted to these loose women, wasting their money, getting drunk and abusing their wives; and two, young girls getting corrupted by this easy way of making money. Dance bars and the dancers were a direct threat to their homes and aspirations, and middle-class women reacted violently.

The demography of the dancers themselves is a topic of much debate. Some scholars have indicated that the women were primarily from traditional dancing/performance communities who had lost the historical patronage of upper-caste landlords. The dance bars became a strategic choice to adapt their traditional skills for a new economy. Others have highlighted that the women were primarily migrants, slum dwellers and unemployed factory workers, for whom dancing at bars, sometimes accompanied with sexual services, was just one among a range of strategies deployed to survive life in a city (Faleiro 2010). The question about the 'skill', or lack of it, of the dancers has been deployed by opposing lobbies to make their point in favour of or against the ban. Often, the exact same point is used strategically by both camps. Was bar dancing an authentic Indian tradition that needed to be saved as a '*kala*' or 'folk art', or was it an unskilled obscenity that could be deployed by anyone to earn some money? (Mazzarella 2015).

While politicians, feminists, lawyers, bar owners and the police came up with contradictory justifications for and against the ban, a handful of ethnographies focused on the aspirations of the women themselves. Perhaps as a response to the dirt and depiction of dance bar girls as moral corrupters, some dancers resorted to predictable boundary work – self-definition to defy and resist this stigma. These women highlighted that their involvement was out of sheer desperation, 'by claiming a moral status as dispossessed mothers, daughters and wives struggling to make a living in a global city' (Lakkimsetti 2017: 464). But not all bar dancers were as selfless.

In her bestselling non-fiction monograph entitled *Beautiful Thing: Inside the Secret World of Bombay's Dance Bars*, Sonia Faleiro (2010) introduces readers to women dancers, like the protagonist Leela, who aspire to be upwardly mobile, shop like rich housewives, receive expensive gifts and be cosmopolitan consumers. 'Every life has its benefits. I make money, and money gives me something my mother never had. Azaadi. Freedom. And if I have to dance for men so I can have it, okay then, I will dance for men.' And so Leela chose *azaadi* (ibid.: 35). Leela is not like the prostitutes in the 'silent bar' (who give handjobs on the side); she is not a victim, she is on top of the hierarchy of pleasure workers – she dances for men, men spend money on her and she is worth it. Faleiro's characters move the debate of such labour in pleasure economies beyond the usual victim/agent binary. For the women, dancing at bars is not just about desperate survival but also mobility and middle-class aspirations and consumption. This mobility and aspiration are not just for her family but, unashamedly, for herself. In some sense, these dance bars challenged the vision of romantic love. Women flirted and dated in order to get money, and the attraction was precisely that – the 'illusion of love', 'sexual tension' and the 'withholding of sex' (Lakkimsetti 2017: 469). Leela's story is not about the romance of resistance nor a celebration of pleasure workers as agents and makers of their own destiny. It does, however, reveal the desires that shape the choices these women workers make amidst all the everyday struggles of surviving a precarious, and now illegal, labour market. Desires that may displease many, but give her and her clients much pleasure.

In this chapter, I focus on the binding thread of these precolonial, colonial and postcolonial instances of pleasure work done by dancing and singing women, not merely out of intellectual enthusiasm. The heterogeneity of their occupations, and yet their tied-up histories, are critical not just for analytical purposes but also for movements towards solidarity. It provides insights into the gamut of heterogenous experiences in surviving precarious, gendered and stigmatized forms of pleasure works, and, at some level, add to

> the modes of action that can be drawn upon for feminist modes of social transformation. It urges us to take seriously, when some middle-class Dalit feminists of Maharashtra vehemently condemn(s) the devadasi tradition that pushed their grandmothers into subjugation. At other times, it compels us to not turn away from newer configurations, such as when women from the devadasi communities of western India, some enrolled as dance bar girls, today collectivize as sex workers to battle against the police. (Gopal 2012: 231)

To continue with the task of unravelling histories, making visible the working women cast off as loose and undesirable, and building connections if not solidarities, we continue our journey to South Africa.

CODIFYING 'TOWN WOMEN' AND PLEASURE WORKERS IN BRITISH AFRICA

The vast and rich scholarship on prostitution in British India has a direct resonance with the one on British-colonized Africa. In Uganda 'prostitution' was legal till 1930, and in songs, folklore and historical writings you get hints of a difference drawn between Malaya (Swahili for prostitutes) and Malaika (the equivalent to the Madonna/whore dichotomy), but who falls in which category is rather ambiguous. Single and urban women are prime suspects as so-called loose women until around the 1920s. In the 1920s there was high rural–urban migration and sex work started flourishing, and this was the time for coding this deviant act – prostitution got listed under offences against morality. In Kampala, Uganda, this contrast between morality–immorality and village–urban women was drawn so sharply that by the 1930s, the category 'town women' came to be equated with prostitution (Davis 2000). When we look at popular Luganda songs, we get a glimpse of the extent to which the urban single woman remains morally suspect. For example, one song is a cautionary tale that relates the story of Naggayi, a city girl who deceives three men into believing each is her only boyfriend. The song goes on to relate how this deception is a monetary strategy that women use to survive in the city of Kampala.

Branding autonomous-minded women as loose or as prostitutes and the 'othering' of single women in Buganda preceded the rise of colonial towns. Two kinds of rural single women who were subject to this 'othering' were *banakyeombekedde* (free women – single women, widows and divorcees) and *bakirerese* (restless people who could not stay in one place for long). Much like the immoral wandering women mentioned in the previous section, restlessness becomes a gendered character flaw. Female *bakirerese* were transients, people who would move between relatives, lovers and friends – whoever was willing to host them. If you look at some of the songs of such free women, a common sentiment among them women used to be, '. . . although men were necessary for a healthy sex life, they were a nuisance in general'. James Ferguson, in his study in Zambia, suggests that this kind of branding of town women as Malaya, in essence, is a local critique of urban capitalist development wherein 'the country' is portrayed as natural, pure, authentic or whole, and these moral images are then contrasted against urban realities conceived as artificial, immoral, corrupt, and anomic' (Ferguson 1997: 138). Within this imagery 'town women' are usually represented as corrupt, money hungry and immoral, in comparison with the hard-working and morally superior village women. In Nigeria again, the 1920s and 1930s reveal some interesting moments around the codification of loose women. For instance, around this time, the Emir declared that under the Islamic law, women would not be allowed to inherit houses or farms, and justified his policy by claiming that women inheritors were more prone to becoming prostitutes (Pierce 2003). Apart from policing women, this proved to be profitable for the state – in the absence of a male heir the property automatically went to the state. The autonomous woman (beyond male patronship) was a *karuwanci* in Hausa, a courtesan – basically a convenient enmeshing of British and Nigerian concerns about two interconnected issues: female immorality and female autonomy. This link between women who are autonomous from men and women who are immoral 'prostitutes' can be observed not just in the language used to describe these women (that I have already mentioned), but also in the laws passed. For instance, Wojcicki writes: 'In 1929, in Sefwi-Wiawso State, Ghana, the Free Women's Marriage Proclamation was issued, ordering that informal sex workers and other independent women working as street hawkers be arrested, locked up in the outer areas of Wiawso, and held there until they were claimed by their husbands or other men' (Wojcicki 2002: 344). In essence, what frightened the state the most was the independence of working women, not so much the work of sex. While this sweeping outline of various former British colonies in Africa might reveal some broad patterns around the ambiguity of 'looseness' in women in colonial Africa, it is far more productive to read deeper into one region – and for that purpose, the focus of the next section will be on South Africa under British rule.

SAILORS AND LOOSE WOMEN IN SOUTH AFRICA

The Cape Colony is an interesting place to start a dialogue with the British Indian case, partly because of the change in governance in the seventeenth to the eighteenth century. During the Dutch East India Company's occupation of the Cape Colony in the seventeenth century, the ports were a node for travelling Company seamen and, not surprisingly, also a hub for sex work. Scholars analysing sex work in this century often provide a functionalist argument – sex work was tolerated as a necessary evil. It kept the morale of the seaman high after their long voyages. Sex work in the Cape ports, however, had other 'functions' even during these times, that gave far more agency to the sex worker than that mentioned in most of the scholarship toeing the functionality line. While many scholars have emphasized the role of 'slave husbands' in 'pimping their wives' in the Company Slave Lodge, India Geronimo Thusi (2015) talks about Lodge, then described as the 'finest little whorehouse', as a place where the slaves also worked as sex workers. He writes: '. . . the motto of the slave sex worker was "Kammene Kas, Kammene Kunte", or "No cash, No cunt." Sex work became a means for some of these sex workers to purchase their freedom' (Thusi 2015: 210).[2] In his book *Diaspora to Diorama*, Robert Shell writes about the vastly different position of such 'Lodge women' and their strategic 'flaunting' of 'European lovers in public – dancing, stark naked even on Sundays, in full aspect', as a way for some slave women to purchase their freedom (Shell 2013: 12). But this was during the seventeenth century. In 1795, the British took control of the Cape Colony and abolished slavery. By then, although prostitution was considered an offence, it was rarely prosecuted (Ross 1999). Yet again we hear the functional argument – it was a controlled release of energies of unruly sailors, prevented the 'unnatural vice' of homosexuality, protected wives from the 'unsavoury desires of their husbands', etc.

While there was not as much formal policing of sex work through laws, sex work was classified and codified far more effectively through public health discourses. The 1860s become pivotal for this analysis especially since much of Britain's colonial policies in Africa were formulated from their experience of governing India, and this attitude towards African colonial governance shifted dramatically after the 1857 'mutiny' in India. There was an urgent need to control the native population, and sexuality emerged as a key access point. The regulation of sex work as a universal and public good could be most effectively argued by labelling sex workers as a 'site of contagion' – and such a label resulted in formal state interventions in the form of the Contagious Diseases Act, passed in England in 1864 and in South Africa in 1868. For this Act the Indian experience was directly translated to the Cape, as it was often the military doctors who had formerly served in India that most vociferously demanded the regulation of prostitutes (van Heyningen 1984). This was an imperial legislation introduced in the Cape Colony without any demand from the colony itself, nor was it based on the local experience. As historian Veronica van Heyningen notes about the anti-contagious diseases campaign in the Cape, 'The campaign achieved its success so rapidly and so easily mainly because there was no real local demand for the Act; it, too, was an exotic with only shallow roots in the Colony' (ibid.: 176). There was 'no public outcry against prostitution, no petitions crying for reform' (ibid.: 173), yet the Act was passed.

Just as the Contagious Diseases Acts have parallels and yet critical divergences across the colonies in Asia, we see a similar trajectory in South Africa. In the Cape Colony, this Act mandated the registration and regulation of sex workers and their 'voluntary' treatment in lock hospitals if found to be carrying infections. The passing of this law did not go unchallenged. While some of the strongest lobbies in the repeal campaign in Britain were led in part by liberal feminists like Josephine Butler, in the Cape the repeal movement had a distinctly white liberal male following with politicians like Saul Solomon in the lead (ibid.). Despite the conflicting pressures from imperial legislations, or the local and global repeal activists, the sex workers in the Cape continued to pursue their trade in relative peace, at least till the late 1880s, when the syphilis epidemic started attracting government attention. The imperial powers used this opportunity to emphasize not just the naivety of the earlier oppositions to the Contagious Diseases Act, but also that prostitution and the infection could possibly poison the entire community. This time the Contagious Diseases Act (of 1885) was passed without a murmur.

Although the mass hysteria around syphilis made prostitutes the most convenient target of state control, the more troubling group was that of the 'occasional prostitutes', mostly all domestic workers who were deemed by the authorities as the most insidious, since they could clandestinely contaminate their employers' (white) families, including children. It was once again the amorphous nature of a contaminating figure that encouraged some extreme recommendations; for instance, 'all servants – especially female servants – should be examined by a doctor and receive a certificate' (van Heyningen 1984: 180). Around this time, the vast majority of the registered prostitutes were identified as 'Coloured', mainly women from farm labouring families who had been former domestics and cooks (ibid.: 182). What also seemed to bind them together was their independent and aggressive behaviour, labelled 'rioters' in van Heyningen's work. These women rioted against the surveillance imposed by the Act, often refusing to subject themselves to the required examination.

The racial demography of these women seldom became the focus of discussions till the influx of European women into the Cape in the 1890s. Then, for instance, members of the British Anti-Contagious Diseases Acts Association (NA) and the Ladies National Association (LNA) pointed out the racialized effects of the Act on dehumanizing Coloured women, formerly part of slave populations. Their renewed attempt to repeal the Act, however, did not pass in the House of Assembly. This period saw a rise in the social purity movement and discussions around the Morality Act – a result of the moral panic around sexual transactions between European sex workers – with a focus on miscegenation and abolition rather than on regulation of such 'vices'. Debates around the Contagious Diseases Act and the Morality Act took an interesting gendered and, as expected, racial turn in the Cape Colony. While African women were known to be involved in sex work, domestic work at that time was not a female domain and in fact was dominated by African men. The presence of an African man or 'houseboy' in the private domain of the white employer, along with the dirt and stigma attached to African sex workers as carriers of contagion, created a panic of a racial and gendered nature – the Black 'houseboys' became likely suspects for bringing VD from the brothels and spreading contagion in white neighbourhoods and households. This fear of Black male sexuality deepened in the first few decades of the twentieth century. For instance, the 1902 Morality Act criminalized relationships between Black males and white female prostitutes in the Cape Colony. The later versions of the Morality Act (of 1927, 1950 and the Sexual Offences Act of 1957) prohibited all forms of miscegenation between all races and regulated the sexual lives of South Africans during apartheid. Worth noting, however, was the side effect of these conversations around the Morality Act on the framing of prostitution *per se* – the prostitutes were no longer the sinners but the victims of profiteering by male pimps. The Morality Act was also instrumental in putting an end to European prostitution in the Cape, where the threat of miscegenation and Black men being solicited by white prostitutes led to most of these women being driven away from the colony.

Several deviants come together in these historical writings – sailors, miners and loose women of various counts. Sailors have long been considered the 'primary carriers of cultural, political, genetic and material cargo' (Trotter 2009a: 701); they are also portrayed as deviant in some ways because of their transient presence on land. Like ports and sailing, a sector that is historically linked with prostitution is mining. Prostitution is not only a side note to historical mining regions but is often one of its defining features. Here too there is a stark association between anxieties around women's autonomy and the need to codify prostitution and prostitutes. In this sector, prostitution often arose due to the exclusion of women from the licit profits of the mining enterprise. For instance, in the nineteenth- and early twentieth-century mining compounds of South Africa, women were often barred from even traditionally female occupations such as domestic work at the mine sites, mostly because of sexual anxieties around the female presence in a masculine space. Sex work often proved the most lucrative, if not the only, means by which a woman could profit from mining, or the only way for women to be 'mining the miners' (Laite 2009: 745). Sex work became a resistive strategy and a means for women to gain access to mining regions. The more functional understanding of prostitution's place in mining communities is that the owners of mines *allowed* the presence of sex workers because it added to 'the miners' masculine work culture and . . . served the company's interests in increasing production' (ibid.: 746). By this argument, sex work was implicitly part of the mining mechanism and not a disruptive act by the women themselves.

The 1920s were an important decade for codification in the area of mining and prostitution. As the mining community grew in population and became more connected to the politics of the larger region, nation or empire, the desire to control independent, young and single women led to demands to repress prostitution and women's migration in southern Africa. This was also the time around which missionaries started expressing fears about the 'dangerous mobility and social disconnection of young women who migrated to mining areas, far away from patriarchal control' (ibid.: 757). The state responded quickly and decisively, and by the late 1930s, physical roadblocks were set up to prevent women from working in mining areas. The same women who were thought to be productively contributing to the masculinist work force's needs were now to be repressed because they led to unruly behaviour by miners. Apart from the roadblocks, the mining companies were able to push the government into passing laws that banned all spaces, like salons and canteens, where sex workers could interact with the miners and even banned the sale of liquor. Native workers' (excessive or unregulated) pleasure was a threat for the mine owners and managers, much like the (uncontrolled) presence of the women pleasure workers. Several scholars have linked the history of mines, miners and beer brewing to the racial and spatial politics of colonial, apartheid and post-apartheid South Africa (Crush and

Ambler, eds 1992). The fact that this history has critical and intrinsic gendered underpinnings has had far less enthusiasm. This is what we turn to next.

Female Beer Brewers, Shebeen Queens and Pleasure Workers

What a helluva mess men are making of this world. And they're so weak-spined and dishonest, they keep blaming their weaknesses on Eve because she gave Adam the apple. . . . Your Aunty Sammy was born for yesterday or tomorrow, but definitely not for today. . . . In those days men and women were very different. The females were all big and strong as oxen, just like me. . . . If I had lived then I would have fitted into life just so easy. . . . It would have been so heavenly to go to cocktail parties without toe-pinching high-heel shoes . . . no bra-straps cutting through my shoulders, no silly narrow skirts to make me walk like a knock-kneed walrus. (Post by Aunty Sammy, Cape Town's famous 'Shebeen' or Tavern Queen, *DRUM*, 1964–67, in Bailey and Seftel, eds 1994)

15 August makes its appearance once again as a critical turning point in the lives and times of post-colonial loose women, this time not for dance bar girls in India but for *shebeen* queens in South Africa. That day in 1962 saw the end of thirty-four years of racialized prohibition in South Africa – the Liquor Act of 1928 that banned the sale of European liquor to Black Africans. *DRUM* reported that it was an end to 'a piece of legislation which never worked, which impressed only to cause misery and the wanton waste of manpower. Only now can the story be told of how it didn't work: how the millions who were supposed to be dry were actually wet' (Bailey and Seftel, eds 1994). As anti-prohibition lobbies victoriously yelled, 'Let the masses drink. They are drinking anyway' (ibid.: 129), less thought was given to what would happen to the flourishing illicit pleasure economy of brewing and selling beer, run primarily by Black South African women – the legendary *shebeen* queens. In this section of the chapter, I demonstrate how the now famous *shebeen* queens, the owners of robust taverns near mines and in apartheid townships, were not a historical or urban aberration but had a clear connection to beer brewing in Africa, which was always and intrinsically about women. I provide a brief historical and global sketch of beer brewing around the world before turning to colonial South Africa when beer brewing was codified as illegal. I argue that, much like in the case of our other category of loose women, the anxiety around female beer brewers and *shebeen* queens – often stigmatized as pimps and prostitutes – was not so much about their 'immoral acts' but their ability to find a niche in the informal urban economy, in direct defiance with white labour laws that dictated certain roles for Black (native) men and women. It was a complex tale of race, space, migrancy and women, and the colonial obsession with the regulation of leisure and pleasure.

Much like with prostitution, the preoccupation with alcohol amongst social scientists has been quite impressive. Anthropologists have been the most prolific in the so-called 'alcohol studies', interested in the interactions of alcohol and human behaviour. A common thread in most early writings from the 1920s to 1980s was to approach alcohol as a social problem (Gefou-Madianou, ed. 1992). Interestingly, deviant anthropologists who emphasized constructive drinking were criticized by other disciplines for focusing excessively on the functionality of alcohol (Douglas 1987). In the last few decades, anthropologists and social historians have started recognizing alcohol's potential to incite conflict and resistance, giving rise to an enthusiastic 'wet' generation of scholars deeply invested in drinking studies (Room 1984). How does this generation talk about women and gender within the study of alcohol and drinking? Men are observed as the primary consumers of alcohol, whether in Europe or elsewhere, and most discussions around alcohol and gender have tended to focus on questions of masculinity, alcohol consumption and men's sociability in public spaces (Gefou-Madinou, ed. 1992). Some exceptions are noted, mostly of defiant and loose women consuming alcohol in public spaces in order to challenge some form of patriarchal supremacy. For instance, Nieuwkerk (1992) talks of 'female entertainers' in Egypt drinking as a way to coopt symbols of masculinity, and Papagaroufali (1992) talks of Greek women in coffee houses drinking as a sign of resistance. Most others, namely good women, drink 'good' alcohol like wine, in private, in all-female gatherings and in moderation. In these tales, women make their appearance as brewers and servers.

Historically and across the globe, beer has been brewed by women, and very often for nutritional purposes. Beer, often with rather low levels of alcohol, was intrinsic to social life and meal customs in various countries around the world. If locally brewed beer was not consumed in the morning, it was consumed during the day as a nutritional supplement. Beer brewing in Egypt dates back to 5500–3100 BC, primarily done by women (Meussdoerffer 2009). This was linked to beliefs around a number of goddesses and their intoxicating powers. Concurrently, as beer brewing took place in the home, it was regarded a female chore. The process of graining grains and producing beer was a time-sensitive and labour-intensive activity. In Burkina Faso, for instance, a woman still needs her husband's permission before she can start brewing, as she may be occupied for several days and unavailable for her other wifely duties (Helmfrid 2013). Wine making on the other hand was a man's job, as it was perceived to be a more complicated process. Traces of beer brewing in Babylon and Mesopotamia can be dated back to 4000 BC. Amidst this rich history of beer brewing in Babylon and Mesopotamia, there is an epoch during which, much like in the South African colonial/apartheid era, women not only brewed beer but also owned the taverns where beer was sold. In *A History of Beer and Brewing*, Hornsey

(2003) states that taverns owned and run by women were places where sex was sold, and often the female tavern owners would act as the madam/pimp. The author uses the term 'loose women' (ibid.: 106); however, there is no definition provided, presumably because readers are expected to know what a 'loose woman' universally stands for! In Peru, Hayashida (2008) argues that before the arrival of the Spanish colonialists, the people residing on the north coast of Peru and in the Andes produced chicha, a local beer brewed from maize. In instances where maize was scarce, other grains or fruits were utilized for the beer brewing. Chicha was produced by 'chosen' (not loose) women and consumed in social and cultural gatherings, including for rituals within various communities. With colonialism, Incan chicha was banned by the colonialist as the local traditional beer was a symbol of the Inca religion. As in the colonies around the world, colonial administrators enforced rules and prohibitions on local traditional beer production and consumption, which then had multiple effects on the (women) workers (ibid.). Women producers have always been at the core of the alcohol economy, yet once brewing becomes more commercialized and women entrepreneurs find ways to use this as a way to access labour markets shaped by colonial laws, this industry becomes severely regulated.

Zoom into the African continent, and here too beer brewing has historically been women's business in rural homesteads (Nelson 1978; Crush and Ambler, eds 1992; McAllister 1992; Redding 1992; Haggblade 1992; Willis 2002; Bryceson 2002). Traditionally African alcoholic brews were made from fruits and grains, in farmlands, and by women, but alcohol *consumption*, whether at social gatherings or in connection with traditional rituals, was primarily an activity for men (Hornsey 2003; Dietler 2006; Meussdoerffer 2009). Female beer brewers were neither synonymous with pleasure work nor with being loose. McAllister (2006) asserts that historically Xhosa beer drinking formed part of ubuntu and moral behaviour; beer drinking was a harmonious cultural ritual. In fact, beer brewing was one of the primary tasks of a quintessential good wife. In Swaziland, a 'good' wife was one who made sure that her husband always had a pot of beer or a fermented porridge in hand. Women who did not brew at least once a month were criticized by their husbands (Crush and Ambler, eds 1992: 371). Colonial governmentality and urbanization changed the dynamics of beer brewing, beer consumption and its gendered political economy (Nelson 1978; Rorich 1989; Crush and Ambler, eds 1992; Bailey and Seftel, eds 1994; Mager 2010). In southern Africa, the selective and racialized access to alcohol was a critical colonial political and economic tool. At the same time, lack of access to this pleasure became one of the most powerful symbols for mobilizing native resistance (Crush and Ambler, eds 1992). In the next few sections, I will focus on the Cape Colony and the major South African mining regions and industrial towns that became pivotal in the story of the battle against liquor laws.

With the abolition of slavery in the Cape Colony after 1834, both the colonial state and white employers had to devise new ways of controlling the native population. As the urban population started expanding in the latter half of the nineteenth century, Black men and Black disorder and drunkenness became points for a renewed focus of anxiety and control. While some in power were swayed by the idea of temperance, the more pragmatic ones were enticed by the revenue potential of distributing liquor amongst native workers. But no concerted state effort was seen till the last decade of the nineteenth century (ibid.). The 1890s saw the rapid expansion of urban migration connected with mining in the areas of Witwatersrand, Kimberley and Natal. While the gendered and spacialized political economy of the three regions had its specific characteristics, there were many parallels.

After a detailed analysis of white and Black alcohol consumption, the 1893 Cape Colony Liquor Laws Commission declared that the entire Black population was incapable of controlling the temptation to get drunk (ibid.: 7). The outcome of the Commission was to restrict the natives from purchasing European alcohol. From 1928 onwards, South Africa saw numerous prohibition liquor laws determined by provinces and their colonial administrations (ibid.; Mager 2010). These reflected the paradoxical position the colonial government found itself in. On the one hand, economically, alcohol consumption by the natives was beneficial for the colonial government as it generated jobs, profits and taxes. It was also an effective means of recruiting workers into the less desired mines. The difference between 'wet' and 'dry' mining compounds was that the former could attract more mineworkers from the rural areas. On the other hand, alcohol consumption was perceived by colonialists as a potential threat towards the colonial project. The colonial subject was considered childlike, and one who would not be able to handle alcohol consumption. Allowing the natives to drink alcohol was thought to result in lazy work attitudes and increased criminal activity, later connected to the apartheid moral panic around *swaart gewar* (Afrikaans for 'Black danger'). By the 1920s, the choice was to follow total prohibition (as in some mines near Johannesburg), run municipal beer hall monopolies (as in Durban), or to employ a combination of domestic brewing and controlled liquor sales. In the Kimberly mining compound, for instance, management convinced the state to pass a prohibition on sale of alcohol to Africans, effectively curbing production of alcohol by Africans in rural areas and its supply to urban areas. In Durban there was a similar impetus to control drinking, but instead of prohibition, the more pragmatic route of municipal monopoly was preferred and the first beer halls were introduced in 1909. The beer halls generated revenue to maintain the residential segregation of workers and also encouraged the workers to spend their time in these townships (Crush and Ambler, eds 1992: 22). The beer halls were mostly dull, gendered and racially segregated spaces, designed to keep all kinds of moral decay in check. To be a leisure activity, drinking requires autonomy (Mager 2010: 3). Drinking in beer halls, under strict surveillance, was like drinking in a cage (Crush and Ambler, eds 1992: 25). The Durban system of beer halls, as it became known, paved the way forward for many municipal administrators, not just throughout the South African provinces, but also across southern Africa. Replications of the Durban system allowed colonial governments across southern Africa to include and exclude its labour force through social engineering and control over the social, economic and cultural life of its subjects. The labourers' leisure time was strictly controlled through draconian liquor laws, while ensuring high profit margins and revenues for the government. Where do women fit into this picture of a masculine state and male mineworkers?

The twentieth-century panic about urban (Black) drinking and drunkenness was as much about worker control as it was about rural–urban migration, especially the urban presence of native women 'deprived of tribal restraints' (ibid.: 7). Urbanization and alcohol were intertwined even in law. For instance, the Native (Urban Areas) Act (a legislation that sought to control the movement of Africans to and from urban areas) contained specific references to alcohol (Gewald 2002: 121). This had obvious implications for women migrants. When African women moved from the rural areas to cities, however transient their move, they used the beer-brewing skills they had acquired back in the village to gain access to the urban economy. Brewing and selling of beer remained in the women's domain, whether in rural or urban settings. In the late nineteenth century, this was recognized in some laws: for instance, although the Act 36 of 1899 prohibited sale or supply of any liquor to Africans, section 4 of the Act 'allowed the sale and supply of Native beer by Native women, according to their usual practice, and not as a permanent business' (la Hausse: 88). As long as the activity remained 'traditional', familial and not overtly entrepreneurial it was deemed acceptable. But not for long.

African women regularly moved from rural to urban areas carrying a variety of agricultural produce, including dagga and beer, for the pleasure and leisure of urban residents. Trains and railway platforms were filled with native women carrying pots of beer. As an example, in just one year, between 1905 and 1906, around 9,000 gallons of such beer is known to have been brought into Durban (ibid.: 86). With economic depression, many male workers found themselves retrenched and very often women continued to bring food on the table precisely by brewing and selling beer. As the crisis deepened, more and more African women used beer sale and supply as a way to make the most of their temporary entry into the cities and to eventually try and make it permanent. Women made informal housing arrangements, some obtained jobs as domestics and washerwomen but there were very few other options. Others preferred to brew and supply beer over these other, more legitimate and gendered, domestic tasks. This floating population of women, especially single women selling beer, started becoming hyper-visible in some cities. For instance, in Durban in the early twentieth century, nearly one in every four Black women was active in the beer trade and in selling beer in urban informal taverns or *shebeens* (ibid.: 91) Women's entrepreneurship in these permanent *shebeens* made the authorities far more anxious than the temporary migration of rural women. It meant the presence of single women or women existing autonomously, free from the control of tribal chiefs and their male kin. It was also a clear and worrying indication of the possibilities of independent Black entrepreneurship. The twentieth-century municipal liquor laws and beer halls thus were as much about worker control as grounds for the expulsion of these undesirable women brewers. The exact nature and trade of these women differed according to the spatiality of the mining trade. While much of what I described till now was in Durban, in Witwatersrand municipality, regulations had a different spatial dimension. For instance, miners who did not live in the company compound were expected to live in 'locations', or nearby slums, where temporary housing was provided in return for rent. This amount was often paid through sale of illicit beer. Black women entrepreneurs were leaders of this brewing and sale – a 'crime' tolerated by authorities as it generated the rent for the housing they provided! But as the depression deepened, and so did the urban housing crisis, Witwatersrand started making a move towards the Durban system of beer halls in order to raise more revenue for urban control (Baker 1992).

While women's presence in general may have been a cause of anxiety, married women joining their husbands in mines was considered a different evil as compared to single women in towns attracting male mineworkers. In Witwatersrand, where mine compounds were not geographically separate as in Natal, the presence of *single* women was the biggest source of concern. On Sundays and mine holidays, mineworkers could easily interact with these single beer-brewing women. Mine owners feared that mineworkers would abandon their mines and contracts to establish unions with these women. In the 1920s, this fear was compounded by the fresh arrival of another set of loose women – single Basotho women who made their living by brewing beer and, sometimes, through (sexual) relationships with men. Much like the prostitutes in colonial India were to blame for all kinds of sin, from contagious diseases to decay of young men's morality, these beer-brewing women became 'symptomatic of a multifaceted crisis of social control' (Bonner 1992: 274). A location manager responding to the crisis wrote: 'Besides being a

menace to the peace and safety of the law-abiding residents of the location . . .
[Basotho women] were responsible for the very unhygienic conditions, and must
have been the cause of a lot of disease, since the place was hopelessly overcrowded.'
In essence, everything from infant mortality, juvenile delinquency, social disorder
and crime was blamed on the presence of these women (ibid.: 278). Authorities
resorted to various acts and laws, expansion of police force in location to assist
with raids and even the extreme strategy of building a physical barrier – a ten-foot,
'man-proof' fence to keep the mineworkers in, and illicit beer and women out!
This proved rather counterproductive as almost immediately, the Basotho women
organized ways of opening up sections of the fence through which the miners
could come out to get their fix. As a result, much of the increased police force
had to be deployed away from the raids within the location to safeguarding the
fence – effectively eroding their ability to do either task properly. By the 1920s,
the phrase 'Basuto women' became a synonym of 'loose' immoral women who
were widows, runaway wives or ones who had had trouble with their husbands.
In 1914, the Basutoland National Council proposed that women be obliged to
carry a pass signed by their husbands or fathers and chiefs in order to cross the
border into South Africa. The first pass laws were thus framed with the related
objectives of suppressing beer brewing and prostitution, and forcing women
on to the domestic labour market as prescribed nannies and cleaners in white
homes. As can be expected from a government that panics over the autonomy
of working women, the pass laws were to also legally mandate the dependence
of women on their male family members.

In Umtata, we notice a similar interlinking of 'loose characteristics', being single,
financially autonomous and a migrant. Here, a floating population of women
brewers and migrant workers returning from Rand mines created a major panic
about crime and prostitution. Before 1913, the government allowed women to
reside in the locations as long as they paid rent, regardless of their marital and
employment status (Redding 1992: 245). But the anxiety about the presence of
single Black women living in towns trumped the profit-making imperative, and the
law was altered to allow only married women to reside in these locations. Women
entrepreneurs responded by finding alternative residences which were outside
the location, but where they could brew their beer with less surveillance. What
is worth noting is that even fines and prison sentences did not deter the brewers,
who returned from prison and got back straight to brewing. As Sean Redding
concludes, this was either because the profits from illicit brewing were so high
or the women were so desperate for a living that all risks were made worthwhile.

Across the country and despite the prohibitions and regulations, brewers
defied the laws and state surveillance by illicitly brewing and supplying beer
near compounds or in townships. Prohibition at no time meant an end to

drinking. Men were determined to drink, and women (and sometimes men) met this determined need by supplying them with all kinds of liquor despite the risk of fines and jail (Baker 1992). The skills of women entrepreneurs lay in not just the hard physical labour of brewing, but also in transporting and selling beer clandestinely. How did women entrepreneurs react to beer halls and municipal attempts to put an end to this illicit pleasure economy? Beer halls were a direct attack on women's entrepreneurship and it took away the hard-earned monthly wages of their male kin to feed the pockets of already rich white employers. The beer halls thus became the symbols of gendered and not just racial and class oppression (Bradford 1992: 208), and as a consequence, the target of what became popularly labelled the 'beer hall riots'. The late 1920s and the early 30s saw a series of protests, which started off as a beer boycott mainly by male migrant workers in Durban, rapidly evolving into a women-led protest movement. Some women protested that their husbands were not bringing enough money home as all the money was spent in these beer halls, while others were as angry because women were restricted from entering these halls. Women raided only those beer halls that barred them from entering as customers. Beer halls situated on the site of the mine, that were mixed gender, did not become targets of the women's ire (Edgecombe 1992). At some point, these protests became so organized that solidarity groups were spreading from urban centres to rural areas. Women organized during church prayer sessions and while singing church hymns. Others armed themselves with assegais (iron-tipped, hardwood spear), chanted war songs, wore men's loincloth and cow tails, and chased men, including policemen, out of the beer halls (Bradford 1992: 221).

But the beer hall riots were just one manifestation of women entrepreneurs reacting to municipality regulations. Across the nation, and despite the prohibition, the illicit brewing and sale of beer continued in *shebeens*. Every fibre of the *shebeens* as cultural institutions challenged the socially engineered machine of the colonial administration. Native beer production was a form of resistance to the tightly controlled wage labour. The sale of native beer generated income which was not accounted for by the government, and as this beer was produced from grain, this entailed that rural native agriculture could survive outside white commercial agriculture (Crush and Ambler, eds 1992). *Shebeens* ranged from the luxurious high-end variety that sold exotic liquor to their grungier counterparts that served illicit and dangerous brews laced with harmful substances. As the nature of the *shebeens* changed, so did the role, strategies and entrepreneurship of the *shebeen* queens. By the 1920s, the nightlife of much of the urban Black population was in highly restricted 'locations', operating under strict curfews. The novel *Marabi Dance*, although set in a later period, describes this subculture of surviving urban life under such restrictions. The *shebeens* were small tenement spaces where women produced and sold not just beer but alcohol laced with chemicals. To keep the spirits up, the hooch drinking was paired with music on the piano, and this is where we find the beginnings of the famous marabi music, inspired by African American jazz and blues, as well as church and African folk music. The *shebeen* queens kept these all-night parties alive by hiring entertainers, supplying the alcohol and keeping the police out.

The 1930s and 40s saw rapid urbanization, and, consequently, a more 'settled' urban working class emerging. To keep up with the demands and desires of its growing clientele, the *shebeens* start getting bigger and more sophisticated. Freehold townships, and some of the first Black suburbs like Western Native Township and Sophiatown, were abuzz with these *shebeens*, music and alcohol. The 1950s witnessed the rapid destruction of these freeholds and the settlement of people in big apartheid townships. This was accompanied by what Christian Rogerson labels 'drinking apartheid' wherein African consumption of alcohol got pushed out of, for instance, central Johannesburg to the official townships. The customers here were factory workers living in hostels, public service employees and nocturnal employees (cleaners, security guards, etc.). In Johannesburg this was the time for the emergence of an organized Black middle class with state approved licenses for starting butcheries and liquor stores. Black men started entering the business scene and the liquor industry, though not yet in large numbers. The all-night parties continued in the *shebeens* in the townships, now with a lot of glamour and attention. The likes of Miriam Makeba, Dolly Rathebe, Dorothy Masuka and Thandi Klaasen are celebrated for their deviant lifestyles and their music, but as actively despised by the churchgoers, and even some union workers, for corrupting the minds and consciousness of their comrades.

The women who established, owned and managed these illegal drinking taverns in urban Black townships were given the title of 'shebeen queens', though sometimes also referred to as 'Aunty' or 'Ma'. They did not always brew the beer in their backyards themselves, but, depending on their wealth and status, hired young men from their community to brew, traffic and run around when the police raided the *shebeen*. *Shebeens* were often set up in the *shebeen* queens' living rooms, which made the drinking taverns homely, as opposed to the cold, institutional and alienating beer halls run by municipalities. *DRUM* is one of the best sources for tales of *shebeen* queens and the nightlives in the variety of *shebeens* that flourished during the thirty-five years of prohibition. *Shebeen* queens were known for their charm, entrepreneurship, sometimes maternal affection and often masculine strength and physical features. As a story goes:

> Even when they possessed pretty faces they had the build and ability to scowl with frightening effect, guaranteed to sober any drunken behaviour. On the other hand

when her costumer gives her no trouble, he was treated with a deliberate show of kindness, to a point of a personal attention. This ability by the Aunty, to scold and love without lasting severity, is the usual hallmark of a close relative. Thus, it seems, the term Aunty became established without semantic strain. (Bailey and Seftel, eds 1994: 11)

Some women ran *shebeen*s to pay their children's school fees and build a respectable life for them. In his autobiography, *Blame Me on History*, William Bloke Modisane writes about his *shebeen* queen mother:

My mother accepted her life, and I suppose, so did the other shebeen queens; they chose this life and accommodated the hazards. . . . My mother wanted a better life for her children, a kind of insurance against poverty by trying to give me a prestige profession, and if necessary would go to jail whilst doing it. (Modisane 1990)

Others did it because this was the best way to gain financial independence. As Es'kia Mphahlele (2013) so eloquently describes in his memoir, *Down Second Avenue*, how a *shebeen* queen carves out a niche of economic independence despite the gendered and raced rules of apartheid:

The same old cycle. Leave school, my daughter, and work, you cannot sit at home and have other people work for you; stand up and do the white man's washing and sell beer. That's right – that is how a woman does it; look at us, we do not sit and look up to our husbands or fathers to work alone; we have sent our children to school with money from beer selling . . .

But not all Aunties were there to selflessly feed their families, or to be affectionate towards their customers. There were others, like Aunty Rose, who flamboyantly flaunted their sexuality and desires and used their 'toy boys', often younger men, for sex and then abandoned them at whim. And the renowned Aunty Peggy was more a 'tour drinker' who bummed hooch off her customers and landed on their laps, whether they liked it or not, by the end of the night. A legendary *shebeen* queen wore specially made ample undergarments to traffic the illicit liquor, while another pushed her supplies in a pram (Bailey and Seftel, eds 1994: 18). Yet another Aunty stripped men of their coats, beat them with her stilettos or chased them down while riding her scooter if they did not pay up for their drinks!

The end of prohibition in 1961 changed the working of the *shebeen*s. The task of a *shebeen* queen was no longer the illicit brewing or sale of liquor but of arranging storage for commercially bought liquor (Mager 2010). Although the illicit nature of their job changed, *shebeen* queens did not have to close shop. As a *shebeen* queen in Johannesburg's western township declared, 'Close up? Never . . . I am here to stay. If I know the drinkers, they'll finish all their bottle store drink on the way home and they be knocking on my door just a few minutes after six, when the liquor shops close' (Bailey and Seftel, eds 1994: 117). The appeal of the *shebeen* and the *shebeen* queens went beyond the supply of liquor. It was a place for political discussions, camaraderie, music and dance. As one interviewee summarized, it was a place for all kinds of conversations, from Picasso to Mariam Makeba (ibid.: 118), and another, talking wistfully of a *shebeen* queen, announced that she 'used to give us life. Chicken lunch on Sundays and a bottle of sealed whiskey for regulars.' As these *shebeen* queens and patrons predicted, women still constitute the overwhelming majority of *shebeen* owners and managers, although the number of men-run taverns have increased over time, especially the high-end kind (Mager 2010).

By focusing on the '*shebeen* queens', my intention here is not to romanticize the story of *shebeen*s. Unarguably, *shebeen* queens operated within a dangerous, illegal and informal labour market. In *Mine Boy*, Peter Abrahams (1989) describes the everyday dangers of being a *shebeen* queen: 'They are the Stockvelt. They are all women who sell beer. And if one is arrested they all come together and collect money among themselves and bail out the arrested one. They are here to collect money for those who were arrested yesterday.' *Shebeen* queens also often provided sexual services to their male clientele or hired young attractive women to work as assistants in the taverns and as sex workers (Edwards 1988). The construction of *shebeen* queens as deviant was not restricted to colonial or apartheid governmentality – a large part of the urban Black African population also cast *shebeen* queens as pimps and prostitutes. But despite the stigma, the *shebeen* queens were (and still are) feared and respected by the community. They were women entrepreneurs who ran the entire pleasure economy of illicit liquor and they did this with full élan. In the words of journalist Jim Bailey (founder of *DRUM*), 'So highly have I learned to respect the shebeen queens, I have been left with a profound question: Would the shebeen queens have preferred to be captains of industry, or in their hearts of hearts, would the captains of industry have preferred to be shebeen queens?'

CONCLUSION

As I write this conclusion, a call for a remarkable special issue catches my attention – *Critical Aunty Studies,* which 'invites submissions that consider the globally ubiquitous and notoriously unruly aunty figures' that appear in various media and in our everyday lives.[3] The 'Aunty' is that liminal figure, often melodramatic and maximalist in her personality and appearance, sometimes asexual and at other times hyper-sexualized, who surveils and yet encourages transgressions of various kinds. Much like the Aunty in this chapter, the 'loose women' involved in various pleasure economies are not just protagonists of this book but also a signpost for a variety of transgressions by women workers across centuries and countries.

The flamboyance of the title 'loose women' is in stark contrast to the mundanity of women's labour. Women have always been workers but have rarely been recognized as such. A 'worker' has historically and erroneously been assumed to be a masculinist title. In this chapter, I argued that the declaration of all financially autonomous women as 'loose' makes women's paid work seem exceptional and ahistorical. It discourages the inclusion of sexuality and gender into mainstream discussions of labour. A focus on the colonial and post-colonial figure of the loose women, and on pleasure economies, allowed us to focus on some inherent anxieties in accepting women as workers, as legitimate occupiers of public spaces and as autonomous citizens. It allowed us to analyse the mechanisms through which these anxieties get codified across continents and across time.

In this chapter, however, we understood dirt and stigma as a mode of disciplining women workers across a gamut of spheres, but also as potential hubs of pleasurable transgressions and communities. Beer-brewing women, *shebeen* queens and Aunties in Southern Africa defied gendered assumptions of (male) dependency. At the same time, they were able to carve out spheres of work outside those mandated for Black African women by the apartheid state. In the Indian subcontinent, such transgressions were as many, whether as dance bar workers in the twenty-first century or courtesans and devadasis in Mughal courts. These pleasure economies were in direct defiance to norms of female respectability. But much like Damodaran (chapter 1, this volume) observes for various forms of precariat labour under capitalist and pre-capitalist systems, the binary of freedom versus unfreedom needs to be treated with caution. For the pleasure economies and the loose women workers analysed in this chapter, freedom and unfreedom are held in constant tension by forces of class, caste, race, and not just gender. Dalit feminists and critical race scholars have warned feminist scholars of reproductive labour against excessive reliance on (Northern) interpretations of choice and bodily autonomy in their understanding of labour, especially labour which is embedded in sexual and moral economies (Rao 2019; Twine 2015).[4] For lower-caste (Dalit) women in India, being able to work is not a privilege or an act of defiance but a necessity, and the real battle is to work with dignity. There lies the inherent paradox of the many pleasure works analysed in this chapter. They have been carved out by women across race, caste and class, through complex negotiation and through sheer defiance of layers of gendered assumptions about legitimate work. At the same time, they have endured through time because they are assumed to be sources of male pleasure. Once we started digging deep into novels, poetry and memoirs, we finally found the words of the Aunties, queens, Mas and dancers who brewed, sang, danced and had sex out of desperation, but also for pleasure.

A special note of thanks to Sepideh Azari, for her generous and thoughtful assistance at various stages of the planning, research and writing of this chapter. A version of this chapter first appeared in the *Journal of Contemporary African Studies*, https://doi.org/10.1080/02589001.2020.1761012

Notes

[1] 'Writ Petition (Civil) No. 576 of 2016', 17 January 2019, available at https://main.sci.gov.in/supremecourt/2016/22533/22533_2016_Judgement_17-Jan-2019.pdf, accessed 20 December 2021.

[2] See Shell (2013); and 'Women of the Slave Lodge', *Ancestors South Africa*, n.d., available at https://www.ancestors.co.za/women-of-the-slave-lodge/, accessed 20 December 2021.

[3] See *Critical Aunty Studies*, available at https://www.criticalauntystudies.com, accessed 20 December 2021.

[4] See M. Rao, 'Surrogacy in India', APU Colloquium Series, *Centre for Law and Policy Research*, 2019, available at https://clpr.org.in/blog/apucolloquium-series-surrogacy-in-india-lecture-by-dr-m-rao/, accessed 20 December 2021; and Twine (2015).

5

'We Just Acted Out Our Gayness'

Male Sex Workers' Performances of Queer Masculinities in South African Prisons

Jan-Louise Lewin

INTRODUCTION

> But while there is no doubt that prison is a strange and removed place in which horrifying acts appear to be commonplace and demanding of specific attention, the connections between what goes on inside prison and in the rest of society need to be engaged with.
>
> – Gear and Ngubeni (2002)

> A sociologist of sex occupies the same status position in sociology as a sex worker in the larger society: a reminder of the seamy unpleasantness of the bodies to which our minds happen to be connected.
>
> – Kimmel (2007)

The mystical world of prison and the Number gangs invite us into a domain where power and performance are staged acts, a play set within grey walls, steel bars, loud-banging gates and endless hours to rehearse a performance restaged on an endless loop. Men's prisons represent a hierarchical, male-dominated space where hegemonic masculinity flourishes through control and command over subordinate masculinities. The constraint of less dominant men is one informed and stylized after extreme hetero-patriarchal and heterosexist traditional masculinities that originate outside the prison walls. The prison setting emulates hierarchical relations among men that contribute to the presentation and reproduction of hegemonic masculinities (Sabo, Kupers and London 2001). The gendered nature of the prison is one where the hegemonic masculinity of the South African prison Number gangs reign supreme.

The Number gangs (also known as The Number, originally The Ninevites) are a complex and intricate organization that has survived for over 150 years

(Steinberg 2004a, 2004b; H.P. Lewis 2010). The Number is made up of the following structures: the twenty-sixes (26s) who control contraband and economic activity; the twenty-sevens (27s) who engage in acts of aggression and also act as mediators between the 26s and 28s (gang law prevents the two from communicating directly); and the twenty-eights (28s) who, acting as henchmen and soldiers, control acts of fighting and war within the prison while also acting as regulators of sex (H.P. Lewis 2010). An additional group, referred to as the 'franse' (pl.), are non-gang members. These inmates have no protection from or against the Number. Their 'Numberless' status renders them invisible within the gang system and open to exploitation. The Number offers a language and moral code that all inmates abide by, whether they are members of gangs or not (ibid.). They offer a history rooted in African folklore and indigenous mythology that appeals to inmates' sense of belonging, brotherhood and need for elevated status within the confines of the prison walls. Thus, the Number provides respectability, honour and a code of brotherhood bound in blood (Steinberg 2004b). The Number is central to informal and underground prison management and the prison economy. This prison economy, in turn, is tied to gendered and sexualized rituals and processes that mainly occur within the Number structures, making them the regulating force and ever-watchful eye overseeing sex in prison (Steinberg 2004a).

PERFORMING GENDER AND SEXUALITY IN SOUTH AFRICA'S PRISONS

In the theatre, one can say, 'this is just an act', and de-realize the act, make acting into something quite distinct from what is real. . . . On the street or in the bus, the act becomes dangerous, if it does, precisely because there are no theatrical conventions to delimit the purely imaginary character of the act.

— Butler (1988: 527)

Sasha Gear introduces an impression of a 'moral economy' operating in South African prisons that has been 'established by hegemonic inmate culture in which sexual interactions are negotiated' (Gear 2005: 195). Under the directive of the Number gangs, these norms uphold a gendered system that value the heteronormative moral code of South African society. The groups within Number gangs each function according to their own hierarchies, laws and structures but are bound by a common 'code' (law) that unifies the three groups. In order to ensure compliance, surveillance by the Number upholds a moral economy that discourages sexual transgression of any gang law. Gear asserts that the gang rituals involved in gender role assignment in prison conform to societal constructions and cultural norms relating to gender. Prison discourses regarding gender construction take leave from the 'outside' by using terms to symbolize heterosexual norms and practices (ibid.).

An alternative view of prison sex culture and sexuality in prison is framed where prisoners perform gendered rituals and complex social scripts that fall quite strictly within societal bounds, which is interesting to note given the conflation of offenders and prisons as being aberrant to society's moral standards. This is particularly important within the total institution of prisons, where every aspect of the inmate's life and daily routine is formally structured and regulated (Goffman 1961). In South African prisons, the Number gangs hold equal (if not greater) authority, for they have the run of the prison for the maximum time of the day (Steinberg 2004b). Not only are prisoners subject to the surveillance of the formal prison system but under that of the gangs who are even more insidious in their totalizing effect of regulating prison life. This form of surveillance can best be described by what Cliquennois (chapter 7, this volume) presents as the 'inverted panopticon', a counter-surveillance measure that to some extent allows prisoners and academic and judicial audiences to monitor prisons and its administrators. Perhaps an extension of this idea, and working in tandem with the inverted panopticon, would be the synopticon, a concept presented by Mathiesen (1997) *where the many see the few*, as a fitting description of the kind of surveillance exerted by the gangs on their fellow inmates.

Queer bodies in this setting are further embroiled in the subtle process of queering as a defying act of countering the surveillance imposed by the prison gangs and the state. Butler's (1990) concept of performativity helps explain how prisoners navigate and subvert the strict social and cultural boundaries in prison, while denoting how gender and sexuality are fluid and constantly up for negotiation. An acknowledgement of gender and sexual orientation as fluid, complex and always changing has promoted research in the field of prison sex culture in the last few decades. While there have been many scholars throughout the 1900s that have written about prison studies, particularly focusing on prison sexualities (Clemmer [1940] 1958; Sykes 1958; Irwin and Cressey 1962; Gibson and Hensley 2013), Butler's theory of performativity in its support of the theatrical metaphor is apt for this study.

Butler asserts that gender is constructed as a performance that the actor and audience believe and attest to over time, giving it a sense of permanence: 'gender is a stylized repetition of acts' (Butler 1988: 519). Gender is neither true nor false; it is not given and stable but, rather, there is no fixed identity by which gender can be measured. The acts produce cultural signifiers of the body as gendered. Heterosexuality, moreover, is an 'imitation', an ideal that cannot be realized because gender (and sexuality) is a social construct imbued with social meaning. Gender is thus an act, an illusion scripted and performed.

Space, however, is imbued with power. It is crucial to consider the restrictions of contested spaces and their effect on the gendered body.

The prisoners' gender and sexuality are influenced by the prison space, and their attitude towards prison sex culture is shaped as a result of their social upbringing but also challenged by the prison. Reality in prison ceases to be the same as reality on the outside. Crossing over from the realities of the outside (normative) society into the prison space exemplifies a confrontation of what outsiders consider 'other' but prisoners would consider 'normal'. Context not only shapes performance but also the experience of the performance for both actor and audience. Further, the reality of post-incarceration means that the movement from the prison to the street (inside vs outside) can be a potentially dangerous setting for the performance of queer sexualities. In a sense, the prison as a stage provides shelter from the outside world, where queer identities can be explored, whereas on the street the 'outside' world can be hostile. An insightful perspective that Perez (chapter 6, this volume) offers is the concept of *marronage* as an alternate mode of being, a queering in this instance, as a way for the subject to subvert the sexualized (and racialized) connotations bound to the body. The prison is the marooning space, a temporary escape, for some more long-term than others.

However, Butler cautions us not to oversimplify the concept of gender performativity as something that can be altered at whim. Performativity is not a radical choice, even though gender itself is an illusive act (Butler 1990). She refers to those who are placed on the margins because their gender and sexualities are regarded as deviant – performances that are subversive and transgressive of the social norm. Very often, these subjects face violent repercussions for their repetition of subversive acts. Subversion is not easy but a necessary act for subjects to embody in order to be written into the social script. The actors must work so much harder to disguise their transgressive sexual persona.

The need to engage in subversive performances is a survival tactic that queer bodies have always had to rely on given South Africa's violent history. This exists quite viscerally in the South African imagination where the long-held idea of 'swart gevaar' vilified Black, African masculinities and sexualities. This idea can partially be attributed to a colonial and apartheid history grounded in racial ideologies that pathologized Black male sexuality and outlawed traditional African sexual practices (Epprecht 2013) – a point also noted by Pande (chapter 4, this volume) when she illustrates the infantilization of the colonial subject by colonialists. The colonial project's intent was to establish ideas of 'immoral savagery' and sexually deviant colonized subjects as signifiers of vice, amorousness and criminality. This is important to note, given the majority Coloured[1] and Black population of men in South African prisons in the present day.

In the precarious space of the prison, where actors are continuously adapting to their roles, the process of 'doing gender' (West and Zimmerman 1987) allows some freedom to navigate these everyday struggles under such strict confines. It is in this context that I attempt to understand where marginal identities fit into the hierarchy, and what methods and performances actors engage in to gain a share of power. I examine the narratives of male prisoners who become sex workers during/post incarceration, to understand how they construct and perform gender and sexuality. The study on which this chapter is based explores male sex workers' experiences of prison sex culture, and how it shapes alternative expressions of gender and sexuality either inside or outside prison.[2] Dominant social discourse portrays sex in prison in a negative light, as only coercive and violent. Focus on prison sex and sexualities is often only foregrounded when cases in the media are part of current affairs or involve high-profile individuals such as local celebrities or politicians. The rest of the time prison sex culture is relegated to the shadows. This study attempts to address that silence and what it means for the people living these realities in prison.

The following section provides a short review of the literature on Gagnon and Simon's (1973) scripting theory, presenting a discussion on the social construction of sexuality, gender and sexual scripts, followed by a brief history of racialization vis-à-vis African men's sexuality and the gendering of the prison space as a way to understand prison sex culture and performances of masculinity. I will outline some of the findings in the upcoming sections.[3]

Reviewing the Literature on Prison Sex Culture

Scripting Theory: A Social Construction of Sexuality

Scripting theory, first developed by Gagnon and Simon (1973), uses the dramaturgical metaphor to depict how individuals experience and perform their sexuality. Sexual scripting is a conceptual framework to understand the social construction of human sexuality. Sexuality and sexual activity are theorized as a sequence of events – much like a script in a play that actors perform – where the subject responds and reacts to a situation that is sexual (Gagnon and Simon 1973; Simon and Gagnon1986; Wiederman 2005).

The interplay between the actors and the script is dynamic. The lived experiences of the actors inform the script in very particular ways, thus making the script real within the context in which it is enacted. Simon and Gagnon (1986) explain that instead of viewing sex as an inherent part of human behaviour, it could be viewed as significant when defined through individual and collective experience. This theory is rooted in the social constructionist perspective, which emphasizes the interplay between cultural and interpersonal interactions as informing constructions of identity (Gagnon and Simon 1973; Simon and Gagnon 1986). This viewpoint enables us to see sex and sexuality as influenced by social and cultural forces.

In the period preceding Gagnon and Simon's (1973) work, sexuality was considered peripheral to the self, located in the sociology of deviance rather than identity formation. Gagnon and Simon (1973) view sexuality and identity as closely and intimately interrelated. Their theory propounds the centrality of sexuality in the construction of the self; they offer an alternative to the historical and biological understanding of the construction of sexuality where 'sexual conduct is learned in the same way and through the same processes: it is acquired and assembled in human interaction judged and performed in specific cultural and historical worlds' (Gagnon 1977: 2, as cited in Kimmel 2007). Sex as it relates to sexual behaviour is social; sex as it relates to sexual identity is an awareness of self, in that identity is constructed in and through sex (Kimmel 2007: xi). Through self-exploration in the form of 'writing and producing' our own sexual scripts, we are both director and producer before being the actors or the audience. The audience comprises the society watching enactments of sexual scripts. Actors make up this audience. A symbiosis operates between the two.

A sexual script is when people interpret, improvise, change and identify whether something is sexual or not: 'scripts are essentially a metaphor for conceptualizing the production of behaviour within social life' (Simon and Gagnon 1986: 98). Sexual scripts are unconventional, whether deviant or non-deviant. People have set ideas of the actions, roles and scripts that are used in the enactment of sexual–social interactions. Five themes guide the formation of sexual scripts: (1) who, as it relates to identities (who does one have sex with?); (2) where, as it relates to location and social context (where do people have sex?); (3) how, as it relates to actions and distractions (how do people have sex?); (4) why, as it relates to meaning (why do people have sex?); and (5) what, as it relates to interactions and methods employed (what do people do when having sex?). These thematic questions allow an insight into the details and meanings people attach to sex and the sexual scripts preceding sexual acts.

Simon and Gagnon explain three levels of sexual scripts. Firstly, cultural scenarios provide a framework through which sex is experienced. These are social norms informed by definitions and behaviours as prescribed by hegemonic social institutions. Cultural scenarios provide the scripts for how to act in a social setting, guiding how actors present themselves and behave in institutional contexts. Second is interpersonal scripts: these are routine patterns of social interaction that guide behaviour in specific settings. Interpersonal scripts are sexual–social exchanges and interactions between people as they engage in sexual activities or performances with and for each other. 'Interpersonal scripts are seen as the ordering of representations of self and other that facilitates the occurrence of the sexual act' (Simon and Gagnon 1986: 97). As the actor moves into a group or joins a collective, he moves from an individual scripted performance to becoming a co-producer of a script shared with others. This leads to the third level: intrapsychic scripts where sexual behaviour and actions are constructed through internalized dialogue with the self – 'the management of desire as experienced by the individual' (ibid.). Intrapsychic scripting is where the subject uses cultural expressions of sexuality and (re)creates them for their own sexual desires, fantasies and expectations, which ultimately play a significant role in the performance of sexuality. Intrapsychic scripting represents the internal struggle to balance and control sexual desires privately and publicly. One can imagine the actor 'trying on' different roles before performing the socially acceptable one publicly. In the case of 'deviant' representations the struggle to hide or disguise part of the self out of fear or shame would add to the inner struggle of the 'internal rehearsal' (ibid.: 99). For the purpose of this study, the focus is mainly on intrapsychic scripting as it focuses on internalized dialogues that the actor has with the self to make sense of the world and his place in it.

The 'I' in Sexuality: Intrapsychic Scripting

The centrality of sexuality in identity formation explores the ways in which different groups develop coherent sexual relationships. Intrapsychic scripting takes on a significant role when social contexts change and the subject finds himself in a setting where a differentiation of sexualities is present. Usually, intrapsychic scripting is limited in a familiar social setting where the performance of self is rehearsed and played out in the same way all the time, becoming supposedly 'natural' and well-rehearsed. When the setting changes or the actor is moved out of his comfort zone/routine, a significant shift occurs and the intrapsychic script is 'kicked into gear'. A 'modification in the self' (ibid.: 100) takes place when the subject enters a new space, especially where multiple alternative genders and sexualities are on display or offered. As he becomes immersed in the culture and society of this new space, questions of self emerge: 'What kind of I am I? What kind of I do I want to be? [These are] Questions that create the illusion of a self distinct from the roles it may be required to play' (ibid.).

The intrapsychic script realizes internal desire and binds it to social life. Meaning is assigned to deep-seated desires, eventually performed in the social setting as the subject becomes acclimatized to the space and finds his voice and place in the collective. The intrapsychic script is able to 'mutate' in order for two important changes to take place. Firstly, the 'I' that the subject is used to performing can be recreated depending on the space the actor finds himself in. A questioning of self begins to take place as the actor's appearance is reflected through others, both actors and audience – i.e. the new strangers on the scene. Goffman (1959) would say the subject begins to model a new and different self through interaction. Secondly, the matter of socialization is not a steadfast one. The intrapsychic script allows an adaptation of self in the new setting in order for the subject to fit in so that the power of social control and socialization is weakened over a period of time, thus not having a hold on the subject and allowing for 'the process of the creation of the self' (Simon and Gagnon 1986: 100).

Simon and Gagnon note that sexual desire is not so much about nature versus nurture but rather that the intrapsychic emerges with autonomy, allowing the subject to express and experience new sexual desires that manifest as a result of interactions and exchanges in and with collective society. In the case of structures and systems where meanings of sex and sexuality are first derived, a crisis can occur in the intrapsychic script when conflict arises between the social world with regard to internal scripts and previous socialization scripts. Crises arise where scripts are not rehearsed – internally and externally – as in the case of sexual coercion, sexual violence and trauma. They warn that the three scripts take on different meanings in different settings – they are not all identical in all settings. Appearance of the self changes in different settings and according to the needs of the subject in any given context. What it means to be a man in one space can be dramatically different in another. This can occur in settings where the collective places value and where deeper meaning and emphasis is on the sexual, or where the performance of the sexual is closely monitored and measured. This plays a major role in the assessment of the individual's worth and value in that setting, placing the intrapsychic script under pressure. However, not all individuals will experience the same level of anxiety or pressure regarding their performances; some may assign greater meaning than others to these sexual encounters and performativity.

The Work of Gender in Sexual Scripting

Sexual scripts are reflective of values, beliefs and morals: to perform sexuality is to participate in a collective drama where actors both contribute to and are recipients of culture. What is deemed acceptable or unacceptable socially and culturally is challenged and negotiated through sex and sexuality (Whittier and Melendez 2004). Through intrapsychic sexual scripting, these social categories inform self-identification and self-awareness. The roles and scripts that people create for their sexual identities are deeply infused with meanings from social and cultural scenarios. Sexual identity informs social and cultural norms as individuals develop cultural norms through everyday activities. However, these meanings are constructed and deconstructed as individuals move from one social context to another. Although intrapsychic scripts take place in the private realm, they are often informed by and, in turn, reinforce the cultural scenarios, stereotypes and stigmas attached to sexuality.

Scripting theory rests on the premise that individuals follow an internalized dialogue to construct meaning out of sexual situations (Gagnon and Simon 1973). There are strict social scripts that guide the management of sexuality. Gender is performed according to cultural expectations and ideals. One of these ideals is that sexuality is conflated with gender performance. Traditional sexual scripts can help us to understand how scripts have progressed in different cultures and to account for its influence on the performance of gender and sexuality (Wiederman 2005). The separate evolution of sexual scripts for each gender historically serves to complement opposing gender roles and to maintain the expectations and dominance of heterosexuality (ibid.).

Traditional sexual scripts for men start at a young age, when boys are taught that it is acceptable to view and play with their genitals, leading to the formation of sexual scripts that regard sexual stimulation in isolation to sexual pleasure. Wiederman (2005) notes that for boys, early experience of sexual stimulation is encouraged and regarded as an ideal gender role act that sets the stage for scripts that are centred on the body. He argues that the common view of traditional male scripts calls for a sexually proactive masculinity that is goal-oriented and assertive. If a man does not display a strong interest in sex, it calls his masculinity into question. Furthermore, this rigid expectation of a binary gender script forces individuals to 'feel compelled to follow the traditional sexual scripts for his or her gender' (ibid.: 499). A conflict may arise between the intrapsychic scripts and traditional gender script, where internal drive and desires may not match the expectations of traditional gender roles. The danger of assigning traditional gender script is that it may be incompatible with the internal sexual script and it also does not allow room for expansion and transformation of sexual desire and expression, thus limiting gender and sexual performativity.

Gagnon and Simon (1973) explain that the lines between heterosexuality and homosexuality are rigidly drawn and closely monitored, making it difficult for alternate performances of gender scripts. This, Schwartz explains, is closely linked to cultural scripts that enforce the binary enactment of gender and sexuality: 'our culture does not want to lose the hard edges of gender, precisely because people depend on the standards of gender enactment to help them delineate heterosexuality from homosexuality' (Schwartz 2007: 85). When homosexuality is openly performed, it is often followed by violence and punishment as a way to preserve heterosexual norms (ibid.).

In the social and cultural realm, scripting of heterosexuality is central to masculinity, with a profound effect on the intrapsychic scripting of the subject who picks up on these cues as a guide to scripting and performing his sexual desires regardless of whether these cues are incongruent with his sexual identity (ibid.). Schwartz explains: 'the cultural prejudice and presumption is that the presence of any homosexual feeling is a dead giveaway of one's sexual essence because homosexual behaviour is somehow more a truth of the body than heterosexuality' (ibid.: 90). It follows that as long as the subject does not 'choose' an alternate sexuality they will be spared rejection. The repercussions of performing a deviant sexual script, no matter how insignificant it may be, can be cause for social exclusion, and, as a consequence, subjects suppress and repress their identity in order to fit into the boundaries of society. As a point of departure, we turn briefly to a discussion of how historically the Black male body has been a site of this repression.

A History of Racializing and Criminalizing Black Male Sexuality in South Africa

A dominant discourse in much of Africa is that homosexuality is a western colonial import, that it is 'un-African' (Msibi 2011; Nyanzi 2013). This argument rests on the notion that same-sex desire is a corruption of African cultures, values and social relations (Msibi 2011). A number of African feminist scholars, historians and postcolonial theorists have argued and documented the various same-sex relations that were in fact present in pre-colonial Africa (Amadiume 1987; Epprecht 1998; Swarr 2004; Lewis 2011; Msibi 2011; Nyanzi 2013). The silencing of these same-sex relations has entrenched a belief that is based on moral discourse, patriarchal and heteronormative standards of sexuality that negate and render invisible historic and cultural practices of indigenous homosexualities (Epprecht 1998; Lewis 2011). Inversely, the 28s prison gang with their acceptance and support of same-sex desire points to the presence of queer sexualities in prison. Here, alterity of masculinity and sexuality – gender and sexuality performances as subversion – lives alongside the social and cultural conventionality of the 'heterosexual matrix' (Butler 1990: 208).

South African literature on prison sex tends to focus on a one-sided narrative that works within a heteronormative framework and understanding of sex. The tendency in South African prison literature to focus on homosexuality, male rape and violence and victimization reinforces stereotypical notions of prison sexuality. There are few studies that address the topics of consensual sex, consenting homosexual sex, gay relationships, bisexuality or queer sexualities in prison (Zungu and Potgieter 2011; Dunkle et al., 2013; Agboola 2015). The current discussion of prison sex is treated in a similar fashion as sex in the mining compounds was in the early 1900s (Niehaus 2002; Epprecht 2013). 'Mine marriages' were a fairly common practice in Johannesburg gold mine compounds in the late 1890s. The practice of *nkotshane*, where younger males engaged in interfemoral sex with older male patrons in exchange for protection, gifts or money, was deeply embedded in cultural norms from the rural countryside that migrated into the cities, albeit under strict censure by colonial authorities (Epprecht 2004; Msibi 2011). The pathologizing of Black sexuality sought to reinforce and legitimate a particular type of unequal power relation in South African society that devalued Black male sexuality, which ultimately shaped moralizing discourses and class divisions around sex and sexuality. This echoes Achmat's argument relating to the similar treatment meted on African bodies by colonial rulers:

> I suggest that the conquest of the body of the African male, and the mapping of different subject positions in terms of race, class, age and gender that arose from colonialism and capitalism, helped establish a new constellation of power relations. These in turn created new forms of disciplined and useful bodies – new pleasures and desires. (Achmat 1993: 105)

There further exists a heterosexist bias in South African literature with a propensity towards only focusing on the negative aspects of prison sexualities and sexual practices. One author who manages to present a nuanced view is Sasha Gear (2002, 2003, 2005). In general, Gear's theorizing attempts to understand male sexuality and victimization in a nuanced exploration that takes into consideration South Africa's history of race, class and gender, and the ways in which these relate to sex and sexuality, and gender construction. She does not treat the prison setting as mutually exclusive or in isolation to the greater social landscape or public discourse of South Africa. Another notable exception is Achmat's (1993) paper, which is the only South African analysis that addresses prison sex and sexuality from the standpoint of desire and pleasure. Alas, Pande (chapter 4, this volume) states, 'there is little place for desire or pleasure in the past and present of the loose women [and men] in the South'. Achmat vehemently contests accounts of sex in the mine compounds and prison sexuality that are established as the prevailing knowledge in the academic community. He calls for a retrospective treatment of contemporary historiography of African sexualities, particularly African (read: Black) male sexuality:

> My engagement with history and anthropology through the work of Van Onselen, Moodie and Harries attempts to recover from the archives a series of local knowledges for queers in contemporary South Africa. In this intervention I want to resist attempts by historians and anthropologists to incorporate 'unnatural vice', 'compound' and 'prison' history into the hierarchies and orthodoxies of the academy. These practices are attempts to neutralize the subversive and destabilizing effects of sex in the compounds, prisons, streets and, through this, to 'normalize' sexual

activity, fix 'cultural' identity, and center monogamous, heterosexual relations. (Ibid.: 108)

This piece deconstructs the historiography of South African prison sex research (dating between 1890 and 1920). However, it was written more than twenty-five years ago and so renews a call for prison sex research that investigates other avenues of sexual expression or performances, especially those that are non-violent and non-penetrative such as homosocial relationships among men and consensual intimate bonds, friendships, partnerships or relationships. Achmat argues that there is a refusal to acknowledge that a contested space such as the prison – which is always regarded as violent, transgressive of social norms and antithetical to society's moral values – can be a place where sexual desire is created and fostered. On the contrary, prison provides a fertile space to explore gender and sexuality in a way that cannot easily be replicated outside. As shown below, there are moments that reveal prison as an incubating space compared to the hostilities faced on the outside when the men entered into sex work post-incarceration.

As I have been showing so far, to speak about this issue is to also speak about the intersections of race, gender and sexuality. The lack of researchers who identify as queer, Black or people of colour (POC) means the majority of Black male prison populace's narratives are told through a predominantly white, heteronormative voice (Lebone 2012). Historically this has promoted reductionist, stereotypical and simplified views of male prison sex culture as merely aggressive, destructive and violent. There are studies that have addressed prison sexualities through – to some extent – applying feminist methodologies (Africa 2010; Boonzaier 2014; Moolman 2015b). Ratele (2013, 2014) claims an impasse has been reached in South African theories of masculinity, specifically Black masculinities that have been positioned in critical light. Ratele (2013), posing a question to theorists, asks us to consider what value feminism may have for Black men. He implores theorists to engage with men to determine how African feminist theorizing can shift prevailing attitudes of Black masculinities in South African discourse.

I turn to the work of three Black feminist researchers who conducted research with diverse prison populations in male and female prison settings in South Africa. The work of these feminist researchers illustrates how women of colour (WOC) position themselves in relation to research that explores prison identities using feminist research methodologies and theories borrowed from African feminism (Moolman 2015a) and Northern Black feminism (Africa 2010; Boonzaier 2014).

Africa conducted a study that focused on the violent crimes perpetrated by women. Her study examined the identity constructions of incarcerated women as they shared narratives about their lives and the crimes they committed

(Africa 2010). Guided by the theories of Northern Black feminism, Africa uses these theories to explain women's violent subjectivities from a Black feminist standpoint. Boonzaier, a feminist researcher who focuses on the differential gender relationship between researcher and researched, worked with male research subjects accused of intimate partner violence (IPV) and addresses the positionalities and power dynamics of the research encounter. She refers to the 'relational dynamics' of the interview encounter where she studied performances of gender during interviews with her participants (Boonzaier 2014: 235). Boonzaier calls this process of feminist work 'reaching across the gender divide' (ibid.: 243), which is the investment of feminist research with/on violent masculinities that pays close attention to social contexts and is vigilant of the ways in which men perform and present their accounts of violence. Guided by qualitative methods, Boonzaier locates her work in critical feminist research, and, similar to Africa, she draws on the work of Northern Black feminists such as Collins (2009) and Crenshaw *et al.* (1995), applying their theories to make sense of power dynamics and shifts in her interviews with perpetrators of domestic violence. For Moolman (2015b), an ethnographic feminist researcher, the journalling method is a way to work through challenges encountered in her research with men. She engages reflectively on her work with men incarcerated for violent sexual offences, writing about her experiences of navigating research with violent masculinities. Describing her research diary as a space to explore a shifting feminist identity, she shares: 'my diary became a space of reflection as I studied the "other". I was simultaneously reflecting my own understanding of power, difference and otherness' (Moolman 2015b: 204).

Gendered relations undoubtedly shape the unfolding narrative between researcher and subject, affecting the performances by both parties. Doing work across the gender divide (Boonzaier 2014) is being mindful of the many challenges this work presents. It draws attention to the gendered identities of the researcher and research subjects. For these researchers, a feminist theoretical approach to understanding discourses of violence contributes to a broader understanding of diverse identity constructions in the South African prison context.

The social locations where the sample population commonly reside, an area commonly known as the Cape Flats, cover a wide geographical area throughout much of the Cape Peninsula. It is an area that was demarcated for 'Coloureds' and 'Black Africans' during the apartheid era, through the implementation of the Group Areas Act of 1950. It has statistically high rates of crime and brutal forms of violence (Lebone 2012), and is known for gangsterism and gang-related violence. Thus, gang culture holds high currency in terms of symbolic and structural value, a likely incentive for recruitment of young men into gangs as the benefits of belonging cater to both material and social needs (Jensen

1999; Salo 2003). In a 2012 study conducted by the South African Institute of Race Relations, it was found that 97 per cent of men make up the total prison population; of that total, Coloured men account for 20 per cent, while nationally the Coloured race only makes up 9 per cent of the total population (Lebone 2012). A rough gauge of these numbers reveals the extent to which the criminalization and incarceration of Coloured men are all-pervasive, and how crime and violence impact socially and materially the lives of these men.

The trope of violent Coloured masculinity is almost always represented as aggressive, criminal and violent. This is depicted in many forms of social engagement, whether it is in the media and news articles or in day-to-day conversations with ordinary citizens. The prevailing message is that Coloured men are gangsters and that gangsterism is a Coloured problem.[4] For Coloured men, the creation of a 'hybridized masculinity' built on complications of racial ambiguity, historic dissociation and societal disregard has resulted in failure to fully understand the complexities of Coloured subjectivities (Adhikari 2009; Lewin and Perez 2018). Discussing race in District Six, Trotter (2009b) argues that early formations of gang subculture provided Coloured men the opportunity to resist and counter the subordinate positions they were categorized into by apartheid. Over time, this subculture became the norm where a sense of belonging and security had been fostered in communities and families (Trotter 2009b). This points to the fact that so many Coloured boys and young men are often caught in the generational web of crime and violence, as their pathways to crime have been paved historically, socially and culturally (Ratele, Shefer and Clowes 2012; Lewin and Perez, 2018). Perez (chapter 6, this volume) does an exemplary job of contextualizing the history of Cape gangs, going back further than District Six in his critique of modern scholarship on gangs in the Cape. He draws continuities linking the racialization and criminalization of Black men to early formations of slave runaway 'gangs' from the colonial seventeenth-century slave period to the modern period of 'hyper-incarceration' of Coloured men in particular. In the next section, I report on findings that demonstrate how hegemonic masculinities and queer sexualities converge in the prison space and the dynamics of these encounters.

PRISON AND THE (RE)NEGOTIATION OF THE SELF

Biographical narratives of participants' life stories yielded data that focused on life events before, during and post-incarceration with their transition into sex work. Participants who had previously been Number gang members were in some cases hesitant to talk about questions relating to sexuality, their engagement in prison sex practices or their experiences of sex work. Euphemism and metaphor dominate the narratives of sex and sexuality, understandably so, given the limited language and spaces available to participants to describe this aspect of their lives. Narrative form lends itself to the dramaturgical form of the study and thus enriches our appreciation of what these men offer through their life stories. The findings presented here are the stories and performances that unfolded in the interview encounter.

'To Be or Not to Be'... a Number

The folklore of the Number gangs is mystical and enchanting; it tells a romanticized story of the gangs and Nongoloza's quest to undermine the authorities.[5] In many of the narratives it emerges that the Number represented much more than commanding power. Sharing experiences of their involvement or their rejection of the Number, the narrative returns to the struggle for recognition and brotherhood. For participants who were part of the Number gangs, prison was a big part of their lives. They were high-ranking members and were involved heavily in gang operations in and out of prison. Prison was (and still is) a significant period in their lives and for them the pinnacle of their masculinity was constructed and performed while inside. For non-Number (*Franse*) prisoners, rejection of the Number was an important marker of masculinity too. Being able to stand their ground against the Number and negotiate masculine performances from the margins is worthy of respect. In other cases, given their proximity to the Number growing up, it had lost its appeal and for them a lifelong commitment to the Number did not fit in their frame of successful masculinity. For others performing marginal masculinities (as *Franse*), a rejection of the Number came as they sought ways to undermine and challenge their authority. These performances were prided on the ability to outwit the Number, to provide for fellow inmates and to hold one's own against a powerful force such as the Number gang. Their performance of an alternative albeit marginal masculinity was positioned in opposition to and dismissal of the Number.

> *Phil*[6]: If I see that you're a stupid Number then I will sabela[7] with you but then I'll see no man you believe what I'm saying . . . okay you're stupid. You keep yourself stupid . . . yeah I've got you . . . I fool many of the guys . . . many!

'Inside You will See Who You Really Are': Performing Masculinity through Subversion

Men in prison have to negotiate various ways to perform their masculinity. These performances are not singular and one-off, they are multiple and nuanced displays of masculinities in prison. Ever-changing circumstances demonstrate the versatility with which these men can transform one facet of their masculine identity to the next. With this mode of shifting, they employ ritual-like behaviours and strategies to manoeuvre their way around other men, mainly those in the Number gangs. Prison is a test that separates the weak from the strong. The men describe being sexually victimized or branded a 'moffie'[8] is seen as a sign of weakness that points to a lack of 'manhood' and essentially failure at adequately performing ideal masculinity.

> *Malik**: The first time I went in I was sitting in the truck. I started to cry cos the way people talk outside. So I experienced when I came inside it's not like the people talk, like you gonna get raped or you gonna be a moffie. It's just who you are . . . like they say 'outside' you can be the strongest man but inside you will see who you really are.

For some, silent performances are also ways of moving around inconspicuously as they try to navigate their way around the gangs. These performances are set against the backdrop of the prison walls where the silent, lone figure attempts to renegotiate a new identity as he begins to figure out how to perform masculinity in moments of power and of vulnerability. Silent performances allow the actor to get by unseen, away from the prying eyes of prison officials and the gangs. Similar to the code of the street where informal rules govern the behaviour of gangs and the management of law and order, so too do the gangs that govern operations and prisoner behaviour lay down the laws in prison. Knowing the rules of prison can be tricky for first-time, unsuspecting offenders; being unprepared places them in a position of vulnerability and, given the limited time to make the 'right' impression, they have to feel out the situation quickly to pass through the scrutiny of the gangs. Participants employ strategies to be alone. This involves not mingling with other prisoners, avoiding contact and generally keeping a low profile, although these tactics are not always met with success. Manoeuvring around the gangs is also a performance of subversion. The performances of peripheral figures such as *Franse* who, in relation to the Number gangs inhabit marginal masculinities, show how participants rescript and undermine totalizing gang power to show that simple moments of subversion and the rituals involved in enacting them are a way of gaining material benefits from gangs.

> *Bobby**: I just laid low. I didn't bother nobody . . . even though I didn't bother nobody, they always find a way to bother you.

> *Eric**: But like I said . . . there you must just be a man . . . like man up.

For others, however, performing a dominant hegemonic masculinity involves taking on a new identity altogether. Fred shares his silent performance of shedding his 'boy' name, along with his childhood memories, in exchange for a hardened, tattooed mask that transforms him into a man. His entry into the Number and '*achieving something in prison*' marks a pivotal moment. With the name, he also escapes the target of being labelled a woman. In order to maintain his power, he has to ensure a steady performance of this masculine identity throughout his prison career so as not to cast doubt on his masculinity. This hardened masculine performance has been ingrained over the years and he has great difficulty negotiating alternative performances. He is one of the few participants who still holds on to the veneer of the Number twenty years later.

> *Fred**: Sweet Boy* . . . that's the name my grandmother was giving me. Because I was a cute little boy man and she gave me that name and on all my photos I was seeing the name Sweet Boy. I grew up with that name. By the time I got to prison that name became my . . . like uhm . . . it was a target name. Sweet Boy is like a girl in prison and I had a lot of challenges in prison before I became a Number, by that name Sweet Boy. Somebody come to me and ask me about sex and that sort of thing because I'm a pretty boy and they want to make me a woman and that sort of things and I fight for it. They started grabbing me and say you not Sweet Boy, you a Tough Guy* . . . see that's why they give me this name Tough Guy [*shows his tattoo*]. See they changed a boy name and I became Tough Guy [. . .] It was giving me power and that time by changing that name it was like I was achieving something in prison.

It is here that the concept of hegemonic masculinity is fundamental to our understanding of the role that men play in relation to women and other men. Connell and Messerschmidt (2005) reveal that hegemonic masculinity uncovers the gendered and social hierarchies of society. Michalski (2015) argues that prison strips men of their gender identities, thus threatening their sense of self. A failure to reconcile hyper-masculinity renders men in a marginal status or relegates them to inferior positions that open them up to exploitation and violence. The stripping process is both a physical and psychological act. In the face of this stripping, Crewe discuss how men wear emotional 'masks' to hide their vulnerabilities. These 'fronts' are part of the emotional geography of prison life that shapes the 'performative masculine culture' (Crewe 2014: 58).

As the men start acclimatizing and 'getting into character' of either dominant masculinity or alternative masculinity, actors start delivering performances of sexuality. The construction of sexuality in prison first and foremost points to a complicated nature with the prison space. Before they can begin to explore their sexuality, there is a period of settling in: learning the rules of prison (codes of conduct), acclimating to the prison space, and then, the crucial test of deciding whether to join the Number gangs or not creates an inner struggle, which all the participants deal with at some point during their period of incarceration.

Ultimately, the proximity of so many men in one place brought about a renegotiation with masculinity and sexuality. Learning the expectations of prison codes of conduct and slowly subverting these rules in subtle ways opened up ways for some of the participants to introduce their own methods of countering the surveillance against the system of policing effected by the gangs and to an extent the prison management, although this is discussed to a lesser extent.

Sex segregation in prison reinforces very specific masculine and feminine roles in single-sex prisons (Pemberton 2013). As a result, the gendering of the prison space contributes to the production of specific forms of masculinity and femininity. This characteristic is quite evident in South African prisons, where gang structures and rituals reinforce and reify heteronormative gender and sex binaries from the 'outside' on to the 'inside'. The Number gang's system emulates outside structures of intimate relations where gendered identities and sexualities are forged in relation to their outside lives, clinging to societal notions of heterosexuality and hegemonic masculinity.

In evaluating the gendered nature of a prison in Kolkata, India, Bandyopadhyay (2006) discovered through ethnographic observations and narrative interviews that dominant masculine traits such as hardness, resilience and strength were re-enacted by men as features permeating the space. She argues that the set-up of men's prisons reinforces the idea of prison as a cold, hard, masculine space – to be tough or be toughened up, to act out aggressions or become aggressive in order to survive, which is attributed as the mark of successful masculinity. She illustrates how subordinate male prisoners negotiate alternative forms of masculinity to cope with competing masculinities, mainly through language and communication styles. She argues that reclamation of agency and a sense of self is a resolute way of constructing a space for oneself in prison. It is in the act of marking territory and making prison a place of their own that queer masculinities are able to assert themselves in that space. In the case of South Africa, Gear (2005) offers an example of subversion of 'wyfies'[9] over their 'husbands' – the dominant partner – when they engage in consensual sex relationships with other non-gang members. The submissive partner – representing alternative masculinity – is able to forge an identity separate to the one imposed on him, creating a space of his own in the landscape of prison sex activity. Wyfies are not passive actors in the heterosexual matrix but instead engage in *ushinthsa ipondo*[10] where they find ways to counter the surveillance placed upon them by the gangs. Any sex for pleasure with a consenting party is a way of subverting the deception made on them when they are forced into 'womanhood' (wyfie status) consummated by a prison 'marriage'. Because prison marriages are based on gang members' rank and seniority, they confer social and symbolic status and are thus a way of showcasing successful masculinity; yet they are also a display of normative views of heterosexuality. Prison is assumed to be an abnormal space, isolated from the norms of society. In contrast to this assumption, I would argue that prisons bring in norms from the outside in mimicry of heterosexuality, as in the production of the heterosexual matrix. Prison sex culture pushes boundaries and opens pathways to new explorations of sex and sexuality that can in some instances be consensual, whilst at the same time also working to defend a heteronormative status quo.

'Are They Really Keeping Humans in Here?': Setting the Stage for Sex and Sexuality in Prison

The confined prison space represents the all-important stage where multiple performances and interactions between actors take place. For many of them prison is the stage where their most successful performances of masculinity are staged, while for others the 'backstage', a behind-the-scenes like setting of prison, is brought to life. Surely a 'backstage' must exist in prison where men are able to perform a bit more freely away from prying eyes – but only to an extent, given that the 'backstage' in this context is occupied by the Number who are ever-watchful. As noted by many of the participants, *'they always know what's going on'*.

Goffman (1959) distinguishes between 'front stage' and 'backstage', the former being the performance presented to an audience and the latter representing a hidden facet, away from public scrutiny. In this context, the 'front' presented to other inmates before either being recruited into gangs, assigned a feminized gender role or being reduced to the status of *Frans* (sing.) is a crucial act in the performance of prison masculinities. Dominant masculinity is associated with strength and virility, i.e. heterosexual men; thus, the assigning of a feminized gender identity to someone who is considered a 'lesser man' involves a redefining of sex roles and status. The redefining of sexuality and gendering of the 'female' partner is a way of distancing oneself from the act of homosexuality that takes place to allow for acceptable sex between a man and a 'woman', not a man and a man (Kupers 2001; Gear 2005; Trammell 2011; Moolman 2015a).

And so, like many actors, these men have rituals that they engage in behind the scenes. These are techniques that they employ to outwit the Number gangs especially. However, given the nature of the prison set-up where overcrowding and limited space mean interaction cannot be avoided, they are soon forced to figure out the code, or risk serious, often violent, consequences. Noting the impact of the prison architecture, Tony shares the following:

Tony: You know what was funny for me? How that place is built. That's not a place for humans actually [*laughs*]. I was sitting in that place and I was looking . . . 'are they really keeping humans in here?' Cos everything is like hard, cold and closed, and dark . . . everything. If the sun go set and there's no light in there it's dark and cold and it's locked up [*laughs*] [. . .] when I sat this one day and looked at how they built this place. That place . . . that's built for dogs or something man . . . for wolves or bears or something man, that they had to keep inside that was wild. It look like that place is built for something like that.

In this vivid picture, Tony expresses his astonishment at the prison environment, stating, '*that's not a place for me*'. By likening it to a zoo, he suggests that it is a place for wild animals. By distancing himself from it and the people in it, he creates a boundary between him and 'them'. He sees himself as a peripheral character, not wanting a part in the grander production, more so by taking refuge way off in the 'backstage' and masking the realities even from himself.

The narratives begin to reveal how sexual identities slowly start shifting for the men. The number one rule in prison is that the performance of masculinity must be overt so as to dispel all thoughts of doubt, for oneself and others. On the flipside, however, while men are trying to renegotiate what it means to be a man in prison, this period is also marked by internal dialogues that reveal how they start to make sense of sexual exchanges and experiences relating to sex in prison as they then attempt to reconcile what these exchanges mean for their shifting sexual identities, particularly for men who are attempting to explore queer sexualities.

*Danny**: Now my real father was gay you check . . . my biological father and I sometimes think I maybe have half of him and half of . . . and that means I'm also gay. Now gay men when I just look at them they suddenly smile I don't know what for . . . or why [*laughs*] that's how this transgender was looking at me [in prison].

At this point in the narratives a shifting and rescripting of identity starts to take shape, and is closely tied to the prison space and code of conduct regarding daily routine and sex practices. Once they are able to figure out the rules and their expected behaviours, they start exploring and getting to know their sexual selves. For some there is a reluctance to explore sexually, while others do so with caution. They are confronted with internalized and repressed sexual desires in prison while trying to shift their views of sex and sexuality. Renegotiating fixed ideas around masculinity and sexuality and coming to terms with changing perceptions of self allow them to slowly open up to questions of sexual exploration.

Renegotiation is an internalized state where the subject, once acculturated to the prison space, begins to question and explore where he fits in, where his place is in the gendered social order. In doing so, he is faced with other choices too that influence the direction he will take. Deciding to join the Number or not is one such key influence. Those who choose to follow the Number take a different path and their gendered and sexual choices are influenced by their group attachment. Those who reject the Number explore gender and sexuality in different ways, having to rely on subversive tactics to navigate their way around the Number as they explore their sexual selves.

> *Fred*: Things you do in the night. Now people think outside that this thing is happening [talks about the Number and its view of sex code]. How can I take you into a camp and you like a woman and you think like a woman . . . how can I make you a soldier? Because the whole Number thing is based on the military . . . now how can you?

Where sex practices contravene gang laws, the implications can be quite startling. Arthur's contemplation to engage in sex failed when he observed what happens when one participates in 'illegal' sex trade in prison. As a non-gang member, he was unwilling to risk engaging in prison sex work. The biggest deterrent for him was the gangs.

> *Arthur*: So my first time in prison I never went there with so a mindset and so, but after a while again when I left there and came back to streets and doing sex work – doing sex work and then I ended up again for theft in prison ja [*laughs*]. I thought of it like [*snickers*] maybe doing sex work like you know [*he talks about seeing other prisoners trade sex for material goods*] so that's when I found out okay so this guy is like having sex with the other men for like tobacco whatever it is, for drugs and then when he like left the room I started like pondering about it, like me going to hook up with him for my surviving in prison . . . [*gang members found out about sex trade in the cell*]. It was a big thing in the room ja, it ended up fighting and luckily me not saying anything about what I was thinking about what I wanted to do to anyone ja so I just kept it to myself, kept quiet so I . . . let me rather not go this way cos I might get hurt you know. By me not being a prison gangster and so I can get – end up more in pain or more hurt than anyone else you know because no one is gonna back me up, so I kept that to myself and nothing happened there.

Sexual relationships built on fragile experiences of sex were linked to loss, trauma, silences and hiding. In cases where men engaged in consensual prison sex, these relationships were shrouded in secrecy as it was viewed as uncommon practice. A large majority of the participants recount personal experiences of sex in prison, some choosing to engage in it despite the risks of being caught by gangs or prison officials, whilst others rejected it for reasons linked to gang affiliation: not wanting to join the gangs, fear of victimization by gangs and, most importantly, what it would mean for their construction of self in relation to their identity.

'So My Pussy I Had to Put on the Table':
Navigating Fragile Prison Relationships

The idea of sex in prison was tightly bound to the gang, so in many cases a rejection of gang membership meant disregarding sex or, in some cases, finding ways to subvert gangs by engaging in sex secretly. Many of the participants described how gay men, 'transgenders' and 'moffies' are seen as sexually enticing in prison. Through these observations, we gain a sense of some of the power peripheral characters hold. Surprisingly, the narratives of the men reveal that a significant proportion of sex in prison is consensual. Another form of consensual sex in this context was a form of sex trade and bartering in prison where men received material goods in exchange for performing sexual duties.

Danny*: I also took my chance with a transgender once in the shower . . .

Malik*: The gay guys always get work in the kitchen, right, so that's how they pay the guys to have sex with them . . . with food . . . if you go to a prison you always see a gay guy, he get first privilege to work in the kitchen.

Bruce*: Because there were also benefits in prison. The same as the benefits one can get out here uhh people also are sexually [chuckles] I dunno whether I should say they're like . . . sexually hungry . . . so there's lots of things happening. People exchange, others use money, others use food, others use all sorts of things just to get the sexual satisfaction in prison.

The Number gangs, however, closely regulate their members' interaction with queer bodies unless there are gains in terms of the larger prison sex economy, turning a blind eye to sexual exchanges for material benefit, particularly for higher-ranking members, as shown by Neil, a senior member in the 26s gang:

Neil*: The only ones I used to fuck in prison was the moffies that wanted to be ladies but not my brothers [. . .] If I see you like a transgender . . . I send someone, 'go there and call that one there'. . . cos me I sleep in the corner, it's closed where I sleep . . . the other inmates don't evens know it.

John*: As a man they gonna mock you. If you want to do something like have sex with a cross-gender, you have to do it quietly. No one have to know. . . it has to be like a secret between you two [. . .] they call a woman [wyfie] the poison because a woman is a thing that can kill you . . . that's just the rules you see.

Engaging with queer bodies in prison poses a huge risk. One has to tread carefully, navigating sex silently and in secret, given the very real threat of personal danger if caught transgressing the rules of the Number gangs. The narratives show how some participants embraced the sex culture in prison as it provided them an opportunity to gain some financial or material benefits. On the other hand, there are narratives of avoidance, given the serious consequences that follow when one is caught. Furthermore, for others, especially gang members, an intense resistance to the idea of sex with other men and contravention of gang codes were reasons for avoiding sex altogether.

PRISON AS A GENDERED SPACE: THE EMERGENCE OF QUEER SEXUALITIES

Contemporary prison studies that investigate queer sexualities in prisons are a fairly recent undertaking, and have mainly been conducted in developed countries like Australia, United Kingdom and the United States of America (Jenness and Fenstermaker 2014; Sexton and Jenness 2016). A recurring theme in this literature is the prevalence of stigmatization by prison officials and fellow prisoners against bisexual, gay and transgender inmates. Jenness and Fenstermaker investigate how transgender inmates accomplish feminine gender performances in all men's prisons. Their findings reveal that successful gender performances were contingent on gender authenticity, where participation and inclusion in prison sex culture depended on their 'pursuit of the "real deal"' (Jenness and Fenstermaker 2014: 5). For transgender participants in this study, being able to perform the role of a 'real girl' (ibid.: 27) illustrates their complicity in gendered practices that embrace and reinforce hegemonic masculinity, heteronormative ideals and hierarchies of race, class and sexuality. The study reveals that transgender prisoners engage in normative social and cultural constructions of gender and sexuality to avoid violence and denigration by a dominantly heteronormative and heterosexist masculine prison population. The authors argue that the performance to attain authentic (feminine) gender identity verifies the agentic power of marginal prison identities. In another study, Sexton and Jenness (2016) explore the experiences of transgender women detained in men's prisons. Their analysis reveals that transgender prisoners identified with a unifying trans community in prison and embraced a collective identity regardless of the representation of a heterogeneous trans community. The findings of this study reveal the complex organizing and structuring of prisoner communities. In the case of prison, there are some, albeit limited, opportunities for shared identities to forge collaborations and create a sense of community regardless of other distinguishing features and characteristics (ibid.). It is the recognition of each other within the community that affirms a sense of self. It is also the recognition of their existence by mainstream prison inmates that affords these smaller communities a location, a space, or role within the larger matrix of the prison system. They are thus granted a place and role in the sexual hierarchy of the prison.

Wyfie status was a marginal (peripheral) identity in this sample population, only embraced by men who openly identified as gay. For the men who engaged in consensual prison sex relationships, it offered them sexual liberation in a way that they did not get outside prison. As a man who openly identifies as gay, Luke's experience of prison sex and his sexuality differed vastly from that of the men in the sample. He shares his experiences of engaging in consensual monogamous relationships with men in prison, where on more than one occasion the relationship continued upon their release.

> *Luke*: I met this African guy . . . Jake*, a 26 gang member . . . prison gang member. So then he accommodated me and then that was the second guy that I met and I lived with in prison [. . .] You know as a 26 he was treating me like his woman and it was cool because you would make the bed and the tent[11] and everything.
> *I*: What does it mean when you say 'woman'?
> *Luke*: He would treat me as his woman, as his girlfriend and we . . . we lovers.

For Luke, wyfie status holds very different connotations than it does for the rest of the men in the study. On the one hand, the view of wyfies as weak and submissive is a fairly general agreement in the narratives. The subversion of heterosexual identity in prison is his reclamation of the wyfie identity, a queer sexual identity he embraces. Wyfies are regarded as the 'other', the unseen, the peripheral character. For Luke, sex is more than a form of survival in prison. Wyfies may not fight like men with their fists, but putting his *pussy on the table* is a way for him to access the benefits that come with other men's hegemonic masculinity.

For Bruce, *'acting out our gayness'* is a rare but transformative moment for alternative performances of sexuality in prison:

> *Bruce*: We were not like sexually attracted to each other but we just acted out our gayness.
> *I*: And what does that mean when you say you 'acted out'? What did you do?
> *Bruce*: We just became like how gay can . . . how gay people are like you know without being afraid like you know whilst we were with these other lots of people in there. You know it's very different . . . you might see or pick up that that one is gay but still he's hiding his feelings you know things like that. Even out of prison there are places where you see and pick up no, one is gay but no, because of the friends he's got he won't act out. Quite a lot of people are like that quite a lot you know.

In this subtle performance, Bruce invites us into an alternative view of prison, as a liberatory space for sexual expression and gender performativity. Participants share experiences of how the prison space gave them the opportunity to explore new areas of their gendered and sexual selves, discovering shifting identity constructs like sexual orientation that could not otherwise be explored as freely on the outside.

In order to engage in homosexual sex in prison, there is a rescripting of the internal intrapsychic scripts so that it mirrors the external cultural scenarios; present in the 'imitative' heterosexual space of the prison, all of which is fabricated in mimicry of the outside. In prison, the taking on of a new role/ character becomes the core of one's existence in that space. For most prisoners there is no before and after, who you become in prison is who you are there and interaction with others is limited to the 'new' self created in prison. It is important to understand what the impact on self is as a result of this reconstruction and renegotiation. This process of stripping away is not solely a passive one. Men are active participants in their construction of masculinity, so much so that they subvert traditional arrangements of gender and masculinity as they work to reconfigure and mould it to the prison space. The renegotiation and reconstruction of multiple masculinities explicitly show that men do not willingly or unwaveringly accept the dominant forms of masculinity available to them even when there are benefits to gain from it – but in fact that competing, alternate masculinities also shape the gender dynamics of the prison space. It shows that there are multiple masculinities on display, not binaries, and that men in prison do in fact contribute to the gendering of the space by constantly shifting their 'maleness' to fit and subvert the dominant hegemonic code that the space lends itself to. This display of agency from inmates in a space that is largely suppressive justifies my claim that the prison setting can in fact be a space that is under constant deconstruction and reconstruction by the subjects/ actors themselves, and that the space is not all-totalizing.

Transitioning to the Outside: Sex Work Post-Incarceration
Pande (chapter 4, this volume) writes about sex work as a disruptive act where 'several deviants come together . . . sailors, miners and loose women'. I would venture that in the coming together of these deviants, (queer) prisoners turned sex workers fall well within this group and are subsequently treated with the stigma attached to this so-called deviant profession.

Male sex work is one of the oldest professions in the world, whether associated with young boys in ancient Greek society or the existence of male brothels in ancient Rome; it has undisputedly been present in many societies throughout history (Foucault 1990; Friedman 2014; Scott and Minichiello 2014). Often misunderstood and targeted as perverts or deviants, male sex workers live and work in a shadowy existence. Historically, research has pathologized men who engage in commercial sex work, relegating their concerns to the margins (Scott and Minichiello 2014). The complex nature of male sex work organizing in its arrangements, processes and structures makes it a challenging topic to undertake. Such is the prevailing consensus in African literature on men who have sex with men (MSM) (Boyce and Isaacs 2014). Knowledge about risky sexual behaviour and MSM lifestyles are limited in the African context (Okal *et al.* 2009; Muraguri, Temmerman and Geibel 2012). There has been significant research into female sex work but very little is known about male sex workers (MSWs) and MSM in Africa (Boyce and Isaacs 2014). A study conducted by Boyce and Isaacs (2014) in five African countries – Kenya, Namibia, South Africa, Uganda and Zimbabwe – explored the social contexts, lived realities, vulnerabilities and sexual risks experienced by MSWs with the aim of centring sex workers' narratives in the research process. They call for continued research into MSWs' experiences, and the development of representations that highlight the subjectivities and first-hand accounts of this exploited group. They present some of the difficulties that sex workers face in their everyday lives. Common themes that exist for male, female and transgender sex workers are sexual abuse and trauma (over the lifespan), financial poverty, high incidence of substance abuse, high risk of HIV/AIDS transmission and homelessness (ibid.). These findings are supported by other studies conducted in South Africa (Needle *et al.*, 2008; Parry *et al.*, 2008; Leggett 2012). Boyce and Isaacs (2014) also note that where research has been conducted in Africa, the data have revealed a limited knowledge of male sex workers' experiences. Further, that most of the research and knowledge about male sex work in Africa has been conducted in Kenya.

Another tendency of the literature is to focus on male sex work in relation to crisis interventions and assessments of drug use and HIV risk as these pose the greatest vulnerabilities (Needle *et al.* 2008; Parry *et al.* 2008; Rispel and Metcalf 2009). International concern about MSM risk practices have been noted in the high rates of HIV positive cases linked to the prevalence of sexual risk in casual sex partnerships, unprotected sex and substance abuse among prisoners post-release and sex workers (Lankenau *et al.*, 2005; Adams *et al.*, 2011). Studies found that these behaviours are particularly evident in the first few days after release from prison where men are exposed to higher risk of escalated drug use, unprotected sex and transactional sex, making the transition from prison back into the community more difficult (Adams *et al.* 2011; Vagenas *et al.* 2016). This is what Mbuba refers to as the 'second cycle of societal retribution' (Mbuda 2012: 231), when offenders experience continued stigma for their criminal status on the outside. The stigmatization of their prison identity coupled with the sex worker status creates further barriers to accessing adequate healthcare, employment, housing or social networks.

For the men in this study, sex work presented an opportunity for change. At least half the group entered sex work post-incarceration. Having very few resources at their disposal, coupled with substance-abuse addiction, unemployment and homelessness, the men for the most part were introduced to sex work by friends or work colleagues post-release. Many of them stated that sex work is a better alternative to unemployment or a life of crime.

> *Chris**: Ja ja it's tough because even if your relatives had to know about it, it sort of taken as taboo like 'how can you do that?' you see ja so it's a strange thing . . . it would be a strange thing.

> *Eric**: Like even friends of yours and they find out you doing like sex work . . . they say you are fokking men and . . . and yorr sometimes they will make a joke but for some people the joke that they make isn't like a joke that everyone understand.

The lead finding in this group is that sex work is an 'act' separate from their real lives. It is a performance they engage in only when doing sex work, and is kept hidden and secret from close family and friends. Where men do disclose their sex work status it is to close, trusted friends or fellow sex workers they interact with in passing. The key insight is that they uphold two realities, moving between two worlds and two separate identities: one as a man (father, brother, husband, son) and one as sex worker. In this performance, sex work is a masquerade – a false show. Here, the analysis reveals that interactions with actors on this stage are performed behind a mask of pretence and concealment.

Several participants shared experiences based on observation of sex work in prison. Malik is one of the few who engaged in sex work as a form of trade in prison. With a lack of financial support and having had some experience with sex work in prison, it became a viable option for him post-release. He has set ideas about his sexuality upon entry into prison. Having to hustle for money in prison, he emphasizes that sex work became the last resort: *'I had to do sex work'*. In stating that it was a 'gay guy' that paid him, he makes a clear distinction on the basis of sexuality. The fact that his client is gay leaves him questioning his own sexuality. He has to grapple with ideas around his sexuality and what it means to his sexual and gendered identity to have sex with men. He, like many of the participants, does not identify strongly with his sex worker status.

> *Malik**: Ja uhh the first time when I went in I was like a . . . like they say a straight guy, then afterwards like my people didn't come to visit me and I had to make money I had to do sex work. A gay guy he give me money that his people send him, then I . . . something like that . . . then afterwards when I came out didn't get a job outside then I started doing this.

> *I*: How do you think it would be viewed if your gang brothers were to know that you are a sex worker?

Bobby*: I think they would discriminate me. They would say I'm a moffie maybe . . . obviously you mos know how it goes [. . .] gangsters don't roll like that . . . you know they tough.

Fear of being judged and ridiculed is one reason for keeping it a secret. For Malik and Bobby, being labelled a 'moffie' implies that they are not 'real men'; that they are not tough like the gangsters who fight back and resist being penetrated by another man. Not resisting sex work in this sense can be compared to prison sex culture where resisting rape in prison is the marker of being a 'real man'. In this case, if, hypothetically, Bobby were to share his sex worker identity with his gang brothers, it would be an admission of his lack of masculinity, which reduces him to the status of a woman, a wyfie and ultimately a 'lesser man'.

The shame attached to sex work is shared by a majority of the men. It is for the most part an identity to remain hidden, especially from family and friends. A deep-seated fear of people finding out that they are sex workers is attached to societal ideas of heterosexual masculinity. For the men, sex work blurs the line between accepted and deviant sexuality. In some cases, coming to terms with a shifting sexuality is made easier by the prison space where sex with men, albeit hidden, is a common practice. On the street, however, public stigma is heightened. The mask they hide behind is a protective factor, as the sex worker identity becomes the self-imposed 'other', an alternate personality created and shrouded in secrecy.

In the end, we know that there are multiple performances of masculinity and sexuality. However, whether they realized this or not, many still preferred to hold on to traditional ideas of tough prison masculinity. This too varied; for some, holding on to hegemonic masculinity meant a determination to maintain heteronormative and heterosexist ideals of gender and sexuality. For a number of the participants a rigid resistance to queer masculinity and sexualities prevailed, where even as MSWs, the idea of having sex with men went against their core beliefs of gender and sexuality. These marginal few choose to hold on to ideals of heterosexism and the binary of male and female gender. Others discussed how the prison space and sex work gave them the opportunity to explore new areas of their gendered and sexual selves, discovering shifting identity constructs like sexual orientation, being fathers to their own children or to other men, and, in other instances, discovering how to be there for other men in non-sexual ways too.

CONCLUSION

Prison is a space for reworking and renegotiating performances of gender. Butler (1990) outlines that gender is an act that is repeated over time and space. The work of Gagnon and Simon (1973) offers a three-tiered model of identity construction. Their analyses of sexual scripting guided the framework of this study by understanding how gender and sexuality are internalized constructions that take place in the personal realm – what they refer to as intrapsychic scripting. The interplay between actor and script is a dynamic process, where the script comes alive in the context in which it is enacted. Intrapsychic scripting allows the individual to have power over his own script; thus, *renegotiation* is performed through a sort of monologue with the self. *Negotiation* is a dialogical process where social scripts are created collaboratively with other actors. Complications arise when scripts are out of sync or where they overlap, or, in some cases, when certain scripts take precedence over others where hierarchies exist between actors.

Gagnon and Simon's argument is that prison sex research has long focused on the deviance of so-called perversions such as homosexuality. The long-running debate on situational homosexuality versus true homosexuality is still a prominent feature of current literature on prison sexualities. Authors such as Eigenberg (2000), Kunzel (2002), and Sit and Ricciardelli (2013) argue that prison, due to its single-gender sex segregation, forces people into homosexual relations – situational homosexuality, which results in heteronormative and homophobic discourses that permeate prison culture. Authors further argue that sexual deprivation accounts for the prevalence of homosexual relations in prison (Gibson and Hensley 2013; Terry 2016). These arguments contend that performances of heterosexual masculinity dominate the prison space. For the most part this is an accurate depiction of sexuality in prisons, but findings in this study show subjects push back on these dominant performances by subtly performing and employing tactics of subversion as they negotiate sex. The findings show how the men renegotiate ideas of sexuality through interactions with others. For some, experimenting sexually or flirting with other queer masculinities was a way to start the exploration into alternative sexuality. For others, a shifting between heterosexuality and queer sexuality marked the beginning of reconfiguring sexual desires. This internal monologue is a period of intense exploration around what it means to be a man and how that translates sexually in the prison space. For many, it marks a period of questioning and renegotiating past beliefs of their gendered and sexual selves. The outcome of this process is the point where men start to explore outside the self as they engage and interact with fellow prisoners through certain sexual exchanges.

Although an insistence on transposing moral codes from the outside world into prison is abided by, social sexual scripts from outside do not effortlessly translate into prison. While outside there may be more spaces to perform queer sexualities as compared to prison, the formal policing of sex work on the outside is enforced more tightly as compared to prison, where regulation of sex work is less rigid (prisoners spend half their day locked up in cells). Findings show a high proportion of consensual sex practices in prison mainly around the organization of an informal sex trade. Men who engaged in these interactions were largely in it for financial reasons. With limited research into this area of prison research this finding highlights the need for future research into this phenomenon.

While findings also show that some men resisted engaging in exchanges of prison sex due to the violent repercussions that followed, it is suggested that the liberating aspect they witnessed through others' engagement of same-sex practices informed their sexual performances upon release from prison into the street. Thus, sexual liberation in prison takes place under certain circumstances. Through processes of renegotiation, they come to have alternative views about their own sexuality and how it can be performed differently on the streets, which is informed by performances of queer sexuality witnessed in prison. Changing attitudes to queer sexualities and sexual practices, informed by their interaction with multiple actors in prison, are translated into their performances on the street. This demonstrates the cyclical nature of sexual scripts, which fuse interpersonal scripts and cultural scenarios.

The complexity of prison as a site for sexual expression and gender performativity promotes performances of queer sexual identity expression and, to an extent, sexual liberation. This claim, while bold and radical, addresses the need for sexual liberation, which this doubly oppressed and marginalized group that occupies peripheral roles in prison and on the street represents. Negotiations with gender and sexuality afford space and time to explore changing and fluid sexual identities to an extent, either privately in prison or publicly on the street. In this instance, prison opens up possibilities for the exploration of multiple constructions of gender and sexuality. Many of the men share the difficulty of having to navigate and renegotiate gender and sexuality on the streets. Their narratives reveal questions regarding their masculinity and sexuality. They struggle with being seen differently as men who have sex with other men, questioning what it says about the fixedness of sexuality – these are murky questions that they must come to terms with as they perform a part of their identity in disguise, in many cases compartmentalizing their identities. These are participants who are aware of the 'act'; they are cognizant that the characters they play as sex workers and the people they are outside of sex work are separate. They lead separate lives and keeping sex work secret is critical. Secrecy follows and plagues them. Having to uphold two realities and keep them apart constantly makes these participants feel particularly vulnerable.

Schwartz (2007) argues that no matter how inconsequential deviant performances of sexual scripts are, the repercussions that follow are cause for social alienation. Actors consciously repress their desire so that it remains internalized, relegated to the subconscious, in order to fit in with societal norms (ibid.). After the relative shelter of prison where freedom to explore queer sexualities was allowed relatively more freely, the shift into the next context – the streets – presents a crisis. Gagnon and Simon (1973) note that crises occur when intrapsychic scripts and cultural scenarios are incongruent. The crisis that sex work presents relates not only to the shifting of context, but also to a discordance between how the individual feels internally and how he performs on the outside. Crises arise because the individual is not able to find harmony between identity (internal script) and performance (external act). The findings show that sex work was a last resort for most of the men. Their narratives reveal how their performances were clouded in secrecy and shame, hiding behind a mask to protect their identity and to deter public stigma and discrimination. This supports the work of Boyce and Isaacs (2014) who highlight the stigma experienced by sex workers across the continent. The 'mask' is an important part of their identity construction as sex workers; it is something they put on and take off for the most part, shifting into an alternate performance with relative and rehearsed ease. This finding is supported by the work of Crewe (2014), which states that a common adaptation to punitive settings, such as prisons and the harshness of the streets, is for men to wear masks as 'fronts' to hide their vulnerabilities. In prison, the spotlight shines on the individual, whereas in the street, moving around incognito seems to be the preferred choice of script.

NOTES

[1] This is based on an apartheid-imposed racial classification system. 'African' refers to Black African and the term 'Coloured' refers to people of mixed-race descent. In the post-apartheid setting, the term 'Black' is an inclusive label to categorize African, Coloured, Indian and Asian.

[2] This qualitative study was guided by feminist methods of research. Sampling was limited to the fulfilment of certain basic criteria. Participants had to have been incarcerated and had to self-identify as male. The data-gathering technique was in-depth, semi-structured interviews with fifteen participants (n =15). Respondents were aged between twenty-three and forty years. The study was open to both South African and African foreign nationals. Three respondents identified as Black and twelve as 'Coloured'. Ten participants self-identified as straight, two as gay and three as bisexual. Six participants were gang members in the Number, seven were *franse* and two chose not to reveal their affiliation to any gang.

[3] Given the volume of rich data that was produced, an extensive number of themes were developed: consensual sex in prison, pathways to prison, physical prison space, performances in prison, prison rituals, entering prison, joining prison gangs, male role models, relationships in prison, wyfies, religion, masculinity, culture and tradition, and, finally, trauma. While these findings are noteworthy, due to the limited scope of this paper, not all of these themes will be discussed below. Rather, this paper focuses on how participants speak more generally of how their performances were surveilled by gangs. Future research will allow for a deeper exploration of these themes, particularly as they relate to implications for performances of queer identities and sexualities.

4 As a cautionary note, Lewin and Perez (2018) problematize the stereotypical view that 'Colouredness' is synonymous with gangsterism. In order to acknowledge the heterogeneity of Coloured identity, this paper attempts to build off the work of key theorists on 'Coloured' identity (see Erasmus 2001a; Adhikari 2009; Salo 2015), while also acknowledging the lived reality of gang culture. As this study, furthermore, is based on the qualitative methodology using a small sample, it is not reflective of the general population. Generalizability to Colouredness in South Africa is not the objective of this study.

5 Nongoloza was the founder of the Number and original head of the 28s gang (H.P. Lewis 2010).

6 To protect identifying information, as per the agreement of informed consent and confidentiality, participants' names have been replaced with a pseudonym and marked with an asterisk.

7 A coded prison language used in the Number gangs.

8 'Moffie' is a derogatory term for a gay man.

9 'Wyfie', meaning 'little wife', is a derogatory term for men in the 28s gangs who serve as 'female' sexual partners, or prison wives (H.P. Lewis 2010).

10 *Ushintsha ipondo* is a type of sexual practice, most common after the prison 'marriage'-type. There is no imposed gender distinction between the two consenting partners. It is outlawed by the gangs as it transgresses their laws pertaining to prison sex and 'marriages'. For a detailed analysis, see Gear and Ngubeni (2002). For a brief overview, see Gear and Ngubeni (2003).

11 A man-made tented structure in the prison cell using sheets to cordon off a private bedroom space. A tent is typically used when inmates want to create privacy for sexual intercourse. South African prison cells usually accommodate a large number of prisoners due to overcrowding (32.25 per cent national average), with Western Cape (the region for this particular study) being the most overcrowded with all twenty-five facilities found to be overcrowded. For more, see Justice Edwin Cameron, *Judicial Inspectorate for Correctional Services Annual Report 2019/2020*, Department of Correctional Services, Republic of South Africa, available at http://jics.dcs.gov.za/jics/wp-content/uploads/2021/01/JICS_AR_2020-LOW-RES_compressed_compressed_compressed.pdf, accessed 20 December 2021.

6

New Chains, New Mountains

Continuities of Defiance against Racialized Criminalization in Cape Town, South Africa

Javier Perez

The South African 'Coloured'[1] population faces highly disproportionate incarceration rates, particularly those living in the working-class communities of the Cape Flats,[2] rendering them a hyper-incarcerated[3] group within a modern prison regime. While the 'Coloured' population makes up only 9 per cent of the total national population, they represent 18 per cent of the total prison population (Jules-Macquet 2014). 'Coloured' men are imprisoned disproportionately at twelve times the rate of white men and double that of Black men (Leggett 2004). The areas of Cape Town collectively known as the Cape Flats have high rates of incarceration, crime and gangsterism. Steffen Jensen (2008) notes, for example, that in one of the Courts in Heideveld, five households out of forty-eight had at least one person incarcerated. High reoffending rates seemingly reaffirm the need for prisons, which in turn productively reinscribe notions of criminality and moral shortcomings on to whole communities in the Cape Flats, effectively pathologizing 'Coloured' areas and families (Gillespie 2002). Baderoon (2018) points to a discourse of 'dirt' that paints 'Coloured' bodies as deserving of punishment. Indeed, just as Pande (chapter 4, this volume) has highlighted that the stigma of dirt associated with sex work powerfully causes women to constantly distance themselves from this identity, a similar fight for respectability continuously beseeches 'Coloured' South Africans to distance themselves from signifiers of the stereotypically dangerous or working-class 'Coloured'.

Just as Pande traces the ongoing signifier 'loose' to its historical role as a colonial tool of disciplining and controlling native women, used to stigmatize the identities of financially autonomous women, the signifier of an unrespectable and criminal 'Coloured' likewise is rooted in colonial discourse. Indeed, the continuity between the slave era and the contemporary is exemplified by the term *'gham'* – a contemporary pejorative label used to describe the 'Coloured' working poor, with connotations of lacking respectability – as alluding to the curse of Ham, a popular biblical justification for African slavery (Adhikari 1992). *Gham* continues to be an important marker and metaphor of the 'other' with deep-seeded connotations that imply a perpetual status of servitude. The contemporary gangster, on the other hand, epitomizes *gham* and yet, despite the clear connection shown here by Adhikari (1992), the considerable literature on gangsterism in the Western Cape is rarely informed by historical contextualization beyond the twentieth century. Many will cite Don Pinnock's seminal work tracing the proliferation of contemporary gangs to the pre-apartheid District Six community and the subsequent role of the Group Areas Act that forced removals (Pinnock 1984). However, they do not delve deeper to explore links to colonial-era racialized criminalization and early gang formations. By falling short of making the sociogenic links between slavery and the current hyper-incarceration of 'Coloureds', we continue to misunderstand the role of gangs within and against the continuities of criminalization and racialized captivity.

This chapter aims to resituate contemporary trends in hyper-incarceration and gangsterism in Cape Town within broader historical contexts traversing colonial slavery until the modern prison regime. Specifically, this paper applies Edouard Glissant's trope of *marronage* – the flight of escaped slaves – within a new framework to revisit the links between colonial-era runaway slaves ('*droster*[4] gangs') and modern Cape gangs, the former being embedded in the wider earliest episodes of 'Coloured' creolization and the latter being descendants of heterogeneous communities such as Khoi and enslaved peoples. It proposes to better understand gangsterism beyond the lexicons of criminality at one extreme and resistance on the other, by positing gangsterism in the Cape as forged productively within and antithetically against particular historical trajectories of racialized criminalization. Whereas the *droster*s took to the mountains to evade oppression and form alternative modalities of being, the descendant gangsters of today go to prisons where they notoriously construct their alternative belongings and identities; in both cases, the lines of flight encompass a condition of becoming in which the fleeing fugitive navigates an economy of survival. I argue that the lives and bodies of the modern Cape Flats gang members are circumscribed by the dual afterlives of slavery and *drosting*, demarcating these gangs as a space for a creative divergence of criminalization.

I take direction from Edouard Glissant's (1997) critical interest in the significance and relevance of maroons, especially as relational spaces where maroons redefine and produce new relational identities within chaotic networks. While Glissant (1989) regarded the maroons as the only indisputable case of complete refusal of systematic opposition, Roberts (2015) insists that maroons were among the first modern subjects to exalt freedom as the highest human good. Indeed, as the only alternative to slavery, *marronage* constitutes a revolutionary oppositional discourse in the light of what Sylvia Wynter (1989) identifies as a central theme across Glissant's oeuvre – *blocking*: the colonial impeding of the colonized subjects' realization of their full potential. Yet *marronage* is equally defined by its complex relation and proximity to the colony, as established maroon communities remained continually dependent on plantations and farms for survival. In *Le quatrième siècle*, Glissant (2001) attributes the decline of 'the glorious Maroon' to the 'despicable bandit' as resulting from a 'historical chain' of colonizers' criminalizing tactics (Cailler 1989: 590). Glissant does not essentialize the maroon as functioning merely in opposition to the colonizer, instead positioning them within more complex networks of relation to plantation slaves, peasants, soldiers, etc.

Here, I further wish to incorporate Alexander Weheliye to allow us to move beyond the 'lexicons of resistance and freedom', both of which he highlights as informed by western Cartesian thought in presuming 'full, self-present, and coherent subjects working against something or someone' (Weheliye 2014: 2–6). More specifically, Weheliye's notion of *assemblage* suggests an ever-shifting and productive – but not necessarily 'liberating' – polyvalent expression of previously non-existent spaces, ideas, etc. These assemblages, manifesting as 'hieroglyphics of the flesh', become adopted by, adapted for and reproduced by succeeding generations. Thus, whilst *marronage* is the embodiment of oppositional discourse, it is not to be understood here as essentially a modality of resistance *per se* but rather as comprised of a 'spasmodic network' between multiple entities, including but not limited to desires of freedom, creative acts of resistance and incorporeal ideas of criminality receptively transformed into flesh. Hence, *marronage* is the embodiment of an alternate modality of being that refuses the racialized perimeters delineating the 'human' and 'non-human' hierarchy; yet it only marks the potentiality of freedom without carrying the onus of being a necessarily liberatory project. Whereas political violence (e.g., systemic criminalization) inscribes racialized assemblages on to the flesh, it simultaneously 'produce[s] a surplus, a line of flight . . . that evades capture' (ibid.: 51) from this surplus, the maroon emerges in exploration of alternative modalities of being, as 'restless pursuit of personal space within the broader confines of slave society' (Barker 1996: 125) and with complete rejection of the racialized human–non-human episteme.

Edward Alpers (2003) identifies two forms of *marronage* distinguished by the length of time of slaves' absences: '*petit marronage*' refers to the temporary absence of runaways who escaped for up to a month, while '*grand marronage*' refers to those who sought successfully more long-term or permanent escapes. Alpers suggests that *petit marronage* reflects how the enslaved mediated the terms of their bondage as well as a coming to terms with slavery, of which some presumably accepted an impossibility of indefinite escape, thus settling for temporary reliefs. *Grand marronage*, on the other hand, encompasses those escapes intended to establish long-term communities or, in some cases, to return to their homeland.[5] The following section will attempt to trace the dialectic of criminalization and *marronage* between the slave era and the contemporary prison regime, drawing continuities that reveal the modern Cape gangs as genealogically linked to the maroon groups of the Cape Colony, i.e. *die droster*s. As such, the continuum between *petit* and *grand marronage* is particularly compelling when applied to the contemporary context where individuals join gangs with similar ambitions of immediate, temporary relief or more long-term goals of going up the ranks within gang structures.

The historical framework used to explore the continuities between the *droster*s and the contemporary Cape gang relies on a concept developed by Ari Sitas *et al.* (2014): anomalic phases. It refers to points in history when public perceptions of increased deviance coincide with two other cyclical processes: Wallerstein's economic B-phase – which alludes to the cycle of contractions of the capitalist world economic system concurrently exhaling 'its poisons' (i.e. elimination of inefficient producers and lines of production), and a cycle of increasing subaltern resistance (ibid.). Historical moments of dissonance give rise to alterity – a group consciousness from below that there is an 'us' and a 'them' – followed by institutional transformation from the world political economy due to economic crises and subaltern resistance. Anomalic phases are instances where, on the one hand, economic and power structures reorganize and reconfigure themselves, and, on the other hand, resistance takes peculiar and pronounced forms. This study pinpoints three anomalic phases in the Cape's history and forms of banditry that correspond to them. The first is *slavery* (1653–1834), its incipient matrix of racialized violence and discourses, and the advent of the archetypal *droster*. The second is *proletarianization* (1835–1994), its crystallization of racial categories within overlapping processes of urbanization, migration and industrialization, and the rise of the *skollie*, the prototypical urban street gang and, ultimately, the birth of contemporary gangsterism on the Cape Flats. Finally, the third is the adjoined *modern prison regime* and the *hyper-ghettoization* of 'Coloured' communities (1994–present), its insistence on rendering 'Coloured' synonymous with gangsterism, and the contemporary trends in gangsterism.

The link I draw between the historical defiance of the *droster*s and that of the contemporary gangsters is one that, I argue, is transmitted through embodied forms of consciousness. We can begin to understand this through Sitas *et al.*'s (chapter 8, this volume) concept of the 'ideomorphic', in which defiant tropes survive across generations, through 'a kind of hyper-habitus produced by the physical and social parameters' of the relevant institution(s), which in this case will be the varying successive systems of criminalization that will be outlined below, as opposed to the university institution Sitas *et al.* poignantly examine. In other words, *marronage* is here treated as an ideomorphic idea that persisted across the different anomalic phases described above, one that shapes the deepest dispositions of gang lives. Added to this is the element of embodiment: the fugitivity of the *droster* gangs is an embodied instinct within the particular racializing conditions initiated through enslavement and carried forward until the present moment.

THE *DROSTER*S OF THE MOUNTAINOUS CAPE

From 1652 until 1808, about 63,000 slaves were shipped into the Cape from ports in four main areas: Eastern Africa (26.4 per cent), India (25.9 per cent), Madagascar (25.1 per cent) and Indonesia (22.7 per cent) (Shell 1997). By the 1760s, Cape-born slaves equalled in population size foreign-born fellow slaves, but it was the shared ordeal of physical torment the slaves experienced as human cargo that encapsulated their quintessential moment of a common collective memory (ibid.). Since that instance, the slave body was highly regulated through a range of institutional, discursive and disciplinary practices and technologies. While the Dutch East India Company (VOC) extended its rights to slaves' bodies post-mortem, for example, by exercising its authority through judicial and public defilement and displays of rotting corpses of those convicted of crimes, masters equally performed control over slaves even after their death by determining slave burials, often executing them 'surreptitiously' in a 'very slovenly manner' (Ward 2007).[6] Prior to the 1820s, the Cape did not consist of a professional police force; thus, policing the slave and serf body took on a more complex set of discursive and violent tactics (Loos 2004).

Foreshadowing the ways in which 'Coloured' masculinities and femininities today are stereotyped, colonial authorities, slaveholders and even anti-slavery activists solidified specific gendered and racialized mythologies: the slave man was a childlike 'man-in-waiting' through his deprivation from becoming a head of a family as well as a 'sexually licentious' figure deeply in need of European intervention to help tame his 'unruly masculinity'; and the slave woman was overly masculine and 'immoral' (Scully 1997). Colonial discourse, moreover, represented the Khoi as noble savages prone to fighting, Southeast Asian slaves as aspiring to whiteness, and West African slaves as epitomizing promiscuity and violence (Gqola 2001). The San were stereotyped as 'incorrigible banditti' (Marks 1972). This hierarchical thinking was predicated on the underlying configuring of slaves as 'wanting in culture and therefore in humanity' (Gqola 2001: 46), inscribing the malleable bodies with varying ideas based on their perceived proximity to either end of the fully-human and non-human scale. Legal regulation, scrutiny and fictions of slave and serfs' sexualities facilitated the inscription of notions of unrespectability, instability and immorality on to the Black body, in contrast to their allegedly civilized European counterparts, forming an imaginary upon which disciplinary and policing practices were both framed and justified.

The fragility and ambiguity of this hierarchal racialization was challenged by slaves who formed bonds on their own terms, as exemplified by communication networks formed to diffuse useful information and create an autonomous sense of family outside the institution of slavery (Vernal 2011). Such alternative social and familial networks and solidarities allowed for the fruition and frequency of *droster* gangs who formed fugitive and autonomous, often mobile communities, on the colonial borderlands (Ulrich 2015). Through this, we witness cases like that of Januarij van Boegies and seven fellow runaway slaves who conjured a plot to escape to a life in the Eastern Cape, a plan that was ultimately unsuccessful when the boat they robbed kept leaking (WCPA, *CJ* 354, 1746, ff. 484–87).[7] Going against popular historiography which frames resistance in the Cape Colony as individualistic or primarily defensive, Ulrich argues that 'the popular classes developed a rich, varied tradition of "direct action" that included desertion and the creation of maroon communities . . . [through which, they] express[ed] *alternative conceptions of morality and justice*' (Ulrich 2015: 17–18). Following a 1751 case of six armed runaway slaves who faced off a commando, another group of twelve slaves were reportedly 'impressed . . . that there had recently been a group of slaves who also taken flight and who had already arrived safely at a free village of blacks or even on Madagascar', demonstrating the symbolic influence *droster*s embodied (WCPA, *CJ* 788, 1750–55, ff. 58–67; WCPA, *CJ* 2485, 1729–59, ff. 130–33).[8]

While initially the term *droster* arose to signify runaways of all sorts and races – slaves, sailors, company soldiers, servants – by the 1750s the connotation more exclusively signified runaway slaves and escapee Khoi servants, reflecting a growing group consciousness of common identity between the slave and the Khoi, who would join these mobile armed bandits living on the outskirts of the colony within striking distance of isolated farms to feed off stolen livestock (Penn 1999). Indeed, by the 1720s, these fugitive gangs had grown considerably in size, frequency and audacity across the Groenekloof, Saldanha Bay, Stellenbosch and Piketberg areas, repeatedly pillaging the fringes and surrounding posts of Cape Town (ibid.). The mountainous landscapes provided natural hiding conditions for *droster*s (Worden 1982: 51):

> In areas such as Franschhoek, Land van Waveren or Hottentots-Holland, the close proximity of mountainous country provided ideal hiding places. Table Mountain and the rocky promontory of Hangklip jutting into False Bay were regular shelters

of droster communities. Inland, remoter regions such as the Roggeveld and Bokke-veld provided opportunities for slaves to escape to the interior, often with the help of the Khoisan.

Many of the documented cases of *drosters* also included foreign-born slaves who had until recently lived a life of freedom. These cases occurred most frequently during the summers when harvesting labour was most strenuous and conditions for life in the mountains relatively easier (Worden 2007). The *drosters* lived precarious lives, living outside the colony but always dependent on it and the surrounding farms. One *droster* group on Table Mountain in the 1770s maintained relations with urban slaves with whom they exchanged firewood for food (Alpers 2003).

The *drosters* forged themselves as figures within the imaginary of both colonizers and the colonized, as exemplified by the largest and longest-surviving group at Hangklip. This group became revered and somewhat glorified among slaves for their notorious banditry,[9] yet their connection with other slaves was even more intimate than reputation alone as several of them shared kinships and meaningful acquaintances with slaves in Town, including the underworld (Ross 1983). This group, furthermore, comprised a diversity of ethnicities – including first-generation South Africans and slaves from Bengal, Malabar, Sri Lanka, Bali, Sumbawa, Sulawesi and Madagascar – typifying the broader creolization within which this marooning was profoundly embedded (ibid.). The white ruling oligarchy, of course, feared the threat the *drosters* posed to the colonial order, increasingly turning from private punishment of captured runaways toward public chastisement and heightened nightly patrol. In 1696, upon discovering numerous slave deserters living with the Griqua, the VOC feared that slaves and Khoi could conspire together to incite a large uprising.

Based on records for a three-and-a-half-year period between January 1806 and June 1809, Worden (2007) estimates that at least 8 per cent of the total slave population had gone missing, of which only 21 per cent either returned or were recaptured. Throughout the colonial period *drosting* was common, and masters used extreme physical violence as both punishment and, more instrumentally, as public spectacle to warn other slaves against further attempts '*tot afschrik van andere*'.[10] When *drosters* were caught attempting escape, the other slaves were often called upon to witness, or even assist, as the *knecht* (Company employees, often sailors or soldiers, hired as overseers) inflicted violence with free rein (ibid.). In his thorough examination of the criminal records of the Council of Justice during the 1730s, Karl Bergemann (2011) highlights that, on the one hand, *drosting* and *aufugie* figure as the largest counts of offences by slaves,[11] and on the other hand, slaves and Khoi were sentenced disproportionally (nearly eight times more than convicted Europeans) to be punished by means of *ledebraken*.[12]

Slave and Khoi offenders were often tortured sadistically and rigorously, with bodily punishments ranging from 'being burnt alive, having body parts chopped off, one's flesh torn with hot iron tongs or *most often a combination of these*' (ibid.: 69). The body was clearly a modality of brandishing: by 1686, recaptured *droster*s had their ears amputated, and by 1711, an additional branding on the cheek was included (ibid.: 89).[13] Furthermore, beyond corporal punishment, slaves and the Khoi experienced the highest (and harshest) instances of capital sentencing. Even prior to punishment, slaves regularly suffered torturous interrogation techniques as courts forced confessions, which not uncommonly resulted in death from unattended wounds (ibid.: 111). By the 1780s, we witness a Thai slave named Spadilje who, recaptured after running away to the infamous Hangklip maroon community and committing a robbery in Simon's Town, was sentenced 'to be exposed with a rope around his neck under the gallows' while being scourged, branded and then sent to work on Robben Island in public works projects (WCPA, *CJ* 795, 1782–89, ff. 239–249).

One peculiar system of policing, criminalizing and controlling maroon activities was the commando system. Farmers and burghers formed commandos 'for self-defence' against banditry of *droster* groups, but they also notably employed the commandos in pre-emptive strikes against perceived 'centres of sedition' (e.g., mission stations) (Worden 2007: 18–19). Commandos were constantly sent out to search for *droster*s along the rural areas, targeting especially the notorious maroon communities who symbolically threatened colonial authority, as with the community at Hangklip who eluded the constant commando raids for over a hundred years and learned to navigate the region clandestinely. The commandos further reflected a characteristically wide level of discretionary powers given to policing forces against racialized groups. Thus was the case when Gerrit Marrits, a colonial authority who would become pivotal in the commando raids against the Khoesan of the Roggeveld, quickly shot and killed a runaway slave named Fortuijn after finding him in the Roggeveld mountains with a group of goats (WCPA, 1/STB 3/11, 1759–82).

Slaves and serfs who ran away were perceived as threatening the very stability and sustainability of the colony. In 1717, Captain de Chavonnes recommended that the colony transition to greater use of European labourers because slaves were costing the Company too much, naming the incidence of runaway slaves as among several high incurred expenses.[14] In the same letter, de Chavonnes argues that European labourers would, in contrast to the slave labouring force, 'bring security' and 'would not have to be divided in order to keep a watchful eye on the slaves' (de Chavonnes 1918: 105). Similarly, in a memorandum about the general state of the colony, it was remarked that farmers apparently made enough income to barely subsist, except that '[n]atives who pour in flocks upon their plantations and forcibly take their cattle from them' makes their financial prosperity impossible (Theal 1897: 169).

The Cape was, of course, also embedded within a larger network of convict transportation that saw political prisoners from the east transported into or via the colony, influencing the Cape's penal ideologies by wider global practices and discourses of the carceral. Clare Anderson argues that the carceral at the Cape was deeply embedded in the broader prerogative of containing the indigenous and managing unfree labour, with the Robben Island prison serving as a central site of confinement throughout the nineteenth century (2016). Robben Island was often used to pacify the Cape through its imprisonment of Black leaders, chiefs, slave rebels and prisoners of the frontier wars (1799–1803 and 1818–19). Like slaves, convicts on Robben Island were forced to participate in a range of labour, including public works, polishing stone, building, quarrying and more. Anderson (2016) interestingly positions Robben Island in a triage of civilizing institutions that also includes mission stations and schools set up for rebel leaders' children. The implicit relationship between the slave trade (and labour expropriation, generally) and carceral regimes was best articulated by the convict labour of Robben Island inmates, labour which contributed immensely to the colony's subsequent urbanized infrastructure (Penn 2008).

With the emancipation of slaves, a significant shift in penal practice occurred: the probation system was introduced for convicts to progress and work their way up from chain gangs to promised freedom. Indeed, emancipation saw a rise in fear over property crime and, without legalized enslavement, new forms of control had to be introduced within the more liberal discourses of 'reforming' so-called criminals. Along with the Caledon Code, which legally obligated Khoekhoe to only walk around with passes and subjugated them to permanent servitude within settler households, the evolving policing and incarceration systems effectively criminalized the movement of ex-slave and ex-serf bodies beyond servitude and submission under colonial rule. Whether the nomadic San, the mobile bandits of the runaway slaves and servants or rebels intent on actual revolt, the commando system was designed and sanctioned to, crudely put, hunt the dissidents who posed such political, social and symbolic threats to the colonial order. These groups, importantly, undermined central colonial understandings of what constituted 'family', creating alternative social and familial networks that destabilized the value system of colony. The marooning *droster*s, I argue, hold a central place within the imaginary and fears of colonial settlers. With emancipation of unfree laborers, subsequent attempts to sustain the racial and class divides established by the Cape would require a new legal and crime control framework that continued to regulate and contain the heterogenous group that would now be recognized racially as 'Coloured'. Amrita Pande (chapter 4, this volume) puts it succinctly: 'With the abolition of slavery in the Cape Colony after 1834, both the colonial state and white employers had to devise new ways of controlling the native population.'

THE ENDURANCE OF CRIMINALIZATION POST-EMANCIPATION

After the abolition of slavery and Khoisan forced labour, the two groups shared a labour pool and single socio-economic status. The immediate years after abolition introduced a transitional period of apprenticeship, designed to keep meeting the agricultural demands of the Cape economy. With the wool boom of the 1840s, followed by diamond and gold rushes, urban migration further reduced group distinctions amongst the heterogenous groups – former slaves and Khoi descendants – that would form a new proletariat class (Adhikari 1992). The elimination of clear slave–master distinctions saw the legal system reorganized to reproduce the previous racial hierarchy based on a paternalism that relegated the 'Coloured' workers to the status of minors (Scully 1989). The new class of free labourers became in effect criminalized. Workers' behaviour such as 'careless work' or 'absence' was defined as misdemeanours under intentionally vague legal codes that allowed magistrates to punish 'behaviour on the part of the "servant" that threatened an employer's authority' (Bickford-Smith 1994: 294). Two amendments to the Masters and Servants Act (1873/1875) triggered new trends of incarceration. They added clauses allowing the arrest of deserting labourers, annulling the need for warrants when dealing with rural workers (Scully 1989).[15] The new *de jure* criminalization of the 'Coloured' labouring class was reinforced on the flesh threefold: direct imprisonment of labourers engaged in an act too reminiscent to that of the *droster*s half a century prior, indirect sanctioning of more intimate violence of bodies by the court's overlooking of farmers' disciplinary measures (e.g., beatings, *dop* system,[16] rape), and discipline through docility-making when wealthier farmers elicited gratitude from workers by intervening 'benevolently' on their behalf in court.

Criminalization of the newly forged proletariat was not unique to the Cape, as new institutions – such as the prison, workhouse and asylum – were formed in the west during its transition from feudalism to capitalism (Foucault 1977). However, as was the case with the Cape Colony's *de jure* slavery, industrialization in the Cape took a different shape than its western counterparts. Linda Chisholm (1986) notes that the United Kingdom's industrialization was based on textile industries with a largely female and juvenile labour force, while South African industrialization focused on extractive industries with an exclusively adult male labour force. Before proceeding, a brief detour into the historical occurrence of the Numbers gangs' creation in the mining compounds is needed. The mineral revolution dispossessed and proletarianized the majority of the Black population in Witwatersrand. Within this context, the Number was birthed as a large set of prison gangs – the 26s, 27s and 28s. Central to their prison gang structures, ideologies and mythical narratives is the tale of Nongoloza, who became a bandit during the colonial era because Blacks were forced off their land and into slavery in the mines (Steinberg 2004b). As historian Charles van Onselen (2001) details, the Numbers originated from a bandit group, the Ninevites, which emerged in the late nineteenth century among Black mineworkers under the leadership of Nongoloza. These mineworkers were put through excruciating conditions, many as convict labourers and others as heavily policed 'free labourers'. Indeed, violence was integral to the mines' production system as white supervisors relied on assault in lieu of financial incentives to motivate workers to meet quotas (Moodie 1994).

From its onset, the Numbers was always a very unique gang model, taking direct inspiration from the colonial military and administrative structures and practices of the time (van Onselen 2001). Under Nongoloza's leadership, the gang was not only highly well-structured – with ranks ranging from generals to colonels, captains, sergeants, soldiers and several other governing positions – but also invoked a considerable level of 'ideological cohesion and social purpose' in its political mission to 'divert Nguni-speaking peasants from wage labour in the compounds to a freer existence', initially directing its campaigns of robbery against the powerful (van Onselen 1985: 66–75). By the 1930s, the Numbers had migrated from the mining camps into South Africa's vast prison system, relying on both its militaristic structure and a highly ritualistic culture that deployed its own language ('sabela'), mythologies (variant tales of its founders, Nongoloza, Kilikijan and the Ninevites), rituals and laws. In the contemporary period, many 'Coloured' men in the Cape are members, know members or have family that are part of the Numbers gangs.

Witwatersrand and Kimberly were the burgeoning industrial centres, while the Cape Colony kept commercial agriculture as its main, though struggling enterprise. It was within this economic context of farmers struggling to retain their labour force and the already generations-deep processes of colonial dispossession and proletarianization that South Africa's first juvenile reformatory, the Porter Reformatory, emerged in the Cape Colony – and not its industrial regions. Thus, unlike the mining compounds[17] and prisons of the latter, the Cape's Porter Reformatory was peculiarly 'shaped by the imperatives of merchant capital and commercial agriculture' (Chisholm 1986: 495), incorporating modified models of forced apprenticeship to train juvenile offenders into wage earners.

In the frequent cases where the boys' parents could not be easily accessed or were deemed 'degenerate' (synonymous for the labouring 'Coloured' poor), the state would easily indenture juveniles into forced apprenticeship. Juvenile convict labour was established as a stable and important source of workers for local dignitaries and farmers. Militaristic in its daily routine and rigid structures, the reformatory aimed to drill inmate bodily habits into docility, discipline, obedience and cleanliness (Chisholm 1986). The practices within Porter also capture the particular racialized and classed discourses developed over the nineteenth-century Cape Colony. Youths convicted of crimes of violence went to gaols and were seen as innately criminal, while boys who committed crimes against property were seen as 'reformable' and sent to Porter, reflecting a discourse of duality between 'respectable'/'reformable'/'disciplinable' and the 'innately criminal'. Inmates at Porter 'included "Coloured Afrikanders" and "Hottentots", who constituted the majority, as well as Africans from the Eastern Cape Transkeian regions, "Mozambiques" generally employed on the docks in Cape Town, Malays and Europeans, who together comprised the remaining quarter of the reformatory population' (ibid.: 487). Simultaneously, during the last quarter of the nineteenth century, many farm workers were migrating to the urbanized towns to join the public works schemes. By 1910, the larger portion of Porter Reformatory inmates came from District Six (ibid.: 485).

By the 1920s, Cape Town's transition into an industrial economy solidified and, following 50 years of large-scale migration, resulted in overcrowded and impoverished urban communities. Between 1928 to 1935, 2,600 'Coloured' youths were imprisoned annually in South Africa – mostly in Cape Town (Pinnock 2016). Just as the term *droster* was used two centuries before, a new term arose here to denote a form of criminality perceived to threaten moral order. '*Skollie*' is Afrikaans best translated directly as 'scoundrel', denoting a violent or thieving criminal (Jensen 2008). Arising first in the context of District Six where young men engaged in petty crime, the underlying connotation of the *skollie* is that he is poor, 'Coloured' and male. A pejorative label with essential racial undertones, the *skollie* represents an existential perception that equated 'Colouredness' with criminality and an untrustworthy nature. In District Six, police pursued these young men labelled *skollies* but soon began treating anyone from the community as such, reflecting a larger criminalization of 'Colouredness' that accompanied the notion of *skollie* (Pinnock 1984). By 1946, a special squad was established to deal with *skollies* using 'wide powers of arrest' (Pinnock 2016), a privilege parallel to the commandos and subsequent police force under the Masters and Servants Act amendments. The police force did not seem to address the issue of rising petty theft. Instead, the Globe Gang (and other street gangs) emerged, with members comprising sons of shopkeepers and businessmen (Pinnock 1984). These first urban gangsters were often regarded (and today, are often remembered and romanticized) as respectable men: they provided protection and order in an otherwise disorderly and overlooked community, policing from within. These gangs also reflected and embodied the basis of the family unit prevalent amongst this community: the extended family.

Pinnock (1984) details how the District Six community developed an important informal economy, to which the first street gangs (e.g., Globe) served as vigilante organizations. The Globe, however, soon turned to criminal activity, including extortion, *shebeens* and gambling rackets, while other gangs such as the Mongrels arose with greater numbers of youth who had experienced the state's only response to youth delinquency: the reformatory. At the same time, police began treating 'Coloureds' with indiscriminate harshness, 'manhandling' innocent and guilty residents alike. Young men were rapidly turning to these prototypical urban gangs which offered money, protection and a sense of community, in what preceded apartheid as a 'spatial reaction to the economic global rise of monopoly capital' (ibid.: 37–42). Simultaneously, in Cape Town, worker resistance was rising and deindustrialization was commencing. The legitimacy of the ruling racial hierarchy had to be reproduced through a production of spaces and discourses that dually served power and capital: the Group Areas Act of 1950. The National Party during apartheid, of course, was notorious for its use of police in extrajudicial state-sanctioned killings and arrests, without warrants in many cases.

By producing the Cape Flats, a particular construction of 'Coloured' identity was imposed that aimed to rearrange 'right' and 'wrong', delegitimizing workers' struggles and shifting the discourse towards a modified perception of 'Coloured' cultural and moral shortcomings (Jensen 2008). The construction of the Cape Flats bears considerable similarities to the hyper-ghettoization of African Americans in the US, a spatial and economic process that Wacquant (2009) reveals to be central to the larger reorganizing of socio-economic order under neoliberal governing: the ghetto is resituated as surrogate prison, functioning to contain the surplus labour no longer needed in a more globalized economic system. The ghettoization of the Cape Flats in the last half of the twentieth century also shares parallels with neoliberal Brazil. Joao Biehl argues that Brazil reconstructed *favelas* as an 'excess population' with no political import and social relevance, as 'zones of abandonment' which the larger society simply cannot or will not absorb (Biehl 2005). By 1980, there were 2,500 'Coloured' youths incarcerated on any given day (Standing 2006). With the aforementioned rise of the Numbers gangs in the prison system nationally, many of these 'Coloured' prisoners either joined or were directly affected by the Numbers. As Lewin (chapter 5, this volume) thoroughly shows us, the Number holds a totalizing and pervasive influence within prison spaces where members and non-members alike must rescript their performances to both survive and subvert the gang's power.

Mountainous Prisons

> We contend that the growing reactive and violent parts of the private security industry are both a reflection of, and a driving force behind, a broader exclusionary political economy. This political economy for human security reflects the long-held, yet historically specific belief that it is possible to pursue an individualized 'political peace' through the enforcement of the law (or law-like rules) and the maintenance of a web of disciplinary power, quite independently from the pursuit of broader projects for 'social' and 'economic peace'. (Kempa and Singh 2008: 341)

The introduction of the new democratic order after 1994 witnessed a huge growth in the tourism industry, which, as Standing (2006) has shown, included vast investments in private and public security, especially in wealthier areas around Cape Town. Privatization of security is exemplified by the 2010 statistics which reveal 'an estimated four security guards for every regular police officer in the country' (Pinnock 2016: 56). Interestingly enough, American police chief William Bratton was brought in to consult on Cape Town CBD's urban revitalization projects, importing with him former mayor Rudy Giuliani's 'broken windows' ideology and rhetoric (ibid.: 48). Consequently, Cape Town underwent several hyper-policing initiatives – including 1998's Operation Clean and Safe, 1999's Operation Reclaim and 2000's Operation Crackdown – which employed hundreds of police to clear the CBD of perceived criminals (ibid.). Hyper-incarceration settled as the status quo, with a 2,197 per cent increase in life sentences between 1995 to 2014 (ibid.: 254). The mid-1990s witnessed worsening conditions within correctional centres, with unprecedented levels of overcrowding: at Pollsmoor Correctional Centre, 'there were twice as many prisoners as the physical structures allowed for' (Centre for Conflict Resolution 2004: 161). Crime steadily intensified post-1994 and the solution has been a militarized police force that often applies shoot-to-kill tactics. Capturing one of the highest police homicide rates, Pinnock underscores that between 2009 and 2010, '2,569 civilians were killed as a result of police action or while in police custody' (Pinnock 2016: 62). It should come as no surprise then that some residents of the Cape Flats view the police as the epitome of corruption, state violence and injustice.

Gangs have fostered important economic interdependence networks with local residents, providing income and occasionally paying off bills for families, echoing the networks formed by *drosters* along Table Mountain who traded firewood for food with town slaves. Of course, gang violence is often turned towards the local inhabitants of the townships, just as – though surely to a greater extent – the *drosters* were also known to direct their violence at Khoi, slaves and free Blacks. Stephen Jensen and Dennis Rodgers attempt to resolve this contradiction by reconceptualizing the gang through Deleuze and Guattari's notion of the 'war machine', defined as 'social phenomena that direct their actions against domination, but without necessarily having well-defined battle lines or standard forms confrontation' (Jensen and Rodgers 2009: 231–32). A war machine destabilizes authority without seeking to establish itself as the governing force or form; its anti-authoritative politics is found simply it its occupation of space in a radically different manner, refusing to settle in the universalized ways of being of the dominant discourses, opting instead for an 'ever-moving', unstable 'line of flight'. Jensen and Rodgers's vision is useful in allowing us to circumvent the binaries of power and resistance with a nuanced focus on 'the potential that [gangs'] existence represents' (ibid.: 233). Yet, the notion still does not sufficiently encapsulate the force or potency of historical processes of racialization and creolization. It does not seize the exceptional role and context of slavery and colonialism, their discursive and racialized continuities and the arena of flesh, which is the 'vestibular gash in the armour of Man' (Weheliye 2014: 44). Here, the oppositional 'line of flight' of gangs is given more direction (though it is still not ideologically based) than Jensen and Rodgers's conception grants.

Edouard Glissant invokes the image of 'the forest into which the slaves escaped and where the maroon communities lived' as one of the first forms of resistance to the 'transparency of the planter' (Britton 1999: 21). Here, *opacity* represents a certain density, mysteriousness, concealment and irreducibility created by the colonized as a liberating experience: a veil from the colonizer. By creating obscurity in one's self, the maroon undermines the colonial dichotomy of 'discoverer' and 'discovered' and resists the colonizers' insistence on a transparent self. Just as Glissant (1997) conceptualized the forest as the embodiment of the maroon communities' pursuit of *opacity*, the Cape *droster*s utilized the mountains to create their opacity. As shown by Steinberg (2005) and Lewin (chapter 5, this volume), the Numbers gang's lore, language, grand historical narratives and rituals have entered the imaginary of young 'Coloured' men from the Cape Flats in such a way that 'Prison Generals walked out of jail demigods' (Steinberg 2005: 283). Within the prison, a dense and complex world was created; Lewin delves deeply into the politics of how precisely this intimate, violent and complex world is staged, performed, negotiated and constantly rescripted. Just as the mountains were a space of impenetrability and opacity for the *droster* gangs, for many 'Coloured' youths, the prison now serves as a space of alternate existence and opacity, impermeable to the current governing forces.

During slavery, slave and indigenous bodies were objectified as property and as carnal signifiers of antithesis to the citizen-human embodied in the European imago; during the contemporary neoliberal order, the former's direct descendants figure as antithesis to the 'respectable' citizenry. The slaves' bondage was justified by the perceived lack they embodied, while the hyper-incarceration of 'Coloured' men is likewise condoned until their communities 'reform' themselves. While the ghost of slavery continues to haunt our imaginaries through the continuities of racialized discourses imprinted on 'Coloured' bodies, the contemporary gang carries the ghost of *drosters* through its continued insistence on opaque structures and alternative modalities of being. Enslaved bodies were inscribed with the lack of value, thus the *droster* regained ownership of their bodies and took to the mountains in constructing an alternate sense of value, or futurities; inhabitants of the Cape Flats are imbued with racist notions of 'Colouredness', thus the gangs' rituals and symbolism emanate from the reappropriation of the body with tattoos, movements and rhythms.[18] Through the latter, marooning continues as a generations-old practice echoed (in part) through the varying types of gangs created under each successive racialized structure of domination; processes of racialization and creolization conflate and diverge in the arena of the flesh, producing a surplus, articulated through escape, movement away, evasion of the oppressors' gaze.

In so far as 'Colouredness' remains ontologically positioned as the incarnation of absence, lack-ness and void, the modern gang on the Cape Flats then figures as an oppositional assemblage. The spirit of slavery is conjured today through the criminalization and stereotyping of 'Coloured' bodies, its undergirding episteme is enfleshed to make an 'inescapable prison house of the flesh' (Hartman 1997: 58). The chains that shackled slaves in the Cape linked to those that bound their descendants not merely in a metaphorical sense, but as inheritance of particular tropes of racialized captivity on the one hand, and defiance on the other. The mountain has previously been alluded to within studies on 'Coloured' men who go to prison, particularly as a metaphor for a rites-of-passage journey comparable to Xhosa rituals for men coming of age (Steinberg 2005; Pinnock 1997). This chapter also deviates from this use of the mountain metaphor. The prison can be framed as the new mountains, but not (solely) for reasons related to masculinities and notions of manhood; rather, I point to the ways in which the mountainous landscape for the *drosters* and the prison for the modern gangs both encompass and have been refashioned around a Glissantian opacity (Glissant 1997).

Conclusion

Stanley Cohen (1986) has detailed how criminology from the mid-1960s – influenced by interactionist sociology of deviance, labelling theory and leftist criminology – attempts to reverse positivist criminology (separation of crime from the state, viewing criminals as 'determined, pathological beings') to emphasize criminality in relation to resistance, rebellion or protest. Stigmatic labels, the political economy of law and punishment (Engels's theft as 'the most primitive form of protest') and discourse of crime within power relations (i.e. Foucauldian approaches) became points of focus. Beyond the problem definition (i.e. criminalization), others questioned the political meanings of criminal behaviour, concluding at one extreme with the criminal as crypto-political actor and crime as an 'embryonic form of social protest'. Notably relevant concepts emerged: Cohen's (1973) *convergence* (i.e. social labelling and behaviour converge); Hobsbawn's *equivalence* (i.e. crime under certain conditions is functionally equivalent to protest/resistance); and *progression* (i.e. crime as primitive precursor for sophisticated political forms) (Hobsbawn 1994). This study does not however fall into a western model of heroic criminality in Africa articulated through the syllogism: 'If "crime is inherently a form of protest" and banditry is "simply a form of criminality common to agrarian societies", then banditry is a form of protest' (Cohen 1986: 474).

Avoiding romanticization, this chapter seeks not to imply blindly that the gang is an inherently political form or that gangsterism is equivalent functionally to political behaviour. This would simply further categorize the bandit/gangster within typologies of who/what constitutes politically self-conscious criminals.[19] Jensen's *war machine* offers a kind of framework that moves beyond a politicized dichotomy of revolutionary and pathological deviant, but even then the emphasis is on the gangster's relation to the political economy. My inquiry, on the other hand, focuses on the gangster's relation to two other forces – racialization and creolization. Creolization here is not reducible to a protest politics – though, surely, many radical traditions and resistance strategies are richly weaved with(in) creolization processes and, as argued by feminism, the personal is always political; rather, it is more complex as a creative praxis that simultaneously fills lacunae and continuously re-envisions ever-unstable epistemological totalities.

This project thus deviates from Jensen's gangs as war machine figures oppositional to political structures, Pinnock's (1997) gangs as sites of 'journeys' where young men pursue brotherhoods and rituals that (re)present desired rites of passage, and Philippe Bourgois's (1996) urban drug dealer as locked into street economies due to a determined search for cultural respect structured symptomatically by institutional racism and life in the depressed 'ghetcolony'. The contemporary gang is situated against the afterlives of slavery and *drosting* within the broader dialectics of racialization and creolization that engender a dialectic of criminalization and marooning, respectively.

NOTES

1 This paper assumes a complex view that sees 'Coloured' identity neither as the product of miscegenation nor as the result of white-imposed conditions, acknowledging rather the role of 'Coloureds' in their own cultural formation as far back as the slave era. More specifically, this paper relies heavily on Zimitri Erasmus's formulation of 'Coloured' identities through processes of *creolization* (Erasmus 2017; 2001).

2 Technically, the Cape Flats encompasses both 'Coloured' and Black apartheid-designated areas, but for the purpose of this paper popular nomenclatures are used whereby the Cape Flats refers to specifically 'Coloured' working-class areas and the townships refer to specifically Black working-class areas.

3 In contrast to the widely used term 'mass incarceration', 'hyper-incarceration' emphasizes the triple selectivity of the carceral state that *finely targets* on the intersecting bases of class, race and place (Rodriguez 2019; Wacquant 2010).

4 An eighteenth-century term referring to runaway slaves and escapee Khoi (indigenous) enserfed servants. When referring to groups of *droster*s, the original Afrikaans court documents use the term *complot*, which is best translated as 'gangs'; see, for example, Western Cape Provincial Archive (WCPA), *Criminal Justice (CJ)* 795, 1782–89, ff. 407–23.

5 Cases of slaves attempting to escape back to their homeland are epitomized by Malagasy maroons whose urge to return home 'drew its power from a deep cultural belief that for the soul to rest one must be buried in the land of one's birth' (Alpers 2003: 63).

6 It should be noted that masters were not *legally* – based on Roman law – permitted to kill their slaves, but as it did commonly occur, slave owners were usually imposed a mere fine for 'accidental death' rather than murder (Ward 2006).

7 The group was sentenced to be whipped and then sent back to their owners to labour in chains for three years.

8 In both these cases, the courts interestingly mentioned the groups' use of Malay words during the encounters – the battle-cry 'amok!' and '*lavang*', which meant 'defend yourself'.

9 The leader, Leander Bugis, was particularly reputable and had earned a general fear among the slaves for his well-known violent character, having killed fellow maroons on occasion.

10 Translated as 'with the intent of scaring the others', from the Council of Justice fiscal, Adriaan van Kervel, in his recommendations for punishment of the slave, Schipio, who transgressed restrictions on where to collect firewood (Bergemann 2011: 55).

11 The latter of these two crimes, '*aufugie*' is difficult to translate and was almost exclusively a crime by slaves: 'It seems to be tied in with runaways and escapees and concerns those incidents where the accused were *drosting* with weapons, although there are times when weapons are mentioned along with the act of *drosting* where *aufugie* was not brought against the accused. For this reasons its exact implications are difficult to monitor. Nonetheless, with more than 60 counts in the 1730s, it too features strongly, tied in with the high number of *drosters* at the time' (ibid.: 14).

12 *Ledebraken* refers to the breaking of limbs by blunt force trauma with the wheel. Bergemann's key finding is how punishments were based less on the crime itself and more on the status of the offender as well as the victim, i.e. a slave convicted of assault received the most brutal punishment in contrast to a European convicted of the same: 'Even murder was recategorized as assault when it came to burghers who murdered their slaves – as if the life of a slave was too inconsequential to usher the crime of murder or manslaughter and therefore the offenders were exposed to wholly different punishments more fitting of assault' (ibid.: 59).

[13] Second-time offenders had their other cheek branded, third-time offenders suffered the worst fate of having their ears and nose cut off.

[14] Specifically, he proposes that 250 European workers would more profitable than 5,600 slaves.

[15] Farm labourers would also often commit petty theft predominantly when the farmer was away, 'suggesting that the farmer's authority was vested in his [physical] person, and not . . . his position as "Master" on the farm' (Scully 1989: 297).

[16] A notorious system used in South African wine farms to pay farm workers in part with daily measures of cheap wine

[17] Gary Kynoch argues the mining industry 'served as an incubator for [a culture of] violence ... that has reproduced itself ever since' (Kynoch 2008: 644–45).

[18] It may be important to note that in both cases, resistance took/takes other forms in a myriad of social, cultural and political practices. It is not to suggest that gangsterism is either the main or essential form of the communities' traditions of opacity making, subversion and, moreover, creolization.

[19] According to Cohen, 'very crudely, there are four possibilities: (i) the "pure-political" deviant whose own account (e.g. in 'rebellion') is accorded legitimacy; (ii) the "pure-ordinary" deviant who offers nor is assigned any type of political motive; (iii) the "unknowing-deviant" who does not show any apparent political consciousness, but awarded this by others (e.g. the juvenile delinquent recruited by criminologists into the class war); and (iv) the "contested-political" deviant own political account is not honoured by others (e.g. the dissenter in the Union labelled as schizophrenia)' (Cohen 1986: 476). Or '(i) unequivocal guerrilla - who is recognised by the party leadership and accepted as such by the peasants; (ii) the unequivocal bandit - individuals and operating under cover of the war, repudiated by the party and feared peasants; (iii) the fighters who are regarded by the party as guerrillas but are not (yet) accorded this legitimacy by the peasants, who see them rather bandits (because they break disciplinary rules, get drunk, are guilty of harassment); (iv) an equivocal category close to social banditry – renegade terrorists accepted and helped by the peasants but not recognize' (ibid.: 478).

7

When Prisoners Bring Their Knowledge to the Academic World and to Judicial Power to Oversee Their Prison Conditions

Gaëtan Cliquennois

Introduction

Penal inflation, which consists in increasing penal sanctions for major offences (especially sexual offences and those related to terrorism), has characterized the majority of penal policies in most states worldwide, and in the United States and European states in particular, since at least 2001. In this regard, since the 9/11 attacks in New York, the European Union (EU) has been urging its member states to adopt repressive measures against terrorism, such as the European arrest warrant,[1] whose legality and compliance with the European Convention on Human Rights is clearly open to discussion (Eckes 2010). The European Council also adopted in 2005 the EU counterterrorism strategy to fight terrorism globally, and radicalization and recruitment to terrorism in particular, in 2008. The strategy was revised in June 2014 in light of evolving trends such as lone-actor terrorism, foreign fighters and the use of social media by terrorists.[2] In December 2014, the Council adopted guidelines for the implementation of the revised strategy by member states. Furthermore, it adopted on 7 March 2017 a directive on combating terrorism that criminalizes acts such as undertaking training or travelling for terrorist purposes, organizing or facilitating such travel, and providing or collecting funds related to terrorist groups or activities.[3]

These punitive European laws have been enacted without being always challenged – either by the European Court of Justice of the EU or by the European Court of Human Rights.[4] In particular, Article 15 of the European Convention on Human Rights, which enables a state to unilaterally derogate from some of its obligations to the Convention (whose scope covers the forty-seven member states of the Council of Europe) in certain exceptional circumstances, has been used by certain member states such as France and the United Kingdom in the context of terrorism.[5] These penal policies have contributed to more convictions, causing prison overcrowding and inhuman prison conditions. In fact, this penal inflation was the main factor responsible for prison overcrowding in most of the member states of the EU, resulting in inhuman prison conditions, healthcare issues, and a rise in incidents of suicide and homicides behind bars.

These human rights violations committed by national prison administrations were progressively and increasingly watched and monitored by international bodies, among which are the United Nations Council on Human Rights, the European Court of Human Rights and the European Committee for the Prevention of Torture (CPT). In this respect, the United Nations' and European judicial and inspectorate bodies that share the general principles and aims of what is now commonly referred to as 'global justice' have gained increasing prominence in the fields of penal and prison policy and practice over time, particularly in recent years. Those bodies work in their diverse capacities to ensure that human rights legislation is observed within the borders of individual nation states.

This process of international monitoring and judicial censure has been extended over time to such an extent that certain prisoners have been progressively in a position to exert some control over their prison conditions by lodging complaints with the European Court of Human Rights and gaining the backing of some NGOs and scholars. Since 2005 at least, this monitoring system has however radically changed, and expanded its scope and obligations imposed on states to such an extent that it could be described as an influential and spreading sociolegal trend that is contributing to the development of modern and democratic societies (Schwartz 2010).

While academic attention has been paid very recently to the impressive rise of the legal framework of human rights in the realm of penal and prison policies in Europe (Van Zyl Smit and Snacken 2009; Van Zyl Smit 2010; Cliquennois and de Suremain 2017; Cliquennois and Snacken 2017; Daems 2017; Daems and Robert 2017), some significant issues have been neglected by the literature. First, human rights conventions, their monitoring and violations need to extend beyond documenting legal and policy issues in the European context. Second, this literature has overlooked non-EU countries such as the United States and Russia which are characterized by a large number of prison policies, the harshness of these policies and large-scale human rights violations. Third, African countries and eastern countries such as Bulgaria and Romania have also been under-researched though they are subjected to international monitoring concerning, notably, their prison overcrowding, inhumane prison conditions, and lack of real and effective domestic remedies. Fourth and last, the process by which prisoners and NGOs are able to monitor prison conditions through international and regional organizations is completely under-researched.

In this regard, the tasks of control and supervision achieved by the United Nations (UN) and the Council of Europe are indeed (according to the Consultative Assembly of the Council of Europe and to the UN Convention on Torture[6]) delegated at a national level to NGOs and human rights groups set up to examine bills in the light of the UN and European Conventions. These bodies prevent and denounce breaches of these Conventions by the member states. In this respect, these national human rights groups, represented since 2003 at the Council of Europe through the International Conference of NGOs and at the UN through the conferences for NGOs and the UN Democracy Fund set up in 2005, may be considered as watchdogs that can inform their respective national human rights structures (such as ombudsmen, human rights commissions and equality bodies) responsible for gathering complaints against violations of human rights, and bring their governments before the European Court of Human Rights (ECHR) and the UN for infringements of human rights (Cliquennois and Champetier 2016). In other words, and also thanks to the role played by these NGOs, human rights groups and legal aid granted to prisoners, is there any evidence in addition to the constant multifaceted supervision of prisoners (as in the hypothesis of Foucault 1975), that national Ministers of Justice and prison administrations are now also efficiently monitored and supervised by the UN and European bodies, NGOs and human rights groups and beyond by prisoners? What are the limits of this monitoring based on human rights 'law' in this context in terms of access to justice for prisoners and persistence of human rights violations in the face of reform?

This phenomenon is such that we assume it leads to the development of an inverted panopticon by which certain prisoners and NGOs are in a position to challenge the authority of national prison administrations. This process fits more broadly within a defiance script through which prisoners can both challenge national authorities and legitimize incarceration (Cartuyvels 2002). The defiance script for prisoners consists in watching professional practices, prison conditions and even potential breaches of human rights, rather than simply being subject to surveillance. While the defiance script to which certain prisoners can adhere might be compliant with national and international human rights and administrative law, defiant prisoners can be stigmatized by prison staff for such monitoring of their prison conditions. It is precisely this fight between both these trends that constitutes the lens of this chapter. More broadly, prison institutions constitute a specific social phenomenon that differs from other kinds of detention such as camps due to its very high level of institutionalization. Prisons are subjected to strain and paradoxical logics from privation of freedom to restrictions on freedom, and constitute an interesting case study for the defiant script in which the inverted panopticon and prison reactions to it take place. The inverted panopticon and the reaction to it by some of its opponents challenges the traditional view on prisons, that are only considered to be a privation of freedom and rights.

It seems important to underline that the inverted panopticon refers to the panopticon that is a technology of power as described by Jeremy Bentham, and constitutes one of the most well-known theses asserted by Foucault concerning prison (Foucault 1975). Foucault indeed stresses in *Discipline and Punish* that the panopticon is a very efficient prison architecture based on the all-seeing eye that does not allow prisoners to check whether wardens are either present or absent (ibid.). Thanks to its conception, the panopticon is turned towards the discipline of the soul and body of prisoners (ibid.). While this theory has been massively endorsed by academic literature to analyse prison architecture and surveillance devices, scant attention has been paid to the opposite process which implies that prison institutions are scrutinized and even overseen by NGOs, human rights groups and prisoners, and through (and thanks to) prisoners by a public audience (Cliquennois and de Suremain 2017). Even though this opposite process is not architectural, it also involves the all-seeing eye in the sense that prison institutions and their staff are subject to public and judicial exposition without the possibility to know exactly when they are exposed or not. In other words, is there any evidence in addition to the constant multifaceted supervision of prisoners (as in the hypothesis of Foucault 1975), that national prison administrations and prison institutions are now also watched by prisoners, NGOs and human rights groups, academic scholars, judges and by a more general public audience?

The lack of study of this trend dubbed 'the inverted panopticon' is quite surprising as it seems to have grown since the 70s due to the rise of a convict criminology (thanks to which prisoners contribute to produce knowledge), prisoners' rights organizations and prison activists such as the Prisons Information Group (or Groupe d'Information sur les Prisons – GIP) to which Foucault himself has contributed. More precisely, we argue that the inverted panopticon is fed and nurtured by prisoners, intellectuals – the first of them being Foucault, and by NGOs and human rights groups representing prisoners and backed by international organizations. Instead of considering Foucault's theory and its effects on prisons as prison literature generally does, we would rather take into account the militant Foucault and his influence and effects on the inverted panopticon that contradicts his own theory on prison. Furthermore, we show that Foucault contributed to a defiant script influenced by NGOs that are backed by international organizations and international human rights law which have been totally overlooked by Foucault.

This is why we study, in the first part of this article, the role played by prisoners and their representatives – NGOs, human rights groups, prisoners as intellectuals through the new school of convict criminology – in the rise of the inverted panopticon and the defiant script. The development of human rights and judicial complaints lodged by prisoners and prisoners' rights groups, which constitutes the second part of this chapter, has also significantly contributed to foster the defiant script and the inverted panopticon.

Prisoners' Voices and Their Insights into Prison Reality through NGOs and the New School of Convict Criminology: the Defiant Script

Prisoners and Prisoners' Rights Organizations: The Role Played by the Prisons Information Group and Human Rights Activists

The role played by NGOs is essential and can been notably be seen in the creation of the GIP. In this regard, the position held by the GIP, notably on behalf of Jean-Marie Domenach, Michel Foucault and Pierre Vidal-Naquet, was to produce critical knowledge and thinking on the prison, which was considered to be a black hole. They were joined in these efforts by other famous intellectuals and artists such as Jean Genet and Jean-Paul Sartre. Similar to other organizations allowing poor social classes to speak (Sitas *et al.* 2014), the main goal of the GIP was to give prisoners the opportunity to express their complaints in their own voice for the first time and to speak about their main concerns regarding detention conditions, poor hygiene and food, abuse, torture, punishment, etc. Prisoners' voices made them actors and their stories constituted critical knowledge from grassroots actors (Artieres, Quero and Zancarini-Fournel 2003) which shed new light on prisons and their daily realities. While prisoners were given access to newspapers and television thanks to the GIP, a more general audience was given a window into their lives and experiences through a journal that frequently published letters written by prisoners. In this regard, this process constituted the premise of the inverted panopticon phenomenon as prisoners' voices were also new insights into prison staff practices and prison officer discretion.

Following the end of the GIP, prisoners' voices were relayed by prisoners' rights organizations and human rights activists in several European countries. For instance, in France, campaigns from prisoners' rights groups were mainly the work of the Multi-professional Prison Group,[7] established and led by Antoine Lazarus (who was very close to Foucault) in 1974; the French section of the International Observatory of Prisons[8] (Observatoire international des Prisons or the OIP, also very close to Foucault), founded in 1996; Ban Public,[9] founded in 1999 by a former prisoner; the Association of Families Fighting against Insecurity and Death in Prisons[10] *(Association des Familles en Lutte contre l'Insécurité et les Décès en Détention – AFLIDD)*, created in 1997 by the widow and son of a prisoner who had committed suicide; the Group for the Defence of Prisoners'

Family Members[11] (Le Collectif de Défense des Familles et Proches de Personnes Incarcérées), created in 2001; and Shed Light on Prisons (Faites la Lumière en Detention – FLD) founded in 2008. These campaigns consisted for the most part of posting information on websites; publishing reports (OIP 2000, 2003, 2005); issuing press releases (recalling, for instance, harsh regime and poor detention conditions); participating in television programmes (by the FLD); organizing protest days against suicide and violent deaths in prison; staging events such as Ban Public's 'The Outdoor Prison Visitors' Room' or FLD's 'Inmate Death in Prison Day' (Lyon, 8 December 2008). French prisoners' rights organizations also refer cases to the CPT, the former French National Commission for Ethics and Safety (Commission Nationale de Déontologie et de Sécurité – CNDS) and the French National Consultative Committee of Human Rights (Commission Nationale Consultative des Droits de l'Homme – CNCDH), whose objectives are to expose administration failures, even those leading to the suicide or murder of prisoners, as well as to request parliamentary investigations. One such investigation, that of 28 October 2002, led to prison visits and public reports on the day-to-day reality of imprisonment.

On a regular basis and on behalf of certain prisoners, some NGOs and members of the French Parliament and independent administrative agencies seize the French Inspector-General of places of deprivation of liberty[12] (Contrôleur general des lieux privatifs de liberté, the French oversight body of detention)[13] to denounce breach of fundamental rights in certain prisons.[14] In reaction, the French Inspector-General of places of privation of liberty can investigate and organize visits in all places of detention to check such fact-finding (notably brought by NGOs and prisoners), and make public reports and statements, recommendations about their visits by pointing out the breaches of human rights they have noticed.[15]

In addition, the development of new information technology such as the internet and smartphone also made it easier to disseminate prisoners' voices. For instance, prisoners' family members and former prisoners have created websites, Facebook accounts[16] and forums, and disseminated pictures of their incarceration to give to society direct access to prisoners' experience in jails and to denounce prison conditions, abuse, punishment and human rights violations. We can find on these websites pictures and even videos taken by the prisoners with their mobile phones.

In this manner, prisoners' voices and insights into the daily reality of imprisonment have been relayed by prisoners' rights organizations and exposed through new information technology to the public. This process, along with the rise of convict criminology, clearly contributes to the development of the inverted panopticon.

The Development of Convict Criminology

Convict criminology is the study of prison by prisoners and ex-prisoners who have become professors or graduate students. While this phenomenon emerged in the American context of mass incarceration with the published works of John Irwin, notably his book *The Felon* (1970), it has expanded its influence beyond the US to Canada, Australia and Europe (Earle 2016). The main aim of convict criminology is to conduct inside research and studies that incorporate the experiences of prisoners and prison workers, with a view to balance the conventional representations of media and governments on prison. In this way, prisoners and ex-prisoners have progressively contributed prisoners' perspective to prison research and criminological knowledge.

The emerging field of convict criminology consists primarily of books and articles written by convicts or ex-convict graduate students and professors, and are based on primary data sources such as interviews and observations of prison reality. The Convict Criminology group nowadays is organized as a voluntary writing and activist collective. Different members inspire or take responsibility for speaking to the media and helping authors with academic articles, research proposals, programme assessments, or mentoring students and junior faculty. Some of these activities are directly funded by private foundations, including the Soros Foundation Open Society Institute (Ross *et al.* 2014). Thanks to this support, some prisoners have brought their first-hand experience of imprisonment to the academic world and beyond, and contributed to the inverted panopticon process, as media stories about convict criminology have appeared in print in the US, Canada, Australia and Europe.

Litigation Undertaken by Prisoners, Their Families and Prisoners' Rights Organizations

Prisoners' rights organizations have progressively used legal action against the prison administration and taken prison cases to courts. At the request of their families or of the prisoners themselves – in particular, men condemned to very long prison sentences and detained in secure closed regimes characterized by closed doors, permanent surveillance and poor visits (as these prisoners have in general nothing to lose except their reputation among prison officers) – several NGOs and prisoners' rights organizations have instructed lawyers to instigate legal proceedings before administrative courts claiming compensation from the prison administration. Generally, certain prisoners condemned to very long sentences play the role of 'jail house lawyers and main litigators' who help other prisoners with practical information, translation, education, writing documents and pre-litigation reports, or making contact with lawyers and NGOs. Sometimes the process of defiance is even more centralized as one or several prisoners are the key litigants and they centralize complaints by serving as go-betweens for prisoners, barristers and NGOs.

For instance, in France the OIP, a pioneer and leader of litigation activities as an NGO, has obtained a hundred rulings returned by domestic courts and several rulings condemning France before the European Court of Human Rights (OIP, Litigation Report, 2012). Litigation activities have also been undertaken by other associations, which include former prisoners such as Robin des lois[17] or Ban Public, which is called the Association for Communication on Prisons and Incarceration in Europe.[18] In their action for inmates' rights, the OIP and Ban Public, which have their own legal teams, have developed a network of lawyers, some of whom are members of the board of directors of these organizations, ready to litigate prison cases and lodge complaints with administrative courts in particular. In this way, a network of lawyers (barristers) dubbed Association A3D (Association of Lawyers for the Defence of Prisoners' Rights) was created in May 2015 on behalf of the OIP, and one year later it brought together nearly 70 members, primarily young professionals ready to undertake prison litigation.[19] The network allows, in particular, through digital tools, to create a collective knowledge source and to share good litigation practices and complaints forms at the national level in the field of prison law in order to be more efficient in terms of litigation and to reinforce the impact of prison litigation. One of the best judicial results obtained by A3D was the judgment ruled in 2020 by the French Council of State that condemned the French state for inhumane conditions of detention and retaliation (such as full strip-searches, forced and inhuman hearings, transfer to a cell located in a specific prison wing, pressures and threats infringing human dignity) by the prison staff against the litigation efforts undertaken by a prisoner.[20]

In the same manner as A3D, the OIP's thinking is that the prison administration is obliged to respect court judgements. According to this optimistic vision of law and human rights, legal challenges can be used to achieve social progress (Scheingold 2004), and to denounce prison conditions and human rights violations committed by the prison administration. Trials also serve as showcases for the OIP and A3D lawyers and barristers: 'It is interesting to see how the prison administration replies publicly to our litigation: it as way to expose their practice and even their so-called legal arguments to public scrutiny', said an OIP lawyer who wishes to remain anonymous. 'The prison administration lacks transparency and our legal action allows us to get more transparency on prisons and conditions of detention', an A3D lawyer commented. Litigation indeed fosters public scrutiny and the inverted panopticon as judgements are often well-publicized by the NGOs and the media.

Nevertheless, it could be misleading to consider the rise of prisoners' rights organizations to be purely a national phenomenon as they are encouraged and promoted by international and European human rights organizations. The tasks of control and monitoring of human rights are delegated by the UN and the Council of Europe to NGOs at the national level. NGOs are in charge of monitoring domestic legal instruments in the light of the 1984 UN Convention against Torture and Other Cruel, Inhuman or Degrading Treatment or Punishment and the 1950 European Convention on Human Rights, and preventing and denouncing human rights violations in their countries.[21] The role played by NGOs is also recognized by the Vienna Convention and the Action Programme adopted at the World Conference on Human Rights of 25 June 1993, according to which NGOs are authorized to inform their national human rights institutions, such as ombudsmen, responsible for gathering complaints related to human rights violations.

The Defiant Script through the United Nations, the European and the African Human Rights Regime

The process of judicial control over many institutions and sectors based on human rights is often described as an influential and growing socio-legal trend that is contributing to the development and reform of modern societies. This seems to be particularly the case for prisons and other penal institutions, as international bodies and the courts have tried to influence prison policies since at least the 1960s. The UN and European judicial and inspectorate bodies that share the same general principles and aims of what is now commonly referred to as 'global justice' have gained increasing prominence in the fields of penal and prison policy and practice in recent years, with each of those bodies working in diverse capacities to ensure that European human rights legislation is observed within the borders of individual nation states. In fact, national penal and prison policies in Europe are increasingly controlled and monitored by the Council of Europe. This increase in monitoring has progressively allowed prisoners to contribute to and foster the defiance script.

United Nations Monitoring: The Development of Independent Ombudsmen
The Convention against Torture and Other Cruel, Inhuman or Degrading Treatment or Punishment adopted on 10 December 1984 by many nations including the USA and most European states, that came into force on 26 June 1987, established the UN Committee Against Torture (CAT) as responsible for monitoring state parties in the implementation of the Convention. In particular, this Convention against Torture set up a monitoring procedure that obliges all state parties to submit regular reports to the CAT on how they are going to implement the rights enshrined by the Convention.

A major change has been the replacement of the UN Commission on Human

Rights by the UN Council on Human Rights in 2006, which resulted in the addition of Universal Periodic Reviews (UPR) to the monitoring apparatus of the Commission. While with the Commission only certain countries were targeted by the UN's human rights monitoring, the UPR has led to regular monitoring of all forty-seven states of the Council of Human Rights. All in all, the reform of the Committee on Human Rights has been accompanied by a significant increase in the monitoring of human rights exercised over the United States and African and European states.

This UN monitoring has been also massively reinforced since the Optional Protocol to the Convention against Torture and Other Cruel, Inhuman or Degrading Treatment or Punishment (OPCAT)[22] of 18 December 2002 created the Subcommittee on Prevention of Torture (SPT), which has a mandate to visit places within states where persons are deprived of their liberty.

A major shift has also been observed in UN monitoring since the introduction of OPCAT to the Convention, in which the US has not taken part, as it fosters independent national monitoring of prisons. This protocol obliges member states to establish independent National Preventive Mechanisms (NPMs) for the prevention of torture at the domestic level. These national preventative mechanisms, which act under the authority of the UN Committee on Human Rights, are charged with performing regular inspections – without informing the prison administration about such inspections to avoid any elaborate preparations – visiting places of detention, hearing appeals by prisoners, making recommendations to their national authorities, submitting proposals and observations concerning existing or draft legislations, and drawing up a public annual report for the relevant parliaments. In response to these international obligations, some African countries such as Congo, Mali, Niger and Nigeria, and South American countries such as Argentina, Brazil and Mexico, have established national ombudsmen in charge of overseeing prison conditions. In the same way, European countries[23] such as France,[24] Germany[25] and the UK[26] have respectively set up the French Inspector-General (Contrôleur général) of Places of Deprivation of Liberty,[27] the German Joint Commission of the Länder[28] and the British Independent Inspectorate for Prisons and Youth Detention,[29] which inspect prisons and issue and transmit annual reports on prison conditions to the Subcommittee on Prevention of Torture.

The European Human Rights Regime

The influence of this European monitoring seems to be both deep and broad, resulting from the interaction between, and the mutual reinforcement of, three distinct organs: the European Court of Human Rights (ECHR), the Committee for the Prevention of Torture (CPT) and the Committee of Ministers (CM). In particular, the ECHR has gained power and developed over time a jurisprudence more and more in favour of prisoners and the inverted panopticon.

The European Court of Human Rights

The ECHR was established in 1953. It allows NGOs and citizens of the forty-seven Council of Europe member states to directly lodge complaints with it. The ECHR has significantly increased its power and influence over time. This increase is due to five factors in particular: the evolution of the ECHR's architecture into a quasi-constitutional court;[30] the power of the ECHR since 2004 to issue pilot and quasi-pilot judgements that bring together groups of similar cases of human rights violations linked to structural and systemic problems, and its power to order governments of member states to implement corrective legislative and/or administrative measures, which must be reported in action plans submitted to the Committee of Ministers of the Council of Europe;[31] the ECHR's increased use of a wide range of bold interpretation techniques to protect the rights of citizens, in particular detainees (Cliquennois, Snacken and van Zyl Smit 2021); the increased interaction of the ECHR with other Council of Europe bodies such as the CPT during its visits to member states and the Commissioner for Human Rights (Morgan and Evans 2001); and the increased interaction of the ECHR with the European Union, which, for instance, funds programmes to improve the implementation of ECHR case law and European penitentiary standards for the prevention of suicide.[32]

This is why protection of the human rights of citizens and, more specifically, of detainees, has been gradually imposed on its member states by the Council of Europe (Mayerfeld 2011) as a 'common European law on detention'. In this respect, the court has increased over time the content of substantial and procedural obligations imposed on states that have committed human rights violations. Procedural obligations are defined as obligations on the burden of states and are supposed to reinforce internal protection of a substantial number of human rights guaranteed by the European Convention on Human Rights. Procedural obligations therefore involve proactive behaviour from national authorities to ensure useful effect of the protected right (Sudre 1995). We give here examples of some rights enshrined by the European Convention which are subject to special protection and attention from the Strasbourg Court, and clearly reinforce the inverted panopticon and oversight of prisons.

The right to life and suicide and homicide prevention in jail (Article 2 of the European Convention). The ECHR considers the right to life to be a priority and stipulates that the right to life should not only be passively respected but the prison administration has an obligation to take practical, suitably adapted steps to protect this right when the risk of suicide and homicide is known or foreseeable on the basis of Article 2. However, this obligation is ambivalent as it involves both an increase of disciplinary and surveillance measures for prisoners and growing control over prison administrations and institutions.

On the one hand, the Strasbourg Court imposes preventive and surveillance measures on national authorities – such as permanent CCTV for prisoners facing suicide crisis, special cells with no anchor points, fireproof mattresses and tear-proof sheets, reinforcement of physical surveillance, removal of all objects or substances that could be used to commit suicide or murder including scarves and bedsheets, particularly intense surveillance, etc. – to respect the right to life and prevent any death (Cliquennois and Champetier 2013; Cliquennois 2010). Consequently, these prevention systems reinforce the punitive approach to prison since prisoners registered on the 'suicide watch list' and designated as 'high risk' are transferred for at least twenty-four hours to special cells with no anchor points and equipped with video surveillance, fireproof mattresses and tear-proof sheets. Prisoners at high risk are also dressed in special tear-proof clothes and are observed by prison staff round the clock.[33] Prisoners assessed at medium risk of suicide are placed under enhanced surveillance by prison staff and offered psychiatric counselling.[34] Prison officers are also required to complete observation forms about each medium-risk prisoner.[35]

On the other hand, national states are required by the ECHR under Article 2 to investigate the death of prisoners in order to give a coherent and true explanation of the death, allowing the court to determine responsibility and liability.[36] According to the ECHR, Article 2 obliges national authorities to conduct investigations into all custody deaths that are formal, independent (in the sense that the investigators are not connected to officials involved in the death), impartial, prompt and effective.[37] The investigations must determine the cause of death (suicide, homicide or accident), the exact circumstances and the liability of individuals or institutions, with appropriate sanctions in the event of suicide.[38] This positive obligation imposed on national governments by the ECHR is derived from the UN's Principles on the Effective Prevention and Investigation of Extra-legal, Arbitrary and Summary Executions, including cases where complaints by relatives or other reliable reports suggest unnatural death in the above circumstances.[39] In addition, the investigation must be based on eyewitness accounts, expert opinions, medical and forensic evidence, autopsies to accurately and fully report injuries where appropriate, and objective clinical analysis including the cause of death.[40] Regarding autopsies, the ECHR applies the UN Manual on Effective Prevention and Investigation of Extra-legal, Arbitrary and Summary Executions that includes a model protocol providing authoritative guidelines for the conduct of autopsies by public prosecutors and medical staff.[41]

The primary purpose of the investigation should be to ensure effective implementation of domestic laws protecting the right to life, and, in cases where national government agents or bodies are involved, to ensure that they are held accountable for the deaths of people under their responsibility.[42] As the ECHR puts it, another aim of such investigation and its promptness is for national authorities to 'maintain public confidence in their adherence to the rule of law and to prevent any appearance of collusion in, or tolerance of, unlawful acts'.[43]

As this procedural obligation of investigation must meet several requirements imposed by the ECHR such as independence, effectiveness, public scrutiny and celerity,[44] these requirements increase, by definition and in practice, policing, medical, psychiatric, judicial and prisoners' insights into the prison reality through interviews of witnesses, prisoners, prisoners' family members and prison staff for investigative purposes; production of autopsies, medical and psychiatric reports; taking videos and pictures of the prison facility, the cells, the body of the prisoner and so forth. In addition, investigations into deaths of prisoners which are often mediatized (Cliquennois and Champetier 2013) oblige the prison administration to carry out internal inspections to foster its defence against prisoners and prisoners' family members, and avoid condemnation pronounced by national jurisdictions and the ECHR. Professional control over the prison is added thanks to this procedural obligation imposed by the Strasbourg Court. The investigation requested by the ECHR therefore leads to an increase of insights into day-to-day prison reality.

Prohibition of torture or inhuman or degrading treatment (Article 3 of the European Convention). Another priority pursued by the court is related to the prohibition of torture or inhuman or degrading treatment, which raises obligations of prevention incumbent on the member states (Prison Litigation Network 2016). These obligations, which also foster the inverted panopticon process, are twofold.

First, they cover investigations and techniques that are necessary to prove human rights violations under Article 3 (ibid.). For instance, evidence of bad and inhuman treatment generated by poor prison conditions involve investigations conducted by surveyors, ergonomists, hygienists and doctors in prison facilities with a view to determining the physical and topological features of prison cells and wings. This new kind of expertise also implies that videos and pictures which increase insights into prison facilities can lead to the renovation and closure of prisons that contravene Article 3; in Italy and France, some prison facilities have been destroyed due to ECHR orders. In some cases, rulings delivered by the European Court have condemned prison architecture deemed to have too much surveillance. In this way, the traditional panopticon is reprehended (ibid.).

Second, the European Court has ordered the implementation of effective domestic remedies which have to meet qualitative criteria such as effectiveness, independence, contradictoriness (by allowing the accused person to defend himself/herself through hearings), adequate motivation of facts and decisions, etc., to give access to justice and the opportunity to complain about conditions of detention for prisoners. According to the ECHR, this last objective can be achieved by equipping the courts with appropriate legal tools, allowing them to consider the problem underlying an individual complaint, and thus effectively deal with situations of massive and concurrent violations of prisoners' rights resulting from inadequate detention conditions in a given facility.[45]

The Committee for the Prevention of Torture
The CPT was established in November 1989 as a consequence of the European Convention on the Prevention of Torture drafted by the International Conferences of NGOs and signed by fifteen states in 1987. Since then, all forty-seven member states have ratified the Convention. Members of the Committee, who are independent and impartial experts from a variety of backgrounds – including lawyers, judges, medical doctors, prison governors and specialists in criminology, prison or police matters – are elected by the Council of Ministers of the Council of Europe from a short list drawn up by the Parliamentary Assembly of the Council of Europe.

The CPT constitutes the inspectorate organ of the Council of Europe, a non-judicial preventive mechanism to protect persons deprived of their liberty against torture and other forms of ill-treatment, and it complements the judicial work of the ECHR. In this respect, the Committee organizes visits to places of detention including prisons, juvenile detention centres, police stations, holding centres for immigration detainees, psychiatric hospitals and centres for the mentally disabled and the elderly, in order to assess how persons deprived of their liberty are treated. To this end, the CPT regularly hears and interviews prisoners to get a more precise insight into the prison institution. It has developed its own standards and methods to protect civilians from torture and inhumane and degrading treatment. After each visit, the CPT sends to the concerned state a detailed public report and requests a detailed response to the issues raised in its report.

The standards and public reports released by the CPT and recommendations issued by the Committee of Ministers, such as the European Prison Rules, have served as evidence and standards for the ECHR. Conversely, the rulings of the ECHR have inspired and enforced recommendations and standards issued by the European Committee of Ministers as well as reports released by the CPT (van Zyl Smit and Snacken 2009; Snacken 2011; Snacken and Dumortier 2012; Cliquennois and Champetier 2013).

The African Human Rights Regime

The African Charter on Human and Peoples' Rights

The African Charter on Human and Peoples' Rights, also known as the Banjul Charter, constitutes an international human rights instrument that is intended to promote and protect human rights and basic freedoms in the African continent.

It was set up by the Organization of African Unity (OAU, since replaced by the African Union), which, at its 1979 Assembly of Heads of State and Government, adopted a resolution calling for the creation of a committee of experts to draft a continent-wide human rights instrument, like those that already existed in Europe and similar to the European Convention on Human Rights and the American Convention on Human Rights. This committee produced a draft that was unanimously approved at the OAU's eighteenth assembly held in June 1981 in Nairobi, Kenya. The African Charter on Human and Peoples' Rights came into force on 21 October 1986, in honour of which 21 October was declared African Human Rights Day.

The Charter recognizes most universally accepted civil and political rights. The civil and political rights enshrined in it cover the right to freedom from discrimination (Article 2 and 18[3]), equality (Article 3), life and personal integrity (Article 4), dignity (Article 5), freedom from slavery (Article 5), freedom from cruel, inhuman or degrading treatment or punishment (Article 5), rights to due process concerning arrest and detention (Article 6), the right to a fair trial (Article 7 and 25), freedom of religion (Article 8), freedom of information and expression (Article 9), freedom of association (Article 10), freedom to assembly (Article 11), freedom of movement (Article 12), freedom of political participation (Article 13) and the right to property (Article 14).

The Charter also enshrines certain economic, social and cultural rights. Overall, it puts emphasis on these rights. It also recognizes the right to work (Article 15), the right to health (Article 16) and the right to education (Article 17).

Oversight and interpretation of the Charter is the remit of the African Commission on Human and Peoples' Rights, which was created in 1987. A protocol to the Charter was subsequently adopted in 1998 whereby an African Court on Human and Peoples' Rights was to be created.

The African Commission on Human and Peoples' Rights

The African Charter created the African Commission on Human and Peoples' Rights, which was inaugurated on 2 November 1987 in Addis Ababa, Ethiopia. The Commission consists of eleven members elected by the African Assembly from among experts nominated by the state parties to the Charter.

The African Commission is mainly in charge of the promotion of human rights, the protection of human and peoples' rights, and the interpretation of the African Charter on Human and Peoples' Rights.

Promotional function. The promotional function of the African Commission consists in sensitizing the population and disseminating information on human and peoples' rights in Africa. To achieve this, the Commission is entrusted under Article 45(1) of the African Charter on Human and People's Rights to 'collect documents, undertake studies and researches on African problems in the field of human and peoples' rights, organize seminars, symposia and conferences, disseminate information, encourage national and local institutions concerned with human and peoples' rights and, should the case arise, give its views or make recommendations to governments'.[46]

The Commission has intensively cooperated with NGOs and intergovernmental organizations to set up a documentation centre used for human rights studies and research, and to organize several seminars, symposia and conferences aimed at promoting human and peoples' rights within the African continent. The Commission has also been collaborating with other human rights institutions (both intergovernmental and non-governmental) in many areas relating to the promotion and protection of human rights. In this regard, in a bid to strengthen cooperation, the Commission has been granting observer status to NGOs since 1988. At its twenty-second ordinary session held in 1997, over 200 NGOs, among which were those aiming at protecting prisoners' rights, received such status. A special status to national human rights institutions has also been granted by the African Commission in order to reinforce their partnership and so that they can function as invaluable partners in the promotion of human and peoples' rights in the continent.

In the same way, the Commission has also drafted and released several human rights documents, including the Review of the African Commission, its annual activity reports, the African Charter and the Commission's Rules of Procedure.

Members of the Commission have been allocated states on the continent for promotional activities. They are entrusted to visit these states and organize lectures with various institutions to discuss the African Charter and the Commission. They report on their intersession activities at each session of the Commission.

The Commission has recruited special rapporteurs on prisons and other places of detention in Africa on arbitrary, summary and extrajudicial executions, and on the human rights of women in Africa. These rapporteurs play a significant role by researching, gathering and documenting information on human rights violations in places of detention. This information is then used by the Commission to formulate advice and recommendations to African states.

The Commission is supposed to 'formulate and lay down principles and rules aimed at solving legal problems relating to human and peoples' rights and fundamental freedoms upon which African governments may base their legislation' (Article 45[1][b] of the Charter). It is also mandated under Article 45(1)(c) to cooperate with other African and international institutions concerned with the promotion and protection of human and peoples' rights.

Intense collaboration and cooperation have also been sought with other regional and international institutions, among which are the ECHR, the Inter-American Commission and the Inter-American Court of Human Rights.

Protection of human rights. The protection of human rights and the interpretation of the African Charter are notably carried out by the African Commission through its responses to the reports that state parties have to submit to the African Charter every two years, on legislative or other measures they have taken to give effect to the rights and freedoms recognized in the Charter. The aim of such monitoring is to ensure the protection of rights and freedoms recognized and guaranteed by the Charter (Article 45 [2]). From this perspective, the Commission studies these reports and makes recommendations at the session dialogues with representatives from the states. NGOs and ordinary citizens are also allowed to request copies of these reports from the Secretariat of the Commission. They can draft counter-reports or recommend to the Commission questions that could be addressed to the state representatives. In this manner, the Commission is required to monitor that citizens effectively enjoy the rights contained in the Charter. The Commission must check on a regular basis that the states do not violate these rights, and if they do, that the rights of the victims are reinstated.

For that purpose, the Charter has established a 'communication procedure', which is a complaint system through which an individual, NGO or group of individuals who allege that their right or those of others have been or are being violated, can petition and take their case to the Commission. A communication can also be made by a state party to the Charter if another state party has violated any of the provisions in the Charter. If the communication meets the criteria set out in Article 56 of the Charter, it will be formally accepted for consideration by the Commission. The defendant state will then be informed about the allegations and invited to submit its comments on them.

Thus, the Commission will rule whether there has been any violation and will make recommendations to the concerned state and to the African Assembly on what the member state should do, and remedy the harm caused to the victim. The Commission also has the option to initiate friendly settlement, whereby the complainant and the accused state negotiate to settle the dispute amicably.

Further, the Commission has sent missions to several state parties to investigate allegations of massive and serious human rights violations. At the end of such a mission, the Commission is able to make recommendations to the states concerned on how to remedy the situation. In emergency situations which imply that the life of the victim is in imminent danger, the Commission might invoke provisional measures and require the state to delay any action pending its final decision on the matter, as per Rule 111 of its Rules of Procedure.

Interpretation of the African Charter. Article 45(3) of the Charter entrusts the Commission with interpreting its provisions on behalf of a state party, an institution of the Organization of African Unity (OAU) or an African organization recognized by the OAU. To date, neither the OAU nor a state party has approached the Commission for interpretation of any of the provisions of the Charter. Nevertheless, some NGOs have sought and obtained, through draft resolutions, interpretations of some provisions in the Charter. Through this method, the Commission has adopted resolutions that give clarity and a broader interpretation to some of the Charter's ambiguous and ambivalent provisions.

The African Court on Human and Peoples' Rights. This is a continental Court established by African countries to protect human and peoples' rights in Africa, as enshrined in the African Charter. The Court was set up by virtue of Article 1 of the Protocol to the African Charter on Human and Peoples' Rights on the Establishment of an African Court on Human and Peoples' Rights, which was adopted by member states of the then OAU in Ouagadougou, Burkina Faso, in June 1998. The Protocol came into force on 25 January 2004. The Court complements and reinforces the functions carried out by the African Commission on Human and Peoples' Rights.

The Court may receive cases filed by the African Commission of Human and Peoples' Rights, state parties to the Protocol and African intergovernmental organizations. NGOs with observer status before the African Commission and individuals can also bring cases directly before the Court as long as the state against which they are complaining has deposited the Article 34(6) declaration recognizing the jurisdiction of the Court to accept cases from individuals and NGOs.

As of July 2021, only nine of the thirty state parties to the Protocol had made the declaration recognizing the competence of the Court to receive cases from NGOs and individuals. These are Benin, Burkina Faso, Côte d'Ivoire, Ghana, Mali, Malawi, Tanzania, the Gambia and the Republic of Tunisia. The thirty states which have ratified the Protocol are: Algeria, Benin, Burkina Faso, Burundi, Cameroon, Chad, Côte d'Ivoire, Comoros, Congo, Gabon, Gambia, Ghana, Kenya, Libya, Lesotho, Mali, Malawi, Mozambique, Mauritania, Mauritius, Nigeria, Niger, Rwanda, Sahrawi Arab Democratic Republic, South Africa, Senegal, Tanzania, Togo, Tunisia and Uganda.

The Court has jurisdiction over all cases and disputes submitted to it concerning the interpretation and application of the African Charter on Human and Peoples' Rights, the Protocol and any other relevant human rights instrument ratified by the states concerned. Specifically, the Court has two types of jurisdiction: contentious and advisory.

Regarding its jurisprudence, in the *Alex Thomas v. United Republic of Tanzania* case, the African Court had to decide on the lawfulness of the imprisonment of over thirty years of a Tanzanian applicant. The Court quashed the sentence pronounced by the Tanzanian court on 20 November 2015, on the grounds that the sentence was unlawful and that the right to liberty was violated.[47] Furthermore, the Court found that the applicant was denied the right to be heard, to defend himself[48] and to get free legal aid to which he was entitled.[49]

In *Lohe Issa Konate v. Burkina Faso,*[50] a case where a journalist was condemned to a one-year term of imprisonment for having denounced in a journal the prosecutor of Faso, the Court required Burkina Faso to have him released immediately or, alternatively, to provide him with adequate medical care. The applicant was backed up by some influent NGOs that intervene in the case as *amici curiae*: the Centre for Human Rights, Comite pour la Protection des Journalistes, Media Institute of Southern Africa, Pan African Human Rights Defenders Network, Pan African Lawyers Union, PEN International and Nation PWN Centres, Southern Africa Litigation Centre and World Association of Newspapers and News Publishers.

As regards provisional measures, the applicant claimed that his health had deteriorated since his detention and that he needed to be provided with medication and adequate medical care. The African Court ruled in favour of the applicant's request for provisional measures on 4 October 2013, by considering that the situation in which the applicant was could cause irreparable harm to him.[51] According to the Court, the applicant had the right to access all medical care that his health condition needed.[52] Consequently, it required Burkina Faso to provide the applicant with medication and healthcare for the entire period of his detention.[53]

On the merits of the application, the African Court decided that Burkina Faso had violated the right to freedom of the applicant, and that defamation should not be punishable by prison sentences and must be decriminalized:[54]

> The Court notes that, for now, defamation is an offence punishable by imprisonment in the legislation of the Respondent State, and that the latter failed to show how a penalty of imprisonment was a necessary limitation to freedom of expression in order to protect the rights and reputation of members of the judiciary.

In this manner, the African Court could significantly orient the penal and prison policy of Burkina Faso, under the pressure exerted by some influential NGOs helping the prisoner. The Court ordered Burkina Faso to amend its legislation on defamation in order to make it compliant with Article 9 of the Charter: by repealing custodial sentences for acts of defamation and by adapting its legislation to ensure that other sanctions for defamation meet the test of necessity and proportionality, in accordance with its obligations under the Charter and other international instruments.[55]

In addition to the African Court, the African Special Rapporteur on Prisons and Conditions of Detention was created during the twentieth Ordinary Session of the Commission, following the Seminar on Prison Conditions in Africa (Kampala, 19–21 September 1996). The Special Rapporteur's remit is to examine the situation of persons deprived of their liberty within the territories of states parties to the African Charter on Human and Peoples' Rights. The various Special Rapporteurs have been active, among others, by holding missions (among which are visits) to the various state parties – since 1997, over twenty missions have taken place and sixteen resolutions on detention adopted.[56]

CONCLUSION

The fight undertaken by Foucault through his participation in the Prisons Information Group has probably changed prison reality, and therefore invalidated his analysis and study of the prison. In this regard, analyses proposed by sociologists, historians, lawyers, etc., tend to integrate the social reality they propose to study and influence it. Foucault has certainly contributed to the development of the inverted panopticon which implies that prisoners have increased their insights and even oversight of their prison administration and facilities. This phenomenon is such that we assume it leads to the development of an inverted panopticon by which certain prisoners and NGOs are in a position to challenge the authority of national prison administrations. This trend has also been fostered by the role played by NGOs, and the development of an international and European human rights regime.

In this regard, the inverted panopticon to which Foucault has contributed through his commitment as an activist, along with other activists, and his fight against the justice and prison administration, could constitute a double paradox. The first paradox is that the inverted panopticon partly relies on human rights, while Foucault was very reluctant to address law and human rights in general. The second paradox is that the inverted panopticon entails not only the all-seeing eye, but also other dimensions that are concerned with the content of incarceration and penal and prison policies.

This process fits more broadly within a defiance script on why prisoners can on the one hand challenge national prison authorities, who are then obliged to make some concessions, and on the other hand legitimize incarceration though their participation as stakeholders in the betterment of prison conditions. The defiance script consists for certain prisoners in watching professional practices and prison conditions rather than simply being subject to surveillance. It constitutes for these prisoners both a cooptation and cooperation with human rights activists and institutions in which prisoners continue to be embedded through the inverted panopticon.

NOTES

[1] '2002/584/JHA: Council Framework Decision of 13 June 2002 on the European arrest warrant and the surrender procedures between Member States – Statements made by certain Member States on the adoption of the Framework Decision', *EUR-LEX*, n.d., available at https://eur-lex.europa.eu/legal-content/EN/TXT/?uri=celex%3A32002F0584, accessed 20 October 2021.

[2] See also the statement by the members of the European Council on the fight against terrorism, 'Timeline: The EU's Response to Terrorism', *European Council*, 12 February 2015, available at https://www.consilium.europa.eu/en/policies/fight-against-terrorism/history-fight-against-terrorism/, accessed 20 October 2021.

[3] 'Directive of the European Parliament and of the European Council on Combating Terrorism and Replacing Council Framework Decision 2002/475/JHA and Amending Council Decision 2005/671/JHA, 23 February 2017 PE-CONS 53/16', European Council, n.d., available at https://data.consilium.europa.eu, accessed 20 October 2021.

[4] ECHR, *Terrorism and the European Convention on Human Rights*, Factsheets, December 2017; ECHR, *A. and Others v. the United Kingdom*, 19 February 2009, no. 3455/05, available at https://www.echr.coe.int/documents/fs_terrorism_eng.pdf, accessed 20 October 2021.

[5] ECHR, *Derogation in Time of Emergency*, Factsheets, November 2017, available at https://www.echr.coe.int/Documents/FS_Derogation_ENG.pdf, accessed 20 October 2021.

[6] Convention against Torture and Other Cruel, Inhuman or Degrading Treatment or Punishment, Adopted and opened for signature, ratification and accession by General Assembly resolution 39/46 of 10 December 1984, entry into force 26 June 1987, in accordance with article 27 (1). Concerning the Consultative Assembly of the Council of Europe, see 'The Consultative Assembly', *CVCE*, n.d., available at https://www.cvce.eu/en/education/unit-content/-/unit/026961fe-0d57-4314-a40a-a4ac066a1801/ddefc8a2-9bbe-40c1-9148-0de02f9af7f9, accessed 20 October 2021.

[7] See *Groupe Multiprofessionnel Prison*, available at https://gmprison.wordpress.com/, accessed 20 October 2021.

[8] See *Ban Public*, available at www.prison.eu.org, accessed 20 October 2021; and *Observatoire International Des Prisons: Section Francaise*, available at www.oip.org, accessed 20 October 2021.

[9] See 'Qui sommes-nous?', *Ban Public*, available at http://prison.eu.org/spip.php?page=rubrique&id_rubrique=5, accessed 20 October 2021.

[10] See Nathalie Guibert, 'décision du conseil d'Etat du 17 déc 2008', *A.F.L.I.D.D.*, available at http://aflidd.over-blog.com/article-25915713.html, accessed 20 October 2021.

[11] See 'Qui sommes nous?', *CDFPPI*, available at http://cdfppi.free.fr/assoc.htm, accessed 20 October 2021.

[12] For instance, the NGO A3D persuaded the Inspector-General of Places of Deprivation of Liberty in December 2019 to denounce the mandatory removal of barristers' underwear in prison. See 'Les avocates et leurs soutiens-gorge ne seront plus interdits de parloirs', *A3D*, 15 December 2020, available at https://www.association-a3d.fr/articles/66572-les-avocates-et-leurs-soutiens-gorge-ne-seront-plus-interdits-de-parloirs, accessed 20 October 2021.

[13] See *Contrôleur général des lieux de privation de liberté*, available at https://www.cglpl.fr/, accessed 20 October 2021.

[14] 'Qui Peut Saisir le Contrôleur Général des Lieux de Privation de Liberté?', *Contrôleur Général des Lieux de Privation de Liberté*, n.d., available at https://www.cglpl.fr/saisir-le-cglpl/qui/, accessed 20 October 2021.

[15] 'Les Derniers Rapports N'ayant Pas Donné Lieu à Recommandations Publiques', *Contrôleur Général des Lieux de Privation de Liberté*, n.d., available at https://www.cglpl.fr/rapports-et-recommandations/dernieres-recommandations/; https://www.cglpl.fr/rapports-et-recommandations/les-rapports-de-visite/, accessed 20 October 2021.

[16] See for instance the Facebook page, *femme de détenu*, available at https://fr-fr.facebook.com/femme-de-d%C3%A9tenu-219014641500198/, accessed 20 October 2021.

[17] See, for example, CE, 29 March 2010, *OIP-SF and Korber*, No. 319043. The association is directed by François Korber, a former prisoner who was at the origin of several appeals during his time in prison. See, for example, CE, 4 November 1994, No.157435; CE, 30 July. 2003, No. 249563; CE, 15 July 2004, No.265594.

[18] See, for example, CE, 24 September 2014, No. 362472. 'Robin Des Lois', *Facebook*, n.d., available at https://www.facebook.com/associationrobindeslois/, accessed 20 October 2021 and *Ban Public*, available at http://prison.eu.org/, accessed 20 October 2021.

[19] See A3D's Twitter page, available at https://twitter.com/associationa3d, accessed 21 October 2021.

[20] Council of State, Decision no. 447141, 16 December 2020.

[21] According to the Consultative Assembly of the Council of Europe held from 18 to 22 October 1971 at the Parliamentary Conference on Human Rights.

[22] The OPCAT was adopted by the General Assembly of the United Nations (57/99) on 18 December 2002 and came into force in June 2006.

[23] In December 2013, among the EU's twenty-seven member states, three had not yet signed the Optional Protocol: Latvia, Lithuania and Slovakia; three signatory countries had not yet ratified the Optional Protocol: Belgium, Finland and Greece.

[24] UN Committee against Torture, Draft Consideration of Reports submitted by state parties (France) under Article 19 of the Convention, Concluding Observations of the Committee against Torture, forty-fourth session (26 April–14 May 2010), CAT/C/FRA/CO/4-6/CRP.1. The Committee welcomes France's ratification of the Optional Protocol to the Convention and 'the subsequent establishment, under the Act of 30 October 2007 (Act no. 2007- 1545), of the post of Inspector-General (Contrôleur général) of places of deprivation of liberty, which constitutes a national preventive mechanism within the meaning of the Optional Protocol'.

[25] UN Committee against Torture, Consideration of Reports submitted by state parties (Germany) under Article 19 of the Convention, Concluding Observations of the Committee against Torture forty-seventh session (31 October–25 November 2011), 12 December 2011 CAT/C/DEU/CO/5. The Committee welcomes Optional Protocol to the Convention against

Torture and Other Cruel, Inhuman or Degrading Treatment or Punishment, on 4 December 2008 and 'the establishment of the National Agency for the Prevention of Torture, composed of the Federal Agency and the Joint Commission of the Länder, which has been mandated to serve as independent national preventive mechanism under the Optional Protocol to the Convention'.

26 UN Committee against Torture, Concluding Observations on the Fifth Periodic Report of the United Kingdom of Great Britain and Northern Ireland, adopted by the Committee at its fiftieth session (6–31 May 2013), 24 June 2013 CAT/C/GBR/CO/5.

27 The Inspector-General of Places of Deprivation of Liberty, who is nominated for six years, has a staff composed of fifteen permanent inspectors and seventeen independent contractors acting as inspectors. See 'Présentation de l'équipe', *Contrôleur général des lieux de privation de liberté*, available at http://www.cglpl.fr/missions-et-actions/presentation-de-lequipe/, accessed 21 October 2021.

28 In addition to the Joint Commission of the Länder, the petitions committees are entitled in some of the Länder to make unannounced visits to places of detention.

29 The UK counts at least three levels of independent inspection for prisons, each one operating independently from the others. At the local level, monitoring boards made up of volunteers recruited from the general population carry out at least two or three visits of the prisons to which they have been designated per week on a continual basis. At the national level, the National Prison Inspectorates carry out programmes of inspections for prisons. In addition, the national prison ombudsmen – and in Scotland, the Independent Prisons Complaints Commissioner – investigate individual complaints lodged by prisoners.

30 See in particular Protocol 11 to the Convention for the Protection of Human Rights and Fundamental Freedoms on the Restructuring of the Control Mechanism established by the Convention, Strasbourg, 11 May 1994. Also see Sadurski, 'Partnering with Strasbourg'; Christoffersen and Madsen, *The European Court of Human Rights between Law and Politics*; Føllesdal, Peters and Ulfstein, *Constituting Europe*.

31 Council of Europe, Resolution (2004)3 of the Committee of Ministers on Judgments Revealing an Underlying Systemic Problem, Strasbourg, 12 May 2004.

32 Criminal justice and human rights programmes funded by the Directorate-General for Justice of the European Commission. For example, JUST / 2013 / JPEN / AG / 4554 funds the implementation of a suicide prevention system in several European countries, in accordance with the case law of the ECHR and as per CPT standards.

33 Memorandum, 15 June 2009; Memorandum, 17 December 2009.

34 Memorandum, 7 July 2009.

35 Ibid.

36 ECHR, *Keenan v United Kingdom*, no. 27229/95: 88, 3 April 2001, available at http://hudoc.echr.coe.int/fre?i=001-59365, accessed 20 October 2021.

37 ECHR, *Paul and Audrey Edwards v. the United Kingdom*, no. 46477/99: 70–73, 14 March 2002, available at http://hudoc.echr.coe.int/eng?i=001-60323, accessed 20 October 2021.

38 ECHR, *Troubnikov v. Russia*, no. 49790/99: 86–88, 5 July 2005, available at http://hudoc.echr.coe.int/eng?i=001-69616, accessed 20 October 2021.

39 'Principles on the Effective Prevention and Investigation of Extra-legal, Arbitrary, and Summary Executions, adopted in Resolution 1989/65', *United Nations Human Rights*, 24 May 1989: 9, available at https://www.ohchr.org/Documents/ProfessionalInterest/executions.pdf, accessed 20 October 2021.

[40] Ibid.

[41] UN Manual on the Effective Prevention and Investigation of Extra-legal, Arbitrary and Summary Executions, adopted in Resolution 1989/65, 24 May 1989: 9.

[42] ECHR, *De Donder and De Clippel v. Belgium*, no. 8595/06: 61, 6 December 2011, available at http://hudoc.echr.coe.int/eng?i=001-107737, accessed 20 October 2021.

[43] ECHR, *Paul and Audrey Edwards v. the United Kingdom*, 14 March 2002, no. 46477/99: 72; *Šilih v. Slovenia*, 9 April 2009, no. 71463/01: 195.

[44] Ibid.

[45] ECHR, *Ananyev and Others v. Russia*, 10 January 2012, No 42525/07 and 60800/08: 219, available at http://hudoc.echr.coe.int/fre?i=001-206363, accessed 20 October 2021.

[46] African Charter on Human and People's Rights, *African Commission on Human and Peoples' Rights*, available at https://www.achpr.org/legalinstruments/detail?id=49, accessed 20 October 2021.

[47] African Court on Human and Peoples' Rights, *Alex Thomas v. The United Republic of Tanzania*, application no. 005/2013, 20 November 2015, available at https://www.african-court.org/cpmt/finalised, accessed 20 October 2021.

[48] Ibid.: 99.

[49] Ibid.: 123–24.

[50] African Court on Human and Peoples' Rights, *Lohe Issa Konate v. Burkina Faso*, application No 004/2013, 5 December 2014, available at https://www.african-court.org/cpmt/finalised, accessed 20 October 2021.

[51] African Court on Human and Peoples' Rights, *Lohe Issa Konate v. Burkina Fasso*, application No 004/2013, Order of provisional measures, 4 October 2013: 22, available at https://www.african-court.org/cpmt/finalised, accessed 20 October 2021.

[52] Ibid.

[53] Ibid.: 23.

[54] Ibid.: 162.

[55] Ibid.: 176.

[56] See 'Special Rapporteur on Prisons, Conditions of Detention and Policing in Africa', *African Commission on Human and Peoples' Rights*, available at https://www.achpr.org/specialmechanisms/detail?id=3, accessed 20 October 2021.

VIGNETTES C

Defiant Dreams and Scripts

8

Students and Youth Defiance

*Ari Sitas, with Abdallah Grifat, Sofia Saeed,
Anubhav Sengupta and Nicos Trimikliniotis*

If you stand among the ruins of war
in the twilight with nothing but wind,
there will sneak in
an odour of jasmine
           – Fusako Shigenobu, 2005

Come mothers and fathers
Throughout the land
And don't criticize
What you can't understand
Your sons and your daughters
Are beyond your command
Your old road is rapidly agin'
Please get out of the new one if you can't lend your hand
For the times they are a-changin'
           – Bob Dylan, 1963

Fusako Shigenobu was not part of the hijacking of the Japan Airlines Flight 351 in 1971 but she was the leader of the Red Army Faction of the Japanese Communist League that did so, allegedly using swords to cart passengers to North Korea. She was to be known as the Red Queen of Terror, one of Interpol's most wanted people, in cahoots with the Palestinian Liberation Organization, responsible for hijackings and bombing in the service – as it was alleged – of the Japanese, the Palestinian and the World Revolution. Shigenobu was a student leader in the 1960s at the prestigious Mej University in Tokyo, cutting her teeth on tuition fees and student everyday issues, a leadership that morphed into the Japanese Communist League – one of the three strands of radicalism in the student movement (Kushner 2011).

She financed her studies by working as a topless dancer in bars, where she hated the men who touched her. She dreamt of becoming a writer, and indeed she did write fascinating manuscripts and poems like 'My Love, My Revolution' in 1974, 'I Decided to Give Birth to You Under an Apple Tree' (2001), and whilst in prison, her collection of poems *Jasmine in the Muzzle of a Gun* (2005). She returned to Japan in 2000 to be arrested and jailed, where she has been kept in a prison hospital ever since, having been diagnosed with colon cancer (Baudelaire 2011).[1]

She and thousands of others were at the extreme end of the ferment of student radicalism in the late 1960s that gripped the whole world: it was vivid in California as much as it was in Ibadan, in Paris, in Mexico City, as much as it was in Delhi and Kolkata. It felt like an enormous spasm of protest action, of street battles, of university closures, of alliances with labour unions – explosive in China in the so-named Red Guard Terror of the Cultural Revolution, dissonant in the Soviet world before the collapse of the Berlin Wall, bifurcated in apartheid South Africa between white and Black students, but on all fronts, militant nevertheless (Fuse 1969; Krauss 1988; Kurlansky 2004).

Immanuel Wallerstein made a fascinating point when he asserted that

> there have only been two world revolutions: one took place in 1848, the second took place in 1968. Both were historic failures. Both transformed the world. The fact that both were unplanned, and therefore in a profound sense spontaneous, explains both facts – the fact that they failed, and the fact that they transformed the world. (Wallerstein 1988)

For the pages that follow, it is only the second that has students at the centre of emancipatory struggles. The 1848 revolution has them mainly on the wrong side of the barricades, in the grip of reaction. We shall return to this at the end of this chapter, but there is no doubt that the 1968 one, or better, the 1964 to 1974 one, created new structures of feeling: it created dispositions for an alternative world beyond the logic of prior anti-systemic movements (socialist or nationalist).

Such structures of feeling and dispositions, the first kind of which we would term 'ideomorphic', are made up of defiant tropes and scripts that survive and have been transmitted through generations of students, dismissed or reworked down the years. Saying this, we are trying to avoid the 'scholastic reason' that Bourdieu (2000) has castigated in his *Pascalian Meditations*: the propensity to read in social actors a manifestation of one's theoretical schema and render them thereafter as ontic realities of one's ontological and often metaphysical discourse. To avoid this, we need to also understand that such reworkings and transmissions occur within students' cultural formations, a kind of hyper-habitus produced by the physical and social parameters of universities as institutions of real and symbolic power. Furthermore, the choice of the word 'ideomorphic', a neologism that Ari Sitas has used in his *Ethic of Reconciliation* (2008), attempts to capture the fact that although neither hegemonic nor dominant in a particular period, such ideas persist and shape behaviour and dispositions in everyday life.

The second, to use Roger Scruton's words, is an alternative structure of feeling: against the 'hooligan behaviour of a middle-class mob' (Wroe 2000), the categorical imperative of order. For example, this was used as a pretext and an alibi to launch neo-conservative and neoliberal movements, and movements of authoritative restoration. In fact, the origins of the new worldwide right were to be found in the moral panic against the student turmoil of the 1960s.

First of all though, we have to invert some of our academic and political common sense. It has been a recent habit of sociology to correlate the figure of the 'student' or the student rebellion of the 1960s in the west and reclassify it as the end of modernism and the move, after Paris 1968, to the new era of the 'post', of a deep and significant cultural revolution (*New Left Review* 1968;[2] Hobsbawm 1994; Kurlansky 2004). And subsequently, to draft further upsurges in the known worlds of the non-west as extensions of the 'spirit of 1968'.

This is a rather partial view because it misses a few important and constitutive social facts. It does not help to even follow Alain Badiou who gives the Chinese Cultural Revolution and its student Red Guards one of the prime spots in his theory of the 'Event'. He then adds Paris and May 1968 as one of the four instances that constitute the exemplars for his philosophy of the Event and Event-ness in history (Badiou 2007). This assertion he generously extends to the Arab Spring as a manifestation, an emanation of his theory as a 'communism in movement', as an ontological rupture that speaks to truth and to the possibility of emancipation. His *The Rebirth of History: Times of Riots and Uprisings* (2012) reads in the enormous challenge of practical action, and inscribes in its gatherings a permanent metaphysical condition.

These 'episodes and repertoires of contention', in Colin Barker's (2018) words (paraphrasing Tilly), involving protests, strikes, riots and occupations always prioritized the west – so much so that the very Vietnam War appears as an externality, something out there, without its own students, without its own imaginaries, who had picked up arms, who had lived through its ruins and traumas. They are absented instead of being at the centre of an interconnected narrative.

There has been a serious interconnection between student life and anti-colonial nationalisms since the heyday of imperialism and the creation of a university system in the majority world, some of it reactive and imitative, some of it imposed – like in the case of the Mej University as part of the Meiji Restoration, Peking University in 1898, or Cairo University in 1905, which spawned student ferment against imperial humiliations: the May Fourth Movement of 1919 in China with its epicentres in Beijing and Shanghai, and what was to become the Zenkaguren movement in Japan, also started somewhere there. And in Africa, where the university system was either established by colonial powers in the post-1945 period (the University of London and the University of Louvain established colleges there, and thereafter, after independence, most of the ferment was to be felt by African students in Europe or North America).

Lin Ping, the party secretary at Tsinghua University during the Cultural Revolution, recalled yet another kind of studentship:

> I had participated in the revolutionary struggle since 1938, and had attended the Anti-Japanese Imperialism University. This University in Yenan was founded by Mao and headed by Lin Piao. Mao Tse-tung taught us philosophy at Yenan; together with the Chairman we studied his works 'On Contradiction' and 'On Practice'. These widely known works constituted the substance of our studies. Lin Piao taught the military courses on the war of resistance, on the war of attack and counter-attack against the Japanese. This was the most progressive University in the world and it was my really good fortune to have studied there. (Macciocchi 1976: 55)

It is hard to tell a linear story, for universities or colleges/institutions of higher learning are old, if not ancient. The story of the Guazijan (Imperial College), for instance, will take us back to 300 CE, to its transformation into Peking University in 1898. Whereas Shanghai University would be a product of nationalist and communist cooperation in 1922, by which time what was the May Fourth Movement would have matured into a complex and modernizing movement. St Petersburg would be as old as 1724, whereas the Pontifical University of Mexico City would date from 1551 before it becomes UNAM in 1910. Fusako Shigenobu would have studied in a very old institution at Mej in Tokyo, but it was an institution that would have changed its thought engines to modernizing gears even though its subcultures were rooted in the past. And even as more and more people identify Humboldt (founded in 1810) in Berlin as the first modern research-intensive university, it would be premature to go that way before we agree on a few critical sociological features.

As an institution, the university offers a familial resemblance to all other institutions that cluster human effort to achieve certain goals. To continue with this train of thought, the university is a remarkable institution which preceded the emergence of a capitalist world economy and which has been refashioned to play a vital role within it (Mielants 2007). What follows is an analysis and an exposition rehearsed before in debates on the university in India.[3]

Knowledge and know-hows were not, and are not, the sole preserve of the university and the system it operated within, but the university had established the right to be the arena that operated their formal accreditation.[4] As an institution there was, and is, a tension between its character, its function, its knowledge project and its practices – and how these are handled. These tensions reproduce and transform its authority in any social formation.

Due to the predominance of European powers in the long period between the fifteenth and late nineteenth centuries, the evolving university system in the world gradually inherited the character, function, knowledge project and practices of the European experience.[5]

Its character: it involved a withdrawal from the world and its contaminations that survived from its old theocratic forms where the hermeneutic study of scripture was encouraged and civilizing languages were learnt – a withdrawal that was reinforced by the emerging scientific spirit of the seventeenth and eighteenth centuries, that used this space of withdrawal to argue its necessary autonomy from the world of the clergy and of immediate aristocratic power (Colish 1997: 267). Peerage trumped interest, and therefore the origins of 'academic freedom' to research and disseminate are to be found there.[6]

Its function: to create the quality of mind necessary to populate the steering and professional strata of society, and therefore play a defining role in class and elite formation in society and to reproduce itself as such a marker (Anderson 2009).[7] This was not only about the quality of mind of its graduates but also about the regimes of rule and discipline to groom such an elite, which always carried a tension between an older apprenticeship system and a hierarchy of control – a tension at the heart of the bureaucratization of the system.[8]

Its knowledge project: the academic community had to research what it taught, and research networks were created out of a range of horizontal activities embedded in scientific and knowledge networks that were trans-institutional and transnational and often quite 'deviant' – for example, four centuries ago, although Descartes was highly respected in scientific and philosophical networks, he had to be in exile in Amsterdam; and Bernier, who was his kindred spirit, was in touch with the Mughal world of science, philosophy and medicine as much as the English, German and Dutch thinkers. Once knowledge interest got normalized as a public good, the networks of science and scholarship and not the specific institution (that is, 'My university') became the definers of, in the words of Kuhn, 'normal science' (Sitas *et al.* 2014).

Practices: within each institution, there are further tensions that finally shape its ethos, and the way it works and educates students (Kuhn [1962] 1974). There is the perennial dissonance that each student and younger academic is considered to be a site of reason and yet the hierarchical professorate demands minimal challenge – rather, it demands patriarchy, loyalty and mimicry (Bordieu [1984] 1990). There is also a dissonance between the relational dissemination of knowledge and the bureaucratic consensus that all should be equal as specific rule-guided 'cases'. The internal tensions and the tensions between autonomy and compliance create sites of contestation. In that, we find differential traditions of freedom of expression and the right to serve non-elite interests and communities (Desreciewicz 2014).

By the late nineteenth century, Britain established its centrality not only as an economic but also a symbolic imperial node in culture, education and technology. Inter-imperial competition led to a transformed curriculum to articulate a civilizational prowess – the 'canon' (the synergy of Shakespeare and Newton), with France and Germany following suit, and the idea of it being the centre of excellence and progress got deeply entrenched.[9] By implication, all colonial spaces had to be validated in and through its circuits of scholarly power (Hobsbawm 1987).

It is fair to say that the majority world's idea of and institutions of higher learning – and the very university system itself – owed in design and purpose to the European model. This is true of settler societies like the USA – Harvard with nine students was established in 1636, the Rio de Janeiro University as a college for armaments and fortifications in 1792 through the British East India Company, the University of Calcutta in 1857 and the Imperial University of Peking in 1898. Most of the universities in the world during the colonial and post-colonial periods reflect a direct influence of the model (Barrington 2006). Similarly, the creation and reproduction of elites and class differentiation relied on a world system of higher education whose apex was the imperial metropole. It was a sign of explicit distinction if from India, you studied in Cambridge, and if from Martinique, you studied in Paris (Selingo 2016).

Since the late nineteenth century, pressure was exerted on the university systems of Europe and North America to become more relevant to corporate and state interests, and a vast array of applied disciplines proliferated (including explicit work for the military-industrial complex in the west and the east!) (Rose 1985). Furthermore, the rise of scientific management in society, the separation of mental and manual labour in mass production, and the need of new types of professionals in industry, commerce and the state stimulated the enlargement of tertiary sectors, whose absolute demographic explosion occurred in the 1950s and 1960s.[10] The idea that universities and disciplines became servants of power gained traction in the 1960s (Baritz 1960). Here, its spatiality and the cultural formations it engenders are vital – the spaces are marked by discord and transgression: not only was it a place where young men and, later, women enjoyed a loosening of family ties and a coexistence with peers in unique forms of accommodation, varied forms of hardship and puritanism, but also as spaces of new carnal and spiritual experiences where for some the 'knowledge interest' became an animating, fervour-producing, paroxysm-generating experience. A hyper-habitus: all-night discussions, explorations and ferment. They are sites for dreaming the 'as not yet' of Bloch's 'anticipatory consciousness', and to the defiant scripts it generated and still generates.

Here, for example, the Humboldt University of Berlin becomes the place and space for the emergence of the Young Hegelians as much as in Japan they spawned the Zengakuren movement, and as Jawaharlal Nehru University (JNU) in Delhi becomes the place and space for radical cohorts of students in the 1970s and 1980s.

Non-elite students who were always, until very recently, in the minority – who made it there despite their perceived cultural deficit and limited educational opportunities, and after so much struggle – would be disappointed that their arrival was not marked by some celebration or acknowledgement. Also, being a foreigner, a member of a marginal ethnicity or religious group, of lower caste or woman (in the first stages), or a Black and/or colonial subject, the tension would be palpable and the dissonance, extreme. Nevertheless, whether poor or rich, dark or light, male or female or somewhere in-between, the experience would produce some measure of disgruntlement. It was life in a specific type of institution with its peculiar ethos, its status claims, its 'culture', and its unwritten codes that could lead to discomfort and alienation.

I am pointing to the inherent tensions *within* the institution, the way it is structured and how it runs its life, its programmes, its timetables, its degrees, its student affairs. Of course, despite the relative autonomy experienced by each institution, even in ones where the state is explicitly directive, the university, despite its 'moats' and its distance from society, it is never immunized from it – the 'outside' infiltrates to haunt the ones 'within' – familial pressures, social, political and religious movements reach over the moat and affect 'being there'.

The very existence of the university – its character with its mix of the monastic and freedom of expression; its functionality or dysfunctionality for elite interests; its knowledge projects; its priorities and paradigms; furthermore, its practices – bureaucratic, authoritarian, medieval and/or anti-democratic – animate students towards grievance and dissonance. Here, bureaucratic rule and sociality coexist – the male lecturer trying to remove your knickers is the one grading your paper; certain types get preferential treatment as opposed to rules of fairness – and animate discord. Ironically, the more democratic and fair, the more rule-guided and constrained an institution seems to feel.

Sometimes the grumbles spill over into 'alterity', a search for an 'us' and a 'them' consciousness which challenges the administration and its academic programmes and challenges the university's complicity with power blocs. Mundane and everyday experience translates dissonance into alterity and produces a variety of collective identities and responses; after a while, universities institutionalize alterity – student representative councils, clubs and societies, levels of participation and voice creating further dynamics and processes. The tensions between individual achievement and success, and collective responsibility, in and by themselves multiply forms of dissonance.

Such alterity may have deeper political hues too: let us say Aime Cesaire in the 1920s at the Sorbonne and student X at the University of Cape Town in the 2010s sense that race becomes the way through which alterity has to express itself and not under the generality of studenthood. The pressure for assimilation into French cultures of excellence which deny you excellence/inclusion even if you achieve it on the real or perceived notions of race, the refusal of assimilation that spills over into deviance, can be generalized to encompass the alterities of marginal groups, Dalits and, in short, subaltern people of all kinds.

On rare occasions, such alterity may turn into a dramatic challenge, nay, a social movement that is both defiant of the rules and laws and begins to rattle the status quo. We can start this account from Russia in 1905, the May Fourth Movement in China in 1919 or the 1964 Free Speech Movement in Berkeley, the Red Guards of the Cultural Revolution in China, the struggle against dictatorship in Brazil, Mexico in 1968, Paris and Frankfurt 1968 or Greece in 1973, and then bring it all the way down to Tiananmen Square in 1991 down to the Arab Spring, the Fees Must Fall movement in South Africa, and in 2016 the Hyderabad and JNU agitations. For Immanuel Wallerstein, the Arab Spring in 2012 was such a challenge and a mere extension of the spirit and legacy of 1968. We think that such emphasis is too restrictive.

If we remain within Europe, at first glance the figure of the student is poised between a youthful Marius defending a barricade in revolutionary Paris straight out of the pages of Hugo's *Les Miserables* – or a Raskolnikov, the existentially conflicted and impoverished student who murders his landlord out of the pages of Dostoyevsky's *Crime and Punishment*. The image of the idealistic leveller, the anguished man suspended between good and evil, might create the wrong impression. Very few of the critical ideas about society emerge out of the university system, although most of the defiant scripts of the nineteenth and twentieth centuries emerge from the pens of university-educated people.

A rigorous study of the university and the figure of the 'student' will indeed find the opposite disposition: in the main, students were about complicity and conservatism. The study will be about children of elite families (and sometimes non-elite families because elite circulation demanded it or affirmative action decreed it) who enter the monastic space to gain competencies and access to elite positions thereafter. The university, as aforementioned, had been the special clearing house for talent and a marker of elite differentiation in class society, where educational and cultural capital was and is procured. And in Europe, one would find students on the wrong side of the barricade in 1848 and mostly on the side of right-wing upsurges and of reaction in the revolutionary years of 1917–26. And most certainly, as part of the rising fascist and Nazi movements in the 1920s and the 1930s (Barlaetti 2005).

There was a marked exception in Germany where at Humboldt, the ideational split between Old and Young Hegelians not only brought into focus religion, German backwardness and civic virtue, but also the idea of a universal class. Animated by the Hegelian claim of the *aufhebung* of mastery and slavery by bourgeois society and the 'universal' state, the hyper-habitus of student life created the imaginings that would make Marx's Philosophic Manuscripts of 1844 possible. (Kolakowski 2004). There were murmurings of defiance in student life but they did not become the backbone of any robust student movement: ferments were to be found outside the university moat.

The link between student life and defiance, therefore, is more easily found during the 1890s–1920s in the non-west and only with rare exceptions in the west. Russian (Raskolnikov's peers), Chinese, Vietnamese, Egyptian, Mexican, Indian, Filipino, Indonesian, Japanese, Iranian and such students were responding in proto-nationalist/anti-imperialist terms and were nurturing defiance, whereas the European experience from the 1890s to the 1930s points the other way: either an imperial and civilizing consciousness, or a sense of a darkening horizon and the birth of proto-fascist movements. To be more precise, there were three waves of student defiance: 1890–1920s, 1960s–1970s and the 2010s to now. The first phase starts from tsarist Russia and spreads to the colonial world in the form of radical nationalist movements; the second starts from the convulsions of the Cultural Revolution in China and the student movements of the USA, Mexico and Europe; the third starts from the so-named Arab Spring and spreads amoeba-like in all directions.

T.K. Oommen (1990) has used the Indian experience to argue for a restrictive definition of a student movement: (i) when it emerges as the result of student needs and interests; (ii) when it is initiated and led by students; (iii) when students are the major participants and actors in the movement; and finally, (iv) when the ideology of the movement is rooted in the consciousness as students. There is no doubt that at first most movements start like that, and he concedes that university students were simultaneously involved in two roles: students and citizens – parts of a real or imagined 'people'. We think that there is no doubt that the institutional life involved in being a student and dynamics within such institutions create the restlessness that may lead to a serious challenge to the status quo.

It is in Russia that we find the first extended case study of a radicalizing student movement in the modern period. It starts in an everyday sense between discord around everyday student life and discord between students and local authorities over their behaviour – i.e. out of their manifold cultural formations qua student-ness. Samuel D. Kassow, in his fascinating study *Students, Professors and the State in Tsarist Russia* (1989), traced the complex emergence of student subcultures and protests from 1899, culminating, not by design, in the 1905 revolution as a radicalizing left. From 1899 to 1911, student strikes and mass demonstrations disrupted higher education and, starting from 1905, caused a closure of the system for two years. The rest has them in the ferment of the Russian Revolution of 1917.

Kassow pointed to the student subculture, the *studenchestvo*, a cultural formation they belonged to as a unique social group. Precisely, we read *studenchestvo* as a hyper-habitus that socializes the meanings of student-ness. As he states, they saw themselves as such:

> a distinct subgroup in Russian society . . . with its own history, traditions, institutions, code of ethics, and responsibilities. This sense of tradition, the consciousness of being part of a unique social group, was at the bottom of most student protest and justifies the term *student movement*. the student movement had an independent identity, quite distinct from the revolutionary left. . . . Student unrest was more likely to break out because of corporate grievances or to protest police repression of fellow students than as a reaction to events outside the universities. Only one major student strike out of six coincided with social ferment outside the universities. Although most of their demands were of a corporate or a liberal character, the students gave (later) their rhetorical allegiance to the radical left. (Kassow 1989: 4)

There is no space here to summarize the depth of Kassow's analysis but to concur: 'belonging to the *studenchestvo* involved accepting a code of behaviour that emphasized upholding the ideals of previous student generations and that stressed student solidarity in the face of government repression' (ibid.: 8). Alongside that, they were animated by their national duty to, on the one hand, overthrow 'backwardness' and not betray their duty and ideals like most West European, and especially German, students had betrayed their ideals. To conclude with Kassow: 'the student movement reflected [also] the anxiety many students felt about following in their fathers' footsteps as ineffectual "Chekhovian heroes", acquiescent civil servants or frustrated professionals vaguely unhappy with the autocratic system but too timid to do anything but accommodate themselves to it'.[11]

The point is simple: everywhere, be it Russia or Japan, the experience of 'being there' has always produced feelings of dissonance in students. There has always been a sense of discomfort about the institution's core modalities. Already the mere selection to it, after merit trumped influence in modernity, brought with it a hope that there would be, in its corridors, lecture theatres, residences, a world of many enticing others to share and enjoy the relative freedoms of youth. Some would be more bookish than others, some more on the edge of sexual and intoxicating encounters, some more religious and some more agnostic than others. Some would join, in the 1930s in Germany, Hitler-inspired power blocs who mourned the loss of Europe's spirit which was usurped by Jews and communists, imposing a process of Nazification and the knowledge project of eugenics.

Yet, the conjunctural intertwining of a student movement in Russia with the Russian Revolution had left an ideomorphic narrative of defiance, often too exaggerated for comfort. Their 'role' was helped by Lenin himself, who at first was quite caustic about the intelligentsia, the professorate and the students though later realizing that they were an important constituency for the revolution (Lenin 1968). But what reached further was his pamphlet on *Imperialism*. It resonated with anti-colonial and anti-imperial sentiments everywhere, most intensely in Asia.

This was further reinforced by many students from the majority world whose educational journeys, or better their 'pilgrimages', found them studying in the metropole: the rising tides of fascism and racism there, the explicit narratives of modern versus traditional, advanced versus backward, civilization versus the lack of it, fanned the flames of disquiet – the first insurgence from the 1890s to the 1920s produced two opposing narratives: the necessity of a social revolution to overthrow the state outside advanced industrial societies so that a new form of state be established in the interests of the oppressed, and the exploited versus the anarchist currents which wanted the overthrow of the state as such.

The ideomorphic and defiant currents were anti-imperialist and abhorred the inter-imperial rivalries that created wars and violence. They also harboured a critique of the 'backwardness' of Russian, Chinese, Egyptian, Indonesian and other similar societies, but differed over whether the past and its traditions were a burden or a vital resource for renewal. It seemed that African proto-nationalists were of the latter variety, eschewing colonial definitions of 'native-ness' and redefining their emerging consciousness as African; and so were the Crescent Moon circles in China's 1919 movements, harking back and drawing inspiration from the Tagores and the Bengali Renaissance; in Egypt they were liberal, chastising the British for moral inconsistency, but also viewed the stirrings of the Muslim trans-border community as a source of pride; the Chinese communists were of the former variety – the past was seen to be too much of a weight to carry. They were in the main ardent dreamers of self-determination and tried to imagine the links between nation, freedom and equality. They were rebelling against their parents' generations who were seen to be Chekhovian, Gogolian, an array of dissonant but acquiescent characters and lackeys.

The post-1945 period witnessed an explosion in tertiary education the world over: led by the USA, imitated by the Soviet Union, steered by the Marshall Plan in Europe to fulfil the escalating needs of governmental and financial bureaucracies, technologically driven workplaces and an exploding service economy, students were recruited in large numbers. The USA was actively taking over from Britain as the world hegemon and the leader in the Cold War's effort to win the hearts and minds of an increasingly decolonizing world. As John Douglass (2000) noted, the public university system of California, a beacon of democratic access, was also seen by its lodestar and vice-chancellor Clark Kerr (2016) as a 'multiversity' and a series of 'knowledge factories'.

Whilst in 1950 only 3.4 per cent of youth went to a tertiary institution, rising gradually to 4 per cent by 1960, thereafter the numbers escalated and continued to do so at an incredible rate. By 1990 there were 25 per cent of youth attending tertiary institutions, which exploded to 40 per cent by 2020, an increase from close to 1,00,000 in 1945 to a staggering 220 million students. This more than reflects, beyond the obvious massification of the system, a vast elite recruitment project from merit-worthy middle-class and upper working-class echelons of society. In short, there was a massive growth in tertiary education, particularly since the end of Second World War, which continues unabated until today. This has reshaped class, gender, ethnicity, sexuality and disability barriers, as persons from less 'privileged' background were included.

This seeming democratization occurs alongside new forms of hierarchization of prestige and the inexorable search for rankings by universities, so the topmost positions in the polity, economy and professions retain their elite character. The puzzling question for Eric Hobsbawm was:

> . . . why did the movement of this social group of students, alone among the new social actors of the golden era, opt for radicalism of the Left? For (if we leave aside rebels against the communist regimes) even nationalist student movements tended to stitch the red badge of Marx, Lenin or Mao somewhere on their banners until the 1980s. (Hobsbawn 1994: 299)

It is uncanny that once again, China appears as an 'externality' in accounts of movements despite the fact that it was and is the most populous country on earth, whose revolution sent tremors throughout Asia and whose people by the 1960s were in the midst of the great Cultural Revolution. It was not only a leftist intelligentsia that became enamoured with this but a whole array of thinkers, planners and development specialists that were spread over Asia to create alternatives to radical land reform and transformation.

Nowhere in the world were such paroxysms of feeling, forms of militancy and rebellion ever encountered. As Mao argued: 'Marxism comprises many principles, but in the final analysis they can all be brought back to a single sentence: it is right to rebel.'[12] This was a statement made in 1939 but it prefigured Mao's and Lin Biao's enthusiastic support of the students' movement later. This was Lin Biao addressing students in 1966: 'We firmly support your proletarian revolutionary spirit of daring to break through, to act, to make revolution and to rise up in rebellion. . . . Overthrow those persons in power taking the capitalist road, overthrow the bourgeois reactionary authorities and all bourgeois loyalists.'[13]

'Your action', Mao enthused the Red Guards in 1966, 'indicates that you are expressing hatred and denunciation of landowners, the bourgeoisie, imperialism, revisionists and their running dogs who exploit workers, peasants, revolutionary intellectuals and parties. Your actions suggest that your rebellion . . . is justified. You have my warmest and fullest support.'[14] The Fourth National People's Congress endorsed the student movement wholeheartedly in 1967: 'Speaking out freely, airing views fully, holding great debates and writing big character posters are a new form of carrying on socialist revolution created by the masses. The state should ensure to the masses the right to use these forms to create a political situation.'[15]

In the words of a militant (1967): 'We will swing a big stick, demonstrate magic, exhibit supernatural power, turn heaven and earth upside down. We are going to throw men and horses off their feet, make flowers wither so that they flow away with the water. We want to heap chaos upon chaos.'[16] In the words too of the Red Guard Collective:

> In June 1966 our great leader Chairman Mao himself launched the great proletarian cultural revolution, a revolution unprecedented in history. Revolutionary teachers and students responded at once and rose up to rebel against the capitalist roaders, exposing and denouncing their crimes. For 17 years, in the literature and art world and in our school, these traitors had tried to create public opinion for the restoration of capitalism in China by protecting, fostering and spreading decadent, bourgeois and revisionist literature and art, and opposing Chairman Mao's revolutionary line on literature and art. . . . What could we use to help inspire the Red Guards in our

struggle against the class enemy? We recalled what Chairman Mao had taught us, that we must 'ensure that literature and art fit well into the whole revolutionary machine as a component part, that they operate as powerful weapons for uniting and educating the people and for attacking and destroying the enemy, and that they help the people fight the enemy with one heart and one mind'. We are music students – our weapon would be music, a battle song for the Red Guards! [17]

Yet, before this revolutionary ferment took centre stage student relations with university authorities were strained: the expansion of university access was undertaken with scant resources, the massification implied met with a rather rigid and authoritarian professorate that demanded high levels of achievement. The socialism implied in the content of educational syllabi clashed with the forms of delivery and assessment, and the voices and grievances of students were not seen to be taken seriously. Like in the case of Russia, what started as tensions within institutions found an outlet in and through the militant wings of the party that demanded a purging of the bureaucratic tendencies in the institutions of the state. The Cultural Revolution was the form given to an increasing radicalized situation from below by those who demanded a renewal from above. Before long, thanks to a powerful new cadre in the party, Mao was to emerge as the epicentre of the ferment.

The adulation of Mao was overwhelming:

> When our struggle was the toughest, we drew strength from these lines of Chairman
> Mao's poem:
>> Only heroes can quell tigers and leopards
>> And wild bears never daunt the brave.
>> Plum blossoms welcome the whirling snow;
>> Small wonder flies freeze and perish. [18]

Their offering to the struggle was a revolutionary song that the revolutionary composer Li Chiehfu set to music, the 'Red Guards' Battle Song' (*Hongweibing Zhan Ge*):

> We are Chairman Mao's Red Guards,
> We steel our red hearts in great winds and waves.
> We arm ourselves with Mao Tse-tung's thought
> To sweep away all pests.

> We are Chairman Mao's Red Guards,
> Absolutely firm in our proletarian stand,
> Marching on the revolutionary road of our forebears,
> We shoulder the heavy task of our age.

We are Chairman Mao's Red Guards,
Vanguards of the cultural revolution.
We unite with the masses and together plunge into the battle
To wipe out all monsters and demons.

[Refrain]
Dare to criticize and repudiate, dare to struggle,
Never stop making revolutionary rebellion.
We will smash the old world
And keep our revolutionary state red for ten thousand generations![19]

Qing Jang was perhaps the most paradigmatic of the revolutionary ferment. She was not just Mao's dog, as she often said, biting when he said bite or heeling when he commanded. She drafted manifestos, developed criteria for the correct performance of opera pieces, scripted pieces on workers' control and on the left of the Chinese Communist Party (CCP), used the Red Guard ferment to attack the 'olds' and the capitalist roaders in the university system and in society. This process saw the tragic end of one of Zhou en Lai's children in the basement of Renmin University, and the subsequent deportation of thousands to the countryside to 'learn' from the peasants and the people (Terril 2012).

The movement ushered through violence was brought to a halt in and through violence. China's official assessment of Mao and the Cultural Revolution was captured on a massive wall poster (1978): 'The Cultural Revolution must be reassessed. Mao Zedong was 70 per cent good and 30 per cent bad.'[20]

The whole experience became an ideo-form of revolutionary as opposed to a conformist response to power. It is precisely this form that travelled. We shall return to this point after our discussion of India's experience. Suffice to state that Paris intellectuals received the Chinese narrative with open ears and arms on the cusp of the ferment there. But it was further afield, in India, that Maoism resonated through the student movement as a serious product of local conditions.

The context of colonialism gave a unique direction and edge to the student movement in India. The vast number of students who joined the Indian freedom struggle were inspired by a commitment to counter the inferior status that a subjugated population is assigned by the 'superior' colonial power. As Altbach (1968: 27) observed, trained in modern, scientific temper, they deployed their intellectual prowess in representing a people who were 'condemned to a pre-modern stage, and a European past'. The student movement assumed an organic relation to a people. Indeed, it saw itself as *representing an emergent people* in and through the Indian National Congress movement.

Before independence, the thrust of student participation in the anti-colonial struggle in India was for the 'emergent nation' and, combined with it, a search of how 'to become the voice of India's people'. Post-independence, the nation remained the concern while the state, with the perceived failure of the Nehruvian model of nation-building,[21] became the terrain of struggle. There was a claim for a unique voice committed to democracy and nation's development, whose own articulation of grievances can give voice to the people who had been wronged by a post-independent state.

One of the most significant instances of student mobilization came in the form of the Naxalite movement. To understand the political subjectivity and disposition of students in the Naxalite movement, the idea of the 'nation' becomes critical. Though the state ended up as the primary target of the organized armed struggle of the Naxalites, students' political subjectivity was overdetermined by the imagination of an alternative nation, made up of *real* people, the very people the post-independent state ignored.

Three separate but adjacent villages – Kharibari, Phansidewa and Naxalbari – erupted on to the political map of India and the subcontinent in the early half of 1967. It was a peasant uprising; however, unlike previous uprisings, it grew in importance for the Indian communist movement. Borrowing the name from Naxalbari village, in 1969, a party was formed which committed itself to Maoism and pledged its allegiance to the CCP. With the party formation, the Naxalbari uprising took the organized form of the Naxalite movement. The movement, an Indian variant of the Maoist campaign, aimed at changing production relations of a 'semi-colonial, semi-feudal' country into socialism. The 'chairman' and principal ideologue of the party was Charu Majumdar, a veteran communist activist even before independence. It drew sizeable participation of students especially in Andhra Pradesh, Bihar and West Bengal. In other states like Punjab, Uttar Pradesh and Odisha, students and youth did participate in armed struggles or stood in solidarity. However, their participation was more spontaneous in nature (S. Ghosh 2010; Banerjee 1980).

It appears that the ideal of an 'alternate nation' continued to inspire students' imagination in the Naxalite movement. This was not surprising given that the initial radicalization of the students began with their disillusionment with the Indian National Congress party and rupture with dominant modes of nationalistic ethos. 'Nation' as political-symbolic order was the locus of ideological articulation. Then, it is understood, this new patriotism also had to mobilize a very different vision of nation. The political subjectivity of students was no longer staged through the trope of the citizen; rather, it was staged through the trope of the 'patriot'. New patriotism was in a way a response to the old Congress-led patriotism. The Nehruvian leadership had only facilitated a 'transfer of power', not independence, with 'people', mostly the rural population, living a slavish life under feudal oppression, no different from colonial oppression. It was by destroying the state (citadel, centres, etc.) and annihilating the 'class enemy' that the nation must be reimagined and restored to the *real* people. No longer being a voice of the people but the opportunity to be an agent in active search for the *real* nation anchored students in Naxalite politics[22] (Samaddar 2012).

Such a commitment lasted way beyond independence. By the 1960s–70s, India witnessed widespread discontent among students. Many of these confrontations turned to violence (Shah 1977). It is not possible here to describe all these confrontations. We shall reflect on two such occasions where the student movement started with issues pertaining to students and campus-specific demands, and then went on to include larger agendas. Students' participation in an anti-price rise movement in Gujarat in 1973–74 is one such instance. It started in the Lalbhai Dalpatbhai College of Engineering in Ahmedabad when the mess bill was increased. Students immediately ransacked the hostel and commenced a strike. In response, police entered the campus and arrested students. This incident agitated students in other institutions and the next day, a procession of thousand students reached the police station and demanded the release of the arrested students. They went to the chief minister's office with the same demand and shouted slogans denouncing the chief minister. Gradually, the movement outstepped the boundaries of educational institutions and linked itself with the anti-price rise demonstration protesting the food crisis in the state (ibid.).

Almost at the same time in Bihar, under the leadership of Jayaprakash Narayan, another student movement emerged. In 1973, Bihar witnessed spontaneous students' agitations for amenities on campuses, reduction in fees and concession in cinema tickets. Jayaprakash Narayan, a revered political figure in the state, soon linked up the student issues with the wider society by asking students, as the future of this country, to leave studies and join the struggle to 'save the democracy'. Another leader, K.V. Sahay, addressed the students and reminded them as youth it is right time that they assumed their political responsibility. The 'political responsibility' was however marked by students' spontaneous anger and violent expressions in looting food storages, vandalizing government building and even arson (ibid.).

In the context of the Bihar movement, where Jayaprakash Narayan gave his famous call for 'total revolution', Shah (1977) observes how the movement never had a vision for an alternative society. In fact, the call was for total revolution consisting of systemic and moral change. And in that scheme, students were perceived as the prime actors. They, Narayan believed, did not inherit their parents' values, class interests or institutions. They were thus ideal actors for social change. However, in all practicality, most of these student protests articulated their grievances against the state from their class and caste positions, and, according to Shah, were far removed from 'total revolution'. In fact, Jayaprakash

Narayan received a cold response to his call to change social customs (ibid.: 701). However, the Indian state did take note of this new political actor. In the period 1965 to 1968, there were at least eleven reports and recommendations that were prepared by various committees, individuals, seminars and conferences, affiliated or initiated by the government, to address the issue of student and youth unrests in India.[23]

Students were seen as a political-ideological force who could break free from the shackles of colonial legacy and create new progressive values: a unique revolutionary force – though not in the case of class – who could take the message of the revolution to the peasantry and the working class. And by doing so, the force could facilitate the emergence of a collective, a class alliance between the peasantry, the proletariat and the middle class (especially the lower middle class, from which most of the students and youths were recruited). Needless to add, this collectivity was seen as an alternate nation. It was to be against the nation of a 'comprador bourgeoisie' and 'jotedars' that the Congress-led nationalism had hitherto produced. It was the nation that became the battleground for students in the Naxalite movement. Consequently, their attacks on Bengali culture, heritage and icons cannot be understood without grasping the symbolic order of the nation, essential to their subjective articulation. Interestingly, Dalit Panthers, another youth movement, enhances the above issues. The movement emerged in the slums of Mumbai in the 1970s in direct relationship with the ideas of the Naxalbari movement. It had a similar imagination of an alternate nation. The former envisioned a nation without 'jotedar-raj'; the latter was aspiring for a nation without Brahmin-raj, or the rule of Brahminism (Omvedt 2002).

EUROPE

The radical explosions of the 1960s and 1970s, which were part and parcel of the so-called 'global sixties' (Chen et al., 2018), had a lasting impact at least on reform in tertiary education if on little else. Moreover, they created a legacy for radicalism even if in reality it was always a vociferous minority of students that made the noise, while most remained compliant and quiet.

As mentioned above, the 1960s and early 1970s were awash with student movements everywhere. They started from specific university-based issues and spread to encompass political and international issues as well. And although there was an intergenerational rift – a critique of parents' perceived materialism and affluence after twenty years of spectacular growth in Europe – as much as there was disquiet about the elitism of the nationalist movement in India and a challenge to the 'capitalist roaders'[24] in China, in all cases the rift was settled by the mid-1970s. Where there still existed anger against the parents' conformity was in Germany, regarding parents' silence about the atrocities of the Nazi period. Both Heinrich Boll in the *The Lost Honour of Caterina Blum* and later Elfriede Jelinek in her writing about Ulrike Meinhof stress this muted or explicit anger. In her recent play, *Ulrike Maria Stuart* (2006), Jelinek dramatizes the struggle for political power between Meinhof and Gudrun Ensslin and Schelling's historical heroines, Mary Stuart and Elizabeth I, to dramatize the restlessness and the futility of their important feminine, anti-fascist and anti-patriarchal struggle that tipped over into chaos.

The German student movement (Sozialistischer Deutscher Studentenbund, or SDS) played a leading role in a range of immediate struggles over university life, but it was not long before issues of war and anti-imperialism were added to their repertoire of contention. And so was a critique of the one-dimensional system (to steal from the very popular Herbert Marcuse, 1964) of their parents. The student movement did not seek alliances because of its view that the working class was a class that could never become a class-for-itself: it was compliant and entrapped by commodity fetishism – the revolution was elsewhere, in tropical humanity, among peasants, with guerrilla movements in tow. The German working class was thickly embedded in the social system and Germany's economic recovery. So, the student movement either petered out or morphed into urban guerrilla violence.

It is within this sway we can witness how a series turns into a group-in-fusion in the Sartrean sense, where serialized individuals created collectivities; how they developed unique forms of protest; and trace their explosive oscillations that may turn to symbolic and real forms of violence. Not only was all this punctuated by the specific university milieu but also by the transient and existential nature of student protest, as the short period of academic life created peculiar 'now' immediacies. Constructing this 'us' in public gatherings and oral rituals of defiance is one side of the story, how administrations and states respond is quite another.

For example, the Berkeley Free Speech Movement led by Mario Savio and Jack Weinberg, who were already involved in supporting the rising civil rights movement, left with it fascinating scripts:

> There's a time when the operation of the machine becomes so odious, makes you so sick at heart, that you can't take part, you can't even passively take part, and you've got to put your bodies upon the gears and upon the wheels, upon the levers, upon all the apparatus, and you've got to make it stop! And you've got to indicate to the people who run it, to the people who own it, that unless you're free, the machine will be prevented from working at all![25]

Whereas in Germany and the USA, the student movement emerged at a remarkable distance from workers and working class organizations, in France it was marked by a new-found proximity. Worker militancy was on the rise since the mid-1960s and the first demonstration of left students after the attempted assassination of Rudi Dutschke in Germany rallied around 200 students. The ferment started from Paris Nanterre University around the expulsion of a young woman and man sleeping together in the dorm. Such were the times that the first demonstration combined issues of sexual freedom and the Vietnam War. The tensions with the police brought Sorbonne students into the equation, and before long a full escalation of street battles and barricades ensued. On 11 May 1968, the General Confederation of Labour (CGT) called for a general strike in solidarity with the students. The largest demonstration, comprising a million or so workers and students, occurred on 13 May, followed by the occupation of the Sorbonne, which had restarted its lectures (Kurlansky 2004).

The strike-wave though outfoxed all party and trade union officials and in a wildcat way led to occupation after occupation, signalling one of the largest ever insurgencies in recent history. Government and big business yielded to a series of reforms in pay, working hours and participatory shop-floor structures, and brought about a settlement which government after government has tried to erode since.

The event has been vividly accounted for. The account by Daniel Singer, *Prelude to Revolution* (2013), is a remarkable guide to those heady days of May. Read along with Mitchell Abidor's oral history of the events, *May Made Me* (2018), a very convincing case is made of its importance and of the impact it had on the lives of activists and students.[26] On the consequences, two books in particular are very important: Julian Bourg's philosophical reflection, *From Revolution to Ethics* (2017), is a vital exposition of the cultural shift and a move to a democratic and post-imperial way of thinking; by contrast, Kristin Ross's *May '68 and its Afterlives* (2004) demonstrates the denuding of the moment of its politics and the construction of a powerful but narcissistic mytheme.

Shifting to Europe's south, the 1973 *Polytechneio* (Polytechnic) uprising against the dictatorship of the colonels in Greece was listed as one of the most violent turning points in the history of student movements around the globe. It became the emblematic and ultimate act of resistance against the dictatorship, the catalyst that led to the downfall of the dictators (Rigos 1999; Tsoukalas 1993).

The *Polytechnio* event was a moment of rupture that would be the iconic and defining moment that legitimized the Third Hellenic Republic in the transition from dictatorship to democracy, known in Greek as *metapolitefsi*, the 'post-authoritarian period in Greek politics and society' (Giannakopoulos 2012). Their slogan, 'Bread, Education, Freedom', was taught to children as a glorious moment from primary school. During the *metapolitefsi*, a new breed of politicians claimed to be speaking in the name of the *Polytechnio* generation. Some of the protagonists of the events did indeed become politicians of the parties of the left (KKE, KKE interior, Synaspismos and PASOK). It is no coincidence that almost every radical student event frames the event as *their very own Polytechnio*.

During such times of ferment, remarkable imaginaries emerged, and so did extraordinary scripts of defiance. Such scripts of the system, the bureaucracy, the machine, the educational policy, capitalism, war and dictatorship got amplified, whilst at the same time voluntarism and action trumped structure, pamphlet and manifesto trumped manuscript, and song and performance trumped the essay.

Colin Barker makes a further vital *cultural* point:

> . . . as well as directly political organizations, the student movement contributed strongly to the development of a 'cultural underground', which both provided some of the *style* of student politics and also acted as a *substitute* for politics for many. The student movement went along with a whole questioning of existing lifestyles and cultural assumptions, which sometimes shocked conservative forces in society (in 'communist' states at least as much as in the 'liberal' west) even more than overt student political action. [. . .] The 'cultural underground' reshaped attitudes to sexuality, not least amongst women. It drew on resources from outside student milieux, from working-class and ghetto life, and fed into other movements of the time: into the wildcat strike movements in American factories around 1970, and the oppositional culture of US soldiers and marines in the later years of the war in Vietnam. It was, too, within student movements that the first serious stirrings of second-wave feminism were heard. (Barker 2008: 84)

On the cultural side, Bob Dylan was a peculiar catalyst, at first playing in local coffee houses to earn money and improve his guitar skills, adopting along the way some of Woody Guthrie's persona, whom he idolized (Shelton 2011: 38). He captured the student movement's imagination and was catapulted into fame by it. From the folk spots of Greenwich Village, he talked-sang, mumbled and twanged himself into fame (Heylin 1991: 24). The student movement met on the way a serious folk music revival which was already growing and looking for new audiences. The expansion of university campuses, and within campuses of student numbers, perfected the match. Dylan's timing was perfect. Not only was he romantically engaged with Suze Rotolo, the daughter of communist parents and victims of the McCarthy era who also worked on issues of race and equality, his own sensibility turned his lyrics into mini anthems (Sounes 2001).

Between 1962 and 1963 Dylan emerges from the 'cultural underground' as a successful and popular political artist. He does not respond to the mood of the times but begins to define it (Heylin 1991). In 1962, his 'Blowin' in the Wind' is made into a national hit by Peter, Paul and Mary, and his LP *Freewheelin' Bob Dylan* becomes the new generation's must-have album. By 1963, *The Times They Are a-Changin'* turns him into a left celebrity and a youth icon: the protest singer, the 'voice of his generation' (Scaduto 1971).[27] Later, in 1963, *The Times They Are a-Changin'* was written and recorded – challenging the establishment and striking political tones, this and 'Blowin' in the Wind' became strident anthems symbolizing the generation gap and the hardships and changes of life, and making Dylan the – albeit reluctant – voice of youth rebellion (Shelton 2011). By the end of 1963, despite Dylan toning down on explicit political commentary, his new work was taken as an emblematic gesture of youth defiance against the American dream.

Thanks to the gramophone and vinyl, TV and radio, youth cultural forms of expression played with intergenerational distance and new countercultural experiments. The countercultural moment of the late 1960s reached everywhere – another example was Mexico with its student subcultures of La Onda, its marijuana and rock, its sensuality and excess, which were 'delegitimizing' the Institutional Revolutionary Party's (PRI) rule. This counterculture and growing radicalism by 1968 spread into student protests and demonstrations that were viciously repressed, with 200 killed and thousands injured, setting off waves and waves of a radicalized and contrary Mexico City whose defiance survives to this day.

Alongside these chimes of freedom, Maoism was also vital. Though many cringed at the personality cult around Mao, they recognized the importance of his 'people first' approach and decried the bureaucratic snares of bureaucracies on all cardinal points of the planet. Many believed that it was imperative to save the 'nation' from the state: this was particularly marked in China and India, whereas in the west, the entire system was in question – its bureaucracies, its commodity fetishisms, its material cultures. In the fray, radical ideas of gender equality, sexual freedom, alternative and experimental lifestyles, alternative education and cultural practices and issues of race proliferated, and support grew for anti-colonial struggles. If there was also a consensus, unlike the previous generation, they were anti-war as such. They saw their parents' generation as an extension of Dylan's Mr Jones.

REACTION

Such forms of defiance generated decisive responses: in the west, moral entrepreneurs created a panic around students' activity – the middle-class hooligans of Paris, the red terror queen in Japan and in Europe – and portrayed it as a manifestation of a deterioration of a 'way of life' and the ineptness of laws and lawmakers and the ineffectiveness of the state and the police. At a deeper level, it started a process of reactive mobilization: in the older days after the 1919 insurgency in China, Chiang Kai-shek started a process of purging the movement of communists. By 1974, Zhou en Lai and a fed-up cohort in the

CCP started taking on Qing Jiang and the Gang of Four, putting an end to the Cultural Revolution and beginning the process that led to a shift towards the Four Modernizations policy. Across the ideological moat, Ronald Reagan's ascendance in California was to fix this mess or, in his words, this 'trash'. It is a similar scream about 'anti-nationals' in India now.

The reaction produced counter-reactions which have turned to extreme forms of violence: the Baader-Meinhof 'gang', the Red Brigades and Red Army factions, the Naxal movement in India, and later, much later, the Taliban and Boko Haram. Again, as Colin Barker intoned:

> from the mid-1970s, however, confidence in the possibility of large-scale transformation from below began to wane. By the late 1970s, there was a widespread mood of rejection of left analyses and prescriptions. A more conservative trend in thought became predominant, marked by the increasing influence of 'post-structuralist' and 'post-modernist' ideas. These involved turning away from global solutions, indeed even from speaking of global problems – even though these problems, in real terms, were multiplying as the long postwar economic boom shuddered to a halt. Left-wing hopes in China ended with Mao's death, the overthrow of the Gang of Four and Deng Xiaoping's access to power. In France, celebrated in the pages of *New Left Review* during the late sixties and early seventies as the world centre of radical thought, the collapse of the Union of the Left went along with the rise of the *nouveaux philosophes*, former Maoist intellectuals who now denounced Marxism as a theory leading to the Gulag. By 1983, Perry Anderson could call Paris 'the capital of European intellectual reaction'. (Barker 2018)

Since we are concerned with the contemporary period, the process of reaction was more than constitutive: Ronald Reagan succeeded to inaugurate a conservative response, a national alternative, a Star Wars programme, neoliberalism (to get the bums off social welfare), and a shift to the STEM model and university managerialism.

If disillusioned Maoists turned the philosophy seminar world into a *jihad* against Marxism and Marxists, purer-than-thou Marxists of Fourth International pedigree turned to neoconservatives as a response to the 'recklessness' of the student movement. Some of them became the ghost workers of Reaganomics and the inventors of value-for-money statism:

> Leaders of the Neoconservative movement included Irving Kristol and Norman Podhoretz, the extended family of each becoming powerful figures in government, journalism, and foundation work. Unlike Old Right Conservatives who wanted to dismantle the welfare state, Neoconservatives assumed the necessity of it but wanted to make it efficient and effective. They also vigorously supported a global

democratic order, a view not found among leaders of the Old Right since they were inherently suspicious of democracy, a suspicion they inherited, they said, from the Founding Fathers. When Ronald Reagan came to power in 1981, most of his staff came from the Neoconservative wing of the movement. (Bloom 1986: 372)

The market and corporatization trend were not the only story. The Cold War provided the alibi to not only unleash a military-industrial complex-linked priority, but an academic one as well. Christopher Simpson's *Universities and Empire: Money and Politics in the Social Sciences During the Cold War* (1999) makes for harrowing reading. And as more documents become declassified in the USA, the complicity of many stellar US institutions of higher learning in propping up oppressive regimes in the developing world is more than corroborated but often wilfully ignored. Here, Inderjeet Parmar's book, *Foundations of the American Century: The Ford, Carnegie, and Rockefeller Foundations in the Rise of American Power* (2012), shows that even the 'soft power' foundations – the Fords, Rockefellers and Carnegies – were implicated in this fight against communism and secular nationalists who sympathized with communists or were too distanced from the west's imperialist rhetoric to become compliant. Many universities appear embroiled in this ferment through networks and conferences, specialist centres and journals, and a whole gamut of indirect activities. But some were involved explicitly: the story of how Michigan State University academics helped and propped up the Viet Minh regime in Vietnam's south and how they assisted in the war is by now explicit. Everywhere, from India to Indonesia, from the Philippines to Egypt, from Africa to Latin America, a concerted effort to win the battle of ideas and culture was under way.

So, when students started their anti-war campaigns in the USA, they did not have to aim far; they could point a finger at important professors, units and centres that were part of the war campaign on their very own campuses. However, their voice and militancy was met with alarm in conservative circles: here was the soft underbelly of a class society with a new vast demographic of questionable academic and patriotic quality, a new enemy *within* challenging the very success of the American dream. It was the very reason Ronald Reagan's rise in California was predicated on the creation of a shrill moral panic about the student movement. His ascendance there and the turning of all this into a national campaign was at the heart of the rise of both neoconservatism and neoliberalism. These universities had to be turned around: they should be about value for money, productivity and measurement, and not rhetoric; they should be about prudent management around the volume of assets under their control.

Corporatization was to follow. Whereas the prior century was a call for universities to be sensitive to the needs of corporations, by now they were seen as corporations themselves. The neoliberal counter-revolution eroded the bases for alternative and radical polices within universities at the practical level of making all accountable to market forces and the value-for-money 'talk', but it was the persistent and psychic challenge by intellectuals of the new right that started edging out the left. Their task was made easier by the obvious totalitarianism of existing socialist societies. The time and opportunity to dream, experiment and/or act to change the world in the spirit of the radical student ethic of the 1960s was being eroded. However, what was simultaneously being eroded was the space, time and energy for students to advance their neoliberal student careerism, in line with the neoliberal ethic of the late 1980s and 1990s. For the majority of students, the expectations of a career ahead became a pathway full of hurdles. With precarity looming in their future career and student years spent in debt or as working poor, the careerist student drive of the 1990s seems to be evaporating (Bourdieu *et al.* 1999). Inertia keeps things going, but the longer-term processes at play are transforming the processes of reproduction as 'homo academicus' (Bourdieu 1984) is mutating.

In the declining and crisis-ridden western Europe of the 1980s, the right-wing turn of social democracy which converged with neoliberalism in the 1980s, 1990s and 2000s (Mitterrand in France, the German SPD under Schroeder and later Blairism in the UK) would complete the game that Thatcher and Reagan had started. The old welfare state would be radically transformed, services would be privatized and students would become 'professionalized' as careerists and 'consumers' in fee-paying educational institutions, replacing the aspiration of universal and free education. The 1980s saw radical departments and centres being reformed, absorbed or closed down.

And then there was the upsurge of the twenty-first century. Students were a driving force in a youthful challenge to a range of issues. There is what occurred and there is no space here to describe it all, there is the presentation of what occurred by those who participated and/or led it, and there is the imagination of what the presentation flairs by those who get inspired by it.

In our terms, the hyper-habitus and its cultural formations that animate student effervescence are common, but their content and the content of each movement differed and differs – and given the horizontal efficacy of this digital generation's messaging, what they do travels. Yet, it is never the content that travels as such but its symbolic visage: its event-ness, its noise and music, its defiant anti-systemic gestures and the violence of the system. The content of the protests in each case gets its character from the specific space and social agglomeration of pressures experienced by this new generation.

The Greek students and scholars in insurrection, the Arab Spring, the Indignados and Podemos and the broader Occupy movement, Rhodes Must Fall/Fees Must Fall and the Indian student movement centred around Jawaharlal Nehru University created a transferrable imaginary. Unlike prior generations, the students' ability to network, upload and share has been remarkable.

We would like to avoid sociological harsh judgements: unlike the generation of 1968, these new insurgencies of defiance lacked coherence, and even when they did get their demands, like in the South African case, they seemed to have dissipated into factional splinters with unexpected rapidity.

Asef Bayat (2013) makes the point explicitly in terms of the Arab Spring: unlike prior generations of the 1960s and 70s, the current movement in the Arab world and beyond lacked ideological coherence and is involved in responsive actions to broader forms of turbulence by getting engaged in a 'refolutionary' (playing with the word reform and revolution) rather than revolutionary dynamic. To return to Immanuel Wallerstein, unlike the revolution of 1968 where even though it failed, it changed 'everything', the current one exacerbates the 'anomalic' and strengthens the power blocs of reaction.

Bayat explains further:

> . . . when I say "revolution without revolutionaries" here I mean revolutions without revolutionary ideas. Those were revolutions in terms of those spectacular mobilizations, those extraordinary protests. They were quite remarkable in terms of the tactics of mobilization – how to mobilize, resist, and manage to bring so many people to the streets. In the Egyptian case, Tahrir square became a global space, it became a model for other movements that emerged in other places later on in some 5,000 cities around the world. But revolution in terms of change, and in terms of having a vision about change, and about how to rest power from the incumbents, that to me was quite lacking. (Bayat 2017: 1)

Nicos Mouzelis (2009: 44) too argued that in the case of Greece, the protests were the product of a 'weak civil society' in what he refers to as 'a partocratic society', speaking of 'the dead-end character of the ensuing mobilizations/riots' which 'led, on the one hand, to the familiar blind violence of anti-state groups, and on the other to more peaceful pupil/student demonstrations'. Mouzelis objects to comparisons with 1968:

> In the former case we observe brainless, nihilistic practices which have been wrongly compared with May '68. The May '68 events may not have changed the political system, but they have shaped to a great extent the social imagery of western societies. In the latter case, the relatively unformed, protean energies of a protesting youth were not channelled in a transformative manner. For neither

the weak civil society nor the discredited parties could play such a constructive, channelling role. (Mouzelis 2009: 44)

Yet, the 2008 Greek uprising and mass rioting, which was initiated by students, had new generations of radicals claiming it as *their polytechnio*. From another perspective, it was read as a highly mobile and globalized student event, 'a mobile Tiananmen' (Gavriilides 2009). Metaphors of events in which students are perceived to be the protagonists, as *deviants* and/or *defiant carriers* of the spirit of revolt and change, are very much part of the symbolic and street wars in the current landscape. Symbolic uses of metaphors of past, present and future were connected to the sense of youthful revolts: 'We are an image of the future' was one of the celebrated graffito on a wall during the 2008 demonstrations. Claiming the specific iconic moment of resistance is very much part of the 'wars of memory' (Fleischer 2003), which is being replayed in contested metanarratives about *what* happened, and *how* and *why* it happened.

Before we claim anything more substantive, we turn to our five examples: Greece, Egypt, Spain, South Africa and India. The economic meltdown of 2008–09 was a creator of new hardships. But such hardships were experienced in unique ways in different spatial and institutional arrangements.

A vital element is the spaces in and through which the ferment originated. Take the Greek case: the inner-city district of Athens, Exarcheia, which is the area around the Polytechnic University deeply enmeshed in the legacy of history as the Greek manifestation of 1968. Various groups of the 'alternative scene', remnants of old radicals, 'urban guerrilla' and anarchist groups are located there, rooting their existence to the spatialized memory as a historic place for revolt.

As Arampatzi pointed out:

Serving as a spatial reference of activism historically and an 'incubator' of political identities, Exarcheia holds a prominent role in the post-war collective imaginary of resistance and representations of social movements-from the Greek civil war battles between the government and the left-wing guerrillas, to the Polytechnio school occupation and the popular uprising against the military junta in 1973. (Arampatzi 2017: 50)

She shows how this area is a very 'global' in spite of its' 'localized' historical references':

The residential character of the area, combined with small-scale retail, the presence of university schools, publishing houses, intellectuals, artists, students and cultural hubs have contributed over the years to the development of an 'alternative milieu' in the area. The historical convergence of social movements in Athens city centre areas, the cultivation of a disobedient alternative culture and the key geographical location of Exarcheia rendered this area a privileged site for activism to flourish. (Ibid.)

This was a far cry from the areas around the University of Cairo, the American University of Cairo and, let us say, the more ancient and theological Al-Azhar University in Cairo. The former, numbering over 2,00,000 students, accommodates only 15,000 in its hostels; the others and the majority of the students are non-locals who are spread in the broader Giza area of the alleys and closer settlements where the majority of their peers are unemployed, semi-employed or casually employed. Used to overcrowded lecture halls and communities, they occupy urban spaces with attitude. It is the Caro of Naguib Mahfouz's *Harafish* with the bazaars and informality. It is working-class Cairo, the difference with Al Adjad's periphery is the thicker concentration of mosques and *madrassa*s, the heart of the Muslim Brotherhood and a growing politics of frugal religiosity. At more than 70,000 pounds a year, the American University of Cairo harbours a more elite cohort, perched on the extreme west of the city, where away from the Nile river it meets the desert's frontier. Whereas the former is thickly embedded in Arabic writing, TV and imagery, the latter is more connected with an Anglo world of 'modernity' and 'modernization'. The worlds of 1968 are to be found in the latter; the toehold of that other generation is scarce elsewhere.

Bayat (2013: 587) highlights that although the uprisings came at a surprising time, they were not inevitable. The Middle East has been ruled for decades by authoritarian regimes. Egypt in particular has a long history of anti-government protests, yet none of those protests had any large-scale impact on the regime structure or the state's political direction. Since the 1960s, the survival of the Egyptian regime relied on providing massive subsidies and public sector employment in exchange for political silencing and minimal public participation. Such socialist socio-economic policies provided employment opportunities in the public sector, which reduced unemployment in countries that had a relatively small working-age population at the time. Moreover, Onn Winckler highlights that the above-described social contract between the Egyptian regime and the people rested on, first, subsidizing basic needs like food and energy products. Second, the authoritarian regime established a large bureaucratic system that provided social services, including healthcare and education. The aim of this bureaucratic system is to expand the regime's control through making the public reliant on the regime's services. Third, to further expand the regime's control and make the public more reliant on its continuity, the regime set up a large number of public sector facilities, companies and factories that provided job opportunities. Lastly, using the conflict with Israel as a justification at that time, the regime expanded the army security services which safeguarded the regime and maintained its stability (Winckler 2017). Yet, those conditions that existed decades ago to maintain the regime's stability had shifted dramatically.

The 2011 events came to question the effectiveness of the 'social contract' highlighted by Winckler. Mahienour El-Massry argues that 'over the years, the lack of political space, and the inclusion of public space in formal politics, resulted in an apolitical environment in Egyptian society. People preached the idea of revolution but no one thought that it would actually happen during their lifetime' (El-Massry and Acconcia 2018). In other words, although it helped to maintain the authoritarian regimes for over thirty years, yet closure of political space was one of the main motivations behind the 2011 uprisings. Police brutality, corruption, lack of accountability, among other manifestations of a rigged system, define the concept of 'closure of political space'.

Traditionally, public resistance to the above conditions remained within the 'practice of public nagging', as Asef Bayat (2013: 588) called it. He further elaborated that when walking around Egypt's crowded streets and public spaces, one can hear the public complaining and blaming the government for the increasing prices, power cuts, police brutality, lack of quality services and even the traffic jams. Although it served a crucial element in formulating and influencing public opinion, yet practising 'public nagging' seem to be a silent feature of the public culture of the Middle East, which for long served as an alternative to a larger organized sociopolitical movement.

In other words, since the 1980s, sociopolitical movements remained active in limited spaces, student movements were forced to remain on university campuses, Islamist groups like the Muslim Brotherhood focused on community work and underground organizing, labour unions launched strikes but not on a level that would challenge the regime's foundation or affect factories and companies owned by the army. Thus, since none of those groups could enforce tangible or real change, the public resorted to non-movement and engaged in 'public nagging'. That was true up until the 2011 uprisings.

Space, tradition and ideomorphic ideas were and are different at JNU in Delhi. It is a green island in the midst of southern Delhi surrounded by shacks, urban villages and malls, and a bustle of traffic and congestion. Although facilities are poor and the hostels (where 90 per cent of the students live) are spartan to the n-th degree, the university provides a highly politicized space. Similarly, most academics, support staff and workers also reside within the campus, creating a vibrant conglomeration. Although there is a hostel segregation between male and female students, the interactions between the sexes go unabated in all its nooks and crannies. Since its inception in 1974, JNU selects a few thousand postgraduate students from the entire country and from across the caste and class system. They were seen by Indira Gandhi, former prime minister of India, as the necessary backbone of creating a national cohort of civil servants and professionals. It prided itself on academic freedom and political pluralism but it has been the home of a student left. The Congress-aligned National Students' Union of India (NSUI) and the saffron-linked Akhil Bharatiya Vidyarthi Parishad (ABVP) are thwarted by the other big three: the Students Federation of India (SFI) – the student wing of the Communist Party of India (Marxist) (CPI[M]), the All India Students' Federation (AISF) of the Communist Party of India (CPI), and increasingly, the All India Students' Association (AISA) of the Communist Party of India (Marxist–Leninist) Liberation (CPI-ML[L]), which since the 1990s has been to the left of all and has been winning most university elections since 2006. The growing Dalit movement has also emerged as a force. The mural wars and the performative arts of the various movements have no parallel in any other university.

The University of Cape Town, by contrast to all, rests on the lower mountainside of Devil's Peak, a site 'donated' to it by Cecil John Rhodes which overlooks the sprawling southern suburbs and their apartheid zoning. It is located as an island in white suburbia and occupied a place of pride in a liberal anti-apartheid discourse of inclusion, whilst modelling itself on the best of British traditions of excellence. Nothing prepared it for the post-apartheid entry of a growing Black student population. The new whispers about 'decolonization' or 'the decolonial' had started in earnest in 2011. The murmurings were clear: something had to be done about the curriculum's, and indeed the system's, Eurocentrism. This was accentuated by US-trained Black academics who had experienced the overlay between race and its manifold tensions in their studies. Although such feelings received a polite nod, student Chumani Maxwele was not so polite: in 2015, he decorated Cecil John Rhodes with bucketloads of shit. The rest, as we all say, was history.

In other words, each institution, despite outward similarities, was informed by a different energy and different tropes of defiance. But by 2008–09, the world was spinning out of joint.

Greece was the first to experience ferment. In December 2008, the assassination of a 15-year-old pupil by the riot police in Exarcheia would lead to the eruption of one of the most violent outbursts of mass protests. Thousands of high school pupils and post-school students all over Greece would take to the streets. Students were at the heart of this eruption and in multiple ways perceived their 'future' as blocked: politics and protest become a daily affair. Since 2008, Greece has seen numerous violent eruptions: May 2010, June 2011, February 2012, with Marfin Bank, Syntagma Square and the generalized implosion of the metropolis.

Anastasakis wrote about 'the general mood of frustration and dissatisfaction' and 'alienation from the political establishment, scepticism towards reform (of the pension system, higher education, employment policies, agricultural sector etc.), and disdain towards instances of political corruption' (Anastasakis 2009: 6). This is what feeds the regularity of public demonstrations and the violence attached to them. However, he speaks of the violence demonstrations, and particularly in Athens, in terms of 'a parallel network of "professional rioters" appear on the scene and test their ability to cause havoc'.

Nonetheless, the messages conveyed and the articulations were always relational and contextual. It is no surprise that the mass participation of students in the 2008 events evoked the famous student uprising against military rule in November 1973. It puzzles some scholars that despite interesting similarities, 1973 was opposing a dictatorship whereas 2008 was an uprising against a democratic state (Kalyvas 2010: 356). What these concerns fail to appreciate is the extent of the legitimacy crisis and the crisis of representative democracy, particularly in Greece, especially amongst the younger generations.

Even if pre-existing social and political organizations are participating in the ad hoc movements each time, in each momentum, they seem to carry the burden of producing the meaning of insurrection. They cannot play any significant role apart from being part of the heterogeneous yet combative multitude; movements are organized horizontally and the quest of any avant-garde is futile. Movements are born in such conjunctures and are generated by the momentum of social, economic, political and cultural processes; how lasting they are depends on different factors, including organizational reasons, ability to adapt and strategy, etc., but the duration of each momentum and of its outcomes is quite uncertain. No guarantee can be provided by any kind of mechanism for long-lasting movements and forms of resistance; ephemerality seems to be the rule for the new-born collective subjects and their endeavours (Trimikliniotis, Parsanoglou and Tsianos 2015).

As such, the 2008 events were romanticized as a living continuation of the left resistance in the long history of struggles against capitalism, authoritarianism and the bourgeois state. But those who saw the 2008 events with unease, if not hostility, also drew from the past to explain what they saw as incomplete modernization (read Europeanization) of Greek institutions and citizens, an interpretation that necessarily underplays the social and economic causes of the riots.

Andreas Kalyvas points out that contrary to the deficient civil society argument, the 2008 demonstrators, and particularly the students, were the effect of the complete opposite, i.e. 'a highly politicized and mobilized informal and dissident civil society' (Kalyvas 2010: 362). A stronger reading goes even further, as the alleged social pathologies of the events are strongly objected to. The first error we must avoid when trying to make sense of the riots that shook Greece in December 2008 is to explain them away as an 'emotional outburst of the youth' or as 'blind violence with no political content'.

The economies of Greece and Spain were teetering for some time, not thrifty enough according to the European troika made up of the European Commission (EC), the European Central Bank (ECB) and the International Monetary Fund (IMF); they had to be buckled to balance the books of Germany's and France's banks. Already their expansion of educational access and opportunities did coincide with a radical constriction of jobs. In Greece, the youths were restless – half were taken in by the talk that somehow migrants were to blame for their economic problems, so many joined right-wing currents centring around Golden Dawn. But not all did so as many abhorred the corrupted state and its 'fatcats', and found easy access to anarchist groups and lore; others were responding to anti-globalization movements and the extremity of intoxicants and petty crimes. The police were pressed in turn to keep the streets clear of protesters lest they frightened off the one successful money route: tourism. The youth, scholar and student insurgence coincided with the meltdown.

The opposite was the case in Egypt. Up to the crunch the economy's GDP growth was rapid. The quasi-pharaonic power blocs around the Mubarak regime played up to capital the way the president played up to the United States. Large injections of aid were converted to serious accumulation schemes that created casual and impermanent jobs. But like Greece, the increase in educational access did not improve life's chances for young people. In Cairo alone, there were 300,000 tertiary students from the elite American University of Cairo to technical and religious colleges. Many post-school graduates were in vulnerable jobs and on a short fuse once the regime responded in a self-serving way when the meltdown happened. Pressures on costs of study and wage freezes followed, and in tandem they broke the camel's back. Tahrir Square was preceded by strikes and student protests since 2009. The Arab Spring followed.

How the Spring was portrayed in social media and how it was expressed during those heady months of 2011 fired the imagination of youths everywhere. Youths in Madrid, Barcelona and Valencia were the first to respond through a variety of movements from Youth Without Future to the resolute Indignados before finally launching a really vibrant movement: Podemos. The propensity to strike or protest in Spain was the highest in Europe. The structural adjustment cuts on public expenditure, on benefits and on institutional funding were declared untenable. The more they articulated disquiet, the more government tightened up policies and laws. In the latter case, the peculiar 'gagging' laws and the fines imposed led to one of the most ingenuous responses: the march of tens of thousands of computer-generated hologram-people outside the parliament, chanting, sloganeering and carrying provocative banners.

Neither India nor South Africa was outside the media loops publicizing the Arab Spring. The 2010–11 Arab Uprisings in North Africa and the Middle East shook the region and had a worldwide impact. The Egyptian uprisings, for example, toppled an authoritarian regime that had for decades been ruling without a visible alternative on the horizon. Similarly, the Spanish 15-M Movement grew in mid-2011 to pose a real challenge to the political and economic system in the country and inspire similar movements beyond Spain's own borders.

The 2011 events were unprecedented, surprising and life-changing for many Middle Easterners and North Africans; even think-tanks and intelligence services of the most advanced states in the world such as the US could not foresee the enormous waves of demonstrations taking over the streets and public spaces in those countries, at least not at the time it happened (Bayat 2013: 587).

Unemployment, poverty and poor service delivery and precarity were the main driving forces behind the 2011 protests. This was evident in many ways including in the slogans, amongst which was the famous revolutionary chants at Tahrir Square of '*Aish, Huriya, Adala Ejtimaie'a*', which translates to 'Bread, Freedom, Social Justice'. Thanassis Cambanis argued in his article in the *Boston Globe* that 'the Arab Spring was a revolution of the hungry' (Cambanis 2015). Similar to Winckler's argument presented earlier, Cambanis too highlighted that one of the main pillars behind the decades-long survival of the Egyptian regime was its ability to control sustenance.

Holding up bread at demonstrations not only sent a powerful message to the government, but also encouraged many people who could relate to the demonstrators' demands and goals to join them. In other words, bread was not only used as a demand, but also as a motivational tool and mobilization instrument. As the uprisings developed, activists learnt how to use different tools and tactics in order to attract and mobilize larger crowds, as well as to share information and enhance and strengthen their positions.

Amongst the most praised instruments that significantly influenced the 2011 uprising's path was creative and clever use of the internet and social media. Access to the internet in general had many benefits. One of its most important contributions was that it became a new tool to resist and raise awareness on an international level through presenting a different reality that opposed and challenged that which was traditionally presented by typical news coverage or, more so, by government-sponsored propaganda agencies (Sarabia 2015).

Similarly, social media gave the protesters a direct line to bypass traditional media platforms and reach a wider audience, to the extent that even large news agencies such as *Al Jazeera* and other independent and international media houses resorted to social media as a communication and reporting means when the Egyptian authorities tried to block their accessibility to cover protests on the ground. Moreover, Asef Bayat highlights that the poor socio-economic and political conditions encouraged the younger generation to get 'involved in civic activism and voluntary work on a scale seen never before. When social media became available for them, the young began to connect, with some getting involved in mobilizing protest actions' (Bayat 2013: 589).

The Egyptian protesters occupied Tahrir Square amongst other public spaces and set up tents and camps for weeks. Some of those tents were turned into mobile clinics to treat the wounded protesters who resisted police attempts to assault and disperse the demonstrators. The 'camel event' on 2 February 2011 was one of the most famous events where such clinics were critically vital and important. On that day, police informants alongside convicted criminals, who had been recently released for the purpose of terrorizing the demonstrators, tried to break into Tahrir Square riding camels and horses. Ten people were killed that day and many others were injured. The 'camel event' taught the protesters how to immediately and quickly share tasks without much time to strategize. Such lessons were significant and useful at later stages at other demonstrations, such as the one organized at Mohamed Mahmoud Street and a demonstration outside the parliament, as well as on the day protesters demonstrated outside the Maspero television building (*The New Arab* 2017).

The Spanish 15-M movement, also referred to as the Anti-Austerity or the *Indignados* movement, was at the heart of the demonstrations that spread across Spain in May 2011 to protest the ways in which the Spanish government was handling the devastating financial crisis that followed the recession of 2008. The protests focused on issues of corruption, private banks' influence over the government's policies, and the unwillingness – and inability – of the political system to represent and respond to the people's needs (Oikonomakis and Roos 2016: 231). Dissatisfaction with the ruling system motivated the public to rally behind the slogan, 'We are not goods in the hands of bankers and politicians', to support the Democracia Real YA (DRY), an independent and decentralized citizen platform that called what became the largest protests in Spain since the start of the financial crisis in 2007–08; close to 150,000 people took to the streets to protest and raise their voices (ibid.). Thus, what 'started [as a] small, inarticulate and youth-centred movement has transformed itself into what some [Spainadors] call the most interesting political development since the death of Franco in 1975' (Beas 2011). And, even if all this had its darker and populist side, as Booth and Baert (2018) assert, its significance in defining defiance cannot be underplayed.

Multiple groups tried to organize demonstrations and strikes since the recession to protest the government's policies. Yet such attempts failed to even change the government's discourse or plans to deal with the financial crisis. However, inspired by the Arab uprisings and the ways in which social media was employed by protesters in North Africa and the Middle East, a number of activists established the online group Democracia Real YA to function as a platform for activists to network, mobilize and organize demonstrations across Spain.

Similar to Tahrir Square in Egypt, Puerta del Sol Square in Madrid became a central space for the Spanish uprising. Tents were set up and occupation of public spaces went on for weeks. Public spaces were used to conduct public general assemblies, where direct democracy was practised. Moreover, Sylvaine Bulle highlights that 'camps and people's assemblies bring together people who are excluded from public space or are victims of the State crises (those without documents, the evicted, citizens of the peripheries, the elderly or the poor, but the middle classes, too)' (Bulle 2012: 4).

Although not by using the same methods but similar to the Egyptian regime, the Spanish authorities tried to stop the demonstrations. For example, on 20 May, a Spanish court outlawed the demonstrations just two days before the national elections. However, such attempts did not stop demonstrators from going on; the idea behind the protests in the first place was to challenge and disrupt the system. Therefore, despite being banned from protest by the Spanish Supreme Court, 'illegal' rallies and demonstrations went on for weeks. In addition, the protesters 'illegally' avoided security and accessed Channel 7 of Murcia to broadcast a manifesto against media manipulation. Continuous 'illegal' actions resulted in clashes between riot police and protesters on 27 May, when over 120 people were injured. In the following month, some protesters blockaded the Catalan Parliament in Barcelona using dumpsters; a number of policemen as well as citizens were injured in clashes that followed the protest. On another occasion, some protesters snuck into the Congress of Deputies to meet the prime minister and present a document titled the 'Book of the People' where the protesters' demands were listed (Global Nonviolent Action Database 2011).

In conclusion, both the Arab and Spanish uprisings provide examples of the effectiveness of public protests and collective action. The two uprisings succeeded not only to shake the economic and political system in their respective countries, but also had a major regional impact. The two had different political histories: Egypt has traditionally been ruled by authoritarian regimes while Spain has been practising democracy for a few decades. Yet, the people in both countries had similar motivations to protest; they both took to the streets aiming to address inequality and injustice, and to change the sociopolitical and economic dynamics in their societies. To do so, they had to resort to new and creative methodologies, mainly the use of the internet and social media as a means of mobilization and an information-sharing platform, as well as to coordinate and build networks and international solidarity campaigns. In addition, one of the highlights of the two uprisings was the creative ways in which public spaces were exploited in order to make political statements. Yet, despite meeting some short-term demands through the massive efforts and sacrifices made by many activists and young people, some analysts argue that the uprisings failed to bring about change, or even have long-term sociopolitical and economic effects.

South Africa's trajectory was different: the student population doubled since the 1994 democratic transition. The rapid entry of Black students into tertiary life had to reach deep into Black working-class households. Although slower in the hitherto white and privileged – and mostly English-speaking – universities, the trend was irreversible. The funding of this increase was propelled through loans that were to be repaid after graduation. The rapid increase and under-preparedness through a struggling basic education system increased the years of study and indebtedness. At the same time, the universities were moving towards corporatization and new forms of managerialism with an emphasis on market-related rewards and opportunities. What did not help was the slow process of institutional transformation to a genuine non-racialism with a new post-apartheid curriculum. The 2008–09 crisis was dealt with decisively by government, business and labour working together to both inject money for recovery and investing in infrastructure keeping labour forces intact. But what has not been explicit is how the government shortened labourers' working hours and, by implication, halved their income – this had a direct effect on Black working-class households whose children were in tertiary education. That Fees Must Fall became a rallying cry for the predominantly Black student movement was obvious; what preceded it though was a Black student rebellion against colonial heritage: Rhodes Must Fall. In short, the ferment demanded not only that Cecil John Rhodes must fall but all Cecil John clones must fall and all Black servants of their enduring power must also fall so that a free, socialist and 'decolonial' system may emerge.

But as the movement in South Africa was entering times of self-doubt, in India students found themselves in the forefront of fighting against the authoritarian turn in India's politics. Here, JNU was marked out as the symbol of such resistance and it was its very perfidy itself that had to be annulled. A moral panic that an institution is cultivating hubris or a mega-deviance is not new. It starts usually with a mobilization identifying perfidies – real, partly real or constructed – and it opens up the space for thousands of actors and moral entrepreneurs to have a field day, add invective, use their 'experience' and insight about the folk devil's, or *shaitan*'s, pelt and wares. Such a panic was being amplified about JNU, about its teachers and its students. For the middle class that supports the ruling Bharatiya Janata Party's (BJP) strategy, JNU was anyway an anachronism in the new knowledge economy and a throwback to the days of isolation and poverty – education had to move on and learn how to be an instrument of corporate success. For other strata of Indian society, this site of perfidy and anti-nationalism had to be smashed and to be shown to be smashed.

Yet, in India, there was another dynamic: the Congress-led government in 2008–09, riding on explosive growth levels, increased social spending and doubled public servant's emoluments, cranking up aggregate demand. It even, in alliance with the left, initiated a rural employment guarantee scheme, tried to dynamize the unregulated sector and facilitate microfinance, and started exploring extensive healthcare reforms. However, it could not forestall the rise of the BJP and its quasi-fascist cells located in the Rashtriya Swayamsevak Sangh (RSS), a right-wing Hindu nationalist paramilitary volunteer organization – the combination of a saffron fundamentalism and buttressing big capital (the Gujarat model), which under Narendra Modi's leadership became decisive. The BJP had had a trial run a decade before but this time around it was much more decisive: it was to intervene and shape all levels of public administration from governance to education. In the latter case, it was to see itself taking control of universities, changing the curriculum and crowding out the Congress and the left. JNU and especially its movements gave it the perfect opportunity to create moral panic around the university. By 2016, the confrontation was unavoidable.

It was on the evening of 9 February 2016 that a few students of JNU decided to hold a protest event. The event was against the capital punishment of Afzal Guru and Maqbool Bhat; both were Kashmiri separatists and had received capital punishment from the Indian state. The event, entitled 'A country without a post office – against the judicial killings of Afzal Guru and Maqbool Bhat', was a cultural gathering of poetry, art and music. It was organized by members of the Democratic Students Alliance (DSU), one of the many left student organizations in JNU. The organizers made all the preparations for the event including seeking permission from the university administration, putting up posters around the campus, and getting the venue and equipment ready. The initial conflict occurred when students of the ABVP, which is a student wing of a far-right Hindu nationalist party and has its affiliation with the RSS, started protesting against the event and approached the university administration to cancel the permission for the event. The JNU student movement began when Kanhaiya Kumar, president of the student union, was arrested on 11 February 2017 – an event that triggered the spontaneous protest of the students. The protest was also sparked by the fact the newly appointed Vice Chancellor of the university allowed the police to enter the campus and arrest Kanhaiya. This was a crucial moment not only for the JNU movement but for student protests across the country in the recent past. Kanhaiya's arrest, however, had an elaborate context.

The students did not lose time in connecting what was going on at JNU with what was going on in other university settings, like at Hyderabad Central University (HCU). The broad-based student protest in HCU began as a spontaneous reaction to an unfortunate event. During January 2017, five students from the Ambedkar Student Association (ASA) were expelled from hostels in relation to their alleged involvement in ransacking the hostel room of an AVBP activist. The first spark of the movement was when these five students started sleeping in the open, protesting their expulsion. It drew support from other organizations; still, it was not yet the movement that it would grow to become. On 16 January 2017, Rohith Vemula, one of the five students, committed suicide.

In JNU, students rallied behind their student union and the union, in turn, led from the front; thus, the JNU student movement was more organized than the Joint Action Committee-led HCU movement. As a student union, it had existed as a legitimate platform for long, while the Joint Action Committee's inception was with the movement and drew legitimacy depending on the success and failure of the movement. In fact, the JNU student union consciously adopted the Joint Action Committee's approach by calling for an 'all organizations' meeting and regularly gathering opinions from other organizations and individual students. Kanhaiya Kumar, upon being released, emphasized the spontaneity in this movement as a positive element: 'JNU has shown the way. JNU stands unshakeable today to state what is right is right and what is wrong is wrong. The best thing about this protest is that it is spontaneous. I am stressing this aspect because everything on *their* part was planned' (Kumar 2016).

In contrast to this unity, Aditya Nigam (2016) has analysed the possibility of unity from the perspective of the protesters. In his view, the entry of students coming from lower caste, Dalit and other marginalized sections of the society has added a diversity to higher education that goes against the ethos of Hindu nationalism. With these two forces finally clashing, a space has opened up to have a dialogue among Dalit politics, old left groups and the women's movement.

The current generation is more attuned to derogations and identity politics of all kinds. Whereas this in India might take a blue and red form (Dalit and left), in South Africa it might take a Black first yet intersectional approach to other sources of inequality; in Greece and Spain it would be more about an enormous US and THEM, against borders and privilege, a mix between the politics of difference and spirituality. And even if vague about what kind of 'other' world might be possible, they all know what they do not appreciate or need. None of their discourses is exactly the same but student activists feel that there is a 'family resemblance' between what they are about. Already, these recent eruptions have become the new mythemes for the future as most of the people involved have graduated, moved on or dropped out but the cultural formations within institutions preserve, enhance and embellish them.

The 2010s were not a continuum of the spirit of 1968 nor were they a 'communism in movement' although many felt they very well might have been; they lacked coherent ideological frameworks, but on closer scrutiny so did most of the movements of the 1960s and the 1910s and 20s. The twenty-first century student movements are technology-savvy and have used the horizontal possibilities of the e-world to the full. Would it be fair to see all their energy as a mere extension of the spirit of 1968 even if many of them invoke it? Will it be fair to see them as an upsurge of communism on the move, as Badiou invited us to do? Would it be cogent to call them 'refolutionary'?

They did not alter the dominant relations of power, and they would have graduated or dropped out by the time many of the changes they would have incubated actually bore fruit. What is important to note are the sociological elements of our analysis: students will always exist in a hyper-habitus which has its own compressed and transitory time scales and forms of restlessness. They will always carry an effervescence, sometimes religious, sometimes spiritual. They will carry past histories, role models and narratives full of mythemes. Within that habitus, anticipatory forms of consciousness emerge, about alternatives to class, national, gender, caste and any forms of oppression.

All social movements bring with them new normative ideas and orientations. The imagined community is one of the 'have-nots' of the hashtag age. They are all convinced that there is the corrupt 1 per cent of business and state, and all those the corrupt have corrupted – and even in India among the leaders of the movement, the BJP is seen not only as a servant of big capital, but as an authoritarian and fundamentalist force. In South Africa, race overlays the notion of the 1 per cent of wealth, and so does colonialism and its enduring differentiations. In India, it has the language of caste and class overlaying visions. In the words of a student leader of Fees Must Fall, Shaeera Kalla:

> The Fees Must Fall Movement is a mass student led movement. This is the first time, post democracy that students were united across political divides and it showed the world that the power of a mobilized youth can shake the core of an unjust system. Student representatives are abused within university structures and this is why we made the decision to shut down the university, to symbolically show our frustration at the system that systematically excludes the poor. (Furlong 2016)

Students do believe that they have been, or are, a catalytic force. Sometimes they are, often they are not. Their impermanence in an institution makes the work of sustained upsurges against a status quo improbable. But the compressed time of their presence in an institution creates what we have termed a hyper-habitus which facilitates defiant ideas and a restlessness to achieve them. Fusako Shigenobu's generation dreamt of a world revolution and of reform of learning institutions; many too dreamt of a more robust status quo and Asef Bayat exaggerates the revolutionary consciousness of prior generations. Students are more of seismograph than the tectonic shift itself – and in Cairo and Madrid, in Johannesburg and Delhi, they have been registering the hardships of their broader generation in these crisis-ridden times.

In Greece, they were part of the groundswell against austerity which, despite the rhetoric of resistance against the fiscal dictatorship of Brussels, led to more austerity and hardship and a swing to the conservative centre. In Egypt, the metaphoric pharaonic dynasty was toppled but the social change and its contours has run away from their defiant dreams. A new social contract has been renegotiated between the powers that be and the 'people'. University-linked issues are being negotiated. In Spain, the rising populism from below has met the mainline socialists and some amelioration is being renegotiated. In South Africa, free university tuition has been achieved but beyond that there seems to be a return to market-friendly priorities, whilst in India, university life is being transformed away from secularism and academic freedom.

Notes

[1] Baudelaire's film, *The Anabasis of May and Fusako Shigenobu,* is an art documentary that tries to capture the relationship between mother and daughter. The daughter has published two books (2002, 2003) about their lives, but alas, I have not been able to access them yet. All of Fusako's books have not been translated yet, but there are samples of her poetry here and there on the internet.

[2] 'Festival of the Oppressed: France 1968: Special Issue', *New Left Review*, vol. 1, no. 52, November–December 1968.

[3] *Café Dissensus* is a critical and vibrant journal for contemporary debates.

[4] See the fascinating study of the seventeenth century in England by Hills, *The World Turned Upside Down.*

[5] All theories of modernization converge on this point from Eisenstadt (1966). See also, Tipps (1973); Knöbl (2003); Delanty *et al.*, eds (2003); and Munck (2018).

[6] See Sitas *et al.* (2014).

[7] See also Soares (2002); Desreciewicz (2014).

[8] Of course, Pierre Bourdieu's work on the French Academy has been illustrative of these patterns of power and elite/class formation: see *Reproduction in Education, Society and Culture,* London: Sage ([1979] 1990) and his *Homo Academicus,* London: Polity Press ([1984] 1990). See also C. Wright Mills's work on elite formation, the middle class and the academy: *The Power Elite; White Collar;* and *The Sociological Imagination.*

[9] During the heyday of the anti-apartheid struggle, many universities in South Africa decided to transform their mandates of 'relevance', with the University of Western Cape trying to make

itself a people's university with a clear anti-establishment agenda. See Gregory Anderson's *Building a People's University in South Africa*.

[10] See Harry Braverman, *Labor and Monopoly Capital*; also see Michael Burawoy, 'A Classic of Its Time'.

[11] The author spends a significant time discussing the tensions between the 'professorate', the state and the students. Such a discussion would take us away from the main thrust of the argument we are trying to develop.

[12] Speech marking the sixtieth birthday of Stalin. 'Stalin, Friend of the Chinese Police', *Marxists*, 20 December 1939, available at https://www.marxists.org/reference/archive/mao/selected-works/volume-2/mswv2_24.htm, accessed 20 December 2021.

[13] 'Quotations: The Cultural Revolution', *Alpha History*, available at https://alphahistory.com/chineserevolution/quotations-cultural-revolution, accessed 20 December 2021.

[14] 'Mao's Letter to the Red Guards at Qinghau (1966)', *Alpha History*, available at https://alphahistory.com/chineserevolution/quotations-cultural-revolution, accessed 20 December 2021.

[15] Ibid.

[16] Ibid.

[17] 'Smash the Old World! How the "Red Guards' Battle Song" was Born', *Morning Sun*, available at http://www.morningsun.org/smash/cr_3_1968.html, accessed 20 December 2021.

[18] Ibid.

[19] Ibid.

[20] 'Mao Denigration Driven by Political Motives', *Global Times*, 22 December 2013, available at https://www.globaltimes.cn/content/833595.shtml, accessed 20 December 2021.

[21] The failure and the reaction that it invoked comes out very evocatively in an account by Johari commenting on the Naxalite movement, 1972, for which he has only contempt. However, he lambasts the Nehruvian state for increasing marginalization of the rural population.

[22] Rabindra Ray (2011) has in-depth insights to offer on this dimension of 'action'.

[23] I have compiled the data from appendices as included in Singhvi, ed. (1972).

[24] See 'China: The Case against the "Capitalist Roaders"'; and Chan, 'The Image of a "Capitalist Roader"'.

[25] https://en.wikipedia.org/wiki/Mario_Savio, accessed 10 May 2022.

[26] There is also a very vivid novel by Olivier Rolin, *Paper Tiger*, which can complement the atmosphere of the times.

[27] 'Bob Dylan 2016 Nobel Lecture in Literature, recorded 4 June 2017, Los Angeles', *YouTube*, 5 June 2017, available at https://www.youtube.com/watch?v=3Zf04vnVPfM, accessed 20 December 2021; 'Nobel laureate Bob Dylan: uneasy "voice of a generation"', *Inquirer.net*, 14 October 2016, accessed 20 December 2020.

9

Tristes Tropiques

Arts in Defiance

Ari Sitas

Suzanne Roussi Cesaire was a real discovery in our attempt to work on her husband Aime Cesaire's (2002) adaptation of *The Tempest*. The Insurrection Ensemble's poets scoured the anti-colonial text but found its drama forced and its storms muted, quite inadequate for the political ferment in South Africa and India that commanded Cecil John Rhodes to fall and mourned Hindutva's rise.[1]

By contrast, some of Suzanne's essays on colonialism and Black aesthetics in the journal *Tristes Tropiques*, published between 1941 and 1943 in Martinique (S.R. Cesaire 2012), and her lost play *Aurora de la Liberté*[2] seemed to be more of a defiant inspiration than Aime Cesaire's *A Tempest*. The temptation of starting a narrative on scripts of defiance from her work was

Fig. 9.1 Cover of Suzanne Roussi Césaire, *Le grand camouflage: Écrits de dissidence (1941–1945)*, first edition, Seuil, 1946.[3]

enticing, but the Martinique of 1941 harboured a walk and a passage of remarkably greater proportions.

The Walk by the Absalon Baths

The tropical rainforest hugging the therapeutic baths provided the setting for an afternoon amble between spirits that were only beginning to find how kindred they were. Aime, Suzanne and their friend Rene Menil led Andre Breton, Jacqueline Lamba (Breton's artist wife, and for a short while also Frida Kahlo's lover), the painter Andre Masson and (this is unclear) the communist writer Anna Seghers, and, most importantly, the Cuban-born painter Wifredo Lam. The proponents of Negritude, surrealism, Afro-cubism, realism (social and socialist), anarchism and communism spent time talking about art and politics in a remarkable setting – all fleeing from Nazi-invaded and Vichy-governed France.

At first, on arrival in Martinique, Andre Breton found a copy of Cesaire's *Return to My Native Land* (1969) at a haberdasher's in Fort-de-France. The long poem was published in 1938 in Paris, but it was a publication that saw the light of day at the wrong time there – as the war sirens began to sound. It was, and is, a spectacular text. Breton was convinced that it was 'nothing less than the greatest lyrical monument of our times' (Breton 2008: 90). Cesaire was back from Paris and teaching in what he later described as a drab classroom, which included students like Frantz Fanon and Edouard Glissant.[4] He defied the curriculum to talk during his classes about the sources of defiance, about Arthur Rimbaud's poetry and about rebellion. After one reading of the poem, Breton, the arch-surrealist, decided that he needed to meet the Black poet of the century for whom surrealism felt like second nature.

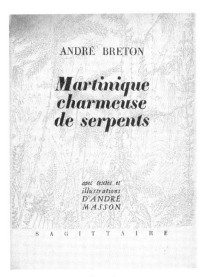

ANDRÉ BRETON

Martinique charmeuse de serpents

avec textes et illustrations D'ANDRÉ MASSON

SAGITTAIRE

FIG. 9.2 Cover of Andre Breton, *Martinique: Charmeuse de Serpents*, designed by Andre Masson, first edition, Paris: Sagittaire, 1948. © Editions di Sagittaire, Paris.

He did. And so, they walked. Breton was trying to get to Mexico or to the USA; he in fact had spent time in Mexico City in 1938 co-penning the *Universal Manifesto for the Freedom of Arts and Culture* with Leon Trotsky, although Diego Rivera agreed to appear as its co-author as the Trotsky brand would have been divisive in the international politics of the day. Breton was to write a celebrated new introduction to Cesaire's masterpiece. He was to also co-pen a text directly linked to his stay there, *Martinique: Charmeuse des Serpents* (Breton 2008).

Andre Masson, who co-wrote part of it and provided some of the most intense lines in the *Snake Charmer*, drew a range of images that defined the manuscript's aura. He was a celebrated and Nazi-listed surrealist. He was trying to reach the USA but was arrested again and again; finally, US customs officials found the drawings he carried with him too pornographic and destroyed them on site.

FIG. 9.3 Andre Masson, *En la tome de sueno*, 1938.
© 2022 Artists Rights Society (ARS), New York /ADAGP, Paris

Masson was to also become an exemplary art lecturer and tutor there; Jackson Pollock was one of his proteges (Poling 2008).

The rainforest and landscape around it extruded some of Breton's finest lines. In the prose-poem 'Antille', for example, we find more than just a description: rather, an exaltation of the heart of redness in the tropical green:

disembowelled earth's arborescent fur, fan of desire, surge of sap, yes, a wheel of heavy leaves in fruity air. Ask the sensitive mimosa tree it will answer no but in the heart of the vaginal shade, red reigns, carnal flower of the canna, blood congealed in its flashy flower. Spermatic lava nourished you, grinding common glass as a fiery hand made it shimmer with living mother-of-pearl. (Ibid.: 41)

FIG. 9.4 Cover of Anna Segher, *Transit*, 1948, design by Curt Georg Becker. © U. Barthelmeß-Weller

Anna Seghers was marked out as a 'degenerate Jewish writer'[5] and, as an active communist, she had already written a novel (Seghers [1944] 2013) about German concentration camps (which would win her the Buchner Prize in 1947). She eventually found her way to Mexico City where she formed the Heinrich Heine Club as an anti-fascist initiative. Her novel *Transit* captured the ordeals of flight, internment and settlement – a kind of autobiography if you please.[6]

Her main character there is Seidler, a man on the run from Nazi Germany, who takes on the identity of another – Weidel, a dead writer, whose character seems as close to a Walter Benjamin as was possible before his suicide. The pseudo-Weidel discovers how hard it is to get to Marseilles, and once there, how hard it is to get a visa alongside all the other desperate people trying to flee the civilizational collapse. Segher's Caribbean stay was to inspire three novels that dealt with betrayal, failure and revolutionary inertia, a thinly veiled allegory for the Stalinist era in the German Democratic Republic (GDR).

Finally, the Cuban Wifredo Lam, Picasso's 'soulmate'. Of Chinese and Afro-Cuban descent, he was already searching for an African language for his cubism, and found the rainforests and Aime and Suzanne Cesaire's friendship a lifelong resource for his art. Fresh from physical combat in the Civil War in Spain, Lam was to make it to the USA, bamboozle audiences in New York with his 'jungle' and his perceived 'primitivism', according to him all inspired by the walk and Cuba's fate.[7]

THE PASSAGE

What carried them across the Atlantic was the last ship from Marseilles to the Americas via Martinique. The ship also carried Claude Levi-Strauss and the legendary Victor Serge. To understand the misery and the fortune this entailed, there is the nuanced work of Eric Jennings (2002) which explores the last exit and the despair attached in the context of France's collapse to Nazi power. What awaited them there after an arduous time of trying to get trans-shipped, travelling in appalling conditions (apart from Levi-Strauss who had a cabin), was to be interned in a lazaretto (a leper's camp turned into a concentration camp) until one by one they were either allowed to move on or stay. To their good fortune, no one was sent back.[8]

We owe stark imagery of the passage to Levi-Strauss and Victor Serge. The by-then famous anthropologist noted that 'although we were all considered "scum"' he did receive better treatment: he was not allowed to be 'quartered like a cow or pig'. He had a cabin unlike 'all other passengers, men, women and children', who 'had to pile into the dark and airless hold, where the ship's carpenters had made a rough scaffolding of beds, one on top of the another, with pallets of straw for bedding' (Levi-Strauss 2012: 26).[9] By the time they reached the tropics, the situation turned 'horrid', so everyone overcrowded the deck.

For Serge, whose recently circulated diaries focused primarily on his life and thoughts in his Mexican exile, the imagery of the 'castaways of Europe on a wrecked ship' was profound (Serge 2013). He crafted the ship as a metonymic Paris with its Champs-Elysees, its Left Bank, its Montparnasse, its Belleville and, in defiance, towards the bow, a place they would come to call Rosa-Luxemburg-Platz, where children were being looked after. Champs-Elysees was between the central deck and the boiler room, where the well-heeled and wealthy migrants including Levi-Strauss were gathered. They were in the main Jews with money and therefore allocated cabins, and stayed aloof, suspicious of everyone (ibid.).

Figure 9.5 Group portrait of European refugees saved by the
Emergency Rescue Committee on board the *Paul-Lemerle*, a
converted cargo ship sailing from Marseilles to Martinique, 1941.
Among those pictured are: Victor Serge, Jacqueline Lamba Breton,
Midi Branton, Mrs Lam, Wifredo Lam, Katrin Kirschmann, Dyno
Lowenstein, Harry Branton, Carola Osner, Walter Barth (in the
background holding a child), Ate Barth, Karl Osner (carrying his
daughter on his shoulder), Emmy Orsech-Bloch, Erika Giepen,
Margret Osner, Karl Langerhans and Hubert Giepen.
© United States Holocaust Memorial Museum Provenance: Dyno Lowenstein.

The Left Bank was the foredeck of the ship, 'slightly more crowded by film-
makers and well-dressed people' behaving as if lounging on a café's terrace.
Montparnasse was the upper deck, 'cluttered with the lifeboats . . . occupied
by the Lams, the Bretons . . . [where] Jacqueline [Breton] sunbathed almost
naked and scorned the world which couldn't care less, and that irked her' (ibid.).
Throughout the passage, Breton, whom he thought poorly of, was pacing there,
restless and inconsolable.

Serge continued: 'Hélène Lam nursed Wifredo, who was ill, with swollen
glands, sad, lying under a blanket, his head in his wife's lap. His eyes like those
of an ancient Sino-African child were full of an animal misery. Even though he
was getting better.' Breton, constantly looking noble and seemingly impassive,
often repeating, 'bastards' under his breath, got a bad press in the diary as a
vacuous artist and a pompous man (ibid.).

Levi-Strauss recalled too that 'Breton was like a blue bear in a velvety jacket,
still concerned about aesthetic beauty and originality' (Levi-Strauss 2012: 27).[10]
Breton for his part recalled how in 'its very fixedness the ship's carcass offers us
no respite from the frustration of being able to move only in slowly measured
paces, in the space between bayonets' (ibid.: 85).

And then there were the proletarian quarters where Serge learnt from Rene

Schickele's daughter about Walter Benjamin's suicide, where there was 'a sort of cowshed on one side, and on the other, the vile shared toilets made of plywood, erected on the deck. Rigging, tools, hordes of kids, washing, bare-chested characters shaving, ladies lying on their deckchairs in the sun' (Serge 2013).

The *Paul Lemerle* ploughed on against the waves in a liminal space between the death camps left behind and the great unknown. In the end, once that speck in the distance received a nod as Martinique, little did they know that, again in the words of Levi-Strauss, the ship was to be remembered as an Eden in comparison to the humiliations that awaited on an island which was a hundred per cent Nazified. Fascism awaited them with its military as if in 'cerebral derangement' (Levi-Strauss 2012: 29) and their abuse: 'humanity was breeding such situations as a sick body breeds pus' (ibid.: 30).

ACUITIES OF THE VERDANT TROPIC

So, there was Martinique: Levi-Strauss was not taken by Fort de France, 'a dead town', he declared, as there was no life in 'the hovel-bordered main square which was planted with palm trees and overrun with rampant weeds, a patch of dead ground' (ibid.). He was outraged by colonial arrogance after observing a case in the local court: 'I was stupefied that a human life could be disposed of so quickly and with such nonchalance. . . . Even today no dream, however fantastic or grotesque, can leave me so entirely incredulous' (ibid.: 34). His discomfort with the dead town was balanced with a sense of the 'exotic': he was taken in by nature, where he came to experience

> . . . a form of exoticism more classical than that found on the mainland of South America: dark tree-agate surrounded by a halo of beaches where the black sand was speckled with silver; valleys deep in a milk-white mist where a continual drip-drip allowed one to hear, rather than see, the enormous, soft and feathery leafage of the tree-ferns as it foamed up from the living fossils of the trunks. (Ibid.: 35)

This was a fascinating contrast to the way Masson's eye scouted the rainforest and Wifredo Lam's awareness absorbed colonial plantations and indigenous foliage in his subsequent work.

Due to Cesaire's, Fanon's and Glissant's fame, Fort-de-France can be redrafted as a hovel-strewn town with Black lives perched against the flats of its administrative centre and its harbour smells, and its wealthy hillside residents of Didier where the melanin hue faded and evaporated into whiteness. Where sixteen-year-olds like Fanon and Glissant studied hard, played hard, hung around in gangs, chased after a football, walked with cigarette in hand on the black sand speckled with silver, cut tree-ferns to shape them into spears, and listened to that 'lizard' of a teacher Aime Cesaire in his green-checked suit, who stood on a chair to orate the defiant strains of 'degenerate' poetry.[11]

Andre Breton, Andre Masson and Wifredo Lam were transfixed by nature and learnt through the Cesaires the meanings of colonialism. Masson's poetic response was highlighted above; here is Breton's:

> Abyss of Absalon – I am here! If the light is the least bit veiled, all the sky's water pierces its canopy, from a rigging of vertigo, water continually shakes itself, turning its tall green-copper organ pipes . . . where, not a minute ago, dance steps spun, taught by two butterflies of pure blood . . . the fern whose mouth is a wheel of time. My eye is the closed violet at the centre of the ellipsis, at the tip of its tail. (Breton 2008: 59)

Here, 'nature in its profusion, shames visual artists' (ibid.: 43). Yet, it enthuses poets:

> . . . we are one with these layered trees, bearing in the elbows of their branches miniature swamps with parasitic vegetation grafted to their supporting trunk: rising, falling back down, active, passive, festooned from top to bottom with *pseudomorphosis* dreams, these impeccable lianas! These branches, what bows drawn for the arrows of our thoughts. (Ibid.: 50)

For the arch-surrealists, the canna flower prefigured all sensations:

> Let us symbolically raise up the canna blossom flowing with blood from the lowest to the highest forms, a chalice brimming with this marvellous ooze. May the canna be emblematic of the reconciliation we are seeking between the obtainable and the wild beyond, between life and dream-wee shall pass through a whole gateway of cannas to continue advancing in the only worthy way: through the flames. (Ibid.: 52)

And for Breton, this floral exuberance lay at the heart of Aime Cesaire's poetry: 'the huge enigmatic canna flower with its triple heart gasping on the tip of a lance' is part of a tropical landscape that amasses form and poetic images 'until they are strong enough to shake the world' (ibid.: 88).

Suzanne Cesaire's writing in *Tristes Tropiques* was very much under the censor's eye in an increasingly Nazi-leaning Martinique. The few essays gathered in *The Grand Camouflage* were mostly consequent to the walk in the rainforest. For her, surrealism should be celebrated because it harboured an affinity of effort: its 'most urgent task', according to her, 'was to free the mind from the shackles of absurd logic and Western reason' (S.R. Cesaire 2012: 35). She confessed admiration for Andre Breton's poetry, especially his 'Mad Love' poem, but for her, the wondrousness of the tropical forest and mountains – the swoons, blues, golds and pinks – were hammock literature: 'far from rhymes, laments, sea breezes, parrots. . . . And to hell with hibiscus, frangipani and bougainvillea. . . . Come on now, real poetry lies elsewhere. . . . Martinican poetry will be cannibal or it will not be' (ibid.: 26–27).

She railed against Breton's and Masson's celebration of nature and what they articulated as '*pseudomorphosis*' (ibid.: 31), and added that 'we have too soon forgotten the slave ships and the sufferings of our slave forebears. Here forgetfulness is tantamount to cowardice' (ibid.: 29).

> Poetry (like Music), helps us move beyond ourselves, and . . . goes further, it leads us into a 'new time', into a new world. The true and real poem, which shows us the human terror, in despair, and in horror even, must pull us out of these hells and lead us to mysterious beaches of consolation. (Ibid.: 14)

It is there, on those coastlines, that a 'liberated, dazzling, and pleasing image of beauty' will be found that is at the same time precisely the most unexpected, the most upsetting of sensations (ibid.: 17). There, 'colonial idiocies will be purified' not by the luminescence of a canna flower but by the scars left and the work of reconstruction 'by the welding arc's blue flame' (ibid.: 38).

In *The Grand Camouflage* essay, Suzanne Cesaire burns through the thicket: 'if my Antilles are so beautiful, it is because the game of hide-and-seek has succeeded, it is then because, on that day, the weather is most certainly too blindingly bright and beautiful to see clearly therein' (ibid.: 46). And here is her incendiary and defiant rub:

> . . . the heliconia shrubs and flowers of Absalon Forest bleed over the chasms, and the beauty of the tropical landscape goes to the heads of the poets passing by. Across the swaying latticed networks of the palms they can see the Antillean conflagration rolling across the Caribbean that is a tranquil sea of lavas. Here life lights up in a vegetal fire. Here, on the hot lands that keep alive geological species, the fixed plant, passion and blood, in its primitive architecture, the disquieting ringing suddenly issue from the chaotic backs of dancers, here the tropical vines rocking vertiginously, take on ethereal poses to charm the precipices, with their trembling fingertips they latch onto the ungraspable flurry rising all through the drum-filled nights. Here the poets feel their heads capsize, and inhaling the fresh smell of the ravines, they take possession of the wreath of the islands, they listen to the sound of the water surrounding the islands, and they see tropical flames kindled no longer in the heliconia, the gerberas, in the hibiscus, in the bougainvilleas, in the flame trees, but instead in the hungers, and in the fears, in the hatreds, in the ferocity, that burn in the hollows of the mountain. (Ibid.: 45)

Martinique then: the site for a creative genius like Levi-Strauss to start penning his critique of notions of European superiority,[12] whose book that revolutionized anthropology took its name from the Cesaires' journal, *Tristes Tropiques*. Behind them a Europe in ruins, ahead the unknown and the Brazilian rainforests through which he was to declare the equality of the entire human species. There, the thinkers around whom the Negritude movement was to flourish, the communists and socialists, the socialist realists and futurists of the 'welding arc', the subliminal and associational connections of surrealism's craft, the angular cubisms of the new modernism, an international of the imagination!

<h2 style="text-align:center">DEPARTURES</h2>

Levi-Strauss did not like Serge:

> . . . the fact that he had been an associate of Lenin was all the more intimidating, because it was difficult to reconcile it with his looks, which were those of a maiden lady of high principles. The smooth and delicate features, piping voice, and stilted, hesitant manner added up to up to the almost asexual character that I was later to encounter among Buddhist monks of the frontier of Burma. (Levi-Strauss 2012: 26)

Serge, as mentioned above, did not like Levi-Strauss either. He was to pip Anna Seghers by a year in completing his requiem to Paris and the misfortunes of flight and escape. His novel *The Long Dusk* was published in 1946. Paris left an indelible and resilient set of images. In the novel's pages, the death of Paris and Serge's anxieties around receiving a visa in Marseilles are sites of a new type of mourning: it was 'as a city of the dead, [of] bereaved house-fronts pierced by windows that were hideous black rectangles with a glacial wind blowing through them. The Seine reflected nothing, as though there were no more sky. A music of fifes and drums blew in gusts over the murdered city' (Serge 2013: 56).

After Martinique and Guadaloupe, Wifredo Lam and Victor Serge boarded a ship to Cuba. Unlike Levi-Strauss, Breton and Masson, they were not welcome in the United States. Serge was to move on to Mexico, Lam was to remain home for a while longer. He had to absorb what had happened to him on that island; his senses did absorb the landscape, its sense, and tropical and excessive and violent beauty. There was already in his very being the visual language of cubism and the struggles for a republican Spain. There was his Sino-African heritage and the deep memory of the sugar plantation and slavery. He understood *The Grand Camouflage*. There was the voice of *Tristes Tropiques* and the presence of the Cesaires and the Menils. And there was the poem, 'Return to My Native Land'. For him surrealism, like cubism, was a contrary and defiant technique for re-becoming African. The poem facilitated an existential 'incendence' into what was deemed by colonialism and expanding fascism as the 'backward', the very African that lurked in his being-in-the-world. His aesthetic acuity was formed, *The Jungle* was to be the transformation's first announcement.[13]

But there we have it, by Absalon Baths: anti-colonialism, anti-capitalism, anti-fascism and a multiplicity of aesthetic forms of expression defined in Nazi Germany as 'decadent art'. Here we have to repeat, an international of the imagination.

Exactly six years before, in Paris, the much-celebrated First International Congress of Writers for the Defence of Culture was held. It brought together all anti-fascist literary sentiment – from Andre Gide to E.M. Forster, from Boris Pasternak to Bertolt Brecht – a plethora of vital writers.[14]

FIG. 9.6 International Congress for the Defence of Culture, Maison du Mutualite, Paris. Photo by Gisele Freund, http://www.gisele-freund.com/, courtesy Dr Ruiter.[15]

If we are to take Walter Benjamin seriously, Paris was the cultural capital of the known world: a city of barricades, boulevards, bohemian life and artistic movements. In exile there from a regime that classified him as degenerate and a university system that scorned him, with a small stipend from his friends of the Frankfurt School led by Max Horkheimer and Theodor Adorno. Crouched there in the College of Sociology, he brought the Paris of his *Arcades Project* into the spotlight.[16] For him, the line from Baudelaire and Rimbaud to Breton and the surrealists was clear. His attempt to flee via Spain after the torment and ruin he expected of the invading Nazi power led to his suicide. Unlike Anna Seghers and Andre Breton, he did not make it.

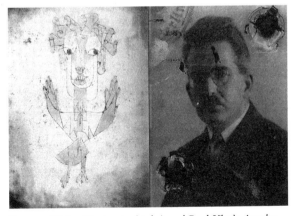

FIG. 9.7 Walter Benjamin (right) and Paul Klee's *Angelus Novus*, 1920 (left). © 2022 ARS, New York.

Benjamin's Paris was defined by its revolutionary currents: 1789, 1830, 1848 and 1872, and how the city itself became an inspiration for art.[17] There are the arcades, there is its street life, there is the bohemian *flaneur* walking the streets and the new moralities that come with that. There are also glimpses of the aura of its cityness and its 'myth' (following Luis Aragon) that were vital, but also what he begins to pick up in the little marginal notes – the 'convolutedness' of the *Arcades*, the aura. Also, how it was the refuge space for many: Marx too was there in 1844 writing his philosophical manuscripts, admiring Balzac. 'The nineteenth century – to borrow the Surrealists' terms – is the set of noises that invades our dream, and which we interpret on awaking' (Buck-Morss 1989: 831). It is sheer modernism that at the same time poses as a permanent antique: 'even the automobile', mused Apollinaire, 'has an air of antiquity here' (ibid.: 82).

We have to also read Paris alongside Pierre Bourdieu's and David Harvey's more sociological accounts. I will only deal with the former because he deals with the aesthetic field and the structuration of art, even though Harvey writes extensively through the eyes of Balzac and Daumier. Bourdieu's account of the emergence of the aesthetic sphere, the artistic forms of life and how they interacted with the social milieu and its class structures, was a challenging intervention. The Paris of the *flaneur* and the bohemian, of Flaubert and the self-displaced creative bourgeois, the patronage of salons and publishers, the competing fields of expression and movements, come to life in a grittier way. He provides the sense of context that explicates the rise of a multiplicity of aesthetic canons, from realism to surrealism, Dadaism to futurism, cubism, impressionism and expressionism.

So, if we follow Bourdieu seriously, for example in his *The Rules of Art: Genesis and Structure of the Literary Field*, he wants to understand Gustav Flaubert so that he may develop a science of the aesthetic sphere. He forces us back to those times in France and, by implication, Europe, where the struggle for independence, where the virtues of the resistance and the revolt against multiple authorities,

Fig. 9.8 Pablo Picasso, *Guernica*, 1937.
© 2022 Estate of Pablo Picasso/ ARS, New York.

led artists and writers to assert themselves clearly in the face of repression, and argue not only for the freedom of expression but about the autonomy of the aesthetic field as such. The right for pure art to express itself, the artist to express himself/herself in any way she deemed fit because art was a special autonomous field, it had its own generative grammar.

Bourdieu's account explicates both symbolic power and symbolic violence. He shows how artists distinguish themselves in relation to money and the market, and yet are orchestrated by publishers who valorize the importance of the book. The market with its successful artists is not enough because its binary opposition is equally entrenched: pure art as art for art itself and not for money sacralizes prestige.

At the same time, it creates multiple lifestyles: the world of salons, where artists meet with power and where privilege is bestowed and rituals of consecration launch games of inclusion and exclusion. Here, a 'proletaroid intelligensia' was and is truly in action – as people who have to live with the poor but have to take on the airs of the cultural critic and take pennies from newspapers to write about art and define this school as important and as the carrier of the new – that reinforces the autonomies of the fields and also the bohemian lifestyles that go with them. 'Bohemia inspires,' according to Bourdieu,

> ambivalent feelings even among its most passionate defenders. In the first place because it defies specification, it's near to the people with whom it often shares misery. It is separated from them by the art of living that defines it socially, in which even if ostentatiously opposed to the conventions and proprieties of the bourgeoisie it is situated nearer to the aristocracy. (Bourdieu 1992: 56)

Within that context, a certain cultural formation exists in the relations between the sexes and within the sexes, where in experiments on a large scale, all forms of transgression are being talked about and permitted, as bohemian lifestyles do. And free love, pure love and eroticism – all these things are active in the nineteenth century.

> For this is known as true for the most destitute members, who stroll in their cultural capital and their authority borne of being taste makers succeeding, providing themselves that he is the cost, with audacities of dress, *their* fantasies, mercenary love and refined measure for all of which the bourgeoisie pay dearly. (Ibid.: 57)

So, in other words, being an artist becomes a life form that is being exported as the way to be. And artists despise, increasingly, the public and the bourgeois. Flaubert thought of the bourgeois as everybody who was involved in the mundane – from the clerk to the bank teller to the rich people to people who were not worried about money – this bourgeois world – and at the same time the public, the vulgar, the this, the that . . . you know, those kind of roles and distinctions. For Bourdieu, it is this Paris that excites him to show how it's got its own dynamics in the various fields it operates in.

Benjamin's and Bourdieu's Paris feel different. Yet, what we can glean from both of them is a city where aesthetic constellations proliferate and matter, where Baudelaire provides both the poetry and the ethos of a *flaneur* to its n-th degree: venal, grimy, in the streets, an irritant to the bourgeois. The way he carries on with his life, the way he writes, the way he attacks religion, resonates. He is there in your face and for art for art's sake. Yet, even he cannot extricate his lines from the lure of the exotic, even if these lines were for his lover, a Black actress and music-hall singer, the epitome of the low and unexalted in the arts of Paris:

FIG. 9.9 Frontispiece of Charles Baudelaire, *Fleur de Mal* (1861), 1917 edition, Paris: Librairie des Amateurs.

> even when she walks she seems to dance, the garments writhe and glisten like long snakes . . . obedient to the rhythms . . . by which a far cry wakens them to grace. . . . Precious minerals from her polished thighs, in a strange symbolic nature, where angels . . . unite where diamond gold and steel dissolve into the light, we see the puppet's sheer majesty . . . (Baudelaire 1998: 33)

Baudelaire's poetry was a rejection of the past, an intense modernity and an intense celebration of the 'cityness' of Paris. But you had to move to Arthur Rimbaud to understand what really moved Cesaire. You sense in Rimbaud's words a total rejection of the west. Not only was he on the barricades of the Paris Commune, but in 'A Season in Hell' and 'The Drunken Boat' he dramatizes his farewell to Europe. Indeed, he packed up his bags and went to Ethiopia where he sold guns to Emperor Menelek. By the turn of the century, Paris was flooded by movements and their manifestos: the cubists, the Dadaists, the surrealists, the futurists, the realists, movement after movement declaring their 'ultra' modernity.

FIG. 9.10 Portrait of Arthur Rimbaud, 1872. Photo by Étienne Carjat.

Bourdieu does not only etch out the trajectory for the development of an autonomous plane for the proliferation of art, but also provides a sociology for the construction of regimes of aesthetic judgement. He asks stridently in *The Rules of Art*:

> What makes a work of art a work of art and not a mundane thing or a simple utensil? What makes an artist an artist, as opposed to a craftsman or a Sunday painter? What makes a urinal or a bottle rack that is exhibited in the museum into a work of art? (Bourdieu 1992: 290)

In his powerful assessment in *Distinction: A Social Critique of the Judgement of Taste*, 'the "eye" is seen as a product of history reproduced by education'. By implication, 'the "pure gaze" is a historical invention linked to the emergence of an autonomous field of artistic production, that is, a field capable of imposing its own norms on both the production and consumption of its products'(Bourdieu 1979: 3). In other words, instead of aesthetic taste, Bourdieu identifies a form of symbolic violence. He argues that 'distinction', that is, the power of a class, a class fraction or an aesthetic elite to differentiate itself from others, depends on the historical cultivation of 'cultural competencies': groups come to possess 'dispositions' and through them 'programmes of perception' that allow them to pass judgements of taste. It also allows them to classify themselves as cultured, distance themselves from necessity or from the vulgar and, through that, colonize behaviour and feeling.

Pierre Bourdieu's castigation of aesthetic gatekeepers, the people of the 'pure gaze', and his attempt in his *The Rules of Art* to insist that 'scientific analysis of the social conditions of the work of art . . . intensifies the literary experience' (Bourdieu 1992: xix), is a serious gesture towards such a sociology – but he shares with Adorno a vision of a working class and popular culture that is colonized: 'it must never be forgotten that the working-class "aesthetic" is a dominated "aesthetic" which is constantly obliged to define itself in terms of the dominant aesthetics' (ibid.: 41). For the dominant, the working class exists as a 'foil' whose sole 'function' in the 'system of aesthetic positions is to serve as foil, a negative-reference point, in relation to which all aesthetics define themselves by successive negations' (ibid.: 57). Such a distance and socialization through what he terms the 'habitus' is deep: it creates a set of 'distinctive features, bearing, posture, presence, diction and pronunciation, manners and usages, without which, in these markers at least, all scholastic knowledge is worth little or nothing', and no schooling can teach these fully or 'define the essence of bourgeois distinction' (ibid.: 91).

Bourdieu relishes the drama this involves:

> The nature against which culture is here constructed is nothing other than what is 'popular', 'low', 'vulgar', 'common'. This means that anyone who wants to 'succeed in

life' must pay for his accession to everything that defines truly humane humans by a change of nature, a 'social promotion', a process of 'civilization' . . . a leap from nature to culture, from the animal to the human, but having internalized the class struggle, which is at the very heart of culture, he is condemned to shame, horror, even hatred of the old Adam, his language, his body and his tastes, and everything he was bound to, his roots, his family, his peers, sometimes even his mother tongue, from which he is now separated by a frontier more absolute than any taboo. (Ibid.: 251)

The alternative is to adjust

. . . their expectations to their chances, defining themselves as the established order defines them, reproducing in their verdict on themselves the verdict the economy pronounces on them, in a word, condemning themselves to what is in any case their lot, *ta heautou*, as Plato put it, consenting to be what they have to be, 'modest', 'humble' and 'obscure'. (Ibid.: 471)

Thus, the Paris of Flaubert, Baudelaire and Rimbaud becomes the aesthetic capital of the world. It becomes so because of the proliferation of avant-garde activity, its multiple and competing schools, its so-called metropolitan physiognomy. Layering on such proliferation the fascination with the manoeuvring agendas and manifestos of defiant groups, these aesthetic groups, playing off each other, with missionary zeal defined and redefined the modern. They hated each other. So, if the establishment of autonomous aesthetic fields was the first phase of the expressive revolution, the development of seemingly exclusive schools, with the banner of modernity hoisted high, was its second animus. Each movement created its own communities of practice and its internationals and each one was being celebrated or listened to beyond its borders.

What is missing in Benjamin's and Bour-dieu's accounts is that Paris was also an imperial capital, a perverse beacon for darker men and women who were supposed to be enthralled by its aura. It was also a racialized space – a space that was to produce Cesaire's *Discourse on Colonialism* and Fanon's *Black Skin, White Masks*. It was a Paris that was to constitute the sense of Black consciousness and anti-colonialism in Leopold Sedar Senghor and Cesaire; a Paris of contradictions with diverse influences such as Stalin's *National Question*, Charles Maurras's fascist evocations of land and soil, Herni Bergson's philosophy of being and time, Black student late-night discussions on the Harlem Renaissance and Georg Frobenius from literally the entire Francophone Afro-Caribbean and Arab worlds.

The rising sense of self-determination was in the air as already networks of Pan-African identity were multiplying after the first Congress in London in 1900; issues of race and racial oppression were also on the boil after the Universal Congress on Race that occurred in 1911. Indian spiritualism as an alternative to western materialism was magnified after the major exhibition of Bengali Renaissance artists like Gaganendranath Tagore and Abanindranath Tagore premiered in Paris in 1914; their relative was to win the Nobel Prize soon after. Simultaneously, in the 1910s, swathes of xenophobic and anti-foreigner feeling spread through Parisian social relations, and infected also the salons and the galleries (Green 2003; Cottington 1998). Moscow and St Petersburg featured heavily, before and after the Russian Revolution; the Harlem Renaissance found serious echoes through Claude McKay's sojourn in Paris after a year in Moscow in 1922–23. Aime Cesaire and Suzanne Roussi were in the midst of restlessness, ignored by Parisian elites, accepted by communists, barely tolerated in the streets, adored in Martinican, Caribbean and Senegalese networks. By 1924, Cesaire, Damas and

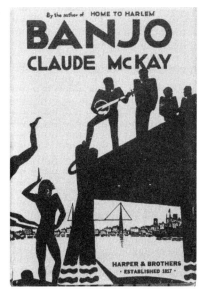

FIG. 9.11 Cover of Claude McKay's novel *Banjo*, first edition, Harper & Brothers, 1929; design by Aaron Douglas. © 2022 Heirs of Aaron Douglas; licensed by VAGA at Artists Rights Society (ARS), NY.

Senghor launched their first magazine, *The Black Student*. Revolutionary Black consciousness had arrived.

It is here, hardly a decade later, that the first texts of Negritude emerge: Jane Nardal, one of the founding members of *La Depeche Africaine*, put out by the Committee for the Defence of the Interests of the Black Race (which had a print run of more than 10,000 copies), published her essays 'Internationalisme Noir' and 'Pantins Exotique' (Exotic Puppets). Aime Cesaire's 'Return to My Native Land' carried the intensity of feeling generated in the city. His 'A Season in Hell' and 'The Drunken Boat', with their rejection of Europe, took Rimbaud's poetry to new levels of expression. Here, the derided backwardness of Africa was embraced, its pasts valorized, colonialism berated and the Caribbean painted with the most extreme forms of colour and pain. It was not just surrealism; it was a revolutionary expression of feeling, as Suzanne Roussi was to assert in 1943, in her essay 'Surrealism and Us'.

It is time now to weave some theoretical strands into the narrative by introducing four concepts that will allow us to get a deeper grip on the processes at hand. We shall see how important *aesthetic constellations* emerge and how they have to be understood in a translocal sense as the making of *internationals of the imagination*. These are linked to large-scale *movements* in society that create unique *aesthetic acuities* that allow for forms to travel and allow people deeply embedded in social spaces to innovate, belong and create new constellations. So, in short, the emergence of subaltern people and classes as collective historical agents have profound implications for aesthetic forms from their most public to their most hermetic manifestations. What emerges in this ferment is what we shall term as the *radical impulse*.

Firstly, it is the concept of an 'aesthetic constellation': it is loosely borrowed from Adorno's work and, if we were to believe him, from Walter Benjamin. The concept of *constellation* is about a diverse universe of concepts and elements that are held together with difficulty by an organizing principle – they include ideological bits, insights, inferences and the like – in our desperate philosophical attempt to bring the non-conceptual into the conceptual and discursive order. *Aesthetic* constellation is about the formal and unformed elements and bits that constitute an artist's universe of creativity which allow her to navigate her art or craft. An artist may be the confluence of many such constellations or a determined follower of one.

Perhaps an ensemble of us might be sitting in Johannesburg listening with total attention to a piece by Cecil Taylor and then one of us, let us say me for example, plays the church organ in the afternoon. Soon I find myself down at the watering hole where some of my friends gather with guitars and sing. Late at night, I might be settling down to earn my real bread by being a politician's speech-writer. I might be going through an intense period of compositional creativity that might bring together all the diversities of sound I encounter or none of them at all. No one ever sets out to create a bad piece of art; artists do what they can within a continuum of diverse impulses.

Here is where the concept *aesthetic acuity* fits in. The distinctions of 'high' and 'low' – the distinction between those who possess the ability to distinguish the 'pure' and the 'vulgar', the 'authentic' and the 'inauthentic', 'good art' and 'aesthetic excellence' and so on – are about the hierarchical structuring of society and not about 'aesthetic acuity'. Put differently, the construction of 'aesthetic dominants' and the 'canonization' of some works and not others is less about aesthetics as such and more about the monopolization of value by aesthetic status groups. This phenomenon is shared from London to Beijing.

'Aesthetic acuity' is the range of aesthetic, visceral and practical sensibilities that accrue in a person by virtue of his or her training, and by virtue of occupying a space in a particular or multiple aesthetic constellations, each of which is constituted by specific symbols/signifiers, grammar and history which influence her or his perceptive responses. For example, an Indian composer listening to Toumani Diabate's kora in Delhi is at the same time imagining the felt connections to local Bengali river music, to the major notes a variety of instruments produce, and perhaps to voices of poetry she once heard. If you are serious about your craft, you are quite open to the 'vulgar' as a poet or a musician. There is no innovation without it – so instead of cultivating class, caste and race bigotry at the gates of the profound, you listen, like, dislike, copy, enhance. The first point, then, is that all artists, writers, composers, photographers and so on have their senses open to multiple figurations – local, national and international. There are relative degrees of openness and closure to the symbolic.

What a poet thinks is wonderful through his or her own acuities, in and through the aesthetic constellations available in his or her visceral reality, is not and was not necessarily what gatekeepers thought was wonderful, and what both artists and aesthetic elites thought or think might be wonderful is not necessarily what power blocs in the state think is powerful or wonderful or what moves artists to create. The process of canonization is a complex one, with those who are 'elevated' finding themselves in school curricula and adorned with prizes by the state or by prestigious foundations. Adoration by aesthetic elites might be the way to a Nobel in literature but it might not be seen as worthy of canonization at all within national borders. For example, Aime Cesaire was only taken seriously by aesthetic elites in Paris *after* Andre Breton sang his praises and again, when Jean Paul Sartre declared, twenty years later, Negritude's verses as the only revolutionary oeuvre of his time. Even there, he was often dismissed alongside all other surrealists as being a victim of a passing fad. But his work was axiomatic for all emerging Black and anti-colonial creative people in Africa and the African diaspora.

The 'international of the imagination' is a concept first utilized in *The Ethic of Reconciliation* (Sitas 2008). It is more a consequence of art and how it has encultured publics and audiences about others – about the refusal of many artists to deal with the 'human abstract' in dealing with what I termed 'living rights' and in working on sensibilities. The 'radical impulse' is a concept Sumangala Damodaran used to understand how it was that a profound cultural movement emerged in India of writers, performers, dramatists and composers as a consequence of the emergence of crisscrossing people's and peasant and working-class movements against the Raj – a movement that was intensively national but infused by real and imagined internationalisms. They were a mixed bag of artists, art-first ones as much as struggle-first ones, belonging to different constellations with competing acuities, who were responding to social upheavals.

In other words, in introducing these concepts, a different path is proposed here through the aesthetic thicket. Part of the emergence of European self-reflection in matters of art is because a sense of a need to define a canon that is transnational and therefore universal is constantly at work. There is also a subcurrent which assumes, without an iota of hesitation, the coincidence between the western and the universal. Here, the sociological imagination too stops short and marks a retreat when asked to provide any insights on the works of the imagination. This is peculiar because the symbolic and the performative, the oral, the scripted and the digital, the narrative, the allegory and the parable are so central to people's everyday lives. And when it comes to comments on the creativity of the non-west, such an imagination becomes remarkably Eurocentric. We need to look no further than Max Weber's *The Rational and Social Foundations of Music* with its powerful discussion of the emergence of the orchestral, the symphonic and its compositional cultures: it is utterly disempowering because the Other's musicality is about a 'nonrational conglomeration of successive and random semitones', best left, one would assume, to ethnography and anthropology. There is a sense of disregard too in works of cultural and literary synthesis like Erich Auerbach's *Mimesis: The Representation of Reality in Western Literature* or Harold Bloom's *The Western Canon*. Exported to the peripheries, if that is ever the correct word, it can only become a study of mimicry and westernization – i.e. a study of artists who may or do have some presence, or pretend to have some presence, in the canon, versus the rest involved in multiple ethnoscapes.

The Frankfurt School did attempt to link sociology to the aesthetic from Theodor Adorno to Jurgen Habermas: their insistence on the creative fields' non-reductive autonomy and Adorno's insistence on understanding the work of art as art, be it music, poetry or the novel, has had some salience; so has Pierre Bourdieu's study and critique of 'taste' and its production, and his attempt to sociologically explicate the emergence of an 'autonomous field' of art and the literary. Yet, not even the Frankfurt School could escape the Eurocentric snare. The most notable of the school's aestheticians, Theodor Adorno, insisted that creative fields could not easily be reduced to social structure and social relations. Adorno in his passionate accounts of having to understanding the work of art as art, be it music (Berg), poetry (Celan) or drama (Beckett), railed against representation, realism, surrealism and jazz, and insisted on the contrariness and irreducibility of a work. For him, Rimbaud in his postulate 'of an art of the most advanced consciousness, an art with technical procedures . . . saturated with the most progressive and differentiated experiences' was a must (Adorno 1984: 33) – an art that rebels against the 'musty and the stagnant' (ibid.: 192), whose expression reveals the wounds of society (ibid.: 237) and brings with it a shudder (ibid.: 20) instead of a message was the only exemplary form. For him too, Andre Masson, in his emerge from the dream worlds of surrealism, found 'a non-representational balance between scandal and social reception' (ibid.: 229). But unlike poetry, fine art ran the serious danger of being 'entombed in the pantheon of cultural commodities, they themselves their truth content – are also damaged' (ibid.: 228–29). Adorno followed the exile path that led to commodification as such:

the culture industry and Los Angeles. He was to never escape the idea that the most progressive was to be redeemed in Europe, beyond Auschwitz. On his return to Paris in 1949, the absence of his friend Benjamin reduced him to tears.

Our concern is in essence about the relationship between changes in aesthetic work and societal change; furthermore, in how social movements and profound events during social upheavals transfigure the arts and how these processes are deeply entangled on a planetary scale. We could have started our story earlier in the entanglements that occurred during the foraging by a number of European powers since the sixteenth and seventeenth centuries to make a relational point. How, at the same point in time, you could have a piano-playing and composing emperor in China and an orchestra of eunuchs with white wigs performing inside the Forbidden City, as Ignatius Sancho (a freed slave) is composing music for the emerging bourgeoisie in England, as guitars are traded for ivory and slaves among the Lunda and the Ethiopian court. We could be looking at the arts and songs of slave rebellions and pirates' shanties in Madagascar, or at earth-shattering events of genocides, revolutions (the American, the French, the Haitian), and at emergent forms and scripts of defiance. We chose to start from Paris.

Aime Cesaire's *Cahier d'un retour au pays natal* (Notebook of a Return to the Native Land) is an exemplary script of defiance. The range of his voice cannot be understood without his sense that it had to reach out to an awakening people blackened by the history of slavery, the plantation and colonialism. For him, this forced diaspora with an umbilicus from the Caribbean to the African continent was finding its Black consciousness, its Negritude. It had to carry through the first Pan-African gathering of the 1900s, the first Universal Congress on Race in 1911, the awakening of alternatives embodied in the Harlem and Calcutta Renaissance, the Mexican and Proletarian Revolutions. Paris allowed for the confluence of these ideas but it is also a monument to colonial racism.

As a man for whom the word and language and their poetic possibilities defined his specific acuity, Cesaire was drawn to Alphonse de Lamartine and to the explosive symbolism of Arthur Rimbaud. But the need to explode the French language itself into a

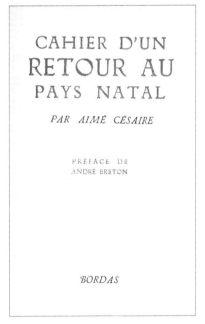

Fig. 9.12 Aime Cesaire, *Cahier d'un Retour au pays natal* (Notebook of a Return to the Native Land), Paris: Bordas, 1947.

magical neologism to capture what he deemed to be 'the inexpressible' nature, exploitation, culture, led him to surrealism. The radical, dreamlike juxtapositions of verbs and nouns, the shifting prepositions and the ritual rhythm of what he imagined an African and oral rhythmic would be created the aesthetic backdrop for the *Notebook* of his return.

Cesaire's *Notebook of a Return to My Native Land* was written in Paris and it is there that the urge to return, to accept his fate, to declare his crimes, to remember, to rediscover his Negritude but also to rediscover the great speech and song that would allow him to give form to his past, to the Black past and to the Caribbean, to declare the slave-ship splitting and himself and his people, upright now on their feet and sailing into the rendezvous of victory.

Surrealism provided the language to express the befuddling contrariness of the Black situation, colonialism, racism and the experience of exploitation. Its extravagant juxtapositions enthralled Cesaire: 'strangle me with your lasso of stars', 'eyelids like rose petals', 'convulsions of a rigid death' and so on – explosive couplets, extravagant claims, overloaded metaphors in one intense and panoramic view of genesis, fall and resurrection. Yet, the form is a means to speak to multitudes of rising people; the loudness and orality of the work, and its pace, are a ritual catharsis but also a call to arms, what he termed later an 'arsenal of the miraculous'.

Indeed, there are the islands: 'at the end of the small hours delicately sprouting handles for the market: West Indies, hungry hail-marked, with smallpox, blown to bits by alcohol, the West Indies shipwrecked in the mud of this bay, wickedly shipwrecked in the dust of this town' (A. Cesaire 1969: 37) And he continues:

> . . . at the end of the small hours: this town, flat, displayed, brought down by its common-sense, inert, breathless under its geometric burden of crosses, forever starting again, sullen to its fate, dumb, thwarted in every degree, incapable of growing as the sap of this earth would have it grow, set upon, gnawed, reduced, cheating its own fauna and flora/at the end of the small hours: this town, flat, displayed. [. . .] At the end of the small hours, this town, flat, displayed [. . .]/it crawls on its hands without the slightest wish ever to stand up and pierce the sky with its protest. (Ibid.: 37, 45)

So he was to leave Europe and return to Fort-de-France, the town, 'flat and displayed', to 'inscend' into the backwardness of colonial 'otherhood' so, 'as there are hyena men and panther men,/so I shall be a Jew man/a Kaffir man/a man-from-Harlem-who hasn't got-the-vote' (ibid.: 48). And as he left Europe he had to clutch to reveries and a restless and tortured memory:

> . . . how much blood there is in my memory. In my memory there are lagoons
> They are covered with death's heads. They are not

covered with water lilies,
in my memory are lagoons. On their banks no
women's loincloths are laid out
my memory is surrounded by blood. My memory
has its belt of corpses.
a volley of rum warmly lacing
our wretched revolts, sweet eyes swooning
drunk with a drink of ferocious liberty
(niggers-are-all-the-same, I tell you
they-have-every-vice-every-conceivable vice, I'm
telling you that/nigger-smell-makes-the-cane-grow
it's like the old saying:
beat-a-nigger-and-you feed-a-nigger)
among the rocking chairs
and my mind upon the voluptuous horse-whip
I go back and forth, an unappeased foal (Ibid.: 64)

In this restlessness he accepts it all, guilty as charged, his crimes:

I declare my crimes and say that there Is nothing to
say in my defence.
Dances. Idols. Relapses. I too have murdered
God with my idleness
my words my gestures my obscene songs
I have worn parrot feathers and
musk-cat skins
I have worn down the patience of missionaries
I have insulted the benefactors of humanity.
Defied Tyre. Defied Sydon.
Adored the Zambezi
The expanse of my perversity confounds me (Ibid.: 57)

Not only does he accept the 'crimes' ascribed to Blackness but also that his pasts could have even been inglorious:

I refuse to pass my swellings off for authentic glories.

And I laugh at my old childish imaginings.

No, we have never been amazons at the court of the King of Dahomey, nor princes of Ghana with eight hundred camels, nor doctors at Timbuctoo when Askia the Great was king, nor architects at Djenne, nor Madhis, nor warriors [. . .]

I wish to confess that we were always quite undistinguished dishwashers, small-time shoeshiners, at the most fairly conscientious witch-doctors, and the only record we hold is our staying-power in wrangling over trifles [. . .] (Ibid.: 66–67)

And the acceptance of it all becomes the way through which creativity and language dawns:

I want to rediscover the secret of great speech and of great burning. I want to say storm. I want to say river. I want to say tornado. I want to say leaf, I want to say tree. I want to be soaked by every rainfall, moistened by every dew. As frenetic blood rolls on the slow current of the eye, I want to roll words like maddened horses like new children like clotted milk like curfew like traces of a temple like precious stones buried deep enough to daunt all miners. (Ibid.: 49)

And alongside the rolling of words and their gallop, he wanted to also discover song to
sing of poisonous flowers
bursting in meadows of fury;
skies of love struck by clots of blood;
epileptic mornings; the white
burning of abysmal sands, the sinking of wrecked ships in the middle of nights rent by
the smell of wild beasts. (Ibid.: 60)

And through the power of the word and song to assert his Blackness and Negritude which at once is a deeply personal and collective experience:

my negritude is not a stone
nor deafness flung out against the clamour of the day
my negritude is not a white speck of dead water
or the dead eye of the earth/my negritude is neither tower
nor cathedral
it plunges into the red flesh of the soil
it plunges into the blazing flesh of the sky
my negritude riddles with holes
the dense affliction of its worthy patience. (Ibid.: 75)

Negritude would allow him to conjure up and gift the islands a powerful form:

You are here and I will not make my peace while the world is on your backs
islands that are scars upon the water
islands that are evidence of wounds
crumbled islands

formless islands
islands that are waste paper torn up and strewn upon the water
islands that are broken blades driven into the flaming sword of the sun
I cast you form
formless islands
on water obedient to the currents of my thirst
absurdly I cast your overthrow and my defiance
stubborn reason will not prevent me [. . .] (Ibid.: 82–83)

And so, to rise with a new-found consciousness:

upright now, my country and I, hair in the wind, my hand small in its enormous
fist and our strength not inside us but above in a voice that bores through the night
and its listeners like the sting of an apocalyptic wasp. And the voice declares that
for centuries Europe has stuffed us with lies and crammed us with plague,

for it is not true that:
the work of man is finished
we have nothing to do in the world
our job is to keep in step with the world
the work of man is only beginning
it remains for him to conquer
at the four corners of his fervour
every rigid prohibition
No race holds the monopoly of beauty, intelligence and strength
there is room for all in the meeting-place of conquest [. . .] (Ibid.: 84–85)

The last two lines should have been translated as beauty, wisdom and power and
that there was room for all in the rendezvous of victory, not conquest! That is how
I remembered it being recited in Black consciousness circles in Johannesburg.

Building towards the end, the rebellion reaches a climax through intense
repetition:

between the torn clouds a sign by lightning:
the slave-ship is splitting open [. . .]
Its belly in spasm ringing with noises
The cargo of this bastard suckling of the seas is gnawing at its bowels like an
    atrocious tapeworm
nothing can drown the threat of its growling intestines
in vain the joy of the sails filled out like a purse full of doubloons
in vain the tricks allowed by the fatal stupidity of the police frigates
in vain does the captain have the most troublesome

nigger hanged from the yard-arm or thrown
overboard
or fed to his mastiffs
In their spilt blood
the niggers smelling of fried onion
find the bitter taste of freedom
and they are on their feet the niggers
the sitting-down niggers
unexpectedly on their feet
on their feet in the hold
on their feet in the cabins
on their feet on deck
on their feet in the wind
on their feet beneath the sun
on their feet in blood
on their feet
and
free
[. . .] and the cleansed ship advances fearless upon the caving waters. (Ibid.: 88–89)

But Paris was the magnet for creative people from all over the world to come and live there somehow, even in the most squalid conditions in Montmartre and Montparnasse throughout the 1920s and 1930s. Whereas the spaces and the bohemian spaces there welcomed everyone, it did not mean that Paris as such and its status group were not xenophobic, as aforementioned. By the 1910s, restrictions in terms of publication and exhibition for foreigners were promulgated. And, as Diego Rivera, the larger-than-life Mexican artist in search of Picasso and cubism was to find out, the initial welcome turned into a distancing and rejection. This created his impulse to transform his cubist leanings through Mexican iconography and colour, and a deeper and deeper grasp of the meaning of revolution. He was to return to become a Mexican institution.

Diego Rivera and David Alfaro Siqueiros reunited in Paris. Siqueiros had already, following his mentor Dr Atl, drafted a manifesto, *Vida Americana*, in 1906, urging for a public and transformative art. Whereas during 1912–17, Rivera tried to paint as if he was a cubist, Siqueiros was more interested in Paul Cezanne's work. And as a loyal party member he embraced socialist realism. He returned to Mexico to join Rivera and Jose Clemente Orozco to decorate a multiplicity of walls with their epic murals.

Something peculiar was happening through the language of cubism: Russians like Kazimir Malevich would transmute his influences into suprematism and

FIG. 9.13 Diego Rivera, *Calla Lily Vendor El Vendedor de Alcatrace*, 1943. *Source*: diego-rivera-foundtion.org (Creative Commons licence).

FIG. 9.14 Kazimir Malevich, *Head of a Peasant Girl*, 1913, The Stedelike Museum, Amsterdam.

constructivism, taking to an extreme the geometrical and multi-perspectival tropes of the constellation which he would carry over into the stage-set design of Vsevolod Meyerhold's productions of Vladimir Mayakovsky's plays. At first he saw his art as an extension of cubo-futurism, turning the adulation of

FIG. 9.15 Gaganendranath Tagore, *Dwarkapuri*, 1925.

FIG. 9.16 Jacob Lawrence, from the *Migration Series*,
1940. © 2022 The Jacob and Gwendolyn Knight Lawrence
Foundation, Seattle, and the ARS, New York.

machines and geometry into a mystical art, as for example in his painting of
the head of a peasant girl.

On the other hand, Gaganendranath Tagore would pull it away from the
mechanical to reach an enhancement of the Indian visual landscape – as in the
painting titled *Dwarkapuri* – and the indigeneity he and his brother sought
through their works.

By contrast still, Jacob Lawrence would define his audacious art around
Harlem and the urban migrations of African Americans from the plantation
south to the industrial north as a dynamic Afro-cubism. Within a similar
family tree, Wifredo Lam would infuse his cubism with a remarkable dose of
Negritude, as in his painting *Zambesia, Zambesia*, 1950.

The walk in Martinique's rainforest signified a possibility that was not to be: the clouds of Nazi power and spreading fascism fashioned the possibility of an international of the imagination that was attuned to radical impulses and provided a range of possible affinities. There was indeed room for all in that rendezvous of history. What the symbolic violence involved in the aesthetic fields in Paris, and the doctrinal idea that there ought to be one appropriate aesthetic for communist culture, was suspended for a while.

At first, Paris was to be a shelter from the interwar storms. Between 1914 to 1939, it played a transformative role. It was no accident that it was to also host the 1935 encounter of all the world's writers who opposed fascism. Alas, the gathering was not without incident, with Andre Breton slapping Ilya Ehrenburg in public for calling surrealists 'pederasts'.

If defiance was a person, she would have had a torrid time in choosing an appropriate script in the early twentieth century, let us say from the 1910s to the 1930s. Discord with what was seen as the modern then led in two directions, a powerful binary: it could celebrate its productive powers, its clocks and technological precision, its rationality and its processes of rationalization, and rail against the fetters that kept its potential trapped in the hands of oligarchies of cash. It would celebrate any strain of anti-traditionalism but castigate the bourgeois. The past was a dead weight, all its solidities had to be vaporized into thin air.

Alternatively, it could celebrate the past and affirm it as that which capitalism, colonialism and imperialism had tried to cover up, and, therefore, search for and fly to and towards a past that would redeem the future. The search for the pre-capitalist and precolonial became a mobilizing trope. Either way, defiance would find plentiful imagery for her generative grammar.

For the majority world, whose ways were deemed traditional or non-modern, backward or underdeveloped, the attraction to head both ways at the same time created untold tensions in the scripts themselves. Aime Cesaire's *Return to My Native Land* tried to, with its Africanism nudging one way and his communism nudging towards the other. The tension was partly resolved by the focus on the chains of slavery and dispossession but leaving the past open and the future uncertain, as a 'rendezvous' of victory where no race held the monopoly of wisdom, beauty or power. At the same time, the authorial voice took on an ecumenical mantle for all oppressions, the Kaffir-man, the Jew-man and then the man of Harlem who did not have the vote. The search for a synthesis haunted most subsequent texts and gets repeated in his plays from Toussaint Louverture in Haiti to Patrice Lumumba in the Congo. *A Tempest* was his most obvious search for a resolution but neither Caliban nor Ariel move beyond the magical nor does the future appear as anything but a threat of insurrection, a distant drumming in the night.

In the industrial west, the binary was replayed in the early twentieth century as the battle between Frederick Taylor's clock time, scientific management and regimentation of work and leisure, which was celebrated as rationality itself – as the triumph of scientific conception and planning and work performance. Its contrary trope was Henri Bergson's philosophy of the *elan vital* of flows and processes and of a different conception of time/*duree*. Many of the protagonists of Negritude and surrealism had read Bergson in detail. In cruder terms, for a while, Taylor was for the Master and Bergson for the Slave.

If that was not enough, there was also – as the international gained traction and the proletarian tremors eventuated in the Russian Revolution – in imperialism's weakest link launching a Soviet world, another binary in the making: there was the Paris mode of competing schools with each one claiming an aesthetic truth for its own constellation, each one seeking its own canonization through the state, the salon or the market, which was emulated far and wide. Then there was the dialectically most appropriate truth, appropriate for the authentic popular. Such currents animated Paris, Moscow, Mexico City, New York, and, by the 1920s, Calcutta and Bombay. It was no accident therefore that Cesaire's voice was operating under different cadences in New York, Dakar or Moscow.

Vladimir Mayakovsky was to follow the one track of the aesthetic binary *in extremis*. Since his student days, he had struggled to express the hyper-scientific modern, a struggle that intensified after the revolution. He had followed suprematism, constructivism and futurism, and his voice was sheer iconoclasm against 'tradition'.

The apotheosis of science and technology, of progress and rational abstraction, was a serious response from areas that felt they had to look up to Paris as the centre of the artistic cosmos. The revolutionary challenge to Tsarist Russia and the social tremors that were to follow released, what Michael Stites termed, 'revolutionary utopias'. A land like Russia, whose modernizing institutions were tenuous, whose inequalities were vast, whose religious conservatism was immense, was witnessing an urban, proletarian insurrection. Through it, working people, craftsmen and artists, professionals and intellectuals learned that soviets might provide an answer to authoritarianism and generate a new society of fundamental freedoms. Fine artists like Malevich, in his defining piece titled 'From Cubism and Futurism to Suprematism', written in 1915, yearned for a society that would allow art to move beyond the 'interrelation of form and colour', and also beyond the 'aesthetic basis of beauty in composition', to arrive at a scientistic moment where art occurred on the 'basis of weight, speed, duration and movement' (Malevich 1915: 24). The obsession with geometry and mathematical form was to reach new heights with Malevich's disciple El Lissitzky, later part of Stalin's machinery of art production, in his famous *Proun* designs.

The motto of Malevich's students at UNOVIS (The Champions of the New Art) in Vitebsk was, 'if you want to study art, study cubism . . . if you don't want to be controlled by Nature start studying cubism' (ibid.: 2). The varied energies – and these were enormous in the post-revolutionary period from Malevich to Alexander Rodchenko, Lissitzky to Mayakovsky – linked a vision of the emancipation of the proletariat and the peasantry to art's capacity to become relevant to life through its own means. This Soviet moment was fascinating in its epic quality: the conviction that art could make a difference and that life could come to be defined by art. Through that a figure, or better a 'force elemental', like Mayakovsky – his passion, his unrequited loves, his hope that his resurrection would be enacted though science – speaks to us down the years. Poems like 'A Cloud in Trousers' and 'Pro Eto', the hyper-modern lover's lament, are blended with a socialist humanism of un-equalled proportions. And all, in a celebration of futuristic, Soviet modernity, its aesthetics hyperbolic

FIG. 9.17 El Lissitzky, *Proun N 89* (*Kilmansvaria*), 1924.

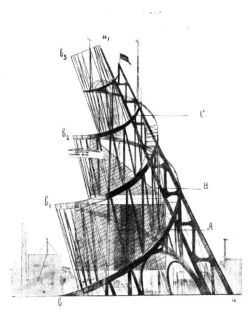

FIG. 9.18 Vladimir Tatlin, *Monument to the Third International*, 1919–20, Shchusev Museum of Russian Architecture.

and syncopated in intense jets of feeling, did not cut well with the 'socialist realists' whose art, and other people's too, had to reflect the real. They yearned for a desacralization of creativity, the creation of workshops, of artist engineers; they got, in turn, a radical rejection by Andrei Zhdanov and his cronies.

The first moment of the New Art has to be traced between Moscow and St

Petersburg, between the revolution of 1905 to the final clamping down of the regime against all experimentation and the triumph of socialist realism. When Maxim Gorky declared the need for 'revolutionary romanticism' in 1928 and Zhdanov declared socialist realism as the state-approved aesthetic of proletarian revolutionary consciousness, the Soviet Union put an end to a tremendous period of social and artistic experimentation and competition.

Between those years, a great, experimental, iconoclastic and public art spread through the country's aesthetic avant-gardes, found a popular audience, flirted with the expressive, idolized science and the modern, prioritized productivism and the practical, and was brought to a halt by Stalin who responded with an iron fist and then switched Soviet priorities to socialist realism. Mayakovsky, then, committed suicide.

The Russian constructivists, the futurists and, later, all the currents that saw in the Bolshevik Revolution the possibility for a New Art stretched to the limits the realm of rationalization. They were all, communists and non-communists alike, self-conscious members of a social and aesthetic revolution against *backwardness*; they searched in turn for a creative language that would craft a rational Parousia of form and content.

For many Paris, by then the obvious pilgrimage point for Russian members of the art and literature world and the navigating beacon of most avant-gardes in the world, was seen as effecting only a *partial* revolution, strapped as it was by its bourgeois essence. For Kazimir Malevich, the true evolution for art was from cubism and futurism to suprematism, which he argued in his manifestos, provided for the most intense rational abstraction of aesthetic form, the true revolution; for Mayakovsky and Rodchenko, the turn had to be about the achievement of a total civility through a celebration of science and technology; the metaphor of the earthly powers of the machine infused their prints, photomontages, objects, paintings and poetry.

Whereas constructivists, those brilliant, abstracted scientists of the aesthetic, were the most scorned, and the Meyerholds and Eisensteins barely tolerated, it was Mayakovsky, brash and excessive, who would survive down the years as the sad emblem of a tragic betrayal. All of them shared a peculiar guru: Frederick Taylor, the master of scientific management, the genius of rational productivism. Sergei Eisenstein praised him as being at the core of his film production; Meyerhold used him to define his theatrical methodology, viz., biomechanics; and the futurists, the celebrators of mechanical and scientific labour, sang his praises. So did Lenin and so did the poets who invaded factories to sing machinofacture's praises.

Without a deeper understanding of the sociological conjuncture of social revolution and its revolutionary dreams; without understanding the repositioning

Fig. 9.19 *'My trebuem mira, no esli tronete . . . V. Maiakovskii'* ('We Demand Peace, but If You Provoke . . . V. Mayakovsky'), poster by Viktor Koretsky, Ukraine, 1950. Permission granted under Rights & Reproductions, Yale University Art Gallery, New Haven, Connecticut.

of a variety of aesthetic elites through this process; without both creating a mythical communication to an emergent people whose consciousness would be defined by art and, in turn, art would be defined by their aspirations; without, too, an understanding of how the venues, contexts and media of aesthetic production were shifted; without an understanding of a competition between schools and currents in the Soviet world of declining resources.

Mayakovsky's appetite for transformation and change was gargantuan, 'stalking the world, handsome' and 'shaking it with the might of [his] voice.' And to the question: '1917 [. . .] October. To accept or not to accept? For me (as for the other Moscow Futurists) this question never arose. It is my Revolution' (Marshall, ed. 1965: 88). Whether bitter at the end, disappointed, reflecting how out of his own volition he 'crushed under foot/the throat of my very own songs' (ibid.: 27), and after processes and conditions made sure that 'the love-boat of life has crashed on philistine reefs' (ibid.: 38), the revolution remained his to the end.

Such reefs and their philistine crafters found in Mayakovsky's hyperbolic arrogance, his intensive lyricism, and his confidence that his aesthetic movement was the only progressive and revolutionary, much timber to rip and chisel at. The new civil service, the new 'ProletKorrect' institutions, whether in film, theatre or poetry, made life difficult for him. He did not take kindly to such people: he was appalled by the hypocrites who posthumously worshipped the artists they had castigated – 'Bread for the living! Paper for the Living!' he incanted (ibid.: 33). He hated the hero-worship and adulation even of Lenin: 'I fear/the mausoleum/

and official functions/established statute/servility/may log/with cloying unction/ Lenin's simplicity' (ibid.: 250).

The mixture of lyricism and modernist intensity was there from the beginning. In 'A Cloud in Trousers': 'If you like – /I'll be furious flesh elemental,/ or – changing the tones that sunset arouses – /if you like – I'll be extraordinarily gentle,/not a man, but – a cloud in trousers!' (ibid.: 99). His lyricism was always 'under the pressure of a million volts/my lips jab into the receiver's molten pitch [. . .] bursting the cable' (ibid.: 165–66). Telephones and wires aflame because 'in the church of my heart the choir is on fire!' (ibid.:105)

He saw himself as the 'only poetry', as 'only the heart' (ibid.: 205) of the revolution and its witness, 'wherever pain is – there I am' (ibid.: 110), but also its bayonet: 'lyrics/we've attacked/with repeated/ bayonet digs/and searched for speech/sharp/and re-doubted' (ibid.: 238–09).

In *Pro Eto*, Mayakovsky concludes with a passionate plea to the future chemical engineer to be resurrected to feel both the world he longed for and fought for, and to fulfil his unrequited love:

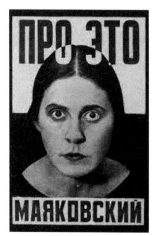

Fig. 9.20 Cover of Mayakovsky, *Pro Eto*, Moscow, 1923.
© 2022 Estate of Alexander Rodchenko; UPRAVIS, Moscow; ARS, New York

It may,
may be,
some time,
some day,
along a pathway of the
Gardens of the Zoo
she too –
for she loved animals –
will also the
Gardens re-enter,
smiling,
like that photo
in the desk of my room.
She is beautiful –
They will for certain resurrect her.
Your
thirtieth century

will leave far behind it
flocks of trifles' heart-rending sighs.

Now love unfulfilled
we are requiting
with the eternal starriness of endless nights.
Resurrect
If only because,
everyday muck-rejecting,
I awaited you,
A poet of strife!
If only for that
resurrect me!
Resurrect –
I want to live out my life!
So that love won't be a lackey there
of livelihood,
wedlock,
lust
or worse.
Decrying bed,
Forsaking the fireside chair,
so that love shall flood the universe.
So as not to be,
by sorrow aged made,
begging in the name of some Christ's birth,
So that,
the very first cry of 'Comrade!'-
Shall spin into one this very earth.
So as to live
Not victims in some home-holes curled.
So that henceforth
all kindred
To each other
our father,
at least, will be the world,
the earth,
at the very least – our mother. (Ibid.: 213–15)

Thanks to Lilya Brik, Stalin rehabilitated Mayakovsky as part of the Soviet pantheon. By then, reactionary artists, influenced by anything from surrealism to futurism, from bourgeois realism or what was seen as reactionary abstraction, were executed, exiled or imprisoned. The most appropriate aesthetic truth for the authentically popular was socialist realism.

Pablo Neruda in his *Memoirs* links his years in Mexico City with the transformation of his very own craft. From the melancholy, neo-romantic strains of his *Residencia en la Tierra* (Residence on Earth) with his anguished cry about the civil war in Spain – 'come and see the blood in the streets/come/ and see the blood/in the streets' – a glimpse of the murals, the exuberance and the popular art they invoked acted as a turning point to a poetry that celebrates these oppressed, magical people, these creatures of nature, these natural forces they embody, these mineral and elemental gravities they struggle through, irreducible to commodities, to things, to create a poetry at once epic and lyrical, with no parallel in the European canon. His vision in the *Canto General* of a new naturalism, a new world, popular revolution and transcendence creates the landscape through which later novelists like Gabriel Garcia Marquez and his generation could emerge. Marquez's work though was to start from the defeat of the dream – what he was left with was the fabulous people and their meanings.

We had mentioned how the young Diego Rivera left Mexico City to find his true vocation in Madrid. To flirt with aspects of cubism and its new formal demands was for him a way of breaking through the conservatism of his prior training. When Pierre Reverdy there apparently insulted his capabilities as a cubist, he was marking the beginning of his marginalization. The rebuke sent him violently back to Jose Vasconcelos and his Mexico. In this counter-repositioning, instead of the slur of 'backwardness', he asserted Mexican precolonial history; instead of the 'primitive', he celebrated the enduring magical, the organic, the natural; and instead of the bourgeois gallery wall, he dreamt of the popular, or the monumental. The track for the mural art of the century was opened.

Growing through the aesthetic schools of Mexico City and the masters of naturalism, the proper canonical art, he had to undertake the pilgrimage to Madrid by 1907; there, he traced the spoor of Picasso and Gris and their move to Paris. And so to Paris he went, where he found a language in analytical cubism by 1913. Then the bust up and the insult by the aesthetic gatekeepers. By then, Jose Vasconcelos's encouragement, the whiffs of rising nationalism, the Zapatistas, popular iconography and his subsequent rediscovery of Renaissance frescoes and, of course, the people: in the crowds, the markets, the festivals, the marching battalions, the workers in the workshops, the fields. His was a break with the past, but not with 'tradition'.

That he was in awe of the 'past' and the rituals of the people – the mystical, the sacrificial, the representations of popular iconography, was always there: in his *Day of the Dead*, or the historical sway of the revolution in the National Palace or even in his Detroit industry murals, the breaking up of the form into geometric elements clearly derived from cubism. And then, the translation of these into the organic forms of his invented neo-traditionalism is lucid and powerful.

Magical realism had, therefore, its own profound antecedents. It has to be searched for in Rivera's, Orozco's and Siqueiros's mural art, which started the figuration of people, their history, their fabulous pasts and legends. It invariably needs to survey the burden of beauty in Frida Kahlo's paintings, so many iconographies of pain, and then focus on the burden: take the calla lily sellers in Rivera's art, feel the weight of the lilies on the peasant men and women, feel the coarse backs and the crude hands and their pleading for hope and you have arrived at a primary moment – these people, Bolivar's hope, were never mobs in the murals, never just crowds, never effaced or defaced; they were there in the thousands, each a face, the arch-line of a back, a gesture, each enduring something. Although the figures were rough-hewn through cubist influence and peasant iconography, there were so many emancipatory markers.

The calla lily sellers, and the kind of empathy that permeates the series and its composition, an empathy for the people, the men and women whose lives were burdened by beauty, speaks of a different disposition. There, the figures of the men and women drawn harshly, simply, beyond representational realism but in a detail that augments and subverts the choice, bearing in silence the enormity of the lily-bunches, speaks of a lyrical acumen far from the machismo of the man.

In short, between Rivera's murals and Marquez's *One Hundred Years of Solitude*, there is a generous bridge: Pablo Neruda's *Canto General*. If Stalin had anything to do with Neruda, it was not about social realism but rather his tract on the *National Question*, the impulse for the colonized towards national forms of self-determination and self-expression. Yet, no one could believe what was to follow: an epic, a cosmogenesis, a history of emergence, a feeling and a sense of nature beyond the contours drawn on Martinique by Masson, Breton and later Lam and Cesaire – this was as if Neruda was speaking for creation itself.

Take the first lines of 'Amor America':

before the wig and the dress coat
there were rivers, arterial rivers: there were cordilleras, jagged waves where
the condor and the snow seemed immutable:
there was dampness and dense growth, the thunder
as yet unnamed, the planetary pampas
and there,
man was dust, earthen vase, an eyelid/of tremulous loam, the shape of clay –
he was Carib jug, Chibcha stone,
imperial cup of Araucanian silica.

Tender and bloody was he, but on the grip/of his weapon of moist flint,
the initials of the earth were written. (Neruda 1991: 13)

And we sense the emergence of the I, 'I, Incan of the loam', in a land without
name, an 'equinoctial stamen, purple lance', 'waiting for the slenderest word
as yet unborn in his mouth' (ibid.: 14).

It is all about an emergence in and through nature, celebrating all sentient
beings, because it was also about 'the twilight of the iguana', in a land where

the monkeys wove
an interminably erotic thread
on the shores of dawn,
levelling walls of pollen
and startling the violet flight
of the butterflies from Muzo (Ibid.: 16)

where,

the puma bolts through the foliage
like a raging fire,
while in him burn
that await me again, and pound
on my door with their starry hands
the jungle's alcoholic eyes [. . .]
next to the depths of the almighty water where the giant anaconda lies [. . .]
(Ibid.: 17)

Neruda is writing in defiance in the same streets where 'gangsters strut', those
men who in the name of Western culture strangle Spain, swing Athens from the
gallows and rape the Americas. 'I am staying here/with words and people and
roads/that . . . pound on my door with starry hands' (ibid.: 398). Because the
tree of the liberators has taken root and it is surging forth: 'the tree/nourished
by naked and where is with the world that Jehovah distributed to Coca-Cola
Inc., Anaconda,/Ford in the lands without a name or numbers, the wind and
rain bring 'celestial threads, and (where) the god of the impregnated altars/
restored flowers and lives' (ibid.: 114).

The abomination is the world that Jehovah distributed to Coca-Cola Inc.,
Anaconda, Ford Motors and other entities: United Fruit Inc., which reserved for
itself the juiciest of the Americas, its 'sweet waist', and on which it unleashed the
'dictatorship of flies' . . . 'Trujilo flies, Martinez flies,/Ubico flies, flies soaked/in
humble blood and jam,/drunk flies that drone/over the common graves/circus
flies, clever flies/versed in tyranny' (ibid.: 179). This ravaging continues as by

the docks' 'sugary abysses', 'a body rolls Today' down, 'a nameless/thing, a fallen number,/a bunch of lifeless fruit/dumped in the rubbish heap' (ibid.: 179).

But his hope was with America's capacity for insurrection: 'Today you'll emerge from the coal and the dew/Today you will come to shake the doors/ with bruised hands, with bits/of surviving soul, with clusters/of expressions that death did not extinguish/with intractable tools/hidden beneath your tatters' (ibid.: 94).

There is so much said and described in the *Canto* from exaltations about the heights of Machu Picchu to the landscapes of Chile, from the lurid processes of colonization to forms of indigenous resistance, to laments about working people and of fugitive lives, of the ocean and flowers. Neruda was to return to these themes with more intensity and often better verse later on, whether in his celebration of ordinary things, of mineral obligations, of birds, of melancholy coastlines and of freedom. Indeed, his androcentrism and his callous description of a rape in his *Memoirs* were commented upon and castigated; yet, the defiant architecture of the *Canto* remains alongside Cesaire's, Mayakovsky's and later Odysseas Elytis's remarkable alternate takes on modernity. The dramatic contrast between the machine-centric Soviet and the eco-centric hues of the *Canto* can only be held together by their radical impulse and their belief in the revolutionary powers of the *pueblo* and/or the working class.

Over and above the creation of aesthetic acuities among creative artists, what emerges are a series of 'artistic cadences' that define a landscape of political feeling that assumes solidarity around issues of unity, solidarity, sorrow, loss, desire and yearning. This is varied but the way it is expressed opens up acuities everywhere. This is in serious tension and complicity with popular market forces precisely because of the commodification of emotions through mass culture.

The movement activity and its crescendos deliver constructions of visual, acoustic or literary archetypes: what are a language of the optic, a repertoire of performance idioms, and a tension between the public and private, the extrovert and introvert of composition – poetic or musical. There is also pressure for deinstitutionalizing art and performance outside dominant spaces and experiments over public spaces, whether participatory or not. Part of the language of the optic is intensified through the new visual media and makes the authentic/ inauthentic undecided. These new ideas and practices are intimately related to the dynamics of space and place and how power disperses and gets centralized.

The rise of New York, and later Los Angeles, was part of the interconnections that we are tracing, and their stories were as close to London, Paris, Moscow or Mexico City as was made possible by the transport systems of the time.

For brevity's sake, we will only articulate their importance and save expansive commentary for another time.

Already, by the 1920s and 1930s, the infrastructure that was to allow the US to think that it could supplant London and Paris as the epicentre for aesthetic value was being put in place – the galleries, the foundations, the concert halls, and in Harlem the clubs and community halls, were gathering energy. Pogroms in Eastern Europe had already sent across the ocean a dynamic and art-loving Jewish community; immigrants of all ethnicities moved in numbers, poor Italians, persecuted Greeks and Armenians, Mexicans; and the most significant and historic migration, of African Americans from the south. This gave New York a mongrel and liberal feel. A certain sense of awe about Europe and, by 1917 of Moscow, animated the rise and support of its cultural life.

We have already touched on the fact that Wifredo Lam was to 'make it' there; we also can trace the fact that Siqueiros was often there or in Los Angeles and that the Harlem Renaissance was in full swing as its jazz was heating up, the writings of Claude McKay and Langston Hughes were being noticed (even though du Bois was furious with McKay's depictions of ghetto vibrancy) – and even though all this made little impact on the USA to start with, Paris and Moscow welcomed both jazz and literature. McKay's *Banjo* was a revelation to Cesaire and his Parisian networks, and the origins of what Paul Gilroy termed the 'slave sublime' was being incubated there.

And so was the Calcutta moment which, however different, was as vibrant and defining: the artists and writers, philosophers and cultural activists that were creating the Bengali Renaissance were cultivating a syncretic and spiritual neo-traditionalism as the path Indian modernity should follow. Research on the expansive networks on the Tagore family is enormous and still growing. Their cultural response to British rule resonated in Shanghai and Tokyo and, after a series of encounters, Paris and London. But Rabindranath Tagore was to prove to be an institution that defies categorization – poet, novelist, dramatist, philosopher, anti-nationalist, nationalist, internationalist, educator . . . the list is voracious, problematic, contested but recalcitrant. His poetry was celebrated to start with and criticized with equal fervour.

It is to his music, his compositional oeuvre of 2,000 and more songs, that I would like to pay attention to. His greatness was to find a structure of feeling outside the *raga* system so that he could play with the system itself, with folk songs and dirges, with European and Anatolian sounds, and combine elements, innovate and create something that was unmistakably Indian, a sung-poetry and *thumri*-like cadence that defined both an elitist and also a cross-class and caste tonality. So, his influence cut in many directions: the formal music of, for example Amjad Ali Khan, the sarod maestro, and the more popular hymnody and song of the anti-colonial nationalist movement. If we separate the music from the mythological figure, we would see how similar and different his craft was from, for example, Verdi, who could create a sense of an operatic nationalism in Italy using a metaphorical orientalism in *Aida* or *Nabucco*, whereas Tagore achieves the opposite with frightening ease: to absorb all that is exotic from a Bengali space into a self-created canon.

Aime Cesaire and Pablo Neruda among others provided a broad canvas that could translate into a Pan-African or Pan-Latin American vision through which specific national imaginaries could be facilitated. Leopold Sedar Senghor could move easily from Negritude to Pan-Africanism (and his idea of African socialism) to a more specific Senegalese anti-colonial nationalism that he could also lead. Creative people were at work in the anti-colonial imaginings that led to a plethora of independent states from the late 1950s onward. The work of the imagination was particularly central as prior policies of segregation and indirect ethnic rule by colonists and the arbitrariness of colonial borders asked for challenging constructions of the new 'we' of belonging. For the communist movement, this was encouraged since Lenin's recognition of anti-imperialist nationalism as an important prop for any socialist future. The idea, taken further by Stalin, created interesting modulations as communist movements were simultaneously trying to bring together an idea of the nation in and through class cleavages.

The variety of nationalisms and their different voices were particularly marked by the time the Bandung Conference attempted to bring them all together in a non-aligned pact, to the ire of Moscow and Washington, in 1955. How colonial independence was followed through by a vibrant literature criticizing postcolonial elites and forms of governance demands a volume in its own right, from African cinema to the poetics of disappointment. Such concerns have taken creative people to the tensions between past and present, or tradition, Christianity and modernity, between the indigenous and the foreign, between the market, the individual and the community, between elites and people, patriarchy and ethnic chauvinism, all cohering around promises made and never kept and the dream of freedom deferred.

What made it possible, then, to think that aesthetic acuities were ready to reimagine a multiplicity of aesthetic constellations in the twenty-first century that could be shared and tied to an emancipatory project? To be crude, there were two: neoliberalism and its global reach, and the rise of authoritative restoration – from neo-fascism, neo-racism and an intensification of religiosity. What was without doubt was that the imaginings that allowed for the vibrant scripts of defiance preceding and consequent to the walk at the Absalon Baths had been scuttled through internal and external factors. Dogmatism of the social realist type, of the authentic in the popular kind in the post-independence movements and the extreme commodification of culture and art did their bit as internal factors. The external ones had as much to do, with the Cold War and its emphasis of a certain narrative in the west and certain orthodoxies from the so-called east.

There was a moment in 1968–74 where such imaginings became possible on the cusp of the student politics of revolt in the west, and the Vietnam War and its solidarities everywhere. Furthermore, there was a rejection of materialism in the youth cultures of the west and a slouching towards the east (especially India), and there was, riding on a new orientalism, an exodus of the east to the west. The new music of the time sang about no borders and no religion too. There was the publication in the English world of a lot of fascinating poetry in translation under the Penguin brand and an explosion of writing circulating in Africa by the Heinemann Africa series. There was also an idea of a Cultural Revolution in China that was advertised in the world as truly revolutionary and different.

But the stagnation of the west's mass-producing economies, the cul-de-sac in China that led to the Four Modernizations policy, the tremors and upheavals in apartheid South Africa, the crisis of the military in Brazil, brought with them India's Emergency, Thatcherism and a serious counter-attack by proxy forces on anything left in Africa, Asia and Latin America. By the early 1990s, the complexity of issues faced by artists and writers were too complex and, even among those sympathetic to the labour movement, responding to trade union attempts to respond to market fundamentalism was not their only preoccupation.

Fig. 9.21 Semsar Siahaan, *Marsinah*, 1993, Singapore Art Museum. © 2022 Siahaan Family

Semsar Siahaan was one of the participants in the 1992 and 1994 attempts to place culture and the arts on the priority list of an emergent trade union movement in the South. The late Indonesian artist had just 'cremated' his teacher's sculptures in public. He was part of the ushering of a grassroots movement against Suharto's New Order. He was an avant-garde artist responding to his time's 'radical impulse', for which he was beaten, arrested and tortured to the extent that one of his legs was permanently damaged. The movement, consisting of a new working-class insurgency around worker study circles, Sufi-inspired creativity, peculiar mixtures of Marx and Islam, was in the throes then of a new dispensation.

The gatherings in Perth brought together creative activists from South Africa, India, Indonesia, Philippines, Thailand, Malaysia, Vietnam and Australia, with China partly present playing a rather subdued and cautious role. The trade union gatherings organized by the Australian trade union movement had to cope with a vast array of traditions – social democratic, socialist, communists of all persuasions from Marxist–Leninist to Maoist. The collapse of the Soviet Union on the one hand, and the emergence of the South and east as epicentres of production and exchange on the other, created the context.

The cultural turn was inaugurated by South African networks in and around the trade union movement. It did not succeed, save some far-flung resolutions, partly because the creative cohorts were not ready to become on-demand adjuncts to trade union work as much as bringing to the gathering a vigorous diversity, a new polymorphy, which was born out of their specific historical challenges.

Fig. 9.22 Semsar Siahaan, *Self Portrait with Black Orchid*, 1999. Courtesy Gajah Gallery. © 2022 Siahaan Family

Semsar Siahaan did not only paint or draw 'struggle' pictures. As *Black Orchid* illustrates, his was a response to a complex aesthetic heritage.

The victory in the west of rights that encompassed the autonomy of the arts and self-expression in the late nineteenth century had a perverse side to it. It spawned, as we have outlined, stellar examples of self-expression with Paris and a range of other European cities functioning as dynamic epicentres. What all this obfuscates is the simultaneous censorship and control in Europe's colonial possessions. As Sumangala Damodaran shows in her chapter in Sitas *et al.* (2014), the censorship of texts and performances in India and the tightening of publication controls escalated in the post-1870s period. The noise of subaltern presses was on the increase everywhere. The Dutch too, not to be outdone in the Dutch East Indies, followed suit and tried to contain the plethora of proto-nationalist texts that started proliferating. What was projected in the colonial world as exemplary culture was being created by absenting the contrary modernist and audacious forms of art in the colonial metropole.

The emancipation of the arts in bourgeois society in the west was significant in another sense too. Many artists and creative people in the majority world saw in modernism's dynamism a sense of 'progress' – a way out of their perceived parochialism, backwardness and traditionalism. This they did from a national perspective – the Bengali Renaissance in the late nineteenth century was a vital case in point, and its importance was not lost to the Chinese or the Japanese emerging modernists as outlined above. Later, for example, notable non-political examples would be the Bombay Progressive Artists' Group (which later migrated to Pakistan) and formed the nucleus around which a national and modernist emphasis in art emerged both in Pakistan and Bangladesh (Akbar 1998). There was something in the language and imagery of European art that enthused creative people in the South.

But after colonialism shifted towards independence (and neo-colonialism in Africa) and the Cold War intensified, a bifurcated reality set in: in the west, art expression was encouraged as a mark of distinction and excellence. In the process, deviance was normalized and the idea of novelty and scandal was often celebrated. The establishment of high art and literature and the generation of a panoply of gatekeepers, canon-makers and experts were part of this enormous effort. To scandalize became a mark of audacity and success, and even artists of left pedigree found appreciation and success. The west as the epicentre of symbolic value provided the magnet for all.

Even though much can be said about the arts and the west, it too succumbed to internal vulnerabilities. The rise of fascism in Europe saw modernism in the arts as an act of decay and the beginning of Europe's marasmus. We do not need to repeat here the enticing discussion of the relationship between National Socialism in Germany and the suppression of 'degenerate' art and artists. Anyone from Paul Klee to Brecht, Benjamin and Anna Seghers were targets. But the period between the 1910s and the late 1930s also saw a convergence of many against the authoritarian tide.

Matters get complicated after the Second World War and the initiation of the Cold War. The McCarthy era between 1950 and 1956 in the USA offered a scary intermezzo: artists from Charlie Chaplin to Aaron Copland and Tom McGrath to Langston Hughes and hundreds more were targeted, not because of the aesthetic content of their work but that through a peculiar 'osmosis' they could be branded as friends of or as actual communists.

The elephant in the room of course was communism. Since the nineteenth century many artists and writers felt a deep attraction to the growing communist or social democratic movement. The movement itself created space for creative people amongst the modernizing elites to work in solidarity with emerging working-class and peasant movements. As an international movement it facilitated the flow of ideas, symbolic forms and creativity. The Second and Third Internationals facilitated movements that harboured defiance, creativity and expression, but also repression and dogmatism. After the Russian Revolution and the initial flourishing of competing schools of art and literature – constructivists, futurists, proletkult-ideologues, realists and so on – the congealing into a socialist realist orthodoxy ushered new forms of repression and marginalization. Such non-revolutionary and reactionary forms of art were castigated in all communist activity the world over.

The Stalin period in the 1930s, and again in the 1950s, was defined by extreme forms of repression, and cultural experts saw deviations and anti-revolutionary forms of art in anything from literature to music. Dmitri Shostakovich was a victim of such 'perfidies' often, celebrated, punished, rehabilitated, marginalized, but at least he survived. At the same time, the very source of dogmatism was tempered through Stalin's *National Question*, as we saw, which in accepting national liberation as a first stage in third-world struggles, became a facilitating way through which indigenous and non-realist elements could proliferate. Sumangala Damodaran's study of the Indian People's Theatre Association (IPTA) musical traditions demonstrates how diverse the mix of anti-colonial and socialist performance work was in India.

The US as part of its Cold War-directed foreign cultural policy pushed a version of modernism defined by abstract, non-representational and existential art as the canonical form against realism and socialist realism that were finding traction in national liberation movements in the South. To fight this communistic tendency a range of art schools and institutes were funded and/or created that propagated art for art's sake and abstract art in particular. A remarkable and successful institute, for example, was the one created in Bandung that produced fascinating work, which was heralded as a beacon of technique, modernism and progress. Siahaan was one of the Bandung Institute's more volatile 'products'.

Repression was not the preserve of Suharto's years. Even during the Sukarno years, the post-colonial state favoured the art and culture of the Soviet-inspired LEKRA movement, which produced writers like Pramoedya Ananta Toer with his socialist realist hues, and banned the modernist Manikebu School. In turn, the violent and bloody overthrow of Sukarno and the decimation of communist supporters that followed ushered Suharto's New Order, which emphasized a national idea of development in search of regional folklore as ballast for nation-building.

The rebellion against Suharto's New Order started from the very Bandung Institute for the Arts where Semsar Siahaan burnt or, in his words, 'cremated' his teacher's sculpture in public. It ushered in the forbidden next: a struggle with heritage, nativism, expression, the personal and the political in a new way. His work has been closer to more complex aesthetic traditions than to the practical theatre of Marxist firebrands of the late 1980s and early 1990s.

By contrast, the Vietnamese and the Chinese were more circumspect in Perth. There was the beginning of a thaw in what was permissible in the arts. The opening of their respective economies to world flows had already begun. In Vietnam after the defeat of the USA, a celebratory nationalist and socialist art culture permeated government policy and was accompanied by the banning of non-patriotic art and bourgeois values. This went together with, as the remarkable novelist Pham Thi Hoai recalls, extensive libraries where the European and socialist classics would be available (2015). So, she could come to know Breton and Ehrenburg! The transition to a Renovation period in Vietnam was marked by a decline, according to her, the emergence of a 'void', as the market did not spend as much time on literature or creative resources as it did on new brands of toilet paper. And although Renovation came with new forms of openness, political work like hers got banned.

China offered a remarkable case study of prohibitions and repressions from an initial Soviet-inspired orthodoxy to an openness when a thousand flowers were supposed to bloom, and then the radicalization of the Cultural Revolution and its extreme rectifications that saw creative people killed, jailed or sent to the countryside to be rehabilitated through hard labour. The orthodoxy of proletarian literature and opera lasted for a decade before a kind of glasnost emerged following the Four Modernizations Policy. This of course applies so far as the art remains apolitical and does not introduce scandalous western avant-garde motifs. An artist like Ai Weiwei is caught between the two and in constant trouble.

But the return to the thousand flowers of the old nationalist movement was hard. The New Cultural Movement of the turn of the twentieth century borrowed heavily from European modernism, from Tokyo's modernizing counterpoint and from the Bengali Renaissance. In no time, Moscow and St Petersburg came into the picture. At first, the rejection of the past went hand in hand with the rediscovery of writers, philosophers and essayists who had rebelled in the past!

On the cusp of the modern story, there were paradigmatic cases during the involution of the older world systems before the rise of capitalism that were brought back into defiance at later stages. Take Li Zhi (1527–1602). His defiant essays loom as large as the title of his books. If the content proved challenging enough for his contemporaries, so were his book titles, like *A Book to Hide* and *A Book to Burn*! The Ming literati and philosophers of his contemporary status quo, admittedly a status quo in its 'autumn years' (Brook 1989), were swift in their caustic and accusatory responses: something had to be done about the 'apostate' and his attack on neo-Confucian philosophy and literature. He was arrested, jailed, and whilst in prison, he took his own life. His deviance was to be celebrated by the New Cultural Movement in China in the 1920s.

Ming prosperity and growth, vividly recounted by Timothy Brook in his *Confusions of Pleasure* (1998), was beginning to stumble. Internal strife based on naked inequalities and resistance to the imperial centre had its toll on governance. It was not long before the Manchu swept southwards to usurp the imperial mantle in 1644, to establish a tentative and nervous hold on Han

China. Similarly, the Mughals, after a period of ascendance, tolerance and syncretic innovation during Akbar's reign, started a downward plunge with his grandson Aurangzeb moving towards a strict Islamic revivalism. Further afield on the Asian map, the Dutch, who could not turn the Ming and Qing into trading vassals, found a declining Malay world as a good opportunity for foraging, settlement and colonization, and the first attempts to impose a Christian puritanism on a tetchy and diverse set of subjects.

As we outlined in *Gauging and Engaging Deviance, 1600–2000* (Sitas *et al.* 2014), panic around dissent in China, overt and covert, launched one of the most ruthless literary pogroms in known history. The people entrusted with tracing sedition and transgression did so in even the most seemingly innocuous and compliant verse.

The New Cultural Movement bifurcated soon enough, with its left centred around Lu Xun and later Guo Muoro, with Shanghai being a remarkable modernizing centre and the followers of the Bengali Renaissance forming a crescent moon movement inspired by Tagore. Here, we do not need to work through the humiliations and violence Guo Muoro experienced during the Cultural Revolution and how his work was shown not to be proletarian enough and how all performance had to be purified to an essential proletarian ethos – how, later, he was rehabilitated and thereafter how more openness to a range of realisms became possible.

The delegation in Perth was uncomfortable with much of the art and performance demonstrated, struggling still with versions of socialist realism. Struggling, too, with the celebration of a new generation of poets back home, like the Misty Poets, whose defiance was against realism and party approval. But it is precisely these poets who have been celebrated in the west as the authentic modernists in China.

Then there were the South Africans, a mix of poets and performers accompanied by progressive art paintings for an exhibition. The poets were a sheer contrast made possible by the manifold currents in anti-apartheid resistance – an established socialist poet and dramatist, on the one hand, part of a broader cultural movement that was flexing its anti-apartheid muscles where class, race and issues

FIG. 9.23 Poster of the Sarmcol Workers' Cooperative for their play, *The Long March*, 1985, designed by Patricia Henderson. © P. Henderson.

of freedom and equality were paramount embodied one dynamic. Another was represented by a mineworker poet who was steeped in oral and indigenous traditions of popular performance. One totally at home in the 'slave sublime' of jazz and the poetry of anyone from Mayakovsky to Neruda, Celan or the Black Consciousness poets. The other, very much immersed in the indigenous languages of the Nguni and the metaphoric language of the *imbongi* tradition.

Both were involved in the workers' theatre movement with its grotesque realism and exaggerated gesture, but what was for one an extension of the folk play was for the other in debate with traditions inaugurated by the existential theatre of Athol Fugard and the serious and sombre theatre of a Black Consciousness movement that flourished in the late 1960s. Theatre work like that was still banned by the South African state and a lot of the performers were being targeted by vigilantes of the civil war in Natal and the broader counter-revolution in South Africa.

Johannesburg under apartheid was not cut off from broader world currents.

Fɪɢ. 9.24 Sfiso M'Kame, *Letters to God*, 1988, Iziko SANG Cape Town. © Sfiso M'Kame.

The city of gold with its wealthy white bourgeoisie and an increasingly restless Black proletariat had significant internal and international dynamics. If you happened to be in music, then the 'blues' of Black experience had its ears tuned to John Coltrane but also to a rich trove of South African Black musicians in exile: Blue Notes, Brotherhood of Breath, Abdullah Ibrahim; and to the poets, the Art Ensemble of Chicago (AACM), the Liberation Music Orchestra and Cecil Taylor. There was a direct influence of Aime Cesaire on Black Consciousness networks and, to a radicalized white cohort, the introduction to Neruda occurred through cyclostyled pieces from the leading Sestiger Afrikaans poet Breyten Breytenbach, who was in Paris. And so were the two canonical Black painters Gerard Sekoto and Ernest Mancoba, the former a realist, the latter an Africanist non-representational dynamo. Through theatre, the works of Beckett and Brecht, Weiss and Genet, circulated beneath the censor's radar. And for the dissenting white youth, there was the world of protest music from Bob Dylan to Woodstock.

The thriving cultural movement, linked to the labour movement in South Africa, emerged in the shadow of three competing traditions: Black Consciousness, that insisted on a serious theatre in new collective venues in the Black communities – mourning the fall from a resplendent past, castigating the present as a purgatory and dreaming of the return of the past; Workshop 71, which had a more people's power perspective, worked collectively and produced plays of the urban and rural working-class experience; and the Junction Avenue Theatre Company, which was more into tapping the traditions and histories of urban and working-class resistance, working collectively and having a non-racial or multiracial cast. The explosion of worker theatre was related to the involvement of activists/creators with talented performers from the trade union movement.

The South Africans were closer to the Indian performers, singers and intellectuals. India, at the time that the Perth gathering happened, was about to enter into a phase where questions of artistic representation were beginning to be asked around issues of tradition, religious practices and 'heritage', and where inter-communal tensions and xenophobic dispositions were being combated through artistic practices. In the aftermath of the demolition of the Babri Masjid in 1992, with communal politics and tensions at their apogee, a number of musicians and other artists began to undertake an enquiry into what kinds of music would be able to address the questions that the political situation in the country had thrown up. At the heart of the communal situation were issues of tradition, heritage, nationalism, religion, tolerance and citizenship. In northern India and especially in the city of Delhi, these questions had simmered for a long time, and violent politics had seen the anti-Sikh carnage of 1984 and Safdar Hashmi's assassination in 1989, both of which involved the Congress Party.

Musicians like Shubha Mudgal and Madan Gopal Singh were reviving

Fig. 9.25: A Jana Natya Manch (Janam) street theatre performance with Safdar Hashmi acting in the foreground.

inclusive traditions of the past in Hindustani and Sufi music, and theatre practitioners like Habib Tanvir were using indigenous forms. Safdar Hashmi was straight out of the people's street theatre traditions. Dancers like Chandralekha and Astad Deboo, to name a few, began studying and performing repertoires that were excavated from the past, often from centuries before. The past needed to be redeemed for the present.

Part of all this was also Sumangala Damodaran's performance and curating work reviving the compositional prowess of the IPTA, where some of the country's top composers and poets responded to both a nationalist and a socialist ferment whose traces went back to the formation of Progressive Writers' Association in Lucknow in 1936, a year after Mulk Raj Anand and others formed the All India Progressive Writers' Association in London. Indeed, Mulk Raj Anand was part of the 1935 gathering in Paris.

In Southeast Asian narratives, India is often contrasted to Pakistan: the former as the land of tolerance, the latter of repression. It is more than accurate that constitutionally India accepted freedom of expression and Pakistan has a long list of interference and repression. But it also harboured a peculiar sense of oscillation between hounding out the left and acceptance of some of its most impressive artists. Faiz Ahmad Faiz, the canonical and radical Urdu poet, despite his incarceration in the 1950s, enjoyed prestige and status in Pakistan in the 1960s, and it was only in the 1970s that his work was

Fig. 9.26 Portrait of Faiz (left) and Iqbal Bano (right) by Shahid Riaz. © 2022 Shahid Riaz.

banned and restricted once again. This did not stop the *ghazal*-diva Iqbal Bano from throwing caution to the wind as she sang his forbidden lyrics in a moving performance that was recorded and released in defiance.

By contrast, India of the present cannot defend artists from attack from a right on the ascendance. As the right is using mobs and the courts to silence dissent and clear out anti-Hindutva and anti-national elements, artists are intimidated and are on the receiving end of violence. A clear example is India's most recognized fine artist M.F. Husain, who had to flee after constant legal and physical intimidation. He was old, celebrated abroad, but had to go into exile.

The Australian participants had the hardest of tasks in communicating with the other creative energies, partly because hitherto Australian official culture had a direct lineage running across the world to the United Kingdom. So, trade union activists prioritized the folk song and the union choir. Some intersection occurred over the legacies of Pete Seeger all the way to the early Bob Dylan and the anti-Vietnam rock movement and more recently Pink Floyd, for example. This was very familiar to primarily Philippines-based groups, but less so among Indians, Indonesians and South Africans. On the other hand, they were represented by a number of Aboriginal creative activists who were into a strong sense of ethnic exceptionalism and this linked up wonderfully with the oral poetry and song of the South African delegation.

This attempt at capturing the creative imagination in the context of a new world dispensing precarity and authoritarianism was centred around the attempts by labour to find a new vocabulary of struggle. It does not stop there; labour's precarity has been amply captured in films and theatre – for example, *Workingman's Death*, the 2005 Austrian and German documentary film by Michael Glawogger, and *Dark Things* (2018), the visual drama directed by Anuradha Kapur and Deepan Sivaraman in Delhi, about the underside of our silk roads. The plight of refugeedom has found ample symbolic force in the decision to have a gigantic refugee puppet, made by the Handspring Puppet Company maestros from South Africa, march from Syria to the heart of Europe so it comes to cross or comes to be stopped from crossing borders. There is also Weiwei's documentary about refugees, or Jenny Reznick's powerful two-hander of a performance of *Every Year, Every Day, I am Walking*, or Maya Rao's *Walk* about defiance against patriarchy and rape.

In short, like in the 1930s, the arts are in defiance of this world and its out-of-jointness. What is missing is the exemplary walk through the rainforest to complete the turning of a symbolic wheel.

There is a long lineage of defiance in literature, in the arts and performance in all social systems and social registers. Often, what was defiant turns out to be canonical and a part of affirmative culture later, and something considered affirmative becomes defiant so much so that a nuanced reader is at a loss of where and how to start 'the' story. Nevertheless, the surviving scripts, visual traces and descriptions of such expressions from popular to elite forms of culture can yield countless examples and figurations. The canvas is large, from everyday subaltern forms of resistance and syncretic innovations to defiant times during the rise of movements and, finally, to individual acts as counter-nomic forms of expression.

We had worked with the idea of articulatory deviance in the first volume (*Gauging and Engaging Deviance*). Given that this was a starting point to understanding artistic defiance, in a further attempt to understand the scripts of such defiance and also to find out whether it is possible for us to arrive at a typology of such scripts, we can ask the following questions. First, we understand that the spoken and printed word, performance and visual art forms were significant categories that were considered to be threatening to existing systems due to what was being expressed and how. What are such forms of expression/articulation? Second, threats perceived due to various articulations are because those doing it are perceived to be violating fundamental principles that a certain dominant group holds dear. What are these principles – forms of representation, definitions of nationhood, culture, religious identity and heritage? Whatever the basis of perceived threat, these defiant people were, and are, seen as violating accepted codes of some sort or the other. Third, are these codes those that are supposedly handed down by tradition or those that are being newly constructed with changing national boundaries, or are they defined in terms of various categories of the 'other'? Fourth, how are these codes laid down and how does the declaration of committed offence happen? What are the specificities/details of what causes offence? What is the range of responses that can be seen in terms of 'reining in' or setting rules? What are the responses from the groups that practise these forms – do they disappear, are they eliminated, do they adjust and normalize, do new forms of expression appear? How do those in positions of domination in turn themselves modify codes in response to how these forms are received by the public? Finally, what are the elements that bring everyday subaltern forms, resolutely defiant forms as well as individual counter-nomic expressions, into relationship with each other?

Although we are very concerned with the arts and forms of expression of subaltern groups in the 'modern' period – First Nations and Adivasis, Dalits and slaves, colonial forms of labour and indenture, all the way to the cultural formations of wage workers and the precariat – we will also have to bring into focus defiant members of the established order. Examples of the first kind are plentiful – from the subterranean innovations of Malay slaves from the Indonesian archipelago in the interstices of the Dutch-controlled Cape in the seventeenth century, to the revelries and processions 200 years later of the poor and their 'sawngs' in colonial Calcutta; from the transgressive performance rituals in the slave plantations of the Americas to the lewd folk art of the rural poor and peasantries. From them come vital structures of feeling – an intimacy with nature from First Nations, notions of freedom from Black slaves in rebellion, forms of equality from 'levellers' everywhere, notions of solidarity in anti-colonial national movements, women and men and their tropes of dissent, lamentation and celebration in song and oral lore.

At times of social ferment and during the rise of social movements, artists with a variety of acuities who belong to a variety of aesthetic constellations are caught up in the maelstrom of a radical impulse which creates contexts that intensify their work. Social movement literature tells us that they are sustained upsurges of people that challenge the power structures or the norms of society, as such artists are not only part of the sustenance of movements but part of the defining groups of new normative orientations. But what is important for our purposes is that such upsurges open up new imaginaries and create important transformations and reconfigurations in their work. Out of this effervescence new constellations emerge, some constellations ossify, some disappear, some are disappeared. Something happens to art.

Notes

1 The final result: Insurrections Ensemble (2017).

2 See also Sharply-Whiting (2002); Rabbit (2013).

3 Disclaimer: Although every reasonable effort was made to trace owners and/or copyright holders of the images in this chapter, in order to obtain permission to reproduce the images, in a few cases such owners/copyright holders could not be reached. Should any infringements have occurred, please make this known, and the publisher undertakes to rectify these in the event of a reprint of this publication.

4 See, for example, Macey (2012); also, Praeger (2003).

5 For a thorough discussion of art's degeneracy, see Wiebke Keim's chapter 'Colonialism, National Socialism and the Holocaust: On Modern Ways of Dealing with Defiance', in Ari Sitas *et al.* (2014).

6 See Wallace, ed. (1998).

7 Ann Eger, 'Wifredo Lam-Chronology 1938-41', *Wifredo Lam*, available at www.wifredolam. net, accessed 20 October 2016.

8 Much of the rescue of artists, activists and Jews was the singular and altruistic work of Varian Fry, an American, whose place in Marseilles became a gathering of some of the best avant-garde spirits in France. See his *Assignment Rescue: An Autobiography*; see also Andy Marino, *A Quiet American.*

9 Claude Levi-Strauss's *Tristes Tropiques* devotes its first part to this journey and his stay in Martinique. I have used the 2012 Penguin rerun of this classic of anthropology (Levi-Strauss 2012).

10 Levi-Strauss 2012: 27.

[11] See Macey (2012).

[12] See Wicken (2010) for the poetic and adventurous in Levi-Strauss.

[13] See Sims (2002). The relationship between Lam, Picasso and Cesaire was celebrated by an exhibition in 2011 at the National Gallery of the Grand Palais in Paris, curated by Daniel Maxinin with the assistance of Sylvie Poujade and Eskil Lam, titled 'Nous nous somnes trouves'. It ran from 16 March to 6 June 2011.

[14] See *Paris 1935: Erster Internationaler Schriftstellerkongreß zur Verteidigung der Kultur, Reden und Dokumente: Mit Materialien der Londoner Schriftstellerkonferenz 1936, Einleitung und Anhang von Wolfgang Klein*, Paris, 1935 (First International Writers' Congress in Defence of Culture, speeches and documents. With materials from the London Writers' Conference 1936. Introduction and appendix by Wolfgang Klein), Berlin: Akademie-Verlag, 1982.

[15] See disclaimer in note 3.

[16] See the powerful reconstruction of Benjamin's project by Buck-Morss (1989). Also, a most useful entry into Benjamin's labyrinthine mind is Steiner (2010).

[17] For an Anglo-speaking audience, *Illuminations* was the first encounter in 1969. A compiled book of his essays on Baudelaire followed, *Charles Baudelaire: A Lyric Poet on the Eve of High Capitalism* (Benjamin 1996). It is only in 2002 that Harvard University Press published *The Arcades Project* in its entirety.

VIGNETTES D

Authoritarian Restorations

10

From Fascism to Post-Fascism

Wiebke Keim

INTRODUCTION

Authoritarians are back: demanding the restoration of community against formalized society and of tradition against the stranger; asking for strong states enforcing law and order, closing borders, preventing dark men from threatening white women; defending traditional family models against individualism and gender pluralism; claiming to represent 'the people'. Today, many denounce the new authoritarians as 'Fascists!'.

Where do these 'fascists' come from? Why are they successful today?

I will take up the argument from the conclusion to my contribution (Keim 2014) to volume I of this book, *Gauging and Engaging Deviance, 1600–2000* (Sitas *et al.* 2014; henceforth volume 1). In that volume, we had defined the 1920s/30s as an anomalic phase. In the chapter on colonialism, National Socialism (NS) and the Holocaust, the fascists (or Nazis, for that matter) had risen in power to become the fixers of that anomalic phase. The whole argument, starting from Cesaire, was around transferring discourses, techniques and practices to identify, classify, administer, re-educate, repress and ultimately exterminate deviants from the colonies into Europe. The end of fascism in Europe was not the achievement of emancipatory struggles but of military defeat. The post-1945 democratic dispositions nationally and internationally turned fascists, the former fixers, into special kinds of deviants by law. The measures to deal with them were denazification, demilitarization, re-education, democratization and reintegration into the international community. Indeed, the few remaining who openly declared their indebtedness to Nazism and fascism were mainly represented as a law-and-order problem. In this sense, they could be considered at first sight as deviants. On several occasions, the readers of our volume 1 questioned our approach to fascists. The critique was that we dealt only with the sympathetic deviants and relegated fascists to a different category. This corresponds to a tendency, erroneous and dangerous in my view, to lend credibility to the fascists' self-declared victimhood of discrimination, witch-hunts and restrictions to their freedom of speech and thought. There is a paradox in this self-reclamation as deviants with democratic rights of organization and expression, although their own relationship with democracy and constitutionally guaranteed fundamental rights is highly problematic. This chapter deals with the dark side of scripts of defiance, contributing to the full picture of their multivocality.

More than that, the conclusion of my chapter in volume 1 outlined continuities and connections between interwar fascists and Nazis post-1945 at the level of foreign relations, administration and bureaucracy, intelligence services and academia, that represented continuities of National Socialist ways of handling deviance in the post-1945 period. Networks of people who preserved and spread fascist ideology through sustained circulation of ideas and who maintained a certain level of organizational capacity persisted. In parallel to the public condemnation of fascism, supposed liberal democrats relied on their special competency and ideological influence against communism. Despite post-1945 dispositions to prevent a re-emergence of fascism, fascist thinking and action remained, although in non-dominant, idiomorphic ways. It adapted to varying conditions and contexts, omnipresent as an ideology with differing degrees of political influence and practical action.

Today, figures, movements and regimes demanding authoritarian restoration of alleged past glory and 'pure' communities are on the rise in many places. A thorough comparative analysis of their resemblances and differences awaits realization.[1] This chapter is focused on the two countries that I know best: my country of origin, Germany, as the direct heir of National Socialism and in continuity with my contribution to volume I; and my country of work, France, as the country that has today, as far as I know, the biggest and one of the most continuous far-right parties of Europe.[2]

In both cases, a diachronic comparison seems tempting. Are the 1930s ahead of us (Granel 1995: 71–74)? *Récidive: 1938* (Foessel 2019) invites us to rediscover the year 1938 in France through its print press, to read in a non-teleological way the rising extremism to revisit how a democracy degenerated at the time. There, authoritarian voices that demanded a stop to welcoming refugees, that argued that the welfare model could not be upheld any longer, that justified violent repression of strikes were on the rise. The three elements – questioning the state of law in the face of a perceived refugee crisis, questioning social policy and increasingly authoritarian institutional practices – appear similar to the current state of affairs in Western Europe. History is not finished,

Foessel argues. The philosopher bases his argument on the idea of an epoch that is not finished and that therefore harbours similar potentials as 1938. The task here is to put the philosophical perspective to a sociological test. That we are still in the same epoch appears, sociologically, as a rather imprecise argument. Which elements allow us to determine the extent and impact of the fascist legacy in the post-fascist society of today? Which actors are working on authoritarian restorationist visions of society, and what underlying causes explain their success?

The post-authoritarian approach in global sociology that Hanafi (2019) calls for comprises at least three levels: a regime level (brutalizing authoritarianism), the level of the political-economic system (neoliberal authoritarianism), and the individual level of the 'authoritarian citizen'.[3] I see this chapter as a complementary contribution, in the sense that it addresses the organizational forms of authoritarian citizens in groups, i.e. collective bottom–up actors of authoritarian restoration (as opposed to the individual, but also to the state and economy levels). In accordance with the idea of scripts of defiance, I will not develop fully insights into the power apparatus of the state and within the neoliberal project that enable continuities in terms of authoritarianism 'from above' or 'from within' – developments in surveillance, biometrics, genetic profiling, methods of data-gathering, repression of public unrest, of lockdowns, curfews and confinement, etc. I also do not take into account the moves and interests of big capital and their links with the current developments.[4] This would require extensions of the project that, though important, I am not able to realize here.

Instead, in accordance with the idea of scripts of defiance, I will focus on the bottom–up mobilizations within the French and the German far right. In the context of the technocratic, expert-led, rather conflict-free neoliberal capitalism of today, those movements and parties could appear as defiant, in the sense of being dysfunctional and disturbing to the political order (Jacquemain and Claisse 2012: 17). This is different from the interwar period, where fractions of the possessing classes who wanted to secure capitalism betted on fascists as being functional in reducing class conflict and limiting the influence of the radical left within the integral nation state.

I have chosen not to use the term 'populist right' as my preferred denomination, first, because it downsizes other very problematic aspects of those groups; and second, because it sounds like a new feature within current politics and a way to differentiate the current 'populist right' from interwar fascism. However, one of the key characteristics of historical fascism was also populism (Griffin 1991). 'Populism' therefore does not appear as an appropriate feature of distinction. In the second section, under 'Political Crisis', I put forth another argument against the use of the term 'populism', based on Collovald's (2004) critique of the term. The structure of the chapter includes an elaboration of criteria that allow qualifying the current far right as post-fascist, in contradistinction to interwar fascism; an outline on multilevel crises in contemporary Western Europe; a description of the current far right in France and Germany, focusing on the Front National (FN)[5] and the Alternative für Deutschland (AfD) and their constituencies. If interwar fascism is largely explicable in the context of multilevel crises to which it provided answers that many considered convincing, I conclude that the current strength of the German and French far right is related to a crisis context but is not explicable in a satisfactory way as a response to multilevel crises. Instead, a thorough understanding is only possible by following down the years the deep roots of the French and German far right, something I do in the following chapter of this volume. The current far right remains unintelligible without considering it as being in direct continuity with its historical predecessors. As we see regarding its major grievances, it grapples with this past. In this sense as well, it can be considered post-fascist.

FROM FASCISM TO POST-FASCISM: DEFINING CRITERIA

Are the current collective far right actors similar to interwar fascists or not? Comparing current cases against historical fascism is in line with parts of public debate about the rise of so-called right-wing populism.[6] In order to tackle this question, we need to define interwar fascism. Based on Reichardt's literature review (2004), I chose Mann's sociological framework for this purpose. In Mann's definition, 'fascism is the pursuit of a transcendent and cleansing nation-statism through paramilitarism' (Mann 2004: 13).[7] The attempt here is to go beyond merely ideological definitions – for instance, against Griffin's (1991) definition of fascism as a political myth – and to include a clear sense of power – power as being exercised through programmes, collective actions and organizations that account for the impact of fascism beyond the level of ideas. Mann's definition therefore contains five key concepts.

Nation-statism corresponds to the exaggeration of two core elements of twentieth-century political ideology. Fascist nationalism was grounded in the idea of the organic, integral nation. Obsessed with unity, fascism therefore constructed a clear distinction between the nation and its internal and external enemies. National Socialism added a particular racial dimension to this organicism. Statism means the worshipping of state power, of the state as the bearer of a project for economic, social and moral development. A strong, hierarchical and authoritarian nation state representing the organic nation was the ultimate political goal and at the same time the organizational form that fascism took once in power. However, fascists were more radical in the formulation of their ultimate goal than in the actual form they gave their states.[8]

Transcendence refers to the goal of transcending class conflict and national divides, in accordance with the idea of the organic nation and its representation by the state. Transcendence would be obtained by repressing or eliminating the revolutionary left and by removing political and racial enemies, on the one hand. On the other hand, corporatist institutions would integrate interest groups, different economic sectors and socio-economic classes into the nation state. This ultimate aim of (class) transcendence was not accomplished, however, due to structural weaknesses in ideology (Griffin 1991: 26–55) and due to change of fascists' strategies through various stages until their accession to power (Paxton 1998). The *cleansing* aspect directly follows from transcendent nation-statism: political opponents as well as strangers within the organic nation could not be accommodated through compromise but were defined as eliminable enemies to be cleansed if the ideal of the transcendent and organic nation was to be achieved.

The cleansing is carried out by bottom–up *paramilitary* organizations. Those militias, structured along male comradeship, represented the key value and organizational form of fascism, and often existed prior to political parties. This particular provocative and aggressive bottom–up organization – one of the reasons to consider fascism a populism – was what clearly distinguished fascism within the political arena of the interwar years, and that sets it apart until today from other forms of authoritarian regimes and dictatorships. It involved a tension between its popular aspect on the one hand, and its inherent elitism and belief in hierarchies on the other.[9] Paramilitarism represented the key value of fascism as far as it is meant to be exemplary for the organic nation, for the hierarchical state it was supposed to create and for the new man that fascism was to bring about. Paramilitarism was to carry out the cleansing. Militias provoked political street violence and simultaneously presented themselves as the guarantors of law and order who sorted out society in order to achieve transcendence. Mann's criteria of cleansing and paramilitarism redress the major weaknesses of purely ideological accounts of fascism in the way they address fascism in action. Ideology, discourse and political myths only became active and harmful once they were harnessed to power organizations: 'Fascism was always uniformed, marching, armed, dangerous, and radically destabilizing of the existing order' (Mann 2004: 16). The next steps in Mann's argument are to show why fascism was successful in half of Europe, offering solutions to multilevel crisis; furthermore, why certain core constituencies were particularly attracted by one or several of the core criteria in Mann's definition.

I will proceed in steps towards a systematization of my argument on post-fascism, with each of the aforementioned five key concepts being my starting points. I have to extend two of them and find it necessary to add a sixth defining key concept: hypermasculinity.

From Nationalism to Exclusive Solidarity

I start from Mann's concept of nationalism in his study amalgamated into nation statism. Nationalism is certainly one of the key concepts to understand today's European far right. However, today's is a different nationalism from that of interwar fascism. Its addition of statism into 'nationstatism' is less obvious (see the next section on statism). More importantly, it seems necessary to extend Mann's concept of nationalism, which is too specific and too narrow for my task, into a broader concept of exclusive solidarity that extends beyond the nation (and in some cases that I will leave out here, also seeks a more reduced frame of reference, such as the regional irredentism of the Vlaams Belang or the former Lega Nord). The more unspecific term 'community', as in Paxton's definition of fascism,[10] comes closer to this than Mann's nationalism.

'Exclusiveness' is adapted from Jacquemain's discussion of the European extreme right as an 'exclusive identitarian project' (Jacquemain 2011: 2). I leave out the aspect of identity since it is not specific to the far right. That solidarity is thought of as something exclusive; in turn, it characterizes the far right's authoritarian restoration as opposed to non-authoritarian and non-restorationist, inclusive narratives of solidarity. 'Solidarity' is adapted from Sitas's idea of the creation of non-class 'horizontal solidarities' through anti-apartheid and anti-colonial forms of nationalism (Sitas 2015). I leave out 'horizontal' because self-perception as an elite or vanguard as well as hierarchical models of society prevail.

Sitas's reflections on non-class solidarities also provide a useful analytical and comparative grid. He argues that '[i]n discussing national or class figurations, i.e. the discursive work of nationalism, articulated by people who attempt to create such historical solidarities, it is important to understand that there are five elements that make the "narrative" cohere' (ibid.: 4). I adapt his table that 'tries to create a heuristic map of them' (ibid.).

The post-fascist far right bases its ideological core on an imbrication of levels of belonging.[12] First of all, there are two slightly distinct invocations of Europe as priority scales of belonging, one of the reasons why 'nationalism' would cut the story short. The first is the idea of 'white Europe', based on white supremacy, sustained by eugenicist and genuinely racist ideologies, and obsessed with the assumption of a natural hierarchy of races and the ultimate ideal of racial purity. Mann's take on nationalism does not represent my insights from volume I around the colonial mindset of National Socialism and its imperial outlook. The legacy of white Europe, however, lives on. It had been invoked in the past, as the section on 'Black Disgrace' in my chapter in volume 1 illustrated, where defence of the white race had become a major European-wide issue. An articulate denunciation of racial miscegenation and decadence related to postcolonial immigration remains limited to small circles of the extreme right. Moral panics

Table 10.1 *Exclusive Solidarities, Analytical Grid*

Historical subject	Originary traumal grievance	Social foundation of alienation	Out-groups	Meta out-groups	Modalities of legitimacy/veracity
White Europe	Postcolonial immigration	Miscegenation/racial decadence	Racialized others		White supremacy (eugenicism, racialism)
The Occident	Islamization	Co-presence of Muslims; oppression of and aggression against women	Racialized others; Muslims	International communism/ Third World nationalism**	(Judaeo-) Christian civilization; Reconquista
# The people of a nation	Globalization; subordination under *Acquis Communautaire*	Loss of national overeignty; Brussel's mandate; 'open borders'	Racialized others; Muslims; immigrants; foreign labour force;		National priority; integrity of the nation;
˙ La Grande Nation	Vichy/Guerre d'Algérie/1968	Cultural heterogeneity and 'anti-French racism'; French Islam	Racialized others; Muslims; immigrants; foreign labour force; communists/leftists		Cultural particularism against universalism of French republicanism; universalism of French republicanism (*laïcité*) against communitarianism
˙ *Volksgemeinschaft*	Holocaust/1968	Parliamentarianism; multiculturalism; culture of remembrance	Racialized others; Muslims; immigrants; foreign labour force; communists/leftists		1000 years of German history; racial organicism

Note: # Denotes subcategory of the historical subjects 'white Europe' and 'the Occident'.
˙ Denotes subcategory of the historical subject 'the people of a nation'.
** Over time, these have evolved to become cosmopolitanism/the EU political elites; 'lying media', 'leftist hegemony'.

Source: Author's own, adapted from Sitas (2015).

around sexual aggression of Muslim refugees against white women, however, echo such historical memories and fears of the dark stranger. In the broader public, what disturbs people is rather the idea of cultural heterogeneity. This makes them call for an exclusive solidarity of white Europeans, across nation states within Europe. This seems all the more logical since the issue of migration is in itself also a transnational phenomenon (Bauman 2017: 17; Sebaux 2016: 387).

A slightly different shade is contained in calls for solidarity at the level of a civilizational 'Occident' (in French) or 'Abendland' (in German). The grievance here is the alleged ongoing Islamization of Judaeo-Christian civilization. This relates to the vision of the Muslim as being highly reproductive, conveying fears of a Muslim settlement and 'takeover' of Europe (Zúquete 2008). The invocation of Christian identity is one of the connecting zones between the conservative, centre-right and factions of the extreme right:[13]

> The increased perception of Muslims, and Islam in general, as an ominous threat to the native communities is in no small part responsible for this evolution. In a few cases, such as that of the National Front, the attention paid to Christianity is an intensified continuation of a previous ideological stance. Thus, when [J.M.] Le Pen defends outlawing large mosques on the grounds that they constitute 'buildings of political-religious conquest' and 'threaten the Christian identity of our country', he is by and large reiterating a familiar theme. (Ibid.: 324–25)

The French President Emmanuel Macron's most recent advances to regulate Islamic life in France, such as his bill against separatism, clearly indicate how such visions dominate large parts of French politics, following the far right's determined strategy to place them on the agenda.

The idea of a civilizational Occident that needs to be defended against Islamization or even the assertion of a necessary re-Christianization of Europe is behind the calls for 'Reconquista!' voiced by identitarian groups today (Keim 2017). They invoke historical antecedents as a legitimate source to eternalize the supposed conflict between Europe and Islam and steer fears that the decadence of Christian Europe is imminent. This version is obviously close to the idea of 'white Europe'. The accent is however more on the co-presence of Muslims and on European values than on racial aspects. In France in particular, both combine in specific ways. Colonial thinking is deeply ingrained in far-right discourses about Islam, where the widely held perception is that any Muslim is Algerian and any Algerian a Muslim. In this sense, moral panics around sexual aggression against French white women are not only related to fear of miscegenation but seen as a threat to civilizational achievements of emancipation. As various feminist groups have pointed out, this argument of Muslims being oppressive against women sounds rather ironic in the sense that the advocates of this version of the Occident otherwise often hold rather patriarchal views. Interestingly, references to the Occident as the historical subject to be defended reaches out beyond the current EU, including Russia. I will discuss below the supposed and known interferences of Russia with the European far right. The Russian philosopher Alexander Dugin features as one of the key ideologues on the continent for the theorization of white and Judaeo-Christian Europe.

We could apprehend those developments beyond nationalism in Mann's sense as emerging post-nationalism in the current far right. I find it more adequate to think about it as intersecting levels of exclusive solidarities. Below the European level, there are calls for solidarity amongst the people of one nation. They vary from country to country. I will develop in more detail the French and German versions below. They share a series of meta-outgroups. In comparison with the interwar years, we observe substantive shifts.

Historically, the originary grievance here was the threat of international communism as well as Third World nationalism during the Cold War and decolonization. Currently, the major perceived threat is the alleged ongoing Islamization of 'Judaeo-Christian' civilization. While historical fascism was decidedly anti-communist (and could therefore gather support from the possessing classes), the consequence of the dilution of communism, class struggle and workers' movements is that post-fascism has lost this anti-communist outlook. The energetic impetus oriented against the Bolshevik threat has given way to a more conservative and reactionary orientation that has lost its attractiveness to wealthy elites who find their interests better protected by the EU and international organizations. Another important transformation concerns the move from imperial aggressiveness towards a defensive anti-immigration stance. Decolonization has thus 'post-colonized' original fascism (Traverso 2015).

Another substantive shift regarding the outgroups is the progressive inclusion, at least in several official discourses of established far-right parties, of the arch-deviance of the Jew (see Keim 2014) into the idea of a Judaeo-Christian Europe.[14] This applies to Western Europe only[15] and has intensified massively with migrations resulting from wars and conflicts in the Middle East, and, most importantly, since the series of violent attacks within Europe claimed by or attributed to the Daesh and related groups. Since then, the deviant figure of the Muslim has been fused with the deviant figure of the terrorist. The discourse and desperate agitation around 'international terrorism' reveals how poorly equipped all concerned nation states are to even intellectually face a non-state transnational army carrying out non-state violence. The call for exclusive solidarity is based on an assumption of national priority[16] and the need to maintain the integrity of the nation. Simultaneously, it inhibits addressing the matter as a class question.

In this sense, exclusive solidarity translates into a 'right to stay amongst us'.

Combined with calls to limit or 'inverse' immigration flows, this right to stay amongst us also translates into policies for spatial segregation and avoiding closeness between supposedly culturally different and incompatible population groups. New right intellectual accounts serve to justify this view. According to Jacquemain, far from an outward-looking rhetoric of sovereignty, from assumptions of racial superiority, from the ideal of an organic nation or from aggressive or imperialist nationalism, nationalism has been re-elaborated to fit better the rising fear of heterogeneity and cultural friction within European societies: '*Il ne s'agit plus ni de dominer, ni de rejeter la domination, mais d'organiser la ségrégation, de refuser la cohabitation. Le projet de la nouvelle extrême droite, c'est la réponse à la mondialisation par la vision d'une sorte d'apartheid généralisé*' ('The question is not any more about domination, or to reject domination, but to organize segregation, to refuse cohabitation. The extreme right's new project responds to globalization with the vision of some generalized form of apartheid') (Jacquemain and Claisse 2012: 22, translated by author).

Europe as the level of identification and belonging does not contradict the national framework as another level for exclusive solidarities. From there, we can identify another shared outgroup. Again, in our day, cosmopolitans are viewed as opposed to patriots. The calls for a European front against the debilitating effects of immigration, outbreeding, globalization or cultural mixture are still expressed under the umbrella idea of solidarity amongst sovereign nations, the 'Europe of fatherlands'.[17] In this sense, the political and administrative framework of the EU functions as a key projection, including political and bureaucratic elites and experts, the new cosmopolitans, that sustain and support it nationally as well as at the European level in order to destroy the nation (d'Appolonia 1992: 23). This is what AfD-Member of Parliament Alexander Gauland expressed when he said, 'It is time that we take the destiny of the German people [*Volk*], in order for it to remain a German people, out of the hands of our Chancellor' (quoted in Borcholte 2015). Far rightists voice conspiracy theories against a political establishment that sells out its population and aims for their nation's decadence through Islamization and racial mixing in order to further US dominance. The Eastern European version is more confident in adding that the US is led by Jewish capital (personified in the name of George Soros). The EU appears here as the opposite of the vision of a 'Europe of fatherlands'. The shared concern about the subordination of the nation under the European *Acquis Communautaire* or 'Brussel's Mandate', including loss of national sovereignty and implementation of the Schengen agreement, i.e. supposedly 'open borders', is but another declination of loss of national sovereignty and specificity.[18]

Apart from Muslim and cosmopolitan elites embodied in the EU, the 'lying media' form another meta-outgroup, as it is supposedly under the influence of 'hegemonic leftists'. In Germany, in particular, reference to *Lügenpresse* clearly is in continuation with NS vocabulary and discourse. Not an outgroup but a common object of outrage is political correctness. This does not only refer to supposed 'anti-national racism' (i.e. affirmative action and non-racist language, for example), but also to what is perceived as 'gender ideology' (*Genderwahn*, *idéologie du genre*) where 'gender mainstreaming' is understood as eliminating gender identities. This has debilitating effects on the healthy development of masculinity and femininity amongst young children, on the reproduction of traditional family models and ultimately of white Europeans – some put forth rather intellectual or cultural arguments, a few insist on the eugenicist implications. The AfD's family policy,[19] for instance, is clearly oriented against the recognition of LGBTQIA+ rights and towards the traditional family model as the 'germ cell of the nation' (Herkenhoff 2016b: 205–06). According to this author, the arguments of the AfD youth league, Junge Alternative (JA), are in continuation with 'core ideologemes of völkisch-nationalist traditions of thought' centred on the idea of the '*Volkskörper*' and eugenic aims of breeding the German people (ibid., referring to Kellershohn 2013). Breeding national Germans is also related to countering 'demographic aberration' in Germany, in direct relation to migration. The aim is to achieve a result where birth rates rise and immigration ceases. In France, the *Manif pour tous* movement against same-sex marriage has been a major mobilizing moment linking the centre-right and extreme right.

Apart from these major sites of struggle, sideshows are taking place in domains where the far right is slowly gaining ground as well. This is the case, for example, in the animal rights and alternative nutrition scene. Far-right activists have been participating in the *Nuit debout devant l'abbatoir* (standing up against slaughterhouses) movement as a means of countering not only animal suffering but *halal* slaughter in French public slaughterhouses. In Germany, a new trade union close to the AfD questions scientific approaches to climate change to accommodate and mobilize workers in the traditional automobile industry. The pandemic context of 2020–21 has again facilitated the profiling of far-right actors in opposition to government policies. On the one hand, they have questioned policy measures and the vaccine strategy based on conspiracy theories, and staged important street protests where they could connect with previously non-rightist groups. On the other hand, growing nationalist discourses about 'each country first' in accessing the vaccines have severely criticized the EU strategy for obtention and distribution of the medication.

Against this background of shared themes, I will look more closely at the two national cases. In France, the appeal to the people is expressed in terms of *grandeur de la France*. The specific originary grievances here are collaboration under the Vichy regime as a consequence of German occupation that discredits the aspirations of the far right within broad segments of the population; the Algerian war and independence, representing loss of empire as the prime expression of France's 'grandeur'; as well as 1968 and the supposed 'leftist hegemony' that followed and against which the far right re-established itself as a counter-force. While earlier far-right orientations insisted on cultural particularism against the universalism of French republicanism, current proponents base their claims on the chauvinist assumption of the universalism of French republicanism against communitarianism (French: *communautarisme*; Stora 1997). The nationalism of today's French far right is hardly distinguishable any more from the mainstream concept of the French nation since, as opposed to former French fascist thinkers who relied on the German idea of *volk*, current representatives refer to the republican heritage and to the political concept of 'the people'. The social foundation of alienation experienced by the French nation is postcolonial cultural heterogeneity, i.e. the presence of 'dark strangers', especially French Islam. This key outgroup is closely related to French colonial history, a chapter that stretches into the metropole and has not been adequately addressed by means of a conscious politics of memory or any reconciliatory attempt. Jean-Marie Le Pen himself declared that '[t]he fight for a French Algeria has prepared the fight for a French France' (cited in ibid.: 24). Colonial assimilationist logic has entered the French mainland and set the bar so high that integration is rendered impossible, justifying measures of social segregation between incompatible population groups.[20]

Those threatening people can rely on the *droit du sol*, i.e. the French nation grants citizenship to those born on its soil, leaving no room for manoeuvre in legally handling those people differently from the 'true French' (*Français de souche*). Proponents of this version of exclusive solidarity agree that assimilation has largely failed, in particular with regard to Muslims. Since strangers who hold citizenship can and do claim all sorts of rights and gain support in rejecting racism and discrimination, far-right actors perceive 'anti-French racism' as being on the increase and feel 'like strangers in their own country'. The latter adds the political left (in prior decades, communists) to the already mentioned outgroups. Their inclusive solidarities are accused of backing claims by undeserving groups. In the end, they are seen as allies to *jihad*ism, as the most recent accusation of *Islamo-gauchisme* (Islamo-leftism) that allegedly dominates French universities insinuates. Those proponents base their claims on the chauvinist assumption of the universalism of French republicanism against communitarianism (French: *communautarisme*). This is particularly evident in recent times in the debate around *laïcité* (see below). While in former times assimilation was the corresponding policy, the French far right today rather argues in terms of multiculturalism. The intellectual new right, realizing the limited chances for racial thinking to gain support, has managed to re-elaborate racial thinking in such a way that cultural differences are supposed to be accepted and are granted a right to existence, but under the condition of remaining within bounded entities, calling for segregation of diverse population groups. This is but a thin veiling of the underlying racism (Shields 2007).

In the German case, the historical subject of the national people would be *Volksgemeinschaft*. There is asymmetry in my categorization since ideas of the greatness of the French nation are much more broadly accepted in France than ideas of *Volksgemeinschaft* in Germany. However, if the aim is to understand national specificities, I believe this distinction still makes sense. I have elaborated on the German concept of *Volk* at length in my contribution to volume I. Suffice it to say here that after a period stretching to the recent past where NS vocabulary had been banned from public spaces but subsisted in rather hidden ways,[21] the AfD has led a strategic struggle to reintroduce NS-laden terms into public debate.[22] This concerns in particular the adjective *völkisch* with clearly historical connotations.

The originary grievance of the *Volksgemeinschaft* ideologues is paradoxically, but without any doubt, the Holocaust, or more precisely, its undeniability. This is what delegitimizes within broad segments of the population any call for the greatness of the German nation and constitutes a major disadvantage in comparison with the far right in other countries. AfD politician Gauland clearly expresses this: 'Hitler has destroyed much more than cities and humans, he has broken the German's spine.' Or again: 'At least in one point we have more difficulty: The British need not struggle with Auschwitz' (quoted in Ulrich and Geis 2016). Since the Holocaust cannot be denied, the far right plays around with ambiguous references to this past, partly to provoke attention, partly to banalize the facts, partly to express their frustration at being strongly disadvantaged with regard to other national far-right movements. While the early post-war far right in Germany opposed parliamentarism and multiculturalism as the main sources of alienation of the *Volksgemeinschaft*, nowadays the German culture of remembrance – in AfD member Björn Höcke's view, a 'shame culture' or 'culture of disgrace' (quoted in Kamann 2017) – is seen as the basic social foundation that inhibits national pride. Höcke's agitation against the German disgrace in terms of its memory politics echoes Joseph Goebbel's outrage against the 'disgrace of Versailles'.

Outgroups are similar to the French case. The modalities of veracity, aiming to overcome the grievance of the Holocaust's undeniability, is the invocation of 1,000 years of German history, within which the NS years appear as no more than 'a bird's shit' (Gauland, quoted in Hebel 2018). Within sections of the German far right that are intellectually versed, racial organicism remains another source of legitimacy of *Volksgemeinschaft* (d'Appolonia 1992: 21; see also Kemper 2016a).[23]

In framing calls for diverse forms of exclusive solidarities, the French and German far right have found their most promising response to ideological crisis (see below). In placing exclusive solidarities above the individual, they aim to transcend internal conflict and to close up spaces of privilege. They represent 'displacement ideologies' that give the illusion of solving social conflict along lines of race, culture or creed (Hammerschmidt 2005). Because exclusive solidarities are essentially based on the exclusion of others and enemies, the potential for violence and coercion is inherent in them.

Statism

In Western Europe, the neoliberal turn, with increased individualization of economic success and material risks, has caused a discursive shift. Against materially based inclusive solidarity, visions of culture-, nation- or race-based exclusive solidarity, until then rather marginal, have gained ground (see below, the sections on crises). Whereas the FN, for instance, was largely Reaganist in orientation throughout the 1980s and had fully assimilated neoliberal ideas (Shields 2007: 192 ff.), the current far right could capitalize on this inversion of trends that accompanied the retreat of the state from its post-war welfare and social security functions in order to attract new voter bases. The trend towards cultural exclusivity and national closure that the far right proposes as a response to the economic and ideological crises of neoliberalism also has another, more macro-level reason: the fact that no state can claim to control its national economy (see 'Economic Crisis' below). With the ascent of neoliberalism and global capitalism, statism in terms of the state as an economic actor itself has been in crisis. The state has appeared as weakened within Western Europe not only in terms of its economic agency but supposedly because of the superimposed EU framework. The 2008 economic crisis and the fact that the state has re-entered the economic field as a major political actor has led to partial reconfigurations within the far right. In addition to cultural exclusivity and various taints of nationalism, some parties reaffirm a strong state against the EU and against globalization. Beyond calls for 'Make X great again' or the metaphor of the closed border, certain economic imaginaries take shape that do not resemble the FN's economic orientation of the 1980s. In their view, a strong state is a free state, where free means mainly free from the subordination of national law and action under the EU treaties, but also free from international legal dispositions and from US domination. The key features of this statism, realized differently by different far-right groups and parties, are six: regaining control over the economy, guaranteeing law and order, bearing national values, guaranteeing true democracy, providing exclusive public services.

Reinforcing the State's Control over the Economy

At the national level, FN[24] demands a strong interventionist state that will re-industrialize the country and renationalize some important companies. In the international sphere, FN favours protectionism. It campaigned in 2017 for France's exit from the Eurozone – reflecting the party's strong anti-EU stance – and bringing back the national currency, until Marine Le Pen shipwrecked the TV duel with Macron when explicating the concrete realization and full impact of such measures. The current evolution of Brexit has made EU exit options less popular and, therefore, electorally unwise. Further, FN asks for stronger taxes on imports to boost national production, and for a strong state against the power of finance and speculation.

The State as Guarantor of Law and Order

Statism plays a role at the level of the largely authoritarian calls for law and order that the far right shares, although often in more exaggerated yet somehow pioneering expressions, with the conservative right. Faced with moral decadence, deviance of all kinds, immigration and the most diverse illegal and illicit activities threatening the security and well-being of spotless citizens, leaders call for more police, more prisons, the introduction of the death penalty, among others. Echoing the moral panic around the Black Disgrace (Keim 2014), any incidence of aggression or violence committed by dark strangers against white women becomes a key event of mobilization (see below, the section on hypermasculinity). The state as the guarantor of law and order applies in particular to the call for reinforced border and immigration controls. Global migration flows that even the sophisticated investments into 'fortress Europe' could not stop is represented as a failure of the state. Far-right thinkers and leaders favour the idea that the state's legitimacy depends on its capacity to ensure the level of law and order that citizens demand (Quent 2016a: 21). The authoritarianism involved is largely directed towards measures against 'insecurity' as represented by migrants/terrorists, not against economic or material insecurity of citizens in the first place (see, however, 'The State as Provider of Public Services' below). In order for the state to be able to guarantee law and order for its citizens, and reflecting the anti-EU position of far-right parties, a related request is to make national law supreme to the *Acquis Communautaire* or to any international law. As former Italian Minister of the Interior Matteo Salvini from the far-right Lega Nord calls for a census of Roma people within Italy in order to be able to more easily expel Roma who are not Italian nationals – whereas 'unfortunately', as he said, Italian Roma will have to stay in Italy[25] (Kirchgaessner 2018) – he still has to realize that Italy cannot expel EU citizens to other EU countries. Nationalist accusations against the EU's vaccine strategy during the 2020/21 pandemic follow the same logic.

The State as Bearer of National Values

Faced with cultural heterogeneity and cosmopolitanism, the far right is putting more emphasis on the state as a bearer of national values and national identity. In

France, a strong state is perceived as the only protector of republican values, and the FN represents itself as the only party that unfalteringly upholds these (Perrineau 2016: 65). In particular, and this is where the far right has gained large portions of public debate, the state is supposed to implement laicity (*laïcité*) at all levels. Through the ideological renewal initiated by M. Le Pen, the FN has imported republican values like *laïcité* and public service (see below). It reinterprets ideas that have been upheld largely by the left and centre left in authoritarian restorationist garb. In the case of *laïcité*, 'that could be understood as a logic of individual emancipation but also as a logic of injunction to conformity' (Jacquemain 2011: 2–3; translated by author), the aim is clearly to demonstrate that Islam is fundamentally incompatible with French republicanism (Perrineau 2016: 65). In order to give shape and visibility to the state as bearer of national values, M. Le Pen has called repeatedly for the creation of a Ministry for the Interior, Immigration and Laicity (*Ministère de l'Interieur, de l'Immigration et de la Laïcité*). In Germany, reflecting the growing hegemony of far-right discourses in the political centre, the former Ministry of the Interior has adopted an additional task, named now Ministry of the Interior, Construction and Homeland (*Ministerium des Inneren, für Bau und Heimat*). The corresponding current minister Horst Seehofer is from Bavaria, where the regional government has had a ministry for *Heimat* prior to the federal one. Similar to the inversion of the formerly liberal-left concept of *laïcité* into an authoritarian one, feminist issues are also instrumentalized. Reinforcing national values is supposed to benefit women – the emancipated amongst us – as opposed to their oppression under Islam. Another claim of the far right is to stop affirmative action, which is seen as anti-national racism.

The State as Bearer of National Solidarity and Morality

Related to the issue of values is the idea of a strong, united state. This combines with the refusal of 'national repentances', in Germany epitomized by what the far right calls 'shame culture'. In France, further, Florian Philippot, for instance, stressed that the republic is indivisible. A strong state leaves no room for strong regionalisms. The Catalonian conflict has increased concerns in this sense, regarding, in particular, Corsica. This aspect shifts the far right's approach to the state closer to Mann's originary meaning of nation-statism.

The State as Guarantor of Democracy

Historical fascism was deeply anti-democratic and anti-parliamentarian. Today's context of established liberal democracies is fundamentally different. Berman draws an optimistic conclusion from this assessment:

But if the similarities are striking, the differences are even more so. Most obvious,

> today's extremists claim they want not to bury democracy but to improve it. They critique the functioning of contemporary democracy but offer no alternative to it, just vague promises to make government stronger, more efficient, and more responsive. Current right-wing extremists are thus better characterized as populist rather than fascist, since they claim to speak for everyday men and women against corrupt, debased, and out-of-touch elites and institutions. In other words, they are certainly antiliberal, but they are not antidemocratic. This distinction is not trivial. If today's populists come to power – even the right-wing nationalists among them – the continued existence of democracy will permit their societies to opt for a do-over by later voting them out. Indeed, this may be democracy's greatest strength: it allows countries to recover from their mistakes. (Berman 2016: 43)

However, this might be a short-sighted assessment of the current situation, and one with a brief memory. That the far right calls for more, better or true democracy sounds paradoxical only at first sight. There is a legacy of claims to 'true democracy' within the extreme right reaching back to NS ideology (Botsch 2017). This is not to say that the relationship of the far right with fundamental democracy is not highly problematic. Regarding the internal functioning of far-right organizations and parties, to start with, it appears that 'politics on the right is characterized by a specific organizational form that builds on strong, personalized leadership rather than citizen participation' (della Porta 2017: 34). This relates to the ongoing debate around the populism of the current far right. According to Della Porta, 'populism is tied to a plebiscitary linkage which does not empower the people as a whole, but rather an individual leader. This plebiscitarian turn can be seen in regressive politics, with leaders appealing to the masses through anti-establishment discourses while manipulating rather than involving "the people"' (ibid.: 36). In this sense, the strategy of far-right leaders, in line with the NS heritage, is directed against representative democracy and oriented towards the ideal of the charismatic leader who embodies the will of the nation. This is what is meant, ultimately, by 'direct' or 'true democracy' within the far right: freeing the direct link between leader and followers from bureaucratic hurdles, democratic procedures and superimposed transnational frameworks. The FN as well favours this direct and exclusive relationship between the public and the charismatic leader (Baier 2016). Furthermore, at a more abstract level, in line with its Euroscepticism, the far right considers a strong state to be the only 'truly democratic' body as opposed to the EU. The latter appears subjugated to the power of cosmopolitan elites, bureaucrats and experts, to global finance and to the rules of the globalized economy at large that play to the detriment of nations and their people. The AfD, for instance, suggests that the German people should decide through direct democratic dispositions according to the

Swiss model (Oppelland 2017). This call for more direct political participation appears in line with the critique of the existing political system (Decker 2016: 11).

Nevertheless, the AfD's claim to represent 'the people' has a different connotation than in the French context. While in France, populism is discursively linked to the *classes populaires*, i.e. the working classes, and therefore the former constituencies of leftist politics, the German *Volk* conveys racial–biological connotations.[26]

The State as Provider of Public Services

Finally, capitalizing on the weakening of precarious classes, the far right also advocates a strong state to ensure better public services for its citizens. Again, this is an exclusive privilege for true nationals. At this level, Herkenhoff gives a precise analysis of the family policies (here as foreseen by the AfD's youth league programme) as an example that ties together the entity of the people, of the German nation and of the state through the 'germ cell' of the family. Accordingly, '[a]s the smallest social entity, only the classic family is able to ensure the survival of the state and therefore is the only form of cohabitation that deserves financial aid' (quoted in Herkenhoff 2016b: 205–06). Since the state is ultimately responsible for providing the conditions under which families reproduce, public school education has become one of the major sites of struggle for far-right anti-gender activists.

To conclude, statism clearly is a feature of the current German and French far right. It does not appear to be a major issue when compared to their blatant racist and anti-immigration discourses. However, their statism does not combine as elegantly as in Mann's account of historical fascism into nation-statism. I have outlined above how exclusive solidarities are articulated within, but also beyond, national frames of reference. The emerging vision of a 'Europe of fatherlands' tries to follow this movement of changing levels of reference and ensures the maintenance of nation-statist ideas.

Transcendence

The kind of strong nationalism explored here does contain some idea of transcendence, in particular the divide between 'the people' and the elites. However, the strong sense of transcendence that was tangible in interwar fascisms has become obsolete in a context where class struggle has nearly come to an end. With the bureaucratization and overall weakening of trade unions, the fragmentation and alienation of the working class through the restructuring, transformation and offshoring of production, combined with the neoliberal narrative of individualization, has led to a situation where class conflict, i.e. conflict over distribution, has given way to 'multiculturalism' as the major site of social friction. And racialized 'others' are an outgroup to far-right exclusive solidarities. The same applies to the supposed divide between corrupt elites and ordinary people. Transcendence is not a necessary option for national renaissance and reintegration.

From Paramilitarism to Vigilantism and Terrorism

Paramilitarism, according to Mann, was a key value as well as the primordial organizational form of fascism. During the interwar years, political violence and paramilitarism as a means of political struggle were widely accepted. Every major political party in Weimar Germany had its militia. Today, the political context in Western Europe is fundamentally different and paramilitarism has largely disappeared from the political landscape. In the case of France, this is a more recent evolution: until the foundation of the FN, paramilitarism remained an important organizational form. The diverse fractions of 'French Algeria', through its major armed expression, the OAS (Organisation Armée Secréte), also present in the metropole, revived paramilitarism after 1945 (Renken 2006; Shields 2007: 90–117).[27]

If Mann defined the paramilitary as one of two key organizational forms of interwar fascism, in the absence of military crisis and in a context where parliamentary democracy is firmly established, the strategic choice by far-right intellectuals and activist networks to bet on a political party within the current political system as the key organizational form has to be considered an opportunistic choice. A party does not, as paramilitarism did for interwar fascism, correspond to both key value and organizational form. Important fractions of both new right intellectuals and networked activist groups on the ground have no affinity whatsoever with parliamentary democracy.

In the current phase, there have been so-called 'lone-wolf' terrorist acts all over Europe.[28] Those deeds, although acted out by single individuals, clearly had right-wing extremist political motivations acquired through socialization and participation in corresponding groups and networks. In every European country as well, we find organized groups that practise extreme right-inspired political violence against leftists, migrants and ethnic minorities, and, within the last few years in Germany, increasingly against representatives of established politics and the state.[29] Because they remain small in size – at least their visible part – do not control territory and do not wear uniforms, we cannot consider them paramilitary. Because organization happens underground and because traditionally state organs are slow in reacting to right-wing violence, it is often difficult to say whether a violent act was carried out by a single individual or by an organized group of people. However, against the commonly held assumption, often expressed in court procedures against perpetrators, that right-wing violence is essentially a spontaneous law-and-order problem involving drunk, jobless and not especially bright youth 'without any definite political orientation' (Oberländer 1993: 177), we can assume that more often than not violent acts depend on some form of organization. In addition, close contact between state organs and right-wing terrorism had also seriously troubled the public with regard to the series of murders by the group National-Socialist Underground (NSU).

Another type of violent organization that often involves far-right motivations is vigilante groups. Rather small in scale, they attack supposed deviants in order to protect the population. In some cases, they do control certain areas, but next to police and state organs that are perceived as deficient. Vigilantism gives shape to the 'dark side' of civil society (Roth 2003). This seems to represent a truly mobilizing activity. According to statistics in Germany, for instance, alongside committed neo-Nazis and right-wing extremists, individuals without prior political experience have joined such vigilante groups in recent years to practise violent self-justice against refugees, as a result of civil society's interpretation of rising numbers of refugees as a failure of the state. The motivation of vigilante groups is not radical change of the system but rather stabilizing the system by defending the old order through exercising self-justice. This can involve, in their view, momentary suspension of the state's monopoly of violence (Quent 2016a: 20). The German group Bürgerwehr Freital/360, for example, pursued the aim of creating 'national liberated zones' until its members were condemned for the creation of a terrorist association in 2018.

If those groups and actions cannot count as paramilitary and remain marginal to the political game, in all the mentioned cases, organized violence is a means to claim agency, to take concrete measures in order to bring order into a social world that is perceived as anomic. They all enact the claim that the state does not sufficiently guarantee the security of its legitimate citizens, defined according to an exclusive identitarian conception. Often, this assumption is combined with conspiracy constructs of an external manipulation of the state. Despite their own illegal action in terms of the state's monopoly of violence, their aim is to reinforce a strong, authoritarian state (Quent 2016a; Waldmann 2011). In many cases, the police have not intervened to prevent their actions. This includes refusing a postulate of fundamental equality between humans to the point where they can legitimately, yet not legally, be intimidated and attacked physically. This violence helps to restore some sense of coherence and expresses claims to privilege. It also has a fundamentally socializing aspect (Roth 2003), as Mann (2004) confirms with his concept of the socializing micro-cage of paramilitary groups.

An interesting additional observation refers to the nearly complete 'speechlessness' of right-wing violence. This sets it apart from left-wing violence that has always sought to provide verbal, elaborate and often strongly theorized justifications of its actions. Right-wing violence, however, hardly provides official justifications 'because the inferiority of certain groups of humans is regarded as *natural.* . . . Theoretically sustained avowals are not deemed necessary in order to legitimate violence, because in their own view, the perpetrators execute the *natural* order and the *true* interest of the people [*Volk*]' (Quent 2016a: 24, emphases in the original).

Cleansing

Cleansing in the sense it acquired in interwar fascism has not appeared as a palpable characteristic of far-right parties. There has been extreme right physical violence and murder of migrants within every single European country. Left-wing locals and activists, at times even established politicians, have also at times been victims of aggression. In some cases those were individual actions, in others, armed organizations were behind the deeds (see the section on paramilitarism). In Germany, some neo-Nazi groups are proud of announcing 'national liberated zones', small territorial entities supposedly cleansed of anyone not considered truly German. However, even the broader far-right movements and official parties have not publicly endorsed those actions. It would be counterfactual speculation to try and guess how far far-right parties would go in their intentions of promoting an exclusive solidarity based on the ideal of a pure and integral nation if they assumed power.

If there has been cleansing, we could argue, somewhat ironically, that it has happened within the ranks of the far right. Marine Le Pen and the French Front National are known to have silenced their connections with violent extreme-right groups and to have expelled them from marches and public demonstrations (*Marine Le Pen: L'héritière*, dir. C. Fourest and F. Venner, 2011).[30] Similarly, the AfD has spent a considerable amount of time with internal disputes around the exposure of overtly Nazi attitudes by some of its key representatives and the necessity to avoid any overt connections. A veritable detective's work even finds out how Björn Höcke, one of AfD's chief politicians, has carefully hidden his intellectual contributions and political activities for the neo-Nazi National Democratic Party of Germany (NPD) (Kemper 2016a). In the political sense, we could debate whether a different form of cleansing has happened within the far right that tries to blur its lineages with interwar fascism, in accordance with its originary grievance, the undeniability of the Holocaust.

Hypermasculinity

To the five criteria put forth by Mann, I add the far right's vision of gender that largely overlaps, although updated, with that of historical fascists. The gender dimension has not been included prominently in theoretical approaches to fascism but I consider it to be an additional key point. I therefore put forth the sixth key concept of 'hypermasculinity' as an extension of Mann's initial framework. Male bonding appears as a key organizational principle involved in extreme-right politicization[31] in the past as well as in the present. To start with, the widespread literature on political far-right parties agrees on the persistence of a gender gap among members as well as among voters (Dubslaff 2017: 160–62; Harteveld *et al.* 2015; Oppelland 2017). This is all the more true for extreme-right fringe groups that were for a long time 'considered as "male" practically by definition' (Blum 2017: 322). Their ideal of masculinity occupies a central place in their world view and so has to be considered as constitutive.[32] Within the far right, this warrior image corresponds to a 'right' or 'true' masculinity within an originary natural order, in the service of the nation and race. Being a 'real man', as insinuated by such visions of hypermasculinity, seems to be one of the key motivations for young men to join the scene. Male aggressiveness is strongly associated with the will to dominate in perceived competition with foreigners for women. The control of women's relationships with unwelcomed outsiders, in particular of their sexuality and potential reproduction, corresponds to defending the nation and the white race. This has no parallel amongst women. It foreshadows an ambiguous vision of those same women.[33]

Hypermasculinity is embedded in the vision of 'gender complementarity'. Gender complementarity is used to mobilize against gender equality, and to restore the original meaning of the family against feminism and gender pluralism. The idea of gender complementarity is often religiously grounded, as is demonstrated in the Vatican's reaction to the 1994 United Nations conference on Population and Development in Cairo (1994) and on Women in Beijing (1995). The Catholic Church, in alliance with Protestants, Muslims and Jews, fought international advances in sexual and reproductive rights as a first step towards international recognition of abortion, as a threat to traditional motherhood and as a legitimization of homosexuality (Paternotte and Kuhar 2017: 263). Alongside the religious justification shared across creeds, within other fractions of the far right, biologistic legitimations of hypermasculinity and gender complementarity prevail (Villa 2017: 104).

In the mobilizations against gender equality and gender pluralism, variously termed 'gender ideology', '*idéologie du genre*' or '*Genderwahn*', political extremisms effortlessly overlap with much wider and more moderate constituencies, including conservative parties, conservative Catholic or broader Salafist constituencies, men's rights movements and homophobic circles. In those mobilizations, gender functions as a 'symbolic glue' that allows the formation of broader coalitions, especially when actors do not share the same ideological framework (Kováts and Pôim 2015).[34] All across Europe, anti-gender movements also address the issue as one of imposition by force through outside, imperial forces – the EU or the UN, for instance.

Furthermore, hypermasculinity clearly opposes the legacy of 1968. The publication by identitarian author Willinger, *Die Identitäre Generation: Eine Kriegserklärung an die 68er* (The Identitary Generation: A Declaration of War on the Generation of 1968, published in 2013), expresses this clearly: 'You have deprived men of their masculinity. Reduced them to feeble teddy bears, with no energy, no courage or strength, in short: no will to power' (quoted in Blum 2017: 326). Opposition to 1968 includes anti-authoritarianism (conceived of as 're-education'), feminism (and related calls for gender-sensitive language and 'political correctness') and sexual liberties, regarded as the foundation of the current dilution of gender roles and family models, and therefore representing a 'threat to social order, shared values and the moral integrity of German society' (Villa 2017: 105). Education is a crucial battlefield. Gender mainstreaming and gender-sensitive education are accused of inhibiting the healthy development of masculinity and femininity amongst young children. As outlined in the section on exclusive solidarity, alongside cultural arguments, we also find more eugenicist visions (Herkenhoff 2016b: 205–06). As a consequence, homophobia is the counterpart to hypermasculinity and is equally shared by both forms of authoritarian restoration (Claus and Virchow 2017: 310–11).

Gender complementarity involves the ideological construction of normative male and female bodies, as well as of a normative, child-producing family. Women partake in these constructions of essentialist gender stereotypes.[35] Hypermasculinity is articulated with constructions of 'total femininity', equally found in both cases. In the case of the Catholic Church's mobilizations against gender equality, much of the ideological substance goes back to Pope John Paul's writings laying the foundations of an anthropology of women (Kováts 2017: 178–79). Restoring the honour of women as mothers, as bearers and educators of the following generation is one of the far right's programmatic ambitions (Köttig 2017: 225–26).

Hypermasculinity is not without its contradictions, however. Despite the ideological limitation of their roles, women are actively taking part in right-wing movements. A woman now leads one of the major European far-right parties, although she owes her status more to her father's nepotism than to her gender. M. Le Pen plays on her femininity as a strategic resource for de-diabolization. However, it was noted that 'she constantly transgresses the "natural" borders of her gender. She uses sexual imagery to defame her political opponents and deny them any kind of masculinity. For her, the former French president, Sarkozy, embodied "hectic impotence" (*impuissance agitée*) and the new president, Hollande, "flabby impotence" (*impuissance molle*)' (italics added). She thus somehow follows the image of a masculine leader, reinforcing visions of hypermasculinity to the point where 'because of this gendered ambiguity, she is celebrated as a homo-icon in certain circles' (Dubslaff 2017: 169). In extremist circles, women have the advantage of being less controlled and persecuted because of widespread gender stereotypes within police and security apparatuses and in the media.[36] Gender ideals are also not unequivocal with regard to political demands. While in Germany, far-right women fight against external childcare in order to restore true motherhood, the FN calls for an expansion of childcare in order to further its policies of national preference and imagines behind governments' insufficient commitment to childcare a conspiracy against French birthing and for increasing immigration levels (Dubslaff 2017).

Regarding the attractiveness of hypermasculinity, recent research shows that the vision of women that the far right propagates accounts much less for their adherence than nationalism, racism and strong conventionalism (Bitzan 2017). Some confusion of categories is also caused by the participation of openly homosexual men and women in some anti-gender manifestations (Paternotte and Kuhar 2017). The public image and dominant ideology tend to hide tensions within the far-right scene, especially around gay members. One skinhead explained, for instance, that 'the struggle against gays is not a struggle against men who go to bed with other men, but a struggle against unmanliness' (quoted in Claus and Virchow 2017: 310–311). Such dismissal of unmanliness partakes in the construction of hypermasculinity; that in turn allows for some expression of homosexuality. Finally, although they propagate decisively anti-feminist ideas in what can be considered an 'ethnicization of sexism', far-right forces often present female emancipation as an achievement of their own country or civilization when it comes to discrediting immigrant cultures or while accusing European Muslims for importing supposedly misogynistic practices (Blee 2017: 196).

Fascism and Post-Fascism: A Certain Family Resemblance

The current far right shares a certain family resemblance with interwar fascism. Both adhere to societal visions based on exclusive solidarity. However, in comparison with interwar fascism, the recent versions of those visions are based less strictly on radical nationalism, let alone nation-statism, but comprise a broader European perspective. In this sense, the current far right is not only post-fascist but also postcolonial. While imperial aspirations are a total taboo in the German case, given the history of the Second World War, the French far right had to fundamentally revise its territorially based concept of 'grandeur' after the end of its last colonial war and the loss of 'French Algeria'. Today's statism is much more moderate than fascist statism. The state is not seen as integrating society based on a corporatist model or as incarnating the organic nation. Rather, it is put in position as a sovereign state against the EU framework, and it has certain functions in the service of national citizens. The criteria of transcendence and of cleansing are not covered any more, although the potential for cleansing is ideologically inherent in far-right societal visions. Paramilitarism has been abandoned as a major organizational form to the expense of party politics out of pragmatic, contextual considerations. At the level of hypermasculinity, both cases overlap to a large extent.

As a result, as well, present authoritarian figures do not appear as innovative, or 'revolutionary' as historical fascism (see the discussion in Griffin 1991). Their programmes are also more limited in scope, ideologically as well as in terms of their potential for political action. The Front National, now Rassemblement National (National Rallye), and AfD and their surrounding networks appear as rather poor copies of their historical predecessors. I therefore argue that they cannot be considered fascists. However, we cannot understand their logic, their functioning and their historical lineage unless we agree they are clearly located in a post-fascist legacy. Post-fascism in this sense not only refers to the fact that the current far right evolves within a broader post-fascist society and has to adapt to those circumstances of context. Qualifying the current far right as post-fascist also acknowledges their own internal process of reflection on their own past and the difficulties they have in tackling it (see the above discussion of their major grievances). Major ideological revisions have taken place and, in many cases, there is an explicitly voiced recommendation not to evoke the semantics of the interwar years in order not to discredit themselves politically. Therefore, although they are not fascists in the sense of interwar fascism, they are not understandable without a thorough following of their lineages into those interwar experiences. If they are definitely not fascists, they are for sure post-fascists.

THE SOCIETAL CONTEXT OF THE FRENCH AND GERMAN FAR RIGHT: A SCENARIO OF MULTI-LEVEL CRISES?

The question now is to find an explanation for the current relative strength of the French and German far right. We argued in volume I that the 1920s and 1930s were an anomalic phase. A return to the structural conditions that explain the rise of interwar authoritarianism and fascism might hint towards the kind of questions we should ask for the present phase. In accordance with his theory on four sources of social power – economic, political, ideological and military – Mann (2004) states major crises at all four levels in interwar Europe as necessary causes for the rise of fascism.[37] Fascism was successful because it offered plausible solutions at all four levels. An important weakness in Mann's account, however, is that he conflates fascists' analysis of crisis and the solutions they offered with sociological and historical analyses of those crises. We shall see below that authoritarians today do offer solutions, but in accordance with the particular, self-tailored analyses of crises they put forth. A rhetoric of crisis is part of their programme.

According to Mann, in the centre, east and south of Europe, as opposed to the north-west, liberal democracy was not entrenched enough to mediate through routine functioning, the four-level crises. Instead, these states proceeded to a first-level escalation of the nation-statist ideology, leading to a more general type of authoritarian nation-statism across half of Europe. The emergence and success of the second-level escalation, fascism, largely depended on the behaviour of old regime powers in dual states, i.e. capitalists, bourgeois conservatives, the church, high-ranking military and landowners largely controlling the state executive in the face of social unrest and perceived disorder led by peasant and labour movements and the left. In the face of the existing example of the Bolshevik Revolution, in many cases they reacted with hysterical, economically and politically irrational behaviour. Favouring a more militarized nation state reinforcing law and order and protecting private property, they would allow the fascists into the political arena. Only weak old regimes allowed for the emergence of fascism. The importance of the conservative parties that, where stable, could ensure government by themselves and thus prevented the coming into power of the bottom-up fascist movements is particularly clear in the works of Paxton (1998) that address fascism praxeologically, as a process in context. Another reason for historical fascists' success was the intensity of their message: fascist militancy. They gained strength in Italy, Germany, Austria, Hungary and Romania, the five countries that Mann studies in more detail.

In focusing on core fascist constituencies in comparative perspective, Mann shows that for many members of fascist organizations, for their followers and voters, fascism represented a reasonable choice. Beyond mere ideological accounts on the one hand and broad class theory on the other, both unconvincing, he distinguished specific social constituencies that particularly favoured nationalism and statism because of their closeness to the nation state: soldiers and veterans, civil servants, in particular teachers and university-based academics, public-sector manual workers, the church and clergy in cases where the church was central to the imagined nation, and, finally, populations in threatened border territories after borders across Europe were redrawn following the Versailles and Trianon treaties with refugees regaining national territories as a consequence. Second, there were core constituencies that favoured transcendence, namely, people in economic sectors that were removed from class conflict: again, civil servants, employees in the public sector and in state-led industries, as well as workers in the service sector and in agriculture. At the margins of urban industrial conflicts, they felt it threatened their social order and divided the nation. Finally, there were two generations of young men who felt attracted by the organizational forms of the paramilitary as total socializing institutions and by their cleansing tasks. These young men included those enjoying considerable levels of secondary and higher education in state institutions preaching morality and national values, on the one hand, and those who had been socialized in the armed forces and were therefore familiar with militarism and violence, on the other hand.

From the theory so far, we deduce the questions that we have to ask for the current phase. Do we have similar broad crises at various levels today? Does the far right address those crises and offer solutions to them? In the following section, we also find out which particular constituencies find their programmes appealing.

Globalization theorists, like the ones who contributed to *The Great Regression* (Geiselberger, ed. 2017), attribute the current situation to the neoliberal policies of the last decades. Neoliberalist deregulation has increased inequalities within and between countries (see the contributions to Wallerstein 2016). The 2008 economic crisis was indeed global in extension and repercussions. The realities of migration that worry the rich parts of the world, and which the far right capitalizes, can be considered – apart from being a reaction to violent conflict, war and climate change – as a major outcome and manifestation of economic crisis. The most promising option for economic upward mobility is migration from poor to rich countries (Korzeniewicz and Moran 2016). Boatcă (2015) interprets migration as a manifestation of and strategy within global economic inequality.

Furthermore, at an abstract level, the weakening of political state apparatuses in the face of economic neoliberalism can be considered a feature of global political crisis. The spread of paranoiac reason in times of terrorism everywhere (Schneider 2010) has furthermore led to a securitization of (international) politics. While it is difficult to assess the current potential for a global military crisis, we certainly can state, again at a very abstract level, a global ideological crisis in so far as neoliberal globalization and its premises are increasingly criticized. This ideological crisis is framed as a variety of perceptions of threat, chaos and instability causing moral panics everywhere: around terrorists and refugees, around western decadence and 'gender ideology', around all sorts of unfaithful and therefore dangerous populations. Such a global outline, however, necessarily remains very abstract. It does not allow for understanding the particular circumstances within specific contexts that refracted the global trends very differently, and in which authoritarian restoration has flourished recently. Let us focus on Europe.

The year 2015 was a dreadful one for Europe in general and for the EU in particular. It started with the terrorist attack against the magazine Charlie Hebdo in Paris and ended with an even more deadly jihadist assault in the same city. In between, the

EU battled an economic crisis in Greece, which threatened the entire eurozone, and endured a staggering inflow of refugees from the Middle East and other war-torn regions. The year 2016 has not been much better. More terrorist attacks have shaken the continent. The refugee crisis has abated slightly, but only because the EU has outsourced the problem to Turkey – a country that is itself experiencing a bout of instability. And for the first time, the EU is set to lose a member, the United Kingdom, as a result of the so-called Brexit referendum. All these developments have helped push populist movements to the center of European politics. The threat of terrorism and anxiety about a massive wave of immigrants from the Muslim world, coupled with the widespread belief that the EU hinders rather than helps when it comes to such problems, have created a perfect storm for populists, especially enhancing the standing of right-wing populists in many countries. (Mudde 2016: 25)

An impression of the growing strength of what is now called 'populism' in Europe from 2008 to 2018 can be inferred from the maps produced by *Euronews* (Harris 2018),[38] which show that in a number of countries,

parties that centre their ideological constructs on the apotheosis of (national or local) identity, on xenophobia and authoritarianism, represent political forces that are rooted in and superior to 10 per cent of the electorate. The other aspect of this implantation is probably more worrying still: It is the way in which the extreme right could impose its agenda in the heart of political debate everywhere in Europe, partly vampirizing the classical right and, favouring ideological recompositions, sometimes reaching out into parts of the left. (Jacquemain 2011: 1)

Mann's convincing argument for the interwar period is that fascism could arise in contexts of multilevel crises in dual states where democratically elected governments were too weak to absorb and refract those crises. Furthermore, he argues that fascism offered solutions to multilevel crises that were appealing for certain sections of the population, its core constituencies. In the following section, I outline an assessment of the past years in Europe as years of multilevel crises – economic, political and ideological. There are no indications of a military crisis in Western Europe today. The military crisis right after the Second World War certainly played a role in the German context, as the reconfiguration of the far right in the immediate post-war years shows (see the following chapter), where the disorientation of formerly high-placed members of the NS army played a role in their newly founded organizations that struggled, among others, for the rehabilitation of the honour of German soldiers. Their competency was also useful for the creation of stay-behind armies and for parts of the national intelligence services. The history of the Front National, in turn, is rooted in France's history as a colonial power and the resulting ideology of 'declinism' of France's grandeur.

Similarly, the military expertise and experience of anti-communist members of the Resistance and of soldiers and high-rank army officials mobilized in colonial wars (Indo–China 1946–54, Algeria 1954–62), connected with the most radical civil nationalist fractions of 'French Algeria', formed one of the core constituencies of the French far right. They were also recycled into French stay-behind structures during the Cold War. A more honourable consideration of veterans continues to be part of the FN programme. The military is therefore a reference for the European far right. But its current strength is not a response to any sort of military crisis and paramilitarism has ceased to be important as an organizational form.

My students have suggested adding media crisis as a major context of emergence. However, I agree with Nachtwey that 'it would be misleading to think of what are – literally – social media as the cause of resentment, rather than as simply the force that gives it shape. To blame the algorithms would be like holding the radio responsible for Goebbels' (Nachtwey 2017: 131). I agree with my students, however, to add an additional section on the alleged refugee crisis as an important contextual element. The situation during the finalization of the manuscript calls for more in-depth research into the effects of the Covid pandemic on the reconfiguration of the political scene, something I am unable to realize due to time constraints.

Economic Crisis

In Europe, the post-war evolutions of the far right occurred in the context of transition from industrial welfare capitalism to post-industrial individualized capitalism. This process went along with the individualization of risks and material uncertainties, and social fragmentation and polarization (Betz 1993: 665 ff.). Indeed, the strengthening of the far right coincided with interdependent recompositions at the economic, political and ideological levels. Throughout the post-war period and into the middle of the 1970s, welfare statism, social security and state interventions to direct and control market forces ensured relative material certainty to large parts of the population. This empowered inclusive solidarities on a given material basis. In the same period, declericalization and secularization, promotion of sexual liberties and the weakening of nationalisms enabled, through broad-based collective redistribution and reassurance, enhanced individual emancipation, culminating in the 1968 movements and the specific values they conveyed. Indeed, 'the aspiration at autonomy, the rejection of institutions experienced as too coercive (think of the evolution of marriage), tolerance and the acceptance of difference . . . have their roots in the profound collective securitisation at the material level' (Jacquemain and Claisse 2012: 23–24, translated by the author). Throughout those early post-war decades, the far right survived in small radical circles around personalities who ensured, in many cases, direct connections with the interwar and war period, with historical fascisms, and, in the case of France at least in pronounced ways, with the colonialists' experience (see the following chapter on deep roots).

From the early 1980s onwards, the neoliberal turn inverted the two trends: generalized competition and the advancement of a meritocratic ideology increasingly individualized the economy, especially the labour market and personal material risks. The individual became fragile, demanding in turn forms and feelings of collectivization at the cultural and symbolic levels. As a result, identitarian questions gained in importance, a trend on which the far right could easily capitalize (Jacquemain 2011: 3).[39] These long-term transformations of the economy do not represent a crisis to the same degree as the interwar economic crisis described by Mann. In addition, at least in the case of France, where the FN was already a stable political force during the high phase of neoliberal transformation, it followed the new economic paradigm in its economic outlook in the beginning. A more welfarist discourse in favour of the national has only recently replaced the Reaganist discourse, a strategy to attract new constituencies amongst the working class and disadvantaged population groups. Today's far right cannot be regarded as a response to those longer-term transformations and the uncertainties they produce.

At the broadest level, one could speak about a crisis of national economies, as in times of global capitalism the national is interconnected to such an extent with transnational and global economic spheres that the very idea of a 'national economy' has become an illusion (Appadurai 2017: 2). National economies have been largely subjected to foreign investors and their influence over national legislation, to outcomes of negotiations at the global level and to the functioning of the global financial market. We find contradictory analyses of the impact of the 2007–08 economic crisis on European societies. The global economic crisis did affect Europe; and it did so in context-specific ways. It might even be hazardous to consider a Europe-wide 'moment' in so far as each national context refracted the global situation differently.[40] Globally speaking, the 2007–08 economic crisis 'with the near meltdown of the global financial order' (Fraser 2017: 40) was an impressive illustration of the structural weaknesses of the global capitalist system. It marked a turning point in at least two respects: politically and ideologically (see below). At the economic level, the outcomes are debated controversially.

One consequence of the 2008 crisis was the realization in mainstream debate that austerity doesn't work (Misik 2017: 123), unsettling mainstream economists' ideological certainty of the last decades. Furthermore, the state has re-entered the economy, unsettling another neoliberal certainty. This has led to a schizophrenic situation where a vast array of commentators have criticized neoliberalism politically and ideologically. Economically speaking, however, it continues (Nachtwey 2017: 134–35). But whereas in the 1980s and 1990s a promise of success and prosperity accompanied and legitimized neoliberalism, in the 2000s and 2010s it is imposed under threat. In the understanding of broad ranges of society, the interpretation of the 2008 crisis is that the state steps in to rescue banks and companies with taxpayers' money when they fail in times of crisis, whereas the benefits remain private as long as the economy does well. This has contributed to discrediting what is perceived as national and European political elites in the service of global economic players (see below, political crisis). The effect of the global economic crisis in Western Europe is therefore more political and ideological than economic in the strict sense of the word. Another reason why we cannot reduce the strength of the far right to economic turmoil is that countries such as Switzerland and Austria, that largely avoided the fallout of the 2008 crisis, still have a high share of far-right votes (Löwy and Sitel 2015: 54).

As far as the response of the far right is concerned, their strength has mainly been to redirect grievances at the economic level to a utopia of symbolic exclusive solidarities. In the face of lack of class conflict, the far right reformulates issues of redistribution. Economic relations are translated into an issue of national sovereignty, European integration is re-politicized, a chauvinistic stance calls for exclusion of those who undeservingly profit from 'our welfare' and thus reassure identitarian claims for the 'right to stay amongst ourselves' as the current expression of exclusive solidarity.

Far-right proponents have always been ambiguous on the economic policy front.[41] Recent experience illustrates once again their incoherence in terms of economic analysis and programmes. M. Le Pen struggled seriously in formulating any meaningful economic policy with regard to France's relationship with the EU, and her plan was to leave the Eurozone in the last election campaign when confronted by Macron. She has now retreated from the former strong Europhobia in terms of economic policy, realizing that many potential voters are not as anti-EU as she had calculated. The starting point of the AfD was the articulation of a Eurosceptic economic stance after the 2008 economic crisis (see below). On the opposite side, a key figure like Gianfranco Fini, formerly declared the heir of Italian fascism, has in the meantime abandoned any allusion to corporatism to become a determined neoliberalist. 'Such evolutions do not contribute to designing an easily readable landscape' of economic orientations within the European far right (Jacquemain and Claisse 2012: 21).

To sum up, the success of the far right is a reaction at the political and ideological levels to processes that have important economic reasons. 'The "anti-system" rhetoric is not aimed against capitalism, which is taken as a given objective, but against the system of liberal representative democracy' (Baier

2016: 51). It is also directed against perceived outsiders in national economies – migrants as well as 'foreign finance capital', an idea with a similar flavour as the NS idea of 'Jewish exploitative capital' (*raffendes Kapital*, see Keim 2014). This corresponds to the second feature of economic crisis: 'the loss of economic sovereignty everywhere produces a shift towards emphasizing cultural sovereignty' (Appadurai 2017: 5). Within the European context, the submission of national politics and economies to the 'dictate of Brussels' represents a particular feature, taken up in the so-called 'Euroscepticism' of most far-right parties.

In contexts where the collective systems of material security have been dismantled, many citizens feel the need for moral reassurance. This may explain partly the support for far-right parties: 'may they give us, at least, the impression that our symbolic order still holds' (Jacquemain and Claisse 2012: 23–24). This is how individualism at the material level combines perfectly with calls for the defence of identitarian values, while it prevents in the same run collective struggles for redistribution. In this sense, economically speaking, the far right does not offer meaningful solutions. It is a particularly weak alternative, if it is even one, economically speaking. The highly theorized economic analyses put forth by the AfD in its founding phase did not characterize the party for long and do not account for its subsequent electoral successes. Rather, on the contrary, far-right programmes transpose economic frustrations and material uncertainties into the political and cultural domains and thus combine perfectly well with economic neoliberalism (Jacquemain 2011: 2). They try to dissolve the left/right dichotomy, not only by mixing up neoliberal and leftist economic policies but also by highlighting cleavages between elites and the people, between outsiders and the people. This goes hand in hand with important parts of scholarly analyses of the 'populist right' that similarly distinguish between educated expert elites as supposed 'guarantors of liberal democracy', on the one hand, and uneducated, authoritarian popular masses as a threat to democracy, on the other hand (Collovald 2004). I conclude that the current strength of the far right is related to long-term, profound transformations of Western European societies at the economic level.[42] However, it does not offer meaningful economic solutions to economic problems. Instead, its success amongst new electoral constituencies can partly be explained by its capacity to translate them into cultural ones.

Political Crisis

The material impact of the 2008 economic crisis in European societies has remained moderate in comparison with the situation in other parts of the world, but its political and ideological impact was profound. Throughout the past decades already, while class conflict has largely disappeared, social and economic inequalities deepened in the most affluent societies of the globe, combined with the erosion of the welfare state and financialization. The ensuing constant climate of economic panic (Appadurai 2017: 6–8) has catalysed a malaise of European liberal democracies at various levels. The term 'malaise' serves to distinguish the depth and degree of problems at the political level from full-fledged political crisis: so far, the basic structures and functioning of the liberal democratic parliamentary systems have not been fundamentally put into question. However, we observe several dynamics that undermine parliamentary democracy from within.

First, in the course of restructuring the economy and the meltdown of trade union organization and labour protest, distributional conflict largely disappeared from European societies despite economic polarization. Instead, it has been 'replaced by a technocratic search for the economically necessary and uniquely possible; institutions, policies and ways of life were to be adapted to this end' (Streeck 2017: 158). This has led to the rise of political, bureaucratic, academic and technical elites and experts as key agents of politics. Reliance on expert knowledge has largely depoliticized many controversial questions, from health and education to the administration of national budgets or European integration.

Second, while experts have taken over and managed issues that should have been subject to major political dispute, the big mainstream parties of the moderate right, left and centre increasingly resemble each other in terms of their external image. Mudde dates the starting point of these transformations back to the 1960s' post-industrial transformations.[43] As governing parties or broad opposition parties, they have also increasingly retreated 'into the machinery of the state as "cartel parties"' (Streeck 2017: 158), acting in a distinctive, narrow arena disconnected from the broad public. Popular criticism suspected that they were obeying big global business.[44] This state of affairs is often described as an 'elite consensus', i.e. 'a common agenda that called for integration through the EU, multiethnic societies, and neoliberal economic reforms' and 'a vision of Europe as a cosmopolitan, business-friendly technocracy' (Mudde 2016: 27). Third, this perceived indistinction of the mainstream parties combined with the impression that the national governing and oppositional parties were largely powerless in the face of supranational (EU) and international (IMF) authorities. Fourth, this has resulted in an overall decline in democratic participation at various levels and in a growing disinterest in politics, in particular at the European level that is perceived as being far more abstract than national politics. Since the 1980s, membership in most established parties has been falling, just as much as participation in elections (Streeck 2017: 158). Democracy fatigue is one aspect of what is analysed in large parts of the literature as a 'crisis of representative democracy'.

Fifth, another consequence is that voting behaviours have changed. Analysts observe an increasing detachment from partisanship with the established, traditional political parties, i.e. voter disalignment, leading to voter volatility. This expresses profound changes in the relationship between voters and those who are supposed to represent them.[45] From 'crisis of representative democracy' we can narrow the issue down to 'crisis of representation'. Tony Blair's and Gerhard Schröder's policies of creating a 'new centre' destroyed the historical party profile of the centre left. Leaving aside politics of redistribution, the centre left has limited itself to agendas in favour of women's, migrants' or LGBTQIA+ rights. In France, even the Communist Party, largely fallen out of favour because of its Stalinist orientation and the 1989 turn, has abandoned references to the working class. The lack of a genuine left in the political spectrum contributed dramatically to the current situation (Della Porta 2017: 36).[46] Positions rather close to those of the Social Democratic 'new centre' were later also adapted by the moderate right, by Angela Merkel and David Cameron, for instance, diluting in turn the classical conservative party profile.[47] The political management of the recent economic crises made things worse:

> Neoliberal deregulation and undemocratic decision-making in the context of strategies to overcome the crisis of European financial capitalism have produced fears of social downward mobility and rejection of hegemonic national and European politics. An unequal burden-sharing in the favour of banks and business and at the cost of broad populations have reinvigorated resentment against the political superstructure of a technocratic market regime in Europe. (Häusler 2016a: 42–43)

As a result, conservative, especially religiously oriented voters and working-class people, have increasingly had the impression that the traditional parties they used to vote for do not represent their interests anymore. This disillusion with the representative link between voters and politicians is highlighted as one of the reasons why the so-called (new) populist right is winning support.

Sixth, all this combines with another more complex process that probably holds the key to understanding an important aspect of the current strength of the far right, and therefore needs to be developed in some detail. Since the 1980s, a specific trend of political alliance has contributed to the particular frustration of conservative and working-class milieus with established politics. The current far right can be interpreted as the rejection of this alliance termed 'progressive neoliberalism'. Frazer provides an elaborate analysis of this development with regard to Donald Trump's election in the US, which I believe can hold for the Western European contexts as well:

> This may sound to some like an oxymoron, but it is a real, if perverse political align-ment that holds the key to understanding the US election results. . . . In its US form, progressive neoliberalism is an alliance of mainstream currents of new social

movements (feminism, anti-racism, multiculturalism and LGBTQIA+ rights) on the one side, and high-end 'symbolic' and service-based sectors of business (Wall Street, Silicon Valley and Hollywood) on the other. . . . the former lend their charisma to the latter. (Fraser 2017: 42)

The rise of 'progressive neoliberalism' put forth a reduced understanding of social emancipation:

Identifying progress with meritocracy as opposed to equality, these terms equated emancipation with the rise of 'talented' women, minorities and gays in the winner-takes-all corporate hierarchy, instead of with the latter's abolition. These liberal-individualist views of progress gradually replaced the more expansive, anti-hierarchical, egalitarian, class-sensitive and anti-capitalist understandings of emancipation that had flourished in the 1960s and 1970s. (Ibid.)

Furthermore:

By the 1960s those excluded populations [women, minorities, LGBTIQIA+] were actively mobilizing against a bargain that required them to pay the price of others' relative security and prosperity. And rightly so! But their struggles intersected fatefully with another front of struggle, which unfolded in parallel over the course of the subsequent decades. That second front pitted an ascending party of free-marketeers, bent on liberalizing and globalizing the capitalist economy, against declining labour movements in the countries of the capitalist core, once the most powerful base of support for social democracy, but now on the defensive, if not wholly defeated. In this context, progressive new social movements, aiming to overturn hierarchies of gender, 'race'-ethnicity and sex, found themselves pitted against populations seeking to defend established life worlds and privileges, now threatened by the cosmopolitanism of the new financialized economy. The collision of these two fronts of struggle produced a new constellation: proponents of emancipation joined up with partisans of financialization to double-team social protection. The fruit of their union was progressive neoliberalism. Progressive neoliberalism mixes together truncated ideals of emancipation and lethal forms of financialization. It was precisely that mix that was rejected in toto by Trump's voters. . . . For these populations, the injury of deindustrialization is compounded by the insult of progressive moralism, which routinely portrays them as culturally backward. . . . What made possible that conflation was the absence of any genuine left. (Ibid.: 43–44).

This combination of neoliberalism with the successes of political activism for the democratic rights of new social and political movements and certain minority groups has made stagnating or descending strata and their dissatisfactions appear to be backward. This also explains the particular aversion of today's far right for issues like migrants' rights and cohabitation of culturally diverse population groups, for alternative family models, for female emancipation, for gender-sensitive language or for the LGBTQIA+'s struggles for recognition.

To sum up, mainstream political parties and elites are perceived as being in close alliance with global capital, on the one hand, and on the other, with groups fighting for the recognition of their particularistic identities and rights, perceived as partial, minoritarian and irrelevant since these issues are far removed from the everyday sorrows and frustrations of majority citizens. The above points describe profound long-term transformations within the political arena that have led to a broad-based political malaise. Those observed trends do not yet fundamentally question the structures and functioning of Western European liberal democratic political systems. They cannot be considered a political crisis in Mann's sense.

However, there is another ingredient in the current phase that changes the picture: until recently, in the face of disillusion with established politics, protest was mainly expressed in the form of social protest outside of established party politics. In the meantime, from the margins of society, dissatisfaction has 'spread through society as flickerings of discontent'. Social movements like CasaPound, Pegida or Bloc Identitaire have expanded 'into potential majorities' that link up with far-right political parties and 'threaten to undermine pluralistic democracy' (Misik 2017: 118). The assault on the Reichstag at the end of August 2020 by opponents to the government's coronavirus measures, foreshadowing the assault on the US Capitol half a year later, expressed symbolically the threat to parliamentary democracy embodied by those developments. In France, the *gilets jaunes* movement, courted by the far right and the left alike but refusing to align with either of them, has diversified the picture of popular unrest.

A meta-level reflection complements this discussion. The observed situation combines with hesitant, at times contradictory and at times reactionary, political attitudes towards the far right. The new far right claims to speak for 'the people'. Its scholarly analysis in terms of 'populism' implicitly confirms this claim. In France, the hegemonic analysis of the 'populist' threat to established democracy mirrors the FN's current strength. Collovald provides us with a sustained, historically informed critique of the emergence of the term 'populism' in its association with the French FN and the political effect this conceptual framing has had on debates of its significance. She decidedly denounces the dominant labelling of the FN as 'populist', as a reactionary response to the far right. Not only is the term 'populism' much less disqualifying than the former labels of 'fascism' or 'right-wing extremism', but more than that, and escaping general debate, the term 'populism' shifts attention from the party establishment (beyond its personified leader), its relationship with other parties, its local anchoring and distinctive significance for a variety of different voters, to the broad-based category of the 'popular' classes giving their vote to the FN. The term 'populism', in the French context at least, has led to blaming 'the people' for the FN's success – mirrored in the broad debates around its working-class character (*classes populaires*, i.e. 'popular classes' being the French term corresponding to the English 'working class') – and thus conceives of 'the people' as the major problem and as a threat to democracy (Collovald 2004: 10). On the other hand, the 'populism' talk erects supposedly neutral experts as the only ones capable of correctly analysing this party as a threat to established democracy. Their expert knowledge transforms 'the people' and, in accordance with the French term *classes populaires*, the most fragile fragments of the population, into a problem to be solved. This discredits in the same vein voices that argue that 'the people' is a political cause worth being defended. Citizens belonging to the so-called 'popular classes' are defined as deficient or bad citizens, epitomized in the frequent talk about their lack of education. This is in line with a long lineage of reactionary responses to democratization since the nineteenth century that pointed to the 'masses', to the uneducated 'majorities', as a threat to political stability. Ultimately, this logic dissolves the left/right divide and therefore suits perfectly our era. It opposes good and bad citizens according to their social, cultural and intellectual levels, on the one hand, and good and bad politicians according to their consent to this new technocratic realism, on the other hand (Collovald 2004: 59 ff.).

In Germany, on the contrary, part of the political establishment and the journalistic counterparts believe that it is time to 'take people's fears and sorrows' seriously. Only a few manage to underline that those fears are largely prejudiced projections in a context of important power inequalities at the political and discourse levels. The far right only expresses in more radical terms what large parts of the conservative right and left, as well as the 'common sense' of mainstream discourse and media, already believe. In this sense, taking such fears seriously rather has the opposite effect: 'It creates the impression that the irrational is rational, the illegitimate is legitimate and right-wing propagandists are only the courageous ones who dared address those problems first. It is not understandable why, under those conditions, voters should not vote for the AfD' (Biskamp 2017: 98).

In this context of political malaise, the frustrated mood amongst voters is partially met by the far right whose ideologues propose a distinctive project in a largely levelled, technocratic political landscape. It was in particular the responses by established mainstream parties to the economic crisis that had recently alienated many voters, and that gave the 'anti-system' rhetoric of the far right new momentum (Löwy and Sitel 2015). Appadurai reminds us that leaders and followers connect only partially.[48] If the leaders 'are typically xenophobic, patriarchal and authoritarian in their styles' (Appadurai 2017: 2), this is not necessarily the political ideal of all those who vote for them (see the section on the constituencies of the AfD and FN below).

Regarding the frustration with elites and experts as key agents of politics, the far right turns the logic around. According to their discourse, ordinary citizens are the only ones who have a sense of reality and are the only legitimate political subjects. This is evidenced in the refusal of far-right representatives to speak to official media, instead directing them towards people on the streets: 'they will tell you' (Richard 2012). As a response to expert knowledge, the far right celebrates the common sense of ordinary people. Furthermore, it voices an anti-elitist, anti-establishment discourse that is directed not only against national elites, but also especially against the 'dictate of Brussels'. The leaders of the movements and parties stage social and political protest as a refreshing alternative against those, and aim, at least in their official discourse, at a mobilization of 'the people'.

As a response to the crisis of political representation, they successfully proceed towards strong forms of representative claim-making (Volk 2017). In this sense, the designation of those movements and parties as 'populist' is justified. Their leaders have managed, despite their own political careers and socio-economic backgrounds, to designate themselves as the voice of 'the people'. In the same move they have redefined, along the lines of widespread racist imaginations, who is legitimately part of 'the people' in terms of exclusive solidarity.[49] Obviously, their talk of 'improving democracy' follows strategic considerations of not publicly appearing anti-constitutional. On the contrary, many of them still espouse the idea of rule by the people, but with their own, particular idea of who and what 'the people' is.[50]

Finally, as outlined above, political leaders from within established far-right networks with deep roots, under the current circumstances, could hit a sensitive nerve in giving voice to stagnating or descending strata that have been regarded by the rich and beautiful as backward or reactionary, as a bothersome residue of past times. This comes with the revenge of denouncing, in turn, the successes of feminists, LGBTQIA+ activists and the presence of self-confident migrants as lack of common sense, values and morality, decadence, intellectualism and reality-denying political correctness that is not only useless and idle but harmful for the integrity of 'the people'.

To conclude, the political landscape was transformed as a result of post-industrial social change, neoliberalism and the rise of technocracy, and more recently, as a consequence of political reactions of established parties to the economic and Euro crisis. Mudde puts it provocatively: 'In essence, the populist surge is an illiberal democratic response to decades of undemocratic liberal policies' (Mudde 2016: 30).[51] Instead, the outlined longer-term developments in the political realm, and in particular the so-called crisis of representation, have to be understood as opening up opportunity windows for the profiling of far-right parties as alternatives to the mainstream. Their recent successes can partly be understood as a consequence of and response to the crisis of representation.

Ideological Crisis

The 2008 economic crisis has had major ideological repercussions. If the economy has taken off again unchanged, the ideological construct that supported global neoliberal capitalism largely unquestioned has been cracking, following a long phase of hegemony. The ideological and cultural response of the far right is not in contradiction with the observed economic trend but thrives on it. Mason illustrates beautifully the ideological shifts through the changing attitudes and actions in his native British working-class town. He shows how 'the culture of resistance to capital has, for some, mutated into a culture of revolt against globalization, migration and human rights. How we got here is not just a story of neoliberalism's economic failure, but the collapse of a narrative' (Mason 2017: 89).

He outlines, for instance, how offshoring had the effect that 'place – the key source of our identity – does not matter' any more. The restructuring of corporations into a value chain of smaller companies had the narrative effect that 'the firm would no longer carry any informal social obligations'. Cutting taxes and moving towards slash progressive taxation signified that 'the post-1945 social bargain was over'. The privatization of public services meant that 'it became logical to plan your life as if only yourself and your close family, not the state and wider community, would be there to catch you if you fell . . . the message to working-class families was clear: You are on your own.' Similarly, through the financialization of everyday life,

> Thatcherism would celebrate the egomaniac of the trading floor. And unlike with the mid-twentieth-century bourgeoisie, which was impenetrable, a pushy, egotistical working-class person could become part of this new entrepreneurial elite. By celebrating the financial predator as a new kind of working-class hero, neoliberalism began to repackage 'working-class culture' as a pro-capitalist ideology. (Ibid.: 91–93)

That every economic restructuring had such ideological effects, especially for the working population, is key to understanding the collapse of the ideological status quo since the most recent economic crises. Since the mainstream conservative and moderate left answers have become discredited in the course of the political transformations described above, and since the radical left remains weak, this has strengthened far-right responses: 'for three decades the function of this was to disrupt and disaggregate working-class resistance to neoliberalism. The problem is, when neoliberalism itself collapsed, it was no longer mainstream conservatism that got oxygenated, but authoritarian right-wing populism' (ibid.).

At the ideological level, we seem to be again in an anomalic phase, similar to the 1920s and 1930s. This is what Foessel (2019) discovers in reading through newspapers from the year 1938: the choice of terminology, the moral panics and the obsessions with a world in decline, where the worst of all cases is regularly imagined, as well as the calls for more authority and the rise of nationalism, resemble our present to astonishing degrees. Of course, the context and the concrete political events are not the same. But the choice of discourse to interpret them are similar. Similar to the 1920s and 1930s, it is not yet clear who will be the fixers on the horizon, and conspiracy theories of all flavours circulate widely.

The success of the far right is essentially explicable with regard to its responses to ideological crises. Economic and political developments as well as the ideological shifts they have promoted have certainly given way to widespread feelings of uncertainty that something might be going wrong. Far-right leaders have succeeded in capitalizing on such fears, in 'activating, bundling, structuring' them in a process that resembles an 'inverted psychoanalysis' (Biskamp 2017: 94–95). It is this structuring exercise that has helped them gain votes in recent elections all across Europe. As a remedy to ideological crises, the far right offers the reinvigoration of exclusive solidarities, combined with the idea of a return to a glorious past – to a former, 'purer' state of an imagined community. While most far-right parties have been underdeveloped in terms of their economic outlook, all of them have excelled with identitarian themes. The first section of this chapter outlined in detail the ingredients that make this narrative of exclusive solidarity coherent.

Refugee Reception Crisis

From 2014 onwards, Europe has been bombarded with media outputs, statements by politicians and a generalized societal debate around the assumption, proclaimed as a certainty, that 'the refugee crisis' would give momentum to the far right all over Europe. Indeed:

> 2014 is the year in which Pegida in Germany was born. This sudden emergence of a . . . determinedly identitarian movement in the public space is no coincidence. It is in direct correlation with a complex geopolitical constellation, characterized by an ultrafast concatenation of politico-religious, economic and socio-demographic destabilizations at a global scale, in particular in the Near and Middle East (emergence of the Islamic State, civil war in Syria). It is in particular explicable through the first consequence of those destabilizations: the uncontrolled increase (or at least this is how it was perceived) of migration flows into Europe, and more specifically to Germany, the 'promised land' of the new migrants. (Sebaux 2016: 389)

Globally, according to the *UNHCR Mid-Year Report 2016*, 64 million people were refugees, many internal or in neighbouring regions. Germany was among the top ten receiving countries for the first time. The figures need to be relativized in various ways though. First, only 3 per cent of refugees did arrive in the EU, not least because of sustained efforts to construct fortress Europe (ProAsyl, n.d.). Regarding the war in Syria, for example, compared to refugee figures in Lebanon, Jordan or other neighbouring countries, the few million who survived their journey to Europe remained a marginal figure within the overall populations of Europe.[52]

Also, the imagined figure of the young single male refugee – perceived as a particular threat for the security of German women and children – proved wrong in statistics. More than a third of the refugees were female and around 36 per cent were minor in age, many children below the age of twelve. Many refugee men were fathers whose hope to have their families follow their trajectory was disappointed with more restrictive handling of family unification. The number of forced expulsions, at 25,000, was also at its highest point in 2016 (ProAsyl, n.d.).

Apart from closing Europe's border to the outside, there is no sustained European refugee policy. As a consequence exists the saddest record of more than 10,000 documented dead on the Mediterrean Sea route between 2016 and 2018 (UNO Flüchtlingshilfe 2019). We need to add another few thousands who had lost their lives on their way towards the coast already. According to a calculation by Doctors without Borders, in 2018 one out of forty-one refugees lost their lives in the Mediterranean, four every day (ProAsyl, n.d.; UNO Flüchtlingshilfe 2019). The figures for the current period, i.e. a relatively marginal number of refugees in the most affluent countries of the world, also have to be relativized with regard to the situation in the immediate post-war years, with much more massive numbers of refugees, homeless, widows and orphans, etc., in an economically and materially collapsed country (see the next chapter on Germany in the 1950s).

Despite these figures, the so-called refugee crisis was a perfect pretext for large parts of the population to fall into states of moral panic. There were cultural fears, especially of that highly deviant religion. There were also more tangible problems. Competition in the labour market was limited because accession to jobs is restricted according to type of residence permit and because more workers were needed. Access to affordable housing was a more serious problem in parts of the country. The policies of downsizing welfare dispositions and social programmes all over were crudely felt at that moment. There has not been much rational debate on the issues at stake such as labour market and housing policies, but also anti-Semitism or gender policies. Instead, xenophobic nationalism transformed rational considerations of unequal competition into a racialized fear and racist hatred against the newly arriving (Biskamp 2017: 93). This succeeded because dominant discourse and in parts legislation had for long established racial prejudice and discrimination all over Europe.

We shall see below that the far right indeed capitalized on the refugee reception crisis. Fractions of it circulated conspiracy theories about Merkel's government flooding the country with immigrants with the aim of abolishing the German nation and race. However, this cannot be considered the major cause of the strength of the far right that preceded it. Rather, this was a societal context in which it could thrive and flourish, and in which it contributed massively to shaping mainstream debate. It was also the context in which organized violence against migrants came to another peak with the creation of vigilante groups as a response to perceived state failure as well as the (re)formation of ultra-right terrorism.

Multilevel Crises: Summing Up the Argument

One of the questions for the following sections will be to evaluate how far reactions to the economic, political and ideological climate of our times are largely emotional, or whether they follow their own rational logic. Emotions have puzzled scholars of historical fascism in peculiar ways. I will outline in the following chapter that the success of the far right is not an effect of pure emotions, although far-right leaders and ideologues have been good in formulating and exploiting sentimental fears about decline, moral decadence and loss of values, *Heimat*, order and direction. Rather, if we consider specific constituencies more closely, it appears that practical, real-world interests do play a role for certain followers. However, while analyses of party programmes and theoretical interpretations and classifications of far-right parties are plenty, the elements we have employed so far in explaining this attractiveness to broader constituencies are still unsatisfactory.

So far, I have applied Mann's framework of fascism emerging out of and responding to major multilevel crises to the current strength of the far right in Western Europe. This endeavour has generated part of the response to the question of why the far right has recently been successful. As a full explanation, however, the responses remain unsatisfactory. Germany and France today are not faced by anything similar to the deep economic, political, ideological and military crises that characterized the interwar period. A military crisis is inefficient in explaining anything at this point. Furthermore, the strength of the far right is not directly caused by the recent economic crisis. Even in the case of the AfD, a party that in terms of its timing could easily be seen as a consequence of and response to the 2008 crisis, we will see that such an argument holds only superficially if we follow the subsequent development of the party. Rather, political reactions to an economic crisis and its ideological impact, just as in the context of the refugee reception crisis, catalysed longer-term transformations at the political and ideological levels. This allowed far-right networks, groups and parties to capture public attention, influence politics across the party spectrum and attract new constituencies. What can be stated for the current phase are difficulties at the political level, what I have called a crisis of representation. Representative claim-making as speaking the voice of the people accounts for the far right's success amongst new constituencies. We also observe deep ideological uncertainties caused through cracks in the ideological hegemony of neoliberalism, in the context of a missing left alternative. This ideological uncertainty favours a climate of moral panics of all sorts. I would argue that these two recent developments are necessary to explain the current strength of authoritarian restoration in Western Europe. The far right does offer some responses to those problems. For sure, its performance at the ideological level has been strongest, taking up the concerns of citizens around the loss of *Heimat*, the threat of mass migration to the nation and to white privilege, as well as the competition of migrants in the domains of cheap housing, education, jobs and women. Qualitative ethnographic studies of the FN vote below illustrate this point. It has also capitalized politically on the representational crisis, claiming to represent the people against corrupt elites and foreigners. For now, however, this remains a limited agenda in a political landscape where liberal democracy remains firmly established.

THE CURRENT STRENGTH OF THE FAR RIGHT IN FRANCE AND GERMANY: AN OUTLINE

We now need to find out what particular constituencies were attracted by the political and ideological offer of the French and German far right. More sustained research would be necessary to uncover all the elements we have used so far in a plethora of publications that would have to be assessed still more systematically and comparatively. I will elaborate first on the recent successes of the FN. The following section is dedicated to the rise of the AfD in Germany, and its political, intellectual and network surroundings. This focus on parties should not obfuscate that it is a real *nébuleuse de tendances* (a nebula of tendencies) that composes today's *fachosphere* in both countries (Jacquemain and Claisse 2012: 21), and that it is difficult at this stage to determine with certainty the alliances and networks between various movements and actors (Köttig 2018). Recent research shows that political far-right parties that have dense connections with non-party nationalist networks are more sustainable than others (Jones 2016).

Recent Developments of the Front National

France hosts one of the oldest, most stable and numerically biggest far-right parties of the continent: the Front National (FN; since 2018, Rassemblement National or RN). The literature on the current far right in France is strongly focused on this single political party. Indeed, the lion's share of the multiplicity of voices and organizational forms of the French far right that existed prior to the FN's foundation in 1972 has successfully been federated under this broad-based party (see the following chapter on deep roots).

The group Générations Le Pen, formed in 2002, is headed by J.M. Le Pen's daughter, Marine Le Pen. While her father had enjoyed the role of anti-system provocateur and political outsider, M. Le Pen constructed a strategy aiming at accession to power from the outset. She competed with Bruno Gollnisch, a former high-ranking official and traditional politician of the extreme right, and with Jacques Bompard, who had maintained a support network to the OAS, been a member of the Tixier-Vignancour committee and of the extreme-right movements Ordre Nouveau and Occident, and was elected mayor of Orange, with a vision to build up local bases of party power (Richard 2012).

I will start the story from January 2011, when M. Le Pen was elected second president of the FN as a result of her father's nepotist party politics. Upon her arrival in the party's top position, its membership increased considerably, starting a regular progression up to the current period, from 13,381 in 2009 to 51,551 in 2015 (Crépon and Lebourg 2015; see also Perrineau 2016: 63). Ideologically, M. Le Pen started a determined strategy to dissociate her party from its former anti-Semitism and denial with regard to the Holocaust. The rhetoric around immigration changed from an argument around cultural and racial difference to one around Islam being incompatible with and antithetical to the values of the French Republic and its fundamental feature of *laicité*, usurping leftist themes.

Politically, in contrast to her father and with the help of Philippot, M. Le Pen aimed at constructing a broad-based party that could eventually take her to power. Philippot as her chief ideologue in the early years of her FN presidency favoured the elaboration of a political programme that went well beyond the narrow focus on anti-immigration. There should be a renewed sense and pride in the country's history, calling, among others, for a focus on education. Schools also needed to spend more time teaching French. National sovereignty would require renegotiating France's treaties with the European Union, including eventually restoring its national currency and controlling its national borders. For the economy, Philippot favoured protectionism as opposed to the former neoliberal outlook.

M. Le Pen's presidential programme for the 2012 elections still had a strong focus on migration: legal immigration should be reduced from 2,00,000 to 10,000 entries per year. In addition, she foresaw the suppression of *ius soli* (citizenship by birth on French soil [as opposed to birth by descendance]) and an in-depth reform of the legislation regarding citizenship. She erected the principle of 'national priority' in all fields. For example, private companies should be encouraged to prefer French nationals with equal skills over foreigners. Another strong point of her programme was security, introducing a zero-tolerance policy throughout the national territory, restoring the death penalty[53] or life imprisonment. But M. Le Pen was only third in the first round of the 2012 presidential elections (with 17.9 per cent of votes, i.e. 64,21,426 voters, 1.5 million more than her father ten years earlier), behind Francois Hollande and Nicolas Sarkozy (Perrineau 2016: 64).

M. Le Pen liked to give the impression that she fundamentally renewed the party not only in terms of ideology but also in its internal organization. Her preferred vision was taken up by the mainstream media who wrote a lot about the party's 'new faces'. Indeed, the FN succeeded in recruiting a few personalities with the academic credentials necessary within the French political elite (Florian Philippot with diploma from HEC and ENA, Philippe Martel from ENA, Aymeric Chauprade from Sciences Po Paris). However, looking at the organizational structures beyond personalities, its organigram, functioning and overall strategies come to light. Most of the changes were not especially characteristic of the FN but common to the evolution of any political party. A critical view therefore attests that there has not been any clear and fundamental change – neither in the organization nor in the ideology of the FN (Dézé 2016).

Another account highlights internal contradictions and frictions within the party. While many members accepted that some renewal was necessary to future success, they also realized that the former right-wing radicalism with its identitarian affirmation, nationalism and anti-system attitudes was also necessary to hold back more extremist members. Further, protected by anonymity, many newly joined members condemned the sanctions against radicals who had been excluded under M. Le Pen for their openly racist attitudes. For the present, the leadership of the president seemed to silence internal criticisms (Crépon and Lebourg 2015: 450). In May 2015, J.M. Le Pen, until then honorary chairman, was suspended from the party with 94 per cent consent from members, and expelled in August the same year. He had refused to attend the disciplinary hearing of the party for his description of the gas chambers as a 'detail' of history.

Since 2014, the FN has become the leading force in terms of electoral results within the country. It has garnered more votes than the centre-right Républicains and the Socialists in each election (Crépon 2016: 14). In the municipal elections of 2014, more than 1,000 FN municipal councillors were elected, and two mayors of big cities, Béziers and Fréjus. A few months later, the FN headed the results of European elections (24.86 per cent, as against 20.81 per cent for the Union for a Popular Movement (UMP) and 13.98 per cent for the Socialists and their allies). The departmental elections in 2015 confirmed the trend: FN candidates received 25.2 per cent of votes, almost as much as the moderate right and left (Perrineau 2016: 65). M. Le Pen's aim to achieve political power had succeeded at various levels of the political system. In the regional elections of December 2015, after the terrorist attacks that shook France that year, the FN achieved 27.7 per cent of votes in the first and 27.1 per cent in the second round, reaching 42.2 per cent in the region Nord-Pas-de-Calais-Picardie and 45.2 per cent in Provence Alpes-Côte d'Azur (ibid.: 66). Despite these clear electoral successes, the FN still did not have a network of elected representatives and high-level cadres necessary for real exercise of power. For instance, in July 2015, it had 51,551 members, compared with 1,70,000 for the Socialist party and 2,00,000 for the Républicains (Crépon 2016: 14). At the municipal level, it still held only eleven municipalities out of more than 36,000, 62 *conseillers départementaux* out of 4,108 in fourteen out of 1,000 departments, two elected Members of the European Parliament (MEPs) out of 577, and two senators out of 348. It did not govern a single region of the country. Despite the success in recruiting some new faces with academic credentials, the deficit in terms of cadres was blatant and the French electoral system clearly detrimental to its realization of political power (Crépon 2016: 14).

M. Le Pen's programme for the 2017 presidential elections resembled the prior one in many respects. After the terrorist attacks, it tailored security concerns even more explicitly than before in Islamophobic terms. The programme foresaw the closing down of all extremist mosques identified by the Ministry of the Interior and prohibiting foreign funding of places of worship and their staff; prohibiting and dissolving organizations of all kinds related to Islamic fundamentalists; a fight against jihadism through deprivation of French nationality; and expulsion and prohibition from the territory of any binational linked to jihadist activities. M. Le Pen came second in the first round after Macron (Macron, 86,56,346 or 24.01 per cent; Le Pen, 76,78,491 or 21.3 per cent), and lost the second round against him (Macron, 2,07,43,128 or 66.1 per cent; Le Pen, 1,06,38,475 or 33.9 per cent). Still, one-third of the voters, more than 10 million, had voted for the FN candidate. And in the meantime, approaching the next presidential elections in 2022, Macron has pushed many of her points on to his policy agenda to compete for voters on the right.

After her failure in the 2017 presidential elections, M. Le Pen aimed at another 'political refoundation', the Rassemblement National, which might mean a return to her father's anti-immigration line while marginalizing the 'Eurosceptic' and social issues, Philippot's preferred strategy to attract different constituencies. In May 2017, Philippot founded the association Les Patriotes within the Front National. Marine Le Pen was critical of this and started to marginalize him from major functions, which led him to declare Les Patriotes an independent party under his leadership. He left with less support from members than Bruno Mégret in 1998, who had taken more than 60 per cent of the FN cadres with him but is hardly remembered today. The FN also lost another of its important figures, Marion Maréchal-Le Pen, M. Le Pen's niece, who has left party politics for the time being to found a higher education institution based on far-right ideas and values. With the election of a clearly right-wing Laurent Wauquiez to the presidency of the Republican party, the stage is set at best for a further absorption of aspects of the FN agenda to the traditional right, and at worst a coalition that would catapult the FN to a place of unprecedented influence on the French political stage (Holiday *et al.* 2018: 38).

Constituencies of the FN: Voters and Activists

Electoral analyses of the progression of the FN hint towards developments within its electoral constituencies over the years. The FN seems to have acquired a more stable and loyal constituency than in its beginnings. It also seems that a move from protest vote to support vote has happened in recent years. Attempts to make the FN appear as a class-based party have had very limited success till today. There has been a broad debate among scholars around the question of whether the FN is a working-class party (*classes populaires*).[54] The attempt to build the image of working-class and popular support has largely failed.[55] If we look at several presidential elections, we see the progression of the debate over time. In the first poll of the 1988 presidential vote, Lajoinie (Communist) gathered 7 per cent of the votes, Mittérand 34 per cent , Barré 17 per cent, Chirac 20 per cent and Le Pen 14 per cent (Lewis-Beck and Mitchell 1993). Shopkeepers and artisans were slightly more represented amongst FN voters, as well as qualified workers and foremen, leading to the notion of the workers' aristocracy supporting FN (Mayer and Perrineau 1990: 166). The hypothesis of specific working-class support, however, did not hold: only 16 per cent of workers declared their intention to vote for FN, a similar percentage as that of the lower middle class and lower than that of the upper middle class.[56] Workers were therefore not drawn to the FN more than other occupational classes, but had predominantly voted for the left candidates Lajoinie and Mittérand.

The Poujadist hypothesis, named after Pierre Poujade's movement in the 1950s, fared slightly better.

> Both movements, so the argument goes, have prospered from *les décompositions* (breakdowns). The Poujadists gained from the failure of the 'Third Force' and the general weakness of the Fourth Republic. In similar fashion, the National Front profits from the divisions on the Left and the impotence of Gaullism. The group especially sensitive to these breakdowns is the petite bourgeoisie. That is, the supporters are small business people, artisans, and perhaps other independents, such as farmers. This group largely made up the Poujadist movement. (Lewis-Beck and Mitchell 1993:116–17)[57]

If it sounds suspicious to anyone familiar with the erroneous yet still widespread belief that National Socialism was a movement of the petty bourgeoisie, the Poujadist argument is at least interesting in so far as it contains a strong element of continuity: one of those Poujadist deputies was Le Pen himself at the starting point of his political career. However, the analyst himself had to admit that 'the Poujadist hypothesis can account for some of Le Pen's support, but not much' (Lewis-Beck and Mitchell 1993: 117). Small business support was far from overwhelming and came from a numerically small population group. As opposed to the moderate left and right who attracted voters with more specific profiles, the conclusion for the 1988 vote was that J.M. Le Pen attracted voters in all population categories, old and young, rich and poor, all religious groups, rural and urban, and across socio-economic groups: 'The Front National disposes of an interclass electorate. This electorate of the FN has no strong sociological specificity' (Mayer and Perrineau 1990: 168).

The data confirm that Le Pen voters in the 1988 elections were slightly less formally educated and had a higher percentage of technical professions than the average. Many were owners of the real estate they inhabited, of a firm or of fortune (ibid.: 166, confirmed in Girard 2017). They were not more unemployed than other parties' voters, and in terms of socio-economic trajectories, more on the rise or stable than descending. They were therefore neither the poor nor those left behind. If there was a politics of resentment and a threat to social decay, it must have been much more imagined than real.

What distinguished FN voters more than the hard variables were indeed specific attitudes – statistically measured as a combination of ethnocentrism and authoritarianism, combined with pessimism. The fact that national identity, immigration and security had become major, overriding issues encouraged the FN vote and is reflected in the attitudes of its electorate (Veugelers 1997). On the ethnocentrism scale, regarding evaluation of the number of immigrants, the power of Jews in France, the rights of Muslims and the feeling of *Heimat* (*se sentir chez soi comme avant*), FN voters scored particularly high. The same was true for the authoritarianism scale, including adherence to the death penalty, to the primordial role of women as mothers, to discipline in schools, and to the societal need for hierarchy and leaders. FN voters most clearly distinguished themselves from other voters by their large acquiescence to reintroducing the death penalty (70 per cent of them fully agree) (Mayer and Perrineau 1990).

What strengthened the assumption that fears were largely imagined more than real was the fact that rejection of migrants amongst Le Pen voters was not correlated with bad relationships with foreigners in the neighbourhood or with a personal experience of insecurity: 'The reactions of those voters are rooted in phantasms and fears', a correlation confirmed again recently for the European-wide far right (Jackson and Doerschler 2018). More than any other group, FN voters had a strong feeling of insecurity even at home: they closed the door with a double lock and extra security measures before 8 pm, and overestimated the number of aggressions and criminal acts. More than others, J.M. Le Pen's voters were anxious. They were amongst the most pessimistic regarding democracy in France or the evolution of living conditions, together with voters of the Communist Party. They were the most numerous in admitting that when thinking about the future, they 'sometimes felt afraid' (Mayer and Perrineau 1990: 175). FN voters were largely pessimistic about the economy, dissatisfied with democracy and expressed a strong anti-immigration attitude. More precisely, unemployment led to high FN vote shares where immigration was high: 'Constituencies with high crime rates, and a pronounced immigration presence in the midst of elevated unemployment, are fertile ground for FN recruiters' (Lewis-Beck and Mitchell 1993: 124). This is taken to be the explanation for particularly high FN vote shares in Marseilles. The colonial connection that I outline in the following chapter is not taken into account here – a large Pieds-Noir population lives in the Mediterranean region, where veterans from the Algerian war are organized in associations and celebrate the memory of their leaders.[58] Interestingly, those negative attitudes correlated with weak social and political resources and networks. FN voters had little trust in institutions, political representatives and administrations, they were reluctant to join civil society groups or collective action such as demonstrations or strikes (Mayer and Perrineau 1990: 175).

Since the change in party leadership, the FN's scores have increased continuously. On the occasion of the presidential elections of 2012, one could note slight changes. M. Le Pen was less successful than her father in attracting the votes of white-collar workers of the Mediterranean and southern regions and in Paris. She gained in spheres with a strong working-class presence (Haute Marne, Pas-de-Calais, Aisne, Meuse, etc.) as well as in some rural areas of the centre. M. Le Pen thus succeeded in presenting herself as the leader for populations in crisis, in professional or livelihood instability, and for those who expressed a lack of trust in established politics (Perrineau 2016: 64). Again, the working-class hypothesis was revived, since workers did increase within her constituency (Veugelers 1997). However, despite evidence that right-wing radical parties have made advances within the working class, it would be short-sighted to blame workers alone for their advance and not reflect the vote shares in other segments of the electorate (Baier 2016). The truth was that the FN advanced in all social milieus, even the most recalcitrant ones like practising Catholics, unionized employees (33 per cent within the trade union CGT, 26 per cent in the CFDT, 34 per cent in FO) and state officials (Crépon 2016: 14).

The regional elections in 2015 reflected the context of the violent terrorist attacks in France. The FN advanced again across all strata and regions. The assumption that it was particularly rooted in 'an alliance of popular strata and independent workers' dominated, although figures indicated a strong presence across all segments (35 per cent within independent professions, 41 per cent among employees, 46 per cent workers, 41 per cent unemployed). Again, no socio-professional category was represented with less than 18 per cent. The FN could progress even in milieus that were traditionally rather weakly represented: salaried middle classes (28 per cent, as against 25 per cent for the moderate right and 25 per cent for the Socialists), farmers (33 per cent) and public-sector employees (30 per cent, as against 26 per cent Socialists and 22 per cent centre right) (Perrineau 2016: 69–70). The attraction amongst people with no formal degree (37 per cent) and with technical degrees (38 per cent) was more pronounced, as compared with 15 per cent among those with tertiary education. Perhaps most interesting and probably related to the violent attacks was the representation by religious group: not only 23 per cent of regularly practising Catholics, 25 per cent without creed, 26 per cent Protestants and 35 per cent of non-practising Catholics, but 22 per cent of Jews as against only 1 per cent Muslims. This is interesting for a party that has open anti-Semitism strongly inscribed in its past, with many of its members still holding anti-Semitic attitudes. The fact that the FN voiced a loud rejection of Muslims – a jihadist had carried out an attack on a Jewish store – seemed to weigh stronger amongst Jews (and Muslims) than anything else (Perrineau 2016: 69–70).

Apart from imputing the high FN scores on workers or the petty bourgeoisie, the 2014 European and 2015 departmental elections were also occasions to analyse the FN results as expressions of crisis. That voters responded to the terrorist attacks in 2015 by voting for a party with a strong law-and-order and anti-immigration programme sounds realistic. However, the interpretation in terms of FN votes as a response to unemployment is less obvious. The regions that had high vote shares for the FN, i.e. mainly the north and north-east of France, the Mediterranean area and diagonal Garonne/Canal du Midi, correspond to the cartography of unemployment in France. Where unemployment was high, the FN scores were high as well (Léger 2015). However, this correlation was not complete. In Alsace or Rhône-Alpes, for instance, unemployment was relatively low compared to the national average, but still the FN was very successful. For the latter, we can advance the colonial heritage as an explanatory factor. Alsace still needs explanation. Eventually, the argument around 'threatened border regions' (Mann 2004) could apply here, although this means reaching back farther into the past than when taking into account the effects of the loss of 'French Algeria'. The influence of the church is also much more strongly felt in the politics of the region (Boumaza 2014). In addition, the Alsatian far right is split between the FN and the regionalists of Alsace d'Abord.

The last big electoral event in France, the presidential elections of 2017, confirmed all of the observed trends so far. M. Le Pen made it to the second round and obtained 34 per cent votes, roughly double the score obtained by her father in 2002. More than 10 million French had voted Le Pen. Macron's victory cannot therefore hide the sustained progression of the far right. A study in the beginning of May 2017 – before the TV duel between Le Pen and Macron – revealed that only 38 per cent of those who intended to vote Macron in the second round did so out of conviction, as against 57 per cent who declared their intent to vote Le Pen due to adherence to her programme (Rouban 2017). Of the remaining 43 per cent who intended to vote for her by default, a third of those who had opted for centre-right candidate Francois Fillon switched to Le Pen, as well as 13 per cent of supporters of the far-left candidate Jean-Luc Mélenchon (Rouban 2017).

The 2017 elections confirmed the trend towards an interclass constituency. While J.M. Le Pen, in 2002, had obtained 11 per cent votes amongst executives (cadres) and 24 per cent amongst workers, his daughter doubled the score amongst workers and tripled it amongst superior staff, and obtained almost four times as many votes amongst the small self-employed category (small and middle-sized farmers, artisans, small shopkeepers – the constituency that had led to the Poujadist hypothesis in the previous elections). She also doubled the vote share among managers of firms with more than ten employees within liberal professions and big farmers. Her attraction amongst young people was considerable. Interestingly as well, while 8 per cent of voters with a tertiary education level chose J.M. Le Pen in 2002, 21.5 per cent of them decided to vote for his daughter in 2017 (ibid.).

Again, the data reveal that the FN vote is not explicable in terms of objective socio-economic distress.[59] Subjectively, however, perceived socio-economic well-being played an important role, confirming the above-mentioned tendency of pessimism amongst FN voters.[60] After synthesizing as far as possible various electoral analyses regarding the FN vote in France with all their difficulties and limitations, the question remains: how to explain the steady progression of cross-class adherence to this far-right party?

Empirical studies that try to qualitatively embed the FN vote into real-world, lived situations, beyond statistical data and beyond the abstract level of political discourse, are rather rare. At least, the French academic landscape has recognized the limitations of purely quantitative electoral analyses with their methodological disconnection of voting behaviour from life circumstances and meaning systems of voters (Collectif Sociologie politique des élections 2016). We find in-depth accounts of one of the constituencies that seems to have joined the FN electorate rather recently and that has led to lively debate around its working-class character:

'The authoritarian populism that is mobilizing a minority of working-class voters across Europe is essentially, a demand for de-globalization. Its reactionary nature lies not only in its preference for racism, Islamophobia and social conservatism but in its complete ignorance of the complexity of the task' (Mason 2017: 97–98). As a result of the socio-economic and related ideological transformations described above, the political landscapes of Western Europe have undergone profound changes that resulted, among others, in sections of the working class becoming one of the new constituencies of the far right. Mason analyses this process from the perspective of his own British working-class background. His account sounds similar to what French studies have brought to light:

> For neoliberalism this was a battle to impose a new narrative on millions of people's lives. A whole generation of workers was forced to behave as if the logic of the market was more important than the logic of place, or class identity - even if they did not believe this to be true. Wages collapsed. Solidarity was eroded. . . . To be frank: it broke us . . . early on, working-class communities adopted a strategy of passive cultural resistance to neoliberalism outside work. In the workplace – where bullying and rampant exploitation now took off – people confirmed to the new rituals, language and norms. But in the private and semi-social spaces – the family home, the social club, the pub – they spoke freely and nursed their grievances. In the 1980s there emerged the beginnings of a working-class culture forcibly separated from work. Then, during the 1990s, it became a working-class culture remote from work, indifferent to work, and centred on a world beyond work. (Ibid.: 91)[61]

In the same volume, Misik agrees that the traditional working class experiences a lack of respect and points towards Eribon for an adequate analysis of the process.[62] In his autobiographical account, Eribon looks back to his original milieu and interprets how sections of the working class have changed their political orientation. In the course of neoliberal ideological reconfigurations, an important fragment of the working class (*classes populaires*) shifted from its traditional support to the Communist Party (PCF) to voting for the FN. Eribon is self-critical about his own leftist, early Marxist and overall sociological perspective on the working class within which he had grown up and from which he had struggled, as an intellectual, to distance himself. In his parents' home, the PCF vote had been the obvious choice. It was about concrete, real-life experience and protest against the powerful. And it was remote from any abstract Marxist category of working-class politics.

As the PCF eroded, in his view as a result of its Moscow orientation and therefore its incapacity for political and intellectual renewal, important sections of former PCF voters gave their vote to Mitterrand, who achieved a victory for the Socialist Party in 1981. However, as described in more general terms in the above section on economic, political and ideological crises, leftist voters were soon disappointed with the 'radical transformation' of the socialist left in what 'was a true metamorphosis of its ethos and its intellectual coordinates' (Eribon [2009] 2017: 120–21). Instead of exploitation and resistance, all the talk was about necessary reforms – meaning reduction of legal protection for workers, cutting back social welfare and mechanisms of social solidarity – and individualization, in very similar ways as Mason described for the UK. Eribon also sensed the violence that these transformations represented for the working class: 'The left parties and their party and state intellectuals . . . took on the standpoint of the governing and disdainfully refuted the standpoint of the governed, and this with a degree of verbal violence that was fully recognized as such by the concerned' (ibid.). However, banning the term 'working class' from public discourse, to speak about only individuals, or eventually about the socially excluded and victims of precarity, did not mean eradicating the collective feeling and identity of those concerned. The above-mentioned 'representation crisis' took shape within the French working class and resulted in a reorientation of sections of them towards the FN:

> This was the reason why, in the course of a new political dealing out, large parts of the underprivileged turned towards the party that seemed to be the only left to care about them and that at least offered a discourse that tried to attribute some sense to their life reality (and this although its leaders were by no means originary from the working class, as opposed to the Communist Party that had always taken care to recruit its cadres from disadvantaged milieus, so that people could recognize themselves in them). (Ibid.: 122)

The FN vote had a very different meaning from the former PCF vote. As opposed to the self-affirmative PCF vote, the FN vote was out of self-defence:

> Through the Communist vote, one reassured oneself, proudly, about one's class identity; one even created this class identity through political support for the 'workers' party'. Through the FN vote, one defended silently and secretly what was left of this identity, what the power politicians of the institutional left, the degree holders from ENA and other technocratic elite schools that produced and taught a dominant, transpolitical ideology, ignored or despised. . . . The relationship to party structures and leaders, to a coherent party program and to its congruence with one's own class identity was strong, even determining in the first case, whereas it was secondary, or inexistent in the second. . . . Whose fault is it, then, that the political rescue option has this face? (Ibid.: 123–26)

This erosion of the traditional proletarian cultural and political milieu accounts, partly, for the current multiple, cross-class constituencies of the FN:

One of the heaviest consequences of the disappearance of the working class and of the worker, of the class-concept as such, from political discourse, was the revocation of the old alliance between workers and other social groups (functionaries, public sector employees, teachers . . .) within the leftist camp. This has led to a new, largely rightist if not extreme right 'historical bloc' (Gramsci), that unites today large parts of the precarious and vulnerable lower class, merchants, rich retirees in southern France, even fascistic former militaries and traditionalist Catholics. (Ibid.: 128)

Girard's ethnographical and interview-based insights into the logics of households' strategies and political attitudes in a peri-urban community gives some clues about another constituency.[63] The term 'peri-urban' designates formerly rural spaces gradually transformed through their relative closeness to urban centres but remaining on their periphery. In the context of the electoral campaign of 2012, the notion of 'modest households of peri-urban areas' appeared in media debates. According to widely held perceptions, modest population groups who had to leave urban areas because of the gentrification of centres and degradation of poorer neighbourhoods typically inhabited those areas. Those predominantly white, working-class households were considered peripheral with regard to the big metropoles that benefited from globalization and were forgotten by established politics. Supposed to be in deep cultural and identity crisis, they were held accountable for the FN vote. Girard's study is much more fine-grained than the blunt assumption of *déclassement* (downward mobility), objective or perceived.

The commune near Lyon where she conducted fieldwork among 2,000 inhabitants was governed by a local mayor, a technician by profession and son of an agricultural worker, and by elected city council members who were also predominantly local workers. The in-depth study revealed that many people in the community were politicized on the far right. However, this was not for ideological reasons, i.e. because people strongly believed in far-right ideologies and discourses. It was not out of socio-economic distress either. Most of those concerned did not correspond to the profile of 'losers' or of households experiencing economic decline. On the contrary, since the 1980s, in quite stable ways, many were qualified workers or employees, well-placed in technical professions, a few of them in the public sector. They were financially stable, had access to property and to their own housing. Rather than social decline, many had even experienced upward mobility. In their self-perception, they represented an in-between segment of the population, and worked hard to distinguish themselves from the 'excluded' and 'socially assisted'. Working hard went without any meaningful reference to a common working-class status, since this category had largely disappeared from political debate. Also, municipal planning had done what was necessary to prevent the flourishing of a working-class culture.

The study reveals the historical background of the village. Municipal decisions regarding land-use planning favoured the development of a local industrial area removed from Lyon's trade union strongholds. Entrepreneurs praised the particularly harmonious social environment, favourable for the establishment of 'excellent social relationships' (Girard 2017b: 15). The concerned industries – in 2011, a total of 3,700 permanent jobs in more than 100 firms, from international groups to small and medium enterprises – underwent deep transformations in the worlds of work, marked by the multiplication of employers, subcontracting and temporary work.

Furthermore, the municipality also chose to favour accession to property in small allotments for single family houses. The planning of industrial development was directly linked to land-use planning, the aim being the maintenance of rural social characteristics with a pacified workforce. Households with rather modest incomes had to search for occupational and marital stability in order to ensure reimbursement of long-term loans. This would also keep them away from trade union activity and collective mobilization. Families could apply for financial support from the state in order to purchase real estate, a feature that contradicts the idea of a 'forgotten' population. This was in line with public policies that aimed at the demobilization of trade union and communist strongholds within the context of big social housing complexes in the major industrial cities.

Following the project for local industrial development and the residential scheme, the working population remained alienated from a trade union-based workers' culture, as in the example described by Mason above. Instead, their social activities centred around massively depoliticized associational activities. Traditional associations included the club named 'friends of the firefighters', a senior citizen's club, a sewing club, a party committee, a flower committee and a hunters' society. The only politically meaningful older organization, in line with the village's far-right potential, was the local branch of the veterans' federation, FNACA (*Fédération nationale des anciens combattants en Algérie, Maroc et Tunisie* or National Federation of Former Combatants in Algeria, Morocco and Tunisia). The more recent associations included an aquarists' club, a dog obedience school, a car tuning and motorbike club, card games, IT, dancing, football, gym, cycling and table tennis. All the associations received financial support from the municipality and enrolled many of the inhabitants (Girard 2017b: 134–35). In such an environment, workers did not socially and culturally constitute themselves as forming part of a working class. If this favoured the FN vote in some cases, the major effect was depoliticization and abstentionism within this population.

However, according to National Social policy targets, the municipality also had to provide for a certain proportion of social housing. Elected members of the city council agreed with many inhabitants of the commune that it was preferable to reserve social housing for the children and descendants of 'originary inhabitants' of the commune alone. In particular, there was broad-based rejection of 'socially assisted' as well as racialized populations. For the municipality, the main concern was to maintain a pacified sociality and the village's reputation, while for the inhabitants the concern was the value of their private real estate property in the first place that depended, among other factors, on the quality of the social environment as well. Many had left the urban centre to escape 'dark neighbours' and were engaged in maintaining their new residential environment closed-up for whites only. The local concern about control of access to housing led the municipality to avoid investments by commercial housing agencies in big social projects. Instead, the social housing apartments were directly owned and administered by the municipality itself (27 per cent social housing, as against 61 per cent privately owned housing in the village in 2004). Access to those apartments was organized through informal contacts and along discriminatory lines as practised by the local administration and encouraged by the municipal authorities. The observed 'racism in action' was not a strongly ideological racism but one related to immediate material concerns (Girard 2017b: 226). The elected members of the city council as well as the mayor also served inhabitants' interests and relied on their proximity to the established households, to which most of them belonged socially and economically, to ensure their re-election. This procedure, and in particular the political attitude of several members of the city council on the matter, gave legitimacy to the political radicalization amongst voters (Girard 2017a). The hope was that supporting the FN could confirm such practices of giving priority to respected members of the community. In turn, the municipal authorities justified their clientelistic and discriminatory practices with the fact that a high percentage in the village voted for the FN and that they did not want to go against the interests of their inhabitants. Interestingly, the reservation of housing for community members in distress as well as important public subventions in the domain of real estate construction more broadly – indicating as well that the commune was not just 'peripheral' with regard to big cities but received quite some public support – was itself not seen as social assistance, a characteristic that was always projected on to non-welcomed 'others'.

For many inhabitants, the future of their children, their schooling and possible social trajectory, also played an important role in their political orientation. The aspiration was not higher education but stable employment in industry and commerce, especially for their sons (see also the section below on firefighters with a very similar argument). These trajectories and corresponding strategies of households then met with the political offer of the FN. The FN vote expressed a demand for social cohesion at the community level related to the 'right to stay amongst ourselves' of the white community. The far-right party made such concerns 'sayable' and legitimate. Finally, the far-right political offer also coincided with other value orientations of many households in the commune. National statistics indicate that families originally from the Maghreb, for instance, access real estate property in much less numbers than the French average. Their only chance to access real estate is through rapid compulsory auctions following the separation and divorce of established couples and families. Awareness of this resonated perfectly with the insistence on the value of traditional family models and marital stability on which the housing and loan schemes were based, and which were simultaneously promoted by the far right (Girard 2017a).

Within this village, the FN vote cannot be taken to be a reaction to objective economic or political crisis. The effects of ideological crisis as outlined above are not abstract but translate into practical concerns. The population of the commune broadly shared feelings of economic and cultural uncertainty regarding the future. They were largely dissatisfied with the moderate left and right who had alternated in the country's government for many years. In particular, the radical discourses of Sarkozy that were not followed, according to interviewees, by coherent action aggravated alienation with regard to established politics and their traditional programmes. This combined with a strong desire to maintain and close up an exclusive solidarity amongst historical members of the commune and control access to it in the form of housing policies. Liberal conceptions of society gave way to a strong wish for a community based on exclusive solidarity at the communal level.

Similar to this study on peri-urban household trajectories, Pudal's (2016) ethnography as a firefighter in the Paris fire brigade generates important insights into the politicization of this particular professional milieu. The figure of 50 per cent support for the FN within the security forces circulated around 2016 (Marin 2016). Pudal's study, although not particularly focused on their potential support for the FN, allows for grasping the logic behind the political orientations of firefighters. Here, as in Girard's study, political opinions appear less as 'a deliberative choice based on free will according to everyday notions of the political game, surveys, and political intellectuals', than as 'variable translations of specific social and professional conditions' (Collovald 2004, quoted in Pudal 2011: 76).

Firefighters were socially located 'in between working and middle classes'; put differently, they formed the upper strata of the working class. They were either professional public-sector employees in the fire brigade or, in the vast majority, full-time manual workers (skilled and unskilled), or technicians, more seldom unemployed or students who acted as voluntary staff and were paid on an hourly basis. The fire brigade was composed nearly exclusively of white men, i.e. in the racial and gender sense it was a largely homogeneous professional group. Many members did not go through a successful schooling experience, resulting in low levels of formal education. As regards the wider household, 'their wives were hairdressers or salespeople, or worked in the city hall, in banks or insurance companies, or as nurses or primary school teachers'. They had one or two children. Most lived in 'modest homes bought on long-term loans, or rent apartments or modern residences that, though "well-kept", were never far from housing projects and rougher neighborhoods' (Pudal 2011: 78–79).

As in the sample of peri-urban households, they were not themselves objectively confronted with socio-economic decline. In fact, they were rather proud of earning a good living despite low educational achievement. However, their perceptions and sorrows resembled those of the population segment analysed by Girard: 'Many worry about the possible decline of their profession, both in terms of income and working conditions. Their fears take the shape of their potential inability to pay back loans, or the disappearance of the status that offers them some amount of protection.' What adds to fears about the future is the constant risk of losing their bodily capital through accidents or injuries specific to their profession. The feeling therefore was, as one quotation expressed it, 'Okay, so we're not the worst off, but if we keep going the way this government is headed, it's going to be rough!' As in the above-mentioned study,

> a particular focus of firefighters' anxiety was what would happen to their children. Parents worried that the public schools that most of their children attended lacked the conditions necessary for academic success, and they often viewed private school as a potential solution. Many of the professional firefighters worked overtime to afford private school tuition, because they did not feel sufficiently protected from the most disadvantaged rung of the working class, composed primarily of immigrants, who were often accused of using the white kids as punching bags. (Ibid.: 80)

They thus expressed their awareness of the importance of good schooling. However, apart from investing money, they had no others means to support their children in their school careers.

For the sociologist, taking into account the professional and social concerns of firefighters was crucial to understand the ways in which they were politicized. In this, the in-between situation of their class-belonging was critical to their interpretation of societal developments and for their political orientations:

> Thus, the personal life of these firefighters is emblematic of the fragmentation of the working class, of which they compose the upper layer: they remain marked by a (strongly resented) proximity to the most disadvantaged of the working-class population with regards to leisure, residence, and their children's education. A

socioeconomic context characterized by crisis, mass unemployment, the devaluation of qualifications, outsourcing, lay-offs, and the changing status and benefits of civil servants fuelled their deep concerns, which they more or less clearly experienced and articulated. Unlike the binary world between 'them' and 'us' described by R. Hoggart, firefighters seem instead to exist in an in-between world. . . . And finally, given that their profession is about helping everyone, especially those who have least, it is understandable that they express anxiety, distrust, and sometimes animosity towards those who appear to them to embody this threat. (Ibid.: 81)

French fire brigades not only extinguish fire but are also called in case of accidents, suicides or to prevent the homeless from freezing outdoors in winter. Facing social misery in their everyday activity, many of them were very critical of the political left. Especially after the 2005 and 2007 riots during which many firefighters were called in behind the police ranks to extinguish burning cars, there was disgust with a left that neglected stronger control and that was seen as supporting the poor and left-behinds without ever asking anything from them in return.[64] But the centre right was similarly attacked, especially after Sarkozy's election, for not living up to the harsh discourses he had promoted during his campaign: "'They act hard on TV, but nothing is changing in the projects [*cités* in the French version, meaning peripheral neighbourhoods with social housing projects and often bad reputation]. They were supposed to clean up the ghettos with water blasters, yeah right, they're all talk like all politicians; when we go to the projects [*cités*] it's not with 300 CRS [riot police] to protect us'" (ibid.: 82).[65]

Furthermore, acting on a day-to-day basis as the state's right hand (order) and left hand (care) at once in a society marked by structural and institutional racism and heavy spatial segregation was important in understanding the firefighters' (self-)critical, profoundly professional and often humorous talk. They were proud of being frank and plainspeaking. This contained a criticism of politicians' and elites' discourse.[66] It is at this level that the FN was attractive to them – in its pretension to be pioneering in taking up popular voices, in understanding and taking seriously the logic of ordinary citizens, in 'saying out loud what everyone thinks anyway', more than in its ideological racism (ibid: 91–92). Its law-and-order discourse and emphasis on statism also valued positions like the firefighters.

Again, the FN vote amongst a small section of firefighters cannot be explained in terms of a concrete economic crisis situation. The perception of political crisis fares better to the extent that many of those concerned intervened in the 2005 and 2007 riots and judged centre-right as well as centre-left politicians for their inability to adequately deal with the social unrest which they had to practically sort out. As Pudal illustrates, the professional environment, action and logic alienated firefighters from the political establishment in any case. The tension between the closeness to but will to segregate from 'socially assisted', poor and racialized population groups distinguishes this group from the peri-urban households in so far as the 'right to stay amongst ourselves' would be an illusion, contradictory to the lived reality of the firefighters at work and of their families. Pudal does not give us hints to understanding how the professional corps is maintained so homogeneously in terms of gender and race. The members of the group project their fears and uncertainties in this regard in particular on to the schooling experience of their children, socially and academically speaking. This translates into a need to distinguish oneself from those much-too-close 'others'. The FN programme of national priority certainly sounds reassuring under these circumstances. Furthermore, the specific relationship to speech, as opposed to action, is a source of seduction by the populist aspects of the FN discourse. Speaking frankly, not being politically correct and daring to talk about things 'as they are', as ordinary citizens see them, is probably compelling for the firefighters.

In comparison with the large number of electoral analyses, there are relatively few studies on the membership and activist base of the FN. In a study inspired by Howard Becker's work on careers of deviant youth, Lafont presented insights from thirty-six biographical interviews with FN activists at the end of the 1990s, i.e. just after the secession from Mégret. Out of the biographies, she chose three to illustrate three different, exemplary trajectories, representative of the 1990s' younger generation of the FN. Those born between 1970 and 1975 and joining the party between 1987 and 1995 were expected to influence its shape in the following decades. The three interviewees were characterized by profoundly different experiences in joining the FN, representing among others the cleavage between working-class members and members of the bourgeoisie within the party. What united them was their feeling of not being represented in established politics and a refusal to situate themselves on a left–right political scale, estimating their struggle to be beyond and on top of this classic division (Lafont 2001: 182–83).

From the outset, the author assumed that family socialization in milieus close to the FN would be the most favourable factor for a career within the party (ibid.: 176). This case was illustrated by an activist originally from an aristocratic, landowning family with many children, who was a student at the time of the interview. His father worked as a farmer in a small town in central France. The student had grown up in a Catholic environment and underwent elitist, authoritarian education at home. His life-story was essentially about continuity and family lineage within the extreme right. The heritage reached far back to a first ancestor who 'engaged for France' under Henry IV, through the royalists and Pétainists including remote ancestors, grandparents, parents, aunts and uncles, and his brothers. His grandfather had participated in the Vichy government, his uncle was killed by the Resistance. His father actively supported Jean-Louis Tixier-Vignancour and participated in OAS actions. He told this as his own story: 'Henri IV . . . *we* had, of course, some problems during the French revolution and this is why *we* left for New York to come back at the right moment, so Louis XVIII, Charles X, then still councillors to the king . . .' (ibid.:185; my emphasis). He inscribed himself into the family tradition, recognizing that it exerted a certain pressure on him to live up to expectations and perform according to the duties his family and religion had imposed on him: 'It is a tremendous continuity. I am trying to make it mine' (ibid.: 186). When he failed to enter a prestigious university, a career within the FN was an option to uphold family honour. The family had always been politically active, and the only legitimate field for their activism was tradition – France of the *Ancien Régime*, anti-modern and anti-democratic. Although extreme in this sense, this case was representative of many amongst the thirty-six who followed the continuity of a family engaged on the far right. Another member traced her lineage to her grandmother who was active against Alfred Dreyfus and Émile Zola. The analysis in terms of continuity has its difficulties since the contexts of society and power have changed radically in the period from Henry IV to the end of the twentieth century, and to meaningfully construct this continuity is no easy task. Since the defeat of Pétain, 'the family has not had any state responsibility' any more but had to join groups outside of the established system, the most traditional of which were within the extreme right (ibid.: 183–87).

The second example in Lafont's study is one of rupture, one that corresponds to the assumption of a fragment of the working class captured by the FN. This activist interviewee had a first university degree but could not complete the next degree and worked as a warehouseman in a small firm. He came from a workers' family in a rural area near Paris. His grandparents were Catholic and communists, his parents voted on the extreme right, and he was early socialized into the Communist Party environment. He grew up with his grandparents, who were not typical industrial proletarians but agricultural workers in the countryside. Then he moved to Paris with his parents to live in a social housing complex in 1983, and was exposed to a new urban reality, to delinquent youth in the neighbourhood and to their violence. The Communist Party in the urban setting did not resemble the more traditional, grounded, rural PCF he had known till then. This provoked in him a feeling of being uprooted and the need to search for his own identity. His political socialization within the PC entered into conflict with his Catholic and rural socialization. The risk of unemployment for young degree-holders at the time was rather high. He engaged with the GUD (Groupe Union Défense) while at university, then did his military service and then joined the FN, where he later also met his future wife. The FN was attractive because it was engaged in social justice for the ordinary, 'small' citizens. His experience of being a victim of uprootedness in the *cité* resonated within the FN. This is a radical case of rupture from extreme left to extreme right; shifts from the centre left occurred more frequently. Also, the experience of rupture due to moving house or due to a rapid change in the living environment was frequent within the sample. Lafont's interpretation is that this corresponded to a social and contextual change rather than to a profound ideological reorientation (ibid.: 190–92).

The third case is that of a young woman born into a Catholic working-class household in the outskirts of a big city. Her family was largely politically indifferent. Her mother had been unemployed and the young woman had thus experienced economic insecurity. She had a professional high-school degree in administration and worked part-time as a cleaner after periods of unemployment and different types of small jobs. She had never had the means to leave the parental home due to her economic instability. This raised doubts in her regarding her autonomy, her capacity for being an adult and being able to set up her own family. Her trajectory illustrated the socialization capacity of the FN out of non-political engagement. In 1995, far from any political terrain, she met her future husband, an FN activist, who was then completing his military service, and engaged with the party through him (ibid.: 193–94). The interviewee spoke little about politics or ideas but rather about the atmosphere within the group of activists to which her fiancé belonged, where she, as the only female, quickly had the role of a collective 'mother'. This was a radical change from her former social isolation and lack of recognition outside of her family home, coupled with anxieties about being able to be a mother. This trajectory of joining the FN's militant circles out of a need for sociality and conviviality was also frequently present in the thirty-six biographies. Especially after a period of unemployment or after retirement, i.e. at a point of time where social 'utility' was put into question and time for activism was plenty, people joined the party's ranks. This third case did not mean that politics were not important. If the party was able to harbour a positive affective and socializing experience, it was precisely because of its ideological orientation and the identitarian values it conveyed. This was coupled in those years with the negative image it projected in society at large, leading to a particularly intense experience for those within against a largely hostile environment outside. Lafont compared the FN to a 'total institution, close to a religious sect', which marked the identity of its members more strongly than other parties or associations could have. In ideological terms, the FN 'offered, in the first place, a place of dreams and a hope for a different, a better future' to its active members (ibid.: 194). In this sense, the integrative function was to transform the group of activists into a 'world by substitution' that allowed 'to compensate desocializing social trajectories and to invert social and political stigmata' (ibid.: 175). This tendency of the FN to provide a space of freedom of expression and for exchange of ideas that were otherwise seen as illegitimate and politically incorrect, as a 'counter-society' where activists created strong social bonds, was highlighted by other analysts as well (Dézé 2016). One noticeable change in more recent years, however, is the increasing willingness of members to publicly identify with the party (Crépon and Lebourg 2015), as opposed to earlier years when this would have been too stigmatizing.

Quantitative analyses have highlighted the cross-class character of the FN's electorate. Qualitative studies, in turn, analyse the significance of electoral support to the FN for different groups of voters and activists. It was with regard to material and social concerns in particular, such as residential and neighbourhood issues, as well as with regard to school education, that the FN's call for national priority and social closure to protect white privileges appeared attractive. Further, for younger members and activists as well as for those who had broken with prior leftist political experiences, the bonding and socializing aspect was important. The following chapter further develops the issue of family traditions.

Germany: The Rise of the Alternative für Deutschland

While the so-called populist radical-right parties (Mudde 2007) had spread over Europe over several decades already, in the context of Federal Germany – apart from small attempts at regional levels – no such party had arisen alongside the more old-style extremist NPD until February 2013, when the Alternative für Deutschland or AfD was formed (Häusler, ed. 2016; Werner 2015). From 2014 onwards, the AfD kept increasing its tally in all the elections (Oppelland 2017). Between 2014 and 2017, it gained seats in fourteen out of sixteen regional parliaments. In 2017, it entered the Bundestag with 12.6 per cent votes (94 seats), and it is currently the largest opposition party against the great coalition between CDU/CSU (Christian Democrats) and SPD (Social Democrats).[67]

At the outset, it looks like the impressively quick rise of the AfD was directly linked to two crisis-contexts. It was in direct reaction to the 2008 financial crisis and the subsequent Euro crisis that the AfD was founded, initially with a decidedly anti-EU agenda, demanding the dissolution of the monetary union and placing restrictions on European integration (Werner 2015: 35). The management of the Euro crisis was but the culminating point of a series of deceptions within established politics in Germany. Thus, the reasons for the foundation and success of the AfD have to be sought in the years that preceded it, and at the level of political transformations rather than in the economic domain proper.

Conservative members of the Christian Democratic Union of Germany (CDU) believed that under Merkel, their party had given up on fundamental conservative positions. Among them was Gauland who later joined the AfD (ibid.: 39).[68] The neoliberal fraction was similarly frustrated, since Merkel's CDU had moved from a strictly neoliberal stance to social-democratic positions in some fields of its economic policy. The 'pain threshold' for liberals and conservatives was reached when the conservative-liberal coalition government agreed to 'rescue packages' for Greece under the European Financial Stability Facility and European Stability Mechanism (ibid.: 35 ff.). The AfD's emergence is thus directly linked to the day in March 2010 when Merkel declared to the Bundestag that European financial aid for Greece would be only a very last resort, and the EU summit the same evening agreed to the first rescue package for Greece, saying that there was no alternative.[69] The party's name 'Alternative for Germany' is explained by this context, reflecting the opinion of leading economists that Europe's financial and rescue politics was not at all without alternative (Decker 2016: 14).

The AfD stepped into an arena of public debate where European integration was highly politicized. Opposition arose against Merkel's politics of first refusing, then finally agreeing to the rescue package for Greece. Among the owning classes, there was widespread fear that the EU would be transformed into a social union with collective liability and redistribution amongst member states. This fundamentally contradicted the ethics of performance of generations of the German middle-sized bourgeoisie (Mittelstand). The self-perception of the Mittelstand was to be *Leistungsträger*, the carriers of performance, in the German economy – the ones who work hard, take risks, create jobs, pay taxes, produce wealth. But in the end, as medium-sized enterprises, they are too small, not 'system-relevant' enough to 'knock on the door of the chancellery' to ask for rescue packages when in trouble (Werner 2015: 46–49). Those Mittelstand-constituencies diverged from the country's big business, represented by the BDI (Bundesverband der Deutschen Industrie, or the Federation of German Industries) that welcomed the rescue packages.

Hans-Olaf Henkel, former president of BDI, turned his back on it at the moment of the Euro crisis and joined the AfD; he later became the member of the European Parliament for the party and one of its 'organic intellectuals':

> The manager Henkel cannot let off the steering wheel. Not when the course taken is so wrong. The final break with the established parties happened when the rescue package for Greece was decided. German tax payers' money for Greek banks. He found it immoral. More so since he – the father fell in the war in '45, the mother struggled to make a living for her family – has all built up himself. He always triumphed in direct competition. Competition has made him big. But the EU changes the rules of the game, helps the weak, sacrifices competition for the rescuing of the Euro. (Ibid.: 46–49)[70]

It was medium-sized and family businesses and their associations that stuck to this kind of argument.

In accordance, the AfD first recruited from amongst the middle classes: 'family entrepreneurs, free architects, tax consultants, lawyers, established medical doctors, managers'. They were not driven by fears of immigration but by lack of respect for their performance, by the opposition between those who create wealth and those who spend taxpayers' money (ibid.: 46–49). Owing to its politics at the time of the Euro crisis, the CDU obtained similar results as the Social Democratic Party of Germany (SPD) with the Hartz reforms: it alienated major parts of its membership base and electorate. This was the precondition for a successful split and establishment of an oppositional party to its right (ibid.: 49), to the despair of the CDU's Bavarian sister party, the Christian Social Union (CSU), that had established long ago that to the 'right of the CSU, there is only the wall'. Obviously, such interpretations of the Euro rescue policies hold only on the basis of ignoring the results of Germany's export orientation, of the consequences of neoliberal economic, financial and labour market policies, and, most importantly, of the dominant role of Germany within the EU. Despite these fundamental aspects of the issue, the AfD could capitalize on the perception of Germany as a victim of uncontrollable European forces, combined with criticism of corrupted national elites. It was this kind of victimization thinking that also enabled a coalition of diverging forces within the party, between liberals, national conservatives and more right-wing populists (ibid.: 111).

On top of the anti-EU outlook, the AfD soon established a more fully-fledged party programme comprising diverging tendencies into what would be its 'winning formula' (Decker 2016: 13). It managed to combine, in its first phase, the concerns of liberal economic professors and the particular interests of medium-sized enterprises against the CDU's crisis policy; of national-conservatives who feared the disappearance 'of cultural institutions considered vital, such as heteronormative marriage and family and the German (mainly Christian) "lead culture" (Leitkultur)', and the populist rightists' appeal to racist and homophobic feelings (Werner 2015: 58–59).[71]

Some further elements are necessary, however, to understand the context of the emergence of the AfD. Discursively, the field had been prepared for its emergence with the debate around *Leitkultur*. CDU deputy Friedrich Merz evoked the idea of a 'lead culture' in a 2010 speech as a counter-model to 'multiculturalism' in the domain of immigration and integration. Simultaneously, in 2010, a book by SPD politician Thilo Sarrazin appeared, entitled *Deutschland schafft sich ab* (Germany abolishes itself). In this book, Sarrazin conjures the decadence of Germany due to a combination, according to him, of low fertility levels, a growing underclass and high immigration levels, mainly from Muslim countries.

The socio-Darwinist and racist overtones of the book have steered fierce public debate.[72]

In terms of its organization and networks, the AfD did not start from scratch either. In the context of the Maastricht Treaty (1993), a Euro-critical party, the Bund Freier Bürger, emerged. This small party (1994–2000) was shaped like the AfD in its beginnings, as a 'professorial party' uniting middle-class members (it had relatively high adherence fees), and favouring a strongly neoliberal financial and labour market and overall economic policy. Nevertheless, it also favoured a nationalist perspective on Germany in the international scene, adhered to elements of a revisionist history of the country, and was close to Vertriebenenverbände (Associations of Exiles) and to networks of the New Right (ibid.: 22). Furthermore, there were a Hayek Society, an Initiative for a New Social Market Economy (Initiative Neue Soziale Marktwirtschaft), the Citizen's Will (Bündnis Bürgerwille) alliance, the Electoral Initiative 2013 (Wahlalternative 2013), as well as the Christian fundamentalist network Civil Coalition (Zivile Koalition). All of these fed into the creation of the AfD in terms of their programmatic agendas and personal networks. Its various predecessors indicated the mix of liberal-economic, social-conservative and nationalist positions that characterized the AfD in its beginnings (Decker 2016: 14). Furthermore, several of its founding and leading members were dissenters from existing political parties, mostly from the CDU and FDP (Free Democratic Party),[73] reacting to the transformations those parties had gone through recently. Those evolutions within the centre right opened up a window of opportunity for the AfD to step in as a more decidedly right-wing party (ibid.: 15).

The initially determining topic of the Euro started to lose importance in public debate and perception around 2015. This was the moment of the second crisis, which explains the rapid rise of the AfD but also its internal transformations. Terrorism, jihadism, Islamization and refugees as major threats to the continuity of the country as *Heimat* and to German identity gained centre stage, and the party was increasingly radicalized on its internal national-conservative and far-right nationalist fronts (Oppelland 2017). Indeed, the successes in the eastern regional parliaments, with a very different agenda from the federal level, led the regional leadership to increasingly question Bernd Lucke's domination over the party. The president of the Saxony branch, Frauke Petry, who had been elected spokesperson alongside Lucke and Konrad Adam, was especially in direct rivalry with Lucke in terms of the party's political orientation.

The Pegida[74] movement catalysed internal conflicts. A brief outline of this extra-parliamentary street movement is therefore necessary here. 'Between late October 2014 and mid-January 2015, political debate in Germany was captured by the rapid emergence of a new political movement, namely the so-called

"Patriotic Europeans against the Islamization of the West'" (Dostal 2015: 523). The movement started with a Facebook page in October 2014 and was followed by a long series of rallies through the city of Dresden on Mondays, mimicking the tradition of mass mobilizations that ultimately led to the fall of the wall in 1989. Pegida represented itself as 'evening walks' by 'concerned citizens' (*besorgte Bürger*). It was initiated by a dozen persons, most of them without prior political experience. Three of them had been active in what represented the conservative scene of the region: one from CDU, one from FDP and one from AfD. They claimed to 'defend the mainstream of German culture and traditions against a liberal elite and political establishment that was alienated from its own people' (ibid.: 524). The rallies grew rapidly, from the first one with 350 participants on 20 October 2014 to up to 25,000 participants by mid-January 2015. Participation rapidly declined afterwards. There were attempts to imitate the movement in other German cities. A 2016 paper counted a total of 239 Pegida marches in forty cities with around 2,27,000 participants in total. More than two-thirds of these occurred in Dresden (Korsch 2016a: 112).

One of Pegida's initial themes was to fight against 'religious wars' on German soil.[75] Another feature was the denunciation of the mainstream media as a 'lying press' (*Lügenpresse*) and established politicians as 'traitors of the people' (*Volksverräter*), terms closely associated with National Socialist vocabulary (Kellershohn 2016: 191). There were also other themes, like the conflict between Russia and Ukraine, the fact that the US secret services had spied on German government officials and later the Charlie Hebdo attacks in Paris, that were taken up by Pegida. The initial image of anxious ordinary citizens constituting the movement's social basis started to change when a picture of one of the initiators and leaders, Lutz Bachmann, circulated where he appears with Hitler's moustache. There was therefore an observable development of Pegida over time:

> It must be stressed that the mobilization was clearly based on right-wing discourses and Pegida leaders frequently stressed that they located themselves to the right of the CDU. One could perhaps go so far to consider Pegida as a kind of prototypical völkisch (ethnic nationalist) movement. Yet this alone cannot explain its initial success, which was due to efforts to put forward demands that were shared by many ordinary citizens. This concerned criticism of the political class for its distance from ordinary people and the voicing of concern about the ongoing refugee crisis in Germany, which derived in turn from the break-up of states in the Middle East and the failure of the European Union to act on this challenge. (Dostal 2015: 526)

In the local context of Dresden, far-right milieus had been particularly strong. The existing structures certainly worked towards shaping the movement, over time, according to their own agenda.[76] The debate within the party about its relationship with Pegida was a complex one, and it evolved over time (Korsch 2016a: 112). Pegida, in turn, kept a distance from the AfD. There were hardly any official connections at the staff level between the organizing team and the AfD. Pegida was determined, from the outset, to present itself as a citizen's movement above party lines. Irrespective of the party's official stance, studies on Pegida's constituencies outlined strong convergences between the movement and the new party.[77]

Further, other actors – on which I will develop more fully below – mediated between Pegida and AfD, and across the far-right scene in the region and beyond. For instance, the New Right intellectual Götz Kubitschek spoke at various Pegida demonstrations and expressed his total refusal to establish a 'pluriethnic' state in Germany (Sebaux 2016: 390). He also lent credibility to the movement by analysing it as 'a revolt of citizens' against 'system elites' in a special issue of the New Right journal *Sezession* (Kubitschek 2015: 10 f., quoted in Kellershohn 2016: 191). Pegida was also accompanied by the Munich branch of Politically Incorrect, a counter-jihadism network (Kronauer 2016: 37). We can therefore conclude that the Pegida movement 'has given wings to the complete right-wing populist and extreme right scene in Germany. Pegida can be seen as the booster detonation of a protest movement that is hostile towards refugees' (Häusler and Virchow 2016: 7).

Returning to the AfD, throughout the year 2015, the internal imbalance between the liberal and the national-conservative sections increasingly swung towards the latter, and the more radical right voices gained ground.[78] While the Euro crisis was the context of its emergence, the rise of Pegida in 2015 and the refugee reception crisis of 2015–16 were contexts of split and radicalization, on the one hand, and of further convergence of several types of forces on the far right, on the other.[79] The 2018 government coalition endowed CSU leader Seehofer with the Ministry of Interior and *Heimat*. From his activities since March 2018, it is obvious that his task within a division of labour is to capture and bring back those voters who have shifted to the AfD in the meantime. While the October 2018 regional elections in Bavaria showed that his strategy had failed, the far right's ideological struggle is succeeding.

In the context of public debate around the refugee reception crisis, the regional elections of March 2016 confirmed spectacular successes for the AfD. In Sachsen-Anhalt, the party became the second largest group in the regional parliament with 24 per cent votes. In Baden-Württemberg, it gained 15 per cent of the votes, confirming that it was not restricted to Eastern Germany. When refugee numbers decreased due to the government's more restrictive handling, so did the AfD tally. In three regional elections in spring 2017, it managed to enter the official scene in all three but with less than 10 per cent votes (Oppelland 2017).

After Lucke's exit, Gauland and Petry favoured a politics of radicalization and polarization within the German party system, especially through integrating more extreme voices on the far right over topics such as immigration, Islam, national sovereignty and family. In 2017, Höcke managed to stage another right-wing radicalization. In a speech to the party's youth branch Junge Alternative in Dresden, in January 2017, he made his famous reference to the Holocaust memorial in Berlin. In his words, Germany was the only country that had established 'a memorial of disgrace' in the middle of its capital. He called for a 180-degree turn in terms of the German culture of remembrance with regard to the National Socialist past, highlighting what I determined as one of the German far right's major originary grievances. Petry, who until then had been a major engine of radicalization against Lucke, initiated a strategy to exclude Höcke from the party, but failed and found herself marginalized, while Höcke emerged with renewed weight, strength and visibility within the AfD (ibid.). After the federal elections of 2017, Frauke Petry, who had been one of the major actors for radicalization in the early phase, left the party together with her husband Marcus Pretzell, former regional party leader of Nordrhein-Westfalen. The still more radical group around Höcke was to mould the party's image from then on. A comment on the 2017 federal elections concluded that:

> With the AfD, for the first time, a flawless right-wing populist party enters the German Bundestag, in terms of its milieu structure just as much as in terms of its staff, its electoral campaign and – apart from a few market-economy-oriented remnants of its liberal founding phase as a Euro-populist professoral party – also in terms of its program. (Vehrkamp and Wegschaider 2017: 60–61)

This is the connecting point with the country's post-war past. In a detective-like 150-page textual analysis of speeches and writings of Björn Höcke in comparison with those of an author writing under the name of Landolf Ladig in various NPD publications, Kemper presents results that make it difficult to doubt that Höcke had been an active member of the NPD before he joined the AfD (Kemper 2016a). As a history teacher in a public school, he could not engage himself under his personal name and therefore had to choose a pseudonym. Höcke, who calls for 'overcoming the neurotic phase in which we had lingered for the last 70 years' (a phrase that was chosen as the title of Kemper's report), has declared on several occasions that he saw the AfD as 'the last evolutionary chance' for this country.

An important fraction of the party's leadership has decisively reconnected with or shifted to the far right. It still hosts people with diverging views and one cannot speak of a homogeneous party structure or a single extreme right programme. But the reconnection of this newcomer on the German scene in a short period of time after its foundation and the marginalization or split of members who did not belong to the tradition of the German far right is evident. Apart from the diachronic contextualization, the current AfD has to be seen within the broader network structure of the German far right. In the following sections, I will develop on Junge Alternative, the New Right and its intellectuals, Gildenschaft, Ein Prozent (One Per Cent), Identitäre Bewegung (Identitarian Movement), vigilantism, the Junker connection and expellees' associations, and how they all connect across the republic.[80]

The AfD's youth branch, Junge Alternative (JA) appears as more radical and more clearly linked to radical-right and New Right circles than the AfD itself. It has played a role as a 'taboo breaker'. Proud of being plainspeaking and mocking political correctness, it has put forth provocative theses regarding the topics of migration, for instance, but also anti-feminist Facebook campaigns and meetings with far-right actors, like its invitation of the UK Independent Party (UKIP) leader Nigel Farage to a meeting in Cologne in 2014. Similar to UKIP, the JA favours Germany's exit from the EU. More than that, it demands 'democratic dissolution' of the European Union (Herkenhoff 2016b).

Not only is the JA compatible at the programmatic level with far-right positions, it is also organizationally connected with the extreme-right scene.[81] It does not hide its affinity with the extremist Alte Breslauer Burschenschaft in Bonn, for instance. This fraternity had provided space for a fair that the journal *Sezession* organized in 2014, and where New Right editors and media exposed their activities (ibid.: 205). The JA converges in its programme with the New Right discourse and there are personal overlaps as well.

The German New Right was largely inspired by the French Nouvelle Droite. It struggles for a metapolitical, culturally discursive hegemony of *völkisch*, racist and nationalist ideas. It has invested considerable efforts into overcoming the 'stigma of National Socialism' (ibid.: 208). The strategy consisted in rehabilitating the intellectual heritage of the Conservative Revolution during the Weimar Republic, i.e. those thinkers that fed into the creation of NS ideology but preceded it, therefore exempt from accusations of directly being linked with NS crimes.[82] Götz Kubitschek, one of the New Right's current key figures, argued that 'with reference to the "Conservative revolution", "the language of the right, under justification constraint since 1945, could be rearmed"' (Kubitschek 2007, quoted in Herkenhoff 2016b: 208). Kubitschek's ambition is the 'provision of a complete argumentative framework' (Wölk 2016: 101). Apart from the literature of the Weimar Conservative Revolution, the writings of French and Austrian identitarians are important references.

The efforts of the New Right are carried out with the material support of a publicist network including the journals *Sezession* (edited by Kubitschek),

Compact-Magazin (edited by Elsässer)[83] and *Junge Freiheit* (edited by Stein), as well as the journals *Blaue Narzisse*, edited by pupils and students, and the Austrian *Die Aula*. *Sezession* has referred several times to the AfD as the 'party-political brick' within a 'milieu of resistance that becomes ever more structurally stable' (quoted in Häusler 2016a: 49). The JA entertains 'privileged contacts' with *Junge Freiheit* that has almost become the informal party publication (Herkenhoff 2016b). The AfD itself has no official party organ and could thus use existing structures and also reach out to potential new constituencies. The *Junge Freiheit*, in turn, increased its readership and achieved the status of a quotable source (Wölk 2016: 100–01). For instance, after the regional elections of 2015 in Sachsen-Anhalt, regional AfD leader André Poggenburg gave his first interview to *Compact*. This obliged mainstream media also to refer to the New Right publication in the first place. The cooperation went so far as authors and editors of *Junge Freiheit* joining the AfD as functionaries and candidates (ibid.). The French think tank GRECE (Research and Study Group for European Civilization) is one of its key references. One of its chief ideologues is Karlheinz Weißmann.[84]

Höcke enjoys the full support of intellectual circles around Götz Kubitschek and Ellen Kositza from Schnellroda Manor, where the far-right think tank Institut für Staatspolitik, the magazine *Antaois* and the journal *Sezession* are hosted. He is even considered Kubitschek's pupil (Kellershohn 2016). Kubitschek spoke at Pegida demonstrations and cordially invited not only authors from identitarian networks but also Höcke as an AfD speaker to activities of *Antaois* at the 2017 Frankfurt book fair. We need not look more deeply into struggles between different sections within the New Right to promote their agenda within the AfD (ibid.: 2016). What is important is the fact that the party has been increasingly captured by a far-right scene that had existed for many years before, and that had been waiting for a political party to carry out its agenda for social and political transformation of the country. In a conversation between Poggenburg, Elsässer and Kubitschek, they revealed that they understood the success of the AfD in the region as a collective achievement.

Another component is the Gildenschaft. If there is a direct connecting line from the NPD to the AfD exemplified by Höcke, there are also long-term continuities in the attempts of the New Right to provide ideological inputs to the party. Interestingly, most of the intellectuals mentioned belong to the Deutsche Gildenschaft, a corporation of far-right intellectuals. This is the case with Dieter Stein, Götz Kubitschek and Karlheinz Weißmann. The *Deutsche Hochschulgilde*, an academic corporation, since the postwar years, 'has seen its space of action in this space between the Union parties and the extreme right'. They had observed the failure of the Republikaner and the Bund Freier Bürger. This space was filled by the emergence of the AfD (Wölk 2016: 100–01). The Gildenschaft has deep roots right into the anti-republican corporations of the 1920s that combined the cult of youth, students and soldiers. In 1933, the Deutsche Gildenschaft committed itself to serve 'the National Socialist revolution' and pledged allegiance to Hitler. Membership in SA or SS became an obligation for its members. Many members became instrumental in the realization of National Socialist rule, mainly in the universities as anthropologists, racial hygienists or *völkisch* theologians. It was refounded in 1958. The aim of the Gildenschaft had always been to form a national elite with *völkisch* orientation to complement, when the time was ripe, a mass movement. It is a tiny group but its qualitative impact on politics and society cannot be overestimated. It has 'provided significant ideological and personal mediation in the zone between conservatism and right-wing extremism' (Kellershohn 2004: 3).

Out of the New Right intellectual circles emerged a new broader movement in 2015, the initiative Ein Prozent für unser Land (One per cent for our country). The name refers to the estimation that one per cent of the population would suffice to create a massive resistance movement on the right, promoting the vision of a 'Germany and Europe organized along völkisch and racist criteria' (Herkenhoff 2016a: 74). Kubitschek defined it as an 'NGO for Germany', i.e. a common platform for all those initiatives and networks that had emerged in the course of the Pegida protests and related activities. Underlying the analysis that led to the creation of this platform are conspiracy theory-like assumptions: Germany is supposed to be in 'lethal danger' in the face of 'the mass flooding with so-called refugees orchestrated by Merkel'. Such visions were elaborated by Elsässer, Kubitschek and Karl Albrecht Schachtschneider, and published among others in *Compact*. Members of the identitarian movement, such as Martin Sellner, leader of Identitäre Bewegung in Vienna, also formed part of the alliance.

The identitarian movement (Identitäre Bewegung) is another scene to which the AfD, like the New Right, is linked. It draws on the French Générations Identitaires and on the Austrian IB. The movement appears as a young hipster movement and constitutes the activist branch of the New Right with which it overlaps ideologically. The leading principles of the identitarians are, 'Neither left nor right – identitarian!', playing again with the fascist motto of neither right nor left; and '0% racism, 100% identity!' (ibid.: 77–78). It has gained publicity mainly through its Islamophobic interventions. At the Frankfurt book fair in 2017, the publishing house Antaios organized a book presentation by identitarians Müller and Sellner, authors of the book *Identitär!* (2017). Reacting against protests by the Antifa, the identitarians and their supporters chanted '*Europa! Jugend! Reconquista!*' (Europe! Youth! Reconquista!) (Keim 2017).

Finally, another scene that needs to be mentioned for the sake of completeness is vigilantism. In the years 2015 and 2016, new vigilante groups emerged such as Bürgerwehr Hannover, Freikorps Bürgerwehr Selbstschutz der Patrioten und unserer Familien and Düsseldorf passt auf (Quent 2016b: 84). They engaged in protecting the population, especially German women, against the alleged influx of and aggression by refugees. This need was based on their analysis of the state's failure to regulate migration and to deal with migrants' criminality. Most of the vigilante groups had merely a virtual presence on Facebook. The few that patrolled on a more regular basis were usually built on top of pre-existing networks such as fraternities or NPD groups. Those are classified as 'vigilantist violent groups', i.e. groups that 'use the vigilantist denomination in order to justify violence against social groups that are marked as deviant' (ibid.: 92). Many of the vigilantes sympathize with Pegida and the AfD. Furthermore, the recent, highly controversial condemnation of members of the NSU apparently has not put an end to far-right terrorist structures. Ongoing investigations around members of Revolution Chemnitz, for instance, indicate that a similar network has reconfigured itself that considered the NSU as a mere 'preschool group' (Machowecz *et al.* 2018).

The AfD's connections also reach out to the Reichsbürger movement. The Reichsbürger consider themselves citizens of the German Reich within its 1942 territorial limits, currently occupied by the Federal Republic government. They do not respect the country's authorities and borders, refuse to pay taxes, and issue their own identity documents or building permits. Their number is growing. In 2021, around 20,000 people counted as Reichsbürger (Rathje 2014).[85] In the context of the coronavirus pandemic, Reichsbürger have spearheaded protests against government measures to tackle the pandemic. They took centre stage in the assault on the Reichstag in August 2020, waving the historical flags of the German empire.

The connection with the Junkers and expellees' associations also merits attention here. In volume I, I had outlined the importance of the German landowning aristocracy, the Junkers, as one of the constituencies who supported National Socialism. Interestingly, there is continuity at this level too within the AfD. Beatrix Amelie Ehrengard Eilika von Storch, born Beatrix Amelie Ehrengard Eilika, Duchess of Oldenburg, is an elected member of parliament for the AfD and former member of the European Parliament (2014–17) (Werner 2015: 54). She started her political career with the creation of the Initiative Göttinger Kreis – Initiative für den Rechtsstaat e.V. This lobbying association reclaimed the rights of aristocratic landowners who had been dispossessed under the Soviet occupation. With the 1989 transformations, the Kohl government did not put into question these dispossessions. The Göttingen Circle demands reparation to those who had been dispossessed by the Soviet land reforms, as well as restitution of land rights to those who then became refugees in Western Germany. This concerns not only aristocratic Junkers but a much broader population group.

Within today's expellee associations, federated under the Bund der Vertrie-benen (BdV, Union of Exiles), although they host heterogeneous forces, nationalist, revisionist and far-right political orientations are still present. These associations have lost in significance and membership in comparison with the immediate post-war decades (membership numbers remain unclear but are estimated at about 25,000; Später and Kotte 2010). After 1989, they had to accept the European ordering. At the same time, as a result of the subsequent European integration process, expellee associations increasingly practise their own 'foreign policy' with eastern Europe (Salzborn 2001). While the older NS staff that had worked towards rehabilitating key National Socialist actors is dying out, the associations persist, funded generously by the federal budget. Erika Steinbach, president of the BdV between 1998 and 2014, was herself born in 1943 in Danzig-Westpreußen, which had been conquered by the Nazis only in 1939. She had to leave her birthplace in 1945. In her defence of 'the right to Heimat', Steinbach mobilizes international human rights dispositions and makes the German occupiers of eastern Europe appear as victims of world history. She left the CDU in 2017 following Merkel's refugee policy and supported the AfD in its electoral campaign. Steinbach is not an AfD member but heads the party's foundation. The BdV has some personal overlaps with the current far right scene, and the refugees and their descendants represent an interesting voters' base.

From this localization of the AfD in the wider far-right context, it becomes obvious that the party's programme and strategy have been increasingly captured by established New Right networks (Häusler 2016a: 47). The group around Höcke and the Erfurt Resolution has played a crucial role in this sense, and has made considerable inroads into pulling the whole party in the nationalist-xenophobic direction. More broadly, the discussion sheds doubts on the term 'populist' in order to adequately characterize recent developments within the AfD, sustained by the Pegida movement during a certain period. Häusler goes far in arguing that we are observing a 'Kulturkampf von rechts', not limited to the parliamentary activities of the AfD but obeying largely the New Right agenda of gaining cultural hegemony.[86] The most recent advances into different sectors of society would need to be interpreted in more detail – such as those networks' exact role in usurping protests against Covid measures; but also their advances in the worlds of work, with the creation of a trade union that denies climate change and seeks to attract workers in the German automobile industry.

The AfD's Constituencies

Membership of the AfD increased rapidly after its creation, moving from 10,000 right after its foundation to 17,000 by the end of the year 2013. At the point of time when Lucke and his followers left the party in mid-2015, the party had 22,000 members, a number that has remained largely stable since then, i.e. the Lucke split did not affect membership numbers in the long term. The party's membership has always been heterogeneous, the only stable characteristic being the strong under-representation of women (only 15 per cent, according to Oppelland 2017), which is still to be explicated.

If the membership is described as heterogeneous, this holds even more true for the electorate (Werner 2015: 65). The radicalization and polarization strategy, it seems, has paid off in terms of electoral results.[87] The party has attracted voters from all existing parties as well as from former non-voters.[88] Electoral analyses confirm that the AfD attracts voters from all socio-economic categories. It is slightly more successful among younger voters. In terms of income and education, AfD voters are situated slightly above the average in the European parliamentary elections and slightly below average in the regional elections. The only hard variable that is significant is gender, with 60 per cent of men and 40 per cent of women voting for the party, similar to the situation of other European right-wing parties (Mudde 2007).

Similar debates to the ones in France focused on the question of whether the AfD attracted in particular workers or the unemployed or, rather, the well-situated middle strata (Bischoff and Müller 2016: 22–23). One opinion research centre declared that AfD voters 'come from a segment of the middle classes that is objectively well-established, but subjectively marked by fears of loss of status and feels squeezed between global capitalism and the proletariat' (ibid.: 25). One wonders what standardized question yielded such results in a country where the proletariat has lost its significance as a reference long ago.[89] Werner is probably right when he states that 'in an early phase of electoral struggle already, a small support basis was identified'. Those persons were attracted to the AfD because 'they recognized the Euro-crisis as the biggest problem of the country, rejected financial aid for indebted EU-member states, saw the future of the German economy with pessimism and were extremely unsatisfied with the current government' (Werner 2015: 65). However, he provides no empirical data to confirm exactly which population sections were concerned.[90]

An analysis of the results of the 2017 federal elections divides the overall population into ten socio-economic and socio-cultural 'milieus', combining social status (household income, education, profession) and orientation (values and attitudes, lifestyles) (Vehrkamp and Wegschaider 2017: 34). The study reveals that the core milieus of the AfD were the precarious, the traditionalists and the bourgeois centre. The precarious are defined as the lower class that struggles for orientation and participation but cumulates factors of social disadvantage, experiences social exclusion and therefore bitterness and resentment. In this milieu, the AfD obtained 28 per cent of votes, its strongest result. This is also where the party gained most support in comparison to prior elections. The party had the merit of strongly mobilizing amongst population groups that had largely abstained in prior elections. The AfD gained double as many votes amongst former non-voters than among former voters. As a result, 'the more social precarious a circumscription, the better the results for the AfD and the higher its increase in votes' (ibid.: 19). While this confirms the AfD's claim to be speaking for the 'silent' (not-yet) 'majority', the analysis does not give us any explanatory elements regarding this milieu's vote. The 'bourgeois centre' was characterized as the bourgeois mainstream, oriented towards performance and adaptation. It generally agrees to the social order, aims at professional and social stability, and at secure, harmonious social relations. Its attitude is characterized by fears of downward mobility. One in five voters of the bourgeois centre voted for the AfD. The party gained 15 per cent in this milieu in comparison with prior elections, the same percentage that the CDU lost. This reveals the competition between AfD and CDU for the population in the centre. It is in line with the founding constituencies of the AfD as outlined above.

The traditional milieu was composed of older generations who strive for security and order. They belong either to the petty bourgeoisie or workers' cultural milieus, and adapt to material necessities through austerity. Traditionalists feel resigned to and left behind by recent developments in society. Among these population groups, the AfD gained 16 per cent, 11 per cent more than in the federal elections of 2013. While the authors conclude that the AfD has 'entered the centre from below' and represents the left-behinds and those who feel squeezed in the middle, they also draw attention to the fact that parts of the upper classes also supported the party. In the 'classical establishment' of the conservatives, characterized by an ethics of performance and responsibility, claims to leadership, consciousness of being upper class and a desire for order, the AfD obtained 10 per cent of the votes. The share was similar amongst the 'hedonists', i.e. the lower-middle class and lower-class sections oriented towards fun in the here and now and with a strong interest in leisure. The 'elevated milieus', however, were represented by only 8 per cent in the AfD (Vehrkamp and Wegschaider 2017). Similar to analyses of the FN's support base, this shows that the AfD draws on multiple constituencies. However, the consulted literature does not provide anything similar to the in-depth qualitative studies on the FN's constituencies and the meaning they attach to the FN vote.

There is one particular constituency that appears surprising. Jewish AfD activists, just like the Jewish FN electorate, do support the party because of what they consider a crisis situation, and for what they consider to be rational motives. Fearing the anti-Semitism of refugees from war-torn regions in the Middle East, they consider the AfD's Islamophobia to be securing their position within

German society. Apparently, they hit a sensitive nerve amongst the Russian-speaking Jewish communities – to the despair of the Central Council of Jews in Germany that openly denounced such attitudes. Wolfgang Fuhl, for instance, an AfD politician in Lörrach, Baden-Württemberg, was a former activist with the Young Social Democrats and former member of the Central Council. Since he is a father and his children experience anti-Semitism in a multicultural schoolyard, he has turned towards the AfD (Rosbach 2016). The Association of Jews in the AfD (JAfD) was founded in October 2018, with twenty-four founding members. A declaration published beforehand gave two motives for the group's formation: the 'uncontrolled mass immigration' of young men from the 'Islamic Kulturkreis' with 'anti-Semitic socialization'; and the 'destruction of traditional monogamic family' through 'gender mainstreaming' and 'early sexualization'.[91]

CONCLUSION: THE CURRENT FAR RIGHT AS A RESPONSE TO MULTILEVEL CRISIS?

Rather than providing explanations, the party-centred, quantitative analyses of electoral results all across Europe present us with a puzzle. The statistical data reveal a largely heterogeneous constituency in both cases; these results therefore remain unsatisfactory to understand the party's recent successes. A heterogeneous voting base simply corresponds to the shape of any party of significant size in current western societies, as a result of voter dealignment, electoral volatility and the crisis of representation regarding mass parties of former times.

The above outline explains how far the AfD fitted the German political landscape at its time of emergence and growth. It also shows how the party was rapidly captured by pre-existing networks that decisively pulled it towards the extreme right. The literature consulted so far does not elaborate qualitatively the question of how far the AfD programme fits the logic and lives of those who sympathize with it, apart from the example of its extremely minoritarian Jewish voters.

The AfD emerged in a specific situation of economic crisis and its political handling by the political establishment, and soon afterwards got radicalized in the context of the refugee crisis. In the initial phase, the AfD emerged as a response to the crisis of representation that affected the German Mittelstand in the face of the political handling of the economic crisis. The 'bourgeois centre' voters correspond to that category. The 'traditional milieus' would rather be those who long for response to ideological crises and moral panics in terms of the AfD's promise of *Heimat* and law and order. Regarding the 'precarious', we might assume, based on our insights from the constituencies of the FN, that their affinity with the party's programme turns around closing up spaces of white privilege against competing strangers in terms of access to affordable housing, education for their children, jobs and women. The party could capitalize on the political representation crisis by representative claim-making, and on a climate of ideological uncertainty and moral panics with narratives of order and security, *Heimat* and the like. Electoral and opinion poll studies, with their rather limited explanatory capacity, seem to confirm rather superficial, imagined moral panic reactions against sociocultural heterogeneity.[92] However, those references to crisis are not sufficient to explain the subsequent development of the party, especially its quick move from liberal economic origins to the far-right scene. An explanation in terms of consequence of and response to crisis does not explain fully the phenomenon of the AfD. I therefore argue that only long-term continuities provide us with the full picture of what has been happening in recent years right in front of our eyes. This will be developed in the next chapter.

The current strength of the FN cannot be sufficiently explained either as a result of or response to crisis. Statistical analyses fail to give clear-cut responses in terms of the far-right vote in France, just like in Germany, as being the vote of the petty bourgeoisie, of a marginalized post-industrial underclass, the result of politics of resentment of globalization losers, the revenge of the working class or of particularly vulnerable populations. The one feature that all recent constituencies do seem to share is experience of representational crisis:

> They all have the feeling that, politically, there is no longer anyone to speak up on their behalf. They all have the feeling that globalization and European integration generate more costs than benefits for them. And in general terms, they are right. . . . All these groups sense that the established progressive parties have generally ceased to be interested in them and that their representatives have themselves joined the global upper class. (Misik 2017: 119–20)

The current strength of the far right is therefore at least partially related to profound socio-economic transformations experienced by West European societies over the last decades. Quantitative as well as qualitative studies also indicate that we cannot reduce the far-right vote to any particular constituency. Whether parts of the German Mittelstand, of the French working class, of populations in peri-urban areas or specific professional milieus, they all seem to share the experience of representational crisis. Each of them has specific reasons related to their lived experiences. Where we can see beyond opinion polls, it appears that their far-right vote is not a result of pure emotions of resentment, but for particular professional, economic, residential, educational and/or family reasons. This provides us with the first part of the explanation. It concerns precisely the relatively 'new constituencies' that account for the parties' recent growth and electoral successes.

But I agree that 'although the threats to security and economic stability that have rattled Europe in the past few years may have spurred the current populist surge, they did not create it' (Mudde 2016: 25). If Mudde traces the origins back to the 1960s, I believe it is necessary to go further back in history. Detailed ethnographic and biographic analyses of FN activists clearly show that the current situation is only understandable if we trace the lineage of the FN back to its deep roots. I argue that the party has remained alive, and has managed to attract new members and voters, only because it could rely on organizational forms and on an ideological tradition that has been sustained by a small, specific circle of people through the decades. In order to understand this, we need to trace its deep roots back to the period before the foundation of the party itself. These long-term continuities and the important role the FN has played for certain people as a political home explain why the FN has survived ups and downs, although it considerably adapted to changing contexts. The attractiveness of the FN and its availability to larger and also more recent constituencies were possible only because the FN has survived in the long term, sustained by silent or open engagements of committed far-right circles in direct continuity with interwar fascism and colonialism. A section of FN activists that the above-mentioned studies highlight personally trace these continuities in their family biographies. I put forth the same argument regarding the recent emergence and success of the AfD in Germany. How an initially 'professorial' party representing the interests and voicing the grievances of the Mittelstand could be captured in a brief time span by far-right networks and actors, and become infused with their discourses, is only intelligible with a determined focus on long-term continuities. I outline this in the next chapter on the deep roots of the West European far right.

NOTES

[1] For an analytical basis to such comparative work, see Keim (forthcoming).

[2] I have chosen the term far right as a concept 'encompassing figures, movements and currents of thought that display some degree of commonality and a core of shared dispositions' (Shields 2007: 10). I prefer 'far right' to 'extreme right' or 'radical right', although those terms might appear at some points in the text, because they situate the phenomenon at the extreme tip of the political spectrum only, whereas 'far right' opens up the spectrum to encompass not only individual actors, groups, movements, think tanks and parties as different types of organizational forms but also indicates that the phenomenon does not necessarily exclude parts of the more moderate forces, i.e. it denominates a larger spectrum of ideological and political influence and of personal networks that reach out beyond the extreme. I also avoid the term 'populist right' for reasons I develop in the subsection 'Ideological Crisis'.

[3] Others have argued similarly: 'Right-wing radicalism, however, is not the only danger that threatens democracy today. The authoritarian means with which austerity policy is being carried out in the EU, the arming of a security and surveillance apparatus under the pretext of fighting terrorism, the anti-Muslim racism amplified by the media, and borders closed

off to immigrants—all not only creates a climate in which right-wing radicalism thrives, but also represents limitations on and threats to democracy and freedom' (Baier 2016: 53).

4 Those were the key points of focus of the workshop 'Rethinking United Fronts and the Far Right', held on 20–21 July 2018 at York University, Toronto. The workshop was organized by Raju J. Das and Robert Latham on behalf of the Critical Scholarship and Social Transformation Program. See 'Critical Scholarship and Social Transformation', *York University*, available at http://criticaltransformation.blog.yorku.ca/, accessed 15 November 2021.

5 The Front National was renamed Rassemblement National/National Rally (RN) at the beginning of 2018. However, since the chapter follows a long-term perspective and most of the consulted literature refers to the former FN, I use the former name and acronym throughout.

6 '"Fascist" has served as a generic term of political abuse for many decades, but for the first time in ages, mainstream observers are using it seriously to describe major politicians and parties' (Berman 2016: 39).

7 Another theoretical approach I considered for this study was Paxton's work on five stages of fascism. According to his definition, 'Fascism is a system of political authority and social order intended to reinforce the unity, energy and purity of communities in which liberal democracy stands accused of producing division and decline' (Paxton 1998: 21). The formulations 'system of political authority and social order' are less precise than the definition given by Mann, but do not contradict it. The idea of 'reinforcing the unity, energy and purity' is contained in Mann's concepts of nation-statism based on the organic nation (unity and purity), in his concepts of transcendence (unity) and of 'cleansing' (purity). 'Energy' does not feature prominently in Mann's definition, though one could translate some of his considerations on paramilitarism as socializing institutions for the New Man and as violent actors of cleansing in this sense. What sets Paxton's definition apart from Mann's are two elements that could have been interesting with regard to the task that this article sets itself: instead of 'nation' and 'state' his definition refers to 'communities', which is a much broader term. As a starting point, this could be more promising for the analysis of the early, still small-scale developmental phases of authoritarian restoration projects. However, I believe Mann's definition is more complete and the potentials Paxton offers are also incorporated in my adaptation of Mann (see below).

8 This corresponds to Griffin's analysis of major structural weaknesses of fascist ideology (Griffin 1991: 26–55) as well as to Paxton's (1998) analysis of fascism as evolving in stages throughout which initial aims were often watered down or betrayed Paxton.

9 Griffin (1991) states the same inherent contradiction between populism and elitism in fascist ideology.

10 'Fascism is a system of political authority and social order intended to reinforce the unity, energy, and purity of communities in which liberal democracy stands accused of producing division and decline' (Paxton 1998: 21).

11 Sitas addresses the various configurations that marked the anti-apartheid struggle as well as political violence and civil war in the KwaZulu Natal-region during the transition period. I am transferring his thoughts to a radically different context. This has led me to adapt the key concept of 'originary trauma', justified for the movements and organizations he studies. It does not apply, however, to the European far right, which tries to play on its traumas that are easily revealed to be invented. Speaking about the traumas of the far right would mean taking seriously and lending credibility to their strategy to establish themselves as victims in a national and international political field, in which they are clearly located on the side of the powerful. Instead, I speak of their major grievances.

12 We shall consider this against the background of a 1985 commission of enquiry of the European Parliament on the rise of fascism and racism in Europe that declared already that 'xenophobophilia' was the new spectre to haunt Europe, that the risk of violence was a reality and that a 'war of races' could break out (d'Appolonia 1992: 27). We have not yet reached that stage but the reworking of exclusive solidarities at various levels in this direction is a fact.

13 See, for instance, the 'short-lived political group of the European Parliament, "Identity, Tradition and Sovereignty" (ITS), a coalition of extreme right parties from six member states that lasted from January to November 2007', that 'had as a founding principle the "commitment to Christian values, heritage, culture". Chairman Bruno Gollnisch stated that one of the goals of the group was to go beyond a narrow euroscepticism (limited to attacking a European superstate) that does not "properly defend Christian values"' (Zúquete 2008). In terms of religious referents, the extreme right also counts pagan groups as well as Celtic or shamanic orientations.

14 'Marine Le Pen, who vowed to "de-demonize" the image of the party, has made overtures to the French Jewish community and, as a member of the European parliament, has registered with the Delegation for Relations with Israel. She was behind the decision to send National Front members to a demonstration in memory of a French Jew killed in a hate-crime, and told the media that she wanted to put an end to a "number of misunderstandings" between the party and the Jewish community who, Marine Le Pen said, "have nothing to fear from the National Front".... "The French community, who are increasingly victims of attacks by Islamic radicals", she said on one occasion, "should be able to turn to us for support".... Guillaume Faye, one of France's New Right main theorists, advocates that those who defend European identity should get rid of an obsessive and "chronic anti-Judaism" because the real danger is colonization from "the third world and Islam"' (ibid.: 328).

15 The Slovene far right, for instance, fuses anti-Semitism and Islamophobia. Quoting from a Slovene rightist weekly journal, Žižek observes the following: 'it brings together anti-Semitism and Islamophobia: the threat to Europe comes from hordes of Muslim refugees, but behind this chaotic phenomenon are the Jews [Soros in the text]' Žižek (2017: 187). See also the collective student portfolio on Hungary (Al Hariri *et al.* 2017).

16 This translates into policy programmes such as obliging companies to give priority to nationals in their employment policies, or reserving social housing or family benefits for nationals, etc., propositions that the FN campaigned with, or practical support for the national poor, such as the programmes put in place by CasaPound in Italy, copied in France by Bastion Social.

17 'Above all, the FN leader consistently laid out the frame that justifies the union of nationalists wherever they are: a totalitarian ideology, advanced by the winners of the Cold War and international organizations, is sweeping across the world, destroying natural identities, ethnicities, diversities and borders in order to create one homogenous, undifferentiated, rootless, artificial creation that can be easily controlled by a world government. Open borders, massive immigration and birth-rate collapse are all part of this plan designed to uproot national identities and solidarities, with the help of treacherous political classes. Nationalists, the last bastions of resistance, are engaged in an all-out war for survival, and they must withstand the tempest together, in solidarity' (Zúquete 2015: 73).

18 This has taken adverse trajectories in France and Germany. The AfD emerged as a Eurosceptic party and was then increasingly captured by the far right. The FN, on the contrary, has recently experienced a controversy over the traditional xenophobic or identitarian line represented by the Le Pens, and the more recent sovereignist line represented by Florian Philippot who tried to instal Euroscepticism more firmly as a key orientation of the party but failed.

[19] On AfD gender politics, see Siri (2016), Kemper (2016b), Jentsch (2016).

[20] See the corresponding sections in Shields (2007) as well as in particular Renken (2006); more in the next section on the deep roots of the FN.

[21] Botsch traces the term '*Volksgemeinschaft*' throughout the post-war history of the German extreme right as being in direct continuity with National Socialism. While from 1949 onwards *Volksgemeinschaft* formed a counter-model to parliamentarianism and pluralism, in the present, it opposes multicultural society (Botsch 2017).

[22] See Luschy (2017).

[23] From work with my students, it has become obvious that it would be crucial to include Eastern European cases in the overall panorama. The originary grievance for ethnic Hungarians, for instance, were the treaties of Versailles and Trianon – the same that animated German National Socialists at the time – that led to the loss of Greater Hungary. This historical experience of Greater Hungary, however, is seen as being the mode of veracity of the ethnic superiority of Hungarians, justifying expansionist discourse and policy practice – like granting ethnic Hungarians in neighbouring countries citizenship and voting rights in order to increase the country's sphere of influence – in recent years. The major internal outgroups, as opposed to Western European concerns about immigration, are Roma – considered a criminal tribe (Damodaran 2014), where 'Roma-crime' has become an established term in national media coverage and has legitimized for a certain period paramilitary structures of defence of the ethnic Hungarian population, for example – as well as Jews, epitomized in the figure of George Soros. Furthermore, the country furthers a determined anti-EU rhetoric, criticizing, not without foundation, the subordination of eastern Europe within the EU framework. These are only preliminary observations that would require far more in-depth analysis.

[24] Apart from the literature on the FN included in the bibliography, the 2018 students' portfolio on the FN has analysed the party's 2012 and 2017 electoral programmes with respect to aspects of statism (Holiday *et al.* 2018: 90–91).

[25] 'Italy to Compile "Register" of Roma People: Matteo Salvini', *The Local Italy*, 18 June 2018, available at https://www.thelocal.it/20180618/italy-register-census-roma-people-matteo-salvini/

[26] Regarding Berman's optimistic assessment that established democracies will withstand the attempts of assault by the far right at direct democracy, the planned prolongation of this study towards the cases of Turkey and India, eventually in comparison with the US, should allow us to understand what can happen, under varying circumstances, once charismatic leaders do gain state power. Erdogan, for instance, then mayor of Istanbul, was quoted in the 1990s as saying: 'Democracy is like a tram. You ride it until you arrive at your destination, then you step off' (quoted in White 2016). This clearly reveals that authoritarians can use democratic disposition in merely instrumental ways.

[27] Absent in Western Europe, we do find truly paramilitary formations in some parts of Eastern Europe. Bulgaria has a strong paramilitary movement, sponsored among others by Russia, to prevent cross-border migration but also to stifle anti-Putin demonstrations (Fromm 2016). The Hungarian Guard, banned recently, was set up to protect the population against 'Roma crime', the Roma defined here as a criminal tribe (Damodaran 2014). László Toroczkai, Mayor of Ásotthalom and vice-president of Jobbik, recently sent out a message via YouTube and social media channels to potential migrants that they should avoid Hungary as a transit country. He proudly declared that he had set up his own border militia which, he says, has captured more illegal immigrants than the state police (Gauriat 2017).

[28] Including, for example, Swedish neo-Nazi John Ausonius who attacked eleven migrants and killed one in 1991/92; neo-Nazi Kay Diesner's attempted murder against book dealer Baltruschat who had his shop in the party locals of the PDS in Berlin and against policemen Grage during his flight in 1997; David Copeland, former member of the British National Party and then of the National Socialist movement who attacked in a series of actions migrants, Blacks and homosexuals in London in 1999; and Anders Breivik who killed 77 participants of the Norwegian youth organization of the social democratic workers party in 2011.

[29] For example, in October 2015, a candidate for the mayoral election of Cologne, Henriette Reker, was stabbed in the street by a right-wing extremist Frank S., near a voting stall of the CDU (Christian Democratic Union, the governing conservative party). She was the head of the Department of Social Affairs and Refugees of the city of Cologne. Frank S. claimed that he had to do that to 'protect you all', since the German political establishment was flooding the country with refugees (Pfahl-Traughber 2015). Reker, who was seriously injured, recovered from the attack and was elected mayor. In the past, the perpetrator had been a sympathizer of the right-wing extremist Freiheitliche Deutsche Arbeiterpartei (FAP), banned by the Ministry of the Interior in 1995 (Stinauer 2015). He had been unemployed for some years and lived on social aid (Hartz IV). Strangely, his Hartz-IV file was declared a secret matter after his arrest, which raised doubts about potential contacts with the Federal Office for the Protection of the Constitution (Wiermer, Meyer and Giesecke 2015). In June 2019, Walter Lübcke, Regierungspräsident (district president) in Nordhessen and CDU politician, was murdered by a former NPD activist.

[30] *Marine Le Pen: L'héritière*, dir. C. Faourest and F. Venner, Nilaya Productions, 2011.

[31] This concerns, for instance, the all-male student organizations or fraternities ('Kameradschaften'; see Köttig 2017: 229), the 'Gildenschaften' (Wölk 2016: 100–01; Kellershohn 2004), the identitarians (Blum 2017: 327) and the far-right parties' youth organizations (Herkenhoff 2016b: 205).

[32] Such an exaggerated vision of manhood based on the 'warrior' figure, reminiscent of the interwar years, combines characteristics such as 'heterosexuality, family breadwinner, intransigence . . . hardness, strength, willingness to make sacrifices, fearlessness, braveness and service to the people and the nation, to the point of self-sacrifice' (Köttig 2017: 225–26, quoting Virchow 2010); or again, 'hardness, power of decision, ability to act following the principles of command and obedience, self-denial and self-sacrifice, and fearlessness in battle as well as heroism' (Overdiek 2014: 6).

[33] See Keim (2014) for a discussion of gender images in the Black disgrace campaign, a historical forerunner to current moral panics.

[34] In the French *La Manif pour tous* movement of 2013 against same-sex marriage, important fragments of the FN marched alongside conservative Catholics, who sought to hide their religious foundations in order to adapt to a largely secularist context (Stambolis-Ruhstorfer and Tricou 2017; Dubslaff 2017). In Germany as well, anti-genderism has become a common theme around which a multiplicity of collective actors converges, including parts of the (neo) conservative and of the far right (Villa 2017: 99).

[35] See, for example, the interview of identitarian Martin Sellner with the blogger of 'Radical and Feminine' (M. Sellner, 'Radikal und feminine: Zwischen Genderwahn und Reconquista: Interview mit Franziska', *Widerstand im Gespräch*, available at https://www.youtube.com/watch?v=T5eXlysYF7I, accessed 31 July 2019.

[36] On the NSU, see Köttig (2017).

[37] In the interwar years, the economy was in crisis. The Great Depression and inflation

exacerbated class conflict. In addition, reactions of old regime powers and possessing classes to labour and the left were over-exaggerated in the face of the threatening model of the Bolshevik revolution. At the political level, while the north-west of Europe had stabilized liberal democracies before 1914 so that it could mitigate shocks and crises, the centre, east and south were in a phase of rapid transition. While installing liberal democracies, old regime powers remained powerful in the executive, leading to dual states with an authoritarian executive alongside liberal-democratic parliaments. The whole of Europe experienced a military crisis after the first total war, with massive demobilization and reintegration of soldiers into societies. The crisis was major in those countries that had experienced defeat and dislocation. Finally, Mann analyses a major ideological crisis all over Europe, with discourses on moral decadence, civil decay and overall corruption through liberalism, secularism and socialism threatening social chaos.

[38] Harris, C., 'Explained: The Rise and Rise of Populism in Europe', available at https://www. euronews.com/2018/03/15/explained-the-rise-and-rise-of-populism-in-europe, accessed 15 March 2022.

[39] A still stronger statement would argue that the former autonomy of the individual has turned into authoritarian attitudes under the pressures of market logics at play since the 1980s: 'The profoundly authoritarian belief in the market is "an anonymous god who enslaves men" because it thinks that there is no alternative to itself. Horkheimer's interpretation turns out to be hugely productive in enabling us to understand the transformation of autonomy into authoritarianism. The absence of alternatives to the market compels the individual to internalize it. . . . The modern individual's naturally acquired autonomy is now tied to his market performance. The winners receive an autonomy dividend; the losers are disciplined and stigmatized. The modern individual is as dependent on institutions as he ever was, but he is now increasingly de-socialized. He is being changed from a citizen integrated in a more or less organized community with institutions of collective solidarity into a market citizen, a customer with rights. However, such disembedded markets produce permanent uncertainty and cause the erosion of many individuals' sense of agency – they no longer believe that they can master current situations, let alone the future' (Nachtwey 2017: 135). Appealing to the critical mind, this hypothesis would need empirical verification, however – just like most other arguments put forth in the consulted literature, it remains largely theoretical so far.

[40] See the country analyses provided by the following student portfolios: Baroni *et al.* (2018); Holiday *et al.* (2018); Al Hariri *et al.* (2017); Berci *et al.* (2017).

[41] Take the FN as an example. Founded in 1972, the rise in unemployment in the wake of the 1979/80 oil crisis was a first moment for reflection on its economic stance. In those years, the famous slogan '*Un million de chômeurs, c'est un million d'immigrés de trop! La France et les Français d'abord!*' ('One million unemployed, that is one million immigrants too much! France and the French first!') aimed at appealing to the working class while remaining solidly anti-communist, transforming a complex economic issue into opposition to immigration. In this same early phase, the FN's economic policy could be characterized as largely neoliberal. Throughout the 1990s, the official 'Neither right nor left' positioning of the party corresponded to its mixed outlook in terms of economic policy, and to the increasing adoption of redistributive, protectionist and interventionist economic principles. This was further accentuated following the 2008 crisis (Ivaldi 2015). In the attempt to broaden the FN's appeal, following 2008 the party's economic policy shifted further left, abandoning its original neoliberal programme and formulating an appeal to 'the forgotten' combined with an anti-globalization and anti-

EU discourse. This further elaborated the far-right reinterpretation of the capital/labour division into one between elites and globalized cosmopolitans on the one hand and 'France from below' on the other. Considering the inconsistencies of its economic outlook over time and the relatively little importance accorded to economic issues over identitarian ones, the question is whether this leftward shift is about substance or just packaging (ibid.: 2015). In fact, the FN's ideologues seemed to be searching for a new 'winning formula' that would ensure them broad political support. According to students' assessment, 'if we look to the 2017 Presidential manifesto, [there is] a line drawn between the real economy and speculative finance. The rhetoric is not one of overcoming internal division, but fighting back invading foreign control of France. The introductory letter to the 2017 presidential manifesto says the election is a decision between the "globalist" choice and the "patriotic" choice. The goal of the patriotic choice being "la protection de notre identité nationale, notre indépendance, l'unité des Français, la justice sociale et la prospérité de tous" [the protection of our national identity, of our independency, of the unity amongst Frenchmen, social justice and prosperity of all]. What is of primary importance is not so much transcending difference – though that is mentioned – but taking back control. Reclamation rather than transcendence seems to be the fundamental message' (Holiday *et al.* 2018, building on Ivaldi 2015).

42 This overlaps with Mudde's conclusion: 'Most conventional explanations of this trend emphasize the importance of two factors: globalization and the economic crises in Europe that resulted from the financial meltdown of 2008 and the subsequent Great Recession. But the current populist moment is part of a longer story and is rooted in the postindustrial revolution that led to fundamental changes in European societies in the 1960s' (Mudde 2016: 26–27).

43 'During those years, deindustrialization and a steep decline in religious observance weakened the support enjoyed by established center-left and center-right parties, which had been largely dependent on working class and religious voters. In the quarter century that followed, a gradual realignment in European politics saw voters throw their support to old parties that had become virtually nonideological or to new parties defined by relatively narrow ideological stances' (Mudde 2016: 26–27).

44 It looks like '[a]ll professional politicians together constituted the field of politics and the professional politician's reference system was other professional politicians. In the eyes of the public, they increasingly formed a separate sphere whose members competed for small advantages but who were bound together in a close complicity. Even worse, it looked to ordinary people as if members of the political establishment were striving to accommodate themselves to the new elite of the global economy' (Misik 2017: 117–18).

45 To complement this, see also the overview of the debate on a legitimacy-crisis in Kriesi (2013).

46 In France, for instance, the high vote share for the FN is among others a result of electoral abstention and demobilization of a left disillusioned by the Socialist Party (PS) and the Front de Gauche (Baier 2016).

47 We will see below that in Germany, for instance, the AfD could fill the void on the right the CDU/CSU opened up in the course of Merkel's development of the party. In the course of a gradual evolution, the centre right has given up on several fundamental conservative positions (regarding gender mainstreaming and same-sex marriage, for example). Since the last federal elections in 2017, CDU/CSU Minister of the Interior and Heimat Seehofer tried to gain back the votes lost to the AfD with radical right rhetoric, a strategy that has not succeeded so far.

48 'The leaders hate democracy because it is an obstacle to their monomaniacal pursuit of power. The followers are victims of democracy fatigue who see electoral politics as the best way to exit

democracy itself. . . . This common cultural ground inevitably hides the deep contradictions between the neoliberal economic policies and well-documented crony capitalism of most of these authoritarian leaders and the genuine economic suffering and anxiety of the bulk of their mass followings' (Appadurai 2017: 8).

[49] This is the critical point about Pegida taking up the call '*Wir sind das Volk!*' (We are the people!), a legacy from the broad opposition movement in the final phase of the German Democratic Republic (GDR). Whereas those opposing the authoritarianism of the former GDR framed 'the people' in terms of inclusive solidarity, the current far right turns the same wording into its opposite, into a call for exclusive solidarity.

[50] On the inherent potential of democracies to reveal their 'dark side' in terms of exclusivist definitions of 'the people', see Mann (2004). See also the section 'The State as the Bearer of True Democracy' above on this tradition within the German *völkisch* right. This seems to be in contradiction with Collovald's critique of the term 'populism' to designate the FN as I have outlined it above, i.e. the problematic political consequences of rejecting representative claims in favour of 'the people' (meaning here: 'the popular classes') as opposed to favouring supposedly neutral experts as true guarantors of democracy. A thorough engagement with democracy theory would be necessary to settle this point. The difference between Mann and Collovald, however, is that Mann starts out from the ideologues and their ideological formulation of 'ideal democracy', claiming to embody the destiny and will of a pure, unified people, as opposed to Collovald, who starts out from the popular (in the sense of ordinary or lay) followers and supporters as supposed and feared adherents to 'populist' programmes.

[51] This is not a political crisis in the sense of Mann. My assessment largely coincides with evaluations in the consulted literature, like the following assessment of political crisis today as compared with the 1920-30s: 'But the more important difference between today's right-wing extremists and yesterday's fascists is the larger context. As great as contemporary problems are, and as angry as many citizens may be, the West is simply not facing anything approaching the upheaval of the interwar period. "The mere existence of privations is not enough to cause an insurrection; if it were, the masses would be always in revolt", Leon Trotsky once wrote, and the same logic applies to the appearance of fascism. In the United States and Western Europe, at least, democracy and democratic norms have deep roots, and contemporary governments have proved nowhere near as inept as their predecessors in the 1920s and 1930s. Moreover, democratic procedures and institutions, welfare states, political parties, and robust civil societies continue to provide citizens with myriad ways of voicing their concerns, influencing political outcomes, and getting their needs met' (Berman 2016: 43).

[52] Germany has never actually practised the broadly proclaimed 'welcome culture' at the juridical level; even in comparison with other European countries the number of newly arriving refugees in Germany has been highest. In 2016, Germany registered more demands for asylum than all other EU countries put together. In relation to the number of inhabitants, Germany was also in first place, with 8 demands for asylum per 1,000 inhabitants. Although this was higher than in any other EU country, 8 in 1,000 just for demands appears still a rather marginal figure. Furthermore, in Germany, about 3,21,000 refugees were registered in 2016, much less than in 2015. But even for 2015, the initial figure of 1.1 million had to be corrected; we ended up with 8,90,000. In 2016, 65 per cent of them came from Syria, Afghanistan, Iraq, Iran and Eritrea, i.e. from countries at war or with massive political persecution. This was recognized in three-quarters of the cases. The ministry in charge of refugees granted some form of protection, thus recognizing legitimate reasons for asylum. However, the protection levels

kept decreasing considerably, often granting only the most basic protection, i.e. non-expulsion, but no right to full-fledged political asylum. This indicated that the decision regarding asylum had grown more repressive in 2016 compared with prior years (ProAsyl, n.d.).

53 In 2015, 60 per cent of FN voters wanted restitution of the death penalty, compared to 28 per cent of voters of the right and 11 per cent of voters of the left (Mayer 2017: 70).

54 See, for instance, the synthesis in Collovald (2004); see also Girard (2017a).

55 As has been the case across Europe: 'Surprisingly for many people, the recent successes of right-wing radical parties across Europe have put the working class back into the locus of wide-ranging analyses. The same working class that many political scientists until recently thought had exhausted its role is now being held responsible for the rise of the radical right. . . . Indeed there is much evidence that rightwing radical parties have made significant advances among the traditionally social democratic working-class electorate. However, these findings remain one-sided as long as the published investigations do not also reflect the vote shares in other segments of the electorate' (Baier 2016: 49).

56 The class cleavage is here operationalized along broad occupational categories: Small business = shopkeepers, little commercial operations, artisans, farmers; workers = blue collar factory, service workers; lower middle = sales clerks, office employees; middle middle = teachers, bureau chiefs, technicians, social workers, middle-level managers; upper middle = liberal professions, top executives (Lewis-Beck and Mitchell 1993: 115).

57 While the middle class predominantly voted for Mittérand and farmers for Chirac, about 31 per cent of small businesspeople voted for Le Pen. They were about twice as likely to vote extreme right than workers, for instance, a share greater than that of any other occupational category. This strengthened the hypothesis that it was the petty bourgeoisie, which largely constituted the Poujadist movement of the 1950s, that was especially attracted by the far right. Hence, '[t]here appears to be a kernel of truth in the notion that Le Pen, heir to Poujade, finds his natural constituency among the shopkeepers' (Lewis-Beck and Mitchell 1993: 117). Why this particular constituency is considered to be 'natural' is not clear. The interpretation that followed was in terms of the politics of resentment, to which the petty bourgeoisie was thought to be vulnerable in the face of government and tax pressures, the emergence of chain stores, and alleged attacks on private property that were supposed to threaten their middle-class status.

58 For a critical account of this, see the insightful film *Mains brunes sur la ville – Quand l'extrême droite est au pouvoir* (French, 2012, dir. B. Richard); also confirmed in Lafont (2001).

59 About 42 per cent of the respondents were economically worse off than their parents, 12 per cent in a similar situation and 46 per cent in a better situation than their parents. This did not translate into FN votes, since 42 per cent of those who were worse off intended to vote for Le Pen, against 47 per cent of those who were in a similar situation and 38 per cent of those who had risen above the socio-economic level of their parents' households (Rouban 2017).

60 Fifty-six per cent of those who estimated that their situation had deteriorated in comparison with that of their parents when they were the same age had decided to vote Le Pen, against 39 per cent of those who believed their situation was similar and 31 per cent of those who believed their situation was better. It was therefore in particular the pessimists, who believed without objective justification that their situation had worsened, that had the highest propensity to vote for Le Pen. It was thus again the perception of a given situation more than its reality that counted in order to understand the FN vote (ibid.).

61 The following is also interesting to note: 'The 52 per cent vote for Brexit was not driven only by white workers; 27 per cent of black people and 33 per cent of Asians voted Leave

according to one exit poll. But the strongest Leave votes took place in small-town Britain, where the residue of working-class culture had now turned into an "identity" whose main characteristic was defiance: not just of globalization but of the liberal, transnational, human-rights-based culture that it had fostered' (Mason 2017: 96).

[62] 'Traditional milieus have the feeling that the members of urban, cosmopolitan groups look down on them and their lifestyles. . . . People from cultural milieus that they could think of as conventional – and therefore hegemonic – only a couple of years ago . . . now suddenly have the feeling that they are no longer respected. And again, they are not entirely mistaken. No one has given such a blunt, unsparing account of these processes as Didier Eribon in *Returning to Reims*' (Misik 2017: 121).

[63] Fieldwork was conducted in 2003 and 2012 (Girard 2017a).

[64] Leading to statements such as the following: 'In any case, all they have to do is make a mess, burn some cars, and you'll see the left saying: poor things, it's not their fault, we need to help them' (Pudal 2011: 82).

[65] The quick answer to the lived experience in the fire brigades would be to take their common talk for expressions of the ethnocentrism and authoritarianism that electoral analyses impute to FN voters. It needed long-term immersion within their workplace culture to understand the subtleties of the humour and cynicism acquired through years of work in the face of accidents, violence, suffering and burning. For example, while showering in the barracks, Pudal confirmed to a colleague that until then the night had been calm but that this could still change. '"And why is that? he said. I don't know, but Algeria is playing tonight [in the football World Cup]." "Oh shit, well yeah, it's over! Either they win and get wasted (wasn't there something in the Qur'an about alcohol? Yeah, well that, there's always a way to get around it, ha!), or they lose, and people get hurt . . . either way, they're bound to make a mess! At the end of the day, I'd rather deal with injuries than see Algeria win! (*À tout prendre je préfère les blessés, ça fait toujours ça de moins!* [lit. I prefer to deal with injured people, so you have something less to deal with]."' Since it was obvious in the interaction that Pudal disapproved such comments, which encouraged someone else to mock him as a sociologist, the conclusion drawn by his conversation partner in the shower was: '"In any case what I was saying has nothing to do with the fact that my wife is a cop and my kid is the only white kid in his class . . . no really, nothing at all!".' Instead of taking this for an expression of blunt racism, Pudal tries to understand what is meant in saying such things: 'What I've written thus far allows, I hope, to reflect the complexity of possible interpretations and offer possible answers: social intermediacy, a desire for social mobility, anxiety about the future, a commitment to public service despite recurrent humiliation, confrontations with urban violence, the underrepresentation of immigrants in the firefighting corps: all of these elements play a role in the development of this kind of political attitude' (Pudal 2011: 89–90).

[66] 'This dimension of the political discourse of firefighters must be highlighted for two important reasons: on one hand, because mastery of language and rhetoric is undoubtedly the prerogative of the wealthy social classes. Although there may be some admiration for this rhetorical prowess, firefighters are primarily convinced that this skill is used maliciously in the service of a continuous lie, a sort of cheating. Consequently, they award a great deal of credit to other forms of verbal virtuosity like puns, jokes, teasing, etc. It's not the baseness or the unacceptability of the language which is the most important thing, but rather the pride of belonging to a group that speaks frankly and "tells it like it is". We can also observe in this a reversal of stigmatism' (ibid.: 91–92).

[67] In October 2018, despite Seehofer's determined strategy to win back voters on the right of the CSU, after decades of single rule, this regional party lost its absolute majority in the Bavarian regional parliament. The AfD instead (but even more, the Green Party) gained immensely in support.

[68] A 2010 'Manifesto against the Leftist Trend' within the party had already criticized 'leftist' social policies in the domains of gender mainstreaming and establishment of quota for women in business, the recognition of same-sex civil unions, abortion rights and the party's official stance towards multiculturalism, the 'threat of Islamization' and a possible accession of Turkey to the EU.

[69] By the way, *Alternativlosigkeit*, the fact that there is no alternative, was voted *Unwort* (a non-word) of the German language later.

[70] Quoting Sydney Gennies, 'Eine Zwischenstation für die AfD: Hans-Olaf Henkels erster Tag im Europaparlament', *Der Tagesspiegel Online*, 7 July 2014, available at https://www.tagesspiegel.de/politik/eine-zwischenstation-fuer-die-afd-hans-olaf-henkels-erster-tag-im-europaparlament/10157066.html, accessed 18 February 2022.

[71] Having said that, in the early phase there were huge divergences between the electoral programme for the European elections and those of the regional parliamentary elections in several eastern regions: 'The contrast between classical right-wing populist rhetoric and the European electoral programme of the AfD could not be greater. While right-wing populism conjures mythical images of unspoiled "Heimat", the AfD carries a demanding arsenal of macro-economic and economic-political scholarly terms that are completely alien to everyday common sense' (Werner 2015 74 ff.). Not least, the topic of Islam was absent from the European programme. The regional platforms for the elections in Sachsen, Thüringen and Brandenburg, in turn were much more oriented towards a refusal of Islam and 'gender ideology'.

[72] Sarrazin continued to provoke with two further publications on the Euro crisis in 2012 and on political correctness in 2014. 'Insofar, he could be considered a sort of spiritus rector of the AfD and one wonders why he has not shifted from the SPD to the right-wing populists long ago' (Decker 2016: 15). In the first volume that sparked massive debate in Germany, Sarrazin puts forth claims such as: the headscarf is getting more and more popular among young Muslim women; the refusal of many Muslim girls to take part in swimming lessons at school is a sign of refusal to integration; compartmentalization of German society keeps increasing with the formation of 'parallel societies'; many immigrants refuse to learn the German language and they themselves as well as their children fail in the education system; 20 per cent of all violent criminal acts in Berlin are carried out by Turkish or Arabic youth. In the meantime, a systematic study has empirically refuted those polemic statements (Foroutan 2011).

[73] The party's founders in 2013 were Alexander Gauland, Bernd Lucke, Konrad Adam and Gerd Robanus (all previously CDU). Frauke Petry was already one of three of the party's spokespersons. Bernd Lucke, professor of economics at Hamburg University and an early leader of the party – coining its initial image as a 'professorial party' until he left the AfD in 2015 – had left the CDU in the context of the Euro crisis. Clearly, 'Lucke had nothing in common with the deep hatred preached by the NPD. But he sees that a gap is opening up between the blatant right-wing extremism of the NPD and the new, totally modernized CDU of Merkel' (Werner 2015: 54). Alexander Gauland, who had been a member of the CDU for forty years, had participated in the Berlin Circle (Berliner Kreis), a group of right-wing members of the CDU in fundamental tension with A. Merkel. The liberal FDP could not capitalize on its oppositional role in the coalition in order to develop an attractive party profile.

Among others, it failed in obtaining tax reductions. Importantly, 'Eurosceptics' in its ranks were outnumbered when the party's membership basis voted for a support to government's rescue policy at the moment of the Euro crisis.

[74] Pegida is short for *Patriotische Europäer gegen die Islamisierung des Abendlandes*, i.e. Patriotic Europeans against the Islamization of the Occident.

[75] Ironically, the experience leading to the perceived threat of Islamization and religious wars being imported to Germany was caused by a pro-Kurdish demonstration against the Islamic State (IS).

[76] Pegida surfaced in Dresden in October 2014, just two months after the AfD was elected into the regional parliament. The AfD maintained a contradictory relationship with the movement. While Lucke and his followers distanced themselves from Pegida as being xenophobic, the Eastern party leaders opted for taking Pegida seriously (Oppelland 2017). Gauland considered Pegida 'natural allies', Petry presented herself as a consultant to Pegida. Björn Höcke, party leader of Thüringen, in turn, in an interview with New Right intellectual Götz Kubitschek, found that 'A state can be happy to have such citizens' (Kellershohn 2016: 191).

[77] Because it was a movement with little formal organization and developed over a short time period, there is not much data on its constituencies (for the following, see the summary of various studies in Dostal 2015: 527–28). A first study found out that Pegida supporters in the streets were typically well-educated, employed middle-class people with an average income slightly above the average of Saxony. Later studies confirmed the above-average educational level, mainly in technical fields. The average age was forty-eight, the movement was clearly dominated by men. Participants often neither belonged to a political party nor to a religious community. They usually located themselves to the centre right but not the far right of the political spectrum. They participated in elections more than the average population, many confirmed they had voted AfD in the last elections, less though NPD. A subsequent study further clarified the political ties: a majority of two-thirds of Pegida supporters could count as moderate rightists; one-third, predominantly the younger and economically less well-off supporters, as extreme right. The AfD enjoyed most support within Pegida, followed by CDU and NPD. A small fraction had voted for Die Linke, whereas voters of the SPD and the Green Party were not represented. 'Crucially, more than three quarters were disaffected from democracy as practised in the Federal Republic of Germany, and more than 90 per cent felt that they were not served by existing parties and politicians. . . . One must conclude, therefore, that most Pegida supporters are not political outsiders but have some connections with the centre ground. However, they are very dissatisfied with the centre-right parties, namely the Merkel-led CDU' (Dostal 2015: 527–28). Not only did many Pegida supporters confirm they voted AfD, a high percentage of AfD voters also supported Pegida's demands, especially with regard to Islam (Korsch 2016a: 113).

[78] Beatrix von Storch caused public outrage when she declared that in the face of the influx of refugees, border authorities might use their weapons to shoot down migrants. She later even insisted that she included women and children as targets in this call for violence. A strange position for someone who was otherwise active in movements for the right to life and against abortion. The party leader of Thüringen, Björn Höcke, initiated the 'Erfurt resolution', signed by himself, André Poggenburg and Alexander Gauland, leaders of the eastern regions of Thüringen, Sachsen-Anhalt and Brandenburg, in order to discredit Lucke's group (Korsch 2016a: 124). Faced with a decisive rightward shift in AfD, Lucke and many of his followers left. Five out of seven AfD members of the European parliament left the party (Oppelland 2017).

79 'The right mobilizes a "national revolt" against immigration and asylum, interculturality and religious diversity. At the same time, populist and extreme right actors find an opportunity for racist mobilization. This mobilization is the expression and propagandist connecting point of a cultural struggle of the right (*rechter Kulturkampf*) with the aim of a reactionary-authoritarian transformation of society' (Häusler and Virchow 2016: 7).

80 The graph also provides some hints about the funding of the party, provided among others by the Verein zur Erhaltung der Rechtsstaatlichkeit und bürgerlichen Freiheiten that provided several million Euro for the AfD's election campaign in 2017. This association was founded in 2016 in a meeting led by Rolf Schlierer, who had led the Republikaner at federal level for twenty years. Much of the association's background remains mysterious. Sarrazin acted as a speaker in 2017, Gauland was present at a meeting in May 2018 (Baroni *et al.* 2018). I do not dispose of sufficient elements to analyse the funding structure more systematically.

81 'By recruiting amongst fraternities and members of the New-Right "identitarians", the youth organization brings a body of thought into the party that is known from the Republikaner, DVU and partly the NPD' (Werner 2015: 56).

82 I have dealt with parts of those currents in my contribution to volume I (Keim 2014).

83 Elsässer had been active for the Maoist Kommunistischer Bund but turned into a 'fervent nationalist' in the course of the war in Serbia. 'Elsässer has remained the revolutionary of the time. He just exchanged his revolutionary subject. The nation has taken the place of the proletariat. And Germany was declared the proletarian nation. It is the old turning point that the Israeli historian Zeev Sternhell has described as the ideological hour of birth of fascism. Through this turn, Elsässer has achieved what he most ardently desires: attention and an increase of his print run' (Wölk 2016: 103).

84 The latter has published in *Junge Freiheit* for many years, co-founded and co-directed (until 2014) with Kubitschek the Institut für Staatspolitik and was editor of *Sezession* for some years.

85 See also 'Reichsbürger und Selbstverwalter: Zahlen und Fakten', *Bundesamt für Verfassungsschutz*, available at https://www.verfassungsschutz.de/DE/themen/reichsbuerger-und-selbstverwalter/zahlen-und-fakten/zahlen-und-fakten_node.html, accessed 17 December 2021.

86 'It is obvious that with the electoral successes of the AfD and the Pegida-protests, new opportunities for articulation of a cultural struggle on the right have emerged; apart from the topics Euro, immigration, Islam and national identity politics, they also feed into public discourse questions of family- and gender-politics' (Häusler 2016c: 1); see also Korsch 2016b: 146.

87 Decker rightly states that this could also be a risk in the long term, since all former attempts to establish a party right of the CDU/CSU (NPD, Republikaner, Bund Freier Bürger, Schill-Partei) have failed in the long run, a historical lesson that Lucke and his followers had understood (Decker 2016: 19–20). In turn, the AfD certainly was an option for voters of formerly existing right-wing parties (Häusler 2016b: 1–2).

88 This is particularly true in Eastern Germany. In the 2014 regional elections in Thüringen, for example, more former voters from the leftist parties (Die Linke, SPD and Green Party) voted for the AfD than from the CDU and FDP. In Brandenburg, it was Die Linke who lost most voters to the AfD, indicating an overall rightward shift within the country's electorate (Decker 2016: 21). In the eastern regions, the fact that overall electoral loyalty to given parties has been less stable than in Western Germany also seems to have been in favour of far-right parties. The electorate of the AfD also needs to be analysed in conjunction with the NPD vote, especially in Saxony, the former NPD stronghold. In 2014, the NPD did not enter the

regional parliament; with 4.95 per cent of votes (81,051) it had not reached the 5 per cent threshold. In the same elections, the AfD received 9.4 per cent of the votes. They were in clear competition for voters: the NPD lost 13,000 votes to the AfD and 10,000 of its former voters abstained. Nevertheless, together they gathered nearly 15 per cent. The analysis of those votes remains a regional specialty since Saxony had been the traditional stronghold of the NPD (Pfahl-Traughber 2016). It is interesting, however, as it shows that in the region, NPD and AfD electorates largely converged with regard to their overall characteristics: both parties were strong amongst young voters, and in both men were much more represented than women. In the NPD, voters with high levels of formal education were under-represented, whereas voters with medium or low formal education were over-represented. This was different within the AfD, where those with medium-level education were strongest and those with high and low levels weaker. The NPD gathered a high percentage of votes among unemployed (11 per cent, i.e. double as many as in the overall voting population). In the AfD the unemployed were slightly stronger represented than in the average. Workers were strongly represented in both parties, less so retired people. The regional strongholds largely overlapped: 'At the level of their party programs, one cannot equate both parties; there are better reasons to do so regarding their electoral basis. If one takes into consideration the recent rightwards shift of the AfD, this party will probably increasingly mobilize the electorate of the NPD' (ibid.). Faced with the threat of prohibition and internal scandals, NPD voters certainly were attracted towards the AfD as a viable alternative (Häusler 2016a: 47–48).

[89] Apart from this methodological concern, this assessment sounds like a reiteration of Mann's analysis of one of the core constituencies of historical fascism, namely those from economic sectors removed from the frontlines of class conflict, attracted by fascism's promise of transcendence (Mann 2004). However, since class struggle has largely disappeared from the current political landscape and transcendence has not been identified as a major feature of the current far right, this parallel appears as merely nominal and the specific motivation of those determined population segments remains unintelligible.

[90] As in France, it was easier to characterize the AfD electorate through opinion polls and studies of attitudes. If the AfD did not appeal neither to any single particular population group in terms of former political affiliation nor to any particular socio-economic group, studies of political orientations and attitudes confirmed more clearly what kinds of people were attracted by it, assuming that the cleavages amongst voters were less material but idealistic. In the 2013 federal elections, it was already evident that a critical stance towards immigration was a strong motive for the AfD vote, more than the party's anti-EU stance. Other studies revealed that dissatisfaction with the existing democracy nourished many AfD votes. Half of voters agreed that 'Germany needs a strong leadership personality that can quickly decide everything' (Decker 2016: 18–19, quoting Berbuir, Lewandowsky and Siri 2015, 168 f.). Although many party leaders had tried to keep a distance from the Pegida movement, 76 per cent of voters sympathized with the protests, as against 22 per cent of the average population (Decker 2016: 18–19).

[91] 'Juden in der AfD: Jüdische AfD-Mitglieder gründen Vereinigung', *Zeit Online*, 7 October 2018, available at https://www.zeit.de/politik/deutschland/2018-10/juden-afd-jafd-vera-kosova?print, accessed 20 December 2021.

[92] Indeed, according to recent statistical research on the far-right vote across Europe, even terms like 'fear of crime' appear to be code words for 'fear of multiculturalism' (Jackson and Doerschler 2018).

11

Deep Roots

The Post-Fascist Legacies of the
Current Western European Far Right

Wiebke Keim

After the end of the Second World War, all over Europe, fascists had to reconfigure. In Italy, the home country of originary fascism, the Resistance movement went public and started to engage in the official politics of the country. The remaining fascists of the Italian Social Republic, if not in prisoner-of-war camps or jail, in turn went underground as the new government banned any attempt to form a fascist organization or party. They also had to fear the revenge of the anti-fascist Resistance fighters who appear to have killed around 2,344 fascists or maybe more (Weinberg 1979: 13). However, following an amnesty in 1946, many fascists became politically active again, claiming continuity with the Social Republic. The main political party they founded was the Italian Social Movement (MSI), represented by the symbol of the tricolour flame over a funeral bier, expressing their commitment to pursue Mussolini's legacy. There was a strong 'continuity with the past', i.e. with interwar fascism, confirming 'the authenticity of the MSI's Fascist credentials':

> One of the most striking features of the Social Movement's history is the extent to which it recapitulates the history of the original Fascist movement. Despite the existence of enormous differences between the two postwar eras and in the distribution of strength of the various social and political forces at work in them, the similarities in Fascist behavior seem impressive. (Ibid.: 71–72)

In other countries, the reorganization after 1945 was more discreet. Oswald Mosley, as soon as he was released from imprisonment, started to reorganize British fascism. He was aware, however, that its appearance needed to change, since the interwar style would not have been acceptable any more. He therefore circulated a letter signed by Alf Lockhart, former British Union of Fascists member, amongst supporters. The letter encouraged the creation of local groups but explicitly asked to avoid the term 'fascist' in their names and publications. As a result, 'many artful names were invented' (Beckman 1995: 16).

This chapter outlines the post-war context in Germany and France, and how former fascists reorganized themselves in it. For the German case, it is necessary to demonstrate how organizational continuity was partly encouraged through external support, due to geopolitical considerations, to a fragmented political scene. For France, the key turning points of the Algerian War and of 1968 led to changes in ideological outlook and political restructuring. I shall conclude by arguing that apart from the current situation of political malaise and ideological crisis, the deep roots of the post-war far right are a second explanatory factor for their current strength. The chapter also includes a digression on its current geopolitical significance.

Post-1945 in Germany: An Overview

In the Federal Republic of Germany, in 1950–51, there were around 8 million displaced persons or refugees (*Vertriebene*),[1] between 1.5 and 2.5 million 'outclassed' public servants, employees of the National Socialist German Workers' Party (NSDAP, or the Nazi Party) and professional soldiers, 2.4 million war widows and orphans, 1.5 million severely disabled, 2 million late returnees from prisoner-of-war camps, 4.5 to 6 million bomb victims, and over 1.5 million unemployed (Stöss 1986: 210–11, quoting Schelsky 1955). In order to avoid shortened memories, these figures should also be kept in mind when debating the relevance of the current refugee reception crisis (see the preceding chapter).

In the face of profound social and economic problems in a divided country, and of diverging views on how to reconstruct nation and society, many citizens adopted oppositional attitudes towards the plans of the occupying powers to consolidate a liberal, capitalist and somewhat democratic project. This opposition was not only nourished by practical, social and economic concerns, by deep feelings of insecurity and disorientation, but also by a more fundamental opposition to pluralistic parliamentary democracy similar to the situation during the Weimar Republic. In this sense, the parallels that Weinberg has noted regarding the situation of Italian interwar and post-war fascism apply to the German case as well. The far-right radical opposition was oriented against the occupying powers and their subordination of the 'German people', as well as against the so-called licence parties, i.e. political parties that had obtained a licence from the occupying powers to stand for elections and that therefore appeared, in the eyes of critics, as extensions of the occupiers. To sum up, 'antidemocrats of all shades regarded the parliamentary-democratic and pluralistic Republic as a form of political order that had failed after 1918 and that had therefore lost its historical legitimation' (Stöss 1986). Former soldiers and National Socialist activists started to organize and took over the ideological leadership of these oppositional forces. It was these groups that ensured organizational continuity for projects of authoritarian restoration in post-war Germany. They developed at first in a contradictory context.

In politics, various 'great men' of National Socialism (NS) history did have a career after 1945. Hans Globke is a key example of personal continuity within the administrative elites. He had 'collaborated and played an active part in carrying out the "Germanization" and extermination policy of the Nazi regime' (Juristen 1963: 7–8). By that time, Globke was chief of Konrad Adenauer's Bundeskanzleramt (Federal Chancellery) and counted as the closest partner of the chancellor. Another prominent example is Christian Democratic Union of Germany (CDU) Chancellor Kurt Georg Kiesinger (1966–69). An NSDAP member between 1933 and 1945, he had started his career as director of the Rundfunkpolitische Abteilung (Broadcasting Policy Department) in the Reichsaußenministerium (Reich Ministry of Foreign Affairs) under von Ribbentrop, maintaining contacts with Goebbels' Reichspropaganda-ministerium (Reich Propaganda Ministry).

A request for information on 'dealing with the NS past' by various Members of Parliament to the German Parliament was answered in December 2011. It stated that due to the need for and high value of 'administrative experience' in the 1950s, there had indeed been a great deal of continuity in terms of contents and staff within German public administration. The 85-page document reveals, among others, that by the end of the 1950s, 77 per cent of staff of the Ministry of Defence were former NSDAP members, 50 per cent in the Ministry of Economic Affairs and one-third in the Foreign Office. Three-quarters of the staff in the Federal Criminal Police Office had been NSDAP members, and more than half, members of the Schutzstaffel (SS). A total of twenty-seven chancellors and federal ministers had been members of NSDAP, Sturmabteilung (SA) or SS, including, for example, the former Minister of the Exterior Hans-Dietrich Genscher (Bundestag 2011). The staffing translated into practice. The Federal Criminal Police Office, for instance, right up to the 1950s, focused on homosexuals as a group and maintained its 'gypsy files', in the tradition of the former Reichszentrale für die Verfolgung des Zigeunerunwesens (Reich Central for the Persecution of the Gypsy Nuisance); only that they changed the name of the file from 'gypsy' to 'people with frequently changing domicile' (Wildt 2014: 54–55).

In the beginning, committed National Socialists formed small groups and parties at local and regional levels, and kept switching, renaming and reorienting in order to comply with structures that were officially possible in the new legal environment of the young republic under western occupation. Figure 11.1

Figure 11.1 *Evolution of far-right parties from pre-war to post-war Germany*

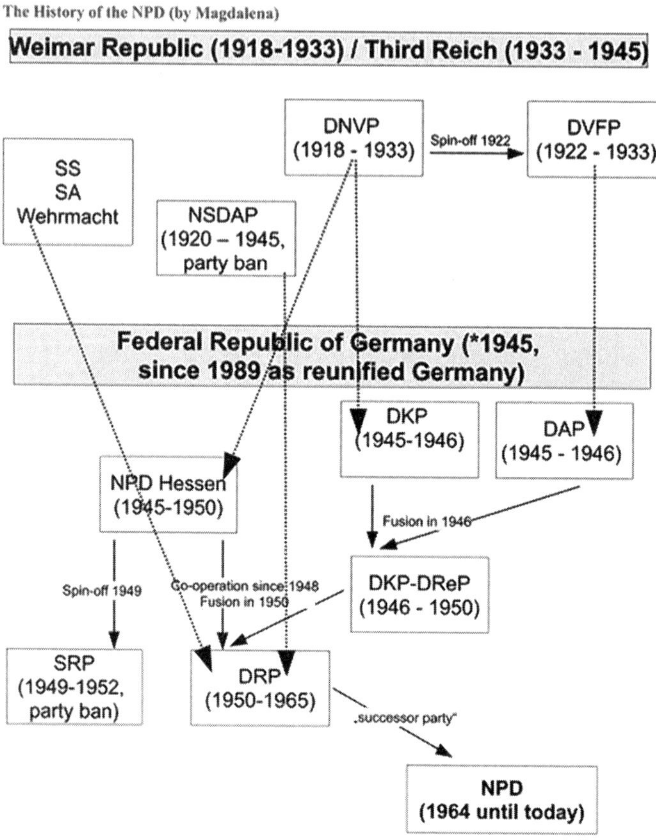

The History of the NPD (by Magdalena)

Weimar Republic (1918-1933) / Third Reich (1933 - 1945)

DNVP (1918 - 1933) — Spin-off 1922 → DVFP (1922 - 1933)

SS SA Wehrmacht

NSDAP (1920 – 1945, party ban)

Federal Republic of Germany (*1945, since 1989 as reunified Germany)

DKP (1945-1946)

DAP (1945 - 1946)

NPD Hessen (1945-1950)

Fusion in 1946

Spin-off 1949

Co-operation since 1948 Fusion in 1950

DKP-DReP (1946 - 1950)

SRP (1949-1952, party ban)

DRP (1950-1965)

„successor party"

NPD (1964 until today)

List of abbreviations (in alphabetical order)

DAP	Deutsche Aufbau-Partei
DKP	Deutsche Konservative Partei
DKP-DR(e)P	Deutsche Konservative Partei- Deutsche Reichspartei
DNVP	Deutschnationale Volkspartei
DRP	Deutsche Reichspartei
DVFP	Deutschvolkische Freiheitspartei
NPD	Nationaldemokratische Partei
NSDAP	Nationalsozialistische Deutsche Arbeiterpartei
SRP	Sozialistische Reichspartei
SS	Schutzstaffel
SA	Sturmabteilung

Own graph based on Botsch 2017

Source: Baroni *et al.* 2018.

outlines their evolution from the pre-war to the post-war period. The post-1945 story could start from the National Democratic Party (Nationaldemokratische Partei [NDP]) that existed between 1945 and 1950 in the region of Hessen. As a right-wing extremist small party, it never obtained the necessary licence from the US occupying force for the whole region. Its leader was Heinrich Leuchtgens, formerly member of the Bauernbund (Farmers' Association), later Hessischer Landbund that collaborated with the Deutschnationale Volkspartei (German National People's Party, DNV). They favoured a strong state, law and order, fight against internationalism, pacifism and social democracy; it was profoundly anti-urban and anti-Semitic. From 1948 onwards, the party increased its social base, integrating more radical Nazis who, because of prior activities for the NSDAP or related organizations, had been banned from political activities and had no chance to obtain a licence for the creation of their own party. Their political ambition went as far as reclaiming the borders of the former German Reich, and their request for a strong state included redistributionist economic ideas. To them, Leuchtgens with his traditionalist view of a feudal-type society appeared as a desperately conservative mind. Although the local branch of the party in Wiesbaden, where the pro-fascists were strongly represented, had been created only in autumn 1947, they achieved 24.4 per cent in the local elections of April 1948. Ideological tensions led to fragmentation of the party. The oppositional, Nazi-minded group joined the Sozialistische Reichspartei (Socialist Reich Party, SRP), and the larger conservative group fused with the Deutsche Konservative Partei-Deutsche Rechtspartei (German Conservative Party – German Party of the Right, DKP-DRP) to form the Deutsche Reichspartei (German Reich Party, DRP) (Schmollinger 1986b: 1892–99).

The SRP (1949–52) was composed of former members of the DRP who had left it or who had been expelled because of their radicalism. It connected directly with the NS ideological line of nationalism, in direct opposition to the political order of the republic and with the ultimate aim of restoring the German Reich. The SRP's leadership, all social scientists, was interesting: Fritz Dorls, the SRP leader, held a PhD in history; Gerhard Krüger had studied history, German philology, sociology, geography and journalism, held a PhD and had been professor at Strasbourg University; and Bernhard Gericke held a PhD in English linguistics. The three had met in a British camp where they had been imprisoned because of National Socialist and right-wing-extremist activities, and had been collaborating since then. They experienced enhanced and accelerated networking as a result of confinement by the 'liberal West'. The SRP was relatively successful politically. In the communes where it presented itself for elections, it obtained around 10 per cent of votes. However, in 1952, the Federal Constitutional Court, in accordance with demands from anti-fascists, and from labour organizations and social democrats, banned the party as unconstitutional, and also prohibited it from creating follow-on organizations. Then, many former members of the SRP joined the DRP and changed its political profile in more radical directions. Many of the former voters, however, joined the more established centre-conservative parties, especially the Deutsche Partei (Schmollinger 1986d: 2274–79).

The DRP (1950–64) was founded in 1950 out of the fusion of a regional fraction of the DKP-DRP (Niedersachsen) and the NDP of the region of Hessen, and was in direct competition with the SRP in its initial phase. Its aim was to fuse the tradition of the Deutschnationale with that of the National Socialists, i.e. it aimed at becoming a broader-based party that could unite the national far right in the Federal Republic with chances to obtain political influence within the existing party system. Ideologically diffuse, largely focused on re-establishing the German Reich, it strategically sought to open up a niche for diverse extreme-right orientations and to attract various constituencies. Furthermore, it opposed denazification and re-education programmes, the political order of the republic, and, importantly, communism and social democracy. Although marginal within the overall party system – many voters had started to support the conservative centre-right parties from the 1953 elections onwards – it nevertheless was the most important and most continuous political party that defended old-style nationalism as the dominant trend within the post-war German far right, in continuity with National Socialism. From 1949 onwards, it was continuously represented in communal and regional parliaments.

Members of the DRP came mainly from Protestant rural areas and small towns of northern Germany – farmers and craftsmen. The leadership was composed of employees, middle-size entrepreneurs, farmers with large land ownership and military staff formerly in high positions, i.e. the upper sections of the middle class. When the block of centre-conservative parties began to erode, the DRP was to form the nucleus of a new, more radical extreme-right party, the Nationaldemokratische Partei Deutschlands (National-Democratic Party of Germany, NPD), which it launched in 1964 and dominated from then on (Botsch 2017; Schmollinger 1986a: 1112–91).

The far right also reassembled in different types of organizations that acted as lobby groups to expellees from Eastern Europe. They have remained an important constituency of the far right to this day, and correspond to Mann's outline of 'threatened border communities' as a core constituency of interwar fascism. A federal association was first founded in 1950 that united most of the anti-communist forces amongst the expellees. Its successor, the current Bund der Vertriebenen (BdV, Union of Expellees), was founded in 1957. The majority of its leading staff had their origins in the political cadres and social elites of the

Eastern European territories occupied by National Socialist Germany, among them former NSDAP and SS staff that had participated in occupational and extermination policies between 1939 and 1945 (Schwartz *et al.* 2013). Within post-war Germany, these associations supported the rapid integration of *Heimatvertriebene* populations – many of whom were not *Heimatvertriebene* in the strict sense of the word; rather, on the contrary, many had to flee because of participation in war crimes. About 90,000 former officials and public employees of NS-occupied territories were integrated smoothly into public service after 1945 (Später and Kotte 2010).

The first big post-war economic crisis hit the republic in 1966/67, giving rise to critical voices against the large coalition government. The NPD gathered a variety of smaller extreme-right groups in the tradition of old-style nationalism. It had representatives in seven regional parliaments between 1966 and 1968. Together with economic recovery, the conservative CDU/ Christian Social Union (CSU), in the opposition since the Social Democrats and Liberals formed a coalition government in 1969, made a considerable rightward shift. This weakened the NPD; they did not even enter Parliament in 1969.

At the same time, within the party, the more national-revolutionary segments criticized the party's leadership for its legalistic, system-conforming strategy, and favoured militant activism against, as they put it, 'the undemocratic and anti-constitutional' politics of the new government. The tone of debate thus had changed; the far right started to appropriate and distort democratic themes in their own interest, a tendency they have displayed to date. Around 1970–71, armed groups emerged within the ambit of the NPD, such as the Volkssozialistische Bewegung Deutschlands (People's Socialist Movement of Germany, VSBD), which was banned in 1982; the paramilitary Wehrsportgruppe Hoffmann that acted as security guards to protect far-right meetings and was banned in 1980; the Deutsche Aktionsgruppen (German Action Groups, DA) that were responsible for bomb attacks; and the Aktionsfront Nationaler Sozialisten (Action Front of National Socialists, ANS), an umbrella organization of neo-Nazis in Hamburg that was banned in 1983. The party leadership officially condemned this militant activism. In March 1978, it decided not to accept the involvement of its members from these groups and of members of its youth organization, the Junge Nationaldemokraten (Young National Democrats, JN). This was paralleled in the Front National's (FN) strategy to make unfavourable radical elements disappear from its public image. Apart from the violent action groups, the more intellectually oriented New Right, inspired by the French Nouvelle Droite, started to make inroads after the cultural shock of 1968, and criticized the party's old-style nationalism. The intellectual developments towards post-fascism started from this impulse.

In 1970, on the occasion of a meeting between Chancellor Willy Brandt with GDR Prime Minister Wilhelm Stoph, the far right experienced a moment of strong extra-parliamentary activity, including within the NPD, intellectual circles (editors of the far-right journal *MUT*, Bernhard C. Wintzek, and of *Deutsche Wochenzeitung*, Alfred Mank) and student groups in the 'National Resistance' movement. After the movement lost momentum, editor Gerhard Frey of the *Deutsche National-Zeitung*, which had a weekly print run of 1,10,000, founded the Deutsche Volksunion (DVU), which collaborated from time to time with the NPD. The Aktion Neue Rechte was also founded in the beginning of 1972. The NPD's assembly of November 1971 led to the withdrawal of former leader Adolf von Thadden. Many members also left party politics or switched to other parties, groups or the Aktion Neue Rechte, whereas voters increasingly shifted towards the centre-right parties that were now in the opposition.

In comparison with its electoral base,[2] the party's leadership still had a peculiar profile:

> The selection of leadership specific to this party is related to the importance of the factor of right-wing extremist organizational experience. If we choose as an indicator membership in the higher leadership ranks of the NSDAP, the SRP and other banned organizations as well as the DRP and other extreme right groups, then for the year 1967, according to information from the Federal office for the Protection of the Constitution, 35% of party members, 42% of party officials at district level, 60% of elected members in regional parliaments, 67% of party officials at regional level, 73% of members of the party executive, 91% of federal chairmen [Bundesredner], and 100% of shareholders in the party publication 'Deutsche Nachrichten' [German News] were part of this group. (Schmollinger 1986c: 1983)

These parties thus accommodated actors with previous organizational experience on the far right, and helped to socialize new recruits into their ranks. Another important constituency was that of displaced Germans from parts of Eastern Europe then under Soviet influence. Linus Kather, one of the activists of associations of displaced persons, was an NPD candidate in 1969; he participated in Aktion Widerstand and in 1980, founded the nationalist working group Aktion Deutschland – two organizations close to the NPD that mobilized against Germany's new eastern policy. The displaced persons, German nationals and ethnic Germans from regions then not part of Germany any more, were already an important constituency for National Socialism (Mann 2004). They were particularly attracted by the idea of a strong nation and a strong state. The far-right parties in question were particularly attractive for them as they aimed at restoring the former borders of the Reich. The previous chapter showed that Alternative für Deutschland (AfD) representative von Storch represents parts of those interests within the party today. These kinds of constituencies are clearly not explicable in terms of any crisis context, but only of long-term continuity of the far right's organizational and ideological nucleus.

In the federal elections of 1972, the NPD experienced a serious electoral failure, and from then on it was a rather marginal party within the German landscape until the beginning of the 1990s (Schmollinger 1986c: 1922–94). Throughout the 1980s, however, the far-right scene was not sustained only by political parties (SRP, NPD, DVU and later Republikaner) – those were even relatively marginal. More importantly, extra-parliamentary armed groups, although considered terrorist, existed without much interference from public authorities. Finally, a much broader neo-Nazi underground with a loose organizational structure subsisted, fed among others by an influential media and cultural landscape. In the 1980s, it had millions of sympathizers among the population, 13 per cent of whom held extreme-right attitudes (Jaenecke 1993: 8). In this phase of weakness of the extreme-right spectrum of the German party landscape, Franz Schönhuber, a CSU dissenter, founded the Republikaner in 1983. He tried to give it a more populist outlook. Schönhuber published his memoirs in which he remembered his activities as a member of the Waffen-SS during the Second World War. In the course of its existence, however, the Republikaner got marginalized. It could not take political advantage of the 1989 turn with the collapse of the Berlin Wall (Betz 1993: 670).

In the German Democratic Republic (GDR), against the official version of its being an anti-fascist state, the far right had started organizing:

> It was thus true what could officially not be: In the GDR as well, while according to article 6 of its constitution it had 'in accordance with the interests of the people and its international responsibilities eradicated German militarism and Nazism on its territory', right-wing radicals were active long before the fall of the wall and, as became obvious at latest in 1987, in close contact with 'comrades' in the West. (Borchers 1993: 121; translated by the author)

Right after the fall of the Berlin Wall, western right-wing radicals engaged in recruiting new members in the eastern parts of the country. Michael Kühnen from the Freiheitliche Deutsche Arbeiterpartie (Liberal German Workers' Party) developed a 'work plan East' with the aim of founding a new political party. This succeeded in 1990 with the founding of the Nationale Alternative that took part in local elections (ibid.: 122–23). The NPD started organizing in the eastern parts of the country and founded the branch Mitteldeutsche Nationaldemokraten (National Democrats of Central Germany, MND). This did not succeed immediately, however. In none of the regional and federal elections held throughout the year did it obtain even 1 per cent of the votes.

Helmut Kohl's CDU, with its nationalistic sympathies and welfare promises, seemed to have caught the attention of the electorate that could otherwise have been attracted by the NPD. In addition, the party was highly in debt at the end of 1990 (Staud 2016). In 1991, a new federal board was elected under the leadership of Günter Deckert. His radicalizing strategy with revisionist speeches did not help reconstruct the party. Deckert himself ended up in prison for Holocaust denial. The NPD could not capitalize, at the beginning of the 1990s, either on the fact that right-wing radicalism had started to flourish or in the context of the asylum debate. Republikaner and DVU were the two parties that dominated the far right at the time. The NPD even kept a distance from militant activist groups such as Neue Front (New Front, GdNF) under Michael Kühnen, the Freiheitliche Arbeiterpartei (Liberal Workers' Party, FAP) and the Nationalistische Front (Nationalist Front, NF). Under continuous threat of being banned, the NPD prohibited its members from joining such groups. However, after a series of extreme-right violent attacks across Eastern Germany in particular, many of these neo-Nazi groups were disbanded. At this point, the NPD changed strategy and opened up to organizationally homeless activists from militant groups. In 1996, Udo Voigt, later a member of the European Parliament for the NPD, followed the former party leader Deckert (then in jail) and welcomed hundreds of militant neo-Nazis into the party. Some of them, like Thorsten Heise (formerly FAP), Jens Pühse (formerly NF) and Thomas Wulff (formerly GdNF), climbed up the internal hierarchy to leading positions. This also led to considerable rejuvenation of the party; the youth league had pioneered this process of opening up to radical members (Staud 2016). This enabled the party to lead several big street demonstrations towards the end of the 1990s and to become a visible political force in the country. It also became influential culturally, with the promotion of right-wing rock groups. In terms of content, Voigt shifted from a rather conservative stance to a more radical ideological outlook, redefining the NPD as a 'revolutionary party'. In addition, capitalizing on growing dissatisfaction with the outcome of the so-called reunification in the eastern parts of Germany, the NPD introduced a new focus on social themes that were attractive for an electorate that was frustrated with its post-1989 existence (ibid.).

As a result of the opening up of the NPD towards militant neo-Nazi groups, the federal government, Bundestag and Bundesrat initiated a procedure to prohibit the party in 2000. Extreme-right violence in the country had grown considerably and spread fear among parts of the population. This first prohibition procedure was suspended by the Federal Constitutional Court, however, because too many members of the party's executive were actually police informers. As a result, much of the verbatim material used in the court files had to be attributed to police informers. They seemed to have dominated the party's leadership in some places, such as at the regional level in Nordrhein-Westfalen (Pilath 2017), shedding light, well before the NSU process, on doubtful connections between state structures and the far right. It turned out that thirty out of 200 party executives at regional and national levels were police spies, i.e. one out of seven had received funding from the Federal Office for the Protection of the Constitution.

The failed prohibition procedure gave the party much public attention. It concentrated its resources in Saxony by moving its publishing business and related jobs for functionaries. In the next regional elections in 2004, the NPD made an agreement with the DVU that only the NPD would present itself in Saxony and the DVU in Brandenburg, which allowed for concentrating far-right votes (the Republikaner did not present themselves). During the campaign, the NPD voiced strong protest against labour market reforms (Hartz IV) promoted by the governing coalition of Social Democrats and Greens – political decisions that count to this day as a disaster for social democracy in Germany.[3] The NPD gained slightly over 9 per cent (Staud 2016). After several decades, the party again sent members to a regional parliament. In the regional elections in Mecklenburg-Vorpommern in 2006, it achieved 7.3 per cent of votes. In 2007, the party had 7,200 members and was considered the strongest far-right political party of the country. It has been losing vote share since then, more so since the AfD started participating in elections (Pfahl-Traughber 2016). Because the NPD hardly managed to cross the 5 per cent hurdle, little documentation exists on its voters' profiles.

The short phase of electoral success at the beginning of the 2000s increased internal tensions between younger militant members and older, more conservative ones. In addition, a series of government programmes against right-wing radicalism were launched. Voigt could contain both factions for a while, and, during the 2010 congress, achieved considerable strategic success by fusing the NPD with the DVU into the Nationaldemokratische Partei Deutschlands – Die Volksunion (National Democratic Party of Germany – The People's Union, NPD–Die Volksunion) after DVU's founder Gerhard Frey withdrew from the party. Financial scandals and debt forced the party to dismiss several functionaries (Staud 2016). In the autumn of 2011, Holger Apfel, a representative of the more moderate faction, succeeded Voigt in the party leadership. Many militant activists left the party.

This was also the time when the terrorist group National-Socialist Underground (Nationalsozialistischer Untergrund, NSU) was arrested and accused of a series of racist murders. The investigations discovered direct connections between members of the NSU and several NPD functionaries. At the end of 2013, the Federal Constitutional Court initiated a second attempt to disband the NPD. Apfel had to leave the leadership after only two years because of accusations of sexual harassment of young militants. In the regional elections of 2014, the NPD could not cross the threshold of 5 per cent necessary to enter regional parliaments. The concurrence of the newly rising AfD contributed to this failure. However, in the European Parliamentary elections of 2014, for the first time, Germany could not impose a threshold any more, enabling Udo Voigt to enter the European Parliament on behalf of the NPD. In 2015, together with Golden Dawn and Jobbik, the NPD formed the Alliance for Peace and Freedom at the European level, gaining access to funding and staff (ibid.).[4] J.M. Le Pen, upon his expulsion from the Front National (see the preceding chapter), joined this alliance.

Even today, the NPD is closely associated with the NS legacy. It is not only closely linked to neo-Nazi movements, but because of its nationalist orientation, the emphasis on the German *Volk* and its welfare chauvinism, and its demands for state control over the economy, it can be considered an 'originary National Socialist party' (*originär nationalsozialistische Partei*) (Kailitz 2007). Its ultimate utopic aim is restoration of the German Reich. In 2017, the new procedure to ban the party as anti-constitutional was refuted by the Federal Constitutional Court. The court recognized the party's ideological closeness to National Socialism and its anti-constitutional orientation, aiming at 'replacing the existing constitutional order with an authoritarian nation-state oriented towards the ethnically defined "Volksgemeinschaft"' (Pilath 2017). It admitted that the party was irreconcilable with democracy and disrespected human dignity. However, the court found that with 5,200 members in the majority of the eastern regions of the country, especially Saxony, the party was too small and insignificant to represent a real threat to liberal democracy in the country. The party's official website summarizes its outlook today as '*Die soziale Heimatpartei*' (The social Heimat-party).[5] Following Kemper's analysis of Björn Höcke, we may assume that parts of the radical energies of the NPD, in the face of an unsuccessful party threatened by prohibition, fused into the rising AfD (Kemper 2016a).

The NPD has remained a small party throughout. Its continued existence throughout up-and-down phases of success and in changing political environments is largely explicable through the biographies of its political leadership, its personal and organizational networks and the ideology they have upheld. The succession of political parties has also maintained throughout the entire period connections with militant groups, at times with the complicity of parts of public authorities. Finally, a cultural sector including not only party publications, but the more intellectual New Right scene, music and youth subcultures, has sustained the continued visibility and appeal of the German far right. The NPD clearly upholds the legacy of National Socialism. It can be considered an organizational form of post-war fascism. In the preceding chapter, we noted the NPD and its surrounding networks as one of the radicalizing agencies within the AfD's short history. Direct continuity is therefore present from the interwar period through the post-war period in the organizational structures and intellectual heritage of the latest far-right party in Germany. This long-term continuity is key to understanding how the AfD, within a brief time span, could make a significant shift towards a far-right stance. Indeed, a small circle of political and ideological cadres, who inscribe themselves clearly in the outlined continuity, have steered these developments. This reality needed separate treatment, independent of societal crisis contexts. Irrespective of existing new electoral constituencies, therefore, their agenda has strongly determined the AfD's rapid evolution and electoral success. This analysis is complementary to that presented in the preceding chapter.

However, as opposed to the NPD, the AfD has streamlined its discourse and adapted it to the new context. This is why many analysts consider it a right-wing 'populist' party. The party corresponds to the intellectual strategy of the New Right. Its members show a different degree of reflexivity about the country's NS past. I therefore conclude that the current situation of the German far right is adequately characterized as post-fascist.

ORGANIZATIONAL CONSISTENCY AND EXTERNAL SUPPORT

During the early post-war decades, the European far right was at odds with the official post-1945 dynamic towards peace, liberal democracy, welfare capitalism and the new international institutional framework. However, these were also the decades of Cold War confrontation. In volume I (Sitas *et al.* 2014), I argued that in parallel to the official landscape, in hidden ways, the direct continuity of National Socialism was upheld within parts of the intelligence services in Germany under the auspices of the Central Intelligence Agency (CIA), and later in coordination with NATO (North Atlantic Treaty Organization), which considered pre-1945 fascists to be qualified and reliable partners against communism (Keim 2014). Apparently, finding refuge and support in intelligence structures was a feature shared by the far right in several Western European countries. If this hidden support does not alone explain why these movements were attractive to their sympathizers, supporters and members, it is an important element in understanding their survival and trajectories.

It was only in 1986 that the US Ministry of Justice admitted that the CIA had recruited SS and Gestapo officer Klaus Barbie in 1947. Barbie, called the butcher of Lyon, had been head of the Gestapo in occupied Lyon (1941–44).[6] Under his leadership, 14,311 people were arrested and tortured, 9,591 deported and 4,342 murdered, among them the Resistance leader Jean Moulin. Despite the fact that France was actively searching for him to try him as a war criminal, he was first recruited by the Counter Intelligence Corps (CIC) as an informant on communist activities in German territories. When the situation became too risky in the face of France's advancements, the CIA, with the support of the Vatican and the Red Cross, had to hide him elsewhere since he knew too much about the functioning of US intelligence. He was allowed to leave Europe through the 'ratline' to Bolivia, as was the case with thousands of other Nazis, and he lived in South America under the name Altmann. He continued collaborating with the CIA against Latin American communism. He was behind the capture and murder of Che Guevara in 1967. From the 1960s onwards, the German foreign intelligence service, Bundesnachrichtendienst (BND, the Federal Intelligence Service for Foreign Intelligence), recruited him as an informant on Latin American communism. In addition, as was the case with many former SS members then, he represented the German weapons industry and negotiated the sale of German arms to Latin American countries. Barbie supported the military coup of Banzer in 1971 and the violent repression of the opposition in the eight years that followed. Beate Klarsfeld, investigative journalist on war criminals, identified Barbie but he was protected by Hugo Banzer from extradition to France. Barbie also supported the 1980 coup by General García Mesa, funded on Barbie's request by his friend, the drug boss Roberto Suárez. For this purpose, he recruited a whole mercenary army composed of former Nazis and fascists, with the complicity of the CIA. After the end of the military dictatorship, Barbie was finally sent back to France – German chancellor Helmut Kohl, during his electoral campaign of 1983, refused to take him back in order to avoid any scandal about collaboration between the BND and NS war criminals. However, German neo-Nazis like Michael Kühnen planned to liberate him from Lyon prison. Publisher Gerhard Frey was ready to provide funding and former Eichmann collaborator Brunner, underground in Syria, was ready to welcome him. All those plans failed and he was sentenced to lifelong imprisonment in 1987. Barbie's case illustrates particularly well the recycling of NS competency in a huge diversity of contexts, as well as the efficiency of their networks.

More systematically, in Allendorf camp in Hessen, where many high-positioned Wehrmacht generals were imprisoned, Franz Halder, General Staff of the NS armies, together with 120 former generals, evaluated their military experience in the East after the end of the war. This evaluation was commissioned by the Historical Division of the US army's Center of Military History. The results of their analyses fed directly into the newly founded Bundeswehr and into NATO (L.A. Müller 1991: 104–10).

The German trajectory was included in my contribution to the first volume (Keim 2014). In the meantime, systematic and detailed research by the Independent Historical Commission has enquired into personal continuities between the NS power apparatus and the post-war German intelligence services. While the Pentagon ordered its intelligence services to detect German Nazis and bring them into the Nuremberg processes for trial, it also recruited select ones for the construction of the German intelligence services.

The BND followed a different path from the Bundesamt für Verfassungsschutz (Federal Office for the Protection of the Constitution, Intelligence of the Interior). In the case of the latter, the Allied powers took care to prevent recruitment of NS staff in the immediate post-war years. It was only from the middle of the 1950s onwards that the Verfassungsschutz got 'National-Socialized': collaborators with an NS past were initially paid on honorary basis and did not form part of the permanent staff. Once the control of Allied authorities weakened, they were recruited (Wildt 2014). This was different from the development of the BND. Probably the most prominent Nazi enrolled in German intelligence was General Reinhard Gehlen. He had been a key figure in the Reichswehramt (Reich Defence Office) for the Nazi information service on Fremde Heere Ost (Foreign Armies East), i.e. he was the chief director of espionage of Eastern Europe from 1941 onwards. He was responsible for torture and murder through starvation of 4 million Soviet prisoners of war. Faced with the defeat, Gehlen voluntarily surrendered in May 1945 to the US body CIC, in charge of tracking down those responsible for NS crimes. He convinced them of his particular competency in combating the Soviets, and he was flown, together with six of his closest colleagues, to Washington, along with data and material gathered during his former functioning as chief of Fremde Heere Ost. Gehlen became the first director of the German foreign intelligence service after the war and constructed this service out of networks of former NS colleagues. The precursor of the BND, the Gehlen organization was initiated in 1945–46 by the American authorities. It was institutionalized in 1947 with the setting up of its headquarters at Pullach. In 1956, the structures were transferred to federal authorities and adapted to the federal institutional landscape (Sälter 2014). The Independent Historical Commission has now published detailed insights into Gehlen's career (Keßelring 2014, 2017; R.D. Müller 2014). The CIA closely controlled his activities, i.e. the German secret service evolved under US control. The presidents of US and Germany had also signed secret protocols in 1955 accompanying Germany's accession to NATO. According to these protocols, the public authorities of the country had to stop prosecution of well-known right-wing extremists.

The Gehlen organization systematically recruited former NS staff from prisoner-of-war camps.[7] Structurally, the Gehlen organization and the early BND, until the end of the 1960s, were staffed by people who had held executive positions within the NS apparatus, and many had war experience as well. Whereas several members were still young of age during the years 1930–45, the leading staff had already had careers under National Socialism, like Gehlen himself. 'In short, [within the BND] the generation Hitlerjugend met the Führergeneration' (Rass 2014: 32). In 1950, 57 per cent of the staff had experience as either members of the NSDAP, the German Labour Front, the Reichsarbeitsdienst, or had been part of the Reich's bureaucracy, police or Waffen-SS. Once experience in the Wehrmacht was added, almost 90 per cent of staff were covered. They were hired through job applications, transferred from other services or recruited directly through BND staff. Allied agencies, the occupation authorities in the first place, additionally channelled about one-third of the staff.

The Gehlen organization consisted of its headquarters and a series of relatively autonomous external units charged with information-gathering. The directors of the external units had autonomy to recruit permanent staff and informants, and were encouraged to recruit 'proven personnel from within their circles of acquaintances' (Sälter 2014: 42). There was no central staff department. Having war experience was particularly valued, which led to a practice where, next to former military staff, National Socialist functionaries were drawn into the organization. 'The recruitment policy, voluntarily or involuntarily, was oriented towards the incorporation of the ruins of the National Socialist security apparatus' (ibid.: 51). Recruitment following the snowball system allowed pre-existing coteries to be recruited wholly. This effect of decentralized recruitment was reinforced by the fact that new recruits were not further examined, since the recruiting director guaranteed their ideological and technical adequacy.[8] Clearly, 'The direction of the BND based its staff policy on the comradeship that had been created during National Socialism' (ibid.: 41). It was only when the BND became a federal body and its staff could aspire to the status of state officials that superior federal authorities imposed minimum control of staff prior to recruitment, problematizing professional career biographies prior to 1945. However, inside Pullach, the leading staff largely resisted such measures and continued to uphold their NS-based ideology with its model of the authoritarian state, of which they felt they were a part. From then on, their energies were more oriented to obscuring existing continuities towards the outside.

Sälter also contextualized his analysis of the BND's staff and recruitment policy within the broader post-war society:

> This form of recruitment was realized in a postwar society in which parts of the old high ranking executives, some under wrong identities, reassembled. Their networking was based on professional friendship, political closeness and complicity. It aimed at collective ideological reassurance, reciprocal economic support and politically, at putting an end to denazification. After 1945, such networks were formed out of people who knew each other either from department of some NS

organization or bureaucracy, or from local cooperation between different institutions in the occupied territories. It also appears that they reorganized themselves and that they expanded their member base in the allied camps of the postwar period, in which, under the pressure of denazification, they experienced a common destiny. In the confusing political situation of the 1940s and 1950s, some of those groups aimed at positions of political influence. (Ibid.: 44)

Recruiting each other into the Gehlen organization and the BND was one such strategy. This practice was backed by Globke in the Federal Chancellery.

The Allied powers considered the Gehlen organization, a sort of 'CIA dependency', as a major tool of information-gathering on the Soviet enemy in the Cold War context. Therefore, the recruitment of guaranteed anti-communist staff with knowledge about the east and with competency in information-gathering outweighed the sensitivity to their NS past (Wildt 2014). The Soviet invasion never happened. However, many of those who had opposed and resisted National Socialism became increasingly suspect again as potential 'collaborators' of the Soviet Union – prominently communists and Social Democrats, but even pacifists and church representatives. Although the Gehlen organization and later BND were charged with foreign intelligence, they abused their position and were also active in the domain of internal affairs. They declared this to be part of their counter-intelligence mission. The fact that they engaged with internal politics was partly due to their aspiration, while 'still in Wehrmacht uniform' to one day become 'the one, the universal German intelligence service' (Henke 2014: 93). Essentially, 'their new enemy was the old one: world revolutionary communism with their fifth columns rummaging everywhere, who were now, on top of this, backed by the victorious Stalin. This obsession did not quit Gehlen until his death' (ibid.). He had decided to continue his fight against communism, in alliance with the US government. The Gehlen organization also collaborated directly on internal affairs with the Federal Chancellery, owing to the close relationship of Gehlen and Globke.[9] One of the aims was to place members of the organization in influential positions within the German state apparatus.

Importantly as well, in the case of the BND, we cannot speak of a direct institutional continuity. Rather, within an organization that had no direct predecessors before 1945, we find a personal continuity of major NS staff. There were only few other organizations, apart from the BND, that offered a post-1945 narrative of anti-communist struggle to their members, and which allowed them to justify and make sense of their own life-stories (Rass 2016: 40). Only when the Social Democrats under W. Brandt governed the country for the first time in 1968 was Gehlen dismissed. He was succeeded by his former adjutant of Foreign Armies East, General Gerhard Wessel, military attaché in Washington since 1945. While the GDR secret service Stasi was dissolved after 1989, the BND was extended. This was reunification.

The Historians' Commission does not establish any link between the BND and Stay Behind Germany. Several times throughout the post-war period and in different parts of Europe, this secret armed network surfaced and caused political scandals. Stay Behind was led by military intelligence services, i.e. only leading executive figures, but neither national parliaments nor populations were informed. It was only after 1989 that the full dimensions of these connections came to light, when Italian Prime Minister Giulio Andreotti, after juridical investigations in the light of terrorist activities in his country, confirmed the existence of secret armies across Western Europe in 1990. In each country, this secret network, also named Gladio after its Italian realization, recruited members who were strictly anti-communist, including moderate conservatives but also right-wing radicals.[10]

In Germany, Stay Behind made its first public appearance in 1952, when former SS officer Hans Otto decided to testify to the Frankfurt criminal police that he formed part of an armed political grouping, the Bund Deutscher Jugend (League of German Youth, BDJ), and headed its 'Technical Service' (Technischer Dienst, TD). The BDJ was the main branch, though not the only one, of Stay Behind in West Germany (Ganser 2005; L.A. Müller 1991; Roth 1992). Otto joined the NSDAP in 1929, became a member of the SA in 1933 aged 20, and pursued a typical Nazi career. In 1934, he joined the SS-Standarte Germania, in 1938 the SS-Junkerschule in Braunschweig; he became SS-Obersturmführer (senior storm leader) in 1940 and SS-Hauptsturmführer in 1942. He fought on several fronts, was a prisoner of war of the French and the Americans, and was released in October 1948. After the war, he worked as a sales representative and started to collaborate with the British secret service in order to make some extra money. But it was not only an issue of money. 'They were looking for new social bonds among like-minded men. They needed new orders, they longed for new fraternities. In organizations like the "Bruderschaft" [fraternity], the old comrades reunited' (L.A. Müller 1991: 74). This secret society was formed in 1950 in a meeting of former officers as 'Deutsche Bruderschaft', with the aim to restore the 'honour of the German soldiers' and to extinguish the 'European disgrace of Nuremberg', i.e. the trials against war criminals. A key figure in this secret fraternity was Alfred Franke-Gricksch – he too had been a member of the NSDAP in 1927, followed an SS career, become SS-Standartenführer and director of the staff department of Himmler's Reichssicherheitshauptamt. There he had been in charge of the 'elaboration of methods of underground work in case of military defeat' (ibid.: 75, quoting Opitz). This fraternity was the recruiting agency for the paramilitary organization TD, that hid behind the BDJ (ibid.: 72–77).

The group's targets, according to Otto, were the communist party, KPD, and the Social Democratic party, SPD. It also led a battle against the communist youth organization, Freie Deutsche Jugend, that operated in the western zones of the country at the time – a struggle that resembled in style and method the street-fighting of the SA in the 1930s (ibid.: 110). Otto confirmed that 'in the case X' (it is unsure whether this referred only to the Soviet invasion or could also refer to mass demonstrations or an electoral victory of the left), it was planned to act out violence against internal aims. The TD drew up death lists of several dozens of leading KPD and SPD members. After Otto's revelations, the regional government directed the case to Berlin, but Adenauer silenced it and prevented investigations. The Federal Constitutional Court decided to release all arrested members of the TD. The BDJ's strategy to actively seek recognition by political authorities within the new Cold War context had proved successful. The regional parliament of Hessen nevertheless issued an investigation in 1953. From the documentation they gathered, 'one can state with certainty that no other youth organization in the Federal Republic had such excellent relationships with highest public authorities, trade associations and former military as the BDJ and that it has succeeded to obtain huge amounts of money through those relationships' (ibid.: 110). The US brought together about 2,000 members of the Nazi BDJ for partisan battles. The report stated, among other things, that the BDJ was 'loosely associated with a political party in Hessen' (quoting a CIA officer); it remains unclear, however, who that was (Ganser 2008: 310).

The next public episode happened in 1981, when forest workers discovered a major secret weapons depot in the Lüneburger Heide. Forest supervisor Lembke, a right-wing extremist, was arrested. The investigations soon revealed connections between Lembke and the neo-Nazi group Wehrsportgruppe Hoffmann, and there seemed to be links to the terrorist attack at the Oktoberfest in 1980, the biggest in Germany since the war. Investigations intensified through the decade. The Social Democrats did not want any revelations just before the 1990 elections. Chancellor Kohl had lied on the issue from 1982 onwards and was scared of the repercussions of a scandal for the elections. Only the Green Party, founded in 1980, insisted on transparency. It was only after the elections, in December 1990, that the German government published a brief report on the matter.

Recruitment for the BND or for Stay Behind ensured not only adequate funding in the difficult post-war context, it also ensured organizational continuity and allowed far-right groups with a more official face, such as the BDJ, to proselytize the far-right ideology and seek political alliance in the new political landscape, while the hidden TD translated this ideology into paramilitary strategy and gave particularly committed individuals a space for militant action, protected by the highest authorities. This combination was only possible because of much broader continuities between the NS bureaucracy and the post-war administration and politics of the country, and, importantly, in the chancellor's office and the security services. It was within this overall societal context that the continuity of active and militant far-right organizations was made possible and even encouraged.

The leadership especially experienced social and ideological uprooting in the post-war years. Many of them, after Hitler's army was dismantled or after they had returned from prisoner-of-war camps, had to follow activities that were much less rewarding than their officers' status during the NS years. In the face of such declassification, the fraternities provided a space to reconnect with the mentality and socialization experience of their former professions. This was even one of its major aims: 'The reunification of former professional militaries from Hitler's army was one of the big aims of the Bund Deutscher Jugend. The freedom of the West was supposed to be secured with the help of those uprooted personalities' (Müller 1991: 103). Apparently, the importance of their activities weakened over the 1970s. Lecorte observes that this was also the phase when the political extreme-right scene in Germany was radicalized, as I have observed above. He therefore assumes that the staff enrolled in the German Stay Behind structures were searching for alternative occupations (Lecorte 2013: 13).

POST-1945 IN FRANCE: AN OVERVIEW

The Front National (FN) is described as 'one of the big European extreme right parties where the lineage with historical fascism is most evident' (Jacquemain and Claisse 2012: 19–20). The French far right traces its roots back to opposition to the 1789 revolution, expressed in anti-republican, royalist and monarchist political ideologies. Anti-revolutionary political movements favoured the Catholic Church as a guarantor of social cohesion and declared the principle of fundamental equality unnatural. Its lineage includes the movements of General Boulanger in the 1880s with its essentially nationalist and authoritarian outlook and virulent anti-Semitism. Following Boulangism, a variety of far-right groups coexisted, claiming 'France for the French'. Their common denominator was a strong Catholic orientation combined with anti-Semitism, with the Dreyfus Affair in 1894 being a culminating point. False accusations of treason against Captain Alfred Dreyfus, of Jewish descent, led to a political and highly mediatized scandal, resolved only in 1906. It caused a division of the country into pro-republican, anti-clerical Dreyfusards on the one hand, and pro-army, mostly Catholic anti-Dreyfusards on the other hand. The far right was then channelled into the Action Française under the leadership of Charles Maurras. Their anti-parliamentary struggle, essentially nostalgic, aimed at restoring a traditional monarchy embodying an integral nationalism. The Action Française lasted until the installation of the Vichy regime. We need to examine this regime briefly before considering the post-1945 period.

The Vichy regime (1940–42) was the first time, and for a short period the only time, that the far right came to power in France, if under peculiar circumstances, under German occupation. Vichy was determined by French military defeat on the one hand,[11] and opposition to the parliamentarianism of the Third Republic on the other. Marshal Pétain as head of state did not follow closely the fascist line, although he approved of La Rocque's authoritarian-nationalist Croix de Feu and its successor Parti Social Français (PSD). Vichy's slogan, '*Travail, Famille, Patrie*' (Work, Family, Homeland), was derived from there. Petain's government can rather be considered as a form of ancient regime despotism. The constitutional law of 10 July 1940, marking the end of the Third Republic and the beginning of the Etat Français, consigned full political authority to Pétain, who pursued a project of 'National Revolution'.[12] His dictates annulled many of the political and social achievements since 1789, replacing the 'Declaration of the Rights of Man and of the Citizen' (1789) with the 'Principles of the Community' (Shields 2007: 17). Under Vichy, far-right actors had large room for manoeuvre (ibid.: 3). In this sense, Vichy can be considered to have been a laboratory for the far right and this experience was to impact its subsequent development. In occupied Paris, for instance, collaborationists who were apologetic of fascism exerted constant public pressure to radicalize, in particular through their presence in the written press and literature. Robert Brasillach was editor-in-chief of *Je suis partout*.[13] Drieu La Rochelle's calls for a strong European federation against the US and the Soviets saw Nazism as the only means of forging European unification. In this sense, even before the end of the Second World War, 'nationalism' had become an 'unstable concept' in the French experience, 'at once buttressed and undermined by the Europeanism which collaboration with Nazi Germany implied' (ibid: 39).

On the ground, there were three major collaborationist organizations, along a variety of parties and movements: Jacques Doriot had founded in 1936 the PPF (Parti Populaire Français), later incorporated into the Wehrmacht, and complemented between 1943–44 by a French Waffen-SS brigade. Both were integrated in late 1944 into the Waffen-SS Charlemagne Division (estimated to have 7,500 members). Marcel Déat had founded in 1941 the Rassemblement National Populaire together with Eugène Deloncle, former leader of Cagoule, with a membership of about 20,000. And Joseph Darnand (Sturmbannführer Waffen-SS), a former member of Action Française and Cagoule, became the leader of the paramilitary police force Milice Française, set up in 1943 as a kind of palace guard, under the aegis of the SS. Its main aim was to combat the Resistance in what resembled a civil war. It had around 30,000 volunteers.

The Liberation gave way to the creation of the Fourth Republic on the bases of the Third Republic, to the triumph of the communists who could present serious Resistance records and who became the most powerful party in the first post-war elections. Collaborators and their organizations were persecuted in trials, their publications banned, Brasillach executed and Maurras put on trial in 1945. At the same time, however, Vichy officials remained in office under the Fourth and later Fifth Republic. It was J. Isorni who defended in court not only Pétain and Brasillach but also Maurice Bardèche, an intellectually influential defender of Vichy who worked towards rehabilitating NS war crimes and formulated attempts at Holocaust denial.

In the largely hostile climate of post-war France, the far right reconfigured. The two sons of a Milice leader executed at the Liberation launched Jeune Nation during the Indo-China war in 1949. P. Sidos became its chief ideologue and later the founder of Occident, and J. Sidos its president. Jean-Louis Tixier-Vignancour was another founding member. They stood as candidates for J. Isorni's Union des Nationaux Indépendants et Républicains (UNIR) party in the 1951 legislative elections. D. Venner, another Jeune Nation activist, would later found Europe-Action. Jeune Nation, the most important fascistic movement of the 1950s, aimed at a national insurrection in order to replace parliamentary democracy with an authoritarian, popular, national and social state. The role of women in society was to be reduced to that of wife and mother (ibid.: 93–95). Its members were in the majority radical-right students and ex-servicemen from Indo-China. Jeune Nation was banned in 1962; some of its members were later integrated into the OAS (Organisation armée secrète).

René Binet, former Waffen-SS Charlemagne Division, launched the Parti Républicain d'Unité Populaire (PRUP) in 1946, which transformed into the Mouvement Socialiste d'Unité Française (MSUF) and was banned in 1949. Charles Gastaut, alias Charles Luca, a relative of Marcel Déat, headed successive militaristic movements between 1947 and 1960, all based on NS ideology (ibid.: 58–59). They all struggled with adapting the former ideology to the new context of the post-war world order, the Cold War and decolonization. Under these circumstances, the neo-fascist International had to have a European perspective. Bardèche, Binet and Luca as the French delegation met like-minded Europeans at an international conference of neo-fascists in Malmö in 1951. Bardèche and Tixier-Vignancour launched the 'Euro-fascist' MSE (ibid.: 124–26). The social climate changed when all the former collaborators were again free, the latest in 1964, after a series of amnesties in 1951, 1953, 1956, 1958 and 1964.

The first attempt to unite the French far right nationally occurred within the Poujadist movement, launched in 1953 as a localized protest by small shopkeepers against the tax system and against government inspectors. Poujade himself was close to Doriot's PPF, then section leader in Vichy's youth movement, Compagnons de France. The Union de Défense des Commerçants et Artisans (UDCA) was founded in 1953. By 1955, it had developed an organizational network all across France and Algeria with the foundation of 'parallel unions', among them the Union for the Defence of French Youth (UDJF), of which J.M. Le Pen was in charge and into which he integrated the JIP (Jeunes Indépendants de Paris), a loose militant grouping he had created within his Law Faculty surroundings upon his return from Indo-China (ibid.: 68–72). In 1956, the newly constituted Poujadist Party Union et fraternité française (UFF, the UDCA's parliamentary group) participated in elections and gained 11.6 per cent, i.e. 52 out of 596 seats, replacing Gaullism as the main right-wing opposition. However, its representatives were ill-prepared for their new institutional role. J.M. Le Pen could all the more excel as their favourite speaker. His attempts to politicize the movement, infusing anti-communism and authoritarian nationalism into its ranks, at first seemed to succeed[14] but was ultimately doomed to fail. Extreme-right elements could not take full control of a movement that was characterized by contradictory political traditions: revolutionary-republican and conservative-nationalist. Poujadism was limited to being a populist movement in defence of lower middle-class interests. In the end, Le Pen and his friend Jean-Maurice Demarquet, on parliamentary leave in 1956 as reservist volunteers in Algeria, turned against Poujade and were excluded in 1957. The Poujadist movement withered away by 1962, and the far right saw confirmation of its marginality in the political game.

The Algerian War (1954–62)

During the Algerian War, colonialist ideology, based on the civilizing mission and racial thinking, was radicalized. France mobilized over 2 million soldiers (Renken 2006: 259–60), the biggest military mobilization outside metropolitan France since the Crusades (Shields 2007: 91). It was the bloodiest of French colonial wars, marked by over 20,000 French and several hundred thousand Algerian deaths. Almost a million *pieds-noirs* (French settlers) fled to metropolitan France after it was over (Renken 2006: 13). During the war, violent conflict was not restricted to Maghreb territories; bloodshed occurred in the heart of Paris. When Superintendent of Police Maurice Papon, responsible for the deportation of more than 1,500 Jews during the Second World War and later tried for collaboration with NS Germany, imposed a curfew over North Africans in Paris on 17 October 1961, the National Liberation Front (FLN) called a protest demonstration in which up to 40,000 Algerians marched through the capital. Papon ordered a break-up of the demonstration (Shields 2007: 105–108). An estimated several hundred Algerian demonstrators were massacred in an incident that has not been officially investigated till today.[15] J.P. Sartre called it a pogrom.

The Algerian War reconfigured the Nationalist scene in the country.[16] It drew new supporters without former extreme-right affiliation into far-right nationalism, including army veterans, soldiers, colonial settlers and committed patriots, since colonialism enjoyed broad support within French society. In defending 'French Algeria',[17] the far right seized a historical chance to promote itself to a position of truly defending the wider interest of the French nation and to move beyond its discredited Vichy past. Indeed, during the Algerian War, nationalist fractions of the Resistance joined the colonialists' camp. During the depressing years of German occupation, Free France had united under the leading figure of Charles de Gaulle and upheld a vision of French 'grandeur' based on its colonial possessions. Not only did the colonies provide important parts of the troops against Germany, the French empire guaranteed the country the position of a world power, despite military defeat on the continent. When France was excluded from the conferences of the victorious powers in 1945 in Yalta and Potsdam, the defence of its colonial possessions became a fight against the humiliation of Yalta. Shortly after, France, still in a bad shape economically, entered a devastating war in Indo-China that ended with its defeat in 1954.

The Algerian War started the same year. It led to major political reconfigurations as a result of two military coups – one successful, leading to the end of the Fourth and the birth of the Fifth Republic, and the return of de Gaulle on the official political scene; the second unsuccessful, leading to the creation of the OAS, a major organizational innovation that fed into the subsequent advance of the French far right. In 1958, the war intensified in the border regions and spread to Tunisia and Morocco, and the French army attacked a Tunisian village. The British and Americans proposed to intervene to negotiate a settlement. The French government went into crisis and dissolved. Simultaneously, the communists reported torture by the French army in Algeria, which sent shock waves throughout the country and alienated left-wing forces – who remembered torture under German occupation and French collaboration – from the country's colonialist ambitions. The Algerian War, in which France was not the dominated nation but the oppressor, broke the strategic alliance between Gaullism and the left. Amongst the defenders of 'French Algeria', and even within the ranks of the OAS, were former fighters of the Resistance who, once again, defended French soil.

On 13 May 1958, right-wing radical civilians, the so-called ultras, assaulted the government buildings in Algiers, formed an oppositional government and demanded the retreat of the central government in Paris. The activists saw Algeria both as an end in itself and as the means of bringing down a hated parliamentary regime in France – a regime they proposed to replace with a 'nationalist, popular, authoritarian and hierarchical State' (ibid.: 92). Political power in Algeria switched to the hands of army generals Jacques Massu and

Raoul Salan, the high ranks of the army supporting a policy of continuing war at any cost and securing French possessions in Algeria. Since Algeria was considered to be part of France, the events equalled a coup. On 15 May, superior commander of the army, General Salan, publicly called upon de Gaulle, who had retreated from the official political scene. On 29 May, under the pressure of running operations to militarily usurp the central government, President René Coty opened the way for a de Gaulle's return to power. This marked the end of the Fourth Republic. De Gaulle obtained full powers for six months. When he travelled to Algeria, he was acclaimed as the saviour of 'French Algeria'. His plans were different though. De Gaulle aimed at restoring French greatness not on the basis of colonial possessions, which he believed would be a burden rather than a viable and profitable endeavour in the future, but on accession to the circle of nuclear powers (Renken 2006: 327). Against all expectations, on behalf of army superiors, he therefore started a move towards ending the war and accepting the self-determination of Algeria. This caused a major rupture between the civil political power and military power that, since 13 May 1958, had entered the political scene as an autonomous force. In the course of those years, right-wing ideologists of the army linked up with civilian extreme-right groups. The army and the settler community of *pieds-noirs* need to be studied further.

During the Algerian War, the army thus entered the field of national politics. Its role was to have a major ideological impact on the development of the French far right. Since the Indo-China war, high-ranking army officials developed the doctrine of 'revolutionary war', based on the key idea that after the end of the Second World War, communism would not increase its global reach through a direct attack on Europe any more. Rather, the new strategy of world communism would be 'subversion from inside', among other things by supporting the national liberation movements against colonialism in the Third World. Thus, the doctrine of 'revolutionary war' was the army's version of the modern colonial war, rejuvenating colonialist ideology. In particular,

> the officers' corps was dominated by a nearby psychotic fear of a further humiliation by a 'communist' guerrilla, after it had to face the fall of the French fortress of Dien Bien Phu under the attack of the Vietnamese Liberation Front on 7th May 1954, that led instantaneously to the loss of the colony of Indochina. (Ibid.: 328)

This experience was taught in military schools and formed the subject of numerous publications in military journals. In the course of the Algerian War, the doctrine of revolutionary war took centre stage within the higher army ranks and led to specific measures, such as the creation of *cinquièmes bureaux* (fifth offices) in charge of psychological warfare and information-gathering, partly in parallel to the official army hierarchy and with the systematic use of torture. Ideologically, in many cases, anti-communism combined with anti-parliamentarianism and a rage against cosmopolitan capitalists, i.e. the key motives of classical fascism. The ideology of revolutionary war was in direct confrontation with de Gaulle's strategy of self-determination for Algeria. In this perspective, the postulate of military obedience was put into question amongst high-ranking officials who attributed to themselves the role of saving the national interest and winning the fight against world communism.

At the beginning of 1961, in a national referendum, the large majority of the French, exhausted by the succession of tenacious wars, expressed their agreement with de Gaulle's policy of accepting Algerian independence. As a direct response, the OAS was founded in Madrid, uniting colonialist militaries with civilian ultras in a desperate fight to keep 'French Algeria'. In April 1961, four army generals, Maurice Challe, Raoul Salan, Edmond Jouhaud and André Zeller, mounted a coup against de Gaulle. Their plan failed because of the resistance of many lower-ranking soldiers and the lack of commitment of other high-ranking military personnel. Challe and Zeller surrendered and were imprisoned, whereas Salan and Jouhaud went underground and took over the leadership of the OAS. De Gaulle reconfigured the army by transferring and dismissing leading figures.

When de Gaulle first mentioned in public the idea of Algerian self-determination, the settler community reacted with radical nationalism. The successful putsch against the Fourth Republic created a unifying atmosphere. The existing splinter organizations, many armed, of the nationalist ultras within the *pieds-noirs* community increased their membership and started to integrate into broader social formations. In 1958, J. Ortiz set up the first umbrella organization, the Front National Français (FNF), of which J.J. Susini soon emerged as leading ideologue. Ortiz also built a uniformed paramilitary formation under the leadership of J.C. Pérez. Alongside the followers of deputy P. Lagaillarde, this paramilitary brigade formed the core of the January 1960 uprising. After the unsuccessful coup of April 1961, those within the army who were convinced by the doctrine of revolutionary war and intended to pursue the fight for 'French Algeria', sought alliances with the civil ultras and their far-right organizations. The result was the creation of the armed secret OAS, founded in January 1961 by Lagaillarde and Susini from Spanish exile. The OAS united the existing currents of Pétainists and of former French Waffen-SS Division Charlemagne. It also recruited from nationalist fractions of the Resistance. Georges Bidault, who succeeded Jean Moulin as the leading figure of the Conseil national de la Resistance, became head of the organization that followed the OAS in 1962, the 'new' Conseil national de la Resistance (Renken 2006: 78–80). In 1961, Salan, the head of the OAS, declared: 'You participate in the OAS as you participated in the Resistance' (ibid.: 78–80). The public image it tried to project was to position itself in continuity with the

Resistance rather than with collaborationism. In the last six months of the war, OAS terror killed three times more civilians than the FLN since 1956. The OAS also maintained a metropolitan branch and carried out terrorist activities in mainland France, including several attacks on de Gaulle himself. But whereas the organization could capitalize on the practical, logistical and ideological support from major segments of the settler community in Algeria, OAS-metropole, under the leadership of P. Sergent, had to manoeuvre in a largely hostile environment, supported only by the most radical far-right groups, like Jeune Nation, which was banned in 1958 but was still active underground (ibid.: 341).

As in the case of Germany, in France as well, the intelligence services partly relied on and partly lent support to far-right structures, an issue that surfaces in the literature in relation to the Algerian War. Ironically, in Germany and France, Stay Behind had its origins in opposing camps. While in Germany it ensured direct continuity with NS structures, in France it was erected on the foundations of the secret service BCRA (Bureau Central de Renseignement et d'Action) that de Gaulle had initiated from his British exile in connection with the Resistance, with the aim of combating the German occupiers. Agents of the BCRA would parachute into occupied territory to lead sabotage against occupation. This was the predecessor of the secret post-war Stay Behind army in France which included many former BCRA soldiers, indicating the fragile nature of the alliance between nationalists and the left that the Resistance under de Gaulle had initiated. It was the anti-communism of former nationalist Resistance members that activated them to join the Cold War Stay Behind army. Although

> almost no documentary sources are available about either the origin or the development of Stay Behind units in France . . . there are indications that already in 1947 certain veterans of the wartime Free French resistance had been asked by the internal security service to organize 'a network for watchfulness and internal protection' – a Stay Behind, as the Anglo-Saxons call it. (Riste 2014: 45–46)

Since there has not been an official inquiry in France to this day, and the archives remain closed, it is difficult to assess Stay Behind activities accurately. The training of secret soldiers seemed to have been organized jointly with French special troops, in particular the parachutists of the 11e Demi-Brigade Parachutiste du Choc, or 11e du Choc, that had been leading secret warfare in Indo-China and Africa, in particular during the Algerian War. When anti-communist violent agitation in the metropole and the war against the FLN in Algeria intensified, the government seemed to have lost control over its secret armies. Charles Cogan, 'who served as station chief in Paris for the CIA in the 1980s' (ibid.), asks 'whether the French stay-behind program "strayed off the reservation", so to speak, as did the Italian one'. He concedes:

If this was the case, the finger would likely point to Service Action, the paramilitary arm of the SDECE [Service de documentation extérieure et de contre-espionnage, i.e. foreign intelligence] and the military unit that supported it, the 11th Choc Regiment. With the Evian peace accords of 1962, the 11th Choc was divided over the question of independence for Algeria, and part of the 11th Choc went over to the Organisation de l'armée secrète (OAS), which opposed the French government's policy. Therefore, it is possible that some elements of the 11th Choc who may have been associated with the stay-behind program undertook terrorist-type actions on behalf of the OAS in Algeria and/or elsewhere. This possibility is alluded to by former DGSE [Direction Générale de la Sécurité Extérieure, successor of SDECE] Director-General Pierre Lacoste in his interview with Jonathan Kwitny: Lacoste still believes that Soviet contingency plans for invasion justified the [Stay Behind] program through his term in office [1982–85]. He acknowledges that some 'terrorist actions' against de Gaulle and his Algerian peace plans were carried out by groups that included 'a limited number of people' from the French stay-behind network. But he says that's the only time it got political. [. . .] Lacoste's statement to Kwitny is categorically denied by the knowledgeable French military source cited above. . . . The statements of Admiral Lacoste concerning the role supposedly played by stay-behind during the events at the end of the Algerian War appear to be unfounded. In any case he [Lacoste] was not at that point connected with Service Action and those who were at the time never heard anything about such a connection. (Cogan 2007: 952–53).

The story is thus not clear. The same is true for the potential role of the French Stay Behind in the face of the 1968 student and workers' revolts.

More than 2 million soldiers had been mobilized in Algeria and returned to metropolitan France after the war. Upon their demobilization, the lower ranks dissolved, and returned to their families and professions. Veterans of Algeria represented around 22 per cent of the male working population in 1962, of whom 60 per cent were from working-class or peasant families (Renken 2006: 259–60).[18] The subsequent role of the higher ranks and professional army staff was different. In particular, the officers' corps largely contributed to the empowerment of colonialist and ultra-nationalist ideas.

In 1962, the *pieds-noirs* community fled to mainland France. As a visible minority, or *rapatriés*, they settled in certain regions of the country, in particular in Provence-Alpes-Côte d'Azur, where they constituted an important support base to those who put forth the 'French Algeria' ideology, forming an organized social and cultural milieu in which a romantic vision of 'French Algeria' and OAS heroes could flourish. Those who remained convinced of colonialist thinking, in particular, integrated in a series of right-leaning 'French Algeria' organizations and associations, whereas more left-wing *rapatriés* were absorbed into the French Communist Party (PCF). Although in the course of the past decades they have been socially integrated into mainstream society, those regions form an important constituency of the FN even today, as the preceding chapter has illustrated.[19] The *rapatriés* embody de Gaulle's sell-out of 'French Algeria'. As opposed to the higher ranks of the army, the *pieds-noirs* are largely a lower middle-class/working-class constituency.

The OAS, in turn, saw about 70 per cent of its former activists, military as well as civilian, fleeing to Franco's Spain;[20] others went underground or were in prison. As opposed to ordinary soldiers who reintegrated into their former lives in French society, many OAS members formed a specific uprooted group, the precondition for the engagement of many of them later in armed groups.[21] The ideological heritage of the putschists and the OAS lasted long after the war. Leading figures like Sergent and Salan published their memoirs. The ideological production of 'French Algeria' was sustained by a publishing house, La Table Ronde, led by R. Laudenbach, who also coordinated the metropolitan OAS's propaganda. After the end of the war and the independence of Algeria, the defenders of 'French Algeria' put forth a 'stabbed-in-the-back' story. According to them, the French army had been victorious against the FLN. It was the central government and de Gaulle that abandoned 'French Algeria' and thus betrayed the military victory.[22] This version of history echoed the 'revolutionary war' doctrine that had inspired larger circles of the army, beyond the OAS. De Gaulle's disloyalty also formed the core of the defence that J.L. Tixier-Vignancour presented in favour of his mandate to General Salan, when on trial as leader of the OAS in 1962. This story, together with other conspiracy theories, remains a constitutive element of the French far right to date (Renken 2006: 407). The OAS was a prominent political actor, and cannot be compared to the marginality of German far-right groups in the post-war decades. And it had a lasting legacy.

Many former activists remained politically active and strengthened the organizational structures of the far right, ensuring the passing down of the OAS's legacy to the next generation. In the end, the foundation of the FN in 1972 was directly based, personally as well as ideologically, on the OAS's experience (ibid.: 389–90).[23] Renken elaborates on the biographies of some leading figures, like R. Holeindre, P. Sergent, J. Fort, J.B. Biaggi, J. Bompard, P. Descaves and J.J. Susini, who joined the ranks of subsequent far-right organizations. Not least, J.M. Le Pen himself upheld his support of 'French Algeria' with pride, and thanks to him, the colonialist legacy persisted within the party during his presidency. In 1985, the FN formed the Centre National des Combattants (CNC), its own veterans' association, that paraded during demonstrations and gave the embodied legacy of colonialism public visibility. The annual celebrations of the CNC provided a platform of exchange between former OAS figures and FN youth (ibid.: 397–98).

Algeria was also a point of connection between far-right nationalism and nationalist Catholicism, represented by people like Georges Sauge and Robert Martel. They interpreted the war as a crusade against communism and its Islamic allies. La Cité Catholique, and its periodical *Verbe*, was a network of militant Catholics and political reactionaries. G. Sauge set up the Centre d'Etudes Supérieures de Psychologie Sociale (CESPS) 'to instruct French army officers in the fight against Marxist subversion'. Officers of the army's *cinquièmes bureaux* welcomed his institution's legitimization of repressive methods of information-gathering (Shields 2007: 98–99).

As in other countries, in the face of leftist radicalism, an anti-democratic, anti-communist, racist, and here decidedly 'pro-French Algeria' association, the Fédération des Etudiants Nationalistes (FEN), was created in 1960 by François d'Orcival (pseudonym of Amaury de Chaunac-Lanzac) and Fabrice Laroche (pseudonym of Alain de Benoist, future ideologue of the Nouvelle Droite GRECE), in order to counter the growing Marxist influence within the UNEF (Union Nationale des Etudiants de France) and against the UNEF's support for negotiations with Algeria. The editorial team and contributors to its *Cahiers universitaires* prefigured some of the leading Nouvelle Droite intellectuals of the future. The FEN tried to take advantage of the war for its authoritarian project. In its 'Manifesto of the Class of 60', the FEN declared its rejection of a democratic conception of man 'which dragged a Bigeard down to the level of the lowest street-sweeper, a Pasteur to that of an illiterate from the Congo, and a mother to that of a prostitute' (ibid.: 95). At times it served as the student branch and a legal cover for the then banned Jeune Nation. Both were involved in OAS terrorism and both constituted training ground for a new generation of post-Vichy activists, like F. Duprat, A. Robert, P. Vial and J.G. Malliarakis, who would lead later organizations like Ordre Nouveau, the FN, the Parti des Forces Nouvelles and Groupement de recherche et d'études pour la civilisation européenne (GRECE). The FEN was banned in May 1958 and recreated in October, the same year as the Parti Nationaliste with its periodical *Jeune Nation* (ibid.: 95–97). The years 1954–62 were a transitional phase between the older generation and up-and-coming activists of the following decades. Just like Jeune Nation, the FEN served as political apprenticeship to some of the most important leading figures of the future.

The Algerian War caused a series of intellectual and political adaptations and modifications within the far-right register. This also concerned the status of nationalism within the far-right ideology. No doubt, the Algerian War, as well as the wider context of the Cold War and decolonization, hardened ultra-nationalism. After the loss of 'French Algeria', the meaning of French nationalism, until then based on territorial coordinates (Alsace-Lorraine, the empire, 'French Algeria'), had to be redefined. Some ideologues, of the FEN in many cases, put forth initial versions of a postcolonial nationalism focused on Europe: French identity, not territorial greatness, was defined in terms of European belonging and supremacism (the latter particularly strengthened by the Algerian War, conceived by Jeune Nation, for instance, as a threat to white Europe) (ibid.: 93–94).

M. Bardèche's *Qu'est-ce que le fascisme?* (1961) was a crucial moment, theorizing a new version of fascism that needed to distance itself from the errors of the interwar past. Against the mistakes of German and Italian fascism (their narrow nationalism that was devoid of a European or universal perspective, their persecution of Jews, their biological racism), Bardèche sought to rescue a timeless, superior fascist essence from political endeavours that aimed at reproducing the interwar heritage. He laid the ground for the Nouvelle Droite and, ultimately, for the electoral strategy of the FN. Interestingly, and hinting at divergences within the far-right camp, he articulated a different view of the Algerian War:

> The defendants [of French Algeria] had never stopped to question . . . whether Algerian nationalism might not itself lead to an Islamic 'fascist' state on the model of Nasser's Egypt, a useful new authoritarian force independent of both Washington and Moscow. 'While the communists immediately posed the Algerian problem in terms of the Communist International, the fascist groups did not for a moment think of posing it in terms of the Fascist International'. (Ibid.: 103, quoting Bardèche)

Simultaneously, Binet modified the racist argument about decolonization, highlighting the primary importance of keeping racially different population groups separate. Both were key arguments in later ideological developments:

> Bardèche's geopolitical and Binet's racist arguments for decolonization pointed the way towards a new anti-colonialism on the extreme right furnishing the rudiments of a rationale that would be elaborated some years later by the Nouvelle Droite. The issue at stake would no longer be French grandeur as measured by colonial power but French identity as defined through European kinship, western culture and racial specificity. This current of thought would dispense with the notions around which much of the debate over French Algeria had turned – 'integration' and 'assimilation' – to insist instead on the preservation of difference, and therefore distance, between ethno-cultural communities. (Ibid.: 104).

These arguments have persisted within the far right of both countries, France and Germany, until today. They inform the ideological core of the FN's and AfD's programmes (see the preceding chapter).

CHANGES IN POLITICAL STRATEGY: MOVING TOWARDS PARTY POLITICS

The loss of 'French Algeria' was also a major turning point in terms of political strategy. It marked the end of paramilitarism as a major organizational form. The Algerian experience had revealed that a direct assault on the regime could not secure political power, and that political activism could not succeed without broad popular acceptance and support. These lessons laid the basis for the later Nouvelle Droite strategy of achieving intellectual hegemony.

Europe-Action, launched in 1963 by D. Venner, former Jeune Nation member, founding member of FEN and author of *Pour une critique positive* (1961), contributed to redefining the far right's strategy post-Algeria. A coherent doctrine was needed and popular support had to be built. Europe-Action functioned as a think tank with its own publishing house, Editions Saint-Just, and bookshop, the Librairie de l'Amitié. Venner's FEN constituted its militant base. For three years, Europe-Action served as a platform of exchange between the former Jeune Nation, OAS and FEN militants, and other fascist-minded personalities (L. Rebatet, M. Bardèche, Vichyites like H. Coston, J. Ploncard d'Assac). Bardèche's *Qu'est-ce que le fascisme?* served as a starting point to promote a doctrine with the potential to unite the far right. Its nationalism had turned Europeanist or occidentalist, defending white heritage with the allure of a pseudo-scientific racism, supportive of segregationist regimes in Rhodesia and South Africa.[24] Europe-Action was committedly anti-Christian, and put forth an aristocratic, neo-pagan ethic free of bourgeois egalitarianism (ibid.: 117–23).

P. Sidos left Europe-Action in 1962 with others from the FEN, following disagreements with D. Venner, and launched Occident, which largely imitated the former Jeune Nation. F. Duprat, G. Longuet, A. Madelin, A. Robert and J.G. Malliarakis were amongst its most prominent members. In the name of the defence of the west, diverging from more recent developments within far-right strategy, Occident continued to promote street violence against left-wing students, PCF offices, migrant organizations and anti-colonialist actors. Its publication, *Occident-Université*, highlighted the 'principle of selection' as opposed to that of election, and articulated hierarchical, authoritarian, deeply anti-egalitarian visions of humanity that combined nationalism and social Darwinism. For Occident, it was 'manifestly clear that men are not equal' (quoted in ibid.: 140). Perplexed in the face of the events of May 1968, Occident, motivated by its anti-communism and by the amnesty granted to many 'French Algeria' diehards, ended up siding with state power against students and workers. In October 1968, after the bombing of a Maoist bookshop in Paris, Occident was the only far-right group that was banned by the government in this period – as compared to fourteen banned leftist groups. It was replaced by Ordre Nouveau (ibid.: 139–42).

Furthermore, the pursuit of electoralism took off from the 1960s onwards, a major rupture with the tradition of anti-parliamentarianism. Initially conceived as a think tank, from 1966 onwards Europe-Action developed the features of a political movement. In October 1964, it set up support committees (comprised of better educated students from Jeune Nation and FEN circles, from Biaggi's PPR and repatriated *pieds-noirs*[25]) to disseminate its journal. In the presidential elections of December 1965, Europe-Action supported the candidate Tixier-Vignancour. The last issue of its journal appeared at the end of 1966. The FEN also disintegrated towards the end of the 1960s (ibid.: 117–23). In the turn towards party politics, Ordre Nouveau played a mediating role (see below).

After the introduction of universal suffrage to elect the president following a referendum in October 1962, anchoring in the Constitution a new form of presidential politics, the change of strategy within the far right led to aspirations to the country's highest political office. J.M. Le Pen and his companions set up a Comité d'Initiative pour une Candidature Nationale (Committee to Initiate a National Candidacy). Participating in presidential elections, Le Pen would argue, 'provided an opportunity . . . to disseminate their message to the taxpayers' expense, to exploit the four hours of television and radio airtime allocated to each candidate, and ultimately to measure popular support for the nationalist cause. Scruples about playing the democratic game were outweighed by such pragmatic considerations' (ibid.: 125).

In November 1963, two years before the elections, J.L. Tixier-Vignanour announced that he would be the first far-right presidential candidate. A former Vichy official and an activist in the student section of Maurras Action Francaise, he had travelled to Spain as part of a parliamentary group in 1936 to congratulate Franco. He represented 'French Algeria' since he had defended OAS activists General Salan, Colonel Bastien-Thiry and others as a lawyer (ibid.: 114–16). He had been involved in various right-wing groups and had led his own short-lived Rassemblement National (RN) in 1954 (the same party name was adopted by M. Le Pen recently while renaming the FN). In addition, Tixier-Vignancour was J.M. Le Pen's daughter Marie-Caroline's godfather. Le Pen acted as secretary general and campaign manager of the Tixier-Vignancour Committee. The campaign was animated by a strong anti-Gaullist stance, accusing Gaullism of the loss of 'French Algeria' and the empire at large, of weakening the army, and of maintaining too close links with world communism (ibid.: 124–26). Against the immense expectations of his supporters, in December 1965, Tixier-Vignancour obtained only 5.2 per cent, i.e. 1.26 million, of the first-round votes. The chapter of 'French Algeria' was indeed over. This far-right vote coincided with the geography of the 'no' vote in the referendum of April 1962 on the Evian Agreements, and had a similar sociological profile as the Poujadist vote in 1956 (ibid.: 127–31).

At the beginning of 1966, Le Pen was excluded from the Tixier-Vignancour movement because of divergences over Algeria and because Tixier-Vignancour accused Le Pen of damaging his campaign through the release of audio recordings of NS speeches. Tixier-Vignancour converted his support committees into a new party, the Alliance Républicaine pour les Libertés et le Progrès (ARLP). Many younger supporters joined the OAS Métro-Jeunes network under P. Sergent, to become the Mouvement Jeune Révolution (MJR). Europe-Action and FEN, in turn, sought autonomy vis-à-vis Tixier-Vignancour and launched the Mouvement Nationaliste du Progrès (MNP) led by D. Venner in 1966. Another semi-secret organization existed behind the MNP, the Centre Nationaliste, under D. Venner's leadership. The Centre Nationaliste articulated diverse nationalist movements, with chosen members from Europe-Action and FEN. The MNP, as the political cover of the Centre Nationaliste, could count on existing organizational structures and an activist base as Europe-Action was integrated into it, as was the FEN in alliance the Algerian repatriate FER. The MNP further pursued the electoral strategy, accepting that in the contemporary context, it was the only political choice. In autumn 1966, the MNP set up the Rassemblement Européen de la Liberté (REL) as its electoral cover. The REL proposed 22 candidates in the March 1967 elections who received fewer than a total of 30,000 votes. (Ibid.: 136–38)

The 1970s were pioneering years of the current configuration of the French far right that directly reaches to the present – through the history of the FN on the one hand, and the Nouvelle Droite's efforts at building cultural and intellectual hegemony, a Europe-wide strategy, on the other hand. The year 1968 proved to be decisive for the development of far-right political and intellectual strategies faced with the influence of the political left in popular and youth culture. But their common grievance was not only the intellectual success of the left throughout the year and especially after May 1968 – the year when, fearing a communist take-over, the French government released all OAS prisoners. The dissolution of the Jeune Nation movement in May 1958, the dismantling of the OAS and the poor showing for extreme-right candidate J.L. Tixier-Vignancour in the presidential election of 1965 added to their frustration.

The year 1968 marked a 'watershed in the evolution of the French extreme right' (Shields 2007: 143). It led to major developments on the intellectual front, at a distance from street violence and electoral politics. The Nouvelle Droite aimed at metapolitics, i.e. at establishing hegemony at the level of ideas in order to prepare a political breakthrough based on broad popular support. Alain de Benoist, who had been active in the FEN, Europe-Action and the MNP, emerged as one of the chief ideologues. His thoughts were influenced by Antonio Gramsci, by the conservative revolution as a predecessor to NS ideology, and by C. Maurras. He became the head of GRECE, launched at the beginning of 1968 (i.e. before May 1968). In accordance with its intellectual ambition, GRECE maintained a publishing house (Copernic) and a series of journals (*Nouvelle Ecole*, edited by A. de Benoist, *Eléments pour la Civilisation Européenne, Etudes et Recherches* and *Nation Armée*, the last which was aimed at the armed forces). Its forty-member founding committee united academics and journalists, among them prominent figures from Europe-Action and the Centre Nationaliste, like A. de Benoist, J. Bruyas, G. Fournier, D. Gajas, R. Lemoine, A. Mallard, G. Schmeltz (alias P. Marcenet), J.C. Rivière, M. Rollet, J.C. Valla, D. Venner, P. Vial, J.M. Zagamé, L. Rebatet, M. Bardèche. Its self-representation as an innovative think tank required conscious avoidance of any overt connection with former fascist endeavours. However, according to Shields, contributions by A. de Benoist or D. Venner to GRECE's journals 'made it easy to trace the ideological lineage of the new movement' (ibid.: 146).

GRECE, against the discourse of the Judaeo-Christian tradition, focused on ancient pagan cultures and their integral, hierarchically organized communities, their bonds of blood and soil. Its major intellectual innovation was to abandon the explicit acceptance of natural or racial inequalities in favour of an emphasis on difference of cultures. As a consequence of this intellectual construction, those who 'destroyed ethnic communities' in the name of equality appeared to them as 'racists' or 'raciophobes' (ibid.: 150). GRECE declared its opposition to colonialism and demanded instead 'reciprocal decolonization', i.e. Europeans' right to preserve their own cultural heritage. However, the assumption behind the emphasis on difference was indeed that of hierarchy. L. Pauwels, one of Nouvelle Droite's leading ideologues and for a certain period even editor of the weekly *Le Figaro Magazine*,[26] expressed this rather crudely: 'different means unequal' (quoted in ibid.: 149).[27] Copernic's publication of Hans Eysenck's *L'inégalité de l'homme* or the collective book *Race et intelligence*, the prominence accorded to Galton, Chamberlain or Gobineau by the Nouvelle Droite, as well as its closeness to periodicals like *The Mankind Quarterly* in Britain or *Neue Anthropologie* in Germany, betrayed such talk. GRECE was also quite outspoken about its anti-democratic beliefs.[28]

The second important body of the Nouvelle Droite was the Club de l'Horloge, founded in 1974. As opposed to GRECE, it sought alliances with the broader right-wing spectrum, with the Gaullist and Giscardian parties; it favoured free-market economics, Catholic conservatism and supported NATO. Nevertheless, both think tanks agreed upon their anti-egalitarian, anti-communist and socio-biologist tendencies. The Nouvelle Droite lost momentum in the 1980s, following the victory of the Socialists in the presidential elections of 1981. From 1983 onwards, the successes of the FN took centre stage within the French far right.[29]

After the banning of Occident in late 1968, activist groups had proliferated, including the Fédération d'Action Nationale et Européenne (FANE, M. Frédriksen), Action Nationaliste (G. Malliarakis), MJR (P. Sergent), Pour une Jeune Europe or JE (P. Saint-Bertais), Jeunesses Patriotes et Sociales or JPS (R. Holeindre), Parti National Populaire PNP (R. Holeindre), L'Oeuvre Française (P. Sidos), and Groupe Union Droit (GUD), that quickly changed its name to Groupe d'Union et de Défense or Groupe Union Défense, and that preserved Occident's violent ethos. Ordre Nouveau, active between 1969 and 1973, was an imitation of Pino Rauti's Ordine Nuovo, confirming the particular appeal of Italian fascism as a model (Mammone 2008: 229). It emerged as a renewed attempt to gather far-right forces:

> The real impetus to 'democratize' would come from a less likely source, the self-styled 'revolutionary' movement Ordre Nouveau, which brought together a younger generation of right-wing radicals with the old guard of the collaborationist and Algérie Française extreme right. Ordre Nouveau applied to political strategy the renovation that Europe-Action and others had brought to ideology. It is examined as a crucial transition between the violent activism and anti-system ethos of its predecessors, Jeune Nation and Occident, and the electoralist vocation of its eventual successor, FN. (Shields 2007: 6)

Ordre Nouveau was formed after exchanges between major figures, like the former Poujadist and Tixierist militant, J.F. Galvaire; GUD leader A. Robert; former leading members of Occident, P. Asselin and F. Duprat; and the former Milicien and editor of *Minute*, F. Brigneau. Ordre Nouveau's national council comprised H. Charbonneau, another ex-Milicien; G. Jeantet, a former Cagoulard and Pétainist journalist; and P. Clémenti, an LVF veteran (ibid.: 159). The organization put forth a rather simplistic programme aimed at unity of a heterogeneous political landscape and launched a series of journals (*Pour un Ordre nouveau, Ordre nouveau, GUD-Occident Université, Jeune Ordre, Travail-Informations*). In June 1970, the majority of its members were university students, i.e. Ordre Nouveau also served as a body that handed down the far-right heritage to the next generation. Its electoral endeavours experienced very limited success. Some of its members took to the streets again in violent activism, setting up a paramilitary group on the basis of GUD with the aim of protecting citizens and ensuring law and order.

The June 1972 supplement of *Pour un Ordre Nouveau* publicized Ordre Nouveau's ambition to become a properly organized party in order to pursue the strategy of a national front in the 1973 elections. However, it was declared, 'only once it had attained a foothold through the democratic process would "all methods" be used to bring about the "popular nationalist revolution" which remained the openly avowed objective of Ordre Nouveau' (ibid.: 163). Similar to its model, the MSI, Ordre Nouveau also aimed at appealing to a larger centre-right constituency. As a consequence, again, the more radical members, especially within the ranks of GUD but also from Pour une Jeune Europe, left and joined Groupe Action Jeunesse (GAJ). Internal friction thus removed, based on the Ordre Nouveau, the Front National was founded in October 1972. This would have a lasting impact on the far-right landscape that remains with us till today. Shields concludes on the outlined continuities:

> While there was less innovation about the Nouvelle Droite and Ordre Nouveau than their names suggested, they represented separately what the FN would seek to combine: ideological renewal and electoral engagement. If this strategy failed to yield any but the most meagre results in the 1970s, it would be vindicated by the unprecedented success which the party would begin to enjoy in the 1980s. (Ibid.: 165)

The first central office of the newly founded FN comprised six members, among them Le Pen, the former OAS member R. Holeindre, and the former Waffen-SS and Ordre Nouveau member P. Bousquet, as well as Ordre Nouveau members F. Brigneau and A. Robert.

In the case of France, the long-term continuities from Vichy, through 'French Algeria', to the creation of the FN, are clearly discernible. Until the FN's foundation, a multiplicity of groups – paramilitary, political and ideological – existed that were strongly connected with one another. They overlapped not only in terms of shared values and ideas, but also in terms of actors. The recurring names of people who shaped this history after 1945 has highlighted this throughout this section. During the Algerian War as well, the French far right played an important role in French politics, in comparison with their sustained marginality on the German scene. The link with colonialism allowed them legitimacy and prominence above and beyond their discredited past, which also allowed them to draw in new activists and broaden their membership base. Some major FN electoral constituents trace their own legacy back to those years. In any case, irrespective of the recent attractiveness of the FN's programme to relatively new voters in a climate of political malaise, representational and ideological crisis, the outlined continuities, the handing down of experience from older to younger generations of leading cadres and activists, are a major explanatory factor in order to understand the party's survival and success. Yet, as in the German case, in the course of their post-war history, the French far right also had to adapt their organizational forms and ideological orientation to changing contexts. From post-war fascism through postcolonial far-right ideology, they developed into what I would characterize here again as post-fascism. Similar to the case of Germany, the representatives struggled with their major grievances (see the preceding chapter). This difficulty in reconstructing a credible narrative after the Holocaust is expressed by Sergent, who 'incidentally mentioned the "Algerian Holocaust" against French Algeria. This lays bare that the invocation of the OAS-legend also serves to downplay the NS-crimes during the second world war' (Renken 2006: 407). In both cases, 1968 proved to be a major point of self-conscious reorientation.

Digression on Geopolitics: Russian and Other Connections

The post-1945 history of the far right also highlighted its relevance within the Cold War geopolitical context. It is surprising, by the way, that geopolitical considerations do not figure more prominently within theories on interwar fascism – after all, this historical period remains unintelligible, for instance, without the outcome of the civil war in Spain, in which the geopolitical constellation and external actors were determining factors.

It seems that the Allied Clandestine Committee (ACC) held a last meeting in October 1990 in Brussels. Interestingly, authors who vehemently argue against Ganser's 'conspiracy theory' indicate that the official dissolution of Stay Behind was not really the end of the story.[30] This already leads to the last section of this chapter on external connections and the geopolitical significance of today's far-right scene. While such external support to the far right for geopolitical motives cannot explain its attractiveness to national voters, it is nevertheless an element necessary for understanding their success.

Russia has played a prominent role in strengthening the far right all over Europe.[31] The aim here is to outline the support that country has lent to Western European far-right actors. This obviously cuts short a much longer story about the Russian position within the international framework, starting from the constellation after the Second World War through the Cold War years – including at least Russia as a reference for anti-colonial struggles, the breakdown of the Soviet bloc and the situation since 1989, and the reconfiguration of global geopolitics between the US, the EU, Russia and China. To illustrate Russian attempts at creating alliances with the European far right does not cover the full background to the story, which would go beyond the scope of this chapter.

Vladimir Putin has become a leading figure of identification for activists from diverse political strands. He has been marketed as a strong, masculinist, national leader in a decadent world, who managed to revive Russian pride after the years of US domination following the end of the Soviet Union. But his appeal reaches far beyond the national domain. Putin also appears today as one who protects European values and successfully opposes US domination worldwide:

> Since at least the middle of the 2000s, 'traditional values' have become the national idea of Russia, deployed internally as a populist ideology to unify Russia, and externally as a kind of exceptionalist-messianic pose to present Russia as the saviour of Europe and the leading defender of true European values (defined through the traditional heteronormative family). . . . Thus the anti-gender position is at the heart of Russia's self-identification in opposition to the decadent West as well as at the heart of Russia's geopolitical strategy to unite like-minded traditionalist forces behind Russia (thereby both gaining international status as a world leader and destabilizing the EU by supporting right-wing dissenting factions in Europe). (Moss 2017: 195)

As opposed to Western Europe, where far-right positions have gained strength but remain non-majoritarian, 'in Russia, the government, the ruling party, the oligarchs, the state church, the state educational and scholarly establishment and the media all speak with one voice' (ibid.: 208–09).

Next to Putin, Konstantin Malofejew, a monarchist Russian oligarch close to the Kremlin and a committed Christian, who uses his media conglomerate to publicize Russian interests, has played a key role in funding networks and events that connect far-right action across Europe, besides funding the war in Ukraine. He has publicly supported the AfD because he wants 'Germany to stay German' rather than resembling an Americanized state 'without traditions and national particularities' (Fromm 2016). Nikolay Shlyamin leads the youth league of the all-Russian National Front (ONF) presided over by Putin himself, a federation of more than 2,000 Russian organizations, among them the ruling United Russia Party. He counts as the direct representative of the Kremlin's interests and maintains connections with the far right across Europe. Finally, Alexander Dugin, philosopher and from 2008 to 2013 head of Department of Sociology of International Relations in the Sociological Faculty of Moscow State University, the State Duma's adviser for foreign affairs, is the single most important intellectual supporting their moves. He is also editor-in-chief of Malofejew's TV channel and an influential voice through his media empire (ibid.). He launched the Eurasian Movement[32] in 2001 (Petsinis 2014: 2).

Dugin's Eurasian perspective valorizes the far-right parties all over Europe[33] as the true alternative to the existing state of Europe as being artificially divided from its natural ally, Russia. These political projects appear to him as 'the second Europe, the Europe of European peoples', and of tradition and values. Apart from their rejection of the EU, they share certain fundamental values: the defence of white and Christian Europe, and the rejection of liberal, capitalist democracy (Fromm 2016; Moss 2017). The defence of traditional gender roles plays a particularly important role. The corresponding 'traditional values' are fully endorsed not only by specific parties or movements on the ground, but by the Russian state, actors in the State Duma and Petersburg's Legislative Assembly, the Orthodox Church, the media and public universities including the Russian Academy of Sciences, where the sociology faculty of Moscow State University plays a leading role.[34] It also circulates internationally through the Paris-based Institute of Democracy and Cooperation or the World Congress of Families. Their mobilizations are funded by Russian oligarchs (Moss 2017: 200).

The Russian policy of alliance with far-right actors has taken concrete shape at certain moments. In preparing a referendum for the annexation of Crimea that did not correspond to international or OECD standards, far-right parties – some far-left parties as well, such as the Communist Party of Greece – from various European countries sent international observers that lent credibility to the event. In the Czech Republic, the People's Republic of Donetsk, i.e. the pro-Russian parts of Eastern Ukraine occupied by Russia, opened up a fictitious embassy in September 2016, an event that was largely publicized and lent legitimacy to an exclave that does not enjoy international recognition. Within national parliaments as well as in the European Parliament, far-right MPs support Putin's politics. In 2016, fifteen out of twenty-four far-right parties across Europe openly defended Russian positions (Fromm 2016).

Apart from particularly strong links with the Eastern European far right, the FN is a prominent example of Russia's influence. The bank of a close collaborator of Putin granted credit to the tune of 10 million for the FN's electoral campaign, as openly admitted by the FN treasurer Wallerand de Saint-Just (ibid.). The AfD is also favoured as a Russian ally in Germany, important among other things to reduce western economic sanctions against Russia. Höcke clearly acted in favour of Russia's foreign politics when he declared that sanctions on Russia were not in German interest. Even the supposedly spontaneous Pegida movement declared it favoured a good relationship with Russia and an end to economic sanctions, and called upon Putin to help them against Islamization of the Occident. Connections at the intellectual level have also been enhanced by the creation of the Centre of Continental Collaboration (Zentrum für Kontinentale Zusammenarbeit) in Munich, a think tank and centre where key Russian actors interact with AfD politicians and German New Right thinkers (Gensing and Stöber 2016). Beyond financial, political and intellectual influence, Russia has also built up considerable militia structures, in particular in Eastern European countries, that are connected with far-right structures. These paramilitary groups, aimed first and foremost against immigration, also serve Russian political interests, such as the attack on demonstrators who criticized Putin by the Bulgarian militia close to the Ataka Party. Apparently, former military staff lead the militarization of the far-right scene. According to estimates, several tens of thousands have joined such armed militias in Bulgaria, Slovakia, the Czech Republic and Hungary (Fromm 2016).

The ideological, political, financial and even military influence of key Russian actors on the European far-right scene is thus evident. In the meantime, Russian initiatives to strengthen the far right have entered into competition with US-based think tanks who have taken up the challenge (Rizzi, Polezhaeva and Chuang 2019). Steve Bannon, former editor of the alt-right platform Breitbart News and former advisor of Trump, has been campaigning across Western Europe after he left the White House, meeting AfD politicians and making an appearance at an FN party convention. The creation of a major US-funded think tank with headquarters in Brussels, initiated in July 2018, is meant to compete with George Soros's Open Society Foundation (Alexander 2018; Doward 2018). The aim, we can assume, is also to make an influence felt against Russia's grip on the scene, denouncing, for instance, Merkel's deal regarding Gazprom. European right-wing structures are increasingly becoming a battlefield for several foreign forces.

Given the sensitive nature of the topic and the fact that it is hard to gather reliable sources and more systematic information, it is difficult to provide a solid assessment of what all this means. A much more consistent research effort would be needed to be able to formulate a thorough third line of argument around the current strength of the far right with regard to its geopolitical instrumentalization.

Conclusion: The Significance of Deep Roots

France and Germany started out from different situations at the turning point of 1945. Both have developed a continuous far-right scene. Today, this resembles interwar fascism only to a certain extent. In Germany, the far right is characterized by its opaque, networked nature and the late success of its political strategy. The German scene has also been particularly struggling with discrediting the NS past. In France, the colonial moment allowed for an early resurgence as a relevant political factor and for overcoming the discredited Vichy past. Ironically, the OAS even inscribed itself in the tradition of the Resistance. The loss of 'French Algeria' has led to postcolonial adaptations of the far-right intellectual baggage. Since the 1970s, the political effort was more concentrated in one single party that has gained much bigger achievements in recent years. Both countries host active ideological production that has adapted classical fascism to changing contexts. It has also led a continuous reflection about how to handle the heritage of historical fascism, since the Second World War and the Holocaust appear as a shared major grievance in both cases. The result is best characterized as post-fascism. The Neue Rechte and the Nouvelle Droite are engaged in an exchange of ideas and have common reference points, such as, ironically, Gramsci's concept of hegemony, the German conservative revolution, Italian fascism, and more recently, Russian and US ideological contributions.

The public image and political strategies of the far right have changed considerably in recent years.[35] Old-style post-war Nazis like the NPD have not been very successful. It is obvious, however, that parts of the NPD have fused with fractions of the currently successful AfD. Similarly, some of Europe's far-right parties today defend Jews and Israel, homosexuals and feminism, laicity and direct democracy. Jacquemain concludes that they therefore reject the legacy of fascism and the 1970s neo-fascism (Jacquemain and Claisse 2012: 21). We have shown that this public rejection is often part of a determined communication strategy. We have also seen that most of these concepts are filled with a particular meaning that fits rather smoothly into classical ideological constructs: Israel and the Jews today are interesting as allies against Muslims and jihadism and a positive reference underlines the distancing from the NS past; homosexuality is not a problem but unmanliness is; feminism and laicity are brought into position against Muslims; and direct democracy implies to free the direct link between a leader and its people from institutional hurdles, constitutional guarantees, the EU and the international framework. Today, they even declare they are not racists, meaning they are defending the white race against all sorts of perceived threats. However, in seizing these discourses, the dividing line between the far right and the classical conservative right, and even parts of the left, has become more permeable.

My explanation of why the far right has been successful in recent years in both countries is twofold, with an indication of a third explanatory element. First, their programmes, adapted to the current context, have been appealing to specific population groups as a result of representative and ideological crisis. A broader trend is observable that indicates disaffiliation of parts of the traditional centre-left and centre-right votes due to the changing faces of the traditional broad-based parties. The far right has managed to put forth credible representative claim-making. Qualitative analyses in the case of France give an idea of how their programmes based on exclusive solidarity, national priority, and law and order resonate with specific population groups in terms of their professional experience, housing situation or anxieties about the education of their children. The reaction to several cases of sexual aggression in recent years in Germany also indicates the enormous mobilizing potential of the call to defend white women against dark strangers. The fact that gender is problematic to them is also evident from the numerous 'anti-gender' mobilizations where the far right meets with more conservative, often faith-based movements (Kuhar and Paternotte 2017). If the assumption of a crisis context cannot explain fully its current strength, the far right has excelled in conjuring moral panics and in proposing solutions to crisis that imply attacking the achievements of earlier deviants' struggles, as we have outlined them in volume I. Their solutions are oftentimes a reaction to emancipation. In this sense, 1968 plays a crucial role as a major grievance. The far right could thus capitalize on a situation of an unattractive left that has abandoned reference to its former working-class constituencies – the losses of the French PCF throughout the post-war period being still superior to the losses of the German SPD after Schröder and his Agenda 2010. This situation combines with the retreat of the post-war welfare state from specific areas, in particular social housing, including for refugees. The understanding of the attractiveness of the far-right programme to relatively new, broadened constituencies is the first part of the answer. An argument around the far right in Europe as essentially a response to crisis remains unsatisfactory, however.

Secondly, I have argued here that despite obvious differences in official rhetoric and style, it is only through existing long-term continuities that we can understand the current resurgence, its strength and transformations. I argue that continuity is another key to understanding. This does not mean to assume an undistorted transmission of an ideological heritage from the interwar years into a completely different context. But the far right has sustained organizational structures that offered spaces for socialization and expression of authoritarian restorationist visions, and allowed a minority of interwar fascists and French colonialists some form of recognition as well as career opportunities. This continuous presence, with changing faces and slogans at times, has allowed fragments of their core constituencies to draw lineages to the past. The fact that in the course of socio-economic transformations at the societal level, in times of crisis, of (however perceived) political or economic hardship or frustrations, new supporters and members joined those movements, organizations and parties, i.e. that new constituencies found their practical, concrete, real-world concerns met by far-right party programmes, has only been possible because of long-term trends. Tracing these long-term continuities does not mean losing oneself in chasing spectres of the past[36] in the face of the current strength of a far right that does not resemble its predecessors any more, and that deals with the historical past in self-conscious ways, as a candidate for power. Searching for the deep roots, instead, is necessary to understand how within changing contexts, and with adapted discursive outfits, a profoundly authoritarian restorationist agenda has been carried through time and adapted to changing circumstances by a small number of committed actors. The presence of far-right agendas today at the intellectual, movement and party levels, whose offer appears attractive for a variety of reasons to a variety of different constituencies, voters and members, has only been possible through their activism and commitment.

A third explanatory element has only been sketched briefly due to lack of more systematic material, and because the broader context could not be developed fully within the scope of this chapter. Concerning the German case, at least for the immediate post-war decades, the issue appears quite clearly though: in fact some of those political actors have been supported, at times, by powerful state and international agencies, as part of much broader geopolitical considerations. This has ensured funding, job opportunities and recognition of their competency.

All this has happened in a contemporary context where the state and capitalism have taken on more authoritarian shapes. This contribution would therefore need to be embedded in a broader perspective on rising authoritarianism at different levels (Hanafi 2019). While the state is developing ever-new forms of surveillance and repression, it simultaneously pursues discursive shifts towards defining parts of humanity as superfluous and eliminable, or at least not worthy of being rescued, and criminalizing those who uphold emancipatory views of inclusive solidarity. The far right, at the same time, plays the liberal party-based game of representative democracy and manages to impose its agenda on ever-bigger parts of the political spectrum.

NOTES

[1] According to the Federal Expellee Law, *Heimatvertriebene* referred to around 12–16 million German citizens and ethnic Germans who left former eastern territories of Germany lost during the war, including former Austria–Hungary, Estonia, Latvia, Lithuania and Poland, and that now formed part, in the majority, of Poland and the Soviet Union according to post-war international dispositions (Vereinigung Demokratischer Juristen [Association of Democratic Jurists] 1963). However, the status of 'expellees', of those who have lost *Heimat*, has also often been instrumentalized to lend legitimacy to former members of the NS-occupying forces in Eastern Europe and to present them as victims of the course of events.

[2] Interestingly, towards the end of the 1960s, already when the party had some electoral success, 'the social structure of NPD-voters . . . had converged to the society of the Federal Republic: its constituency was socially diversified' (Schmollinger 1986c: 1981). The NPD was particularly strong in economically weak regions amongst all professional groups, more so amongst professional groups affected by economic crisis. Its membership, however, had a specific profile, featuring in particular members of the old and new middle class and self-employed. One-third of the members were workers, more than half of them working in medium-sized enterprises that were especially affected by the economic crisis. The more typical profile of party members was therefore men in middle-class occupations and who had grown up under National Socialism.

[3] More precisely, 'structural factors . . . have been building up since the 1990s in the context of neoliberal economic restructuring. In particular, the decision of the then SPD and Green party government to severely retrench the welfare state (the so-called "Hartz reforms" after 2002) produced large-scale demoralization of the centre-left SPD's electoral base. This triggered in turn a permanent disengagement of disadvantaged milieus from the political system. Notably, the SPD lost half of its electoral support after the Hartz reforms and has never since been able to recover' (Dostal 2015: 530).

[4] Current member parties, apart from the NPD, are the Belgian Flanders Identitists Nation Movement, the Czech Workers' Party of Social Justice, the Greek Golden Dawn, the Italian

Forza Nuova, the Romanian New Right, the Slovak Kotleba and the Spanish National Democracy.

5 *NPD: Die socialize heimatpartei*, available at https://npd.de/, accessed 10 March 2018.

6 The following is based on Müller and Mueller (2015).

7 This was the case with Ebrulf Zuber, former Waffen-SS, head of division in the SS-Hauptamt in 1942, fighting in 1944 in a tank regiment. In 1947, while still in US internment, he was recruited into the Gehlen organization, undertook a brilliant career and received an award for forty years in service as early as 1980, since his activity for Reichsarbeitsdienst and Waffen-SS were counted as well (Rass 2014: 26 ff.). It was also the case of Josef Heinrich Reiser, member of the NSDAP since 1932, former Gestapo, then chief of the security police in occupied France where he led the unit 'defence against communism-Marxism' as SS-Hauptsturmführer and in 1942–43 headed the special command 'Red Orchestra'. Released from French war captivity, he joined the Gehlen organization in 1951 as an undercover agent, responsible among others with investigations on the residues of the 'Red Orchestra'.

8 'Until 1947, new staff was not examined [in terms of their biography and past], since everybody knew one another anyways' (Sälter 2014: 41).

9 See also Hechelhammer (2014).

10 It is somehow difficult, at this stage, to write about Gladio. Ganser, the author of a PhD thesis on the complete European Stay Behind network (2005), has been harshly accused of promoting conspiracy theories (Hof 2009; Kaplan 2006; Riste 2014; Cogan 2007). I try, in this section, to review only those points on which nobody in this fierce debate seems to fundamentally disagree. All authors agree that Stay Behind structures existed all over Western Europe and that they existed outside of parliamentary control (Hof 2009). Their origins, developments, outlook, size and staffing differed from country to country (Riste 2014). None of them denies that the fear of Soviet aggression or a communist takeover was a common motivation; that they were all, at some point, in contact with NATO through a committee with changing names (Coordination and Planning Committee, Allied Clandestine Committee) located within SHAPE (Supreme Headquarters Allied Powers Europe). It is the chronology as well as the exact nature of the link with NATO that is disputed.

11 The new regime tried to present military defeat as a victory: 'Four months on from total military and political collapse, France had contrived its salvation as self-appointed partner in the Nazi project of constructing a "new European order"' (Shields 2007: 16).

12 'The "National Revolution" ushered in by Pétain owed much to a French right-wing tradition of anti-parliamentarism dating back to the Revolution of 1789. It repudiated the liberal, humanistic rationalism of the Enlightenment and preached a reactionary, authoritarian nationalism. It drew inspiration in particular from the ideas of Charles Maurras and his Action Française movement, with their sustained assault on the democratic values and institutions of the Third Republic as inimical to the culture, traditions and interests of the French nation' Shields (2007: 16). Furthermore, 'The National Revolution, in sum, was to restore order and greatness to France, promoting national unity to the detriment of individualism, authority to that of liberalism, hierarchy to that of equality' (ibid.: 22–23).

13 See also Foessel (2019).

14 'The transformation of Poujadism over this period [1953–57] can be seen as a gradual slippage from anti-fiscalism to anti-parliamentarism, from patriotism with strong Republican resonance to a narrow nationalism with xenophobic tones, from anti-capitalism to anti-Semitism' (Shields 2007: 83).

[15] For a brief collection and comparison of the number of deaths as estimated by different reports and studies, see Riché (2012).

[16] The section on the war in Algeria is based essentially on Renken (2006).

[17] '. . . the much conjured "French Algeria", *l'Algérie française*, was as French, as South Africa under apartheid was white. *L'Algérie française* was no reality. It was a political slogan that the representatives of big *colons* used to ideologically bind the mass of *pieds-noirs* and to demoralize the Muslim majority' (Renken, 2006: 47).

[18] An organizational network representing their interests as veterans had developed already before the end of the war, having them accused of treason by radical defendants of 'French Algeria'. The FNACA was to become their most important representative structure. In its early years, it seemed to be under the influence of the Communist Party, supporting the independence of Algeria and demanding the end of the war. Later on, it became a more depoliticized body of lobbying for the lower rank veterans' interests, such as reparation payments.

[19] Electoral analyses of the 1984 European elections showed that the support of *rapatriés* associations to Le Pen pushed the left out of the position of leading opposition in several southern cities, like Toulon or Aix-en-Provence. Le Pen remained the leading figure of 'French Algeria' (Renken 2006: 392–97).

[20] Since many *pieds-noirs* were of Spanish immigrant origin, 50,000 *pieds-noirs* also took refuge on the Iberian Peninsula.

[21] For biographic accounts on many OAS members, see Harrison (1989).

[22] On the 'Dolchstoßlegende', i.e. stab-in-the-back story of National Socialism, see Keim (2014).

[23] Some of those most committed to 'French Algeria', like P. Arrighi, P. Sergent, J.P. Reveau, P. Descaves, E. Frédéric-Dupont, R. Holeindre were among the thirty-five FN deputies elected to the National Assembly in the 1986 legislative elections (Shields 2007: 113). In the 1992 elections still, several former members of the OAS headed electoral lists in various places (Stora 1997: 17–19).

[24] 'The nationalism of Europe-Action was not geopolitical but racial. It proclaimed "race" to be "the new patrie", the "patrie of the flesh" which should be defended with an animal-like ferocity.' Furthermore: 'It advocated racial segregation and denounced miscegenation as "genetic suicide"; it supported colonialism (synonymous with "civilization") and decried "universalism" and "globalization"' (Shields 2007: 122).

[25] There were over 200 Algerian repatriate associations in the mid-1960s. The most solid amongst them, the Fédération des Etudiants Réfugiés (FER), was captured by Europe-Action and FEN.

[26] Launched in 1978 by the renowned daily newspaper *Le Figaro*; see Mammone (2008).

[27] 'As Maurice Bardèche approvingly observed, the "substitution of the idea of culture for the idea of heredity" allowed the right finally "to recognize, and even to assert, the diversity of races" while at the same time "being able even to call itself anti-racist". As Bardèche also observed, this was more a change of style than a change of substance' (Shields 2007: 149).

[28] 'There should be leaders and led. The error in liberal democracies, according to GRECE, was that these leaders should emerge through popular election, with all the arbitrary results and distortions to which this gave rise. The only sure means of appointing the best to lead was to apply scientific criteria free of arbitrariness, opportunism and corruption. Therein lay the role of biology and educational psychology for GRECE' (ibid.: 152).

[29] Nevertheless, years later, the initial aim of achieving intellectual hegemony seemed to be

succeeding: Sarkozy during his presidency (2007–12), although officially upholding the 'cordon sanitaire', nearly doubled the FN on its right with a discourse that was 'a blueprint' of the FN's. During his time as Minister of the Interior already, Sarkozy had introduced a compulsory 'social integration contract' for immigrants, obliging them among others to follow educational measures to learn Republican values such as *laicité* (Zúquete 2008). His campaign based on immigration and security issues allowed him to capture part of Le Pen's electorate.

[30] More than that, some even consider that the concept is again timely in the face of the recent moves of Russia: 'Even after the end of the Cold War and the dissolution of the Soviet Union, some officials were concerned that cashing in a "peace dividend" might be premature. In 2014, those concerns no longer seem fanciful. Russian incursions into Georgia in 2008, Russia's occupation and annexation of Crimea in March 2014, and Moscow's central role in fomenting violent rebellion in eastern Ukraine after the annexation of Crimea have sparked grave anxiety among some new NATO members, especially Poland and the Baltic countries, which want to strengthen allied defenses against Russian military power and expansionist moves. In effect, those states now feel the need for some of the same elements of reassurance that gave rise to the Stay Behind networks of the Cold War' (Riste 2014: 58–59). Or elsewhere: 'Given the specter of Russian irredentism in Eastern Europe, threatened countries such as Estonia, Latvia, Lithuania, Moldova, Georgia, and even Kazakhstan must reevaluate their national defence strategies for their ability to conduct resistance or unconventional warfare on all or parts of their sovereign territory. Historical analysis can inform this process. Unsurprisingly, the Russian military draws upon its historical experience in the Russian Civil War and Soviet Cold War for the components of its hybrid warfare model. Similarly, at-risk states can review the Cold War period and, through the careful study and analysis of appropriate historical resistance and unconventional warfare cases, can assess previously used concepts for possible adaptation, application, and integration into a national resistance strategy' (Stringer 2017: 112).

[31] The following is largely based on the documentary *Putin's völkische Freunde* (Fromm 2016).

[32] In his 1997 publication *Principles of Geopolitics*, he developed a foreign policy doctrine shaped by cultural essentialism and historical revisionism as the basis of his Eurasian vision. His is not a strictly statist approach but he aims at embedding Eurasianism within a 'political infrastructure that goes beyond the role of states as the main actors in international politics' (Petsinis 2014: 3). This builds on a fundamental distinction between continental Europe (Russian, Eurasian), the Atlantic powers (Western, US, NATO) and the 'Arab/Islamic' sphere in what sounds like a repetition of Huntington's 1996 *Clash of Civilizations*. In 2012, he published his *Fourth Political Theory* in which he aims at establishing the foundations of a fourth integrative ideology beyond communism, fascism and liberalism. Dugin is careful not to equate Eurasianism with any imperialist notion of 'Greater Russia' but conceives of it as a transnational, inclusionary mosaic of national identities that coexist with Russia.

[33] Dugin 'has often acknowledged he maintains close connections with the leaders of Jobbik (Gábor Vona), Ataka (Volen Siderov) and Golden Dawn (Nikolaos Michaloliakios). . . . He regards such parties as a potential vanguard or "fellow-travellers" in the European revolution against the Atlantic imperium' (Petsinis 2014: 6). What unites them politically is their hard Euroscepticism: 'Most importantly, the Russian thinker views the EU as a mere instrument through which Atlanticism promotes its geopolitical interests within the European space' (ibid.: 7–8).

[34] 'Moscow State University's Faculty of Sociology is home to several prominent pro-"traditional

family" scholars, and its psychologists have helped define "propaganda of non-traditional sexuality". . . . One of the chief ideologues of the Russian attempt to re-establish a bipolar world is Alexander Dugin, who was described at the time of the invasion of Crimea as "Putin's Brain". . . . Dugin was head of the Department of Sociology of International relations at the Sociology Faculty of Moscow State University until he was relieved of his position for saying that the way to deal with Ukraine was to "kill, kill, kill"' (Moss 2017: 200–01).

[35] The turnaround is perhaps most evident again in the Italian case. G. Fini, former coalition partner of Berlusconi, declared in 1994 still that Mussolini was the most important man of Italian twentieth-century history. Soon afterwards, his MSI has transformed into Alleanza nazionale, and has abandoned its openly fascist lineage. Mussolini's daughter, one of the MSI's key figures, left the party (Jacquemain and Claisse 2012: 19–20).

[36] 'In order to face this evolution, and not to find ourselves helpless in front of an adversary who has moved while we were still chasing their historical spectres, it is urgent to update our analytical framework' (Jacquemain and Claisse 2012: 17; translated by the author).

Conclusion

Since 2008, the state has returned in earnest, trying to regulate and channel human action. The very institution that is supposed to have weakened through globalization's flows is back in the sociological and analytical frame. The belief in the market's invisible hand needed the return of a more determined fist. Yet, this was not about a transition or a more social-democratic dispensation. The financial meltdown necessitated an intervention but, contrary to popular opinion, it was in the main to save the market's errant institutions (the banks) to start with. It also moved to forge new forms of cooperative interconnection: the G7, G20, BRICS. It was in China that such an intervention was uncontested, where the state spent to grow and increase aggregate demand, knowing full well that its banks held the world economy together.

The pandemic in turn has given the institution of the state more than fists and teeth. It has also handed over all the technological and surveillance functions possible in this world 'out of joint'. These technologies were refined over the war on terror and over forms of surveillance around refugee and migrant 'mobilities', as Trimikliniotis has described the phenomena in his chapter. Such panopticons and since the invention of mega spying acoustic devices, such 'pan-autica' as well, have been put in the service of Covid-19 responses, tracking movements and tracing interlocking patterns of behaviour that might or might not lead towards authoritarianism beyond the temporary declarations of states of exception.

In tandem, the very social movements (against neoliberal globalization) that clustered around the World Social Forum have been on the decline since. There was a high point during the Mumbai moment and a low during the Nairobi moment that followed. The funding was to run short of aspirations and the energies were quite dissipated.

The fiscal turbulence did not hamper social protest and new movement activity. The way power elites responded to the 2008 meltdown unleashed new forms of discontent and people were once again on the streets everywhere, from China to Tunisia and from South Africa to France. Taken in by the World Social Forum euphoria, Michael Hardt (2002) tried to articulate what was 'new' in the new movements: they owed their uniqueness to the new tech-based network logic of the system that facilitated new forms of horizontal communication. Yet, he warned at the same time, however interconnected, their struggles were different, unique and 'untranslatable'. Their emerging imagined community had to be diverse.

This remains rather abstract because it does not go deep enough to explain what happens within such networking processes. Both gestures (read also symbolic figurations) and methodologies of mobilization have been more than transferable despite the limits of language and/or translation. Whereas in the past, people had to follow physical tracts to visit and learn from sites of action, write about it and send it back 'home', or attend an international event that highlighted certain issues that demanded solidarity, the mix between imagery and content move fast. As was emphasized in the chapter 'Students and Youth Defiance', gestures and methods hopped from locale to locale and hopped over borders and barricades. So, a striking workforce in Pretoria in South Africa occupies a shop floor, wears mujahideen-like djellaba, fashions wooden AK-47s and puts on trial-discarded mannequins – all elements defining a radical gesture: an assemblage of images from afar, all mobilized for a local issue. The fall of the Rhodes statue in Cape Town ignites multiple attacks on statues elsewhere. It would be a remarkable study to gauge which symbolic figurations travel and which do not.

Furthermore, similar crises in one locale solicit different responses: a young woman from an artisanal family in Cape Town may find answers to her alienation and a sense of belonging by joining the ISI Khalifate or, like her cousin, from joining a grassroots women's movement with manifold links to global feminist-inspired networks. You could find also in South Africa left movements advocating compliance to Covid regulations, whereas right-leaning movements advocating defiance against compliance and, even if Black, circulating white supremacist/patriotic views from the USA. Finally, as one industrial worker joins pogroms against foreigners, another forms coalitions to protect them.

The sociological vignettes presented here throw some light on which defiant narratives and dispositions propel social action down the years, despite dominant institutional discourses and ideologies. The fact that 150 million workers put down tools in January 2019 in India, involving ten trade union centres and other federations in the manufacturing, mining, energy, transportation, banking, public services and construction sectors, alongside farmworkers who have been marching in their tens of thousands since 2018, signifies troves of defiance in the formal economy of India, whose very existence is in the main without formal norms of employment. The fact, too, that there is a large network involving labour federations of the South (SIGTUR, or the Southern Initiative on Globalization and Trade Union Rights, which includes Argentinian, Brazilian, South African, Filipino, Indonesian, Indian and Australian trade unions) means that the older forms survive alongside new associations of precarious and variegated work. The fact that the pandemic has amplified care work and large swathes of reproductive women-led care activity has brought about new tropes of defiance.

This volume is not a departure from our first one but rather an 'enhancement'. Our discomfort with the accepted sociological canon was aired in the first volume. What these vignettes do is amplify the points about this peculiar entanglement that has produced what we mis-name as modern or postmodern, colonial or post-colonial phases. Whereas we dealt explicitly with Durkheim, Weber and Foucault in the first volume, we did not focus on the enduring influence of Karl Marx and strands of Marxism in our work around the dynamics of a capitalist economy and its consequences on social life. As Sumangala Damodaran traces in the first essay, although in theory, capital ought to have been independent of social categories of race, gender, caste, religion or ethnicity, capitalism has utilized any social derogation possible, including slavery and neo-bondage, to achieve its short- and long-term goals. It is precisely extensive struggles for autonomy, dignity and freedom by working people that have altered the balance of power in relations of production everywhere. The precarity that followed market fundamentalism has been a new challenge and a terrain of new struggles.

Adjacent to this has been Immanuel Wallerstein's work on the world system and his contention that the contemporary world is out of joint; indeed, the last crisis possible in a capitalist world system, plummeting into a series of disruptions that are bound to lead to a new systemic configuration. Whereas we are conscious of the manifold crises in institutions and communities, in the relationship to our very eco-habitat and the discontent they have produced, a transition to something new is hardly detectable despite a move towards a multipolar world system, as the USA is losing the capacity to be the hegemon after the Soviet world collapsed.

Central to the dystopian view is the work of Giorgio Agamben: the erosion of democracy through the continuous creation of states of exception as a response to security threats, wars, refugeedom and migrations, and now viruses, and the need to control miasmic deviants. Such processes are enhanced by the democratic trust of authoritarian/populist movements and the removal of life-and-death decisions from the public sphere. Such processes have been reducing our species into a zoonotic entity – in his words, a 'bare life'. Like in Wallerstein's case, there is much to observe through the idea of a 'state of exemption' and to refine our analytical prowess about what and how power is exercised, but the entire volume points another way. Between deviance and defiance there would be creative forms of agency in and through and despite social systems.

Our reading of the entanglement that produced the 'contemporary' has been influenced by a contrary reading of the very idea of 'progress' – since Aime Cesaire's and Edouard Glissant's works, there has been no innocent reading of that entanglement. European foraging, settlement and colonization, so absent in the sociological canon, was a tremendous sociocultural disruption that haunted everything from migration to gang life, from inclusion to exclusion, from wealth to poverty, inequality to famine. It affected the rise of major national sentiments in the university systems of the colonial world as Ari Sitas and others show in the chapter on youth defiance, the symbolic acts of prisoners in and through apartheid South Africa as Javier Perez has been outlining, and the everyday imaginaries of the mobile communities of the new migrants. It touches on the character of the refugee dissensus that Trimikliniotis is warning us about, and animates the rise of movements of authoritative restoration in France and Germany as Wiebke Keim makes clear in her two chapters. Similarly, Amrita Pande takes inspiration from Gayatri Chatterjee to wade into the thin line between intimate labour and the work and representation of women as loose and deviant on both sides of the Indian Ocean. It is a panoramic view from the Mughal courts to colonial India, from the Basotho Highlands to the outskirts of the mining camps of the Witwatersrand where beer-brewing was to mutate into the famed shebeen queens of the high apartheid period.

We offered here four sociological vignettes to amplify what had been elaborated in our first volume, *Gauging and Engaging Deviance, 1600–2000* (Sitas *et al.* 2014). We started work on a second volume by trying to move our accounts from deviance to a concern about scripts of defiance: the many ways through which subaltern people, castes and classes construct cultural formations and articulate defiant ideas. Such ideas and scripts of defiance have not been dominant; they were and continue to be, in the words of Ari Sitas, ideomorphic. They become part and parcel of a counter-habitus that subsists despite systems of domination.

There were two enormous challenges that haunted us: one, that from cardinal points of the planet the general disquiet was being translated into an enormous movement of authoritative and authoritarian restoration, amplifying crises and panics and demanding decisive forms of action that had the echoes of past forms of fascism. So, we started wondering, what were the continuities and departures from the past? We hope we have provided some ideas.

No matter what our differences from such diverse parts of the planet, we can agree that the promise of sociology was to explicate an unequal, interconnected, patterned and evolving sociality. It was accepted within the disciplinary repertoire of institutions because it was to explicate, to predict, to understand in order to control or channel deviant behaviour. Can it shift out of this carapace so that it may explicate in order to facilitate human flourishing? We may disagree about what such flourishing might mean, but the rub would be there: critically engaging such differences in order to make what is potential become actual.

In presenting these vignettes, we understand how dispositions are structured by both institutional and socializing pressures, but also by 'experiential' dimensions. Pressures and socializations might lead one sister towards the right, the khalifate, and another towards the left, to a radical and egalitarian movement. Structure and conditioning are vital, but so is that intangible nexus of living and acting in society. There is no one-to-one correlation between structures and dispositions – institutions are constraining artefacts that produce a plethora of forms of disquiet, grumbling and incongruity. There has been an attempt to theorize and dramatize the experiential intangibilities: take the Fanonian 'gaze' through which your 'racing' is inscribed; take the theories of 'cultural trauma'; take the claims of a Badiou-like 'event-ness' of certain events that make phenomenological work hard; the Heideggerian 'being thrown' in the world; or the Goffman theatricality of everyday life, crawling towards the side of the stage.

The second challenge is that the 'event-ness' of large-scale occurrences, their psychic intensity, cannot be measured: Hiroshima and Nagasaki, the Rwandan genocide, the Battle of Stalingrad, the earthquake, but also everyday encounters affect dispositions in many directions. The worker sent miles underground by syndicates to scratch out the last vestiges of gold in disused mines, the undocumented migrant who survives a near-death drowning experience, the woman who survives a stoning for her looseness, the student living in a turbulent hyper-habitus, the artist who is beaten for being anti-national, all may lead to forms of defiance that are of a different range of intensity.

Bibliography

Abidor, M. (2018), *May Made Me*, London: Pluto Press.

Abrahams, P. (1989), *Mine Boy: The First Modern Novel of Black South Africa*, Portsmouth: Heinemann.

Abrams, L.S. and B. Anderson-Nathe (2012), *Compassionate Confinement: A Year in the Life of Unit C*, New Brunswick, NY: Rutgers University Press.

Achmat, Z. (1993), '"Apostles of Uncivilized Vice": "Immoral Practices" and "Unnatural Vice" in South African Prisons and Compounds, 1890–1920', *Social Dynamics*, vol. 19, no. 2: 92–10.

Adams, J., C. Nowels, K. Corsi, J. Long, J.F. Steiner and I.A. Binswanger (2011), 'HIV Risk after Release from Prison: A Qualitative Study of Former Inmates', *Journal of Acquired Immune Deficiency Syndrome*, vol. 57, no. 5: 429–34.

Adhikari, M. (1992), 'The Sons of Ham: Slavery and the Making of Coloured Identity', *South African Historical Journal*, vol. 27, no. 1: 95–12.

—— (2009), *Burdened by Race: Coloured Identities in Southern Africa*, Lansdowne: UCT Press.

Adorno, T.W. (1966), *Negative Dialectics*, London: Routledge.

—— (1974), *Minima Moralia*, London: New Left Books.

—— (1984), *Aesthetic Theory*, London: Routledge and Kegan Paul.

Africa, A. (2010), '"Murderous Women"? Rethinking Gender and Theories of Violence', *Feminist Africa: Rethinking Gender and Violence*, no. 14: 79–92.

Agamben, G. (1998), *Homo Sacer: Sovereign Power and Bare Life*, Stanford, California: Stanford University Press.

—— (2005), *States of Exception*, Illinois: Chicago University Press.

—— (2020), 'Invention of an Epidemic', *Quodlibet*, 26 February.

—— (2020), 'Contagion', *Quodlibet*, 11 March.

—— (2020), 'Clarifications', *European Journal of Psychoanalysis*, 17 March.

Agboola, C. (2015), 'Consensual Same-Sex Sexual Relationships in South African Female Prisons', *Gender and Behaviour*, vol. 13, no. 2: 6658–67.

Agnes, F. (2005), 'Bar Dancers and the Issue of Livelihood, *Asian Age*, Mumbai edition, 14 June.

Aguiar, L. and A. Herod, eds (2006), *The Dirty Work of Neoliberalism: Cleaners in the Global Economy*, London: Blackwell.

Ahuja, R. (2013), 'A Freedom Still Enmeshed in Servitude: The Unruly "Lascars" of the SS City of

Manila or, a Micro-History of the "Free Labour Problem"', in R. Ahuja, ed., *Working Lives and Worker Militancy: The Politics of Labour in Colonial India*, New Delhi: Tulika Books: 97–133.

Al Hariri, M., G. Italia, H. Kuhlfelt, A. Olmati and S. Yosef (2017), 'Hungary', Research Portfolio, students' coursework for the course 'Fascisms: European History, Current Challenges', taught by Wiebke Keim within the MA Programme Euroculture, Strasbourg.

Cambanis, T. (2015), 'The Arab Spring Was a Revolution of the Hungry', A. Al Khateeb, trans., *Sasapost*, 1 September.

Al Sayyad, N. (2021), 'A History of Tahrir Square', *Midan Masr*, 2018, available at http://www.midanmasr.com/en/article.aspx?ArticleID=140, accessed 20 December.

Alexander, H. (2018), 'Steve Bannon Announces Plan for European Foundation to Back Right-Wing Political Groups', *The Telegraph*, 21 July.

Alonso, S. and S. da Fonseca (2012), 'Immigration, Left and Right', *Party Politics*, vol. 18, no. 6, November: 865–84.

Alpers, E. (2003), 'Flight to Freedom: Escape from Slavery among Bonded Africans in the Indian Ocean world, c. 1750–1962', *Slavery & Abolition*, vol. 24, no. 2: 51–68.

Altbach, G.P. (1968), *Student Politics in Bombay*, Calcutta: Asia Publishing House.

Amadiume, I. (1987), *Male Daughters, Female Husbands: Gender and Sex in an African Society*, London: Zed Books.

Anandhi, S. (1991), 'Representing Devadasis: "Dasigal Mosavalai" as a Radical Text', *Economic and Political Weekly*, vol. 26, no. 11–12: 739–46.

Anastasakis, O. (2009), 'The New Politics of the New Century', in S. Economides and Monastiriotis Vassilis, eds, *The Return of Street Politics? Essays on the December Riots in Greece*, London: Hellenic Observatory and LSE: 5–8.

Anderson, C. (2016), 'Convicts, Carcerality and Cape Colony Connections in the 19th Century', *Journal of Southern African Studies*, vol. 42, no. 3: 429–42.

Anderson, G. (2002), *Building a People's University in South Africa: Race, Compensatory Education, and the Limits of Democratic Reform*, Bern: Peter Lang International Publishers.

Anderson, R.D. (2009), *Universities and Elites in Britain Since 1800*, Cambridge: Cambridge University Press.

Anderson, R.N. (1996), 'The Quilombo of Palmares: A New Overview of a Maroon State in Seventeenth-Century Brazil', *Journal of Latin American Studies*, vol. 28, no. 3: 545–66.

Anthias, F. (2020), *Translocational Belongings: Intersectional Dilemmas and Social Inequalities*, New York: Routledge.

Anthias, F. and N. Yuval-Davis (1992), *Racialized Boundaries: Race, Nation, Gender, Colour and Class and the Anti-Racist Struggle*, New York: Routledge.

Anthias, F. and G. Lazaridis, eds (1999), *Into the Margins: Migration and Exclusion in Southern Europe*, Avebury: Ashgate.

Appadurai, A. (2017), 'Democracy Fatigue', in H. Geiselberger, ed., *The Great Regression*, Cambridge: Polity Press: 1–12.

Arampatzi, A. (2017), 'Contentious Spatialities in an Era of Austerity: Everyday Politics and "Struggle Communities" in Athens, Greece', *Political Geography*, vol. 60, September: 47–56.

Arendt, H. (1973), *The Origins of Totalitarianism*, New York: Harcourt, Brace & Jovanovich, 1951.

Aresti, A. (2012), 'Developing a Convict Criminology Group in the UK', *Journal of Prisoners on Prisons*, vol. 21: 148–65.

Arrighi, G. (2007), *Adam Smith in Beijing: Lineages of the Twenty-First Century*, London: Verso.

Arthur, J.W. (2003), 'Brewing Beer: Status, Wealth and Ceramic Use Alternation among the Gamo of South-Western Ethiopia', *World Archaeology*, vol. 34, no. 3: 516–28.

Artieres, P., L. Quero and M. Zancarini-Fournel (2003), *Le Groupe d'Information sur les Prisons: Archives D'une Lutte*, Paris: IMEC: 1970–72.

Ashe, S.D. and B.F. McGeever (2011), 'Marxism, Racism and the Construction of "Race" as a Social and Political Relation: An Interview with Professor Robert Miles', *Ethnic and Racial Studies*, vol. 34, no. 12: 2009–26.

Ashforth, B.E. and G.E. Kreiner (1999), '"How Can You Do It?": Dirty Work and the Challenge of Constructing a Positive Identity', *Academy of Management Review*, vol. 24, no. 3: 413–34.

Ashour, O. (2015), 'Rabaa's Massacre: The Political Impact', *Al Jazeera*, 14 August.

Axtell, J. (2016), *Wisdom's Workshop: The Rise of the Modern University*, Princeton: Princeton University Press.

Baderoon, G. (2018), 'Surplus, Excess, Dirt: Slavery and the Production of Disposability in South Africa', *Social Dynamics*, vol. 44, no. 2, May: 1–16.

Badiou, A. (2007), *Being and Event*, London: Bloomsbury.

—— (2012), *The Rebirth of History: Times of Riots and Uprisings*, London: Verso.

Baier, W. (2016), 'Europe on the Precipice: The Crisis of the Neoliberal Order and the Ascent of Right-Wing Populism', *New Labor Forum*, vol. 25, no. 3, August: 48–55.

Bailey, J.R.A. and A. Seftel, eds (1994), *Shebeens Take a Bow! A Celebration of South Africa's Shebeen Lifestyle*, Lanseria: Bailey's African History Archives.

Baker, J. (1992), 'Prohibition and Illicit Liquor on the Witwatersrand, 1902–1932', in J. Crush and A. Ambler, eds, *Liquor and Labor in Southern Africa*, Athens: Ohio University Press and Pietermaritzburg: University of Natal Press: 139–62.

Bakewell, O. (2007), 'Keeping Them in Their Place: The Ambivalent Relationship between Development and Migration in Africa', International Migration Institute Working Papers, University of Oxford, Paper 8.

Bale, T. (2008), 'Politics Matters: A Conclusion', *Journal of European Public Policy*, vol. 15, no. 3: 453–64.

Bales, K. (1999), *Disposable People: New Slavery in the Global Economy*, Berkeley: University of California Press.

Balibar, E. (2015), 'Borderland Europe and the Challenge of Migration', *Open Democracy*, 8 September, available at https://www.opendemocracy.net/can-europe-make-it/etienne-balibar/borderland-europe-and-challenge-of-migration, accessed 20 December 2021.

Balibar, E. and I. Wallerstein (1991), *Race, Nation, Class, Ambiguous Identities*, London: Verso.

Bandyopadhyay, M. (2006), 'Competing Masculinities in Prison', *Men and Masculinities*, vol. 9, no. 2: 186–203.

Banerjee, A. and E. Duflo (2011), *Poor Economics: A Radical Rethinking of the Way to Fight Global Poverty*, New York: Public Affairs.

Banerjee, Shoumojit (2016), 'All You Need to Know about the FTII Students Strike', *The Hindu*, 22 April.

Banerjee, Sumanta (1980), *In the Wake of Naxalbari: A History of the Naxalite Movement in India*, Kolkata: Subarnarekha.

—— (1993), 'The "Beshya" and the "Babu": Prostitute and Her Clientele in 19th Century Bengal', *Economic and Political Weekly*, vol. 28, no. 45, 6 November: 2461–72.

Baritz, L. (1960), *Servants of Power: A History of the Use of Social Science in American Industry*, Middletown, Connecticut: Wesleyan University Press.

Barker, A.J. (1996), *Slavery and Antislavery in Mauritius, 1810–33: The Conflict between Economic Expansion and Humanitarian Reform under British Rule*, London: Macmillan Press.

Barker, C. (2018), 'Some Reflections on the Student Movements of the 1960s and Early 1970s', *Revista Critica de Ciencias Siocials*, vol. 81.

Barlaetti, S.C. (2005), *Hitler Youth: Growing Up in Hitler's Shadow*, Wilkins: Scholastics Inc..

Baroni, G. *et al.* (2018), 'Is there Fascism in Germany?', Research Portfolio, students' coursework for the course 'Fascisms: European History, Current Challenges', taught by Wiebke Keim within the MA Programme Euroculture, Strasbourg.

Barrington, L.W. (2006), *After Independence: Making and Protecting the Nation in Postcolonial and Post-Communist States*, Ann Arbor: Michigan University Press.

Baudelaire, C. (1998), *Flowers of Evil*, Berkeley: West Margin Press.

Bauer, A. (2011), 'Life is Too Short for Faint-Heartedness: The Archaeology of Andrew Sherratt', *Journal of World Prehistory*, no. 24: 99–105.

Bauman, Z. (2000), *Liquid Modernity*, Cambridge: Polity Press in association with Blackwell.

—— (2005), *Liquid Life*, Cambridge: Polity Press.

—— (2011), *Collateral Damage: Social Inequalities in a Global Age*, Cambridge: Polity Press.

—— (2017), 'Symptoms in Search of an Object and a Name', in H. Geiselberger, ed., *The Great Regression*, Cambridge: Polity Press: 13–25.

Bayat, A. (2013), *The Arab Spring and its Surprises, Development and Change*, vol. 44, no. 3: 587–601.

—— (2017), *Revolution without Revolutionaries: Making Sense of the Arab Spring*, Stanford: Stanford University Press, 2017.

Beas, D. (2011), 'How Spain's 15-M movement is Redefining Politics', *The Guardian*, 15 October.

Beckman, M. (1992, 1995), *The 43 Group: Antifaschistischer Kampf in Großbritannien 1946-1950*, Berlin: Harald-Kater-Verlag.

Bengtsson, T.T. (2016), 'Performing Hypermasculinity: Experiences with Confined Young Offenders', *Men and Masculinities*, vol. 19, no. 4: 410–28.

Benjamin, W. (1969), *Illuminations*, London: Schocken.

—— (1996), *Charles Baudelaire: A Lyric Poet on the Eve of High Capitalism*, London: Verso.

Bennett, J. (1991), 'Misogyny, Popular Culture and Women's Work', *History Workshop Journal*, vol. 31, no. 1, March.

Berci, G., M. Geniola, M. Page and C. Pescara (2017), 'Italy', Research Portfolio, students' coursework for the course 'Fascisms: European History, Current Challenges', taught by Wiebke Keim within the MA Programme Euroculture, Strasbourg.

Bergemann, K.J. (2011), *Council of (in)Justice: Crime, Status, Punishment and the Decision-Makers in the 1730s Cape Justice System*, Cape Town: University of Cape Town.

Berggren, E., B. Likic-Brboric, T. Toksöz and N. Trimikliniotis (2007), 'Irregular Migration, Informal Labour and Community: A Challenge for Europe', Maastricht: Shaker.

Berman, S. (2016), 'Populism is Not Fascism: But It Could Be a Harbinger', *Foreign Affairs*, vol. 95, no. 6: 39–44.

Betz, H.G. (1993), 'The Two Faces of Radical Right-Wing Populism in Western Europe', *The Review of Politics*, vol. 55, no. 4, August: 663–85.

Bhabha, H. (2019), 'The Burdened Life: Ambedkar, Hannah Arendt and the Perplexity of Rights', in V. Rodrigues, ed., *Conversations with Ambedkar*, New Delhi: Tulika Books.

Bhagwati, J. (1998), 'The Capital Myth: The Difference between Trade in Widgets and Dollars', *Foreign Affairs*, vol. 77, no. 3, May–June: 7–12.

—— (2003), 'Borders Beyond Control', *Foreign Affairs*, vol. 82, no. 1, January–February: 98–104.

Biao, L. (1966), 'Comrade Lin Biao's Speech at the Celebration Rally', *Marxists.org*, 1 October, available at https://www.marxists.org/reference/archive/lin-biao/1966/10/01.htm, accessed 1 December 2018.

Bickford-Smith, V. (1994), 'Meanings of Freedom: Social Position and Identity Among Ex-Slaves and Their Descendants in Cape Town, 1875–1910', in N. Worden and C. Crais, eds, *Breaking the Chains: Slavery and its Legacy in the Nineteenth-Century Cape Colony*, Johannesburg: Witwatersrand University Press: 289–312.

Biehl, J. (2005), *Vita: Life in a Zone of Abandonment*, Berkeley: University of California Press.

Bigo, T. and A. Tsoukala, eds (2008), *Terror, Insecurity and Liberty: Illiberal Practices of Liberal Regimes after 9/11*, London and New York: Routledge.

Bischoff, J. and B. Müller (2016), 'Rechtspopulismus in der "Berliner Republik" und Europa: Ursachen und Hintergründe', in A. Häusler and F. Virchow, eds, *Neue Soziale Bewegung von rechts? Zukunftsängste, Abstieg der Mitte, Ressentiments, Eine Flugschrift*, Hamburg: VSA Verlag: 19–31.

Biskamp, F. (2017), 'Angst-Traum "Angst-Raum": Über den Erfolg der AfD, "die Ängste der Menschen" und die Versuche, sie "ernst zu nehmen"', *Forschungsjournal Soziale Bewegungen*, vol. 30, no. 2: 91–100.

Bitzan, R. (2017), 'Research on Gender and the Far Right in Germany since 1990: Developments, Findings, and Future Prospects', in M. Köttig, R. Bitzan and A. Pető, eds, *Gender and Politics: Gender and Far Right Politics in Europe*, Cham, Switzerland: Palgrave Macmillan: 65–78.

Blee, K. (2017), 'Similarities/Differences in Gender and Far-Right Politics in Europe and the USA', in M. Köttig, R. Bitzan, and A. Pető, eds, *Gender and Politics: Gender and Far Right Politics in Europe*, Cham, Switzerland: Palgrave Macmillan: 191–204.

Bloom, A. (1986), *Prodigal Sons: The New York Intellectuals and Their World*, New York: Oxford University Press.

Blum, A. (2017), 'Men in the Battle for the Brains: Constructions of Masculinity within the "Identitary Generation"', in M. Köttig, R. Bitzan and A. Pető, eds, *Gender and Politics: Gender and Far Right Politics in Europe*, Cham, Switzerland: Palgrave Macmillan: 321–34.

Boatcă, M. (2015), *Global Inequalities beyond Occidentalism: Global Connections*, Farnham: Ashgate.

Bonner, P. (1988), '"Desirable or Undesirable Sotho Women?" Liquor, Prostitution and the Migration of Sotho Women to the Rand, 1920–1945', Johannesburg: African Studies Institute, African Studies Seminar Paper to be presented in RW 4.00 p.m., May.

—— (1992), 'Backs to the Fence: Law, Liquor, and the Search for Social Control in an East Rand Town, 1929–1942', in J. Crush and A. Ambler, eds, *Liquor and Labor in Southern Africa*, Athens: Ohio University Press and Pietermaritzburg: University of Natal Press: 269–305.

Boonzaier, F.A. (2014), 'Methodological Disruptions: Interviewing Domestically Violent Men across a "Gender Divide"', *NORMA*, vol. 9, no. 4: 232–48.

Booth, J. and P. Baert (2018), *The Dark Side of Podemos*, London: Routledge.

Borchers, A. (1993), 'Wiedervereinigung und Neonazismus: von der Zionskirche bis Hoyerswerda', in M. Leier, ed., *Un-Heil über Deutschland. Fremdenhaß und Neofaschismus nach der Wieder-vereinigung*, Hamburg: Gruner und Jahr: 120–35.

Borcholte, A. (2015), 'Seehofers "Notwehr"-Sprüche: Rhetorisch Braun', *Der Spiegel*, 9 October.

Boris, E. and R.S. Parreñas, eds (2010), *Intimate Labors: Cultures, Technologies, and the Politics of Care, Stanford*, California: Stanford Social Sciences.

Botsch, G. (2017), *Wahre Demokratie und Volksgemeinschaft: Ideologie und Programmatik der NPD und Ihres Rechtsextremen Umfelds*, Edition Rechtsextremismus, Wiesbaden: Springer VS.

Boumaza, M. (2004), 'Les Élections Régionales et Cantonales 2004 Vues du Front', *Research Gate*, January, available at https://www.researchgate.net/profile/Magali_Boumaza/

publication/278809985_Les_elections_regionales_de_2004_vues_du_Front/links/
55e07b4f08aecb1a7cc45524/Les-elections-regionales-de-2004-vues-du-Front.pdf, accessed
20 December 2021.

Bourdieu, P. (1979, 1990), *Reproduction in Education, Society and Culture,* London: Sage.

—— (1979), *Distinction: A Social Critique of the Judgement of Taste,* London, Routledge.

—— (1984), *Homo Academicus,* P. Collier, trans., Stanford: Stanford University Press.

—— (1996), *The Rules of Art: Genesis and Structure of the Literary Field,* Cambridge: Polity Press.

—— (1997, 2000), *Pascalian Meditations,* Stanford: Stanford University Press.

—— et al. (1999), *The Weight of the World: Social Suffering in Contemporary Society,* P.P. Ferguson,
S. Emanuel, J. Johnson and S.T. Waryn, trans., Cambridge: Polity Press.

Bourg, J. (2017), *From Revolution to Ethics: May 1968 and French Thought,* Toronto: McGill-
Queens.

Bourgois, P. (1996), *In Search of Respect: Selling Crack in El Barrio,* Cambridge: Cambridge
University Press.

Boyce, P. and G. Isaacs (2014), 'Male Sex Work in Southern and Eastern Africa', in V. Minichiello
and J. Scott, eds, *Male Sex Work and Society,* New York: Harrington Park Press.

Bradford, H. (1992), '"We Women Will Show Them": Beer Protests in the Natal Countryside,
1929', in J. Crush and A. Ambler, eds, *Liquor and Labor in Southern Africa,* Athens: Ohio
University Press and Pietermaritzburg: University of Natal Press: 210–34.

Brass, T. (1999), *Towards a Comparative Political Economy of Unfree Labour: Case Studies and
Debates,* London: Frank Cass.

Braverman, H. (1974), *Labor and Monopoly Capital: The Degradation of Work in the Twentieth
Century,* New York: Monthly Review Press.

Breman, J. (1976), 'A Dualistic Labour System? A Critique of the "Informal Sector" Concept:
III: Labour Force and Class Formation', *Economic and Political Weekly,* vol. 11, no. 50, 11
December: 1934–44.

—— (1996), *Footloose Labour: Working in India's Informal Economy,* Cambridge: Cambridge
University Press.

Breton, A. (2008), *Martinique: Snake Charmer,* Austin: University of Texas Press.

Brinkbäumer, K. (2007), 'The Onslaught of the Poor. The New Mass Migration', *Der Spiegel,*
24 January, available at https://www.spiegel.de/international/spiegel/the-onslaught-of-the-
poor-the-new-mass-migration-a-461120.html, accessed 20 December 2021.

Britton, C.M. (1999), *Edouard Glissant and Postcolonial Theory: Strategies of Language and
Resistance,* Charlottesville: University Press of Virginia.

Brook, T. (1989), *The Asiatic Mode of Production in China,* New York: Armonk.

—— (1998), *The Confusions of Pleasure: Commerce and Culture in Ming China,* Berkeley:
University of California Press.

—— (2009), *Vermeer's Hat: The Seventeenth Century and the Dawn of the Global,* New York:
Bloomsbury Press.

Brown, W. (2009), *Walled States, Waning Sovereignty,* Cambridge: Zone Books.

Bryceson, D. (2002), 'Pleasure and Pain: The Ambiguity of Alcohol in Africa', in D.F. Bryceson,
ed., *Alcohol in Africa: Mixing Business, Pleasure and Politics,* Portsmouth: Heinemann: 267–91.

Buck-Morss, S. (1989), *The Dialectics of Seeing: Walter Benjamin and the Arcades Project,* Massa-
chussets: MIT Press.

Bulle, S. (2012), 'Why Does the Street inspire Revolt? Riot Skills and Social Transformation
Plan in the Worldwide Occupation Movement (Spain, Israel, USA)', *Justice Spatiale / Spatial
Justice (JSSJ).*

Burawoy, M. (1996), 'A Classic of Its Time', *Contemporary Sociology*, vol. 25, no. 3: 296–99.

—— (2005), 'American Sociological Association Presidential Address: For Public Sociology', *The British Journal of Sociology*, vol. 56, no. 2: 259–94.

Butler, J. (1988), 'Performative Acts and Gender Constitution: An Essay in Phenomenology and Feminist Theory', *Theatre Journal*, vol. 40, no. 4: 519–31.

—— (1990), *Gender Trouble*, New York: Routledge.

Cailler, B. (1989), 'Edouard Glissant: A Creative Critic', *World Literature Today*, vol. 63, no. 4: 589–92.

Caldwell, C. (2010), *Reflection on the Revolution in Europe: Immigration, Islam and the West*, London: Penguin Books.

Cambanis, T. (2015), 'The Arab Spring was a Revolution of the Hungry', *Boston Globe*, 23 August.

Camus, J. and N. Lebourg (2017), *Far-Right Politics in Europe*, Cambridge, MA: Harvard University Press.

Carens, J.H. (2013), *The Ethics of Migration*, Oxford: Oxford University Press.

Carr, M. (2012), *Fortress Europe, Inside the War Against Migration*, London: Hurst and Company.

(1996), *Voices from Indenture. Experiences of Indian Migrants in the British Empire*, London: Leicester University Press.

Carter, M. and J. Ng Foong Kwong (1997), *Forging the Rainbow: Labour Immigrants in British Mauritius*, Mauritius: Alfran Co. Ltd.

Cartuyvels, Y. (2002), 'Réformer ou supprimer: le dilemme des prisons', in O. de Schutter and D. Kaminski, eds, *L'institution du droit pénitentiaire: Enjeux de la reconnaissance des droits aux détenus*, Paris: LGDJ: 113–32.

Castles, S. (2004), 'Factors That Make and Unmake Migration Policies', *The International Migration Review*, vol. 38, no. 3, Fall: 852–84.

Castles, S., H. de Haas and M.J. Miller (2014), *The Age of Migration: International Population Movements in the Modern World*, fifth edition, London: Palgrave Macmillan.

Castles, S. (2015), 'International Human Mobility: Key Issues and Challenges to Social Theory', in S. Castles, D. Ozkul and M.A. Cubas, eds, *Social Transformation and Migration: National and Local Experiences in South Korea, Turkey, Mexico and Australia*, London: Palgrave Macmillan, Springer: 3–14.

Centre for Conflict Resolution (2004), 'Prison Transformation in South Africa', in M. Balfour, ed., *Theatre in Prison: Theory and Practice*, Bristol: Intellect Books: 161–76.

Cesaire, A. (1969), *Return to My Native Land*, Harmondsworth: Penguin.

—— (2002), *A Tempest*, London: Theatre Communications Group.

Cesaire, S.R. (2012), *The Great Camouflage: Writings of Dissent (1941-45)*, Middletown: Wesleyan University Press.

Chan, S. (1979), 'The Image of a "Capitalist Roader": Some Dissident Short Stories in the Hundred Flowers Period', *The Australian Journal of Chinese Affairs*, no. 2: 77–102.

Chase-Dunn, Ch. K. (1991), *Global Formation: Structures of the World Economy*, London, Oxford and New York: Basil Blackwell.

Chatterjee, G. (2008), 'The Veshya, the Ganika and the Tawaif: Representations of Prostitutes and Courtesans in Indian Language, Literature and Cinema', in R. Sahni, K. Shankar and H. Apte, eds, *Prostitution and Beyond: An Analysis of Sex work in India*, New Delhi: Sage Publications: 279–300.

Chebel d'Appolonia, A. (1992), 'Les parties d'extrême droite et l'Europe', *Cultures et Conflits*, vol. 7: 17–30.

Chen, J., M. Kirasirova, M. Klimke, M. Nolan, M. Young and J. Waley-Cohen (2018), *The*

Routledge Handbook of the Global Sixties: Between Protest and Nation-Building, Abingdon: Routledge.

Chetail, V. and C. Bauloz, eds (2014), *Research Handbook on International Law and Migration*, Cheltenham: Edward Elgar Publishing.

Chisholm, L. (1986), 'The Pedagogy of Porter: The Origins of the Reformatory in the Cape Colony, 1882–1910', *The Journal of African History*, vol. 27, no. 3: 481–95.

Chouliaraki, L. and M. Georgiou (2019), 'The Digital Border: Mobility beyond Territorial and Symbolic Divides', *European Journal of Communication*, 2019, vol. 34, no. 6: 594–605.

—— (2017), 'Hospitability: The Communicative Architecture of Humanitarian Securitization at Europe's Borders', *Journal of Communication*, vol. 67, no. 2: 159–80.

Christoffersen, J. and M.R. Madsen (2011), *The European Court of Human Rights between Law and Politics*, New York: Oxford University Press.

Cisneros, S. (1995), *Loose Woman: Poems*, reprint, New York: Vintage.

Claus, R. and F. Virchow (2017), 'The Far Right's Ideological Constructions of "Deviant" Male Sexualities', in M. Köttig, R. Bitzan, and A. Pető, eds, *Gender and Politics. Gender and Far Right Politics in Europe*, Cham, Switzerland: Palgrave Macmillan: 305–19.

Clemmer, D. (1940, 1958), *The Prison Community*, New York: Holt, Rinehart and Winston.

Cliquennois, G. (2010), 'Preventing Suicide in French Prisons', *British Journal of Criminology*, vol. 50, no. 6, 1023–40.

Cliquennois, G. and B. Champetier (2013), 'A New Risk Management for Prisoners in France: The Emergence of a Death-Avoidance Approach', *Theoretical Criminology*, vol. 17, no. 3: 397–15.

—— (2016), 'The Economic, Judicial and Political Influence Exerted by Private Foundations on Cases Taken by NGOs to the European Court of Human Rights: Inklings of a New Cold War', *European Law Journal*, vol. 22, no. 1: 92–126.

Cliquennois, G. and S. Snacken (2017), 'European and United Nations Monitoring of Penal and Prison Policies as a Source of an Inverted Panopticon?', *Crime, Law and Social Change*, vol. 69, no. 1–2, 20 November: 1–18.

Cliquennois, G. and H. de Suremain (2017), *Monitoring Penal Policy in Europe*, London: Routledge.

Cliquennois, G., S. Snacken and D. van Zyl Smit (forthcoming), 'The European Human Rights System and the Right to Life Seen through Suicide Prevention in Places of Detention: Between Risk Management and Punishment', *Human Rights Law Review*, https://doi.org/10.1093/hrlr/ngab023, accessed 20 December 2021.

Coddington, K. and M. Alison (2014), 'Countering Isolation with the Use of Technology: How Asylum-Seeking Detainees on Islands in the Indian Ocean Use Social Media to Transcend Their Confinement', *Journal of the Indian Ocean Region*, vol. 10, no. 1: 97–112.

Cogan, C. (2007), '"Stay-Behind" in France: Much Ado about Nothing?', *Journal of Strategic Studies*, vol. 30, no. 6: 937–54.

Cohen, S. (1972), *Folk Devils and Moral Panics*, New York: Routledge.

—— (1986), 'Bandits, Rebels or Criminals: African History and Western Criminology', *Journal of the International African Institute*, vol. 56, no. 4: 468–83.

Cohen, S. and L. Taylor (1972), *Psychological Survival: The Experience of Long-Term Imprisonment*, New York: Pantheon.

Cole, J.A. (1985), *The Potosi Mita, 1573–1700: Compuslory Indian Labour in the Andes*, Stanford: Stanford University Press.

Colish, M.L. (1997), *Medieval Foundations of the Western Intellectual Tradition, 400–1400*, New Haven: Yale University Press.

Collectif Sociologie Politique des Élections (2016), *Les sens du vote: Une enquête sociologique (France, 2011–2014)*, Res Publica, Rennes: Presses Universitaires de Rennes.

Collins, P.H. (2009), *Black Feminist Thought: Knowledge, Consciousness, and the Politics of Empowerment*, second edition, New York: Routledge.

Collovald, A. (2004), 'Le "Populisme du FN". Un Dangereux Contresens', Bellecombe-en-Bauges: Éditions du Croquant.

Comaroff, J. and J. Comaroff (1992), *Ethnography and the Historical Imagination Boulder*, Boulder, Colorado: Westview Press.

Comfort, M. (2002), '"Papa's House": The Prison as Domestic and Social Satellite', *Ethnography*, vol. 3, no. 4: 467–99.

Connell, R.W. and J.W. Messerschmidt (2005), 'Hegemonic Masculinity: Rethinking the Concept', *Gender and Society*, vol. 19, no. 6: 829–59.

Costello, C. (2015), *The Human Rights of Migrants and Refugees in European Law*, Oxford: Oxford University Press.

Cottington, D. (1998), *Cubism in the Shadow of War: The Avant-Garde and Politics in Paris 1905–1914*, New Haven and London: Yale University Press.

Cowen, Deborah (2014), *The Deadly Life of Logistics: Mapping Violence in Global Trade*, Minneapolis: University of Minnesota Press.

Crenshaw, K., N. Gotanda, G. Peller and K. Thomas, eds (1995), *Critical Race Theory: The Key Writings that Formed the Movement*, New York: The New Press.

Crépon, S. (2016), 'La progression électorale du FN et ses limites', *Hommes et Libertés*, vol. 173: 14–16.

Crépon, S. and N. Lebourg (2015), 'Le Renouvellement du Militantisme Frontiste', in S. Crépon, A. Dézé, and N. Mayer, eds, *Les Faux-semblants du Front National: Sociologie d'un Parti Politique*, Paris: Sciences Po Les Presses: 435–51.

Crewe, B. (2014), 'Not Looking Hard Enough Masculinity, Emotion, and Prison Research', *Qualitative Inquiry*, vol. 20, no. 4: 392–403.

—— (2009), *The Prisoner Society: Power, Adaptation and Social Life in an English Prison*, Oxford: Oxford University Press.

Crewe, B., J. Warr, P. Bennett and A. Smith (2014), 'The Emotional Geography of Prison Life', *Theoretical Criminology*, vol. 18, no. 1: 56–74.

Crush, J. and A. Ambler, eds (1992), *Liquor and Labor in Southern Africa*, Athens: Ohio University Press, Pietermaritzburg: University of Natal Press.

Curtis, A. (2014), '"You Have to Cut it Off at the Knee": Dangerous Masculinity and Security Inside a Men's Prison', *Men and Masculinities*, vol. 17, no. 2: 120–46.

Daems, T. (2017), 'Slaves and Statues: Torture Prevention in Contemporary Europe', *British Journal of Criminology*, vol. 57, no. 3: 627–43.

Daems, T. and L. Robert, eds (2017), *Europe in Prisons: Assessing the Impact of European Institutions on National Prison Systems*, Cham, Switzerland: Palgrave Macmillan.

Dalrymple, W. (2009), *The Last Mughal: The Fall of Delhi, 1857*, London: A&C Black.

Dalwai, S. (2016), 'Dance Bar Ban: Doing a Feminist Legal Ethnography', *Socio-Legal Review*, vol. 12, no. 1.

—— (2019), *Bans and Bar Girls: Performing Caste in Mumbai's Dance Bars*, Delhi: Women Unlimited.

Damodaran, S. (2007), *Regulations, Labour Rights and Violations – A Study of G4S*, Delhi: Service Employees International Union.

—— (2014), 'Deviance and the Making of Modern India', in A. Sitas, W. Keim, S. Damodaran,

N. Trimikliniotis and F. Garba, *Gauging and Engaging Deviance, 1600–2000*, New Delhi: Tulika Books: 75–108.

Damodaran, S. and A. Sitas (2016), 'The Musical Journey: Re-centring AfroAsia through an Arc of the Blues', *Critical Arts*, vol. 30, no. 2.

Dasgupta, H. and H. Adhikari (2008), *Bharatiya Upomohadesh er Chatra Andolan* (Student Movements in the Indian Subcontinent), Kolkata: Radical.

Dasgupta, R. (2014a), '#Hokjolorob: The Politics of Making Noise', *Kafila*, 29 September.

—— (2014b), 'Goodbye Politics, Hello Social Science: A Reply to Ranabir Samaddar and Others on Recent Students' Politics in Jadavpur', *Kafila*, 27 October.

Davies, B. (2014), 'Unique Position: Dual Identities as Prison Researcher and Ex-Prisoner', in D. Drake, R. Earle and J. Sloan, eds, *The Palgrave Handbook of Prison Ethnography*, Palgrave Studies in Prisons and Penology, Basingstoke: Palgrave.

Davis, P.J. (2000), 'On the Sexuality of "Town Women" in Kampala', *Africa Today*, vol. 47, no. 3/4, Sexuality and Generational Identities in Sub-Saharan Africa, Summer–Autumn: 29–60.

de Carvalho, A.V. (2007), 'Archeological Perspectives of Palmares: A Maroon Settlement in 17th Century Brazil', *African Diaspora Archaeology Newsletter*, vol. 10, no. 1, March.

de Certeau, M. (1984), *The Practice of Everyday Life*, Berkeley: University of California Press.

de Chavonnes, C.D. (1918), 'Rapport van De Chavonnes en Raad (Report of De Chavonnes), 1717', in *Reports of Chavonnes and His Council, and of Van Imhoff, on the Cape*, Cape Town: Van Riebeeck Society for the Publication of South African Historical Documents: 87–128.

Decker, F. (2016), 'Die "Alternative für Deutschland" aus der vergleichenden Sicht der Parteienforschung', in A. Häusle, ed., *Die Alternative für Deutschland*, Programmatik, Entwicklung und politische Verortung, Wiesbaden: Springer VS: 7–24.

Degenhardt, T. and F. Vianello (2010), 'Convict Criminology: Provocazioni da Oltreoceano: La Ricerca Etnografica In Carcere', *Studi Sulla Questione Criminale*, vol. 5: 9–23.

della Porta, D. (2017), 'Progressive and Regressive Politics in Late Neoliberalism', in H. Geiselberger, ed., *The Great Regression*, Cambridge: Polity Press: 26–48.

Dembour, M. and Kelly, T., eds (2011), *Are Human Rights for Migrants? Critical Reflections on the Status of Irregular Migrants in Europe and the United States*, London and New York: Routledge.

Derrida, J. (1997), *Spectres of Marx: The State of the Debt, The Work of Mourning, and the New International*, London: Routledge.

—— (2001), *On Cosmopolitanism and Forgiveness*, London: Routledge.

DESA (2017), *International Migration Report 2017: Highlights*, Department of Economic and Social Affairs of the United Nations Secretariat, available at https://www.un.org/en/development/desa/population/migration/publications/migrationreport/docs/MigrationReport2017_Highlights.pdf, accessed 9 September 2021.

Desreciewicz, A. (2014), *Excellent Sheep: The Miseducation of an American Elite*, New York: Simon and Schuster.

Deutscher Bundestag (2011), 'Antwort der Bundesregierung auf die Große Anfrage der Abgeordneten Jan Korte, Sevim Dagdelen, Ulla Jelpke, Weiterer Abgeordneter und der Fraktion DIE LINKE: Umgang mit der NS-Vergangenheit (No. Drucksache 17/8134)', Berlin, 14 December, available at http://dipbt.bundestag.de/dip21/btd/17/081/1708134.pdf, accessed 20 December 2021.

Dietler, M. (2006), 'Alcohol: Anthropological/Archaeological Perspectives', *Annual Review of Anthropology*, vol. 35: 229–49.

Diminescu, D. (2012), 'Digital Methods for the Exploration, Analysis, and Mapping of e-Diasporas', *Social Science Information*, vol. 51, no. 4: 451–58.

Doezema, J. (1999), 'Loose Women or Lost Women? The Re-emergence of the Myth of White Slavery in Contemporary Discourses of Trafficking in Women', *Gender Issues*, vol. 18: 23–50.

Dostal, J.M. (2015), 'The Pegida Movement and German Political Culture: Is Right Wing Populism Here to Stay?' *The Political Quarterly*, vol. 86, no. 4: 523–31.

Douglas, M. (1987), *Constructive Drinking: Perspectives on Drink from Anthropology*, Cambridge: Cambridge University Press.

Douglass, J. (2000), *The California Idea and American Higher Education*, Stanford: Stanford University Press.

Doward, J. (2018), 'Steve Bannon Plans Foundation to Fuel Far Right in Europe', *The Guardian*, 21 July.

Drake, D., R. Earle and J. Sloan, eds (2014), *The International Handbook of Prison Ethnography*, Basingstoke: Palgrave.

Drakopoulou, A. (2016), 'Hotspots: The Case of Greece', *Searching for Solidarity in EU Asylum and Border Policies: A Collection of Short Papers following the Odysseus Network's First Annual Policy Conference*, Université libre de Bruxelles, 26–27 February: 19–22.

Dubslaff, V. (2017), 'Women on the Fast Track: Gender Issues in the National Democratic Party of Germany and the French National Front (1980s–2012)', in M. Köttig, R. Bitzan and A. Pető, eds, *Gender and Politics: Gender and Far Right Politics in Europe*, Cham, Switzerland: Palgrave Macmillan: 159–78.

Duncan, F. (2010), 'Immigration and Integration Policy and the Austrian Radical Right in Office: The FPÖ/BZÖ, 2000–2006', *Contemporary Politics*, vol. 16, no. 4: 337–54.

Dunkle, K.L., R.K. Jewkes, D.W. Murdock, Y. Sikweyiya and R. Morrell (2013), 'Prevalence of Consensual Male-Male Sex and Sexual Violence, and Associations with HIV in South Africa: A Population-Based Cross-Sectional Study', *PLOS Medicine*, vol. 10, no. 6: 1–11.

Dézé, A. (2016), 'Le Changement dans la Continuité: L'organisation Partisane du Front National', *Pouvoirs*, vol. 157, no. 2: 49–62.

Earle, R. (2014), 'Insider and Out: Making Sense of a Prison Experience and a Research Experience', *Qualitative Inquiry*, vol. 20, no. 4: 429–38.

—— (2016), *Convict Criminology: Inside and Out*, Bristol: Policy Press.

Eckes, C. (2010), *EU Counter-Terrorist Policies and Fundamental Rights: The Case of Individual Sanctions*, Oxford: Oxford University Press.

Edgecombe, R. (1992), 'The Role of Alcohol in Labor Acquisition and Control on the Natal Coal Mines, 1911–1938', in J. Crush and A. Ambler, eds, *Liquor and Labor in Southern Africa*, Athens: Ohio University Press and Pietermaritzburg: University of Natal Press: 187–207.

Edwards, I. (1988), 'Illicit Liquor and the Social Structure of Drinking Dens in Cato Manor', *Agenda*, no. 3: 75–97.

Ehrlich, P. (1968), *The Population Bomb*, New York: Ballantine Books.

Ehrlich, P. and A.H. Ehrlich (2009), 'The Population Bomb Revisited', *The Electronic Journal of Sustainable Development*, vol. 1, no. 3: 63–71.

Eigenberg, H.M. (2000), 'Correctional Officers and Their Perceptions of Homosexuality, Rape, and Prostitution in Male Prisons', *The Prison Journal*, vol. 80, no. 4: 415–33.

Eisenstadt, S. (1966), *Modernization, Protest and Change*, Englewood Cliffs, NJ: Prentice Hall.

El-Massry, M. and G. Acconcia (2018), '"From the Revolution, We Learned to Be United": Leaving Politics Behind: An Interview with Mahienour el-Massry', *Open Democracy*.

Epprecht, M. (1998), 'The "Unsaying" of Indigenous Homosexualities in Zimbabwe: Mapping a Blindspot in an African Masculinity', *Journal of Southern African Studies*, vol. 24, no. 4: 631–51.

—— (2004), *Hungochani: The History of a Dissident Sexuality in Southern Africa*, Montreal: McGill-Queen's University Press.

—— (2013), *Sexuality and Social Justice in Africa: Rethinking Homophobia and Forging Resistance*, London: Zed Books.

Erasmus, Z. (2001), 'Re-Imagining Coloured Identities in Post-Apartheid South Africa', in Z. Erasmus, ed., *Coloured by History, Shaped by Place: Perspectives on Coloured Identities in Cape Town*, Cape Town: Kwela Books: 13–28.

—— (2017), *Race Otherwise: Forging a New Humanism for South Africa*, Johannesburg: Wits University Press.

Eribon, D. (2009, 2017), *Rückkehr nach Reims: Edition Suhrkamp Sonderdruck*, Berlin: Suhrkamp.

Estanque, E. and R. Bebiano (2008), 'Memória e Actualidade dos Movimentos Estudantis', *Revista Crítica*, no. 81.

Eurostat (2017), 'Asylum Quarterly Report, Third Quarter 2017', 12 December, available at http://ec.europa.eu/eurostat/statistics-explained/index.php/Asylum_quarterly_report, accessed 20 December 2021.

Faleiro, S. (2010), *Beautiful Thing: Inside the Secret World of Bombay's Dance Bars*, Delhi: Hamish Hamilton.

Fanon, F. (2008), *Black Skins, White Masks*, London: Grove.

Fangen, K. and M.R. Nilsen (2021), 'Variations within the Norwegian Far Right: From Neo-Nazism to Anti-Islamism', *Journal of Political Ideologies*, vol. 26, no. 3: 278–97.

Fekete, L. (2009), *A Suitable Enemy: Racism, Migration and Islamophobia in Europe*, London and New York: Pluto Press.

—— (2018), *Europe's Fault-lines, Racism and the Rise of the Far Right*, London: Verso.

Ferguson, J. (1997), 'The Country and the City on the Copperbelt', in A. Gupta and J. Ferguson, eds, *Culture, Power, Place: Explorations in Critical Anthropology*, Durham: Duke University Press.

Fiddian-Qasmiyeh, E., G.L. Elena, K. Long and N. Sigona, eds (2014), *The Oxford Handbook of Refugee and Forced Migration Studies*, Oxford: Oxford University Press.

Fleischer, H. (2003), 'The Past Beneath the Present: The Resurgence of World War II Public History After the Collapse of Communism: A Stroll Through the International Press', *Historein*, vol. 4: 45–130.

Føllesdal, A., B. Peters and G. Ulfstein (2013), *Constituting Europe: The European Court of Human Rights in a National, European and Global Context*, Cambrigde: Cambridge University Press.

Foroutan, N., ed. (2011), *Sarrazins Thesen auf dem Prüfstand: Ein empirischer Gegenentwurf zu Thilo Sarrazins Thesen zu Muslimen in Deutschland (2. Aufl.)*, W-Serie: No. 1, Berlin: Humboldt-Universität zu Berlin.

Foster, J.B. (1998), 'Malthus' Essay on Population at Age 200: A Marxian View', *Monthly Review*, vol. 50, no. 7, December: 1–18.

Foucault, M. (1975), *Surveiller et Punir*, Paris: Gallimard.

—— (1977), *Discipline and Punish: The Birth of the Prison*, London: Vintage.

—— (1990), *The Use of Pleasure, Volume 2: Of the History of Sexuality*, New York: Vintage Books.

—— (2008), *The Birth of Biopolitics: Lectures at the Collège de France, 1978-79*, M. Senellart, ed., G. Burchell, trans., New York: Palgrave Macmillan.

Frank, A.G. (1998), *ReOrient: Global Economy in the Asian Age*, Berkeley: University of California Press.

Frankenberg, G. (2014), *Political Technology and the Erosion of the Rule of Law: Normalizing the State of Exception*, Cheltenham: Edward Elgar.

Fraser, N. (2017), 'Progressive Neoliberalism versus Reactionary Populism: A Hobson's Choice', in H. Geiselberger, ed., *The Great Regression*, Cambridge: Polity Press: 40–48.

—— (2016), 'Contradictions of Capital and Care', *New Left Review*, vol. 100.

Friedman, M. (2014), 'Male Sex Work from Ancient Times to the Near Present', in V. Minichiello and J. Scott, eds, *Male Sex Work and Society*, New York: Harrington Park Press.

Furlong, A. (2016), 'Interview with Shaeera Kalla of #FeesMustFall', *Ground Up*, 16 February.

Fuse, T. (1969), 'Student Radicalism in Japan: A Cultural Revolution?', *Comparative Educational Review*, vol. 13 no. 13.

Fry, V. (1992), *Assignment Rescue: An Autobiography*, Madison, Wisconsin: Demco.

Fœssel, M. (2019), *Récidive: 1938*. Paris: Presses Universitaires de France.

Gabriel, C. and H. Pellerin, eds (2008), *Governing International Labour Migration: Current Issues, Challenges and Dilemmas*, London and New York: Routledge.

Gagnon, J. and W. Simon (1973), *Sexual Conduct: The Social Sources of Human Sexuality*, Chicago: Aldine Publishing Company.

Ganser, D. (2005), *NATO's Secret Armies: Operation Gladio and Terrorism in Western Europe*, Contemporary Security Studies, London and New York: Frank Cass.

—— (2008), *NATO-Geheimarmeen in Europa: Inszenierter Terror und Verdeckte Kriegsführung*, Zürich: Orell Füssli.

Gauriat, V. (2017), 'Inside Hungary's Far-Right Movement', *Euronews*, 23 November, available at http://www.euronews.com/2017/11/23/hungary-s-fear-factor, accessed 20 December 2021.

Gavriilidis, A. (2009), 'Greek Riots 2008: A Mobile Tiananmen', in S. Economides and V. Monastiriotis, eds, *The Return of Street Politics? Essays on the December Riots in Greece*, London: The Hellenic Observatory and LSE: 15–20.

—— (2010), 'Kathigites tou Tipota-Anti-Exeghersi os Politiki Epistimi', *Theseis*, vol. 113, October–December.

Gear, S. (2005), 'Rules of Engagement: Structuring Sex and Damage in Men's Prisons and Beyond', *Culture, Health and Sexuality*, vol. 7, no. 3: 195–208.

Gear, S. and K. Ngubeni (2002), 'Daai Ding: Sex, Sexual Violence and Coercion in Men's Prisons', Braamfontein: Centre for Study of Violence and Reconciliation.

—— (2003), 'Your Brother, My Wife: Sex and Gender Behind Bars', *SA Crime Quarterly*, no. 4, June: 11–16.

Gefou-Madianou, D., ed. (1992), *Alcohol, Gender and Culture*, New York: Routledge.

Geggus, D. (1983), 'Slave Resistance Studies and the Saint Domingue Slave Revolt: Some Preliminary Considerations (Paper #4)', *Florida International University (FIU)Digital Commons*, LACC Occasional Papers Series (1981–1990), available at http://digitalcommons.fiu.edu/laccops, accessed 12 August 2021.

Geiselberger, H., ed. (2017), *The Great Regression*, Cambridge: Polity Press.

Georges R.A. and M.O. Jones (1980), *People Studying People: The Human Element in Field Work*, Berkeley: University of California Press.

Georgiou, M. and R. Zaborowski (2017), *Media Coverage of the 'Refugee Crisis': A Cross-European Perspective*, Council of Europe Report, DG1(2017)03, available at https://edoc.coe.int/en/refugees/7367-media-coverage-of-the-refugee-crisis-a-cross-european-perspective.html, accessed 20 December 2021.

Gewald, J. (2002), 'Diluting Drinks and Deepening Discontent: Colonial Liquor Controls and Public Resistance', in Windhowek, Namimbia', in D.F. Bryceson, ed., *Alcohol in Africa: Mixing Business, Pleasure and Politics*, Portsmouth: Heinemann: 117–38.

Ghosh, S. (2010), *Naxalbari: Ekti Mulyayan* (*Naxalbari: An Assessment*), Kolkata: People's Book Society.

Giannakopoulos, G. (2012), 'Metapolitefsi: From the Transition to Democracy to the Economic Crisis', *Historein*, vol. 13, no. 3.

Gibson, L.E. and C. Hensley (2013), 'The Social Construction of Sexuality in Prison', *The Prison Journal*, vol. 93, no. 3: 355–70.

Giddens, A. and P.W. Sutton (2021), *Sociology*, ninth edition, Cambridge: Polity Press.

Gillespie, K. (2002), *Bloodied Inscriptions: The Productivity of South African Penal Institutions*, Chicago: University of Chicago.

—— (2008), 'Moralizing Security: "Corrections" and the Post-Apartheid Prison', *Race/Ethnicity: Multidisciplinary Global Contexts*, vol. 2, no. 1: 69–87.

Gilroy, P. (1987), 'The Myth of Black Criminality', in P. Scraton, ed., *Law, Order and the Authoritarian State*, Milton Keynes: Open University Press: 47–56.

Girard, V. (2017), *Le vote FN au Village: Trajectoires de Ménages Populaires du Périurbain*, Vulaines-sur-Seine: Editions du Croquant.

Glaser, B.G. and A.L. Strauss (1967), *The Discovery of Grounded Theory: Strategies for Qualitative Research*, Illinois: Aldine Publishing Company.

Glissant, E. (1989), *Caribbean Discourse: Selected Essays*, Charlottesville: University Press of Virginia.

—— (1997), *Poetics of Relation*, Ann Arbor: University of Michigan Press.

—— (2001), *The Fourth Century*, Lincoln: Bison Books.

Global Nonviolent Action Database (2011), 'Spanish Indignados Protest Austerity Measures, 2011: The Movement and Its Vision', *Open Democracy*.

Glueck, S. and E. Glueck (1934), *Five Hundred Delinquent Women*, New York: Alfred A. Knopf.

Goffman, E. (1961), *Asylums: Essays on the Social Situation of Mental Patients and Other Inmates*, New York: Anchor Books.

—— (1963), *Stigma: Notes on the Management of Spoiled Identity*, New York: Simon and Schuster.

—— (1969), *The Presentation of Self in Everyday Life*, London: Penguin Books.

Goifman, K. (2002), 'Killing Time in the Brazilian Slammer', *Ethnography*, vol. 3, no. 4: 435–41.

Goldberg, D.T. (1993), *Racist Culture, Philosophy and Politics of Meaning*, Oxford: Blackwell Publishers, Oxford.

—— (2002), *The Racial State*, Oxford: Blackwell Publishers.

Goldin, I., G. Cameron and M. Balarajan (2011), *Exceptional People: How Migration Shaped Our World and Will Define Our Future*, Princeton: Princeton University Press.

Gopal, M. (2012), 'Caste, Sexuality and Labour: The Troubled Connection', *Current Sociology*, vol. 60, no. 2: 222–38.

Gqola, P. (2001), '"Slaves Don't Have Opinions": Inscriptions of Slave Bodies and the Denial of Agency in Rayda Jacob's "The Slave Book"', in Z. Erasmus, ed., *Coloured by History, Shaped by Place*, Cape Town: Kwela Books: 45–63.

Granel, G. (1995), *Etudes: Collection La Philosophie en Effet*, Paris: Galilée.

Green, C. (2003), *Art in France, 1900–1940*, New Haven: Yale University Press.

Griffin, R. (1991), *The Nature of Fascism*, London: Pinter Publishers.

Groenendijk, K. (2004), 'Legal Concepts of Integration in EU Migration Law', *European Journal of Migration and Law*, vol. 6, no. 2: 111–26.

—— (2012), 'Integration of Immigrants in the EU: The Old or the New Way?', in Y. Pascouau and T. Strik, eds, *Which Integration Policies for Migrants? Interaction between the EU and Its Member States*, Nijmegen: Wolf Legal Publishers: 3–14.

Habermas, J. (2020), 'In This Crisis, We Must Act in the Explicit Knowledge of Our Non-knowledge', *Archyde*, Interview, 10 April, available at https://www.archyde.com/in-this-crisis-we-must-act-in-the-explicit-knowledge-of-our-non-knowledge/, accessed 1 January 2022.

Haggblade, S. (1992), 'The Shebeen Queen and the Evolution of Botswana's Sorghum Beer Industry', in J. Crush and A. Ambler, eds, *Liquor and Labor in Southern Africa*, Athens: Ohio University Press, Pietermaritzburg: University of Natal Press: 395–412.

Hall, S. (1992), 'The West and the Rest Discourse and Power', in S. Hall and B. Gieben, eds, *Formations of Modernity*, Cambridge, Mass: Open University and Blackwell: 275–95.

—— (1996), 'New Ethnicities', in D. Morle and C. Kuan-Hsing, eds, *Critical Dialogues in Cultural Studies*, London: Routledge: 442–51.

Hall, S., C. Critcher, T. Jefferson, J. Clarke and B. Roberts (2013), *Policing the Crisis: Mugging, the State and Law and Order*, London: Palgrave Macmillan.

Hall, T.D. and P.N. Kardulias (2010), 'Human Migration over Millennia: A World-Systems View of Human Migration, Past and Present', in T. Boulder and E. Mielants, eds, *Mass Migration in the World-System: Past, Present and Future, Political Economy of the World-System*, Boulder: Paradigm Press: 22–37.

Hammerschmidt, M. (2005), 'Ist der Islamismus eine Abart des Faschismus?', *Telepolis*, 25 November, available at http://www.heise.de/tp/artikel/21/21397/1.html, accessed 20 December 2021.

Hanafi, S. (2019), 'Global Sociology: Towards New Directions', *Global Dialogue: Magazine of the International Sociological Association*, vol. 9, no. 2.

Hardt, M. (2002), 'Porto Alegre: Today's Bandung?', *New Left Review*, no. 14, March–April.

Harney, N. (2013), 'Precarity, Affect and Problem Solving with Mobile Phones by Asylum Seekers, Refugees and Migrants in Naples, Italy', *Journal of Refugee Studies*, vol. 26, no. 4: 541–57.

Harris, C. (2018), 'Explained: The Rise and Rise of Populism in Europe', 15 March, *Euronews*, https://www.euronews.com/2018/03/15/explained-the-rise-and-rise-of-populism-in-europe, accessed 10 May 2022.

Harrison, A. (1989), *Challenging de Gaulle: The O.A.S. and the Counterrevolution in Algeria, 1954–1962*, New York, Westport and London: Praeger.

Harteveld, E., W. van der Brug, S. Dahlberg and A. Kokkonen (2015), 'The Gender Gap in Populist Radical-Right Voting: Examining the Demand Side in Western and Eastern Europe', *Patterns of Prejudice*, vol. 49, no. 1–2: 103–34.

Hartman, S. (1997), *Scenes of Subjection: Terror, Slavery, and Self-Making in Nineteenth-Century America*, Oxford: Oxford University Press.

Harvey, D. (1997), *A Brief History of Neoliberalism*, Oxford: Oxford University Press.

Hausse, P. (1988), *Brewers, Beer Halls and Boycotts: A History of Liquor in South Africa*, Johannesburg: Raven Press.

Hayashida, F.M. (2008), 'Ancient Beer and Modern Brewers: Ethnoarchaeological Observations of Chicha Production in Two regions of the North Coast of Peru', *Journal of Anthropological Archaeology*, vol. 27, no. 2: 161–74.

Hebel, S. (2018), 'Vogelschiss', *Frankfurter Rundschau*, 5 June.

Hechelhammer, B. (2014), 'Die "Dossiers": Gehlens geheime Sonderkartei', in J. Dülffer, K.D. Henke, W. Krieger and R.D. Müller, eds, *Studien / Unabhängige Historikerkommission zur Erforschung der Geschichte des Bundesnachrichtendienstes 1945–1968*, Vol. 2, *Die Geschichte der Organisation Gehlen und des BND 1945–1968: Umrisse und Einblicke; Dokumentation der Tagung am 2. Dezember 2013*, Marburg: Unabhängige Historikerkommission zur Erforschung der Geschichte des Bundesnachrichtendienstes 1945–1968: 83–92.

Heidegger, M. (1973), *Introduction to Metaphysics*, G. Field and R. Polt, trans., New Haven and London: Yale University Press.

Helmfrid, S. (2013), 'Thirsty Men and Thrifty Women: Gender Power and Agency in the Rural Beer Trade in Burkina Faso', in S.V. Wolputte and M. Fumante, eds, *Beer in Africa: Drinking Spaces, States and Selves*, Berlin: LIT Verlag: 195–22.

Henke, K.D. (2014), 'Der Auslandsnachrichtendienst in der Innenpolitik: Umrisse', in J. Dülffer, K.D. Henke, W. Krieger and R.D. Müller, eds, *Studien / Unabhängige Historikerkommission zur Erforschung der Geschichte des Bundesnachrichtendienstes 1945–1968*, vol. 2, *Die Geschichte der Organisation Gehlen und des BND 1945–1968: Umrisse und Einblicke: Dokumentation der Tagung am 2. Dezember 2013*, Marburg: Unabhängige Historikerkommission zur Erforschung der Geschichte des Bundesnachrichtendienstes 1945–1968.

Herkenhoff, A.L. (2016a), 'Neurechte Netzwerke und die Initiative "Ein Prozent für unser Land"', in A. Häusler and F. Virchow, eds, *Neue Soziale Bewegung von rechts? Zukunftsängste, Abstieg der Mitt, Ressentiments, Eine Flugschrift*, Hamburg: VSA Verlag: 73–83.

—— (2016b), 'Rechter Nachwuchs für die AfD – Die Junge Alternative (JA)', in A. Häusler, ed., *Die Alternative für Deutschland: Programmatik, Entwicklung und politische Verortung*, Wiesbaden: Springer VS: 201–17.

Herrera, L. and N. El-Sharnouby (2018), 'Alain Badiou on the Egyptian Revolution: Questions of the Movement and Its Vision', *Open Democracy*.

Heylin, C. (1991), *Bob Dylan: Behind the Shades*, Berkeley: University of California: Viking.

Hills, C. (1972), *The World Turned Upside Down: Radical Ideas during the English Revolution*, Harmondsworth: Penguin.

Hobsbawm, E.J. (1994), *The Age of Extremes: A History of the World, 1914–1991*, Harmondsworth: Penguin Books.

—— (1987), *The Age of Empire, 1875–1914*, London: Weidenfeld & Nicolson.

Hof, T. (2009), 'Daniele Ganser: Nato-Geheimarmeen in Europa', *Sehepunkte*, vol. 9, no. 4, available at http://www.sehepunkte.de/2009/04/14558.html, accessed 20 December 2021.

Holiday, E., S. Zanaz, N. Tousch, R. Roberts, S. Morris and A. Gomelauri (2018), 'France', Research Portfolio, students' coursework for the course 'Fascisms: European History, Current Challenges', taught by Wiebke Keim within the MA Programme Euroculture, Strasbourg.

Hollifield, J.F., P.L. Martin and P.M. Orrenius, eds (2014), *Controlling Immigration: A Global Perspective*, third edition, Stanford: Stanford University Press.

Hornsey, I.S. (2003), *A History of Beer and Brewing*, Cambridge: The Royal Society of Chemistry.

Hruschka, C. (2020), 'Hot Returns Remain Contrary to the ECHR: ND & NT before the ECHR', *EU Immigration and Asylum Law and Policy*, 28 February, available at https://eumigrationlawblog.eu/hot-returns-remain-contrary-to-the-echr-nd-nt-before-the-echr/, accessed 20 December 2021.

Hui, W. (2020), 'The Revolutionary Personality and the Philosophy of Victory: Commemorating Lenin's 150th Birthday', *China Dream*, 22 April.

Hunter, M. (2005), 'Cultural Politics and Masculinities: Multiple-Partners in Historical Perspective in KwaZulu-Natal', *Culture, Health and Sexuality*, vol. 7, no. 4: 389–403.

Huntington, S. (1996), *The Clash of Civilizations and the Remaking of World Order*, New York: Touchstone.

Hung, H.F. (2011), *Protest with Chinese Characteristics: Demonstrations, Riots, and Petitions in the Mid-Century Qing Dynasty*, New York: Columbia University Press.

Häusler, A. (2016a), 'Die AfD – Eine Rechtspopulistische "Bewegungspartei"?', in A. Häusler and F. Virchow, eds, *Neue Soziale Bewegung von Rechts? Zukunftsängste – Abstieg der Mitte – Ressentiments, Eine Flugschrift*, Hamburg: VSA Verlag: 42–51.

—— (2016b), 'Einleitung', in A. Häusler, ed., *Die Alternative für Deutschland. Programmatik, Entwicklung und Politische Verortung*, Wiesbaden: Springer VS.

Häusler, A., ed. (2016), *Die Alternative für Deutschland. Programmatik, Entwicklung und Politische Verortung*, Wiesbaden: Springer VS.

Häusler, A. and F. Virchow (2016), 'Einleitung: Formierung Einer Neuen Rechten Bewegung', in A. Häusler and F. Virchow, eds, *Neue Soziale Bewegung von Rechts? Zukunftsängste, Abstieg der Mitte, Ressentiments, Eine Flugschrift*, Hamburg: VSA Verlag: 7–9.

Illouz, E. (2017), 'From the Paradox of Liberation to the Demise of Liberal Elites', in H. Geiselberger, ed., *The Great Regression*, Cambridge: Polity Press: 49–64.

ILO (2005), *A Global Alliance Against Forced Labour: Global Report under the Follow-up to the ILO Declaration on Fundamental Principles and Rights at Work, 2005*, Geneva: ILO.

—— (2009), *The Cost of Coercion: Global Report under the Follow-up to the ILO Declaration on Fundamental Principles and Rights at Work*, International Labour Conference, 98th Session 2009 Report I(B), Geneva: ILO.

Insurrections Ensemble (2017), *The Storming*, Cape Town: South African History Online, Centre for Humanities Research, University of the Western Cape.

International Organization for Migration (2019), *World Migration Report 2020*, available at https://publications.iom.int/system/files/pdf/wmr_2020.pdf, accessed 20 December 2021.

—— (2021), *World Migration Report 2020*, available at https://worldmigrationreport.iom.int/wmr-2020-interactive/, accessed 20 December 2021.

Irwin, J. and D.R. Cressey (1962), 'Thieves, Convicts and the Inmate Culture', *Social Problems*, vol. 10, no. 2: 142–55.

Irwin, J. (1970), *The Felon*, Englewood Cliffs, NJ: Prentice Hall.

Isin, E.F. and G.M. Nielsen, eds (2008), *Acts of Citizenship*, London and New York: Zed Books.

Ivaldi, G. (2015), 'Du Neoliberalisme au Social-Populisme? La Transformation de Programme Economique du Front National (1986–2012)', in S. Crépon, A. Dézé and N. Mayer, eds, *Les Faux-semblants du Front National: Sociologie d'un Parti Politique*, Paris: Sciences Po les Presses: 161–84.

Jackson, L. (2019), *Palaces of Pleasure: From Music Halls to the Seaside to Football, How the Victorians Invented Mass Entertainment*, New Haven: Yale University Press.

Jackson, P.I. and P. Doerschler (2018), 'Radical Right-Wing Parties in Western Europe and Their Populist Appeal: An Empirical Explanation', Session of Research Committee RC18 Political Sociology, 19th ISA World Congress of Sociology, Toronto, 18 July.

Jackson, W. (2013), 'Dangers to the Colony: Loose Women and the "Poor White" Problem in Kenya', *Journal of Colonialism and Colonial History*, vol. 14, no. 2, Summer.

Jacobson-Hardy, M. (2002), 'Behind the Razor Wire: A Photographic Essay', *Ethnography*, vol. 3, no. 4: 398–415.

Jacquemain, M. (2011), 'L'extrême Droite Nouvelle Est Arrivée', *Démocratie*, May: 1–3, available at http://hdl.handle.net/2268/91396, accessed 20 December 2021.

Jacquemain, M. and F. Claisse (2012), 'Que Ont Les Fachos Devenus?' *Politique, Revue de débats*, vol. 75, May–June: 16–25.

Jaenecke, H. (1993), '"Der Feind Steht Rechts": Das Gilt Noch Immer', in M. Leier, ed., *Un-Heil über Deutschland. Fremdenhaß und Neofaschismus Nach der Wiedervereinigung*, Hamburg: Gruner und Jahr: 7–11.

Jefremovas, V. (1991), 'Loose Women, Virtuous Wives, and Timid Virgins, Gender and the

Control of Resources in Rwanda', *Canadian Journal of African Studies*, vol. 25, no. 3: 378–95.

Jenness, V. and S. Fenstermaker (2014), 'Agnes Goes to Prison: Gender Authenticity, Transgender Inmates in Prisons for Men, and Pursuit of "the Real Deal"', *Gender and Society*, vol. 28, no. 1: 5–31.

Jennings, E. (2002), 'Last Exit from Vichy France: The Martinique Escape Route and the Ambiguities of Immigration', *Journal of Modern History*, vol. 74, no. 2.

Jensen, S. (1999), 'Discourses of Violence: Coping with Violence on the Cape Flats', *Social Dynamics: A Journal of African Studies*, vol. 25, no. 2: 75–97.

—— (2008), *Gangs, Politics and Dignity in Cape Town*, Johannesburg: Wits University Press.

Jensen, S. and D. Rodgers (2009), 'Revolutionaries, Barbarians or War Machines? Gangs in Nicaragua and South Africa', *Socialist Register*, vol. 45: 220–38.

Jentsch, U. (2016), 'Die "Lebensschutz" Bewegung und die AfD: Nur ein Teil der Bewegung Ergreift Partei', in A. Häusler, ed., *Die Alternative für Deutschland: Programmatik, Entwicklung und Politische Verortung*, Wiesbaden: Springer VS: 99–107.

Jewkes Y. (2014), 'An Introduction to "Doing Prison Research Differently"', *Qualitative Inquiry*, vol. 20, no. 4: 387–91.

—— (2014), 'Autoethnography and Emotion as Intellectual Resources Doing Prison Research Differently', *Qualitative Inquiry*, vol. 18, no. 1: 63–75.

John, M.E. (2017), 'The Woman Question: Reflections on Feminism and Marxism', *Economic and Political Weekly*, vol. 52, no. 50, 16 December.

Jones, R.S., J.I. Ross, S.C. Richards and D.S. Murphy (2009), 'The First Dime: A Decade of Convict Criminology', *The Prison Journal*, vol. 89: 151–71.

Jones, S. (2016), 'Mapping Extremism: The Network Politics of the Far-Right', Political Science Dissertations', *Scholar Works @ Georgia State University*, available at https://scholarworks.gsu.edu/political_science_diss/42, accessed 20 December 2021.

Judis, B.J. (2016), *The Populist Explosion: How the Great Recession Transformed American and European Politics*, New York: Columbia Global Reports.

Juhász, A. (2018), 'Hungary after the Election: Continuing on Orbán's Path', *Heinrich Böll Stiftung*, 12 April, available at https://www.boell.de/en/2018/04/12/hungary-after-election-continuing-orbans-path?dimension1=ds_focus_hungary, accessed 20 December 2021.

Jules-Macquet, R. (2014), *The State of South African Prisons: Edition One*, Cape Town: National Institute for Crime Prevention and the Reintegration of Offenders (NICRO).

Juss, S., ed. (2013), *The Ashgate Research Companion to Migration Law, Theory and Policy*, London and New York: Routledge.

Kailitz, S. (2007), 'Die nationalsozialistische Ideologie der NPD', in U. Backes and H. Steglich, eds, *Extremismus und Demokratie: Vol. 17: Die NPD. Erfolgsbedingungen einer rechtsextremistischen Partei*, Baden-Baden: Nomos: 337–54.

Kalyvas, A. (2010), 'An Anomaly Kalyvas? Some Reflections on the Greek December 2008', *Constellations*, vol. 17, no. 2: 351–65.

Kalyvas, S. (2008), 'Why is Athens Burning?', *New York Times*, 11 December.

Kamann, M. (2017), 'Was Höcke mit der "Denkmal der Schande": Rede Bezweckt', *Welt Online*, 18 January, available at https://www.welt.de/politik/deutschland/article161286915/Was-Hoecke-mit-der-Denkmal-der-Schande-Rede-bezweckt.html, accessed 1 January 2022.

Kaplan, L.S. (2006), 'Review of: NATO's Secret Armies: Operation Gladio and Terrorism in Western Europe by Daniele Ganser', *The International History Review*, vol. 28, no. 3: 685–86.

Karatzogianni, A., O. Morgunova, N. Kambouri, O. Lafazani, N. Trimikliniotis, G. Ioannou and D. Nguyen (2016), 'Intercultural Conflict and Dialogue in the Transnational Digital Public

Sphere: Findings from the MIG@NET Research Project (2010–2013)', in A. Karatzogianni, D. Nguyen, and E. Serafinelli, eds, *The Digital Transformation of the Public Sphere: Conflict, Migration, Crisis, and Culture in Digital Networks*, London: Palgrave Macmillan.

Kasparek, B. (2017), 'Routes, Corridors, and Spaces of Exception: Governing Migration and Europe', *Near Futures Online*, available at: http://nearfuturesonline.org/routes-corridors-and-spaces-of-exception-governing-migration-and-europe/, accessed 10 April 2018.

Kassow, S.D. (1989), *Students, Professors and the State in Tsarist Russia*, Berkeley: University of California Press.

Keim, W. (2014), 'Colonialism, National-Socialism and the Holocaust', in A. Sitas, W. Keim, S. Damodaran, N. Trimikliniotis and F. Garba, eds, *Gauging and Engaging Deviance, 1600–2000*, New Delhi: Tulika Books: 109–88.

—— (2017), 'Mitschrieb zu den Veranstaltungen des Antaios-Verlags auf der FF Buchmesse', Frankfurt.

—— (forthcoming), 'The Rise and Strength of Authoritarian Restoration – Constructing a Comparative Logic for Research', in O. Giraud and M. Lallement, eds, *Decentring Comparative Analysis*, Leiden and Boston: Brill.

Keim, W., E. Çelik and V. Wöhrer (2014), *Global Knowledge Production in the Social Sciences: Made in Circulation*, London: Ashgate.

Kellershohn, H. (2004), 'Im "Dienst an der Nationalsozialistischen Revolution": Die Deutsche Gildenschaft und ihr Verhältnis zum Nationalsozialismus', available at http://www.diss-duisburg.de/Internetbibliothek/Artikel/kellershohn--gildenschaft-und-ns.pdf, accessed 20 December 2021.

—— (2016), 'Risse im Gebälk. Flügelkämpfe in der Jungkonservativen Neuen Rechten und der AfD', in A. Häusler, ed., *Die Alternative für Deutschland. Programmatik, Entwicklung und Politische Verortung*, Wiesbaden: Springer VS: 181–200.

Kempa, M. and A.M. Singh (2008), 'Private Security, Political Economy and the Policing of Race', *Theoretical Criminology*, vol. 12, no. 3: 333–54.

Kemper, A. (2016a), *'Die Neurotische Phase Überwinden, in der Wir uns Seit Siebzig Jahren Befinden': Zur Differenz von Konservativismus und Faschismus am Beispiel der 'Historischen Mission' Björn Höckes (AfD)*, available at http://www.th.rosalux.de/fileadmin/ls_thueringen/dokumente/publikationen/RLS-HeftMissionHoecke-Feb16.pdf, accessed 20 December 2021.

—— (2016b), 'Antiemanzipatorische Netzwerke und die Geschlechter- und Familienpolitik der Alternative für Deutschland', in A. Häusler, ed., *Die Alternative für Deutschland. Programmatik, Entwicklung und politische Verortung*, Wiesbaden: Springer VS: 81–97.

Kennedy, L. (2013), '"Long Termer Blues": Penal Politics, Reform, and Carceral Experiences at Angola', *Punishment and Society*, vol. 15, no. 3: 304–22.

Keßelring, A. (2014), *Die Organisation Gehlen und die Verteidigung Westdeutschlands: Alte Elitedivisionen und neue Militärstrukturen, 1949 – 1953*, Studien, *Veröffentlichungen der Unabhängigen Historikerkommission zur Erforschung der Geschichte des Bundesnachrichtendienstes 1945–1968*, Nr. 3, available at http://www.uhk-bnd.de/wp-content/uploads/2013/05/UHK-BND_Bd3_online.pdf, accessed 20 December 2021.

—— (2017), *Die Organisation Gehlen und die Neuformierung des Militärs in der Bundesrepublik. Veröffentlichungen der Unabhängigen Historikerkommission zur Erforschung der Geschichte des Bundesnachrichtendienstes 1945–1968: Vol. 6*, Berlin: Ch. Links Verlag.

Kimmel, M, ed. (2007), *The Sexual Self: The Construction of Sexual Scripts*, Nashville: Vanderbilt University Press.

Kinnes, I. (2000), *From Urban Street Gangs to Criminal Empires: The Changing Face of Gangs in the Western Cape*, Cape Town: National Institute for Crime Prevention and Reintegration of Offenders (NICRO).

Kirchgaessner, S. (2018), 'Far-right Italy Minister Vows 'Action' to Expel Thousands of Roma', *The Guardian*, 19 June.

Kissler, S.M., C. Tedijanto, E. Goldstein, Y.H. Grad and M. Lipsitch (2020), 'Coronavirus: Projecting the Transmission Dynamics of SARS-CoV-2 through the Post-Pandemic Period', *Science*, vol. 368, 860–68, 22 May.

Knöbl, W. (2003), 'Theories that Won't Pass Away: The Never-Ending Story', in G. Delanty and E.F. Isin, eds, *Handbook of Historical Sociology*, London: Sage.

Kolakowski, L. (2004), *Main Currents of Marxism*, New York: Norton.

Kolar, C.V. (2015), 'Resistance in the Congo Free State: 1885–1908', Southern Illinois University Carbondale, *Southern Illinois University*, 1 June, available at https://opensiuc.lib.siu.edu/uhp_theses/399/, accessed 12 August 2021.

Korsch, J. (2016a), ''Natürliche Verbündete?'' Die Pegida-Debatte in der AfD zwischen Anziehung und Ablehnung', in A. Häusler, ed., *Die Alternative für Deutschland. Programmatik, Entwicklung und politische Verortung*, Wiesbaden: Springer VS: 111–34.

—— (2016b), 'Stichwortgeber in Nadelstreifen. Personelle und Inhaltliche Konvergenzen Zwischen AfD und Pegida', in A. Häusler, ed., *Die Alternative für Deutschland. Programmatik, Entwicklung und politische Verortung*, Wiesbaden: Springer VS: 135–47.

Korzeniewicz, R.P. and T.P. Moran (2016), 'Economic Inequality, Stratification and Mobility', in I. Wallerstein, ed., *The World is Out of Joint: World-Historical Interpretations of Continuing Polarizations,* vol. 1, London: Routledge: 23–38.

Kostakopoulou, D. (2010a), 'The Anatomy of Civic Integration', *The Modern Law Review*, vol. 73, no. 6: 933–58.

—— (2010b), 'Introduction', in R. Van Oers, E. Ersboll and D. Kostakopoulou, eds, *A Re-definition of Belonging?*, Leiden: Koninklijke Brill: 1–23.

Kováts, E. (2017), 'The Emergence of Powerful Anti-Gender Movements in Europe and the Crisis of Liberal Democracy', in M. Köttig, R. Bitzan, and A. Pető, eds, *Gender and Politics: Gender and Far Right Politics in Europe*, Cham, Switzerland: Palgrave Macmillan: 175–89.

Kováts, E. and M. Pőim, eds (2015), *Gender as Symbolic Glue: The Position and Role of Conservative and Far Right Parties in the Anti-Gender Mobilizations in Europe*, Budapest: Foundation for European Progressive Studies.

Krauss, E.S. (1988), 'The 1960s Japanese Student Movement', in G.L. Bernstein and H. Fukui, eds, *Japan and the World*, Zurich: Springer.

Kriesi, H. (2013), 'Democratic Legitimacy: Is There a Legitimacy Crisis in Contemporary Politics?' *Politische Vierteljahresschrift*, vol. 54, no. 4: 609–38.

Kronauer, J. (2016), 'Die internationalen ''Counter-Jihad''-Netzwerke', in A. Häusler and F. Virchow, eds, *Neue soziale Bewegung von Rechts? Zukunftsängste, Abstieg der Mitte, Ressentiments, Eine Flugschrift*, Hamburg: VSA Verlag: 32–41.

Kronsell, A. (2005), 'Gendered Practices in Institutions of Hegemonic Masculinity', *International Feminist Journal of Politics*, vol. 7, no. 2: 280–98.

Kuhar, R. and D. Paternotte, eds (2017), *Anti-Gender Campaigns in Europe: Mobilizing against Equality*, London: Rowman and Littlefield International.

Kuhn, T.S. (1962, 1974), *The Structure of Scientific Revolutions,* Illinois: Chicago University Press.

Kumar, K. (2016), 'English Translation: Full Text of Kanhaiya Kumar's Electrifying Speech at JNU', *The Wire*, 4 March.

Kunzel, R.G. (2002), 'Situating Sex: Prison Sexual Culture in the Mid-Twentieth-Century United States', *GLQ: A Journal of Lesbian and Gay Studies*, vol. 8, no. 3: 253–70.

Kupers, T.A. (2001), 'Rape and the Prison Code', in D. Sabo, T.A. Kupers and W. London, eds, *Prison Masculinities*, Philadelphia: Temple University Press: 111–17.

Kurlansky, M. (2004), *1968: The Year that Rocked the World*, New York: Ballantine Books.

Kushner, H. (2011), 'Shigenobu Fusako (1945–)', in G. Martin, ed., *The Sage Encyclopedia of Terrorism*, Thousand Oaks, California: Sage Publishers.

Kutay, A. (2014), 'Theoretical Perspective: Governmentality and Discursive Formation of European Civil Society', in A. Kutay, *Governance and European Civil Society*, London: Routledge: 17–44.

Kynoch, G. (1999), 'From the Ninevites to the Hard Livings Gang: Township Gangsters and Urban Violence in Twentieth-Century South Africa', *African Studies*, vol. 58, no. 1: 55–85.

—— (2008), 'Urban Violence in Colonial Africa: A Case for South African Exceptionalism', *Journal of Southern African Studies*, vol. 34, no. 3: 629–45.

Köttig, M. (2017), 'Gender Stereotypes Constructed by the Media: The Case of the National Socialist Underground (NSU) in Germany', in M. Köttig, R. Bitzan and A. Pető, eds, *Gender and Politics: Gender and Far Right Politics in Europe*, Cham, Switzerland: Palgrave Macmillan: 221–34.

—— (2018), 'A Biographical and Family Historical Approach in Researching Gender and Right Ming Movements', Toronto: RC47 Social Classes and Social Movements, July.

la Hausse, P. (1992), 'Drinking and Cultural Innovation in Durban: The Origins of the Beerhall in South Africa, 1902 – 1960', in J. Crush and A. Ambler, eds, *Liquor and Labor in Southern Africa*, Athens: Ohio University Press and Pietermaritzburg: University of Natal Press: 78–114.

Laclau, E. (1982a), 'Towards a Theory of Populism', *Politics and Ideology in Marxist Theory: Capitalism, Fascism*, London: Verso.

—— (1982b), 'Fascism and Ideology', *Politics and Ideology in Marxist Theory: Capitalism, Fascism*. London: Verso.

—— (2005), *On Populist Reason*, London: Verso.

Lafont, V. (2001), 'Les Jeunes Militants du Front National: Trois Modeles D'engagement et de Cheminement', *Revue Française de Science Politique*, vol. 51, no. 1: 175–98.

Laite, J.A. (2009), 'Historical Perspectives on Industrial Development, Mining, and Prostitution', *The Historical Journal*, vol. 52, no. 3: 739–61.

Lakkimsetti, C. (2017), '"Home and Beautiful Things": Aspirational Politics in Dance Bars in India', *Sexualities*, vol. 20, no. 4: 463–81.

Lal, B.V., D. Munro and E.D. Beechert, eds (1993), *Planters, Workers, Resistance and Accommodation*, Honolulu: University of Hawaii Press.

Langa, M. and A. Sitas, eds (2016), *Gwala, Mafika Pascal: Collected Poems*, Woodstock: South African History Online.

Lankenau, S.E., M.C. Clatts, D. Welle, L.A. Goldsamt and M.V. Gwadz (2005), 'Street Careers: Homelessness, Drug Use, and Sex Work among Young Men who Have Sex with Men (YMSM)', *International Journal of Drug Policy*, vol. 16: 10–18.

Lara, S.H. (2010), 'Palmares and Cucaú: Political Dimensions of a Maroon Community in Late Seventeenth-Century Brazil', available at http://www.yale.edu/glc/brazil/papers/lara-paper. pdf, accessed 12 August 2021.

Larson, M. and J. Piche (2013), 'Preface from the Managing Editors: Convict Criminology and the Journal of Prisoners on Prison', *Journal of Prisoners on Prison*, vol. 21: 1–2.

Lawrence, E. (1982, 2005), 'In the Abundance of Water the Fool is Thirsty: Sociology and Black 'Pathology', Centre for Contemporary Cultural Studies, ed., *The Empire Strikes Back: Race and Racism in 70s Britain*, London and New York: Routledge: 93–139.

Lazaridis, G. and A.M. Konsta (2015), 'Identitarian Populism: Securitization of Migration and the Far Right in Times of Economic Crisis in Greece and the UK', in G. Lazaridis and K. Wadia, eds, *The Securitization of Migration in the EU: Debates since 9/11*, London: Palgrave Macmillan: 184–207.

Lean, N. (2017), *The Islamophobia Industry: How the Right Manufactures Hatred of Muslims*, second edition, London: Pluto Press.

Lebone, K. (2012), 'South Africa Survey 2012: Crime and Security', South African Institute of Race Relations: 679–788.

Lecorte, T. (2013), *Stay Behind - wieviel Verschwörung ist dabei?*, March, available at http://www.lecorte.de/wp/wp-content/uploads/2013/03/Lecorte-Stay-Behind-wieviel-Verschw%C3%B6rung-ist-dabei.pdf, accessed 20 December 2021.

Lefebvre, H. (1996), *Writings on Cities*, Oxford: Blackwell.

—— (1971), *Everyday Life in the Modern World*, London: Allen Lane and New Brunswick, NJ: Transaction.

—— (2002), *Critique of Everyday Life*, London: Verso.

Legg, S. (2014), *Prostitution and the Ends of Empire: Scale, Governmentalities, and Interwar India*, Durham: Duke University Press.

Leggett, T. (2004), 'Still Marginal: Crime in the Coloured Community', *South African Crime Quarterly*, no. 7: 21–26.

—— (2012), 'Drugs, Sex Work, and HIV in Three Southern African Cities', *Centre for Social and Development Studies*, vol. 32, no. 1:101–09.

Lenin, V.I. (1968), 'The Student Movement and the Present Situation', *New Left Review: Special Edition*, vol. 1, no. 52, May.

Lerche, J. (2007), 'A Global Alliance against Forced Labour? Unfree Labour, Neo-Liberal Globalization and the International Labour Organization', *Journal of Agrarian Change*, vol. 7, no. 4, October: 425–52.

Levi-Strauss, C. (2012), *Tristes Tropiques*, J. Weightman and D. Weightman, trans., New York: Penguin Books.

Levine, P. (2000), 'Orientalist Sociology and the Creation of Colonial Sexualities', *Feminist Review*, vol. 65: 5–21.

—— (2003), *Prostitution, Race, and Politics: Policing Venereal Disease in the British Empire*, New York: Routledge.

Lewin, J. and J. Perez (2018), 'Pilgrims of Belonging: Family, Gang, and Religious Script(ure)s to Live By', *African Journal of Gender and Religion: Advancing Theory and Methods in Gender and Religion*, vol. 24, no. 2, December: 95–119.

Lewis, D. (2011), 'Representing African Sexualities', in S. Tamale, ed., *African Sexualities: A Reader*, Cape Town: Pambazuka Press: 199–216.

Lewis, H.P. (2010), *God's Gangsters? The Number Gangs in South African Prisons*, Cape Town: Ihilihili Press.

Lewis-Beck, M. and G. Mitchell (1993), *French Electoral Theory: The National Front Test, Electoral Studies*, vol. 12, no. 2: 112–27.

Liebling, A. (1999), 'Doing Research in Prison: Breaking the Silence?', *Theoretical Criminology*, vol. 3, no. 2: 147–73.

—— (2001), 'Whose Side Are We On? Theory, Practice and Allegiances in Prisons Research', *British Journal of Criminology*, vol. 41: 472–84.

—— (2014), 'Postscript: Integrity and Emotion in Prisons Research', *Qualitative Inquiry*, vol. 20, no. 4: 481–86.

Lombroso, C. and G. Ferrero (2004), *Criminal Woman: The Prostitute, and the Normal Woman*, M. Gibson and N.H. Rafter, trans, Durham: Duke University Press, .

Loos, J. (2004), *Echoes of Slavery: Voices from South Africa's Past*, Cape Town: David Philip Publishers.

Luschy, C. (2017), *Between Past and Present: The Rhetoric of the Alternative für Deutschland: Instrumentalization of National Socialist Vocabulary in Today's Germany. A Political Strategy?*, MA thesis, Master Euroculture, University of Strasbourg/Uppsala University.

Luyt, R. and D. Foster (2001), 'Hegemonic Masculine Conceptualization in Gang Culture', *South African Journal of Psychology*, vol. 31, no. 3: 1–11.

Léger, J.F. (2015), 'Le Chomage, terreau du vote Front National?', *Population et Avenir*, vol. 723, no. 3: 40–70.

Löwy, M. and F. Sitel (2015), 'The Far Right in France: The Front National in European Perspective', in L. Panitch and G. Albo, eds, *The Politics of the Right: Socialist Register 2016*, New York: NYU Press, Monthly Review Press: 51–67.

Macey, D. (2012), *Frantz Fanon: A Biography*, London: Verso Books.

Macciocchi A. (1976), *Everyday Life in Revolutionary China*, New York: Monthly Review Press.

Machowecz, M., P. Middelhoff, Y. Musharbash and H. Stark (2018), '"Revolution Chemnitz": Zum Umsturz bereit', *Zeit Online*, 3 October, available at https://www.zeit.de/2018/41/rechtsterrorismus-revolution-chemnitz-telegram-neonazi-gewalt?print, accessed 20 December 2021.

Mager, A.K. (2010), *Beer, Sociability, and Masculinity in South Africa*, Cape Town: UCT Press.

Maguire, M. (2014), 'Inside Job: Research Dilemmas, Exploits and Exploitation of a Prison "Insider"', in D. Drake, R. Earle and J. Sloan, eds, *The International Handbook of Prison Ethnography*, Basingstoke: Palgrave.

Malevich, K. (1915), 'From Cubism and Futurism to Suprematism', Art Institute of Chicago, available at https://www.artic.edu/artworks/199128/from-cubism-and-futurism-to-suprematism-ot-kubizma-i-futurizma-k-suprematizmu, accessed 4 June 2016.

Malik, K. (1996), *The Meaning of Race*, New York: Palgrave Macmillan.

—— (2009), 'Book Review: Reflections on the Revolution in Europe: Immigration, Islam and Europe by Christopher Caldwell', *New Humanist*, 16 July, available at http://newhumanist. org.uk/2093/book-review-reflections-on-the-revolution-in-europe-immigration-islam-and-europe-by-christopher-caldwell, accessed 13 October 2021.

Mammone, A. (2008), 'The Transnational Reaction to 1968: Neo-Fascist Fronts and Political Cultures in France and Italy', *Contemporary European History*, vol. 17, no. 2: 213–36.

Mandel, E. (1976), 'Introduction', in K. Marx, ed., *Capital*, vol. I, London: Penguin Books: 11–86.

Mann, M. (2004), *Fascists*, Cambridge: Cambridge University Press.

Mantoux, P. (1928), *The Industrial Revolution in the Eighteenth Century: An Outline of the Beginnings of the Modern Factory System in England*, London: Jonathan Cape.

Macey, D. (2012), *Frantz Fanon: A Biography*, London: Verso Books.

Marantzidis, N. (2009a), 'La Farce Grecque: Bilan D'une Fausse Révolte', *Le Monde*, 28 April.

—— (2009b), 'Ola Thimizan Ena Kseperasmeno Parelthon' (Everything Reminded of a Bygone Era), To Vema, 6 December.

Marcia L.C. (1997), *Medieval Foundations of the Western Intellectual Tradition, 400–1400*, New Haven: Yale University Press.

Marcuse, H. (1964), *One Dimensional Man: Studies in the Ideology of Advanced Industrial Society*, London: Routledge and Kegan Paul.

Marin, G. (2016), 'Pourquoi le FN n'a pas Encore Gagné? Débat et controverses', *L'Humanité*, 7 October.

Marin, L.A. (2001), *Alcohol, Sex, and Gender in Late Medieval and Early Modern Europe*, New York: Palgrave Macmillan.

Marino, A. (1999), *A Quiet American: The Secret Work of Varian Fry*, New York: St Martin's Press.

Marks, S. (1972), 'Khoisan Resistance to the Dutch in the Seventeenth and Eighteenth Centuries', *The Journal of African History*, vol. 13, no. 1: 55–80.

Marshall, H., ed. (1965), *Vladimir Mayakovsky's Poetry*, New York: Hill and Wang.

Martin, A.L. (2001), *Alcohol, Sex and Gender in Late Medieval and Early Modern Europe*, New York: Palgrave Macmillan.

Marx, K. (1976), *Capital*, vol. I. London: Penguin Books.

Massey, D.S. and M. Sánchez, *Brokered Boundaries: Immigrant Identity in Anti-Immigrant Times*, New York: Russell Sage Foundation, 2010.

Massey, D.S., J. Arango, G. Hugo, A. Kouaouci, A. Pellegrino and J.E. Taylor (1993), 'Theories of International Migration: A Review and Appraisal', *Population and Development Review*, vol. 19, no. 3, September: 431–66.

—— (2008), *Worlds in Motion, Understanding International Migration at the End of the Millennium*, Oxford: Clarendon Press.

Mason, P. (2017), 'Overcoming the Fear of Freedom', in H. Geiselberger, ed., *The Great Regression*, Cambridge: Polity Press.

Mathiesen, T. (1997), 'The Viewer Society: Michel Foucault's "Panopticon" Revisited', *Theoretical Criminology*, vol. 1, no. 2: 215–34.

Maurer, J.L. (2010), 'The Thin Red Line between Indentured and Bonded Labour: Javanese Workers in New Caledonia in the Early 20th Century', *Asian Journal of Social Science*, vol. 38, no. 6: 866–79.

Mayer, N. (2017), 'Les Électeurs du Front National (2012–2015)', in F. Gougou and V. Tiberj, *La Déconnexion Électorale: Un État Des Lieux de la Démocratie Française*, Paris: Fondation Jean-Jaurès: 69–76.

Mayer, N. and P. Perrineau (1990), 'Pourquoi Votent-ils pour le Front National?', *Pouvoirs – Revue Française D'études Constitutionnelles Et Politiques*: 163–84.

Mayerfeld, J. (2011), 'A Madisonian Argument for Strengthening International Human Rights Institutions: Lessons from Europe', in L. Cabrera, ed., *Global Governance, Global Government: Institutional Visions for an Evolving World System*, Albany: SUNY Press.

Mazzarella, W. (2015), 'A Different Kind of Flesh: Public Obscenity, Globalization and the Mumbai Dance Bar Ban', *Journal of South Asian Studies*, vol. 38, no. 3: 481–94.

Mbembe, A. (2008), *Johannesburg: Elusive Metropolis,* Duke University Press.

Mbuba, J.M. (2012) 'Lethal Rejection: Recounting Offenders' Experience in Prison and Societal Reaction Post Release', *The Prison Journal*, vol. 92, no. 2: 231–52.

McAllister, P. (1992), 'Beer Drinking and Labor Migration in the Transkei: The Invention of a Rural Tradition', in J. Crush and A. Ambler, eds, *Liquor and Labor in Southern Africa*, Athens: Ohio University Press and Pietermaritzburg: University of Natal Press: 252–68.

—— (2006), 'Xhosa Beer Drinking Rituals: Power, Practice, Performance in the South African Rural Periphery', Carolina Academic Press: Durham, North Carolina.

Mccurdy, J. (2014), 'The Heartbreaking Poetry of an Apple Factory Worker in China Who Took His Own Life', *In These Times*, 17 November.

Meussdoerffer, F.G. (2009), 'A Comprehensive History of Beer Brewing', in H.M. Resslinger, ed., *Handbook of Brewing: Processes, Technology, Markets*, Weinheim: Wiley-VCH Verlag GmbH and Co., KGaA: 1–42.

Mezzadra, S. (2017), 'Digital Mobility, Logistics, and the Politics of Migration', *Spheres: Journal of Digital Cultures*, no. 4, June, available at http://spheres-journal.org/digital-mobility-logistics-and-the-politics-of-migration/, accessed 20 December 2021.

Mezzadra, S. and B. Neilson (2013), *Border as Method, or, the Multiplication of Labor*, Durham: Duke University Press.

Michalski, J.M. (2015), 'Status Hierarchies and Hegemonic Masculinity: A General Theory of Prison Violence', *British Journal of Criminology*, vol. 57, no. 1: 1–21.

Michel, J.D. (2020), 'Covid-19: Fin de Partie ?!', *Anthropo-logiques*, 18 March, available at http://jdmichel.blog.tdg.ch/apps/print/305096, accessed 24 April 2020.

Mielants, H. (2007), *The Origins of Capitalism and the 'Rise of the West'*, Philadelphia: Temple University Press.

Mills, C.W. (1956), *The Power Elite*, Oxford: Oxford University Press.

—— (1959, 2000), *The Sociological Imagination*, New York: Oxford University.

—— (2002), *White Collar: The American Middle Classes*, fiftieth anniversary edition, New York: Oxford University Press.

Minderhoud, P. and N. Trimikliniotis (2009), *Rethinking the Free Movement of Workers: The European Challenges Ahead*, Nijmegen: Wolf Legal Publishers.

Mishra, P. (2017), 'Politics in the Age of Resentment: The Dark Legacy of the Enlightenment', in H. Geiselberger, ed., *The Great Regression*, Cambridge: Polity Press: 104–16.

Misik, R (2017). 'The Courage to Be Audacious', in H. Geiselberger, ed., *The Great Regression*, Cambridge: Polity Press: 117–29.

Mitsilegas, V. (2007), 'Immigration, Diversity and Integration: The Limits of EU Law', in P. Shah, ed., *Law and Ethnic Plurality*, Leiden: Brill: 31–45.

Mitsilegas, V. and S.H. Yewa (2018), 'The Criminalization of Irregular Migrants', in T. Basaran and E. Guild, eds, *Global Labour and the Migrant Premium: The Cost of Working Abroad*, London and New York: Routledge: 60–68.

Modisane, W.B. (1990), *Blame Me on History*, New York: Touchstone Books.

Moodie, D. (1994), *Going for Gold: Men, Mines and Migration*, Berkeley: University of California Press.

Moolman, B. (2015a), 'Carceral Dis/Continuities: Masculinities, Male Same-Sex Desire, Discipline, and Rape in South African Prisons', *Gender & Behaviour*, vol. 13, no. 2: 6742–52.

—— (2015b), 'Ethnography: Exploring Methodological Nuances in Feminist Research with Men Incarcerated for Sexual Offences', in D.H. Drake, R. Earle and J. Sloan, eds, *The Palgrave Handbook of Prison Ethnography*, London: Palgrave Macmillan: 199–213.

Morcom, A. (2017), '"The Cure is Worse than the Disease": Mumbai Dance Bars, and New Forms of Justice in the History of Female Public Performers in India', *Cultural and Social History: The Journal of the Social History Society*, Special Issue: Rethinking Gender and Justice in South Asia, vol. 14, no. 4: 1772–2013.

Morgan, R. and M. Evans (2001), *Combating Torture in Europe: The Work and Standards of the European Committee for the Prevention of Torture*, Strasbourg: Council of Europe Publishing.

Moss, K. (2017), 'Russia as the Saviour of European Civilization: Gender and the Geopolitics of Traditional Values', in R. Kuhar and D. Paternotte, eds, *Anti-Gender Campaigns in*

Europe: Mobilizing against Equality, London: Rowman and Littlefield International: 195–214.

Moten, F. (2013), 'Blackness and Nothingness (Mysticism in the Flesh)', *The South Atlantic Quarterly*, vol. 112, no. 4: 737–80.

Mouzelis, N. (2009), 'On the December Events', in S. Economides and V. Monastiriotis, eds, *The Return of Street Politics? Essays on the December Riots in Greece*, London: The Hellenic Observatory, LSE: 41–44.

Mphahlele, E. (2013), *Down Second Avenue*, New York: Penguin Books.

Msibi, T. (2011), 'The Lies We Have Been Told: On (Homo)Sexuality in Africa', *Africa Today*, vol. 58, no. 1: 54–77.

Mudde, C. (2000), *The Ideology of the Extreme Right*, Manchester: Manchester University Press.

—— (2007), *Populist Radical Right Parties in Europe*, Cambridge: Cambridge University Press.

—— (2013), 'Three Decades of Populist Radical Right Parties in Western Europe: So What?', *European Journal of Political Research*, vol. 52, no. 1: 1–19.

—— (2016), 'Europe's Populist Surge: A Long Time in Making', *Foreign Affairs*, vol. 95, no. 6: 25–30.

Mudde, C. and C.R. Karlwasse (2016), *Populism: A Very Short Introduction*, Oxford: Oxford University Press.

Müller, L.A. (1991), *Gladio, das Erbe des Kalten Krieges: Der Nato-Geheimbund und sein Deutscher Vorläufer* (Rororo Aktuell), Reinbek-bei-Hamburg: Rowohlt.

Müller, R.D. (2014), 'Frühe Konflikte: Annäherung an eine Biographie Reinhard Gehlens', in J. Dülffer *et al.*, eds, *Studien / Unabhängige Historikerkommission zur Erforschung der Geschichte des Bundesnachrichtendienstes 1945–1968*, Vol. 2: *Die Geschichte der Organisation Gehlen und des BND 1945–1968: Umrisse und Einblicke; Dokumentation der Tagung am 2. Dezember 2013*, Marburg: Unabhängige Historikerkommission zur Erforschung der Geschichte des Bundesnachrichtendienstes 1945–1968: 15–24.

Munck, G.L. (2018), 'Modernization Theory as a Case of Failed Knowledge Production', *The Annals of Comparative Democratization*, vol. 16, no. 3.

Muraguri, N., M. Temmerman and S. Geibel (2012), 'A Decade of Research Involving Men Who Have Sex with Men in sub-Saharan Africa: Current Knowledge and Future Directions', *SAHARA-J: Journal of Social Aspects of HIV/AIDS*, vol. 9, no. 3: 137–47.

Murray, D. (2018), *The Strange Death of Europe: Immigration, Identity, Islam*, London: Bloomsbury.

Myers, R. (2015), 'Barriers, Blinders, and Unbeknownst Experts Overcoming Access Barriers to Conduct Qualitative Studies of Juvenile Justice', *The Prison Journal*, vol. 95, no. 1: 66–83.

Nachtwey, O. (2017), 'Decivilization: On Regressive Tendencies in Western Societies', in H. Geiselberger, ed., *The Great Regression*, Cambridge: Polity Press: 130–42.

Nagy, B. (2015), 'Hungary's Hypocritical Migration Policy', *Heinrich Böll Stiftung*, 29 May, available at https://www.boell.de/en/2015/05/29/hungarys-hypocritical-migration-policy, accessed 20 December 2021.

—— (2016), 'Hungarian Asylum Law and Policy in 2015–2016: Securitization Instead of Loyal Cooperation', *German Law Journal*, Special Issue Constitutional Dimensions of the Refugee Crisis vol. 17, no. 6: 1033–182.

Naidoo, A. (2014), 'Long Reign of the South African Shebeen Queen', *Media Club South Africa*, 12 August.

Nair, J. (2008), '"Imperial Reason", National Honour and New Patriarchal Compacts in Early Twentieth-Century India', *History Workshop Journal*, no. 66, Oxford University Press: 208–26.

Naqvi, A. (1998), *Image and Identity: Fifty Years of Painting and Sculpture in Pakistan*, Karachi and New York: Oxford University Press.

Needell, J. (2010), 'American Counterpoint: New Approaches to Slavery and Abolition in Brazil', The 12th Annual Gilder Lehrman Center International Conference at Yale University, co-sponsored with the Council on Latin American and Iberian Studies at Yale, New Haven, Connecticut: Yale University, 29–30 October.

Needle, R., K. Kroeger, H. Belani, A. Achrekar, C.D. Parry and S. Dewing (2008), 'Sex, Drugs, and HIV: Rapid Assessment of HIV Risk Behaviors among Street-Based Drug Using Sex Workers in Durban, South Africa', *Social Science Medicine*, vol. 67: 1447–55.

Nelson, N. (1978), 'Female-Centered Families: Changing Patterns of Marriage and Family among Buzaa Brewers of Mathare Valley', *African Urban Studies*, vol. 3, Winter: 85–103.

Neruda, P. (1991), *Canto General*, Berkeley: University of California Press.

Nettleton, S. and J. Watson, eds (1998), *The Body in Everyday Life*, London: Routledge.

New Left Review (1968), Special Issue on France, vol. 1, no. 52, May.

Newbold, G. and J.I. Ross (2013), 'Convict Criminology at the Crossroads', *The Prison Journal*, vol. 93: 3–10.

Newbold, G., J.I. Ross, R.S. Jones, S.C. Richard and M. Lenza (2014), 'Prison Research from the Inside: The Role of Convict Autoethnography', *Qualitative Inquiry*, vol. 20, no. 4: 439–48.

Niehaus, I. (2002), 'Renegotiating Masculinity in the South African Lowveld: Narrative of Male Sex in Labour Compounds and in Prisons, *African Studies*, vol. 61, no. 1: 77–97.

Nietzsche, F. (1974), *The Twilight of the Idols*, Harmondsworth: Penguin Books.

Nieuwkerk, K. (1992), 'Female Entertainers in Egypt: Drinking and Gender Roles', in D. Gefou-Madianou, ed., *Alcohol, Gender and Culture*, New York: Routledge.

Nigam, A. (2016), 'Insurgent Ambedkar and a New Moment in Politics', *Kafila*, 28 March.

Nissen, A. and B. Siim (2021), 'The Danish "New Right": Replacing "Old" Welfare Chauvinism with a Neoliberal Far Right Agenda', *C-REX - Center for Research on Extremism*, 15 April, available at https://www.sv.uio.no/c-rex/english/news-and-events/right-now/2021/the-danish-new-right.html, accessed 20 December 2021.

Noll, G. (2016), 'Failure by Design? On the Constitution of EU Solidarity, Searching for Solidarity', in *EU Asylum and Border Policies: A Collection of Short Papers following the Odysseus Network's First Annual Policy Conference*, Brussels: Université libre de Bruxelles, 26–27 February: 3–4.

Nyanzi, S. (2013), 'Dismantling Reified African Culture through Localized Homosexualities in Uganda', *Culture, Health & Sexuality*, vol. 15, no. 8: 952–67.

Oberländer, H. (1993), 'Wie die Justiz mit Neonazis umgeht', in M. Leier, ed., *Un-Heil über Deutschland. Fremdenhaß und Neofaschismus nach der Wiedervereinigung*, Hamburg: Gruner und Jahr: 174–82.

Oikonomakis, L. and J. Roos (2016), *A Global Movement for Real Democracy? The Resonance of Anti-Austerity Protest from Spain and Greece to Occupy Wall Street*, Amsterdam: Amsterdam University Press.

OIP (2012), *Litigation Report: Ten Years of Litigation*, internal document.

Okal, J., S. Luchters, S. Geibel, M.F. Chersich, D. Lango and M. Temmerman (2009), 'Social Context, Sexual Risk Perceptions and Stigma: HIV Vulnerability among Male Sex Workers in Mombasa, Kenya', *Culture, Health and Sexuality*, vol. 11, no. 8: 811–26.

Omvedt, G. (2002), 'Ambedkar and After: The Dalit Movement in India', in G. Shah, ed., *Social Movements and the State*, New Delhi: Sage Publications.

Oommen, T.K. (1990), *Protest and Change: Studies in Social Movements*, New Delhi: Sage Publications.

Open Education Sociology Dictionary, 'Society', *Free Online Sociology Dictionary*, available at https://sociologydictionary.org/society/#definition_of_society, accessed 10 October 2021.

Oppelland, T. (2020), 'Kurz und Bündig: Die AfD', *Bundeszentrale fur Politische Bidung*, 26 October, available at http://www.bpb.de/politik/grundfragen/parteien-in-deutschland/211108/afd, accessed 20 December 2021.

Overdiek, U. (2014), 'Männliche Überlegenheitsvorstellungen in der Rechtsextremen Ideologie', *Bundeszentrale fur politische Bidung*, 27 November, available at http://www.bpb.de/politik/extremismus/rechtsextremismus/197016/maennliche-ueberlegenheitsvorstellungen-in-der-rechtsextremen-ideologie, accessed 20 December 2021.

Pajnik, M. and F. Anthias, eds (2014), *Contesting Integration, Engendering Migration: Theory and Practice*, London and New York: Palgrave Macmillan.

Pande, A. (2009), 'Not an "Angel", Not a "Whore": Surrogates as "Dirty" Workers in India', *Indian Journal of Gender Studies*, vol. 16, no. 2: 141–73.

—— (2014), *Wombs in Labor*, New York: Columbia University Press.

—— (2017), 'Gestational Surrogacy in India: New Dynamics of Reproductive Labour', in E. Noronha and P. D'Cruz, eds, *Critical Perspectives on Work and Employment in Globalizing India*, Delhi: Springer: 267–82.

—— (2020), 'Visa Stamps for Injections: Traveling Bio-Labour and South African Egg Provision', *Gender and Society*, vol. 34, no. 4: 573–96.

Papadopoulos, D., N. Stephenson and V. Tsianos (2008), *Escape Routes. Control and Subversion in the Twenty-First Century*, London: Pluto Press.

Papadopoulos, D. and V. Tsianos (2013), 'After Citizenship: Autonomy of Migration and the Mobile Commons', *Citizenship Studies*, vol. 17, no. 2: 42–73.

Papagaroufali, E. (1992), 'Uses of Alcohol among Women: Games of Resistance, Power and Pleasure', in D. Gefou-Madianou, ed., *Alcohol, Gender and Culture*, New York: Routledge.

Parkin, J. (2013), 'The Criminalization of Migration in Europe: A State-of-the-Art of the Academic Literature and Research', *CEPS*, Paper no. 61, 25 October, available at https://www.ceps.eu/system/files/Criminalisation%20of%20Migration%20in%20Europe%20J%20Parkin%20FIDUCIA%20final.pdf, accessed 20 December 2021.

Parmar, I. (2012), *Foundations of the American Century: The Ford, Carnegie and Rockefeller Foundations in the Rise of American Power*, New York: Columbia University Press.

Parry, C., P. Petersen, S. Dewing, T. Carney, R. Needle, K. Kroegerm and L. Treger (2008), 'Rapid Assessment of Drug-Related HIV Risk among Men Who Have Sex with Men in Three South African Cities', *Drug and Alcohol Dependence*, vol. 95: 45–53.

Parry, R. (1992), 'The "Durban System" and the Limits of Colonial Power in Salisbury, 1890–1935', in J. Crush and A. Ambler, eds, *Liquor and Labor in Southern Africa*, Athens: Ohio University Press and Pietermaritzburg: University of Natal Press: 115–38.

Parsanoglou, D. (2015), 'Organizing an International Migration Machinery: The Intergovernmental Committee for European Migration', in L. Venturas, ed., *"Migration Management" in the Early Cold War: The Intergovernmental Committee for European Migration*, Corinth: University of the Peloponnese: 55–86.

Parsanoglou, D. and G. Tourgeli (2017), 'The Intergovernmental Committee for European Migration (ICEM) as Part of the post-WWII "World-Making"', in E. Calandri, S. Paoli and A. Varsori, eds, *Peoples and Borders: Seventy Years of Migration in Europe, from Europe, to Europe (1945–2015), Journal of European Integration History*, Special Issue, Baden-Baden, Germany: Nomos: 37–55.

Parsanoglou, D., G. Tourgeli, V. Tsianos and N. Trimikliniotis (forthcoming), *Towards Theorizing the Emergence of Post-Migrant Society*.

Pascouau, Y. (2012), 'Mandatory Integration Schemes in the EU Member States: Overview and Trends', in Y. Pascouau and T. Strik, eds, *Which Integration Policies for Migrants? Interaction between the EU and Its Member States*, Nijmegen: Wolf Legal Publishers: 129–40.

Pascouau, Y. and T. Strik, eds (20120, *Which Integration Policies for Migrants? Interaction between the EU and Its Member States*, Nijmegen: Wolf Legal Publishers.

Passmore, K. (2014), 'L'historiographie du 'fascisme' en France', *French Historical Studies*, vol. 37, no. 3: 469–99.

Paternotte, D. and R. Kuhar (2017), 'Anti-Gender Movement in Comparative Perspective', in R. Kuhar and D. Paternotte, eds, *Anti-Gender Campaigns in Europe: Mobilizing against Equality*, London: Rowman and Littlefield International: 253–76.

Paxton, R.O. (1998), 'The Five Stages of Fascism', *The Journal of Modern History*, vol. 70, no. 1: 1–23.

Pemberton, S. (2013), 'Enforcing Gender: The Constitution of Sex and Gender in Prison Regimes', *Signs: Journal of Women in Culture and Society*, vol. 39, no. 1: 151–75.

Penn, N. (1999), 'Rogues, Rebels, and Runaways: Eighteenth-Century Cape Characters', Cape Town: David Philip Publishers.

—— (2008), '"Close and Merciful Watchfulness": John Montagu's Convict System in the Mid-Nineteenth-Century Cape Colony', *Cultural and Social History*, vol. 5, no. 4: 465–80.

Perez, J. (2020), 'The Maroon as Abolitionist: The Embodied Fugitivities of "Coloured" Gangsters as Inhabited Abolitionism in Cape Town', in D. Scott and M. Coyle, eds, *The Routledge International Handbook of Penal Abolitionism*, London: Routledge.

Perrineau, P. (2016), 'Montée en Puissance et Recomposition de L'électorat Frontiste', *Pouvoirs*, vol. 157, no. 2: 63–73.

Petsinis, V. (2016), 'Eurasianism and the Far Right in Central and Southeast Europe', *Central Eastern European Review*, vol. 8, no. 1: 1–10.

Pfahl-Traughber, A. (2015), 'Der Anschlag auf Henriette Reker. Eine Auseinandersetzung im Lichte der Terrorismusforschung', *Humanistischer Pressedienst*, 20 October, available at https://hpd.de/artikel/12310, accessed 20 December 2021.

—— (2016), 'Wer wählt eigentlich rechtsextrem? Eine Fallstudie anhand des NPD-Landtagswahlergebnisses in Sachsen 2014', *Bundeszentrale fur politische Bidung*, 2 March, available at http://www.bpb.de/politik/extremismus/rechtsextremismus/222304/wer-waehlt-eigentlich-rechtsextrem, accessed 20 December 2021.

Philips, O. (2011), 'The "Perils" of Sex and the Panics of Race: The Dangers of Interracial Sex in Colonial Southern Rhodesia', in S. Tamale, ed., *African Sexualities: A Reader*, Cape Town: Pambazuka Press: 101–15.

Phillips, C. (2012), *The Multicultural Prison: Ethnicity, Masculinity and Social Relations among Prisoners*, Oxford: Oxford University Press.

Phizacklea, A. and R. Miles (1980), *Labour and Racism*, London: Routledge and Kegan Paul.

Piche, J. and K. Walby (2010), 'Problematizing Carceral Tours', *British Journal of Criminology*, vol. 50: 570–81.

Piche, J., B. Gaucher and K. Walby (2014), 'Facilitating Prisoner Ethnography: An Alternative Approach to "Doing Prison Research Differently"', *Qualitative Inquiry*, vol. 20, no. 4: 449–60.

Pierce, S. (2003), 'Farmers and "Prostitutes": Twentieth-Century Problems of Female Inheritance in Kano Emirate, Nigeria', *The Journal of African History*, vol. 44, no. 3, Cambridge: Cambridge University Press: 463–86.

Pierre, B. (1984, 1990), *Homo Academicus,* Cambridge: Polity Press.

Pilath, M. (2017), 'NPD Wird Nicht Verboten', *Zeit Online*, 17 January, http://www.zeit.de/

politik/deutschland/2017-01/bundesverfassungsgericht-lehnt-npd-verbot-ab, accessed 20 December 2021.

Pinnock, D. (1984), *The Brotherhoods: Streets Gangs and State Control in Cape Town*, Cape Town: David Philip Publishers.

—— (1997), *Gangs, Rituals, and Rites of Passage*, Cape Town: African Sun Press.

—— (2016), *Gang Town*, Cape Town: Tafelberg.

Poling, C. (2008), *Andre Masson and the Surrealist Self*, New Haven: Yale University Press.

Poovey, M. (1993), 'Anatomical Realism and Social Investigation in Early Nineteenth-Century Manchester', *Differences*, vol. 5, no. 3: 1–20.

Praeger, M. (2003), *The Imaginary Caribbean and the Caribbean Imaginary*, Lincoln: Nebraska University Press.

Premo, B. (2000), 'From the Pockets of Women: The Gendering of the Mita, Migration and Tribute in Colonial Chucuito', *The Americas*, vol. 57, no. 1: 63–93.

ProAsyl (n.d.), 'Überblick: Fakten, Zahlen und Argumente', available at https://www.proasyl. de/thema/fakten-zahlen-argumente/, accessed 20 December 2021.

Prison Litigation Network (2016), *Final Research Report on the European Prison Litigation Network*, Brussels: European Commission, September.

Pudal, R. (2011), 'Politics in the Fire Station: An Ethnographic Approach to Relationships to Politics in the Firefighting World', *Revue française de science politique*, vol. 61, no. 5: 75–101.

—— (2016), *Retour de Flammes. Les Pompiers, des Héros Fatigués?* Paris: La Découverte.

Punch, K. (2005), *Introduction to Social Research: Quantitative and Qualitative Approaches*, second edition, London: Sage Publications.

Puri, J. (2016), 'Sexualizing Neoliberalism: Identifying Technologies of Privatization, Cleansing, and Scarcity', *Sexual Research and Social Policy*, vol. 13: 308–20.

Quent, M. (2016a), 'Selbstjustiz im Namen des Volkes: Vigilantistischer Terrorismus', *Aus Politik und Zeitgeschichte*, vol. 66, nos. 24–25: 20–26.

—— (2016b), 'Vigilantismus - die Inszenierung rechter Bürgerwehren', in A. Häusler and F. Virchow, eds, *Neue Soziale Bewegung von Rechts? Zukunftsängste, Abstieg der Mitte, Ressentiments, Eine Flugschrift*, Hamburg: VSA Verlag: 84–94.

Quijano, A. (1998), 'The Colonial Nature of Power and Latin America's Cultural Experience', in Roberto Briceno-leon and Heinz R. Sonntag, eds, *Sociology in Latin America*, Montreal: International Sociological Association.

Rabbit, K. (2013), 'In Search of the Missing Mother: Suzanne Cesaire, Martiniquaise', *Research in African Literatures*, vol. 44, no. 1, Spring.

Ramberg, L. (2014), *Given to the Goddess: South Indian Devadasis and the Sexuality of Religion*, Durham: Duke University Press.

Rancière, J. (2004), *Disagreement: Politics and Philosophy*, Minneapolis: University of Minnesota Press, .

—— (2006), *Hatred of Democracy*, London: Verso Press.

—— (2010a), *Dissensus on Politics and Aesthetics*, New York: Continuum.

—— (2010b), 'Racism, a Passion from Above', (a translation of his talk given in Montreuil on 11 September 2010, during the conference on 'Les Roms, et qui d'autre?', published as 'Racisme, une Passion d'en Haut' by *Mediapart*), *Monthly Review*, 23 September.

—— (2014), *Moments Politiques: Interventions 1977–2009*, New York: Seven Stories Press.

Randeria, S. (2007), 'The State of Globalization Legal Plurality, Overlapping Sovereignties and Ambiguous Alliances between Civil Society and the Cunning State in India', *Theory, Culture & Society*, vol. 24, no. 1: 1–33.

Rao, M. (2019), 'APU Colloquium Series', *Centre for Law and Policy Research*, available at https://clpr.org.in/blog/apucolloquium-series-surrogacy-in-india-lecture-by-dr-m-rao/, accessed 20 December 2021.

Rass, C. (2014), 'Leben und Legende: Das Sozialprofil eines Geheimdienstes', in J. Dülffer, K.D. Henke, W. Krieger and R.D. Müller, eds, *Studien / Unabhängige Historikerkommission zur Erforschung der Geschichte des Bundesnachrichtendienstes 1945 – 1968*, vol. 2: *Die Geschichte der Organisation Gehlen und des BND 1945 - 1968: Umrisse und Einblicke; Dokumentation der Tagung am 2. Dezember 2013*, Marburg: Unabhängige Historikerkommission zur Erforschung der Geschichte des Bundesnachrichtendienstes 1945–1968: 26–39.

—— (2016), *Das Sozialprofil des Bundesnachrichtendienstes: Von den Anfängen bis 1968*, Veröffentlichungen der Unabhängigen Historikerkommission zur Erforschung der Geschichte des Bundesnachrichtendienstes 1945–1968, Berlin: Ch. Links Verlag.

Ratele, K., T. Shefer and L. Clowes (2012), 'Talking South African fathers: A Critical Examination of Men's Constructions and Experiences of Fatherhood and Fatherlessness', *South African Journal of Psychology*, vol. 42, no. 4: 553–63.

Ratele, K. (2013), 'Of What Value is Feminism to Black Men?', *Communicatio*, vol. 39, no. 2: 256–70.

—— (2014), 'Currents against Gender Transformation of South African Men: Relocating Marginality to the Centre of Research and Theory of Masculinities', *NORMA*, vol. 9, no. 1: 30–44.

Rathje, J. (2014), *'Wir Sind Wieder da': Die 'Reichsbürger': Überzeugungen, Gefahren und Handlungsstrategien*, Berlin: Amadeu Antonio Stiftung.

Reber, N. (2015), 'Reading Colourfully: Traveling through the World's Literature', *Pank Magazine*, 10 August.

Redding, S. (1992), 'Beer Brewing in Umtata: Women, Migrant Labour, and Social Control in Rural Town', in J. Crush, and A. Ambler, eds, *Liquor and Labor in Southern Africa*, Athens: Ohio University Press and Pietermaritzburg: University of Natal Press: 235–51.

Reichardt, S. (2004), 'Was mit dem Faschismus Passiert ist: Ein Literaturbericht zur Internationalen Faschismusforschung seit 1990, Teil 1', *Neue Politische Literatur*, vol. 49, no. 3: 385–406.

Reiter, K. (2014), 'Making Windows in Walls Strategies for Prison Research', *Qualitative Inquiry*, vol. 20, no. 4: 417–28.

Renken, F. (2006), *Frankreich im Schatten des Algerienkrieges: Die Fünfte Republik und die Erinnerung an den letzten großen Kolonialkonflikt*, Göttingen: V&R Unipress.

Rhodes, L.A. (2002), 'Psychopathy and the Face of Control in Supermax', *Ethnography*, vol. 3, no. 4: 442–66.

Ricciardelli, R., K. Maier and K. Hannah-Moffat (2015), 'Strategic Masculinities: Vulnerabilities, Risk and the Production of Prison Masculinities', *Theoretical Criminology*, vol. 19, no. 4: 491–513.

Riché, P. (2012), 'Guerre des Chiffres: Combien de Morts le 17 Octobre 1961?', *L'Obs*, 18 October, available at https://www.nouvelobs.com/rue89/rue89-explicateur/20121018.RUE3272/guerre-des-chiffres-combien-de-morts-le-17-octobre-1961.html, accessed 20 December 2021.

Rigos, A. (1999), 'Student Movement and Dictatorship', in G. Athanasiatou, A. Rigos, S. Seferiadis, eds, *I Dictatoria 1967–1974: Poliktikes Praktikes – Ideologikos Logos – Antistasi (The Dictatorship 1967–1974: Political Practices – Ideological Reason – Resistance)*, Kastaniotis, Athens.

Rispel, L.C. and C.A. Metcalf (2009), 'Breaking the Silence: South African HIV Policies and the Needs of Men who Have Sex with Men', *Reproductive Health Matters*, vol. 17, no. 33: 133–42.

Riste, O. (2014), '"Stay Behind": A Clandestine Cold War Phenomenon', *Journal of Cold War Studies*, vol. 16, no. 4: 35–59.

Rizzi, A., M. Polezhaeva and H. Chuang (2019), *European, US and Russian Connections Across the Current Far-Right*, students' coursework for the course 'Fascisms: European History, Current Challenges', taught by Wiebke Keim within the MA Programme Euroculture, Strasbourg.

Roberts, N. (2015), *Freedom as Marronage*, Chicago: University of Chicago Press.

Rodriguez, D. (2010), 'The Disorientation of the Teaching Act: Abolition as Pedagogical Position', *The Radical Teacher*, no. 88: 7–19.

—— (2019), 'Abolition as Praxis of Human Being: A Forward', *Harvard Law Review*, vol. 132, no. 6: 1575–612.

Rogerson, C. (1992), 'Drinking Apartheid and the Removal of Beerhalls in Johannesburg, 1939–1962', in J. Crush and A. Ambler, eds, *Liquor and Labor in Southern Africa*, Athens: Ohio University Press and Pietermaritzburg: University of Natal Press: 287–303.

Rolin, O. (2007), *Paper Tiger*, Lincoln: University of Nebraska Press.

Room, R. (1984), 'Alcohol and Ethnography: A Case of Problem Deflation?', *Current Anthropology*, vol. 25, no. 2, April: 169–91.

Rorich, M. (1989), 'Shebeens, Slumyards and Sophiatown: Black Women, Music and Cultural Change in Urban-South Africa c 1920–1960', *The World of Music*, vol. 31, no. 1: 78–104.

Rosbach, J. (2016), 'AfD-Politiker Wolfgang Fuhl. Rechtspopulistisch und Jüdisch', *Deutschlandfunk*, 11 April, available at https://www.deutschlandfunk.de/afd-politiker-wolfgang-fuhl-rechtspopulistisch-und-juedisch.1773.de.html?dram:article_id=350918, accessed 20 December 2021.

Rose, M. (1985), *Industrial Behaviour: Theoretical Development since Taylor*, Harmondsworth: Penguin Books.

Ross, J.I. and S.C. Richards, eds (2003), *Convict Criminology*, Belmont, California: Wadsworth/Thomson Learning.

Ross J.I., S. Darke, A. Aresti, G. Newbold and R. Earle (2014), 'Developing Convict Criminology Beyond North America International', *International Criminal Justice Review*, vol. 24, no. 2: 121–33.

Ross, K. (2004), *May '68 and Its Afterlives*, Illinois: Chicago University Press.

Ross, R. (1983), *Cape of Torments: Slavery and Resistance in South Africa*, London: Routledge and Kegan Paul.

—— (2004), *Status and Respectability in the Cape Colony, 1750–1870: A Tragedy of Manners*, Cambridge: Cambridge University Press.

Roth, K. (2017), 'The Pushback Against the Populist Challenge', Preface, *World Human Rights Report 2018*, London: Human Rights Watch.

Roth, K.H. (1992), 'Stay behind - in Germany', in *Newsletter/Hamburger Stiftung für Sozialgeschichte des 20. Jahrhunderts*: 7–23, available at https://www.digizeitschriften.de/de/dms/toc/?PID=PPN885562747_0001_2, accessed 20 December 2021.

Roth, R. (2003), 'Die dunklen Seiten der Zivilgesellschaft', *Forschungsjournal Neue Soziale Bewegungen*, vol. 16, no. 2: 59–73.

Rouban, L. (2017), 'Le Front national 2002–2017: Du Vote de Classe au Vote de Classement', *The Conversation: Academic Rigour, Journalistic Flair*, 8 May, available at https://theconversation.com/le-front-national-2002-2017-du-vote-de-classe-au-vote-de-classement-77303, accessed 20 December 2021.

Rowe, A. (2014), 'Situating the Self in Prison Research: Power, Identity, and Epistemology', *Qualitative Inquiry*, vol. 20, no. 4: 404–16.

Roy, A. (2020), 'The Pandemic as Portal', *Financial Times*.

Sabo, D., T.A. Kupers and W. London (2001), *Prison Masculinities*, Philadelphia: Temple University Press.

Sadurski, W. (2009), 'Partnering with Strasbourg: Constitutionalization of the European Court of Human Rights, the Accession of Central and East European States to the Council of Europe, and the Idea of Pilot Judgments', *Human Rights Law Review*, vol. 9: 397–453.

Salo, E. (2003), 'Negotiating Gender and Personhood in the New South Africa: Adolescent Women and Gangsters in Manenberg Township on the Cape Flats', *European Journal of Cultural Studies*, vol. 6, no. 3: 345–65.

—— (2004), *Respectable Mothers, Tough Men and Good Daughters: Producing Persons in Manenberg Township, South Africa*, Atlanta: Emory University.

Salzborn, S. (2001), *Heimatrecht und Volkstumskampf: Aussenpolitische Konzepte der Vertriebenenverbände und ihre praktische Umsetzung*, Hannover: Offizin.

Samaddar, R. (2012), 'Banglar Bidrohi Jubo-Chatra Andolon: 1966–1970' (The Militant Student Movement of Bengal: 1966–70), in A. Aharya, ed., *Sattar Dasak (Vol. III): Shaat-Sattarer Chatra Andolon* (The Decade of Seventies (Vol. III): The Student Movements of the Sixties-Seventies), Kolkata: Anustup.

—— (2014), 'Elitist Protest in Jadavpur', *DNA*, 22 October.

Sarabia, J. (2015) 'Art IS Resistance: The Role of the Artist in the Arab Spring and Other Uprisings', *Pangaea Journal*.

Sartre, J.P. (1974), *Being and Nothingness*, London: Methuen & Co.

Sassen, S. (1996), *Losing Control? Sovereignty in an Age of Globalization*, New York: Columbia University Press.

—— (2008), *Territory, Authority, Rights: From Medieval to Global Assemblages*, Princeton: Princeton University Press.

—— (2014), *Expulsions, Brutality and Complexity in the Global Economy*, Cambridge, MA: The Belknap Press of Harvard University Press.

Saul, M. (1981), 'Beer, Sorghum and Women: Production for the Market in Rural Upper Volta', *Africa: Journal of the International African Institute*, vol. 51, no. 3: 746–64.

Saull, R., A. Anievas, N. Davidson and A. Fabry (2014), *The Longue Durée of the Far-Right: An International Historical Sociology*, London and New York: Routledge.

Scaduto, A. (1971), *Bob Dylan: An Intimate Biography*, New York: Grosset and Dunlap.

Scheingold, S. (2004), *The Politics of Rights: Lawyers, Public Policy, and Political Change*, Ann Arbor: Michigan University Press.

Schept, J. (2014), '(Un)Seeing Like a Prison: Counter-Visual Ethnography of the Carceral State', *Theoretical Criminology*, vol. 18, no. 2: 198–223.

Schierup, C.U., P. Hansen and S. Castles (2006), *Migration, Citizenship, and the European Welfare State: A European Dilemma*, Oxford: Oxford University Press.

Schmitt, C. (2005), *Political Theology: Four Chapters on the Concept of Sovereignty*, Illinois: Chicago University Press.

Schmollinger, H.W. (1986a), 'Die Deutsche Reichspartei', in R. Stöss, ed., *Parteien-Handbuch: Die Parteien der Bundesrepublik Deutschland 1945–1980*, Schriften des Zentralinstituts für Sozialwissenschaftliche Forschung der Freien Universität Berlin: Bd. 39., Opladen: Westdeutscher Verlag: 1112–91.

—— (1986b), 'Die Nationaldemokratische Partei', in R. Stöss, ed., *Parteien-Handbuch: Die Parteien der Bundesrepublik Deutschland 1945–1980*, Schriften des Zentralinstituts für Sozialwissenschaftliche Forschung der Freien Universität Berlin: Bd. 39., Opladen: Westdeutscher Verlag: 1892–921.

—— (1986c), 'Die Nationaldemokratische Partei', in R. Stöss, ed., *Parteien-Handbuch: Die Parteien der Bundesrepublik Deutschland 1945–1980*, Schriften des Zentralinstituts für Sozialwissenschaftliche Forschung der Freien Universität Berlin: Bd. 39., Opladen: Westdeutscher Verlag: 1922–94.

—— (1986d), 'Die Sozialistische Reichspartei', in R. Stöss, ed., *Parteien-Handbuch: Die Parteien der Bundesrepublik Deutschland 1945-1980*, Schriften des Zentralinstituts für Sozialwissenschaftliche Forschung der Freien Universität Berlin: Bd. 39., Opladen: Westdeutscher Verlag: 2274–336.

Schneider, M. (2010), *Das Attentat: Kritik der paranoischen Vernunft*, Berlin: Matthes and Seitz.

Schneider, M., A. Post, M. Buddrus and M. Holler (2013), 'Funktionäre mit Vergangenheit: Das Gründungspräsidium des Bundesverbandes der Vertriebenen und das "Dritte Reich"', München, Germany: Oldenbourg Verlag München, available at http://search.ebscohost.com/login.aspx?direct=true&scope=site&db=nlebk&db=nlabk&AN=757896, accessed 20 December 2021.

Schwartz, P. (2007), 'The Social Construction of Heterosexuality', in M. Kimmel, ed., *The Sexual Self: The Construction of Sexual Scripts*, Nashville: Vanderbilt University Press.

Schwartz, R.D. (2010), *Law, Not War: Legal Evolution from the Ancient Empires to the Emerging World Society*, New York: Xlibris.

Scott. J. and V. Minichiello (2014), 'Reframing Male Sex Work', in V. Minichiello and J. Scott, eds, *Male Sex Work and Society*, New York: Harrington Park Press.

Scully, P. (1989), 'Criminality and Conflict in Rural Stellenbosch, South Africa, 1870–1900', *The Journal of African History*, vol. 30, no. 2: 289–300.

—— (1997), *Liberating the Family? Gender and British Slave Emancipation in the Rural Western Cape, South Africa, 1823–1853*, Cape Town: David Philip Publishers.

Sebaux, G. (2016), 'Pegida: Émergence, Sens et Influence d'un Mouvement Identitaire (trans) national Dans L'espace public Allemand', *Revue d'Allemagne et Des Pays de Langue Allemande*, vol. 48, no. 2: 387–99.

Seghers, A. (2013), *Transit,* New York: New York Review Book.

Selingo, J.J. (2016), 'Our Dangerous Obsession with Harvard, Stanford and Other Elite Universities', *Washington Post*, 5 April.

Sellner, M. (2017), 'Radikal und Feminine: Zwischen Genderwahn und Reconquista. Interview mit Franziska'.

Senior, P. (2011), 'In and Out of the Belly of the Beast', *International Journal of Offender Therapy and Comparative Criminology*, vol. 55: 1015–19.

Serge, V. (2013), 'Mexican Notebooks, 1940–1947', *New Left Review*, vol. 82, July–August.

Sexton, L. and V. Jenness (2016), '"We're Like Community": Collective Identity and Collective Efficacy among Transgender Women in Prisons for Men', *Punishment and Society*, vol. 18, no. 5: 544–77.

Shachar, A. and R. Bauböck (2014), 'Should Citizenship Be for Sale?', EUI Working Paper, available at http://cadmus.eui.eu/bitstream/handle/1814/29318/RSCAS_2014_01.pdf, accessed 20 December 2021.

Shah, G. (1977), *Protest Movement in Two Indian States: A Study of the Gujarat and Bihar Movement,* New Delhi: Ajanta Publications.

Shah, S.P. (2003), 'Sex Work in the Global Economy', *New Labor Forum*, vol. 12, no. 1, Spring: 74–81.

—— (2014), *Street Corner Secrets: Sex, Work and Migration in the City of Mumbai,* Durham and London: Duke University Press.

Sharpley-Whiting, T.D. (2002), *Negritude Women,* Minnesota: University of Minnesota Press.

Shell, R. (1997), *Children of Bondage: A Social History of the Slave Society at the Cape of Good Hope, 1652–1838,* Johannesburg: Witwatersrand University Press.

—— (2013), *From Diaspora to Diorama: The Old Slave in Cape Town,* Cape Town: NagsPro Multimedia.

Sheller, M. and J. Urry (2006), 'The New Mobilities Paradigm', *Environment and Planning A: Economy and Space,* vol. 38, no. 2: 207–26.

Shelton, R. (2011), *No Direction Home: The Life and Music of Bob Dylan,* Minnesota: Hal Leonard Corporation.

Shepherd, V. (1994), *Transients to Settlers: The Experience of Indians in Jamaica 1845–1950,* Coventry: University of Warwick Press.

Shields, J. (2007), *The Extreme Right in France: From Pétain to Le Pen,* London and New York: Routledge.

Silverman, D. (2013), *Doing Qualitative Research: A Practical Handbook,* fourth edition, London: Sage Publications.

Simon, W. and J.H. Gagnon (1986), 'Sexual Scripts: Permanence and Change', *Archives of Sexual Behavior,* vol. 15, no. 2: 97–120.

Simpson, C. (1999), *Universities and Empire: Money and Politics in the Social Sciences During the Cold War,* New York: The New Press.

Sims, L.S. (2002), *Wifredo Lam and the International Avant-Garde, 1923-1982,* Austin: University of Texas Press.

Singer, D. (2013), *Prelude to Revolution,* London: Haymarket Books.

Singhvi, L.M., ed. (1972), *Youth Unrest: Conflict of Generations,* Delhi: Institute of Constitutional and Parliamentary Studies.

Siri, J. (2016), 'Geschlechterpolitische Positionen der Partei Alternative für Deutschland', in A. Häusler, ed., *Die Alternative für Deutschland. Programmatik, Entwicklung und politische Verortung,* Wiesbaden: Springer VS: 69–80.

Sit, V. and R. Ricciardelli (2013), 'Constructing and Performing Sexualities in the Penitentiaries: Attitudes and Behaviors among Male Prisoners', *Criminal Justice Review,* vol. 38, no. 3: 335–53.

Sitas, A. (2004a), *Theoretical Parables,* Pretoria: University of South Africa Press.

—— (2004b), *Voices that Reason: Theoretical Parables,* Leiden: Brill.

—— (2008), *The Ethic of Reconciliation,* Durban: Madiba Press.

—— (2010), *The Mandela Decade,* Pretoria: University of South Africa Press.

—— (2015), 'Variations on a Zulu Theme', in E. Webster and K. Pampallis, eds, *The Unfinished National Question: Left Thought under Apartheid and Beyond,* Johannesburg: University of the Witwatersrand Press.

—— (2016), 'Freedom's Blind Spots: Figurations of Race and Caste in the Postcolony', *South African Review of Sociology,* vol. 47, no. 4: 121–31.

Sitas, A., S. Damodaran, W. Keim and N. Trimikliniotis (2016), 'Deviance', in I. Wallerstein, ed., *The World is Out of Joint: World-Historical Interpretations of Continuing Polarizations, Vol. 1,* London: Routledge.

Sitas, A., W. Keim, S. Damodaran, N. Trimikliniotis and F. Garba (2014), *Gauging and Engaging Deviance 1600–2000,* New Delhi: Tulika Books.

Smit, D. and S. Snacken (2009), *Principles of European Prison Law and Policy: Penology and Human Rights,* New York: Oxford University Press.

Smith, A. (1974), *The Wealth of Nations,* Harmondsworth: Penguin Books.

Smith, M. (2004), 'Labouring to Choose, Choosing to Labour: Coercion and Choice in the Potosi Mita', *Past Imperfect*, vol. 10: 21–44.

Snacken, S. (2011), *Prison en Europe: Pour une pénologie critique et humaniste*, Brussel: Larcier.

Snacken, S. and E. Dumortier (2012), *Resisting Punitiveness in Europe? Welfare, Human Rights and Democracy*, London and New York: Routledge.

Soares, J.A. (2002), *The Power of Privilege: Yale and America's Elite Colleges*, Palo Alto: Stanford University Press.

Solomos, J. (2014), 'Racism and Migration', in Anderson, B. and Keith, M., eds, *Migration: A COMPAS Anthology*, Oxford: COMPAS.

Solomos, J. and M. Bulmer, eds (2014), *Multiculturalism, Social Cohesion and Immigration: Changing Conceptions in the UK*, London and New York: Routledge.

Soneji, D. (2012), *Unfinished Gestures: Devadasis, Memory, and Modernity in South India*, Chicago and London: University of Chicago Press.

Sounes, H. (2001), *Down the Highway: The Life of Bob Dylan*, New York: Grove Press.

South African History Online (1962), 'The Liquor Laws Amendment Comes into Effect', 15 August, available at https://www.sahistory.org.za/dated-event/liquor-laws-amendment-bill-comes-effect, accessed 24 January 2019.

South African Union Liquor Report (1957), Chapter 3: 'Supply of Liquor to Non-Whites'.

Sparks, R., A.E. Bottoms and W. Hay (1996), *Prisons and the Problem of Order*, Oxford: Clarendon Press.

Sparks, R. (2002), 'Out of the "Digger": The Warrior's Honour and the Guilty Observer', *Ethnography*, vol. 3, no. 4: 556–81.

Später, E. and H.H. Kotte (2010), 'Historiker Erich Später: "Konzentration auf Steinbach Lenkt ab"', *Frankfurter Rundschau*, 11 February, available at https://www.fr.de/politik/konzentration-steinbach-lenkt-11717562.html, accessed 20 December 2021.

Srivastava, R. (2005), 'Bonded Labor in India: Its Incidence and Pattern', ILO Working Paper, Cornell University Library, available at https://hdl.handle.net/1813/99630, accessed 12 August 2021.

Srnicek, N. (2016), *Platform Capitalism*, London: Polity Press.

Stambolis-Ruhstorfer, M. and J. Tricou (2017), 'Resisting "Gender Theory" in France: A Fulcrum for Religious Action in a Secular Society', in R. Kuhar and D. Paternotte, eds, *Anti-Gender Campaigns in Europe: Mobilizing against Equality*, London: Rowman and Littlefield International: 79–98.

Standing, A. (2006), *Organized Crime: A Study from the Cape Flats*, Pretoria: Institute for Security Studies.

Staud, T. (2016), 'Mehr als 50 Jahre Rechtsextrem', *Bundeszentrale fur politische Bidung*, 7 March, available at http://www.bpb.de/politik/extremismus/rechtsextremismus/222499/mehr-als-50-jahre-rechtsextrem, accessed 20 December 2021.

Steinberg, J. (2004a), 'Nongoloza's Children: Western Cape Prison Gangs during and after Apartheid', monograph, Centre for the Study of Violence and Reconciliation, July.

—— (2004b), *The Number: One Man's Search for Identity in the Cape Underworld and Prison Gangs*, Jeppestown: Jonathan Ball Publishers.

Steiner, U. (2010), *Walter Benjamin: An Introduction to His Work and Thought*, Chicago and London: Chicago University Press.

Stepputat, F. and N. Sørensen (2014), 'Sociology and Forced Migration', in E. Fiddian-Qasmiyeh, G. Loescher, K. Long and N. Sigona, eds, *The Oxford Handbook of Refugee and Forced Migration Studies*, Oxford: Oxford University Press: 86–97.

Stern, S.J. (1988), 'Feudalism, Capitalism, and the World-System in the Perspective of Latin America and the Caribbean', *The American Historical Review*, vol. 93, no. 4, October: 896.

Stierl, M. (2016), 'A Sea of Struggle – Activist Border Interventions in the Mediterranean Sea', *Citizenship Studies*, vol. 20, no. 5: 561–78.

Stiglitz, J.E. (2019), *People, Power and Profits: Progressive Capitalism for an Age of Discontent*, London: Allen Lane.

Stinauer, T. (2015), 'Angriff auf Reker - Das wissen wir über Frank S. Attentäter Sympathisant der rechtsextremistischen FAP', *Kölner Stadt-Unzeiger*, 17 October, available at https://www.ksta.de/23015348, accessed 20 December 2021.

Stoler, A.L. (2009), *Along the Archival Grain: Epistemic Anxieties and Colonial Common Sense*, Princeton: Princeton University Press.

Stora, B. (1997), 'L'onde de Choc des Années Algériennes en France: L' "Algérie Française" et le Front National', *Esprit*, vol. 237, 11 November: 13–28.

Streeck, W. (2017), 'The Return of the Repressed as the Beginning of the End of Neoliberal Capitalism', in H. Geiselberger, ed., *The Great Regression*, Cambridge: Polity Press: 157–72.

Stringer, K.D. (2017), 'Building a Stay-Behind Resistance Organization: The Case of Cold War Switzerland against the Soviet Union', *Joint Force Quarterly*, vol. 85 (2nd Quarter): 109–14.

Stöss, R. (1986), 'Einleitung: Struktur und Entwicklung des Parteiensystems der Bundesrepublik – eine Theorie', in R. Stöss, ed., *Parteien-Handbuch: Die Parteien der Bundesrepublik Deutschland 1945–1980*, Schriften des Zentralinstituts für sozialwissenschaftliche Forschung der Freien Universität Berlin: Bd. 39, Opladen: Westdeutscher Verlag: 17–309.

Sudre, F. (1995), 'Les "Obligations Positives" dans la Jurisprudence Européenne des Droits de L'homme', *Revue Trimestrielle des Droits de l'Homme*, no. 23: 362–84.

Sundar, N. (2016), *The Burning Forest: India's War in Bastar*, New Delhi: Juggernaut.

Sunder, R.R. (2003), 'The Prostitution Question(s): Female Agency, Sexuality, and Work', in *The Scandal of the State: Women, Law, and Citizenship in Postcolonial India*, Delhi: Permanent Black.

Swarr, A.M. (2004), 'Moffies, Artists, and Queens', *Journal of Homosexuality*, vol. 46, no. 3–4: 73–89.

Sykes, G.M. (1958), *The Society of Captives: A Study of a Maximum Security Prison*, Princeton: Princeton University Press.

Szczepanik, R. and S. Siebert (2015), 'The Triple Bind of Narration: Fritz Schütze's Biographical Interview in Prison Research and Beyond', *Sociology*, vol. 50, no. 2, 26 February: 285–300.

Sälter, G. (2014), 'Kameraden: Nazi-Netzwerke und die Rekrutierung Hauptamtlicher Mitarbeiter', in J. Dülffer, K.D. Henke, W. Krieger and R.D. Müller, eds, *Studien / Unabhängige Historikerkommission zur Erforschung der Geschichte des Bundesnachrichtendienstes 1945–1968*, Vol. 2: *Die Geschichte der Organisation Gehlen und des BND 1945–1968: Umrisse und Einblicke ; Dokumentation der Tagung am 2 Dezember 2013*, Marburg: Unabhängige Historikerkommission zur Erforschung der Geschichte des Bundesnachrichtendienstes 1945–1968: 40–51.

Tambe, A. (2005), 'The Elusive Ingénue: A Transnational Feminist Analysis of European Prostitution in Colonial Bombay', *Gender and Society*, vol. 19, no. 2: 160–79.

Tazzioli, M. and W. Walters (2016), 'The Sight of Migration: Governmentality, Visibility and Europe's Contested Borders', *Global Society*, vol. 30, no. 3: 445–64.

Terril, R. (2012), *The Life of Madame Mao*, New York: New World City Inc.

Terry, A.N. (2016), 'Sexual Behavior in Prison Populations Understood through the Framework of Rational Choice and Exchange Theory', *Inquiries Journal/Student Pulse*, vol. 8, no. 10: 1–10.

The Fourth National People's Congress, 'Article 13', *Constitution of the Republic of China, 1975*, available at http://www.npc.gov.cn/englishnpc/constitution2019/201911/1f65146fb6104 dd3a2793875d19b5b29.shtml.

Thompson, E.P. (1974), *The Making of the English Working Class*, Harmondsworth: Penguin Books.

—— (1980), *Customs in Common*, New York: The New Press.

Theal, G.M. (1897), *Records of the Cape Colony from February 1793 to December 1796*, London: William Clowes and Sons.

Thusi, I.G. (2015), 'Policing Sex: The Colonial, Apartheid, and New Democracy Policing of Sex Work in South Africa', *Fordham International Law Journal*, vol. 38, no. 1.

Tilly, C. (1987), 'The Contentious French: Four Centuries of Popular Struggle', *Journal of Peace and Research*, vol. 24, no. 1, March: 101–02.

—— (2006), *Regimes and Repertoires*, Chicago: University of Chicago Press.

Tipps, D.C. (1973), 'Modernization Theory and the Comparative Study of National Societies: A Critical Perspective', *Comparative Studies in Society and History*, vol. 15, no. 2: 199–226.

Toscano, A. (2011), 'Anti-Sociology and its Limits', in P. Bowman and R. Stamp, eds, *Reading Rancière: Critical Dissensus*, London: Continuum: 217–37.

Trammell, R. (2011), 'Symbolic Violence and Prison Wives: Gender Roles and Protective Pairing in Men's Prisons', *The Prison Journal*, vol. 91, no. 3: 305–24.

Traverso, E. (2015), 'Spectres du Fascism: Les Métamorphoses des Droites Radicales au XXIe Siècle', *Revue du Crieur*, vol. 1, no. 1: 104–21.

Triandafyllidou, A., ed. (2016), *Routledge Handbook of Immigration and Refugee Studies*, Abingdon and New York: Routledge.

Triandafyllidou, A. and R. Gropas, eds (2022), *European Immigration: A Sourcebook*, second edition, Research in Migration and Ethnic Relations, Global Governance Programme, Cultural Pluralism, Ashgate: Aldershot, 2014, retrieved from Cadmus, European University Institute Research Repository, available at http://hdl.handle.net/1814/30557, accessed 1 January.

Trimikliniotis, N. (1999), 'New Migration and Racism in Cyprus: The Racialization of Migrant Workers', in F. Anthias and G. Lazaridis, eds, *Into the Margins: Migration and Exclusion in Southern Europe*, Avebury: Ashgate: 139–78.

—— (2007), 'Populism, Democracy and Social Citizenship: Discourses on "Illegal Migration" or Beyond the "Fortress" versus "Cosmopolitanism" Debate', in E. Berggren, B. Likic-Brboric, T. Toksöz and N. Trimikliniotis, eds, *Irregular Migration, Informal Labour and Community: A Challenge for Europe*, Maastricht: Shaker: 351–71.

—— (2009a), 'Exceptions, Soft Borders and Free Movement for Workers', in P. Minderhoud and N. Trimikliniotis, eds, *Rethinking the Free Movement of Workers: The European Challenges Ahead*, Nijmegen: Wolf Legal Publishers: 135–54.

—— (2009b), 'The Use and Abuse of Undeclared and Unprotected Labour: Migration, Europeanization and the Role of Trade Unions', in A. Neergaard, ed., *European Perspectives on Exclusion and Subordination: The Political Economy of Migration*, Maastricht: Shaker: 177–99.

—— (2009c), '"Race" and Ethnicity in the Era of Global Insecurity: Legacies, Contestations and Transcendence', in H. Fagan and R. Munck, eds, *Globalization and Security: An Encyclopaedia*, London: Praeger Press: 321–36.

—— (2010), 'The Case of Cyprus', in M. Kamali, *Racial Discrimination: Institutional Patterns and Politics*, London and New York: Routledge: 193–207.

—— (2012), 'The Instrumentalization of EU Integration Policy: Reflecting on the Dignified, Efficient and Undeclared Policy Aspects', in Y. Pascouau and T. Strik, eds, *Which Integration*

Policies for Migrants? Interaction between the EU and its Member States, Nijmegen: Wolf Legal Publishers: 109–28.

—— (2013), 'Migration and Freedom of Movement of Workers: EU Law, Crisis and the Cypriot States of Exception', *Laws*, vol. 2, no. 4: 440–68.

—— (2014), '"The Only Thing I Like Integrated is My Coffee": Dissensus and Migrant Integration in the Era of Euro-Crisis', in M. Pajnik and F. Anthias, eds, *Contesting Integration, Engendering Migration: Theory and Practice*, Basingstoke: Palgrave Macmillan: 64–85.

—— (2016), 'Parties and the Politics of Exclusion and Exploitation: Migrants and Dissensus After the End of the Cyprus Economic Miracle', in C. Christophorou and G. Charalambous, eds, *Party–Society Relations in the Republic of Cyprus: Political and Societal Strategies*, Abingdon and New York: Routledge.

—— (2020a), 'Covid, Re-Racialization of Migrants and the "Refugee Crisis"', in M. Lavalette, V. Ioakimidis and I. Ferguson, eds, *Social Work and the Covid-19 Pandemic*, Bristol: Bristol University Policy Press.

—— (2020b), *Migration and Refugee Dissensus in Europe: Borders, Insecurity and Austerity*, London and New York: Routledge.

Trimikliniotis, N., D. Parsanoglou and V. Tsianos (2016), 'Mobile Commons and/in Precarious Spaces: Mapping Migrant Struggles and Social Resistance', *Critical Sociology*, vol. 42, no. 7–8, 26 October: 943–46.

—— (2015), *Mobile Commons, Migrant Digitalities and the Right to the City*, London and New York: Palgrave Macmillan.

Trimikliniotis, N. and C. Demetriou (2012), 'Racist Discourse and the Rise in Racial Violence: A Case Study on the Far Right Attack against a Multicultural Festival', in *The Interaction between Racist Discourse and the Rise in Racial Violence in Cyprus*, ACCEPT Pluralism Research Project, Fiesole: European University Insititute, Robert Schuman Institute for Advanced Studies: 10.

Trimikliniotis, N. and M. Souroulla (2012), 'Informalization and Flexibilization at Work: The Migrant Woman Precariat Speaks', in F. Anthias, M. Kontos and M. Morokvasic, eds, *Female Migrants in Europe: The Paradoxes of Integration*, New York: Springer: 59–78.

Trimikliniotis, N., C. Demetriou and S. Stavrou (2016), *On-the-Move: The Reality of Free Movement for Young European Citizens Migrating in Times of Crisis*, Cyprus National Report, December.

Trotter, H. (2009a), 'Soliciting Sailors: The Temporal Dynamics of Dockside Prostitution in Durban and Cape Town', *Journal of Southern African Studies*, vol. 35, no. 3, pp. 699–713.

Trotter, H. (2009b), 'Trauma and Memory: The Impact of Apartheid-Era Forced Removals on Coloured Identity in Cape Town', in M. Adhikari, ed., *Burdened by Race: Coloured Identities in Southern Africa*, Lansdowne: UCT Press: 49–78.

Tsianos, V. and J. Karakayali (2014), 'Rassismus und Repräsentationspolitik in der postmigrant-ischen Gesellschaft (Racism and Representation Politics in Post-Migrant Society)', *Aus Politik und Zeitgeschichte (APUZ)*, vol. 13: 33–39.

Tsianos, V. and H. Sabine (2010), 'Ethnographische Grenzregimeanalyse als Methodologie: Von der Ethnographie zur Praxeographie des Grenzregimes', in S. Hess and B. Kasparek, eds, *Grenzregime Diskurse, Praktiken: Institutionen in Europa*, Hamburg: Assoziation A: 243–64.

Tsianos, V., D. Papadopoulos and N. Stephenson (2012), 'This is Class War from Above and They are Winning It: What is to Be Done?', *Rethinking Marxism: A Journal of Economics, Culture & Society*, vol. 24, no. 3: 448–57.

Tsoukala, A. (2007), 'The Terrorism-Immigration Nexus in the EU, in the Post-11 September Era: An Analysis of the Political Discourses in the British Press', in E. Berggren, B. Likic-

Brboric, T. Toksöz and N. Trimikliniotis, eds, *Irregular Migration, Informal Labour and Community: A Challenge for Europe*, Maastricht: Shaker.

Tsoukalas, C. (1993), ' Ekeino Pou den Yparhei Pia: 1968' (That Which No Longer Exists: 1968), *To Vema*, 25 May.

Twine, F.W. (2015), *Outsourcing the Womb: Race, Class and Gestational Surrogacy in a Global Market*, New York: Routledge.

Ueno, C. (2006), 'The Place of "Comfort Women" in the Japanese Historical Revisionism', *Sens Public*.

Ullrich, M. (2017), 'Media Use During Escape: A Contribution to Refugees' Collective Agency', *Spheres: Journal of Digital Cultures*, 23 June, available at http://spheres-journal.org/media-use-during-escape-a-contribution-to-refugees-collective-agency/, accessed 20 December 2021.

Ulrich, B. and M. Geis (2016), '"Hitler hat den Deutschen das Rückgrat Gebrochen": Interview mit Alexander Gauland', *Zeit Online*, 14 April, available at https://www.zeit.de/2016/17/alexander-gauland-afd-cdu-konservatismus/komplettansicht?print, accessed 20 December 2021.

Ulrich, N. (2015), 'Cape of Storms: Surveying and Rethinking Popular Resistance in the Eighteenth-Century Cape Colony', *New Contree*, no. 73: 16–39.

United Nations (2017a), Department of Economic and Social Affairs, Population Division, *Trends in International Migrant Stock: The 2017 Revision*, available at http://www.un.org/en/development/desa/population/migration/data/index.shtml, accessed 20 December 2021.

—— (2017b), *International Migration Report 2017*, available at http://www.un.org/en/development/desa/population/migration/publications/migrationreport/docs/MigrationReport2017.pdf, accessed 20 December 2021.

United Nations High Commissioner for Refugees (UNHCR) (2020a), 'Key Legal Considerations on Access to Territory for Persons in Need of International Protection in the Context of the COVID-19 Response', *RefWorld*, 16 March, available at https://www.refworld.org/docid/5e7132834.html, accessed 20 December 2021.

—— (2020b), 'Why "Undocumented" or "Irregular"?', *UNHCR: The UN Refugee Agency*, available at https://www.unhcr.org/cy/wp-content/uploads/sites/41/2018/09/TerminologyLeaflet_EN_PICUM.pdf?fbclid=IwAR3uGdVJdy7zmUfRQE-z6pYnHD5A5N0RahoEZ54a7ia6FiR-WG7VjfopXIU, accessed 20 December 2021.

—— (2021), 'Figures at a Glance', *UNHCR: The UN Refugee Agency*, 18 June, available at https://www.unhcr.org/figures-at-a-glance.html, accessed 10 October 2021.

UNO Flüchtlingshilfe (2019), *Flüchtlingskrise im Mittelmeer*, available at https://www.uno-fluechtlingshilfe.de/hilfe-weltweit/mittelmeer/, accessed 20 December 2021.

Urry, J. (1999), *Sociology Beyond Societies: Mobilities for the Twenty-First Century*, London: Routledge.

—— (2003), *Global Complexity*, Cambridge: Polity Press.

—— (2007), *Mobilities*, Cambridge: Polity Press.

—— (2016), *What is the Future?*, Cambridge: Polity Press.

US Department of State (2011), *Trafficking in Persons Report: June 2011*, Washington DC.

Vagenas, P., A. Zelenev, F.L. Altice, A. Di Paola, A.O. Jordan, P.A. Teixeira, P.M. Frew, A.C. Spaulding and S.A. Springer (2016), 'HIV-Infected Men who Have Sex with Men, Before and After Release from Jail: The Impact of Age and Race, Results from a Multi-Site Study', *AIDS Care*, vol. 28, no. 1: 22–31.

Van der Linden, M., ed. (2008), *Workers of the World: Essays toward a Global Labor History*, vol. 1, Leiden: Brill.

van Heyningen, E.B. (1984), 'The Social Evil in the Cape Colony 1868–1902: Prostitution and the Contagious Diseases Acts', *Journal of Southern African Studies*, no. 2: 170–98.

van Kersbergen, K. and A. Krouwel (2008), 'A Double-Edged Sword! The Dutch Centre-Right and the "Foreigners Issue"', *Journal of European Public Policy*, vol. 15, no. 3, April: 398–414.

van Onselen, C. (1985), 'Crime and Total Institutions in the Making of Modern South Africa: The Life of "Nongoloza" Mathebula', 1867–1948', *History Workshop*, no. 19: 62–81.

—— (2001), *New Babylon New Nineveh: Everyday Life on the Witwatersrand, 1886–1914*, Cape Town: Jonathan Ball Publishers.

van Zyl Smit, D. (2010), 'Regulation of Prison Conditions', *Crime and Justice*, vol. 39, no. 1: 503–63.

van Zyl Smit, D. and S. Snacken (2009), *Principles of European Prison Law and Policy: Penology and Human Rights*, Oxford: Oxford University Press.

Vanni, I. and T. Marcello (2005), 'On the Life and Deeds of San Precario, Patron Saint of Precarious Workers and Lives', *Fibreculture Journal*, no. 5.

Vaïsse, J. (2010), *Neoconservatism: The Biography of a Movement*, Cambridge, Massachusetts: Harvard University Press.

Vehrkamp, R. and K. Wegschaider (2017), *Populäre Wahlen: Mobilisierung und Gegenmobilisierung der sozialen Milieus bei der Bundestagswahl 2017*, Gütersloh, available at https://www. bertelsmann-stiftung.de/fileadmin/files/BSt/Publikationen/GrauePublikationen/ZD_ Populaere_Wahlen_Bundestagswahl_2017_01.pdf, accessed 20 December 2021.

Vereinigung Demokratischer Juristen (1963), *Dr. Hans Maria Globke. Tatsachen und Dokumente*, available at http://www.profit-over-life.org/books/books.php?book=40&pageID=1&expand=no&addPage=0, accessed 20 December 2021.

Vernal, F. (2011), 'Discourse Networks in South African Slave Society', *African Historical Review*, vol. 43, no. 2: 1–36.

Veugelers, J. (1997), 'Social Cleavage and the Revival of Far Right Parties: The Case of France's National Front', *Acta Sociologica*, vol. 40, no. 1, 31–49.

Viannello, F. (2013), 'Daily Life in Overcrowded Prisons: A convict Perspective', *Prison Service Journal*, no. 207: 27–33.

Victor, S. (1946), *The Long Dusk,* New York: Dial Press.

Villa, P.I. (2017), '"Anti-Genderismus": German Angst?', in R. Kuhar and D. Paternotte, eds, *Anti-Gender Campaigns in Europe: Mobilizing against Equality*, London: Rowman and Littlefield International: 99–116.

Viney, R. (1999), 'A History of Masculinities in South Africa: Context and Parameters', *New Contree*, no. 45: 85–97.

Volk, S. (2017), '"Wir sind das Volk!" Representative Claim-Making in Pegida's Populist Discourse', MA thesis, Rijkuniversiteit Groningen/University of Strasbourg, MA Programme Euroculture.

Von Holdt, K., M. Langa, S. Molapo, N. Mogapi, K. Ngubeni, J. Dlamini and A. Kirsten (2011), *The Smoke that Calls*, Johannesburg: The Centre for the Study of Violence and Reconciliation.

Wacquant, L. (2002), 'The Curious Eclipse of Prison Ethnography in the Age of Mass Incarceration', *Ethnography*, vol. 3, no. 4: 371–97.

—— (2009), *Punishing the Poor: The Neoliberal Government of Social Insecurity*, Durham: Duke University Press.

—— (2010), 'Class, Race and Hyperincarceration in Revanchist America', *Daedalus*, vol. 140, no. 3: 74–90.

Wald, E. (2009), 'Defining Prostitution and Redefining Women's Roles: The Colonial State and

Society in Early 19th Century India', History Compass, vol. 7., no. 6, November: 1470–83.

Walters, W. (2012), *Governmentality: Critical Encounters*, New York: Routledge.

Wakeman, S. (2014), 'Fieldwork, Biography and Emotion: Doing Criminological Autoethnography', *British Journal of Criminology*, vol. 54, no. 5: 705–21.

Wallace, I., ed. (1998), *Anna Seghers in Perspective, German Monitor Series*, Amsterdam: Rodopi.

Waldmann, P. (2011), *Terrorismus: Provokation der Macht*, revised edition, Hamburg: Murmann.

Wallerstein, I. (1974), *The Modern World System: Capitalist Agriculture and the Origins of the European World Economy in the Sixteenth Century*, New York: Academic Press.

—— (1988), 'Comments on Stern's Critical Tests', *American Historical Review*, vol. 93, no. 4, October: 873–85.

—— (1989), '1968, Revolution in the World-System: Theses and Queries', *Theory and Society*, vol. 18, no. 4, July: 431–49.

—— (2000), *The Wallerstein Reader*, New Haven and London: Yale University Press.

Wallerstein, I., ed. (2015), *The World is Out of Joint: World-Historical Interpretations of Continuing Polarizations*, Boulder: Paradigm Publishers.

—— (2016), *The World is Out of Joint: World-Historical Interpretations of Continuing Polarizations*, vol. 1, London: Routledge.

Walters, W. (2015), 'Reflections on Migration and Governmentality', *Movements: Journal for Critical Migration and Border Regime Research*, vol. 1, no. 1, available at https://movements-journal.org/issues/01.grenzregime/04.walters--migration.governmentality.html, accessed 20 December 2021.

Ward, K. (2006), 'Defining and Defiling the Criminal Body at the Cape of Good Hope: Punishing the Crime of Suicide under Dutch East India Company Rule, circa 1625–1795', in S. Pierce and A. Rao, eds, *Discipline and the Other Body: Correction, Corporeality, Colonialism*, Durham and London: Duke University Press: 36–60.

—— (2007), 'Knocking on Death's Door: Mapping Spectrums of Bondage and Status through Marking the Dead at the Cape', in N. Worden, *Contingent Lives: Social Identity and Material Culture in the VOC World*, Cape Town: University of Cape Town: 391–413.

Weber, M. (1969), *The Rational and Social Foundations of Music*, Carbondale: Southern Illinois University Press.

Webster, E. and K. Von Holdt, eds (2005), *Beyond the Apartheid Workplace: Studies in Transition*, Pietermaritzburg: University of KwaZulu-Natal Press.

Weheliye, A.G. (2014), *Habeas Viscus: Racializing Assemblages, Biopolitics, and Black Feminist Theories of the Human*, Durham: Duke University Press.

Weinberg, L.B. (1979), *After Mussolini: Italian Neo-Fascism and the Nature of Fascism*, Washington, D.C.: University Press of America.

Werner, A. (2015), *Was ist, Was will, Wir Wirkt Die AfD?*, Köln: ISP Verlag.

West, C. and D.H. Zimmerman (1987), 'Doing Gender', *Gender and Society*, vol. 1, no. 2: 125–51.

Western Cape Provincial Archive (2005a), '1/STB 3/11, 1759-1782', in N. Worden and G. Groenewald, *Trials of Slavery: Selected Documents Concerning Slaves from the Criminal Records of the Council of Justice at the Cape of Good Hope, 1705-1794*, Cape Town: Van Riebeeck Society for the Publication of South African Historical Documents: 481–82.

—— (2005b), 'Criminal Justice 354, 1746, ff. 484-487', in N. Worden and G. Groenewald, *Trials of Slavery: Selected Documents Concerning Slaves from the Criminal Records of the Council of Justice at the Cape of Good Hope, 1705–1794*, Cape Town: Van Riebeeck Society for the Publication of South African Historical Documents: 259–60.

—— (2005c), 'Criminal Justice 788, 1750–1755, ff. 58-67', in N. Worden and G. Groenewald,

Trials of Slavery: Selected Documents Concerning Slaves from the Criminal Records of the Council of Justice at the Cape of Good Hope, 1705–1794, Cape Town: Van Riebeeck Society for the Publication of South African Historical Documents: 294–97.

—— (2005d), 'Criminal Justice 795, 1782–1789, ff. 407–23', in N. Worden and G. Groenewald, *Trials of Slavery: Selected Documents Concerning Slaves from the Criminal Records of the Council of Justice at the Cape of Good Hope, 1705–1794*, Cape Town: Van Riebeeck Society for the Publication of South African Historical Documents: 561–65.

—— (2005e), 'Criminal Justice 2485, 1729–1759, ff. 130–33', in N. Worden and G. Groenewald, *Trials of Slavery: Selected Documents Concerning Slaves from the Criminal Records of the Council of Justice at the Cape of Good Hope, 1705–1794*, Cape Town: Van Riebeeck Society for the Publication of South African Historical Documents: 293–94.

White, J. (2016), 'Democracy is Like a Tram', *Turkey Institute*, 14 July, https://www.turkeyinstitute.org.uk/commentary/democracy-like-tram/, accessed 20 December 2021.

Whittier, D.K. and R.M. Melendez (2004), 'Intersubjectivity in the Intrapsychic Sexual Scripting of Gay Men', *Culture, Health and Sexuality*, vol. 6, no. 2: 131–43.

Wicken, P. (2010), *The Poet in the Laboratory*, London: Penguin Books.

Wiederman, M.W. (2005), 'The Gendered Nature of Sexual Scripts', *The Family Journal: Counseling and Therapy for Couples and Families*, vol. 13, no. 4: 496–502.

Wiermer, C., O. Meyer and S. Giesecke (2015), 'In Berlin will man jetzt Klarheit Die V-Mann-Spur des Reker-Attentäters – Quelle', *Express*, 21 October, available at https://www.express.de/koeln/in-berlin-will-man-jetzt-klarheit-die-v-mann-spur-des-reker-attentaeters-23028094, accessed 20 December 2021.

Wildt, M. (2014), 'Kommentar', in J. Dülffer *et al.*, eds, *Studien/Unabhängige Historikerkommission zur Erforschung der Geschichte des Bundesnachrichtendienstes 1945–1968: Vol. 2. Die Geschichte der Organisation Gehlen und des BND 1945–1968: Umrisse und Einblicke; Dokumentation der Tagung am 2. December 2013*, first edition, Marburg: Unabhängige Historikerkommission zur Erforschung der Geschichte des Bundesnachrichtendienstes 1945–1968: 52–56.

Willis, J. (2002), 'For Women and Children: An Economic History of Brewing among the Nyakyusa of Southwestern Tanzania', in D.F. Bryceson, ed., *Alcohol in Africa: Mixing Business, Pleasure and Politics*, Heinemann: Portsmouth, NH: 55–73.

Wilson D., R. Spina and J.E. Canaan (2011), 'In Praise of the Carceral Tour: Learning from the Grendon Experience', *Howard Journal of Criminal Justice*, vol. 50, no. 4: 343–55.

Winckler, O. (2017), 'The "Arab Spring": Socioeconomic Aspects', *Middle East Policy Council*, vol. 20, no. 4.

Wojcicki, J.M. (2002), 'Commercial Sexwork or Ukuphanda? Sex-For-Money Exchange in Soweto and Hammanskraal Area', *South Africa Culture, Medicine and Psychiatry*, vol. 26: 339–70.

Worden, N. (1982), 'Violence, Crime and Slavery on Cape Farmsteads in the Eighteenth Century', *Kronos: Journal of Cape History*, vol. 5: 43–60.

—— (2007), 'Revolt in Cape Colony Slave Society', in E.A. Alpers, G. Campbell and M. Salman, eds, *Resisting Bondage in Indian Ocean Africa and Asia*, New York: Routledge: 10–23.

Wroe, N. (2000), 'Thinking for England', *The Guardian*, 28 October.

Wynter, S. (1989), 'Beyond the Word of Man: Glissant and the New Discourse of the Antilles', *World Literature Today*, vol. 63, no. 4: 637–48.

Wölk, V. (2016), 'Jenseits der "Lügenpresse". Mit wem AfD, Pegida und Co. sprechen', in A. Häusler and F. Virchow, eds, *Neue Soziale Bewegung von Rechts? Zukunftsängste, Abstieg der Mitte, Ressentiments, Eine Flugschrift*, Hamburg: VSA Verlag: 95–104.

Zerubavel, E. (2006), *The Elephant in the Room: Silence and Denial in Everyday Life*, Oxford: Oxford University Press.

Zizek, S. (2016), *Against the Double Blackmail: Refugees, Terror and Other Troubles with the Neighbors*, London: Allen Lane.

—— (2017), 'The Populist Temptation', in H. Geiselberger, ed., *The Great Regression*, Cambridge: Polity Press: 185–97.

—— (2020), *Pandemic!: COVID-19 Shakes the World*, Cambridge: Polity Press.

Zungu, R. and P.J. Potgieter (2011), 'The Prevalence of Consensual Sex in South African Male Correctional Centres', *Acta Criminologica: Southern African Journal of Criminology*, vol. 24, no. 2: 60–74.

Zúquete, J.P. (2008), 'The European Extreme-Right and Islam: New Directions?', *Journal of Political Ideologies*, vol. 13, no. 3: 321–44.

—— (2015), 'The New Frontlines of Right-Wing Nationalism', *Journal of Political Ideologies*, vol. 20, no. 1: 69–85.

VIDEOGRAPHY

'Anirban returns to JNU's Freedom Square – Full Speech', Stand with JNU, 18 March 2016, https://www.youtube.com/watch?v=tbedwP41ZkM&t=849s.

Baudelaire, E., dir., *The Anabasis of May and Fusako Shigenobu, Masao Adachi, and 27 Years without Images*, 2011.

'Exclusive Release, Umar Khalid Speech on 22 Feb. 2016, Umar Khalid Enters JNU, Addressing Students', Dirty Politics, 21 February 2016, https://www.youtube.com/watch?v=XQ3vbTSFc1I.

Fourest, C. and F. Venner, dir., *Marine Le Pen: L'héritière*, Nilaya Productions, 2011.

Fromm, R. dir., *Putins völkische Fans. Europas Rechte auf Kreml-Kurs*, MDR Television, 2016.

Gensing, P. and S. Stöber, dir., 'Pro-russische Netzwerke. Moskautreue Rechte', ARD, 29 April 2016, https://www.tagesschau.de/inland/neurechte-russland-101.html.

Müller, P.F. and M. Mueller, dir., *Mein Name sei Altmann. Das zweite Leben eines, Kriegsverbrechers*, Filmfabrik/WDR, 2015, https://www.arte.tv/de/videos/051086-000-A/mein-name-sei-altmann/.

Naidoo, A., *Long Reign of the South African Shebeen Queen*, Brand South Africa, 12 August 2014, https://www.brandsouthafrica.com/people-culture/long-reign-of-the-south-african-shebeen-queen.

'Nation Wants to Know with Surgical Strike Interview, Arnab Goswami Nation Wants to Know', Arnab Debate Live, 30 September 2017, https://www.youtube.com/watch?v=vJVTj6eOlIQ.

'Out of Jail, Kanhaiya Kumar Attacks PM Modi in Speech on JNU Campus', NDTV, 3 March 2016, https://www.youtube.com/watch?v=8jkQhAE-j8s.

Richard, B., dir., *Mains Brunes Sur la Ville – Quand L'extrême Droite est au Pouvoir*, La Mare Aux Canards, France, 2012.

'Shehla Rashid Shora: "This is an Attempt to Depoliticize the University"', *The Wire*, 12 March 2016, https://www.youtube.com/watch?v=JdaJZ8Di1WI.

'Tribute to Afzal Guru at JNU – Students Crossed All Lines?: The Newshour Debate', Times Now, 10 February 2016, https://www.youtube.com/watch?v=oGN2KOJMaeM.

'Umar Khalid Returns to JNU's Freedom Square – Full Speech', Stand with JNU, 18 March 2016, https://www.youtube.com/watch?v=XChGhQ44Mr4.

'Video Showing JNU Students Chanting Anti-India Slogans Goes Viral, JNU-Afzal Guru', India TV, 15 February 2016, https://www.youtube.com/watch?v=U1RuAcP4OXM.

Contributors

SEPIDEH AZARI was born in Iran and raised in Norway. She holds a postgraduate degree from the University of Cape Town and is completing her PhD on issues of race thinking in the South African Academy. She has worked on issues of migration and on refugees, and worked as a coordinator for the 'Other Universals' project of the University of the Western Cape, Cape Town.

GAËTAN CLIQUENNOIS holds a law degree, a Master's in criminology from the Free University of Brussels, and a dual PhD in the sociology of law from L'École des hautes études en sciences sociales (EHESS), Paris and Facultés Université Saint-Louis (FUSL), Brussels. He has worked on human rights in penal and prison matters. He was a visiting scholar at the University of Cambridge and the London School of Economics, UK. Since 2013 he has been working as a permanent research fellow at the French National Centre for Scientific Research (CNRS), University of Strasbourg (SAGE: Societies, Actors and Governments in Europe), and since 2018 at the University of Nantes (DCS: Law and Social Change) where he has been director of a programme on Law and Social Change. He has co-edited *Monitoring Penal Policy in Europe* (2018).

DINA DABO is from Zanzibar and holds a postgraduate degree from the University of Cape Town. She is the founder of Tanzania Facilitation Services Ltd. (TFS) and managing director of Girls in Tech Tanzania, an NGO focused on inspiring Tanzanian girls and women to pursue education in STEM. She has worked in areas of historical sociology, migration and cultures of possession in Zanzibar.

SUMANGALA DAMODARAN teaches at Ambedkar University Delhi (AUD) and works in the areas of development studies and popular music studies. She is also a musician and composer who has archived and written about Indian resistance music traditions, and done collaborative performative and scholarly work on music with poets, musicians and academics. She was involved as a consultant with the National Commission for Enterprises in the Unorganized Sector (NCEUS), Government of India, from March 2008 to March 2009. From 2016 she has been co-leading, with Ari Sitas, the Re-Centring AfroAsia Project 700–1500 CE, which involves seven universities and scholars from a range of countries.

ABDALLAH GRIFAT is from Palestine and studied sociology at the University of Cape Town for his postgraduate degree. He was the public relations coordinator of the Al Mezan Palestinian Human Rights Institute and Al Sharq Youth.

WIEBKE KEIM did a PhD in sociology at the University of Freiburg (Germany) and Paris IV-Sorbonne (France). She led the research project, 'Universality and Acceptance Potential of Social Science Knowledge: On the Circulation of Knowledge between Europe and the Global South' (2010–14) at the University of Freiburg, and has been a CNRS (French National Centre for Scientific Research) researcher at SAGE (Societies, Actors and Governments in Europe), University of Strasbourg, since 2013. Her publications include 'Vermessene Disziplin: Zum konterhegemonialen Potential afrikanischer und lateinamerikanischer Soziologien' (transcript, 2008), *Global Knowledge Production in the Social Sciences: Made in Circulation* (2014), *Gauging and Engaging Deviance, 1600–2000* (2014), and *Universally Comprehensible, Arrogantly Local: South African Labour Studies from the Apartheid Era into the New Millenium* (2017). Her focus areas of research are history and epistemology of the social sciences, knowledge circulation, sociology of science and knowledge, fascisms and post-fascisms.

JAN-LOUISE LEWIN is an African feminist, researcher and teacher. She has lectured in the gender studies department at the University of Cape Town where her teaching focused on the intersections of race and gender. Her research specializes in prison masculinities, prison sex culture, street and prison gangs, and coloured identity politics.

AMRITA PANDE is an associate professor in the sociology department at the University of Cape Town. She is the author *of Wombs in Labor: Transnational Commercial Surrogacy in India* (2014). Her research focuses on the intersection of globalization and the intimate. She has published widely in well-known journals and edited volumes. She is also an educator-performer touring the world with a performance lecture series, 'Made in India: Notes from a Baby Farm', based on her ethnographic work on surrogacy. She is currently leading a large National

Research Foundation (NRF)-funded project exploring the 'global fertility flows' of eggs, sperms, embryos and wombs, connecting the world in unexpected ways.

Javier Perez is a San Salvadorian raised in the United States. He completed his doctoral studies in sociology at the University of Cape Town. He is also a poet, dramatist and cultural activist based in Cape Town.

Sofia Saeed is from Pakistan and studied for her Master's degree in the Global Studies Programme (Freiburg, Cape Town, Delhi). She is pursuing a second Master's in visual anthropology.

Anubhav Sengupta is an assistant professor in sociology at the Manipal Centre for Humanities (MAHE), Manipal, Karnataka. He holds a PhD in sociology from Jawaharlal Nehru University, New Delhi. His scholarly interests span student and youth movements in India, left-radical revolutionary movements, subjectivity studies, and political sociology and theories.

Ari Sitas is a poet, dramatist and sociologist, and a recipient of the Order of Mapungubwe for his scientific and creative work. He is Emeritus Professor at the University of Cape Town and Gutenberg Chair at the University of Strasbourg. He has published extensively in the areas of historical sociology, labour and social movements. He has been involved with Sumangala Damodaran, Nicos Trimikliniotis and Wiebke Keim on a range of scholarly projects. His latest work that combines his skill-range, *Notes for an Oratorio: on Small Things that Fall (like a screw in the night)*, was published in 2020. At the end of 2021 he directed a musical and pluri-media production, *Giraffe Humming*, which premiered in Cape Town. He has just completed his tenure as the Chair of South Africa's National Institute for the Humanities and the Social Sciences.

Nicos Trimikliniotis is a professor at the School of Social Sciences, University of Nicosia. He heads the Cyprus team of experts for the Fundamental Rights Agency of the European Union. He has researched on sociology and law of the state, ethnic conflict, migration, asylum precarity, citizenship, racism, labour and discrimination. His publications include *Migration and the Refugee Dissensus in Europe: Borders, Security and Austerity* (2020) and *Mobile Commons, Migrant Digitalities and the Right to the City* (2015). He is currently director and principal investigator for a research project, 'Mobile Citizenship, States of Exception and (non)Border Regimes in Post-Covid-19 Cyprus', awarded by the Hellenic Observatory at the London School of Economics and Political Science, funded by the A.G. Leventis Foundation.